D1523702

ASPECTS OF
THE LANGUAGE OF
LATIN POETRY

PROCEEDINGS OF THE BRITISH ACADEMY · 93

ASPECTS OF THE LANGUAGE OF LATIN POETRY

Edited by
J. N. ADAMS & R. G. MAYER

Published *for* THE BRITISH ACADEMY
by OXFORD UNIVERSITY PRESS

Oxford University Press, Great Clarendon Street, Oxford OX2 6DP

Oxford New York
Athens Auckland Bangkok Bogota Bombay
Buenos Aires Calcutta Cape Town Dar es Salaam
Delhi Florence Hong Kong Istanbul Karachi
Kuala Lumpur Madras Madrid Melbourne
Mexico City Nairobi Paris Singapore
Taipei Tokyo Toronto Warsaw
and associated companies in
Berlin Ibadan

Published in the United States by
Oxford University Press Inc., New York

British Library Cataloguing in Publication Data
Data available

ISBN 0–19–726178–7
ISSN 0068–1202

Phototypeset by Intype London Ltd
Printed in Great Britain
on acid-free paper by
Creative Print and Design Wales
Ebbw Vale

Contents

vi CONTENTS

Stylistic and Generic Variation

Notes on Contributors

J. N. Adams was until 1995 Professor of Latin at the University of Manchester, and then held the Chair of Latin at the University of Reading. Since January 1998 he has been a Fellow of All Souls College, Oxford. He has published widely on the history of the Latin language, most recently on aspects of the operation of Wackernagel's law. He is currently writing a book on bilingualism in the Roman Empire.

Robert Coleman is Emeritus Professor of Comparative Philology in the University of Cambridge. He has published widely in classical and Indo-European linguistics, and also in Greek and Latin literature, which he taught for many years at Emmanuel College, where he has been a Fellow since 1960. He is currently working on IE dental preterites and dialectal differentiation in Oscan, and on the History of the Latin Language.

Woldemar Görler is Professor of Classics in the Universität des Saarlandes, Saarbrücken. He is author of the section on the language and style of the *Aeneid* in the *Enciclopedia Virgiliana* (1985) and of a number of articles on Roman poets and poetical diction; he has also written books and numerous papers on Hellenistic philosophy including Cicero's philosophical writings and on Greco-Roman comedy.

H. D. Jocelyn taught Latin in the University of Sydney between 1960 and 1973 and in the University of Manchester between 1973 and 1996. He has published an edition of the fragments of Ennius' tragedies (Cambridge 1969), and notes and essays treating all the genres of poetry cultivated at Rome in the archaic and classical periods. He has not ignored prose. He is working now in a desultory way on an edition of Plautus' *Pseudolus*.

E. J. Kenney is Emeritus Kennedy Professor of Latin in the University of Cambridge. His new translation, with introduction and notes, of Apuleius' *Golden Ass* was published in Penguin Classics in May 1998. He is currently preparing articles on Ovid for the classical encyclopaedia *Der neue Pauly* and Brill's forthcoming *Companion to the Study of Ovid*.

David Langslow is University Lecturer in Latin Philology and Linguistics in the University of Oxford, and a Fellow of Wolfson College, Oxford, and is Professor Elect of Classics in the University of Manchester. He has published a series of articles, and is about to publish a book, on the language of the Latin medical writers; he is also preparing an annotated translation of Wackernagel's *Lectures on Syntax*.

Robert Maltby is Senior Lecturer at the University of Leeds. He has contributed entries to the *Thesaurus Linguae Latinae*, and is the author of *Latin Love Elegy* (1979), and *A Lexicon of Ancient Latin Etymologies* (1990); he has written articles on Roman and Greek Comedy and Roman elegy. He is preparing a commentary on Tibullus, a translation and commentary on Terence's *Phormio*, and a monograph on ancient etymology.

R. G. Mayer holds a personal Chair of Classics in the University of London at King's College London. He has published commentaries on Lucan VIII, Seneca, *Phaedra*, and Horace, *Epistles I*; he is currently editing with commentary Tacitus, *Dialogus* for the Cambridge Greek and Latin Classics series.

R. G. M. Nisbet was Corpus Christi Professor of Latin in the University of Oxford from 1970 to 1992. He has published commentaries on Cicero, *In Pisonem* and (with Margaret Hubbard) on Horace, *Odes* I and *Odes* II. His *Collected Papers on Latin Literature* appeared in 1995.

John Penney is a Fellow of Wolfson College, Oxford and University Lecturer in Classical Philology (since 1972); he has research interests in Indo-European philology, with a special concern for the Italic languages. His publications include a chapter in *CAH* IV (2nd ed.) 1988 on 'The languages of Italy'; he is currently at work on a handbook on the development of Latin and the other Italic languages from Indo-European.

Hubert Petersmann is Professor Ordinarius of Latin and Greek in the University of Heidelberg. Besides numerous articles on linguistic phenomena of Latin and Greek he has published a commentary on Plautus' *Stichus*, a study of Petronius' urbane style, and, together with his wife Astrid, a survey of Latin Poetry from its beginnings to the end of the Republic. At the moment he is mainly doing research on the history of the Latin language, especially as spoken.

J. G. F. Powell is Professor of Latin at the University of Newcastle upon Tyne, and is the author of commentaries on Cicero, *Cato Maior De Senectute* (Cambridge 1988) and *Laelius De Amicitia* and *Somnium Scipionis* (Warminster 1990). He edited *Cicero the Philosopher: Twelve Papers* (Oxford 1995) and is co-editor, with Professor A. J. Woodman, of *Author and Audience in Latin Literature* (Cambridge 1992). He is currently preparing a new text of Cicero, *De Republica* and *De Legibus* for the Oxford Classical Texts series.

David Sedley is Professor of Ancient Philosophy at the University of Cambridge, and a Fellow of Christ's College. He is co-author (with A. A. Long) of *The Hellenistic Philosophers* (Cambridge 1987), and has recently published with the Cambridge University Press *Lucretius and the Transformation of Greek Wisdom* (1998). His other recent work includes a papyrological and philosophical edition of the anonymous commentary on Plato's *Theaetetus*, and articles on Plato, Platonism, Aristotle, Epicurus, Stoicism, and Brutus and Cassius.

Proceedings of the British Academy, **93**, 1–18

Introduction

J. N. ADAMS & R. G. MAYER

THE MUSES WERE NOT warmly welcomed by the peoples of ancient Italy. The Etruscans, for instance, who clearly had a dramatic poetry, never produced a literature that we know of. Other peoples in Italy too, though they doubtless composed songs and performed dramas, for instance the Atellan farces, have not left a written literature of texts. (It is significant that Ennius, who claimed to have three hearts — Greek, Latin and Oscan — did not undertake to produce Oscan poems in writing.) The Romans too sang panegyrics, according to Cicero (*Brutus* 75), but of the Italic peoples only they in the course of time embarked upon the enterprise of committing newly composed poems to writing as texts, and that only after their city had been a political and social organism for some five centuries.

To some degree they owed this change of heart to accident; as chief city of the peninsula in the third century, Rome proved a magnet for literary (among other) talents, and some of her earliest authors were *semigraeci*, according to Suetonius, *Gramm.* 1, brought up in the Hellenic tradition of writing. Their first steps were not taken in vain, and for about two hundred and fifty years thereafter Latin-speakers developed an impressive verse literature, generally modelled upon the Greek. Their task was by no means easy, since their medium, the Latin language, was not a match for the suppler forms of Greek, varied by distinct dialects, especially the Attic (Quintilian in the late first century AD still reckoned that Latin was no match for it in comedy: *mihi sermo ipse Romanus non recipere uideatur illam solis concessam Atticis uenerem, Inst.* 10.1.100). Indeed, the heart of the problem was that Latin lacked altogether an artificial, yet universally received, poetic diction and syntax, such as we find in Homer and Hesiod (cf. Jocelyn (1969*a*: 38) 'in third-century Latium there seem to have been no commonly recognised traditions of public poetry ... in place of the three very distinct vocabularies of the Attic stage they offered one'). The language did however have traditional resources of high style, for instance, alliteration, lexical and morphological archaism, which had long been exploited in prayers and the terminology of law (cf. Jocelyn (1969*a*: 39 with notes)). What the first writers of Latin poetry had above all to do was to develop the resources of their language, and so far as possible create the impression of a poetic medium out of what lay to hand. They thus remained true to the character of the native language as they perceived it; for example, poetic compound words were in general more restricted in both frequency and type than in Greek (Palmer 1954: 102–3). But they elaborated it into a medium that satisfactorily ranged from satire and invective through elegy, drama and lyric, to the grandest heroic epos. The study of this process of linguistic development in verse and its results has long occupied professional students of the language (there is a convenient summary in Palmer (1954: 95–118)). But since there are still new things to be said about the ways in which the poets used the Latin language, we decided to organize a symposium at which philological aspects of poetic usage in the classical period would be discussed. The British Academy generously undertook to host the sessions and to publish the proceedings.[1]

We have tried to group the essays together so far as their themes suggest relationships within the collection. The order is as follows.

First, R. G. G. Coleman tackles the topic at the heart of the symposium and broadly surveys the concepts of poetic diction, discourse and register. Many of the issues he touches upon, e.g. archaism and the debt to Greek, recur in the later essays, but he widens the focus to include the use of metaphor and of specifically poetic syntax. There follow two studies on word order by J. N. Adams and R. G. M. Nisbet; the former concerns the relationship between ordinary usage and certain 'poetic' patterns, the latter the highly artificial structures of Horace. The influence of Greek and the use of technical vocabularies are the themes of the papers by R. G. Mayer on the concept of grecism, D. R. Langslow on scientific language and D. Sedley on Lucretius' philosophical language; the latter two complement each other. W. Görler and J. H. W. Penney focus upon syntactic matters, Görler upon unexpected usages of transitive verbs which may amount to metaphor, Penney upon features that derive from the oldest stratum of the language's usage. The remaining studies are all concerned with stylistic variation within particular authors or genres: H. Petersmann and J. G. F. Powell on satirists, H. D. Jocelyn on Catullus, R. Maltby on elegists and E. J. Kenney on Ovid.

---

[1] Dr S. J. Harrison delivered a paper on Virgil's etymologizing of names, but, on learning of the imminent publication of J. J. O'Hara's *True Names: Vergil and the Alexandrian Tradition of Etymological Wordplay* (Ann Arbor 1996), decided that his own contribution did not advance the matter sufficiently beyond O'Hara's to justify its inclusion in this volume.

We now attempt neither a summary of the content of the papers published nor a general definition of 'poetic language', but rather seek to highlight some of the recurrent themes of the volume and to clarify some of the terminology used.

Terms such as 'common parlance' (Kenney p. 402), 'ordinary discourse' (Jocelyn p. 343), 'everyday language' (Jocelyn p. 342), 'ordinary language' (Jocelyn pp. 350, 351), 'speech, spoken language' (Coleman p. 33, Adams p. 98), 'colloquialism' *et sim.* (Coleman pp. 38, 39, 43, 84) and even 'Vulgar Latin' (Coleman pp. 40, 46) abound in the volume. Since they may either overlap or be used inconsistently, it is appropriate to offer an overview here.

The 'language' of Latin poetry was of course Latin (note the remarks of Coleman p. 25), though admittedly a Latin which sometimes took elements of vocabulary, syntax, morphology, word order and even sound from Greek, or in the case of satire from other languages or dialects of Italy (Petersmann pp. 292, 308–9). It is easy to exaggerate the differences between the varieties and registers of extant Latin. Terms freely used such as the 'language of medicine', 'legal Latin' have the effect of diminishing the common elements shared by technical, colloquial and other varieties of the language. Indeed despite the currency of the capitalized expression 'Vulgar Latin' it is well to remember that in the active voice, at least, a good deal of the verb morphology found in the high literary language of the classical period passed on into the Romance languages; the masses of ordinary speakers were using much the same verb system as the small literate élite, and not a grossly simplified, or different, language. And in poetry there are no extensive differences between the morphology and syntax of the various poets.

'NEUTRAL' TERMS

Powell (p. 324) notes that any language is bound to contain a large number of words and constructions that are neutral as regards register (cf. p. 325: 'much of Juvenal's vocabulary, and more of his sentence construction than is often supposed, is simply neutral for register'). 'Neutrality' seems to us to be a useful concept to embrace the words, morphology and syntax shared at any one time by different forms of writing and speech. If one were to assess the distribution and stylistic level of the words that make up the first seven lines of the *Aeneid* (some 50+), one would find that no more than a small handful of terms (about four) were not 'neutral' Latin, though the issue is complicated by the fact that words in combination have syntax, order and morphology, and in all three areas there are departures

from the strictly neutral in the seven lines. Not that morphological departures amount to much: only *superum* has an ending which is not standard
Latin, and even that is not particularly striking (Coleman p. 41, Petersmann
p. 305).

We believe that when Kenney (p. 402), speaking of a use of *infundo*
in Ovid, attributes it to 'common parlance (rather than colloquial) ... in
Ovid's day', he was thinking of our neutral Latin. And elsewhere (p. 405),
commenting on *famam ... tenebo*, he notes that it is difficult to detect
anything in either diction or the combination of words that tends to place
a phrase such as this in a specific register: '*In this sense its literary effect
can be classified as "neutral"*' (our italics).

'PROSAIC' TERMS

There may be a difference between words that are 'neutral' Latin, and
those that are 'prosaic'. If a word were avoided entirely by poets, but used
for instance by Cicero in his speeches, it might in theory qualify for some
such designation as 'prosaic', 'unpoetic' or the like. But words belonging
to the common stock of the language, at home as well in verse as prose —
in *Aen.* 1.1–7 note for example *arma, uir, primus, ora, fatum, uenio, litus,
multum* (adverbial), *ille, terra, iacto*, etc. — cannot reasonably bear such a
designation. Thus, while we agree with the gist of Coleman's observation
(p. 55) on epigram 85 of Catullus (*odi et amo*) that it is the 'most remarkable case in Latin of a sequence of prosaic [*sic*] words combining to create
a powerful effect' (and cf. his later remark, 'every word here is prosaic'),
we would suggest that most of the words in question are not 'prosaic' in
the restricted sense defined above, but neutral.[2]

'FORMAL' SPEECH OR PROSE

Another example of Kenney's may be used to introduce a slightly different
category of usage, which further suggests the need for a refinement of the
blanket term 'prosaism'. At *Her.* 17.37–40 Ovid has the construction *non
quo ... sed quia*, noted by Kenney (p. 407) as a favourite of Cicero's, and
found apparently nowhere else in Latin poetry. Here *par excellence* is a
'prosaism' (Kenney p. 407), but in this case one might feel that that is too

---

[2] Mayer (1994: 16 with the references in n. 57) briefly tackled this issue of designating words
in poetry as prosaic, by pointing out that the English word bears connotations that do not
satisfactorily describe the usage of formal Latin prose.

imprecise a term, since in English 'prose' embraces a vast spectrum of texts or utterances from the most mundane piece of conversation to highly formal rhetoric. The construction was perhaps more at home in *formal* prose or speech (and its attestation in Cicero's letters as well as his speeches does not invalidate that suggestion) than in non-elaborate, functional or colloquial prose or speech. By its very nature it is overtly rhetorical, in that it tends to contrast an actual reason with an attributed or rejected reason (Kenney p. 407), and as such it is a more complex manifestation of the type of opposition which takes the form of 'not A but B'.[3]

Kenney (p. 412) accounts for Ovid's admission of this usage of what we might label 'formal' prose or speech from the more 'adversarial tone of these epistles as compared with the single *Heroides*'.

The Latin language had resources of word order and collocation for expressing effects carried in English by, say, intonation. Focused terms were typically placed at the head or end of a colon, and an initial focused term could be further highlighted by attaching to it certain types of enclitic, such as focusing particles, e.g. *quidem*, the copula (which statistically is more common after the predicate in the order subject-predicate-copula), or alternatively a nominative personal pronoun (*ego*, *tu*), even when that pronoun was not motivated by its own emphasis. This type of placement of *ego/tu* was certainly at home in formal speech or prose, and indeed it seems to have given rise to certain hackneyed oratorical collocations such as *credo ego*, which opens Cicero's *Pro S. Roscio* and is found in speeches in Livy (Adams p. 105). It probably occurred across a wider spectrum of speech than the *non quo . . . sed quia* construction, but the categories we are setting up do not have absolutely clear-cut boundaries and the evidence is inadequate to determine how far down the scale of formality a construction such as *credo ego* extended. Certainly the presence of the structure in, say, Catullus would seem to reflect an attempt to catch the tones of formal speech in certain types of verse (hendecasyllabic, elegiac).

COLLOQUIALISM AND ORALITY

Educated speakers may admit in informal utterances or writing 'colloquial' usages which they exclude from their formal performances and tend to associate with the lower social dialects (see Cic. *Fam.* 9.21.1 on *plebeius sermo* as appropriate to epistles). Two cases in point might be Cicero's

---

[3] Compare again the remarks of Mayer (1994: 18) on Hor. *Ep.* 1.8.4 *haud quia*, a poeticization of the Ciceronian formula.

use of *uenire in buccam* in the letters, where *bucca* has the sense of *os* and anticipates, e.g. Fr. *bouche* (see Powell (p. 328)), and Lucilius' use of *demagis*, whence Sp. *demás* (see Petersmann (p. 305)). The colloquial usage of the educated does not however overlap completely with that of the uneducated.

There is another dimension to the colloquial. We refer to various forms of imperfect performance which are associated with oral delivery. Recently attemps have been made to identify universal features of oral performance (Koch 1995), features alluded to by Coleman (p. 24) as 'false starts, nonce mispronunciations, abrupt and ungrammatical transitions, anacolutha, rambling pleonasm and banal repetition, not to mention mere noise'. There is a difference between the deliberate use in colloquial speech, or indeed high literature for that matter, of an item belonging mainly to the lower, non-literary registers (e.g. *bucca* = *os*, *demagis*), and the failure under conditions of stress or in a heated spoken exchange to complete an utterance according to accepted norms of correct grammar. A usage of the first type may be called a 'colloquialism', but features of unsuccessful oral performance are not deliberate, and they may occur even in formal surroundings when the speaker is intent on avoiding colloquialisms. Features of this second type are of limited interest to classical scholars, because real Latin speech does not survive. Nevertheless, even in poetry attempts are sometimes made to reproduce unprepared speech, and it is in such attempts that the imperfections of orality are likely to be found, as for example the aposiopesis in Neptune's speech in *Aen.* 1.135 *quos ego . . .* or the agitation of Nisus at 9.427. In the conversation which Catullus constructs in *c.* 10 certain features typical of oral performance seem to have been incorporated. At 10.29–30, for example, there is a case of what has been called 'segmentation', whereby a noun which begins a sentence is left suspended, to be picked up by a pronoun: *meus sodalis . . . is sibi parauit.* Koch (1995: 135), claiming the phenomenon as a universal of oral delivery, illustrates it from Plautus and the *Peregrinatio Aetheriae*, and there are comparable examples to be found in the letters of Claudius Terentianus (P. Mich. viii.468.27–8), which were probably dictated to scribes. Jocelyn (p. 361) describes some repetitions of *paro* in the same conversation as 'studied unconcern', an expression which we would interpret as descriptive of (deliberately) imperfect oral performance. On repetitions and orality, see Koch (1995: 138); though it has to be said that the determinants of verbal repetition are complex, and cannot be assigned *en bloc* to the imitation of oral performance (Wills (1996)).

Catullus' second speech in the poem also has several pieces of 'syntactic incoherence' (28–9, 32; see in general Koch (1995: 133–4)). There can be no doubt that Catullus was seeking in this poem to capture linguistically not only the tones of conversation, but more specifically the confusion inflicted by the encounter with the woman and its effects on his syntax and sentence structure.

It can be assumed that, if in a written text such as a poem, a writer admits such incoherence, he will have special reasons for doing so. Oral features introduced into what on the surface is a narrative text (as distinct from a reported conversation) are potentially more interesting. We note in passing that Freudenburg (1993: 13 with notes), arguing that Horace intended to construct *Sat.* 1.1 in accordance with a 'conversational logic', draws attention to one or two features which independently have been ascribed to oral performance.

Linguistic usages associated with oral performance occupy only a marginal place in Latin poetry. Rather more extensive are ordinary colloquialisms, but these are far from easy to classify and their motivation is not always easy to grasp. An obvious function of colloquialism in poetry was to impart a conversational style appropriate to a particular context, or more generally to a genre or type of writing. The dialogue in Hor. *Sat.* 1.9 naturally has colloquialisms, such as the intensive *misere* (14) and *si me amas* (38; familiar from Cicero's letters, and now in a letter from Vindolanda, *Tab. Vind.* ii 233), but it would be difficult to sustain the view that Horace has tried to distinguish the speeches from the narrative portions of the satire in this respect; the whole poem, like the *Satires* in general, has a colloquial veneer. As Coleman (p. 39) remarks, 'in satire . . . occasional echoes of *sermo cottidianus* were appropriate'. And so it is that colloquialisms 'from the ordinary language' in Catullus 10 (Jocelyn p. 363) are not merely to be found in the conversation itself, but in the body of the (hendecasyllabic) poem, which is by this means, as by others which Jocelyn discusses, distinguished from, e.g. the lyric poems (cf. Jocelyn p. 364).

Colloquialisms may be more striking in a 'poetic' setting. Powell shows that one of Juvenal's constant tricks was to introduce what he calls a 'mismatch of registers' (p. 326), 'either between one word and another in the same passage, or between sentence structure or verse structure and vocabulary, or an incongruity between the content and the level of language used to express it'. This procedure may involve the use of a colloquialism in an inappropriate context, as e.g. the deflating *caballus* with *Gorgoneus* of Pegasus, and the cluster of everyday words alongside epic mannerisms in the description of the man killed in the street by the collapse of a cartload of marble (Powell pp. 326, 327).

A factor which sometimes determined or justified the use of a colloquialism was the influence exerted by the traditions of a genre. Coleman (p. 38) notes that at *Aen.* 6.779 Virgil uses *uiden* in Anchises' solemn address to his son. The colloquial pronunciation which underlies this form might be justified from the fact that it is located in a speech, albeit a solemn one, but an additional influence noted by Servius was that the usage was Ennian (see *Ann.* 622 Sk with Skutsch's n.). Why Ennius used the colloquialism is another question, since the context is lost, but where Virgil was concerned the presence of a colloquialism in an elevated context could obviously be defended from an ancient precedent (Coleman p. 38).

It is a curious fact brought out by Coleman (p. 43) that sometimes literary prose usage distanced itself more sharply from colloquialism 'than poetic usage felt the need consistently to do'. A nice illustration is provided by an aspectual nuance which could be given to the perfect, particularly the perfect infinitive. A perfect infinitive dependent on a modal verb such as *uolo* may refer to future rather than to past time; that is, it envisages a hypothetical act as already a concrete, accomplished reality at an indeterminate future time. This usage is familiar in prohibitions in early laws, such as *neiquis eorum Bacanal habuise uelet* in the *S.C. de Baccanalibus*, where its motivation has been well described by Daube (1956: 37–49). It seems to be absent from classical prose, and one might be tempted to see it as an archaism as used in Augustan verse, particularly in the second half of the pentameter, where the metrical utility of the *-uisse* form is especially clear (for a discussion see Smith's note on Tibull. 1.1.29–32). However, in a letter from Vindolanda written by a *decurio*, the linguistic level of which is shown by the substandard forms *habunt* = *habent* (whence Fr. *ont*) and *rediemus* (future), there is now a vivid use of the perfect infinitive *fecisse* in unambiguous reference to future time,[4] and the possibility opens up that the perfect infinitive had never lost this aspectual potentiality in spoken colloquial Latin, though it was considered unacceptable for some reason in ordinary literary prose.[5]

Another case in point is discussed by Penney (pp. 258–9): *dico* + subjunctive, a construction which is old and seems to be inherited, is admitted in poetry, but in prose is confined to informal letters, both literary and sub-literary. (This construction perforce will be most likely to appear in speech rather than narrative.)

We would suggest, following Coleman, that the Latin poetic language was not a register whose syntactic, phonetic or morphological norms were determined either by the norms of the educated language at the time of composition, or by the norms obtaining at a particular social or stylistic

---

[4] See Bowman and Thomas (1996: 324): *cras quid uelis nos fecisse, rogo, domine praecipias* (Inv. no. 93.1544).
[5] There are a few examples in Livy, though sometimes clear imitations of legal language, e.g. at 39.14.8, and others in artificial Imperial prose writers such as Pliny the Elder (see Kühner–Stegmann (1955: ii 1.133–4)).

level of the language at any one time. Poets in most genres were more tolerant than orators or historians of usages across a wide stylistic spectrum, from the archaic to the colloquial. A colloquialism, as noted above, might of course have the function of giving an appropriate tone to a genre or a particular context, but equally some colloquialisms which cannot be accounted for in this way may simply have been raised to acceptability because they were potentially useful (e.g. metrically), or because some other factor gave them respectability in the poet's eyes. Thus in the case of the completive use of the perfect infinitive Coleman suggests (p. 83) that 'Greek influence also helped to re-establish the purely aspectual distinction between infinitives in the complements of certain verbs'.

It seems likely, for example, that poets embraced various phonetic colloquialisms, that is colloquialisms of pronunciation, for the sake of metrical convenience (Coleman p. 33 'the great majority of phonetic devices for overcoming unmetricality can be directly linked to known facts of ordinary Latin speech'), though the evidence is difficult to assess. Latin had a strong stress accent, and unaccented vowels, particularly those in final syllables, were subject to various types of weakening (Coleman p. 36). The shortening of long *o* in final position in verbs no doubt began in words of iambic structure (Coleman p. 38), but in Augustan poetry it is found in words (including verbs) of other structures as well (Coleman p. 38). In Cicero on the other hand in clausulae the *-o* ending of the first-person singular generally seems to be treated as long (e.g. *Fam.* 9.7.2 *exspecto tuas litteras*, where long *o* would give a double cretic; cf. Fraenkel (1968: 164 with n. 4, 166–7, 170) for various verb-endings treated as long), and in the Vindolanda writing tablets (early second century AD) scribes quite often mark the final *o* with an apex, both in iambic (e.g. *rogo*) and other types of verbs. This habit at the very least betrays a lingering awareness well after the Augustan period among careful scribes that a long *o* in this position was more 'correct', however they actually pronounced such words. There is then a possibility that in the Augustan period, in non-iambic words at least, shortening of the final *o* was more a feature of colloquial than of careful formal speech. The fact that in Seneca's later plays short final *o* shows some increase in verbs[6] suggests that in the first century AD the status of final *o* in verbs had not crystallized in the judgement of the educated; and this in turn implies a certain boldness on the part of earlier poets in exploiting developments which had not fully percolated through to the educated language. Coleman (p. 38) remarks that 'what is characteristic of the poetic register is not so much the intro-

---

[6] For discussion see J. G. Fitch, *AJP* 102 [1981], 289ff. and Nisbet (1995: 299–300).

duction of the shortened forms but the retention side by side with them of the older forms'.

Coleman (pp. 36–40) discusses various other possible phonetic colloqui- alisms, but, as he implies (p. 52), it must always be allowed that a development which one might be inclined to see as colloquial, non-stan- dard or informal might in fact by the time of its entry into poetry have become a general trend in the language. Similarly Jocelyn (p. 351) is non- committal about the status of iambic *meae* in Catullus at the time of writing, and (e.g.) dactylic *commoda* (p. 361). On balance the shortened forms such as *comparasti*, *audissem*, *complerunt*, in which *w* was lost with resultant vowel contraction, commented on by Coleman (p. 39) and Jocelyn (p. 361 with n. 127), seem for the period in question to reflect a widespread speech habit (as distinct from a substandard, non-formal pronunciation), despite Jocelyn's reluctance to commit himself (see Cic. *Orat.* 157 with Coleman p. 39).[7]

ARCHAISM

Archaism is dealt with in several papers, e.g. by Coleman (pp. 34–5, 43–4), Penney *passim*, Petersmann (pp. 293, 304). To poets earlier poetry was a reservoir which could be freely drawn on (Coleman (p. 33)), and the poetic register is thus bound to contain usages which at any particular time of writing were old-fashioned. Again Coleman (p. 43 with p. 84) notes that poetic language may align itself with vulgar usage rather than that of educated prose, since a construction which had archaic precedent may have been dropped from the educated language while surviving in lower- class speech. Penney (pp. 251–2) discusses syntactic archaisms used for effect, but particularly important is his demonstration that an 'archaism' may in fact represent an innovation: that is, a genuinely archaic pattern may be used in a slightly different way from its correspondent in early Latin (pp. 253–4). He refers for example to a new use of *ne* + present imperative, which in early Latin had an inhibitive meaning ('stop doing . . .'), but in later poets can 'function as a prohibitive with future reference' (p. 253). It is a moot point whether such developments should be seen as deliberate innovations, or as misunderstandings of earlier idiom. On archaisms which were of uncertain interpretation by the classical period see Coleman (p. 58).

The motivations of a poet in using an archaism may be many-faceted.

---

[7] Mayer (1994: 17) drew attention to the fact that such contracted forms are found in Horace's conversational satires, but are absent from the more 'documentary' style of his epistles.

The archaism gives a suitably stately tone to its context, but the poet may have additional reasons for using it. Penney (e.g. p. 255) discusses several cases where a construction might be attributed as well to Greek models as to the influence of earlier Latin. But we would draw particular attention to his observation (p. 260) that various possible features of 'archaic' syntax 'have in common that they make for a denser texture to the sentence, without explicit markers of subordination'. The well-known taste of poets for using various oblique cases in a range of functions unsupported by the prepositions which would have been the norm in prose may look like a carry over from an earlier, 'Indo-European' stage of the language, but in reality the main determinant may have been a desire to keep function words to a minimum. A general aim of this type might on the one hand have the effect of introducing 'archaisms', but equally it might lead to the admission of a current 'vulgarism' (e.g. *dico* + subjunctive; see above p. 8).

THE INFLUENCE OF GREEK

Since poetry was recited, the sounds of the language, and particularly devices such as alliteration and assonance which were achieved by the collocation of appropriate words, were a potential sphere of the poet's inventiveness. Although various inherited potentialities of the Latin language of the types referred to were fully exploited, it is well recognized that foreign, i.e. chiefly Greek, sounds also contributed to the texture of Latin poetry (see Coleman pp. 45–6). The sounds of Greek were in various respects admired by Latin speakers (Quint. 12.10.27–8): Greek was supposedly 'sweet' in sound, Latin 'harsh' (Biville (1990: i.71)), and the poet who wanted his *carmen* to sound *dulce* should adorn it with Greek *nomina*: *itaque tanto est sermo Graecus Latino iucundior ut nostri poetae, quotiens dulce carmen esse uoluerunt, illorum id nominibus exornent* (Quint. 12.10.33). It was obviously a Greek word which was *not* integrated into Latin which would most strikingly retain the 'sweet', or in satire peculiar, sounds of Greek, and into that class fall *par excellence* proper names, which were often inflected as Greek by Latin poets; for that reason Quintilian is likely to have meant chiefly 'proper names' by *nominibus* here (see R. G. Austin's commentary ad loc., and cf. Quint. 12.10.27). Quintilian in another context was of the view, shared by Messala, referred to there, that Greek names should be Latinized in oratory (1.5.58ff.); for him then poetry was a special case in this respect. The exotic character to Latin ears of certain distinctive Greek sounds cannot be underestimated. There is an anecdote at Quint. 12.10.57 (see Biville (1990: i.158)) about an uneducated person who was asked in court whether he knew *Amphionem*. He said 'no', but when the speaker dropped the aspirate, shortened the *i*, and said *Ampionem* he recognized the man.

On names inflected as Greek in Latin verse see Coleman (pp. 46, 47), Jocelyn (p. 352). On the other hand the Latinizing of an exotic name might be significant, as *Serapim* in the highly colloquial poem Catullus 10 (Jocelyn (p. 362)). In elegy Greek inflections are rare (Maltby (p. 380)), and in Horace there is generic variation (Mayer (p. 158)). The whole question of the use of Greek inflections in Latin poetry (which inevitably has a textual dimension) merits a systematic study.

It was not of course only by inflection of proper names that Greek sounds could be imported into Latin verse. An accumulation of Greek words in a line of verse would no doubt have an exotic sound which might take on a symbolic significance. Sedley (pp. 242–3) observes that the almost Greek line Lucr. 2.412 *ac musaea mele, per chordas organici quae* contrasts with the Latin line that precedes: 'Where Greece has given us sublime music, Rome's more characteristic noise is the shrieking sawblades of a workshop' (Sedley (p. 243)). Similar in effect to the Lucretian line is Tibullus 2.3.60 *barbara gypsatos ferre catasta pedes* (Maltby (p. 381)).

The relationship between Greek syntax and Latin is a complex one, much debated and variously described. There can be no doubt that poets consciously imitated Greek syntax, as readers in antiquity frequently noted (see Mayer *passim* on the comments of scholiasts particularly). Sometimes a particular purpose can be discerned in a special context, as perhaps Catullus 4.2 *ait fuisse nauium celerrimus* (see Coleman (p. 84)), but more usually the borrowed syntax was simply a means of distancing poetic language from the banal. Syntactical grecism is thus arguably one of the factors which contributed to Latin the specifically poetic syntax it lacked from the start. Nevertheless many 'grecisms' turn out on closer inspection to be traceable back at least partly to certain native structures which had been extended or revived under Greek impetus: see Penney (p. 263): 'these [phenomena] could be seen as purely analogical Latin developments, or one might accept that there was reinforcement from Greek'; see further Penney (pp. 255, 256, 262–3), Coleman (p. 79 (adverbial neuter), p. 80 (some uses of the genitive), p. 81 (an accusative use), p. 83 (perfect infinitive; cf. above p. 8)).

Greek words are as interesting in their avoidance as in their use. Petersmann (pp. 301–2) notes the absence of Greek from a Roman context in Lucilian satire (a context enhanced by archaism), and Maltby (p. 380) notes that Tibullus is more sparing in his use of Greek words than both Propertius and Ovid; Propertius on the other hand has more mundane Greek words from humble spheres than the other elegists. Petersmann (pp. 299–300) discusses similar features in Lucilius, 181–8M; but in general

Petersmann addresses himself to the way in which early satire provides evidence of the social tensions surrounding the use of Greek in Roman daily life, and its reflection in literature. He draws attention to the rising tide of linguistic purism in Rome (p. 292 on Ennius) which deprecated at least on formal occasions the employment of Greek. Lucilius carries the debate on further (Petersmann (pp. 298–301)), and is far from indiscriminate in his interweaving of Greek into the Latin texture of his satires.

The papers of Langslow and Sedley are complementary. Both deal to some extent with 'technical terminology' in poetry, terminology which in Latin is often of Greek origin (see Sedley (p. 228) for a definition of the expression 'technical term'; Langslow (p. 190) prefers to speak of 'special vocabulary'). Petersmann (pp. 300–1) draws attention to the vast technical vocabulary — mainly literary critical — borrowed from Greek by Lucilius. But there seems to have been some feeling against the admission of banal (Greek) technical terms in some genres of poetry, at least as used literally within a technical context or to evoke a technical discipline (see below). Lucretius does not borrow, or in Sedley's terminology 'transliterate', the technical terms of Greek philosophy (though Lucilius had: see Petersmann (p. 301)), nor does he even attempt to find a similar Latin term instead of the Greek (Sedley (p. 230)). Instead he uses a *range* of metaphors for a single Greek term (Sedley (p. 230): see below). In using non-technical Greek words he acted not out of 'caprice' (Sedley (p. 238)), but 'to conjure up for the readers a Greek or an otherwise exotic context' (Sedley (p. 238)). The avoidance or use of Greek is thus functional rather than ornamental or merely learned. On the one hand Lucretius enhanced his philosophical aim, by 'making Epicurean philosophy . . . at home in his own native language', as a result of which 'he proves to us its true universality' (Sedley (p. 246)), while on the other he sought to give particular colour to certain contexts.

Langslow notes generic variations in the admissibility of 'special' vocabulary, with the more conversational genres such as comedy, satire and epigram showing no restriction in the use of banal technical terms not allowed in epic (pp. 191–2). Technical (often Greek) vocabulary is not however completely avoided in the 'higher' genres, but it tends not to be banal; Langslow lists (p. 195) three different purposes for which more exotic technical terms are used *sensu proprio* in these genres, particularly epic. On the other hand the desire to avoid terms felt to be inappropriate for some reason provided poets with an opportunity of displaying their inventiveness (Langslow (pp. 195–7)). Lucan, for example, avoids conventional disease names, Latin as well as Greek, and produces some clever periphrases (Langslow (p. 196)).

Langslow (pp. 198ff.) makes the interesting case that in (high) poetry

(Greek) technical vocabulary is often exploited in *metaphorical*, as distinct from literal, usage (see below). In theory the poet who paraphrases a medical term in its literal sense may admit that term as a metaphor. This insight has the additional benefit of opening the way to the identification of technical terms current within various disciplines: the metaphor will depend for its effect on the reader's familiarity with the source domain and its phraseology (Langslow (p. 198)), and the phraseology must therefore be current.[8]

METAPHOR

Ordinary speech in any language tends to be shot through with systematic sets of metaphors, and it has even been suggested that human thought processes are highly metaphorical. Cicero was well aware that metaphors were commonplace in peasant speech (Coleman (pp. 68–9.)). If there is anything 'poetic' about metaphor, it does not lie therefore in the use of metaphors as such, though it was the practice in formal oratorical prose for the speaker to qualify a metaphorical expression with a modest pronoun or adverb or both, e.g. *uelut quidam*, a practice unknown to poetry. 'Density' of metaphor might well be thought to characterize poetry, but claims about the incidence of such an elusive phenomenon as metaphorical usage are bound to be unreliable.

A distinction can usefully be made, in the manner of Lakoff and Johnson (1980) (and cf. Lakoff and Turner (1989)), between a metaphorical concept, and the potentially unlimited number of surface realizations of that concept. Lakoff and Johnson paraphrase metaphorical concepts in the form 'A is B' (e.g. 'argument is war'), and under headings of this sort they list examples of particular realizations. Any discussion of the 'originality' of a metaphor might attempt to draw a distinction between the originality of the concept and that of the realization. A good deal of Fantham's book (1972) consists in effect in the identification of metaphorical concepts. Originality or inventiveness is far more likely to be displayed in the devising of new or unusual realizations than of new concepts. The person who first used 'exocet' metaphorically, as in a sentence such as 'the next speaker delivered an *exocet* in the form of a telling counter-example which left his opponent floundering', was operating with a familiar metaphorical concept (Lakoff and Johnson's 'argument is war'; or more specifically, 'arguments are weapons'), of which he invented a striking new manifestation. Certain metaphorical concepts may occupy a significant

---

[8] Langslow's observation is relevant to the material assembled by Fantham (1972: 16 n. 8).

place in a particular genre of poetry. An obvious example is the metaphor 'love is slavery' (also 'love is warfare'), which is at the heart of elegy.[9]

Görler looks at the nature of some so-called verbal metaphors from a fresh angle, noting that thanks to its highly restricted vocabulary Latin poetry, especially Virgil's, worked several verbs very hard. These verbs he suggests (p. 282) are in themselves fairly colourless, and form a sort of common denominator in a number of expressions which might be deemed at first glance metaphorical (pp. 282–5). On closer analysis, however, a shift of specific grammatical objects is seen to actualize latent potential in the verb (n. 20), which enhances for the reader the precision of the picture and so produces an 'effect of alienation' (p. 282). Thus perhaps the expression is not best described as metaphorical at all. At any rate he warns against a too easy acquiescence in the use of this term.

The point is often made (see Kenney (p. 401 with n. 11); Coleman (p. 55 n. 52)) that, merely to list, in the manner of Axelson, allegedly 'unpoetic' words without consideration of their function and collocations in particular contexts is to reveal nothing of their true character. This point may be further illustrated in relation to metaphor, from part of Langslow's paper. Disease names, as we saw, tend to fall within the category of mundane entities avoided by poets in the higher genres. But, as Langslow shows (see above), there *are* such terms in poetry, but they are generally used metaphorically or figuratively. A case in point is Horace's use of *hydrops* figuratively in reference to avarice (Langslow (p. 199)). The underlying metaphorical concept is in fact banal: it might be paraphrased conceptually as 'vice is disease' (for the spread of this concept see Nisbet and Hubbard on Hor. *Odes* 2.2.13). Langslow's observation has various ramifications. In the first place, the underlying metaphor presumably ceases to be mundane once it is given a new surface realization; we do not know of *hydrops* used as a manifestation of this metaphor until a much later date,[10] and it is perhaps an invention of the poet's, though with an oratorical precedent, in that the Latin *intercus* had already been used metaphorically by Cato, *Orat.* 62. It may be a feature of poetry that metaphorical concepts are reinvigorated by the use of unexpected variants in the vehicle of the metaphor, though it would be rash to suggest that such inventiveness was exclusively the preserve of poets. Secondly, *hydrops*, which a poet might well have found unacceptable *sensu proprio*, was clearly capable of a different resonance in metaphorical usage.

Across the full range of technical disciplines, as much today as in antiquity, metaphor is one of the most fruitful sources of new terms (see

---

[9] See Wyke (1989).
[10] See *TLL* vi 3.3.37.84.

Coleman (pp. 69–70)). Lucretius indeed creates a technical terminology of Epicurean philosophy by means of metaphors, but paradoxically it is a technical terminology which avoids in a curious way the stamp of technicality. Coleman (p. 69) remarks: 'What is characteristic of scientific metaphors is their permanence and univocality. Once the new meaning is assigned, it remains purely referential within the register; there is no ornamental function, no contextual variation and no emotive accumulation from previous occurrences.' Sedley (pp. 230–1, 233), however, shows that Lucretius renders single Greek technical terms not by a single Latin metaphor, but by what he calls 'metaphorical diversification': that is, he uses a range of metaphorical terms for a single technical term. This can be seen as a form of subtlety by means of which a wider range of associations could be embraced than would be possible through a single term; and it was also a means of avoiding in poetry a stereotyped technical vocabulary.

WORD ORDER; HYPERBATON

Forms of hyperbaton emerge from the symposium as among the most distinctive features of Latin poetic usage. Powell (p. 323) notes: 'In Latin, the most obvious feature of poetic register as regards word order is persistent hyperbaton of noun and adjective.' Both Jocelyn (p. 355 n. 91) and Powell (pp. 323, 324) remark that much work remains to be done on the subject. Powell (p. 323) recommends as a topic for research an attempt 'to determine a hierarchy of register for different types of hyperbaton'.

To some extent hyperbata (in interlacing patterns) may be seen as reflecting patterns adopted by Hellenistic poets (Nisbet (p. 137); Mayer (p. 159) notes in passing some word orders characteristic of Greek and borrowed by Latin poets), but there were types which were rooted in native Latin speech, as for example when a demonstrative, e.g. *hic* with *ego/tu* attached, was separated from its noun (Adams (p. 127)). A native pattern such as this, well represented in prose, is obviously not a defining characteristic of poetic language. Where some poets, such as Ovid, differed from prose writers was partly in their readiness to take an inherited pattern and increase its complexity (Adams (pp. 130ff.)), and partly in the much greater frequency of hyperbata which they allowed (see Nisbet (p. 137)). Forty per cent of Horace's adjectives are separated from their nouns (Nisbet (p. 137)), and there is an extraordinary incidence of such separations in Catullus 64 (Jocelyn (p. 355)). In Catullus generic variations are discernible, with separations not so common, it seems, in hendecasyllables (Jocelyn (p. 365)).

In prose hyperbaton is often functional, in that (e.g.) inherently emphatic adjectives such as *magnus* are often separated from their noun, or, in exploitation of the emphatic potentialities of the final position in a clause, a focused or climactic noun is left to the end. An expectation of its eventual use is created in the reader/hearer by the use of an adjective or genitive which demands, but does not immediately receive, an associated noun (Adams (pp. 128–30)). Nisbet (p. 139) draws attention similarly to the way in which in Horace 'the ear is kept waiting for the corresponding noun', which 'sometimes ... may surprise the reader'. Horace in this respect was again no more than drawing on a pragmatic resource of the language, rather than of 'poetic language' in particular. Nevertheless his exploitation in the *Odes* for the purpose of emphasis not only of emphatic positions in clauses and sentences in the conventional sense, but also of significant positions in the line of verse, is a phenomenon of greater complexity than anything in prose (Nisbet *passim*; note e.g. p. 145 for the suggestion that 'when the pronoun [out of the Wackernagel postion] follows the central diaeresis in the Asclepiad line, . . . it is usually emphatic and perhaps always so').

It has been argued that 'since speaking is correlated with time and time is metaphorically conceptualized in terms of space, it is natural for us to conceptualize language metaphorically in terms of space. Our writing system reinforces this conceptualization. Writing a sentence down allows one to conceptualize it even more readily as a spatial object' (Lakoff and Johnson (1980: 126)). It seems likely that some Latin poets had, up to a point, a spatial concept of the structure of their verses. Thus the device of 'vertical responsion', whereby 'a word in one line is sometimes picked up by a corresponding word at the same place in a following line' (Nisbet (p. 146)). The relationship between the words is reinforced by their identical position in the pair of lines viewed as a spatial object. Paradoxically a separation (hyperbaton) may have the effect of juxtaposing (artificially by the norms of prose) two words which enter into some sort of relationship in the meaning of the line. The spatial contiguity underlines the semantic relationship. So at Hor. *Odes* 1.3.10–11 *qui fragilem truci commisit pelago ratem* the double disjunction of the adjectives from their nouns, which creates what is known as a golden line, produces also the juxtaposition of *fragilem* and *truci*, such that 'the fragility of the boat is set against the savagery of the sea' (Nisbet (p. 139)). At *Odes* 1.5.3 *grato, Pyrrha, sub antro* the vocative intrudes into the prepositional phrase and finds its place next to an adjective appropriate to the person named: 'the cave is welcome to Pyrrha' (Nisbet (p. 140)). There may be more to it than that: Pyrrha is enclosed by the cave, spatially in the words of Horace, and in the world he describes. Also worth mentioning here is the phenomenon which Sedley (p. 236), following David West, calls 'syntactical onomatopoeia': that is, 'intellectual contortion is symbolized by contorted grammar'. Sedley gives two examples from Lucretius, though perhaps the term 'grammar' is less than appropriate in the context: it is rather the (contorted) order of words that may arguably have symbolical significance.

It would not do, however, to make too much of spatial symbolism in the structure of verses. Hyperbaton in verse seems usually to be purely mechanical, without any semantic function in a particular context other than to create a recognizably 'poetic' disjunctive pattern.

Finally, we wish to express our gratitude to the institutions which enabled the symposium to take place (in April 1995) and to the many individuals who supported the undertaking and made it such an agreeable occasion for all who attended. We thank first and foremost the British Academy for supporting the undertaking from the beginning, and for lodging the symposiasts; Rosemary Lambeth's cheerful and ready help was particularly welcome. The Institute of Classical Studies hosted an afternoon session at Gordon Square, and provided refreshments afterwards; we thank the then Director, Professor Richard Sorabji, for his hospitality. The Classics Department at King's College London also hosted a drinks party at the Academy, and we thank the then Head of the Department, Professor Michael Silk, for making this possible. (The College itself however made no contribution from its research funds to this symposium.) The University of Manchester also contributed to that party, and in addition paid the fare of one of the symposiasts, a generous donation. The Swiss Cultural Fund in Britain and the German Embassy generously contributed towards the cost of lodging their symposiasts in London.

Individual colleagues were very supportive, and some who did not give papers acted as chairmen. We are grateful for this service to Sir Keith Thomas PBA, Dr John Briscoe and Professors K. Coleman, E. Fantham, G. J. P. O'Daly, M. D. Reeve, M. Winterbottom. All of the papers were refereed anonymously, either by members of the symposium or by colleagues who generously responded to our appeal; we wish to thank them too for their help.

GENERAL

Proceedings of the British Academy, **93**, 21–93

Poetic Diction, Poetic Discourse and the Poetic Register

R. G. G. COLEMAN

Summary.   A number of distinctive characteristics can be identified in the language used by Latin poets. To start with the
lexicon, most of the words commonly cited as instances of
poetic diction — *ensis, fessus, meare, olle, -que . . . -que* etc. —
are demonstrably archaic, having been displaced in the prose
register. Archaic too are certain grammatical forms found in
poetry — e.g. *aulāī*, gen. pl. *superum, agier, conticuere* — and
syntactic constructions like the use of simple cases for prepositional phrases and of infinitives instead of the clausal
structures of classical prose. Poets in all languages exploit the
linguistic resources of past as well as present, but this facility
is especially prominent where, as in Latin, the genre traditions
positively encouraged *imitatio*. Some of the syntactic characteristics are influenced wholly or partly by Greek, as are other
ingredients of the poetic register. The classical quantitative
metres, derived from Greek, dictated the rhythmic pattern of
the Latin words. Greek loan words and especially proper
names — *Chaoniae, Corydon, Pyrrha, Tempe, Theseus,
Zephyrus* etc. — brought exotic tones to the aural texture, often
enhanced by Greek case forms. They also brought an allusive
richness to their contexts. However, the most impressive characteristics after the metre were not dependent on foreign
intrusion: the creation of imagery, often as an essential feature
of a poetic argument, and the tropes of semantic transfer —
metaphor, metonymy, synecdoche — were frequently deployed
through common words. In fact no words were too prosaic to
appear in even the highest poetic contexts, always assuming
their metricality. Native too are the aural figures of alliteration
and assonance, and the exploitation of word-order variation for

pragmatic effects. Many of these characteristics can be found occasionally in literary prose; it is their frequency and accumulation that define the poetic register. Nor is this register merely a code for translating prose discourse into poetic form. It is the vehicle for distinctively poetic modes of argument. This is why we can hope to recover what a poem meant to the author who conceived it, including the occasional ambiguities and ambivalences that are in the text and not merely imposed by our own ignorance, incompetence or cultural preoccupations, only if we have some notion of what the poetic register was in detail and what its relationship was to contemporary prose usage. To attempt to articulate such a notion is the purpose of this essay.

INTRODUCTION

1.1. ON A NARROW DEFINITION poetic diction can be viewed simply as the words that are used exclusively or primarily in poetry or used in meanings that are not normal to them in prose discourse. A broader definition would include also phonetic characteristics, the patterns of sound that are created in the choice and organization of the vocabulary, most conspicuously those dictated by metrical conventions, and grammatical distinctions exhibited in the choice of morphological forms and syntactic structures.[1] In general the distinguishing characteristics are not the presence or absence of a particular linguistic phenomenon but its relative frequency in comparison with prose.

1.2. The dividing line between the registers is often hard to draw. Some poetry can be classified as such only from its metrical form. Aristotle's judgement on Empedocles may have been too severe — οὐδὲν δὲ κοινόν ἐστιν Ὁμήρῳ καὶ Ἐμεδοκλεῖ πλὴν τὸ μέτρον, διὸ τὸν μὲν ποιητὴν δίκαιον καλεῖν, τὸν δὲ φυσιολόγον μᾶλλον ἢ ποιητήν (*Po.* 1447b) — but there are certainly passages in the Sicilian philosopher, as in his illustrious Latin admirer Lucretius, that can only be described as versified prose.[2] However, the important qualification that Aristotle apparently made to his judgement on Empedocles, — δεινὸς περὶ τὴν φράσιν γέγονεν, μεταφορητικός τε ὢν καὶ τοῖς ἄλλοις τοῖς περὶ ποιητικὴν ἐπιτεύγμασι χρώμενος (*ap.* D.L. 8.57) — applies far more aptly to Lucretius. A didactic poem that is concerned primarily with conveying information and expounding basic scientific or philo-

---

[1] The importance of *all* areas of linguistic usage in defining the poetic register is well stressed by Janssen (1941: 14, 35).
[2] A clear distinction is drawn in Sanskrit between scientific treatises in verse and true poetry *kāvyam*.

sophical theory simply cannot operate, like Virgil's *Georgics*, at a consistently high poetic level. The effective style must be objective and univocal, not metaphoric, allusive and subjective. Coleridge was right to insist[3] that the fundamental distinction is between poetry and science, not poetry and prose.

1.3. To take an example from English, the couplet *True Wit is Nature to advantage dress'd, / What oft was thought, but ne'er so well express'd* (Pope, *Essay on Criticism* 297–8) may seem little more than a versified alternative to *True Wit is Nature dressed to advantage, What was often thought, but never expressed so well*, as Johnson's paraphrase *Wit is that which has been often thought, but was never before so well expressed*[4] clearly reveals. The sentiment is not especially poetic and the only properties of the poetic register are the use of *oft* and *ne'er* for *often* and *never*, the reminder in the spelling of *dress'd* and *express'd* that the archaic variant of syllabic *-ed* was still available to poets as in *learned* beside *unlearn'd* (*ibid.* 327), and the placing of the two participles in phrase-final position, a poetic order in itself but here used to secure the rhyme that is essential to the verse form. There are many couplets like this in Pope but few readers would subscribe to Matthew Arnold's description[5] of Pope and Dryden as 'classics of our prose'.

1.4. On the other side we can point to many passages of high literary prose that have more in common with the poetic register. The links are explicit in the view expressed by Antonius in Cic. *De or.* 2.34, *qui enim cantus moderata oratione dulcior inueniri potest? quod carmen artificiosa uerborum conclusione aptius?* and Quintilian's famous description of historiography as *proxima poetis et quodam modo carmen solutum* (10.1.31), following the line taken by 'Antonius' again in the discussion of *historia* at *De or.* 2.51–64. The comparison is of course stylistic, but it applies also to the subject matter of historiography, which has replaced epic as the medium in which the myths and ideologies of a society are projected on to that society's past by some of its major creative writers.[6]

1.5. It is interesting that Aristotle (*ap.* D.L. 8.57 again) described Empedocles as the inventor of ῥητορική, in view of the modern tendency to

---

[3] The most comprehensive exposition is in *Biographia Literaria*, especially chapter 14.

[4] *Lives of the English Poets: Life of Cowley* (World's Classics edn., Oxford 1952) I.13.

[5] *The Study of Poetry. Essays in Criticism, Second Series* (London, 1905) 42. The remark must be seen in the context of Arnold's general argument that poetry was replacing religion and philosophy as the complement to science, continuing the viewpoint held by Wordsworth and Coleridge.

[6] For poetry as the intellectual nucleus of prehistoric society see Meillet (1965: 121–3) and Watkins (1982: 1989). This nucleic status is recoverable in a number of poetic words and phrases in Latin, Greek, Sanskrit, Old English etc. that can be traced back to Proto-Indo-European. See the detailed discussions in Schmitt (1967) and Watkins (1982, 1989).

polarize ῥητορική and ποιητική and both with φυσιολογία (cf. the Aristotle citation in §1.2). In fact many important discussions of the ingredients of the poetic register are found in works on rhetoric, modern as well as ancient. Nor should we be surprised, since poetry and prose alike share the three classic aims of linguistic communication, to be pursued severally or in combination — *ut doceat, ut moueat, ut delectet.*

1.6. Even outside the literary registers the boundaries between prose and poetry are often hard to draw. In many cultures the rhetoric of religious prayer, secular proclamations etc. have a strongly poetic character. In Latin the *Carmen Fratrum Arualium* (*CIL* I²2) is clearly composed in verse triads of some sort, but the corrupt text prevents useful analysis. No less clearly the prayer at the *lustratio agri* cited by Cato (*Agr.* 141) is in prose: *Mars pater, te precor quaesoque uti sies uolens propitius mihi domo familiaeque nostrae . . . uti tu morbos uisos inuisosque uiduertatem uastitudinemque calamitates intemperiasque prohibessis defendas auerruncesque, utique tu fruges frumenta uineta uirgultaque grandire beneque euenire siris . . .* This rhythmic and formulaic prose, enriched with alliteration, assonance, rhyme and etymological word-play (cf. §§16–18), can be paralleled in the ritual passages of the Umbrian Iguvine Tables, and so belongs to the Italic liturgical tradition. The rhythmic prose of the Christian *Te Deum*, composed in the fifth century AD belongs to the same tradition.[7]

1.7. The same very rhythmic character is found in political rituals, recalling the close connection between the religious and the secular in earlier societies. For instance the *Formula Patris Patrati* for declaration of war (Livy 1.32.7ff): *audi Iuppiter et tu Iane Quirine deique omnes caelestes uosque terrestres uosque inferni audite. ego uos testor populum illum iniustum esse neque ius persoluere . . . si ego iniuste impieque illos homines illasque res dedier mihi exposco, tum patriae compotem me numquam siris esse.*[8] It is not surprising to find such productions classed as *carmina* in classical Latin.

1.8. It is worth reminding ourselves at this point that in the linguistic characterization of the elevated registers that we have been looking at both stand well apart from the *sermo cottidianus* of the mass of the population. This is not so much because the characteristic features of ordinary conversation — false starts, nonce mispronunciations, abrupt and

---

[7] Traditionally attributed to St Ambrose and St Augustine, it is probably the work of Bishop Niceta of Remesiana or a contemporary. For the rhetorical shaping of Christian collects see Coleman (1987: 45–7).

[8] See Gordon Williams (Kenney–Clausen (1982: 53–5)). The use of *carmen* of the Twelve Tables, however, more likely refers to its mode of recitation by schoolboys: the fragments show plenty of formulaic composition but nothing rhythmic enough to parallel the versified laws of certain early Germanic societies.

ungrammatical transitions, anacolutha, rambling pleonasm and banal repetition, not to mention mere noise, the Latin equivalent of '*er*... *um*...
ah...' — have not survived. Even in a living language such phenomena,
ruthlessly exposed in oral recording, are usually edited out of transcripts.
It is rather that even the most realistic passages of Roman comedy, say,
are already creative adaptations of what such transcripts would have
looked like. In fact we do not possess a single example of real everyday
conversation from any language before the invention of the phonograph.
Even the most vulgar Pompeian graffiti were after all written by literates
and subject to conventional literacy pressures.

1.9. The gap is considerable. Every sample of a language at whatever
level of performance, whether it is intended for ephemeral communication
at the oral level or for permanent accessibility in written form, belongs
ultimately to the same linguistic system and must be taken account of in
any description of the language claiming to be comprehensive. There is a
fashion among some linguists for giving more attention to the ephemeral
or casual discourse as being more representative of the way most native
speakers use their language. Telephone conversations then become more
important than contemporary works of literature. This view is mistaken if
we are concerned to explore the full communicative resources available
in the phonology, grammar and lexicon of the language. We can properly
lament the absence of transcripts from the conversation of Latin farmers
or artisans, but the surviving text of the *Aeneid* yields far more information
about the character and potentialities of the Latin language.[9] The higher
literary registers may well be deviations from the norms of ordinary written
Latin and of the spoken Latin that we can only infer from it, but they are
ultimately much more revealing to philologists and linguists.

2.1. Any attempt to define the poetic register and the nature of poetic
diction runs into a number of practical problems. Apart from the differences between poetic and prose discourse, which is the chief concern of
this essay, there are for instance the variations between the poetic genres
themselves that are stressed by ancient theorists. *Sua cuique proposito lex,
suus decor est, nec comoedia in cothurnos adsurgit nec contra tragoedia
socco ingreditur*, writes Quintilian (10.2.22), summarizing the doctrine of
stylistic *decorum*, τὸ πρέπον, already alluded to in Plato's *Laws* 700a–b.
The classic statement for later ages was Horace's (*A.P.* 73–98). The conven-

---

[9] Throughout this essay examples are taken mostly from the central classical authors, Lucretius and Catullus, Propertius and Ovid and above all Virgil and Horace, who as a group
represent the Latin poetic register at its richest.

tions were not of course totally rigid for all times, but as with, say, the sonnet form or the nineteenth-century symphony, innovations were generally made in the context of adherence to what had gone before.

2.2. Poetic discourse is of course an occasional mode of communication. It is not the way poets talk or write all the time but the product of a consciously creative process that is activated only on particular occasions. Yet there must always be a considerable input from their own normal and largely unconscious linguistic habits. If we have no other representative of their idiolectal practice, there is a very real danger of confusing these linguistic habits with the linguistic peculiarities of the poetic register in which they are composing.

2.3. Sometimes we have the chance to compare a poet's Latinity in different literary registers, e.g. Seneca's tragedies, philosophical treatises and letters. Again there may be an opportunity to compare contemporaries or near contemporaries writing in the same genre, as for instance the Augustan elegists, where we are also able to make comparisons between *Amores* and *Metamorphoses*. Where material is more sparse the problems become more acute. We have perhaps good reason to infer that Lucretius was an archaist, Catullus an innovator, but what is the norm against which these classifications are made?

2.4. Even more vexing is the situation in the early decades of the second century BC, a formative period for the Latin literary register. We have the comedies of Plautus and the fragments of Ennius' work in divers genres, many of them cited by later authors precisely because they exhibit linguistic eccentricity or provide a precedent for some anomalous usage in a classical author. (It is striking how much less strange most of the citations made by literary commentators, antiquarians or orators turn out to be.) But there is nothing much beside, not even in prose, except for a few inscriptions, including the *Senatus consultum de Bacchanalibus*, which certainly deserves a place in the history of literary Latin as the most elaborate piece of *oratio obliqua* before Caesar. Non-epigraphic prose is represented by Cato's *De agri cultura*, which hardly counts as literature, and the fragments of history and oratory by various authors (as well as the material cited in §§1.6, 7) which certainly do. But the latter have been too corrupted in the manuscript tradition and by ancient editorial revision to provide as firm a basis for comparison as is needed. So there is no real touchstone by which to distinguish the early Latin poetic register from early Latin as a whole. What sort of a picture would we have of Augustan Latin, say, if all that survived were the elegies of Propertius, some fragments of Horace and a handful of inscriptions?

2.5. The diachronic problems are of course even more imposing. For the history of English or French we have a sufficiently large and varied body of material to be able to plot changes in the phonology, grammar and lexicon with some degree of confidence. But for Latin the first surviving attestation of a phenomenon must generally be interpreted as an innovation only with the utmost caution. Conversely what is found at an early date but is then not attested for several centuries can be classed at its reappearance as an archaism only on the assumption that its intervening absence from the records is accidental. Finally what is distinctly poetic at one period may not have been so at an earlier or later stage in the language. Much of what follows must be read with these important qualifications in mind.

2.6. One area of linguistic behaviour that does not impinge upon the literary registers is that of dialect. There is no trace of a Latin Robert Burns, let alone anything like the ancient Greek association of regional dialects, artificial and selective to be sure, with specific literary genres. Sappho's Aeolic, the Doric of Alcman and Theocritus, the Ionic of Archilochus etc. not only characterized their own poetry but the subsequent tradition of the respective genres as well. Popular regional poetry there must have been in Latin, but no record of it survives, and ambitious poets from the regions came to Rome for their education and wrote in the *sermo urbanus* of the capital.[10] Whatever Pollio meant by *patauinitas* (Quint. 1.5.56), the peculiarities of Livy's magnificent prose owe nothing to Padua. Dialect forms like Lucilius' *Cecilius pretor* (1130) are satiric and merely underline the disdainful attitude of *urbanitas* to *rusticitas*. Most of the major Latin authors from Plautus and Ennius onwards were Italians or provincials, not Romans, but in literature as in so much else in the Roman culture centralization came early and remained, being receptive to external influence only from Greek.

SOUNDS AND PATTERNS OF SOUND

3.1. The first and most clear-cut definition of the poetic register is phonetic.[11] Poetry was distinguished from prose by the recurrence of regular rhythmic patterns that marked the boundaries of verses and groups of verses, and influenced the choice of word order within the verse.

---

[10] Cicero's reference to *Cordubae natis poetis, pingue quiddam sonantibus atque peregrinum* (*Arch.* 26) seems to be a comment on regional pronunciation rather than on departure from *urbanitas* in the Iberian Latin poets' habits of composition.

[11] The relevance of the sound of Latin to all aspects of poetry and literary prose is abundantly demonstrated in Wilkinson (1963).

3.2. Oratorical prose was also highly rhythmical. The classical *clausulae*, marking the cadences of clauses and sentences, have been well researched, but one can often detect rhythmic patterns extending over large sections of the sentence, which can hardly be coincidental. Cicero cites a sentence from Crassus in which the *numerus* appears to be *non quaesitus*: 'nam ubi lubido dominatur, innocentiae leue praesidium est' (*Or.* 219). The sequence of third paeon, dactyl and trochee (an echo here of the hexameter cadence mischievously hinting at the *licentia* of poets?), two trochees, dactyl and choriamb is deploying aural effects redolent more of lyric poetry than of any prose idiom. Or consider the rhythmic structure of one of Cicero's youthful tricola: *nam commoditati ingenium, grauitati aetas, libertati tempora sunt impedimento (Rosc. Am. 9)*, with its sequence of spondee, anapaest and choriamb, anapaest and spondee, two spondees, choriamb, cretic and spondee. Phrases like *uersus... propemodum* and *numeros quosdam* were not lightly used to describe the best prose style (*De or.* 3.173).

3.3. The effect of such rhythmic sequences delivered in the mannered style that characterized public oratory must have been comparable to that of a poetic recitation (cf. Cic. *Or.* 55–60, Quint. 10.1.16–17). Nevertheless the fundamental division remains: verse rhythms, as Cicero explicitly recognized (*Or.* 195), fell into finite, regularly repetitive patterns.

4.1. From Plautus and Ennius onwards the literary metres were all Greek. Although syllabic weight, based on vowel length and consonontal content, was a phonological property of Latin as of every human language, its use as the basis of metre was adopted along with the verse forms themselves from the Greek tradition. The binary classification into light and heavy syllables was an oversimplification and a matter of convention, as indeed was the placing of syllable divisions; cf. *pa-tris* with a light initial, *pat-ris* with a heavy (see §6.2) but only *lap-sus*.

4.2. The only difference between the two languages that had a bearing on versification was that of accent. The Greek tonal accent was of no metrical significance, though of course it provided a melodic line, both in poetry and prose, that was foreign to Latin. Against this the Latin stress accent did have metrical implications, since it had some effect upon vowel length (see §§10–11) and, more importantly, set up a dynamic pattern that corresponded only partially and accidentally to the pattern of quantitative rhythm. Thus we can represent a line like *Tityre tu patulae recubans sub tegmine fagi* as

To this typical interaction between stress and quantity we must return (§4.6). For the present we need only note this as a new element in the adopted Greek metres, just as the quantitative basis probably was in Latin versification.

4.3. The native verse forms seem to have been based, like the Germanic ones, on a fixed number of syllables and word-stresses in each verse. Thus the Saturnian verse would have been divided by a caesura into two parts, a seven-syllable group with three stresses and a six-syllable group with two stresses, or something of the sort;[13] e.g. Livius Andronicus' *uírum míhi Caména ínsece uersútum* and *tópper cíti ad aédis uénimus Circái*, where it is assumed that the initial syllable stress had already been replaced by 'the rule of the penultimate', and Naevius' *nóctu Troíad exíbant capítibus opértis*, alongside the earliest surviving Scipio epitaph (*CIL* I²9), *hónc oíno ploírume coseńtiont R[ománe]*etc.

4.4. It was presumably in Saturnian verses that the *clarorum uirorum laudes* recited at banquets before Cato's lifetime (Cic. *Brut.* 75, Varro *ap.* Non. s.v. *assa uoce*) were handed down, to find their way via the annalists into the pages of Livy.[14] How long Saturnians survived in epigraphic *elogia* we do not know, but the rejection of the old metre for the elegiac couplet on the epitaph for Scipio Hispanus (*CIL* I²15, after 139 BC) may be significant. The replacement of Saturnians by the dactylic hexameter for narrative poetry in the *Annales* of Ennius was certainly decisive.

4.5. In fact the abandonment of a stress-based system of versification for a quantitative one was facilitated by accidental similarities in the stress patterns of the two major verse forms concerned. For many of Ennius' hexameters are characterized by a similar stress pattern to that assumed

---

[12] The choice of musical notation does not imply that Latin poetry was normally sung or chanted, though there is evidence that some pieces were sung — e.g. the distinction between the metrically freer *cantica* and the more strict *diuerbia* in Plautine comedy — and some maybe even mimed (Don. *Vita Virg.* 26). The musical notation has been used here because the interaction of stress patterns and temporal units is for modern European readers more familiar in music than in poetry.

[13] Basically this analysis derives from Lindsay (1893). Fixed syllable verses occur in Gatha-Avestan, combined with set quantitative patterns in Vedic and Aeolic Greek, with set stress patterns in Germanic. For further discussion of the Saturnian metre with different conclusions see Pasquali–Timpanaro (1981).

[14] Niebuhr's hypothesis has never quite recovered from Schwegler's criticisms. See Momigliano (1957) for a modern critical but sympathetic discussion. The certified parallels in other Indo-European cultures and the absence of any other obvious vehicle for the stories of Romulus, Horatius etc. to have survived into the historiographical tradition have ensured that the hypothesis retains its sympathizers.

for the Saturnian;[15] e.g. *Músae quae pédibus mágnum pulsátis Olúmpum* and *transnáuit cíta per téneras calíginis aúras* and *tália tum mémorat lácrumans, extérrita sómno* (*Ann.* 1, 18, 35 Sk). The increased number of syllables in the dactylic hexameter (the three examples cited have respectively 14, 15 and 16) made a limit of five stresses untenable and the frequency of a penthemimeral main caesura altered the distribution of stresses between the two 'halves' of the verse. Nevertheless the stress patterns that were a distinctive feature of the native poesy remained the distinguishing feature of Latin hexameters against their Greek models.

4.6. The interaction between word stress and syllabic quantity in the Latin hexameter yields three possibilities, for which there would be no precedent in Greek. First a homodyne pattern, in which the stress coincides with the fixed heavy syllable of the foot, as in *Músae* and *pulsátis Olúmpum*. Homodyne rhythms are frequent in the first and fourth feet of classical hexameters, almost invariable in the fifth and sixth.[16] Indeed in some of the more vulgar epigraphic verses that survive it is only the concluding rhythm to each line ⊲ ⌣ ⌣ ⊲ - that confirms the composer's metrical intentions. Secondly a heterodyne pattern, in which the stress falls on the second or third syllable of the foot, as in *quae pédibus mágnum*. Heterodynes were most frequent in the second and third feet, as here. Thirdly a neutral pattern, which has either no stress at all within the foot, as in *magnùm pùlsatis*, or two stresses, as in *arma uirúmque cáno*.

4.7. Homodynes obviously underlined the time signature of the metre, heterodynes obscured it. Virgil, perhaps uniquely, seems to have employed varying patterns of distribution of the three possibilities for expressive effect. Thus in *ímpius haéc tam cúlta nouália míles habébit?* (*E.* 1.70) the six homodynes, four of them dactyls, seem expressive of agitated despair. By contrast in the well known onomatopoeia of *quádrupedánte pútrem sónitu quátit úngula cámpum* (*A.* 8.596) the prevalent dactylic rhythm, strongly marked by the first and fifth-foot homodynes, is blurred by the neutral second foot and the heterodyne third and fourth, and the aural effect is — perhaps appropriately — more confused. All this presupposes of course retention of the normal Latin accent in the recitation of verse.[17]

---

[15] For a partial anticipation of this view see Bartalucci (1968), who however sees the similarities as due to the influence of one metre upon the other.

[16] For the hypothesis that in Indo-European poetics the latter part of the verse was more regular metrically than the earlier part see Lotz's discussion of metric typology in Sebeok (1960: 135–48, esp. 136).

[17] For an argument in favour of a metrical ictus of some sort distinct from word accent, based on the possibility of resolving the second but not the first heavy syllable of each hexameter foot except the last, see Allen (1978: 92–4). For a general discussion of Latin hexameter rhythm see Allen (1973: 335–59).

5.1. Very few Latin lexemes are unmetrical in all their grammatical forms, if one does not confine eligibility to dactylic metres. Pacuvius' line *Nerei repandirostrum incuruiceruicum pecus* is a regular trochaic tetrameter, though the two adjectival compounds censured by Quintilian (1.5.67) are ineligible for dactylic verse. Because dactylic metres, employed in hexameter and elegiac poems, were so prominent in classical literature, a large number of words that could in no other sense be considered unpoetic were excluded by their syllabic composition. Thus *cognitio* and *uoluptas* are acceptable in all their cases, *notio* and *suauitas* in none.

5.2. Frequently it was only particular grammatical forms that were excluded. While *audimus* and *audit* were acceptable, *audiunt* was not; nor was *audio* without clumsy elision into a following light syllable. Tribrachs were more easily elided, e.g. *agere*, but were intractable in prefinal position, e.g. *celeritas*.

5.3. Various expedients were adopted to overcome this problem. One was to employ a synonym.[18] Where the meaning is very close, nothing is lost in the process. The well established functional convergence between the originally distinct action nouns in *-tio* and *-tus* enabled Lucretius to use for instance *iniectus* in place of *iniectio animi* to translate Epicurus' ἐπιβολὴ τῆς διανοίας without creating any semantic problems. In contrast to the classical and post-classical periods *-tu-* had been the more prominent in early Latin. So the metrically acceptable variant also contributed to the archaic tone that the poet consistently sought in promoting this very unRoman philosophy and projecting a high seriousness that distanced his work from the *nugae* of the contemporary *poetae noui*.

5.4. Again nothing is lost when a cretic rhythm is avoided by a tmesis, which recalls the precompounding stage of the language, e.g. *inque pediri* (Lucr. 3.484) or *inque salutatam linquo* (Virg. A. 9.288), where the archaic effect is enhanced by the presence of the uncompounded finite verb, and *inque ligatus / cedebat* (A. 10.794–5), where the figure is combined with the old meaning of *cedere*. On the other hand the replacement of *imperator* by the archaic *induperator* imports an archaic tone that the poet may not want. Characteristically Juvenal exploits the satiric possibilities against Domitian (unnamed of course) in *Sat.* 4.28–9, *qualis tunc epulas ipsum gluttisse putamus / induperatorem*, combining the mock-heroic grandiloquence of the archaic form with the distinctly subliterary verb *gluttire*.

5.5. Substitution may however blur a semantic distinction, as when the intractable *ārbŏrēs* 'trees' is replaced by the plesionym *arbusta*, plural of the collective *arbustum* 'a cluster of trees'. The peculiarly Roman connotations of *imperator* are lost when it is replaced by the less specific *ductor*

---

[18] See Leumann (1959: 147–8).

or *dux*, and there is again a loss of precision. We may contrast the nice use of the more generic word in Lucretius' *ductores Danaum* (1.86) to recall Δαναῶν ἡγήτορες (*Iliad* 11.816).

5.6. Even clearer examples are to be found in Lucretius' use of *maximitas* (2.498) to replace *magnitudo*, where a comparative implication 'the state of being largest' is introduced irrelevantly. The intensive force of the *-tare* suffix (cf. *dicto, dictito* with *dico*) is weakened by its use to maintain metricality, e.g. *nominitamus* (Lucr. 3.352; cf. *CIL* I²1221). The problem was of course particularly troublesome for a poet confronted with the highly nominalizing terminology of philosophical discourse and compelled into neologisms like *differitas* for *differentia* and *uariantia* for *uarietas* (and *uariatio*), neither of which however poses the same semantic queries. (For unmetrical inflections see §§13.4, 14.1–3).

5.7. The use of tropes like metaphor and metonymy for metrical purposes can gain advantage from the semantic imprecision (see §§29, 32). Thus the metonymy of *thalamus, thalami* for *nuptiae* (Virg. *A.* 4.550, Ov. *M.* 6.700) offers the poet both an evocative image and at the same time the exotic colour of a Greek loan-word.

6.1. Phonetic expedients are sometimes adopted to cope with the unmetrical. The most radical, employed almost exclusively with proper names, is to alter a vowel length. Thus *Itălĭam* has its initial vowel lengthened in Virg. *A.* 1.2 etc., following Callimachean precedent (*H.* 3.58), as Catullus had already done with *Ītalorum* (1.5). It is worth noting that Virgil (*A.* 3.185) chooses the long vowel in *Ītala regna* to secure the plural phrase where the normal *Ĭtalum regnum* could have been accommodated in a hexameter. The similar device in Greek, e.g. Σῑκελίδᾱν (Theocr. *Id.* 7.40) beside Σῐκελούς (Hom. *Od.* 20.383) would have been a reassuring precedent for Latin poets. So we find *Sīcelides* and *Sĭculis* in Virg. *E.* 4.1, 2.21. The impossibility of accommodating the cretic *Scipio* or any of its cases is overcome by the use of the Greek patronymic suffix, *noster Scipiadas*[19] (Lucil. 1139), *geminos . . . Scipiadas* (Virg. *A.* 6.843), which of course has the additional effect of associating the family with the Homeric heroes. *Pollio* can appear in dactylic verse only in the nominative, and then only by a harsh elision (for unattested substitution of the glide *i̯* see §9.2), e.g.

---

[19] *-as* is strange. *-άδᾱς* (or *-άδᾱ* in some early W. Greek inscriptions) would be the regular Greek form outside Attic-Ionic, and if the suffix became known first from Italian Doric dialects, it would have been early enough to have undergone assimilation to Latin *-adă*. We should expect therefore either *Scipiadēs* (metrical) or *Scipiadă* (unmetrical). On Greek inflection see §§15, 27.

Pollio et ipse, Pollio et incipient (Virg. *E.* 3.86, 4.12), or by shortening the final vowel, *Polliŏ* (Hor. *S.* 1.10.42; cf. *C.* 2.1.14).

6.2. There is no evidence for any specifically poetic pronunciations apart from those just noted, though we may infer from the accounts of oratorical delivery supplied by Cicero (*Or.* 57) and Quintilian (1.8.2; cf. §3.3) that poetic verses were also delivered with distinctly artful and unprosaic intonations. Synizesis and vowel contraction, as in *dī, īs* for *dĕī, ĕīs*, and *ădicere* for *adiicere* (cf. Manil. 4.44 with Gellius 4.17.1–8) are likely to have begun in colloquial usage. Some instances however, like *eādem* (Lucr. 4.744), *aureā* (Virg. *A.* 1.698), are likely to have been inspired as much by Greek models. In fact the great majority of phonetic devices for overcoming unmetricality can be directly linked to known facts of ordinary Latin speech. Even the variation in the treatment of 'mute plus liquid' clusters between, for instance, the normal *uólu-crem* and the occasional *uolúc-res* (Virg. *A.* 11.858, 4.525; see Quintilian 1.5.28) may be a reflection of contemporary speech variants rather than a contrast between current and archaic metrical conventions. Elision, for instance, was certainly a feature of the spoken language, though in educated usage the elided syllable was rarely totally omitted.[20]

7.1. Examples occur of pronunciations that were obsolete in current speech being preserved in poetry. This is merely a special case of the general distinguishing characteristic of the poetic register, that all earlier poetry is, or can be made by poet or reader, contemporary poetry. The language of earlier poets is thus a reservoir on which each new generation of poets can draw.

7.2. The early Latin treatment of final -*s* following a short vowel is instructive.[21] Before *c.* 240 BC it was regularly omitted in writing before a following initial consonant, e.g. *Cornelio L. f.* on the earliest surviving Scipio epitaph, *CIL* I²8. All the available evidence indicates that the consonant was retained where a vowel followed, — a situation complementary to that of -*m*, which was lost before a vowel and retained, at least as a nasal adjunct to the vowel, before a consonant. Examples certainly occur in the comic poets at verse ends, a well-known location for archaisms, e.g. *occidisti(s) me* (Pl. *Ba.* 313), *tempu(s) fert* (Ter. *Ad.* 839).[22] However, it is likely that the phenomenon also occurred elsewhere in the verse, but

---

[20] The whole subject of elision in Latin poetry is fully treated by Soubiran (1966).
[21] For further examples and discussion see Leumann (1977: 227–8).
[22] See Lindsay (1922: 126–135).

because of the range of permissible metrical variants certification is impossible.

7.3. Final *s* is consistently written in inscriptions from the end of the third century BC onwards, assisted no doubt in literary texts and official epigraphy by Greek models. It continues to be written throughout the classical and post-classical periods. Its restoration in pronunciation, though guaranteed for educated speech by classical verse, may not have been universal in the dialects. Cicero (*Or.* 161) describes its omission as *iam subrusticum* but *olim politius*, citing Ennius' *omnibu(s) princeps.*

7.4. This last example is typical of Ennius' *Annales*, e.g. *suauis homo facundu(s) suo contentu(s) beatus* (280 Sk), though there are a few exceptions, e.g. *uolauit auis. simul* (87 Sk), *Laurentis terra* (30 Sk). The omissions in lines like Lucilius' *uita illa dignu(s) locoque* (cited in Cic. *Or.* 161), *laterali(s) dolor, certissimu(s) nuntiu(s) mortis* (cited by Marius Victorinus 6.217 K) are unlikely at this date to be reflections of colloquial urban usage and are better taken as echoes of Ennian epic.

7.5. In poetry of the late republican period omission is very rare. Catullus' unique *dabi(s) supplicium*, a special case with its successive sibilants, occurs at the end of some invective against Gellius (116.8) for rejecting the poet's neoteric interests. The piquancy of the usage here comes from the disdain of the *poetae noui* for such archaisms (cf. *Or.* 161 again).[23] As befitting the epic style of didactic poetry, -*s* is occasionally omitted by Lucretius, e.g. *ex omnibu(s) rebus, infantibu(s) paruis* (1.159, 186), and by Cicero, e.g. *lustratu(s) nitore, Aquiloni(s) locatae* (*Arat.* 92, 97). However, neoteric prejudice prevailed and even Virgil's passion for archaism and for specific echoes of Ennius did not induce him to employ what was now felt to be altogether too *subrusticum* for poetic usage.

8. Another group of archaisms involves the revival of long vowels in final syllables. Like the omission of -*s* this had the effect not of accommodating unmetrical words but of enabling metrically acceptable words to stand in places where it would not otherwise have been possible to place them. So Ennius could write (*Ann.* 108 Sk) *o pater, o genitōr, o sanguen dis oriundum*, taking advantage of the original long vowel, probably a recent archaism at this date, to place the word immediately before a vowel. The traditional label 'lengthening under ictus' misclassifies the phenomenon, which is rooted in the history of the language, with the *poetica licentia* of *Ῑtaliam* etc. (§6.1), which is not. There is moreover no evidence that ictus was a phonetic reality in classical antiquity, whatever its role may have

---

[23] The frequency of *qui sit* in Cicero and other prose writers may represent *qui(s) sit* or *quī sit.*

been in later conventions of reading quantitative verse (see §4.7 fin.) Some
of the instances are in any event not 'under ictus'. Thus Ennius has *essēt
induperator* and *ponebāt ante salutem* (*Ann.* 78, 364 Sk). The lengthening
is frequent in Plautus, e.g. *non uxōr eram* and *alienum arāt, incultum*
(*Asin.* 927, 874). The archaism survives into the classical poets, including
Lucretius and Virgil, who has many instances, e.g. *aberāt. ipsae* (*E.* 1.38)
uidēt, hominesne and *pauōr et plurima* and *amittebāt oculusque* (*A.* 1.308,
2.369, 5.853). Outside the epic tradition the variant may be used to evoke
Antiquity, as in Propertius' description of early Rome (4.1.17) *nulli cura
fuīt externos quaerere diuos*. Here *fuīt* < *fueit* (cf. *fuǐt* < *fuet*), but some
instances of lengthening are merely analogical, as *manusque sinīt. hinc* and
frater, erīt? o quae (*A.* 10.433, 12.883), unless we envisage the vowel being
checked by final *-t* before a pause.

9.1. Sometimes advantage is taken of free variants available in the ordinary
spoken language, in particular the ambivalence of *i* and *u*, which may be
consonantal or vocalic. So Virgil's *abịete* for *ăbǐětě* and *Lauinịaque* for
Lauīnǐăquĕ (*A.* 2.16, 1.2) to accommodate otherwise unmetrical words,
Ennius' *auịum* and *insidịantes* (*Ann.* 89, 425 Sk) and Horace's *principịum*
for *princǐpǐum* (*C.* 3.6.6 Alcaics), to enable particular placings in the verse.
Ennius has *quattụor* for *quattŭor* (*Ann.* 88 Sk), Catullus has the archaisms
solŭit and *peruolŭent* (2.13, 95.6) for the usual *solụit, peruolụent*, which
are of course not in themselves unmetrical. Lucretius uses *tenụia* for
unmetrical *tĕnŭǐă* (4.66) and conversely *sŭadent* (4.1157), Virgil *genụa*
for *gĕnŭă* (*A.* 5.432), Horace *silŭae* for *silụae* (*Epod.* 13.2). Palatalized
forms in Romance like *grace, prezzo* (<*gratia, pretium*) imply a shift from
tǐ to *tị* to *tš*, which is attested in isolated vulgar forms from the imperial
period, and was already acceptable in educated speech by the late fifth
century, as we can see from manuscript and epigraphic confusions of
e.g. *condicio* and *conditio*, set beside statements by grammarians such as
Papirianus (*ap.* Cassiod. 7.216 K).

9.2. It is surprising that, given the precedent of Ennius' *insidịantes* and
Virgil's *abịete*, the consonantal variant was not used to overcome the
unmetricality of *oratio, auditio* etc. (cf. §5.1, 3). It may be that *orātịo* etc.
in classical times had still a hint of vulgarism, and the few instances of
comparable phenomena perhaps confirm this, e.g. from Pompeii *otịosis
locus hic non est. discede, morator* (*CIL* IV.813) and the spellings *ActIani,
ClaudIanum* beside *digredIens, facIo*.[24] Whatever the reason, occasional

---

[24] See Väänänen (1966: 34–6).

substitutions of - ˘ for ˘ ˘ ˘ (*abiete*) and of - - for - ˘ ˘ (*principium*) were acceptable, but - - for - ˘ - (*Pollio, otiosi*) was not.

10.1. One particular example of the introduction of current habits of pronunciation has attracted much scholarly attention: the so-called iambic shortening by which unstressed final vowels are regularly shortened in *bene, duo, ego, modo, nisi, scio, uolo* etc., often also in *fero, mihi, uide, ubi*. In fact it is verse texts that enable us to plot the distribution and history of this and related phenomena in Latin, though of course the earliest attestations provide only a *terminus ante quem* for the respective changes in ordinary speech (cf. §2.5). Instances abound in the classical poets. In early Latin verse the phenomenon is even more widely attested, e.g. *domĭ* (Pl. *Mil.* 192), *abĭ, darĭ, lupŏ* (Ter. *Ph.* 59, *Ad.* 311, *Eun.* 832) and *sicutĭ, quasĭ* (Enn. *Ann.*, 522, 542 Sk).

10.2. Phonetically this change belongs with the general reduction of unaccented vowels that is typical of languages with a strong stress accent. In Latin this reduction had led at a time when the stress apparently fell on initial syllables to such changes as **konfăkiont* > *conficiunt, *exkaidet* > *excīdit, *obklaussom* > **occlūsum*. Such shortening affected both pre- as well as post-accentual long vowels, resulting for instance in an initial tribrach in *amicítiam* (Pl. *Merc.* 846). That the tendency continued into post-classical Latin is confirmed by Consentius (5.392 K), who like St Augustine (*D.Chr.* 4.10.24) regards *ŏrător* as *uitium Afrorum* along with the lengthenings in *pīper, pīces*. It is not surprising to find so many examples of *breuis breuians* in the comic poets, *apud quos, nisi quod uersiculi sunt, nihil est aliud cottidiani dissimile sermonis* (Cic. *Or.* 67), but its occurrence in the tragedies of Ennius[25] shows how close poetic discourse in general was to common speech.

10.3. This phonetic shortening of long vowels was extended however to the treatment of heavy syllables adjacent to the accent as metrically light. Thus the light syllables underlined in <u>ĕx</u> ŏre orationem (Enn. *tr.* 258J), sĕn<u>ĕx</u>, uĕ<u>lĭnt</u> (Pl. *Mo.* 952, *Cu.* 268), ă<u>dĕst</u> (*tr.* 41J) uŏ<u>lŭptă</u>tĕs, gŭbĕr<u>nă</u>bunt (Pl. *Am.* 939, *Mi.* 1091). These extensions cannot be attributed to any plausible phonetic reality.[26] The only way to lighten such syllables would have been to reduce the consonant cluster following the vowel, e.g. **ades* or **uolutates*.

10.4. In fact Ritschl proposed just such an explanation for pyrrhic *uelĭnt, ferŭnt* etc., citing *dedrot, dedro* from the Pisaurian dialect (*CIL*

[25] The tragic fragments are cited from Jocelyn's edition (1969), as those of the *Annales* are from Skutsch's (1986: 59–61).
[26] As Lindsay (1922: 7) already observed.

I²378, 379). Other early forms like *dedron* from Rome and *coraueron*, *dedero* from Praeneste (*CIL* I²30, 59, 61) might also be cited, but the restoration of *-nt* at Rome and the survival of the nasal into Romance justifies Lindsay's scepticism. In any case Ritschl's hypothesis would not account for anapaests like *bŏuĕs qūi* (Pl. *Ps.* 812) or pyrrhics like *bŏnĭs* in Terence's *ex Graecis bonis Latinas* (*Eun.* 8), which is surely calculated to suggest the vulgarism of Latin-speaking *barbari*. Even a shortening of the long vowel in *-ēs*, *-īs* would still have left *bouĕs qui*, *bonĭs Latinas*, where we should have to assume the same loss of *-s* as after an original short vowel (§7.2–4) or some other equally unattested development. Praenestine *sueq. ede* for *sueisque eisdem* (*CIL* I²62) is inconclusive as to the length of the monophthong, and in any case we should need attestations from Rome to account for the massive literary incidence. The extension is much more likely to have been an artificial one, metrically motivated, and as such never belonged to the spoken language and did not survive into the classical poetic register.

10.5. At this point it is perhaps worth raising the question whether some of the instances of *breuis breuians* may in fact conceal peculiarities in early Latin pronunciation, for which we do have other evidence. Thus *duas secum* (*Rud.* 129) may be scanned not ⌣ ⌣ - - but ⌣ - - with *dų* for *dŭ*, *ille qui* (*Rud.* 1240) not ⌣ ⌣ - but - -, with apocope of *-e*. Sometimes an archaic form may have disappeared in the tradition. Thus *potest fieri prosus* (*Trin.* 730) may well conceal *pote fieri* with ellipse of *est* as in *Aul.* 309.[27] However, the volume of hard evidence is too large and its range, including all the pre-classical dramatic poets, too extensive to be greatly whittled away by alternative hypotheses. The shortening of final long vowels in dissyllabic words with which we began undoubtedly reflects ordinary speech habits: *benĕ*, *duŏ*, *egŏ* etc. were standard in classical poetry. Where the word belonged to or was in its usage associated with a paradigm, the length was retained: thus adverbial *citŏ*, *modŏ* but ablative *citō*, *modō*; *benĕ* but *probē*; *pută* 'for instance', *cauĕ sīs* 'look out please', all with specialized senses that detached them from the verbal paradigms to which they had originally belonged.

10.6. Sometimes poets exploit the availability of alternative forms, the one current, the other archaic, for metrical convenience or for expressive effect (cf. §12). The latter is seen in Virgil's *ualē ualĕ* (*E.* 3.79), the

---

[27] C. F. W. Müller (1869) based his Iambenkürzungsgesetz largely on metrical analysis, as did most of his successors, including even O. Skutsch (1934). It is surely time that the vast body of data assembled by Müller and the scholars who subsequently refined and modified the initial account was re-examined in the light of modern research both in early Latin metrics and more particularly in Latin historical linguistics. For a detailed examination of the relevant phonology see Allen (1973: 179–99).

former in Lucretius' *idque sibī solum per se sapit et sibĭ gaudet* (3.145) and
Propertius' *prora cubile mihī seu mihĭ puppis erit* (2.26.34), both rather
laboured lines, Catullus' *tepēfaciet* beside *madēfient* (64.360, 368), Ovid's
liquēfaciunt but *liquĕfiunt* (*M.* 7.161, *Pont* 1.2.55).

10.7. The extension of *-ŏ* beyond verbs of iambic shape like *ago, fero,
scio* is again to be seen as reflecting current speech. Thus we find in place
of cretic words with ⌣ ⌣ -, impossible in dactylic verse (see §6.1), *nesciŏ*
(Cat. 85.2), *dixerŏ, mentiŏ* (Hor. *S.* 1.4.104, 93), *desinŏ* (Tib. 2.6.41), *Polliŏ*
and *Scipiŏ* (Ov. *Ars* 3.410); even for spondaic words, ⌣ -, *findŏ* (Prop.
3.9.35), *tollŏ, estŏ* (Ov. *Am.* 3.2.26, *Tr.* 4.3.72); and thence for spondaic
ends to longer words *imagŏ, soluendŏ* (Sen. *Ag.* 874, *Oed.* 942), *properabŏ*
(Stat. *Th.* 2.342). The range of occurrence goes far beyond the genres in
which we should expect colloquialism. A striking instance of the early
adoption of a very colloquial pronunciation into the tradition of high
poetry is the use of *uidĕn*. The form reflects *uidḗsne > uidĕ́n > uídĕn*)
and is already attested in comedy, e.g. Pl. *Mil.* 219. It is used in highly
excited passages by Catullus (61.77, 62.8) and by Virgil in *A.* 6.779, where
the colloquial tone is enhanced by the indicative verb in the dependent
ut- clause. Virgil's context is Anchises' solemn address to his son, and
Servius notes the usage as Ennian, adding the interesting comment *adeo
eius est immutata natura ut iam ubique breuis inueniatur.* This situation
cannot have come about by the influence of Ennius and Virgil. It is
simply that between Virgil and Servius the boundary dividing literary from
colloquial had shifted, and it was no longer necessary, as it had been for
classical poets, to justify the presence of colloquialisms in elevated contexts
from ancient precedent. The use of a subjunctive in the *ut* clause by
Tibullus (2.1.26) and Silius (12.713) suggests a desire to tone down the
colloquialism. Finally, what is characteristic of the poetic register is not so
much the introduction of the shortened forms but the retention side by
side with them of the older forms, *egō, mihī* etc. and of course *canō* etc.,
where the analogy of other 1st sg. forms retarded the spread of *-ŏ;* a
reminder that in the poetic register nothing is ever obsolete.

11.1. Syncope of unstressed vowels was a feature of the spoken language
at all periods, with or without reduction of the resultant consonant clusters.
Prehistorically **dŭíiugai > bīgae, *ópifakīna > opifícīna* (Pl. *Mil.* 880) >
offícīna, *pósino > pōnō etc. In imperial Vulgar Latin *dóminus > domnus*
(perhaps already in Plautus, *Cas.* 722) *uíridis > uirdis, comparare > com-
prare* etc. Even in educated usage new examples continued to appear:
Augustus preferred *caldus* to *calidus* as being less *otiosum* (Quint. 1.6.19),
and *caldu* became the regular form in Vulgar Latin, whence *caldo* and

chaud. Quintilian himself preferred *audacter* to the unsyncopated form, which he regarded as *molestissima diligentiae peruersitas* (1.6.17 and 19), and the exclamatory *ualde* (< *ualide* Pl. *Am*. 1062) was normal in classical Latin alongside the adjective *ualidus*. The grammarian Caper (7.108K) regarded *balneae* as more correct than *balineae*, which was in fact the older form.

11.2. The availability of syncopated and unsyncopated forms, whether or not they were both current outside the poetic register, again provided useful metrical variants. Thus Plautus has colloquial *ardos* (*Pers*. 266) beside *aridi* (*Rud*. 574), and *surpuit* (*Capt*. 760), which must have been formed in the period of initial stress, from **súbrapuet*, like *captibus* from *capitibus*, if this is the correct form at Enn. *Ann*. 511 Sk; conversely archaic *dexteram* beside *dextras* (*Merc*. 149, 965), an alternation that survives into the classical poetic register, e.g. Horace's *dexterā* and the usual *dextrā* (*C*. 1.2.3, 2.17.29).

11.3. This variation not surprisingly became confused with that between forms with and without an anaptyctic vowel, e.g. again from Plautus *periculo* and *populi* beside the older *periclum* and *poplo* (*Capt*. 687, *St*. 492, *As*. 617, *Ps*. 125). Variants like *saeclum* and *saeculum*, *uinclum* and *uinculum* are normal in classical poetry, the anaptyctic forms being obviously favoured in the nom.-acc. plural. The archaic tone of *saecla*, however, justifies its choice in Virg. *E*. 4.46 in preference to the metrically acceptable *saecula*.

11.4. Shortened forms like *dites* beside *diuite* (Prop. 3.4.1, 3.5.4) are due not to syncope but to the loss of *w* between like vowels and subsequent contraction. The phenomenon, well attested in Plautus, was especially frequent in the *w*- perfects, *audissem, complerunt* etc., and was analogically extended to give Plautine *amarit, noram* etc. The forms were convenient for poets, e.g. *admorunt* in Virg. *A*. 4.367, *nossem* with *audissem* in Tib. 1.10.11–12. The latter, like *complerunt*, imply derivation from -*ĕrunt* rather than -*ērunt* (see §§14.3–4). In prose such forms were accepted by Cicero (*Or*. 157) and treated as the norm by Quintilian, who recommends *uitauisse* etc. only for *compositio* (1.6.17, 9.4.59). So here again the poets are in line with general trends in the language.

11.5. The acceptability in literary language of the shorter variants, of whatever origin, enabled the poets to adopt them occasionally without incurring charges of colloquialism. In satire of course occasional echoes of *sermo cottidianus* were appropriate. So we find Horatian *caldior* (*S*. 1.3.53), for *călĭdĭor, soldum* (*S*. 2.5.65) and even *surpite* (*S*. 2.3.283), which like Lucretius' *surpere* (2.314) extends syncopation beyond the perfect forms to which Plautus seems to have confined it. Only *calidĭor* is metrically impossible; the rest would be positionally restricted. This last consideration

accounts for the rare examples in Horace's odes, e.g. *lamnae* (2.2.2). There
are a few where the unsyncopated form would be metrically impossible.
Thus *surpuerat* (4.13.20) and, much more remarkable *puertiae* (1.36.8),
which cannot be motivated phonetically from *pŭĕrĭtĭae* and would have to
be an otherwise unattested archaism, reflecting *pŭĕrĭtĭae*! This is surely out
of the question, and the form must be put down to the poet's boldness in
innovation. Nothing quite comparable is to be found in other classical
poets, who follow established precedent.

11.6. Forms like *posta* for *posita* (Lucr. 1.1059), which were metrically
convenient rather than necessary, originated in colloquial Latin (e.g.
expostus in Cato, *Agr.* 151.2), where the influence of the noun *postis* may
have assisted the verbal syncope. They were regular in Vulgar Latin, as
the Romance reflexes *imposto, compote* etc. show. However, they had
entered the poetic tradition as early as Ennius, whose precedent for Virgil's
repostum (*A.* 1.26), where for once the full form is indeed unmetrical, is
reported by Servius. Lucretius also has *reposta* (1.35) along with many
other syncopated compound forms that are used by Virgil. The latter often
serve to emphasize an alliteration. Thus in *placida compostus pace* and
imposta Typhoeo and *expostaque ponto* (*A.* 1.249, 9.716, 10.694), *-pos-* falls
in a homodyne position.

11.7. Factors other than mere metrical convenience can also be discerned elsewhere; e.g. in *Paridis direxti tela* (*A.* 6.57), where the longer
variant *direxisti* would be uneconomical of metrical space and phonetically
less harsh. The importance of tradition is clear in Virgil's choice of *porgite*
(*A.* 8.274). Servius on 1.26 again reports Ennian precedent, and the form
occurs in Cicero's *Aratea* 211. The established status of *-postus* is illustrated
further by Propertius' *imposta* (4.2.29) alongside older and more widely
established shortenings like *duxti* and *consumpsti* (1.3.37)[28] and by Silver
epic examples like *repostam* (Val. Flacc. 2.286), *imposta, expostus* (Stat.
Th. 1.227, 5.551). Rare examples of apparent extensions are to be found,
like Statius' *replictae* (*Silv.* 4.9.29) in place of the unmetrical *replicitae* or
the alternative innovation *replicatae*. The classical reluctance to admit what
was so prominent a feature of Vulgar Latin, except where archaic precedent within the genre conferred respectability, was thus strictly
maintained.

12.1. Poets were not conspicuous innovators in pronunciation or morphology, being content to adopt selectively what was already current in

---

[28] Again likely to have begun at the time of initial stress: *doúxistei* rather than *douxístei*,
unless *-tei* was older than *-istei* in sigmatic perfects.

educated use. However, they did take full advantage of archaic grammatical forms which, though rare or even obsolete outside poetry, were
established in the poetic tradition and so not alien to cultivated readers.[29]
Sometimes an archaism provided a briefer form. Thus *deum* for *deorum*
in the urgent sequence of angry questions . . . *quare / templa ruunt antiqua
deum*? (Hor. *S.* 2.2.104), with the archaic form juxtaposed to *antiqua*, or
the even more archaic *diuom* in *tuis flexus Venerisque gratae / uocibus
diuom pater* (Hor. *C.* 4.6.21–2), which contributes to the heroic context
not only the old case form but also the archaic form of the root, which
adds to the Ennian alliterative effect.

12.2. Some examples suggest that the poet had Greek -ων in mind, as
magnanimum heroum (Virg. *A.* 6.307) and *Danaum Euboico litore mille
rates* (Prop. 2.26.38), where the toponymic adjective following *Vlixēn* in
the previous line provides a strong Hellenic tone,[30] while the archaism of
a locatival ablative without a preposition and the metonymy of *rates*
form a rich poetic context for the genitive. The use of the old genitive
forms in technical terms of law and the trades, e.g. *fabrum, iugerum,
sestertium, socium*, well illustrates the parallels that are possible between
the subliterary registers of the language and that of poetry.

12.3. The a-stem gen. pl. *-ārum* was as ancient as thematic *-um*. Hence
forms like *caelicolum* (Enn. *Ann.* 445 Sk, Virg. *A.* 3.21) and *agricolum*
(Lucr. 4.586) must be analogical, like the converse *-āī* for *-ās*. In proper
names the influence of Greek *-ῶν* must again be admitted, as in Lucretius'
Aeneadum genetrix hominum diuomque uoluptas, where the forms *Aene-
adum*[31] and *diuomque* reflect the association of heroic Greece and ancient
Rome. The appropriate Greek resonance of Virgil's *optume Graiugenum*
(*A.*8.127) in Aeneas' address to Evander contrasts with the more native
Latin *Graiugenarum* (Lucr. 1.477).

12.4. At other times the chosen form may be longer, more weighty,
like the archaic gen. sg. *-āī*. The inherited *-ās*, which it replaced, survives
in the legal phrase *pater familias* and as an archaism already in Livius'
escas (*poet.* 12M), Naevius' *Terras* (*FPL* 8B) and Ennius' *uias*[32] along with
the ancient nom. sg. *aquilā* (*Ann.* 430, 139 Sk). In fact *-āī* was already

[29] For archaic morphology see Leumann (1959: 143–5).
[30] In view of the attested Greek variants Ὀλισεύς and Οὐλιξεύς and the recharacterization of ἱερē, acc. sg. of ἱερēs (<ἱερεύς), *Vlixēn* may be a genuine Greek form in spite of Housman (Diggle–Goodyear (1972: 2. 834–5)).
[31] The early Latin nom. sg. would have been *Aeneadă*; cf. archaizing *Aeacidā* (Enn. *Ann.* 475 Sk).
[32] *auras* for *aurae*, reported by Servius as an *antiqua lectio* at *A.* 11.801, turns up in the ninth-century *Bernensis d* and may be due not to Virgil's archaizing passion but to the interference of *auras* (799).

archaic by the early second century. Monosyllabic -ai (usually written -ae in our MSS) is much the more frequent in Ennius, who tends to keep the dissyllabic form for verse ends, e.g. the aptly toilsome *siluai frondosai* and in the wholly spondaic line *olli respondit rex Albai Longai*, where the form of the pronoun adds to the antique tone (*Ann.* 179, 31 Sk). Plautus has -*āī* in parodic phrases like *filiai nuptiis* (*Aul.* 295), and *magnai rei publicai gratia* (*Mil.* 103).

12.5. Lucretius has many instances, again especially at verse ends (*animāī, materiāī* etc.), and the overall total in fact exceeds that for -*ae*. But Virgil uses the variant more freely, if much less frequently. Thus in *A.* 3.354, *aulai medio libabant pocula Bacchi*, the opening archaic genitive dependent on an unprepositioned locative ablative (cf. the normal classical idiom *in media aula*), the metonymic *Bacchi* for *uini*, appropriate to the strict sense of *libabant* with which it is linked by assonance, and the contrasting heterodyne and homodyne patterns in the otherwise metrically symmetrical halves of the verse all combine to celebrate this emotional high point in Aeneas' narrative. The genitival archaisms both occur together in the description of Turnus' army, *diues equom, diues pictai uestis et auri* (*A.* 9.26). The use of the genitive rather than ablative case with *diues*, the archaic forms of the two genitives and the stately spondaic rhythms provide tones worthy of the heroic scene. The use of -*āī* declines in imperial epic. When it does occur, it is probably a Virgilism.

13.1. The interaction of *i*-stem and consonant stem nouns and adjectives had begun prehistorically with the transfer of *i*-stem nom. pl. -*ēs* and dat.-abl. pl. -*ibos*. However, in the historical period it is generally at the expense of *i*-stems, with **mentim, *mentī, mentīs* replaced by *mentem, mente, mentēs*.

13.2. The encroachment of *imbre* on *imbrī, parte* on *partī* etc., as well as reverse confusions like *couentionid* for **couentione*, are attested in early Latin (cf. Pl. *Mo.* 142, Ter. *HT.* 57, *CIL* I²581). In the first century BC, where -*e* was spreading rapidly in educated usage, retention of the older forms provided useful metrical alternatives, e.g. *finī, finĕ* (Lucr. 1.978, 4.627), *ignī, ignĕ* and *currentī, rubentĕ* (Prop. 1.9.17, 3.5.36, 4.5.12, 3.10.2); cf. *caelestī, caelestĕ* (Ov. *Pont.* 3.5.53, *M.* 15.743). In only a few instances were the newer forms metrically difficult — *celere* for instance required elision into a heavy syllable — but the availability of options once more enabled greater variety in placing the word, varying the proportion of long vowels and creating patterns of assonance, e.g. the opening juxtaposition in *Sigea igni freta lata relucent*, and the repetition of *tī* in *cristasque rubentis/ excipiam sorti* (Virg. *A.* 2.312, 9.270–1). For increased syllabic weight innovative -*ī* was used in *maiorī* (Luc. 7.162), and *capiti* (Virg. *E.* 6.16) avoids *capite*, which would have needed elision.

13.3. That the distinction between *ĕ* and the *exilis uox* of *ĭ* mattered to the educated Latin ear is plain from Probus' discussion of the relative merits of *urbīs* and *urbēs*, *turrim* and *turrem* and Gellius' reflections thereon (*N.A.* 13.21). Because such pairs are not metrically distinct, we have no way of recovering their distribution from the manuscript tradition, which was inevitably corrupted by the phonetic confusion between the reflexes of classical *ĭ* and *ē* in the late Empire. Appeal to Virgil's autograph is made by Probus to show that the poet made his choices *arbitrio consili-oque usus auris*. So we have the assonance of *urbisne inuisere, Caesar* (*G.* 1.25) but the appropriately *pinguior* ('fuller') *uox* in *centum urbes habitant magnas* (*A.* 3.106). Similar observations are reported on *turrim* and *securim* (*A.* 2.460, 224), and Gellius cites the alternation between *tres* and *tris* in successive lines (*A.* 10.350–1).

13.4. Finally the difficulties posed by gen. pl. -*ium* following a heavy syllable, as in present participles and many *i*-stem nouns and adjectives. These were overcome in the participle by reviving the consonant stem forms that made up the original paradigm of the -*nt*- participle, the *i*-stems having been introduced from the remodelled feminine *ferentī (cf. Skt *bharantī* and Gk φέρουσα <*bherontiə). Virgil's *cadentum* (*A.* 10.674) and the remarkable sequence including the verse-final rhymes *ruentum, parentum* (*A.* 11.886–7) would have seemed distinctly archaic, especially if the older spelling *lacrumantum* is authentic. Later but still pre-classical is the extension of consonant-stem genitives from participles to *i*-stem adjectives, especially when used substantivally like *caelestum* (Enn. *var.* 23V; cf. Virg. *A.* 7.432) and *agrestum* Virg. *G.* 1.10). The metrically useful forms, though not so likely to have had an archaic tone, since confusion of the two paradigms was clearly widespread in the colloquial register, nevertheless distinguish poetic discourse from literary prose usage, which here, as sometimes elsewhere, distanced itself from the colloquial more sharply than poetic usage felt the need consistently to do.

14.1. Older forms of the imperfect tense like *scibas* (Enn. *tr.* 272J), *insanibat* (Ter. *Ph.* 642) were useful to dactylic poets avoiding tribrachs and cretics, e.g. *stabilibat* (Enn. *Ann.* 42 Sk), *audibat* (Ov. *F.* 3.507), in place of the more recent forms *stabiliebat, audiebat* which were preferred in prose. Now and then the archaic form is preferred to a metrically possible alternative for positional and phonetic reasons. Thus in Virg. *A.* 8.436, *certatim squamis serpentum auroque polibant*, the verb form contributes along with the metrically unavoidable *serpentum* to the aural effect of a verse in which the only dactyl is *aurōquĕ pŏlibant* with *auroque* in hendiadys with *squamis*. This ability to make a virtue of metrical necessity can also be seen in Cat. 64.319, *uellera uirgati custodibant calathisci* with its dignified central spondees.

14.2. Of the three classical variants of the third person plural perfect, inherited *-ēre*, innovative *-ĕrunt* (<*-is-ont*) and *-ērunt*, a conflation of the two, the first is notably more frequent in poetry than in prose. It is in fact the oldest of the three forms, but it was its trochaic ending that enabled it to overcome the prejudice reported by Cicero (*Or.* 157) against a form wrongly believed to be shortened from *-ērunt*. The frequency at all periods of the shortened forms *cessarunt, norunt*, which must have replaced *cessauĕrunt, nouĕrunt*, not the forms in *-ērunt*, suggests that the former were much more frequent than is often supposed. They are certainly the starting point for the Romance forms, It. *-arono* etc. Even in Ciceronian clausulae the short penult sometimes offers a better rhythm; e.g. *mortem dŏlŭĕrunt, mŏuĕrunt respóndĕō, dē mănĭbŭs āmĭsĕrunt* (Cic. *Cael.* 24, 27, 64). In dramatic verse, *-ĕrunt* can be certified only at the end of a verse or hemistich, e.g. *meruĕrunt* (Pl. *Mo.* 281), *emĕrunt* (Ter. *Eun.* 20), but there are many other positions in which *pĕpŭlĕrunt, dīxĕrunt* etc. would be as acceptable as the *-ērunt* forms that are usually assumed.[33]

14.3. The heavy final syllable of most perfect stems severely restricted the incidence of *-ĕrunt* in dactylic metres. Thus Virgil has *tŭlĕrunt, miscŭĕruntque, stĕtĕruntque* (*E.* 4.61, *G.* 3.283, *A.* 2.774) but *implērunt, nōrunt* (*E.* 6.48, *A.* 6.641) for *implēuĕrunt, nōuĕrunt*. The shortened forms were supported by *implesti, nosse* etc. (see §11.4). In Lucretius, combined with the small number of *-ĕrunt* forms, they outnumber *-ērunt*. They are also notably more frequent in the *Metamorphoses* than in the *Aeneid*.

14.4. However, *-ēre*, which is the most frequent of the three in Lucretius, remains the distinctively poetic form in classical Latin. Virgil uses it in all positions even where it is not metrically necessary; e.g. at the end of *A.* 1.398, *et coetu cinxere polum cantusque dedere*, where the rhyme with *cinxere* is clearly important, and in the famous opening to Book 2, *Conticuere omnes intentique ora tenebant*, where the light syllable is actually elided to usher in the rhythmic gravity of the central section of the verse.

14.5. Finally an archaism which, though not frequent, is remarkably persistent in all genres of classical poetry, the medio-passive infinitive *-ier*. Its origin is probably the same as that of *-ī*,[34] with which it is in allomorphic

---

[33] See Pye (1963) for further discussion and relevant statistics.

[34] viz. a gerundial *-iĕ̆*: *uṛtiĕ̆* > *uortiĕ̆* (cf. Skt *vṛtyă̆*) *uortī* or *uortie+r*. The *-ī* form could also reflect *-ei* (cf. *agī* with Skt *nir-aje*), but there are no examples before monophthongization to test this, and it would not account for *agier* etc.

variation in early Latin. The tendency for -*ier* to be placed at the end of the verse in republican drama suggests that it was already archaic. In classical verse it offered useful metrical alternatives to iambic and pyrrhic endings. In practice the first of these, exemplified in, say, *agier uentis*, is rarely if ever attested, the second widely, e.g. *nitier* (Cat. 61.68), *accingier* (Virg. *A.* 4.493), *labier* (Hor. *Epist.* 2.1.94), *spargier* (Hor. *C.* 4.11.8), all followed by a vowel.

15.1. One notable difference between Latin poetry and literary prose is the higher frequency of Greek sounds. This is true of all poetic genres, even when the subject matter is not specifically Greek, though the pleasure that was got by educated Latin speakers from the exotic sounds cannot be dissociated from the cultural associations of the words that contained them (see §§27, 28).

15.2. The introduction of Greek sounds into Latin by Greek speakers was of course, like their inability to cope satisfactorily with distinctive Latin sounds such as [kʷ], [w] and [f], a mark of incompetence (cf. Quint. 1.4.14). As in other societies, unless the speaker belonged to one of the prestigious artistic or learned professions, the defect was a social handicap, looked down upon by educated native speakers. By contrast the occasional deliberate injection of a distinctively Greek word, sound or idiom into the discourse of an educated Latin speaker, provided it was kept to conventional limits — one thinks, for instance, of the contrast between the poetical and epistolary Cicero and the Cicero of the formal literary prose — was viewed as the natural outcome of what since the second century BC had been a self-consciously bilingual culture. This bilingualism accepted after some resistance the introduction of Greek technical terms into the learned vocabularies of rhetoric, grammar, philosophy, science and technology,[35] but the influx there was much more a prose phenomenon and a relatively late one, as the pages of the *Ad Herennium*, Celsus and Vitruvius show.

15.3. Quintilian extols at some length (12.10.27–34) the aesthetic superiority of Greek *y* and *z*,[36] the two *peregrinae litterae*, and the aspirated stops *ph, th, ch.* (It is not clear whether his omission of the aspirated allophone of *r* is significant or not.) Instead Latin has the *horridae litterae, f, w* (the *Aeolica littera!*), *qu* and final -*m*. Of ζέφυρος he writes *si nostris litteris scribentur, surdum quiddam et barbarum efficient.*

---

[35] See Coleman (1989).
[36] Greek υ was originally [u] everywhere and remained so in some dialects until the spread of [y] from Attic-Ionic in the Hellenistic period. ζ was originally [dz] or [zd], perhaps both, depending on the dialect, but in Hellenistic Greek had become [z:] generally.

15.4. In early Latin the convention seems to have been, as in English until recent times, to naturalize all foreign words, including proper names.[37] Thus *ampora* < ἀμφορέα (acc.), reflected in the diminutive *ampulla* beside classical *amphora, carta* < χάρτης and *massa* < μᾶζα, *tumba* < τύμβος, *tus* < θύος, in which the *peregrinae litterae* were never restored. This practice seems to have continued in Vulgar Latin, where e.g. *colpus* < κόλαφος, *balneus* < βαλανεῖον, *spada* (cf. class. *spatha*, but dim. *spatula*) < σπάθη.

15.5. Traces of the early Latin convention are discernible in the MS tradition of Plautus and Ennius. Thus *sonam* (*Po.* 1008 ms. A), *carmidi* (*Trin.* 744 A), *sumbolum* (*Ps.* 716 A), *Sibulla* (*Ps.* 25 A), *scema* (*Am.* 117 ms. J), *baratrum* (*Ba.* 149 P). From Ennius *Andromaca* (*tr.* 102 J test.), *cartis* (*Ann.* 458 Sk), *poinice* (*tr.* 258 J test.), *tyeste* (*tr.* 307 J test.) *maceriis* for *maceris* (*Ann.* 519 Sk) < *macaireis*. It is probable that before *c.* 150 BC all Latin poets wrote (and pronounced) *Ampitruo, numpa, Smurna, teatrum, Tuestes*.

15.6. The first datable use of the digraphic representation of Greek aspirates occurs in *Achaia* and the unetymological *triumphans* beside *Corinto* on Mummius' dedication of 145 BC (*CIL* I² 626). At what date *y* and *z* were introduced we do not know, but it is likely that they were systematically pronounced and written by the neoteric poets in *charta, nympha, Rhodope, tympanum, zephyrus, Zmyrna* etc.

15.7. It was not just the individual Greek sounds in *cithara, cyathus, delphinus, rhythmus, lychnus* etc. that brought exotic colour. There were also the unLatin combinations of familiar Latin sounds, as in the diphthong in *Eurus*, the vowel sequences in *āēr, Chāos, Trōilus*, the initial clusters in *psallere, Xanthus*, the medials in *cycnus, Lesbia*, the final syllables of *Actaeōn, Corydōn*.

15.8. The exotic effect was further enhanced by the increasing retention in poetry of Greek case forms in Greek nouns, which also provided metrical variants, e.g. the accusatives *lampadăs* (Lucr. 2.25), *lampada* (Virg. *A.* 6.587) and nominative *lampadĕs* (Ov. *Ep.* 14.25). Ennius had already adopted acc. *ait(h)era* and nom. *Aiacidā* (*Ann.* 545, 167 Sk), but it was probably Accius who established the practice, at any rate in proper nouns according to Varro, who also notes (*L.* 10.70) the currency of mixed declension and complete Latinization, which was the norm in common nouns of Greek origin. Catullus has for instance in 64 and 66 voc. *Theseu*, acc. *Amphitritēn, Minōa*, nom. pl. *Nereidĕs*, gen. *Locridos Arsinoĕs* and the variant datives *Minoidĭ* and *Thetidī, Peleî* and *Peleō*, where the metrically necessary but unLatin contraction gives the latter form a distinctly Greek quality. The usage was maintained and extended in Augustan and later

---

[37] For a comprehensive account of the whole subject see Biville (1987).

poetry, Lucretius' *Tityon* (3.984), and *cinnamon* and *Patroclon* in Propertius (3.13.8, 2.8.33).

15.9. The effects of this Greek colouring were recognized explicitly by the ancients themselves. Cicero, having stated that poets are governed by sound rather than sense, cites as an instance a verse that is *locorum splendidis nominibus illuminatus*; the text is uncertain but it clearly contained *Helles, Tmolum* and *Tauricos* (*Or.* 163). Other examples are discussed in §§27–28.

16.1. The phonetic figures[38] of alliteration, assonance and rhyme are a well-known feature of Latin poetry, though by no means exclusive to the register. The most famous of all Latin alliterations was after all Caesar's *ueni uidi uici*, reported by the Elder Seneca (*Suas.* 2.22), which shows that it was typical of conversational epigram, though the figure is conspicuously absent from the *Commentarii*. All three figures can have expressive functions in poetry, as in ritual texts and even legal formulae, though with the possible exception of onomatopoeia, it is often impossible to dissociate interpretation of any such phonetic effects from the perceived meaning of the words themselves. Examples can be noted and analysed precisely and objectively, but anything beyond that must be to some extent subjective and influenced by the reader's own linguistic culture.[39]

16.2. Alliteration, even more than the other two, also has a powerful cohesive effect in binding together words that the author wishes to associate closely, whether or not they are adjacent or belong together syntactically. In Horace, *C.* 2.3.1–4, *aequam memento rebus in arduis / seruare mentem, non secus in bonis / ab insolenti temperatam / laetitia, moriture Delli*, the alliterative link between *memento* and *mentem*, with its characteristically Horatian etymological word-play, and the unnerving *moriture* contribute significantly to the effect of the exhortation.

16.3. Alliteration is a striking feature of early Latin literary composition, no doubt assisted by the initial stress accent. This coincidence of alliteration with stress is also seen in Old English poetry with alliteration of two or three stressed syllables in each line: e.g. *oft Scyld Scēfing sceaþena þrēatum / monegum mǣgþum meodosetla oftēah* (*Beowulf* 4–5) 'Often Scyld son of Scef from bands of enemies, from many races, the mead-benches took away'.[40] We find in prayers formulae like *quod felix faustum*

---

[38] For more detailed discussion see Hofmann–Szantyr (1965: 699–721).

[39] For some salutary remarks on the significance of alliterations see Goodyear (1972: 336–41).

[40] Whatever rules there may have been, comparable to those in Germanic and Welsh alliterative poetry, have disappeared with the lost texts. For an unsuccessful attempt to recover such rules in extant Latin poetry see Evans (1921).

fortunatum siet (Cic. *Diu.* 1.102) and *pastores pecuaque salua seruassis* (Cato *Agr.* 141), and in dedicatory inscriptions various combinations of *donum* with *datum, donatum* and *dedicatum*, which show that the figure survived in the religious register. In early poetry Naevius has *eorum sectam sequontur multi mortales* (*FPL* 6B), Ennius *Apollo puerum primus Priamo qui foret / postilla natus temptare tollere; / eum esse exitium Troiae, pestem Pergamo.* (*tr.* 59–61 J) and the virtuoso sequence *machina multa minax minitatur maxima muris* (*Ann.* 620 Sk).

16.4. There is nothing on this scale in Greek poetry, nothing either in surviving Latin prose, though some remarkable alliterations can be found. For instance Cicero, *Tusc.* 1.118–19: *tum incideret in mortis malum sempiternum; portum potius paratum nobis et perfugium putemus. quo utinam uelis passis peruehi liceat! sin reflantibus uentis reiciemur*.... This highly alliterative and sustained nautical metaphor comes at the emotionally charged conclusion of a long exposition. Even Nepos sometimes indulges, e.g. *illum ait Magnesiae morbo mortuum neque negat fuisse famam uenenum sua sponte sumpsisse* (*Them.* 10.4). The two examples are significant in not being drawn from high oratory; a reminder of the stylistic common property shared between poetic discourse and literary prose generally.

16.5. The archaizing Lucretius was of course greatly addicted to alliteration. As a result the functional power of the figure is greatly diminished. Catullus by contrast sets the appropriately archaic tone for his epic theme of Peleus and Thetis with *Peliaco ... prognatae ... pinus, Neptuni nasse* and *fluctus et fines* (64.1–3); but the figure is reserved in the personal poems purely for expressive effects, as in *lepidum nouum libellum* and *pumice expolitum* (1.1–2), *senum seueriorum* (5.2), *fidem ... foedere fallendos* (76.3–4).[41] The contribution of *cedente carina* and *languida ... litoribus* to Propertius' depiction of the deserted heroine (1.3.1–2) is all the stronger because he alliterates so infrequently. Similarly in 2.22.1–2, *scis here mi multas pariter placuisse puellas; / scis mihi, Demophoon, multa uenire mala*, the alliteration of *m, p, l* combined with the repetition of *scis* and the colloquial *here* and *mi* convey a vividly dramatic effect. Finally in Virgil's *et pro purpureo poenas dat Scylla capillo* (*G.* 1.405) the juxtaposition of the visual image of crime and its punishment is reinforced by the same alliteration which unites the syntactic unit of epithet and noun, underlined by the grammatically conditioned homeoteleuton. As often in poetry one feature accompanies others.

---

[41] For the relatively high frequency of alliteration in the dialogue love poems, Catullus 45 and Horace *C.* 3.9 see Wilkinson (1963: 26–7).

17. Assonance is also employed for expressive and cohesive purposes. It is often combined with alliteration, as in Lucretius' *linquitur ut merito maternum nomen adepta / terra sit, e terra quoniam sunt cuncta creata* (5.795–6), with its characteristic word-play between *maternum* and *terra*, and the use of recurrent patterns of linguistic *elementa* to reflect the syntheses of cosmic *elementa*.[42] In *C.* 3.4.69–71 Horace gives a didactic, almost pedantic, emphasis to the mythological *exemplum* of *uis consili expers*, which *mole ruit sua*, by the repetition of *te, ti* in *testis mearum centimanus Gyges / sententiarum*. This is continued in the repeated *t* and *i* through the rest of the stanza to the final *domitus sagitta*. The opening stanza of *C.* 4.13.1–4 is even more striking, with the repeated *exilitas* of *ī, ĭ* and *ē* expressing contempt for the hapless Lyce. The use of assonance merits attention, even if interpretation of it must often remain speculative.

18.1. Rhyme has been an important structural feature of Western vernacular poetry since the Middle Ages and has a strong cohesive role in such varied genres as the *terza rima* of Dante's *Divina Commedia*, the heroic couplet of Chaucer's *Canterbury Tales* and the sonnet forms of Petrarch and Ronsard. The need to provide the specified rhyme can be constricting and the use of the figure has declined in modern poetry. The earliest surviving pieces of rhymed Latin verse are Christian hymns, though in most of the pre-medieval hymns the rhymes, even when frequent, are not systematic. Moreover we cannot be sure of pronunciation. In Fortunatus' *Vexilla Regis* was it assumed that congregations would rhyme *prodeunt* with *mysterium*, as they would *uestigia, gratia, hostia*? In Insular Latin, where pronunciation was more conservative, we have in fact some of the earliest systematic rhymes, as in the *Lorica* attributed to Gildas and St Columba's *Altus Prosator* (*Anal. Hymn.* 51.262 and 216).

18.2. The two areas where rhyme is to be found in pre-Christian Latin are in popular incantations, where the correspondence was systematic and obviously magical, and in high rhetorical prose, where homeoteleuton or sequential rhyme was occasional and calculated for special effect. Thus *terra pestum teneto. / salus hic maneto* (Var. *R.* 1.2.27), and *est igitur haec, iudices,   non scripta sed nata lex,   quam non didicimus, accepimus, legimus, uerum ex natura ipsa arripuimus, hausimus, expressimus,   ad quam non docti sed facti, non instituti sed imbuti sumus* (Cic. *Mil.* 10), where the rhythmic structure also reveals careful composition.

18.3. Such examples indicate an awareness of rhyme as a possible

---

[42] See Friedländer (1941) for the exposition of this idea generally in Lucretius.

stylistic device, and, given the obvious frequency of good rhymes offered by the grammatical morphology of a highly inflected language, it is perhaps surprising that the possibilities were not taken up and developed in the educated poetic tradition. One reason may have been that in contrast to alliteration and assonance, which can affect lexically as well as grammatically significant syllables, rhyme affects only the inflections, unless it is dissyllabic, as in Chaucer, or even more intricate, as in the fantastic hexameter couplets of the twelfth-century Bernard of Cluny's *De contemptu mundi*:[43] *Hora nouissima, tempora pessima sunt, uigilemus. / ecce minaciter imminet arbiter ille supremus.*

18.4. The great majority of verse-end rhymes in classical poetry are unsystematic. Many seem to have no significance, which is surprising, given that the poet's choice was unconstrained. Now and then however we can see some significance, as in Ovid's *amnis harundinibus limosas obsite ripas, / ad dominam propero. siste parumper aquas* (*Am.* 3.6.1–2). Here the rhyming links the exhortation closely to the relevant descriptive phrase. Even the echo in the imperative *siste* of the rare vocative *obsite* may also be calculated. Again in Horace, *A.P.* 99–100, *non satis est pulchra esse poemata. dulcia sunto. / et quocumque uolent animum auditoris agunto*, the archaizing legalistic imperatives, unexpected in this context, are emphasized by their position, and the rhyme is supported both by the assonance of *pul- dul-* and perhaps *uol-* and by the alliteration in both verses.

18.5. There is good evidence for the occasional cultivation of internal rhyme with the syllable before the principal caesura. This is particularly notable in the Propertian elegiac pentameter, and can be seen as an easy extension of a tendency to place two concordant members of a noun phrase in these positions.[44] Thus in 1.1 we find *suis ... ocellis* (1), *castas ... puellas* (5), *nullo ... consilio* (6) with the grammatically comparable *nullis ... Cupidinibus* (2), *constantis ... fastus* (3) and *impositis ... pedibus* (4). An exceptional sequence, but there are plenty of similar individual verses, and even a few dissyllabic rhymes like *Tyrrhena ... harena* (1.8a.11). Now and then two weakly rhymed words are not even in grammatical concord, as *irasci ... tibi* (1.5.8) and *urgenti ... dedi* (4.3.12), though these are at least syntactically linked.

18.6. In the well known sequence in Horace, *C.* 1.1.6–10, the rhyming words in *terrarum dominos euehit ad deos* (6), which are also linked by

---

[43] Which includes the *Name of the Rose* line: *nunc ubi Regulus? aut ubi Romulus? aut ubi Remus? / stat rosa pristina nomine, nomina nuda tenemus.*

[44] For a detailed classification of the data on juxtaposed homeoteleuton see Shackleton Bailey (1994).

alliteration, are syntactically unconnected,[45] as they are also, for instance, in 1.36.12, *neu morem in Salium sit requies pedum*. But the rest of the passage shows strict grammatical concord from *mobilium ... Quiritium* (7) to *Libycis ... areis* (10), with only the alliterative *certat tergeminis tollere honoribus* (8) unrhymed. Elsewhere in Horace internal rhymes of this kind occur often enough to suggest intention, e.g. in *C.* 1.22 *uenenatis ... sagittis* (3), *silua ... Sabina* (9), *curis ... expeditis* (11) etc., in contrast to the concordant but unrhymed *Syrtis ... aestuosas* (5). Ovid uses such rhymes more sparingly after early instances like *Ep.* 1.6, which has two rhyming and two non-rhyming concords. Perhaps the figure itself was considered too naive and monotonous for fastidious poets, though Martial still has examples now and then of both rhyming and unrhyming concords.

18.7. In dactylic hexameters, while internal rhyme is frequent enough for obvious grammatical reasons, it seldom marks the two 'halves' of the verse. Examples are therefore the more noteworthy, as in Virg. *A.* 4.652–8, *uixi et quem dederat cursum Fortuna peregi / et nunc magna mei sub terras ibit imago, / urbem praeclaram statui, mea moenia uidi, / ulta uirum poenas inimico a fratre recepi, / felix, heu nimium felix, si litora tantum / numquam Dardaniae tetigissent nostra carinae.* Here five rhyming first person verbs are placed one in verse-initial, three in verse-final position and one before a principal caesura, as is the rhyming first person pronoun *mei.* The queen's proud statement of her own achievements, thus powerfully emphasized, contrasts poignantly with the closing couplet in which she is the passive victim, and there is no first person verb, only the alien and hostile *tetigissent.*

THE LEXICON

19.1. The lexical ingredients of the poetic register — the choice of words and the way they are employed — are clearly important for its definition. Indeed poetic diction often consists of words that in origin belonged to ordinary prosaic usage but because of their adoption and reiteration in poetic contexts acquired a distinctive status.

19.2. Words like *formosus, mollis* and *tener* were all thoroughly at home, say, in rustic or horticultural contexts — *porcus formosus, asparagi molles, tenerae gallinae* etc. But in poetry of the Callimachean connection *mollis* and *tener* were polarized with *durus* and *seuerus* over a wide metaphoric range (Prop. 3.1.19–20, Ov. *Am.* 2.1.3–4 etc.) and through their

---

[45] See Nisbet–Hubbard ad loc. For rhyme in the Odes see Skutsch (1964).

frequent occurrence in such contexts acquired like *formosus* connotations that in turn coloured new contexts. Keywords[46] of erotic poetry they certainly became, but the continued use of *tener* and *mollis* outside the genre in their older more prosaic denotations hamper their classification as poetic diction.

19.3. The case of *formosus* is more complicated. It is well known that whereas Virgil often uses the adjective in the *Eclogues* (e.g. 1.5, 2.1, 3.79), where it is appropriately *molle atque facetum*, he uses it only once in the *Georgics*, in its old sense, *formonsa*[47] *iuuenca* 'a well shaped heifer' (3.219), and never in the *Aeneid*. Dido is always *pulcherrima*, never *formonsa*. The ancient *pulcher*, used as a near synonym of *formosus* in Cic. *Fam.* 9.14.4, *nihil est . . . uirtute formosius, nihil pulchrius, nihil amabilius*, retains an elevated tone in both classical verse and prose usage. *Bellus*, originally the diminutive of *bonus* (or rather **duenos*), was used by Plautus and indeed Cicero to mean both 'fine' and 'pretty', but it never quite rivalled *formosus* in erotic poetry. Its lexical profile includes Catullus, Lucretius, Tibullus, Horace *Sat.*, Persius and Martial, which certainly does not mark it as 'unpoëtisch', unless we confine 'poëtisch' to the highest poetical genres. However, the two words prevailed in Vulgar Latin and are reflected in Romance, *beau, hermoso* etc. *Pulcher* disappeared without trace from the spoken language.

19.4. Words may of course rise and fall in literary as well as social status over the years and the emergence of a particular word in Vulgar Latin at one period is no guarantee of its literary humility at another.[48]

19.5. Sometimes ancient testimony on the status of a word raises more questions than it answers. When Andromache says, referring to Ascanius, *ecquid . . . et pater Aeneas et auunculus excitat Hector*? (*A.* 3.342–3), Servius says of *auunculus*: *humiliter dictum in heroico carmine*. The word is certainly rare in poetry, but is this merely because poets did not normally talk about uncles? Perhaps Virgil is being bolder than he seems in introducing a homely colloquial tone into epic dialogue? Equally infrequent in poetry is *patruus*. It is used satirically by Catullus (74) of Gellius' debauchery and also occurs in the Sibyl's conversation with Charon (*A.* 6.402), *casta licet patrui seruet Proserpina limen*. The fact that Pluto, who had raped Proserpine, was the brother of her father Jupiter, is bitterly underlined by the juxtaposition of

---

[46] See Delatte (1967), who records *tener* as the most frequent adjective in Tibullus, *formosus* and *mollis* in Propertius.

[47] Presumed to be the original form of this as of other adjectives in *-osus*. Virgil may have been exceptional in retaining *-ns-*. For the change of *Vns* to *V̄s* generally see Allen (1978: 28–9, 65–6).

[48] The point was well made by Ernout (1947) in reviewing Axelson (1945), who in this as in other matters did not always see the significance of the patterns in his own statistics.

patrui with *casta* and its alliteration with *Proserpina*. Like *auunculus* the noun is used with characteristic semantic precision, as was not perhaps the case in Servius' day, when the use of *auunculus* of paternal as well as maternal uncles may already have been consigning *patruus* to oblivion.

20.1. The rise and fall of words needs to be plotted with some care. Thus *plorare* and *lacrimare* certainly ousted *flere* in Vulgar Latin, but both are well attested in classical poetry. The start of Ovid's lament for Tibullus, *Memnona si mater, mater plorauit Achillen* (*Am.* 3.9) is surely a place for solemnity; nor does the chiastic structure of the line, with the Greek accusatives of Homeric names at either end, seem an appropriate setting for the unpoetic or colloquial. As for *lacrimare*, its membership of the lexical group *lacrima, lacrimosus* ensured its survival in all registers of the language.

20.2. When Juno complains to Aeolus (Virg. *A.* 1.68) that her enemy sails the Tyrrhenian Sea *Ilium in Italiam portans uictosque penatis*, the verb has its normal classical sense of 'carrying a burden', and its subsequent semantic expansion to replace its hyperonym *ferre* in Vulgar Latin is irrelevant. Again, although (*de*)*fessus* was replaced in Vulgar Latin by *lassus*, little can be inferred from this for classical poetry. Ovid prefers *fessus* in his elegies, *lassus* in the *Metamorphoses*, but this is not merely a matter of idiolectal whim. Virgil in the flower simile describing the death of Euryalus has (*A.* 9.436–7) *languescit moriens lassoue papauera collo / demisere caput*. The preference for *lasso* over the metrically identical *fesso* may have been motivated by the resultant *la-* assonance, which binds together two central words in the simile. However, given the long tradition of the flower simile from *Iliad* 8.306–8 and Sappho 105c LP, it is unlikely that Virgil would have been so motivated, if it had meant introducing a word with distinctly subliterary associations.

20.3. In contrast to *fera*, the noun *bestia* is rare in poetry. It is sporadically reflected in Romance (e.g. Fr. *biche*) and must therefore have become established at some time in Vulgar Latin. Its occurrence in *B.Afr.* 81.1 but not in Caesar might suggest an early date, but it is used by Livy and often by Cicero; so its literary acceptability is secure for the classical period. Not vulgar then, but perhaps not poetical either. This would make its rare occurrence in Catullus 69.8 all the more striking: *hunc metuunt omnes neque mirum; nam mala ualde est / bestia nec quicum bella puella cubet.* The syntax and the vocabulary — *ualde, bella* — are colloquial but not vulgar, and *bestia*, with its contrastive alliteration with *bella*, is certainly vituperative (cf. *mala tu es bestia* in Pl. *Ba.* 55), but again not necessarily vulgar.

20.4. It is of course rare that a lexical profile is homogeneous, wholly poetic or wholly prosaic, and there are many other cases where the details of a heterogeneous profile are illuminating. Consider for instance the word *lābrum*,[49] a shortened form of *lauābrum* (cf. §11.4). The formation type is ancient, being paralleled in *cribrum, delubrum, uelabrum* etc. but it is not productive in the historical period. The unshortened form occurs once, where Lucretius warns against lingering in hot baths — *si calidis . . . cunctere lauabris* (6.799). In this, its original sense, it seems to have been replaced by *lauatio* (originally 'the act of washing'; cf. §32.1) and especially by the Greek loan-word *balineum*, whence Romance *bagno, bain* etc. In Cic. *Fam.* 14.20 *lābrum* is clearly something that can be placed inside a *balineum*, presumably a 'tub' or 'basin'. In agriculture *lābrum* is used of a tub for mixing oil (Cato, *Agr.* 66.2) or making wine (Virg. *G.* 2.6, Col. 12.15.3). This certainly looks prosaic, and the impression is confirmed by the diminutive *lābellum* (Col. 12.38.3), which is also used of a decorative bowl on a tomb (Cic. *Leg.* 2.66) and survives in Italian dialect words for 'trough' and 'coffin'. Nothing very poetic here either.

20.5. However, the word is twice found in the *Aeneid*. At 8.22 it appears in the simile of turbulent water in a cauldron, adapted from A.R. 3.756ff., where the corresponding word λέβης is unmarked as to register. The distinctly unepic Latin word and the image of which it forms part are perhaps not inappropriate to the unheroic predicament of a very indecisive Aeneas. Again in 12.417, *labris splendentibus* introduces a homely detail into the lofty heroic diction, reminding us that the high and mighty have humble domestic objects around them, even if they are grander versions than ours. The poetic effect in both instances depends precisely on the unpoetic status of the word, for which plenty of parallels can be found in the homely details of other epic similes.

20.6. Similarly in Ovid's use of the plural *lābra* of the bath of Diana in *Ep.* 21.180, *F.* 4.761 and *Ib.* 479, a reference to the goddess' 'bath-tub' is deliberately irreverent, and even the trochaic plural seems belittling. In the very next line of *Fasti* there is a reference to Faunus *medio cum premit arua die*. The image of the god applying pressure to the croplands is distinctly satiric, whether or not there is an allusion to his midday sexual activities. There may even be a parody in *labra Dianae* of the *labrum Venerium* 'teazel', a plant described by Pliny (*Nat.* 25.171) as *in flumine nascentem*. Diana, behaving in the myth like an excessively prim maiden lady, is treated like one. There is a lot going on here, but the presence of *lābrum*, while it is essential to the witty poetic effect, does so again

---

[49] What follows is developed out of an attempt to answer a query from Professor Kenney.

precisely because it is not in itself poetic. Nor does it acquire the status of poetic diction as a result of its contribution here.

20.7. The most remarkable case in Latin of a sequence of prosaic words combining to create a powerful poetic effect comes from Catullus. Not one of the bawdy pieces sprinkled with coarse vocabulary — *Ameana defutata* and the rest — which were designed to shock conventional sensibilities, but the famous epigram, *odi et amo. quare id faciam fortasse requiris. / nescio sed fieri sentio et excrucior* (85). Every word here is prosaic and there is not a single trope or figure to enrich their sheer ordinariness. Contrast for instance a couplet like Propertius' *in me nostra Venus noctes exercet amaras / et nullo uacuus tempore defit Amor* (1.1.33–4). Sustained plainness of diction characterizes all Catullus' epigrams, but this one is an extreme case.

20.8. There is an almost unbelievable density of verbalization — nine finite verbs and an infinitive in fourteen words. All the finite verbs except one are in the present tense, all except one in the first person. Only one is a subjunctive, and the mood there is purely rule-governed. The opening paradox *odi et amo* is compounded by the choice of the ergative *faciam* to denote a passive state, a choice that is not unparalleled (cf. Hor. *S.* 1.1.64, 94),[50] though it is here promptly 'corrected' by the passive *fieri*, with the two contrasted verbs in alliteration with the prosaic adverb *fortasse*,[51] which introduces the only tentative note in the couplet, referring however not to the poet but to the reader. The progression from the opening paradox through the puzzled question and his puzzled answer to the reiteration of the emotion and the pain caused by it, is articulated in the starkest and most austere lexical material. Poetic diction is clearly not essential for a powerful poetic effect: *series iuncturaque* certainly are.[52] Nevertheless it is doubtful whether this power could be sustained through a poem much longer than an epigram solely by such unenriched prosaic vocabulary, however artfully arranged the words might be.

20.9. Once again a walk-on part in a highly charged poetic context does not confer the status of poetic diction. The fourteen words in Catullus' epigram revert thereafter to their former prosaic status. Similarly with Horace's *odi profanum uulgus et arceo*, which acquire their full metaphoric sense only when we have read the rest of the stanza. The individual words

---

[50] On *ut scias me recte ualere quod te inuicem fecisse cupio* at Vindolanda see Adams (1995a: 123).

[51] The grammarian Cledonius noted (5.66 K) that *forsan* and *forsitan* are both more poetic than *fortasse*, which certainly never occurs in the more elevated passages of Virgil and Ovid.

[52] Axelson (1945: 98) by labelling *idoneus, ordinare, praesidium* etc. as unpoetic fails to account for their successful appearances in poetry, most notably Horatian lyric. As Ernout (1947: 69) and Marouzeau (1949, 1954 *passim*) insisted, context is of critical importance.

retain no particular poetic charge; their effect hereafter is recoverable only in a context that alludes specifically to this verse. In fact Horace constantly uses plain prosaic phrases within richly elaborated contexts as an instrument of poetic argument. The summary *dulce et decorum est pro patria mori* (*C.* 3.2.13) derives its impact from the vivid images of bravery and violence that surround it. The homely *iam dudum apud me est* (*C.* 3.29.5) is carefully contrasted with the grand and luxurious imagery that precedes it. Poetic effects do not depend upon consistency of lexical texture.

21.1. We often find that a pair of synonyms is divided between literary prose and the higher genres of poetry but both words occur in the less elevated poetic contexts. Consider for instance the 'poetic' words *ensis, letum, coniunx* and *amnis*. The ancient noun *ensis* was synonymous with *gladius* (Quint. 10.1.11), which supplanted it in general usage before the classical period and was in its turn later supplanted in Vulgar Latin by the Greek loan-word *spatha*. For *letum*, a nobler synonym of the ancient *mors*, Varro cites (*L.* 7.42) an old legal formula *ollus leto datus est*, though the legal register normally has *mors*. No less ancient than *mors* is *uxor*, which is again regular in legal texts, though *coniunx* is generally preferred in sepulchral inscriptions. While *amnis*, frequent in early Latin, is rare in classical prose — only once even in the archaist Sallust — it is frequent in Livy, another instance of *historia proxima poetis*. Of course *gladius, mors, uxor* and *flumen* are often found in the higher poetic genres; the significant fact is rather the very rare occurrence of *ensis, letum, coniunx* and *amnis* in prose.[53] It is not irrelevant either to note that all four 'poetic' words disappeared eventually from the spoken language and have left no direct traces in Romance.

   21.2. There are many other instances of such synonymic pairs: cf. *pulcher* and *formosus* (§13.3), *uirgo* and *puella* (§26.1), *meare* and *ire, celsus* and *altus, natus* and *filius* etc. The effect of a combination of two such elevated synonyms can be seen in the solemn words of Virgil's Sibyl, *Tróius Aeneas pietáte insígnis et armis / ad genitorem imas Erebi descéndit ad úmbras* (*A.* 6.403–4). The identical quantitative rhythm of the two verses produces an incantatory effect, which avoids monotony by the different patterns of homodynes (indicated by the accents). The Greek sound of *Trōĭŭs Aēnēās* is balanced by the gravity of *genitorem imas*, in

---

[53] For further discussion of the 'poetic lexicon' see Marouzeau (1962: 193–8), Leumann (1959: 155) and for Indo-European Schmitt (1967) and Watkins (1954: 193–8).

contrast to *patrem* and the unmetrical *infimas*. Another instance of the great poet making a virtue of necessity.

22.1. The retention of archaisms, words that have become obsolete in ordinary usage, is a feature of the poetic lexicon that has already emerged in the preceding paragraphs. *uerba a uetustate repetita*, says Quintilian (1.6.39), *adferunt orationi maiestatem aliquam non sine delectatione*. Not only do they have *auctoritatem antiquitatis* but also *quia intermissa sunt, gratiam nouitati similem parant*. In 8.3.24, writing of the *dignitas* conferred by *antiquitas*, he continues *eoque ornamento acerrimi iudicii P. Vergilius unice est usus*; a good example incidentally of the close relation between rhetoric and poetic in the ancient theorists.

22.2. Quintilian's examples of Virgil's archaisms include *moerus*, which was presumably not merely a relic of the old orthography *moirus*[54] but also intended to carry with it the archaic pronunciation and so underline the connection with *moenia*. Other words cited with approval[55] are *olli*, the older equivalent of *illi*, also found in Lucretius and rarely on official inscriptions, *quianam*, attested outside the *Aeneid* only in Naevius, Ennius and Accius, and *pone*, which as an adverb is found in Virgil, Propertius and Silver epic as well as Suetonius and Apuleius, but as a preposition has far too wide and heterogeneous a lexical profile generically and diachronically to even qualify as an archaism. Indeed *pone* occurs in a passage (*Rhet. Her.* 4.14) illustrating the *cottidianus sermo*!

22.3. Not all archaisms were approved. In 1.6.40 Quintilian refers disparagingly to words *ab ultimis et iam oblitteratis repetita temporibus*, citing various examples (beside those in 8.3.25–7), which end with *Saliorum carmina uix sacerdotibus suis satis intellecta*. These were still to be heard in his own day and unlike the revival of old words with which we are principally concerned here, they represent an unbroken tradition, preserved but progressively garbled over the centuries. As for the other words cited, it is not clear whether the objection is to attempts to revive them or to the idea of doing so. The first, *topper*, is not attested after Accius and Coelius Antipater, *antegerio* which *nemo nisi ambitiosus utetur* (8.3.25), is not attested at all, *exanclare*, well attested in early Latin, is not found between Cic. *Luc.* 108 and Apul. *Met.* 1.16, and *prosapia*, described by

[54] Which may indeed be what Quintilian wrote; cf. the MS variants *mus, mis. moerus* is due to Ribbeck.

[55] One of them, *porricere*, Haupt's correction of *pollicerent*, is problematic, since after Plautus, although it appears in a proverb quoted in Cic. *Att.* 5.18.1, *inter caesa et porrecta*, and in a conjecture for *porrigit* in Var. *R.* 1.29.3, there are no certain poetic or indeed literary attestations at all.

Quintilian in 8.3.26 as *insulsum*, is used by Cicero (*Tim.* 39) with the explicit label *uetus uerbum* and later by Suetonius and Apuleius. It is also used by Sallust (*Iug.* 85.10), whose taste for archaizing was notorious (Suet. *Aug.* 86.3 *Gramm.* 10).

22.4. There is no evidence in any case that any of these words was revived by any of the classical poets. What is important, however, is that for poets there is no such thing as an obsolete word. Any word can be resurrected for a specific poetic purpose, though to be effective it must obviously be intelligible and its traditional connotations recognizable to the educated reader. It looks as if there was already in classical times uncertainty about the meaning of *topper*, as of *caluitur* and *pedem struit* in the Twelve Tables. Such doubts would certainly have been a deterrent to revival.

23.1. Archaisms rarely appear in isolation from other ingredients of the elevated style. Take Catullus 64.35–6, *deseritur Cieros,*[56] *linquunt Pthiotica Tempe / Crannonisque domos ac moenia Larisaea.* The archaism *linquunt* which like other uncompounded forms, *cedere, fidere, gradi, solari* etc., was a particular feature of the higher poetic genres, is surrounded by the exotic sounds of toponyms appropriate to the narrative and to Achilles, who was born in Phthia. The strange coupling of Phthia with Tempe is implied in Callimachus, *H.* 4.105, 112, and the chiastic structure of 36 with its concluding double spondee is very much in the grand style.

23.2. In Virgil, *A.* 1.254, Jupiter's reassurances to Venus are introduced with appropriate majesty: *olli subridens hominum sator atque deorum.* The verse contains the archaism *olli* and the poetic use of *sator* as a synonym for *pater.* In the speech itself we find *fabor enim, quando haec te cura remordet, / longius et uoluens fatorum arcana mouebo* (261–2), with etymological word-play between *fata* and the archaic verb *fari.* In 2.54 *fata deum,* the passive participle of the middle verb, itself an archaism, is combined with the archaic genitive plural.

23.3. Ovid, *M.* 14.806, has *casside* in place of the usual classical word *galea.*[57] Unlike Virgil Ovid does not employ archaic words very much, even in this epic-scale work. However, the whole sentence is laden with archaism: *posita cum casside Mauors / talibus adfatur diuumque hominumque parentem.* Though not itself archaic, the presence of *cum* in the

---

[56] Meineke's correction of *Scyros*, the form which lies behind the actual manuscript readings, is adopted by most modern editors.

[57] As Leumann (1959: 143) noted, observing Ovid's reduction in archaic vocabulary, compared with Virgil and Horace.

opening phrase reminds readers of the comitative sense out of which the absolute construction developed. Straightforward archaisms are *posita* for *deposita*, *Mauors* for *Mars*, *adfatur* for *adloquitur*, *diuum* for *deorum* and the inherited *-que... -que*, the retention of which in poetry was no doubt assisted by Greek τε ... τε. Finally there is the descriptive phrase substituted for a proper name that was such a feature of Latin poetic discourse, though not always as unambiguous as it is here and in Virgil, *A.* 1.254 above. All these details combine to distance the sentence from normal prose usage, e.g. *galea deposita, Mars patrem deorum hominumque allocutus est.*

24.1. Some poetic paraphrases are metrically constrained, like *ter quattuor, bis senos* for *duodecim* (Enn. *Ann.* 88 Sk, Virg. *E.* 1.43) and other numeral substitutes. No such problem was posed by *caseus*, but cheese, like uncles, seldom needed to be mentioned in poetry. An exception is supplied by Virgil. In *E.* 1.34, *pinguis et ingratae premeretur caseus urbi*, the perennial down-to-earth complaint of the farmer against the city, an important motif of the poem, places the prosaic word in a carefully crafted alliterative 'golden' line. Later in the poem in an inviting rustic bill of fare we find a more conventional poetic periphrasis, *mitia poma, / castaneae molles et pressi copia lactis* (80–1). The contexts dictate the variation.

 24.2. At the start of Anchises' cosmological lecture (*A.* 6.725) *lucentemque globum lunae Titaniaque astra*, the periphrasis for *solem*, itself of course not unmetrical, not only counterbalances the description of *luna* but also alludes in a demythologizing context to the older religious view that made Helios the son of the Titan Hyperion. This kind of periphrasis is an important didactic vehicle in the *Georgics*, continually associating the old mythology with science as complementary elements in a unified world view. So we get *fratris radiis obnoxia... Luna* and *Tithoni croceum linquens Aurora cubile* (*G.* 1.396, 447). These periphrases contribute more than embellishment to their context (see §§29–30).

25.1. Various lexical formants can be singled out as to some extent characteristic of the poetic register. The first is the diminutive suffix, which has an interesting role in the history of the lexicon as a whole.[58] Always an ingredient of the colloquial register, some diminutives came to replace their base forms in late Vulgar Latin, e.g. *agnellus, masculus, uetulus.* Others, like *anulus, calculus* had already replaced their base forms in early

---

[58] See Ernout (1947: 67–9).

Latin. In the case of *uitulus, ancilla* the bases themselves had disappeared, though *anculus* is reported by Festus without attribution. Others like *bellus, flagellum, osculum* and *ampulla* had become distanced from their bases. It is doubtful whether any of these should be classed as live diminutives in the classical period. The diminutive form could be used in both a literal sense — *castellum, sacellum, tabella* etc. — and an emotive sense, connoting affection or contempt. The latter is a feature of satiric writing, e.g. *deteriore ... forma muliercula* (Lucr. 4.1279) and *furtiuae ... aurum / pelliculae* (Juv. 1.11) of the golden fleece. Its colloquial associations kept it from the higher genres of poetry and of prose. It may be that the epic preference for *uirgo* dates from a time when *puella* was still felt to be the diminutive of an obsolescent *puera*.

25.2. Lucretius has examples of diminutives used referentially; *particula, tantulus* etc. were obviously useful for discussing atomic theory. In 2.153–4, *nec singillatim corpuscula quaeque uaporis / sed complexa meant inter se conque globata*, we have besides *corpuscula* the old adverb based on the diminutive of *singuli* and the archaic tmesis of *conque globata*, both metrically necessary variants, and the epic archaism *meant*: in all a typical sample of the poet's purest didactic style. Sometimes the diminutive form has technical connotations, as *uitis ... nouellas* (Virg. *E.* 3.11); cf. *uineas nouellas* (Var. *R.* 1.31.1). On the other hand both literal and emotive senses seem appropriate to many of the Bucolic contexts e.g. *gemellos* (1.14), *agelli* (9.3), *capellae* (10.77).

25.3. The purely emotive use was especially associated with the discourse of love and already a target for satire in Plautus (*As.* 666–8). However Catullus does not restrict diminutives to personal erotic like *turgiduli ... ocelli* (3.18) or erotic satire like *rosea ista labella* (80.1). He has a number of them in poem 64: Ariadne on the shore *maestis Minois ocellis prospicit* (60–1), the grim detail in the picture of the Parcae, *laneaque aridulis haerebant morsa labellis* (316). This neoteric initiative in bringing elements of the lower genre into at least the more abbreviated forms of epic composition was not developed by the poet of the *Aeneid* or his successors in the epic genre. This may be due not to stylistic disdain — Virgil was content to include *lābrum* and *auunculus* — but to the fact that epic has few occasions when diminutives, whether literal or emotive, would be appropriate. Where they do seem appropriate, Virgil does not hold back. The poignancy of Dido's lament in *A.* 4.328–9 is deepened by the diminutive: *si quis mihi paruulus aula / luderet Aeneas ....*

26.1. If the diminutive suffix was fed from colloquial usage, the use of compound words has different orientations. Quintilian, after quoting Pacu-

vius' *repandirostrum incuruiceruicum pecus*, concludes his discussion of
compounding *sed res tota magis Graecos decet, nobis minus succedit*
(1.5.70). This observation accords with Livy's comment on the word *androgyni* (27.11.5), *uulgus, ut pleraque, faciliore ad duplicanda uerba Graeco
sermone appellat*. Latin was certainly not a compounding language comparable to Greek, Sanskrit or modern German, but the process was already
established in common Italic. Compounding simple verbs with preverbs, as
in *aduenio, anticipare circumferre, praeterire*, was an ancient and expanding
formative process.

26.2. Compound nouns and adjectives reflecting various kinds of predicate — determinatives like *princeps* (cf. *primum capere*), possessives like
nundinum (cf. *nouem dies*) etc. — already existed in Latin[59] and provided
a precedent on which Greek influence could expand. Thus in the areas of
trade and craft, law, politics, war and religion we find, for instance, *aedifi-
care, artifex, auspex, biennium, iudex, mancipium, sacerdos* and *sestertius*,
as well as some, like *hospes, manifestus* and *uindex*, whose analysis was
obscured by the passage of time. Semantically transparent compounding
of this sort remained a property of technical registers, where it received
additional stimulus from Greek models, especially in philosophy, science
and linguistic studies.[60] Thus Celsus, a purist in Latinity, willingly employed
Greek loan-words like *cataplasma, emplastrum, habrotonum* and *leth-
argicus* as well as calques like *auripigmentum, exulcerare, febricitare*.

26.3. Many poetic compounds are clearly formed on Greek models. In
epic and tragedy Homer, Pindar and the choral odes of tragedy were
influential, and the spread of compounding into Hellenistic epigram, most
notably Meleager, accounts for its presence in Augustan elegy. Genre is
important. Horace (*AP.* 93–98) sees *sesquipedalia uerba* as the norm for
tragedy, from which a Telephus or Peleus might depart *si curat cor spec-
tantis tetigisse querela*, while on the other hand the *tumidum os* of an angry
Chremes represents a departure from the norms of comedy. The frequency
of compounds in the surviving fragments of tragedy — *beniuolentia, miser-
icordia, uitisator* (Accius), *caprigenus, grandaeuitas* (Pacuvius) etc., most
of them metrically impossible for epic (see §5.1), confirm the realism of
Horace's precept.

26.4. Many of these early compounds were calques on Greek originals.
Thus Ennius' *altitonans* is modelled on ὑψιβρεμέτης, *frugifer* on καρποφόρος.
Sometimes the relation is more complex. Thus *magnanimus* in a Plautine
parody of the elevated style (*Am.* 212) seems to be modelled on μεγάθυμος

---

[59] See Bader (1962). More recently there has been intensive study of Latin word formation,
especially in France, reflected in the numerous writings of F. Biville, M. Fruyt and C. Kircher.
[60] On which see Coleman (1989).

but with a native stimulus in the phrase *magno animo*; Ennius' *caelicolae* on οὐρανίωνες, assisted like Naevius' *siluicola* by native *incola*; Lucilius' *grandaeuus* certainly on μακραίων. Livius however chose *uersutus* for πολύτροπος rather than *multimodus* (cf. *multimodis*, the substantival ablative used adverbially).

26.5. The process of compounding in poetry became cumulative. Lucretius follows earlier poets in using *frondifer* (Naev.), *laetificus* (Enn.), *lucifer* (Acc.) etc., but has also the earliest attestations of *suauidicus, montiuagus, siluifragus, turicremus* etc. Though first attestations can be misleading (cf. §2.5), a diachronic pattern of retention and innovation is unmistakable. Thus *omnipotens* is first attested in Ennius and Plautus and may well be independent of παγκράτης, *ignipotens* does not appear before Virgil, *auricomus*, calqued on χρυσοκόμης, is first found in Virgil, *aurifluus* not before Prudentius; *suauisonus*, calqued on ἡδύφωνος, is found as early as Naevius, *dulcisonus* not until Sidonius Apollinaris. Because of the domination of dactylic metres Livius' *quinquertĭō*, calqued on πένταθλος, and *inūmĭgāre* as well as eccentricities like Catullus' *lasarpicifer* were not taken up. In general the most productive classes were the determinatives, with verbal second components — *laniger, armisonus, belligerens* etc. — and, some way behind, the possessives — *longaeuus, aequanimus* etc.

26.6. Sometimes, inevitably, the compound becomes a cliché and its semantic distinctiveness is eroded.[61] Accius' *quadrupedantum sonipedum* (*tr.* 603) is the first attestation of the calque on Hesiod's καναχήπους. The aural image is clearly prominent, as it is in Virgil's *stat sonipes ac frena ferox spumantia mandit* (*A.* 4.135). But in Valerius Flaccus' *quemque suus sonipes . . . portat* (1.431) the word has become just an anapaestic synonym for *equus*, a piece of 'poetic diction' in the pejorative sense of the phrase. The same is even more true of the choriambic *quadrupedes*.

26.7. The poetic associations of compounding can be confirmed indirectly from two sources. The first is its occurrence in Plautus, who like Aristophanes employs it for comic and specifically parodic purposes. Some examples, like *magnanimus, caelipotens*, are simply lifted from contexts of high seriousness and survive in that tradition; others, like *multibiba, unoculus, turpilucricupidus*, reflecting the formation of nicknames like the cognomen *Crassipes*, do not outlast their immediate comic role.

26.8. The second source is the effect of occurrences of known poetic compounds in prose contexts. Thus *suauiloquens* is attested first in Ennius' praise of Cethegus (*Ann.* 304 Sk) and recurs appropriately in Lucretius' *suauiloquenti carmine Pierio* (1.945–6). However, it is also used once in classical prose by Cicero, who cites the Ennian passage for Cethegus'

---

[61] What follows is developed from Ernout (1947: 56).

suauiloquentiam at *Brut.* 58; in *Rep.* 5.11, a certain *suauiloquens iucunditas* is attributed to Menelaus. Far from being diminished here, the poetic connotations are especially apt for Cicero's context: an epic epithet for an epic hero. Another example: in *Tusc.* 5.79, *non montiuagos atque siluestris cursus lustrationesque patiuntur?* Cicero takes over *montiuagus* from Lucretius, who uses it, as Cicero does, in analogies between human and animal behaviour (1.404, 2.597). But the poetic tone is again stylistically appropriate, since the context is the emotional conclusion of the Stoic argument, and the whole clause forms a rhythmic and grandiloquent finale to a tricolon. Finally *ueridicus*, which first occurs in Lucr. 6.6 and Cat. 64.306, is again taken up by Cicero, *ueridicae uoces ex occulto missae esse dicuntur* (*Diu.* 1.101), and then by Livy, *ueridica interpres deum* (1.7.10), where the poetical tones are appropriate respectively to the antique tale of Faunus' prophecies and to Evander's account of Hercules and Cacus. Subsequent attestations in the elder Pliny and Martial suggest that the word soon lost its high poetic status, but its effectiveness in Cicero and Livy still depends upon that status.

26.9. Compounds were also, as we noted in §26.2, a feature of technical registers. Lucretius, who was cited for poetic compounds, also exemplifies the technical usage, as one would expect of a truly didactic poet. Thus *ex alienigenis rebus constare* (1.865), *genitales auctificique motus* (2.571–2), *sensifer unde oritur... motus* (3.272), *modis multis multangula* (4.654). The patterns of formation are identical with those in §26.5, and this is true for the scientific, technological and learned compounds generally, as witness the following, taken from the pages of Pliny's *Natural History*: *aquifolia*, the hybrid *aurichalcus, internodium, lapicidinae, multiformis, proportio, saxifragum, triangulus, unicolor* and *uitifer*. In both registers the intention is the same, to present an object or concept in clear and economical terms. The difference is that the technical compounds, recurring in contexts where their effectiveness depends upon univocal precision, do not have and must not have the evocations and allusiveness that come from the succession of emotive contexts in which poetical compounds recur and on which *their* effectiveness depends.

27.1 We have already noted (§15) the phonetic contribution of Greek words to Latin poetic contexts, but of no less importance is their semantic input to these contexts.

27.2. Macrobius notes (*Sat.* 6.4.17) *lychnus* as a graecism used by Ennius, Lucretius and Virgil. Attestations in Statius confirm the poetic profile for the word. But in contrast to *lucerna, lanterna* etc. it is used of hanging lamps, and as the regular word for this luxury item of furniture it

is found in Cicero, *Cael.* 67. The association with grandeur and wealth
gives the word its passport into epic, but it is not in itself poetic. Virgil's
fondness for Greek words for drinking vessels is also noted by Macrobius,
who cites (*Sat.* 5.21.1) *cantharus, carchesium, scyphus*, but what these words
tell us is not that the poet preferred Greek names to Latin ones but that
he preferred the imagistic detail of Greek utensils. In this he was merely
extending the precedent of *amphora, cadus, crater* etc.

27.3. Many Greek words had in fact become so familiar in Latin as
to have almost surrendered their foreign connotations. Thus *balineum,
bracchium, carta, machina, massa* and *purpureus* had undergone Latin
sound changes, *ampulla, gubernator* and *spatula* had acquired Latin suffixes. The entry status of *aer, barbaricus, corona, dracuma, ostreum* and
stola, all attested already in Ennius, cannot be determined, but they certainly have no specifically poetic connotations in classical Latin. When
Horace, characterizing spring, writes *trahuntque siccas machinae carinas*
(*C.* 1.4.2) it is precisely the unpoetic character of *machinae*, characteristically juxtaposed with the poetic synecdoche of *carinas* in an alliterative
sequence that injects the workaday detail into the image. By contrast in
C. 1.1.29–34 the counterpoint of Greek and Latin words brilliantly enacts
the synthesis of the two poetic cultures that Horace is proclaiming as his
vocation. Thus the *hederae* that crown learned brows place him among *dis
superis*, the *Nympharum . . . cum Satyris chori* are what *secernunt populo,
Euterpe* does not constrain the Latin *tibias* nor *Polyhymnia* refuse to tune
Lesbōum . . . barbiton. The hybrid phrase *lyricis uatibus* (35) sums it all
up, and the self-mocking deference of the conclusion does nothing to
destroy the effect.

27.4. Apart from Greek words there is little evidence of direct borrowing into the poetic register of words from other foreign sources. There
is ancient testimony to Italic origins for *cascus, crepusculum, dirus* and
famulus, to which we can add *bos* and the very unpoetic *multa*; from
dialectal Latin *testis, uerna* and possibly *sol*. None of these is likely to have
entered Latin through poetry.

28.1. It is of course proper nouns and their derivative epithets that are
most often used for poetic effect, above all those that relate to mythological
incidents and geographical locations.

28.2. Propertius boasts (1.9.5) that not even *Chaoniae . . . columbae* can
surpass his power to prophesy in amorous matters. The phrase also occurs
in Virgil, *E.* 9.13, and refers with conventional obliquity to the oak-tree
cult of Zeus at Dodona and the oracular *columbae* (πελειάδες) associated
with it. But *columbae* are after all *Veneris dominae uolucres, mea turba*

(3.3.31); so they have a special relevance, the poet would have us believe, to erotic prophecy. Learning and wit are the characteristics of such mythological allusions.

28.3. In the much discussed opening similes of Propertius, 1.3, the three sleeping beauties are given identifying epithets. The local epithet *Cnosia* (3), juxtaposed with *desertis* recalls the treachery to her family, now punished by the treacherous *Thesea carina* (1); *Andromede* (4), with the exotic colour of the Greek nominative, needs no further specification and the patronymic epithet *Cepheia* alludes to the story of her sacrifice; *Edonis* (5) identifies the third woman as a member of the Thracian tribe famous for Bacchant worship, or as a Thessalian devotee behaving like one beside the river, *Apidano* (6). In each instance the actual descriptive details look back to events before the sleep — *desertis . . . litoribus, libera . . . cotibus, fessa choreis* — so that the triad form a poetic argument fashioned in myth and imagery but highly relevant to the following autobiographical scene. This use of a group of mythological *exempla*, already employed in 1.2.15–24 occurs elsewhere in Propertius, e.g. 1.13.21–24.

28.4. An interesting example of a Graecism used apparently to distance the familiar comes in Virg. *A.* 8.72, *tuque o Thybri tuo genitor cum flumine sancto*, a line which we learn from Macrobius (*Sat.* 6.1.12) is adapted from Ennius' *teque, pater Tiberine, tuo cum flumine sancto (Ann.* 26 Sk). Having referred to the god of this Etrusco-Latin river as *deus . . . Tiberinus* (31), Virgil subsequently has the god identifying himself as *caeruleus Thybris, caelo gratissimus amnis* (64). The Hellenized version of the name (for the more usual Greek Θύμβρις) is set between a very poetical colour adjective and an allusion to its supposed etymology. The exotic form of the name is enhanced by the choice of the Greek vocative case, adding the majestic *genitor* in place of *pater*, which was the normal address even in Latin prayers. The tribulations of Aeneas, *Laomedontius heros* (18), like those of Priam, *Laomedontiades* (158), are the penance that Laomedon's descendants must pay for his impious crime (cf. 4.542). Now suddenly a potentially hostile river god with a Hellenized name announces the presence of friendly Greeks at the site of Rome and an offer to conduct the harassed Trojans to unexpected allies. *Thybris* is after all propitious in its distancing.

28.5. Similarly significant is the epithet in Horace's *C.* 3.29.1. *Tyrrhena regum progenies* has a grandeur above the more matter-of-fact address, *Maecenas atauis edite regibus*, in 1.1.1. Again the Etrusco-Greek form is preferred to *Tuscus* or *Etruscus*, which is used of the *mare Tyrrhenum* later in the ode. Its transfer from *regum* to *progenies* gives the phrase a more characterizing force compared with 1.1.1, but the form of the epithet well characterizes the Hellenophile Etruscan. Appropriate too is the sybar-

itic Greek detail of *pressa tuis balanus capillis* (4), βάλανος amidst the
homely Latin hospitality promised. The warning that follows against
the perils of fashionable Tusculum is wittily presented in the learned
allusion of *Telegoni iuga parricidae* (8), which we can set beside the
Circaea... moenia of *Epod.* 1.30. Three illustrations in two stanzas of
the allusive potentialities of Greek words in Latin contexts.

28.6. A frequent and colourful use of Greek names, whether of natural
phenomena or of mythological persons, is to form geographical periphrases. In Catullus, 64.3, the Greeks sail not to *Colchis* but *Phasidos ad
fluctus et fines Aeeteos*. The river Phasis, provided with a Greek case form,
and the derivative noun from the name of Medea's father, with its unLatin
spondaic vocalism, provide appropriate exotic colour and enclose an old-
fashioned alliterative phrase in which *fluctus* 'waves' suggests a substantial
flumen. The periphrasis adds *grauitas* to the remote oriental region, but
before readers can appreciate this, they do need to know what the references are. There is thus a loss in accessibility.

28.7. Catullus at the end of 66 uses the form *Ŏărĭōn*, echoing Callimachus' 'Ωαρίων (*H.* 3.265), appropriately, since the poem is an adaptation
of the Greek poet's *Coma Berenices*. The short iota provides respectable
precedent for modifications of *Ōrīōn*, which is not in itself metrically
difficult. So Virgil has *nimbosus Ŏrīōn* (*A.* 1.535), reminding us of the
importance of the heavenly bodies as clock, compass and calendar in
the premodern world. Much that strikes us as esoteric astronomical
learning would have been less unfamiliar to ancient readers, Quint. 1.4.4
notwithstanding. Similarly the identification of the constellation with the
mythical hunter giant would have been familiar to educated readers; and
Horace can cite as an *exemplum* of *uis consili expers* (*C.* 3.4.65) *notus et
integrae / temptator Orion Dianae* (70–1). The ancient myths provided an
accessible store of paradigms of good and ill, appeal to which was a
characteristic of Greek and thence Latin poetry. Accessibility could be
endangered by the tendency to make the allusions more and more oblique.
But Greek words certainly had far more than the ornamental effect noted
in §15.3.

28.8. Not all allusive epithets are mythological. In *C.* 3.5. Horace presents Regulus as an *exemplum* of self-sacrificing patriotism, following
Pindar's paradigmatic citation of the exploits of Greek mythical heroes.
The poem ends with the depiction of the Roman hero in happier times
tendens Venefranos in agros / aut Lacedaemonium Tarentum. It is not
known whether Regulus had ancestral estates near the Samnite town and
what associations he had with Tarentum (nearby Brundisium had been the
site of his earlier consular triumph). But *Lacedaemonium* alludes to
the Spartan foundation that Tarentum had long claimed. It evokes the

Greek state with which traditional Romans preferred to identify their own civic ideals,[62] specified by Cicero, *Flacc.* 62–3, but only after his own Athenian preferences. Moreover, if Livy's belief (38.17.12) that contemporary Tarentines retained little of the proverbial Spartan qualities was widely shared, the phrase mirrors summarily the decline from Regulus' Rome to the Rome castigated in this and other Horatian 'laureate' odes.

28.9. The next ode provides an important example of a non-Greek allusive epithet. Horace contrasts with the degenerate Augustans (3.6.17ff., 45ff.) those who had made Rome great, *rusticorum mascula militum / proles, Sabellis docta ligonibus / uersare glaebas et seuerae / matris ad arbitrium recisos / portare fustis* (37–41). The homely unglamorous imagery, created out of very prosaic vocabulary, evokes a way of life remote from Augustan *urbanitas* and *luxuria*; but it is rural Italy, not rural Latium that is extolled. The synecdoche in *Sabellis* may have a subversive edge when used to extol traditionally 'Roman' virtues. For the epithet refers strictly to non-Latin speaking, especially Oscan, regions of Italy (cf. *Sabellus ager* in Liv. 8.1.7). We can compare his fellow Italian's *pubem . . . Sabellam* (*G.* 2.167).

29.1. The allusiveness that we have observed constantly in the preceding paragraphs depends upon readers learned enough especially in Greek poetry to respond to the references. This is why it is particularly associated with the higher genres of epic, didactic and public lyric. By contrast metaphor and other lexical tropes of semantic transfer,[63] which are, with the creation of imagery, the most powerful and distinctive of the poet's communicative vehicles, yield their effect to anyone who knows the language and has imagination. Various tropes employing semantic shifts away from the current meaning of a word are widely attested in poetry. The most prolific is metaphor, which, at least since Aristotle's *Poetics*[64] has been recognized as the most important of all the poet's verbal skills. Aristotle also remarks in *Rh.* 3.2.5 that everyone uses metaphor as well as literal meaning — κύριον καὶ τὸ οἰκεῖον — in ordinary discourse, resorting to metaphors in order to repair deficiencies in the lexicon but thereafter

---

[62] See Rawson (1969: 99–106).

[63] This area of lexical usage has been much discussed in recent years both by literary critics and theorists and by linguists; e.g. Nowottny (1962), Henry (1971), Ortony (1979), Lakoff and Johnson (1980), Levinson (1983 esp. 147–62).

[64] The most important Graeco-Roman discussions of metaphor that survive are Arist. *Po.* 22.1458b-59a, *Rh.* 3.2.6–15, 1404b-1405b, Cic. *De or.* 3.155–69, Longin. *Sublim.* 32.1–7. The examples cited and the discussions of them all repay close attention.

retaining them for ornamentation. To quote Cicero (*De or.* 3.155), *uerbi translatio instituta est inopiae causa, frequentata delectationis.*[65]

29.2. The ornamental function of metaphor, which gives pleasure to readers, does not displace other poetic functions. By suggesting a similarity between dissimilars, especially between the less familiar, and the more familiar, authors are able to convey to their readers new perceptions of the world and to move them by associations thus made, while delighting their imagination. Aristotle stresses that metaphor is of great effect in both prose and poetry (*Rh.* 3.2.7), and Cicero, whose concern is the education of orators, nevertheless chooses examples of metaphor and other semantic transfers from poetic as well as prose writings.

29.3. The use of metaphor to supplete a limited vocabulary is well illustrated in the linguistic habits of children and remains, as Aristotle noted, a feature of adult discourse in all languages. Along with neologisms and loan-words metaphor and other transfer tropes provide the tools for dealing with new objects, experiences and concepts and are the major vehicle of semantic change in the lexicon. Sometimes the shift is permanent and the original sense is lost. The Romance reflexes of *caput* are almost wholly metaphorical, *capo di famiglia, Capo dello Stato, chef de cuisine, chef d'oeuvre* etc., while the original meaning has been replaced by reflexes of *testa*, the slang use of which in turn completely ousted its older meanings. There are numerous parallels in Latin, e.g. *animus* *'breath, wind', *audax* *'insatiable, eager', *scire* *'to cut' etc.

29.4. It is not always easy to ascertain the direction of metaphoric shift without an abundance of documentation for the periods in question. Of the three instances of rustic metaphor[66] adduced by Cicero (*De or.* 3.155), *gemmare uitis, luxuriem esse in herbis* and *laetas segetes* two are misleading. For *gemma* originally meant 'bud', as in Cato, *Agr.* 42, and it is 'gem' that is the metaphoric extension, first attested for us in Cicero's own *Verr.* 4.39. The original meaning of *laetus* was 'lush, sleek, in good condition', as in Cato's contrast between *agro laeto* and *agro sicco* (*Agr.* 61.2), so that the more familiar meaning is again the metaphoric one.

29.5. This is also true of *felix*, cognate with *fecundus, felare, femina* and meaning 'fruitful', as in Cato's definition (Festus 81), *felices arbores quae fructum ferunt*. Only *luxuries* really belongs here, being used of plants running wild and of uncontrolled growth. Virgil's *si luxuria foliorum exuberat umbra* (*G.* 1.191) exploits the extension to human behaviour as a term of moral disapproval. The tree is squandering its resources; the harvest of

---

[65] For an important discussion of *De or.* 3.155–68 see Fantham (1972: 176–80).

[66] cf. the rustic metaphors like γελᾶν τὰ φυτά and ἱλαρὰ εἶναι, cited in the Homeric Scholia (*Iliad* 23.598, ed. H. Erbse).

nuts will suffer. It is characteristic of a *doctus poeta* in any language to exploit semantic layers in the history of a word. Virgil surely had in mind too Dido's childlessness when he gave her the epithet *infelix* (cf. 4.68 with 595 etc.). In such words the original meaning may lie dormant for a period, to be reactivated by a poet confident in the knowledge that readers will be familiar enough with earlier literature to appreciate that what to the uninitiated can only appear as a metaphor is in fact a semantic reversion.

29.6. Many other words retain their original sense while acquiring various metaphoric uses permanently. Thus OE *hēafod* has retained its anatomical meaning along with a host of extensions, which fill over eighteen columns of the *Oxford English Dictionary*. Similarly in Latin we have *clarus* 'loud' etc., *comprehendere* 'to take hold of' etc., *uirtus*, 'manliness' etc.

29.7. Such metaphors affect the semantic fields of words in a permanent way. For this reason they are conspicuous in scientific and technical registers. New inventions and discoveries demand new linguistic resources. One has only to think of the vocabulary of modern computer technology — *gateway, menu, mouse, software, virus, to back, go down* etc. Latin architects gave new metaphoric senses to existing words, like *ordinatio, membrum, principium, reticulatus, surdus*. What is characteristic of scientific metaphors is their permanence and univocality. Once the new meaning has been assigned, it remains purely referential within the register; there is no ornamental function, no contextual variation and no emotive accumulation from previous occurrences. This univocality is far removed from literary metaphor, which is very often a nonce phenomenon; no one since Macbeth has called life *a walking shadow* except with reference to the famous soliloquy.

29.8. There are on the other hand many poetic metaphors that, once invented, are taken up and extended by later authors. Macrobius (*Sat.* 6.4.3) cites Ennius' *et Tiberis flumen . . . uomit in mare salsum* (*Ann.* 453 Sk) and Virgil's *mane salutantum totis uomit aedibus undam* (*G.* 2.462). The image of a river god spewing water into the sea is certainly not ornamental, and the later poet has exploited the unattractive image in a context of repugnance, using a chiastic word order around *uomit* to enhance the image. Here, unlike most reworked metaphors, the poetic effect does not depend very much on the reader's recognition of the original source.

30.1. Scientific and poetic metaphors naturally appear side by side in didactic poetry. To the scientific category belongs Lucretius' *elementa* (1.827), calqued on στοιχεῖα. The aptness of the metaphor, for which Cicero

(*Ac.* 1.26) seems to claim the credit, is underlined by the use of the word in its literal sense 'letters' in the course of an analogy with the atoms out of which things are composed (1.197). Another Lucretian calque is *simulacra* (1.1060) for εἴδωλα, the Epicurean term for the images given off by objects, which account among other things for *simulacra* in the ordinary sense, 'ghosts' (1.123). The use of *materies* for ὕλη is especially appropriate to Epicurean metaphysics, given its usual sense 'building timber' and the etymological connection with *mater* (see §30.6).

30.2. More poetic is, for instance, the use of *lacessere* of colliding atoms (2.137), a personification, since the word was originally used of challenging to a contest. A particularly Latin source of such metaphors is the legal and political registers. Thus Horace declares (*C.* 3.29.54–6) his choice of Poverty rather than dependence on Fortune in the legal terminology of gift repayments, *resigno quae dedit* (sc. *Fortuna*), and marriage contract, *probamque / Pauperiem sine dote quaero*.

30.3. But some of the most striking examples occur once again in Lucretius. The concept of natural law is presented anthropomorphically (1.76–7) in terms of the definition of constitutional power: *refert nobis . . . / . . . finita potestas denique quoique / quanam sit ratione* (cf. *infinita potestas* granted to Pompey: Cic. *Agr.* 2.33). This metaphor, combined with the *qu* alliteration that is not uncommon in legal phraseology, is followed immediately by another, taken from land tenure, . . . *atque alte terminus haerens*. Nature assigns powers and fixes their limits. The two metaphors come towards the end of a passage (63–79) rich in metaphor — the crushing weight of the monster *Religio*, Epicurus' breach of the *arta / Naturae . . . portarum claustra* and advance beyond the *flammantia moenia mundi*, the outcome of his victory, which *nos exaequat . . . caelo*, and much else. The powerful appeal to imagination and emotion well illustrates how much more than mere ornament metaphor can bring to a poetic — and a proselytizing — context.

30.4. There are references elsewhere to *foedera Naturai* (1.586), Nature's treaties, the pacts that define the relations between different parts of the universe. The use of *concilium* to depict the combinations of atoms to form sensible objects was no doubt inspired by Epicurus' ἄθροισμα, but the Latin term has much stronger political and constitutional connotations. The term is introduced in a passage (1.182–3) that itself illustrates the difficulties than can arise in identifying a metaphor: *primordia quae genitali / concilio possent arceri*. The verb *ordiri* is used by Pliny (*Nat.* 11.80) of a spider weaving its web, and this may be the original sense of the verb, which would make Pacuvius' *machinam ordiris nouam* (*tr.* 379) a bolder metaphor than it seems. It would also make Lucretius' *primordia* and *exordia* not 'initial particles' but 'threads' from which the world's fibres are woven. Pliny again (*Nat.* 7.61) has the phrase *profluuium genitale* of menstruation, so it is possible that a notion of biological reproduction was prominent in Lucretius' use of *genitalis*. The notion that atoms could be held together in a 'generative council' is certainly strange, but no more so perhaps than, say, *creatrix Natura* (1.629) or *daedala Tellus* (1.7). Stoics could indeed define *Natura* as that which *contineat mundum omnem eumque tueatur* (Cic. *Nat.* 2.29) and so provide a context for Nature's creativity in a literal sense. But its introduction even metaphorically in an Epicurean poem seems bold.

30.5. The personification of *Natura* belongs with a number of other metaphors that exploit traditional religious concepts. Especially notable is the reference to *Terra*, who has earned her *maternum nomen* when she *genus . . . creauit / humanum* and *animal . . . fudit / omne quod in magnis bacchatur montibu(s) passim* (5.821–5). In an author not given to using Greek words *bacchatur*, like *daedala Tellus*, has a distancing effect, but the emotive power of *Mater Terra*, like that of *Pater Aether*, with whom she is coupled in 1.250–1, is great and helps to conceal the awkward gap in the rational argument between inanimate and animate modes of being. The poet again comes to the philosopher's rescue.

31.1. Personification is of course a form of metaphor more easily available in languages that assign animate gender to inanimate objects or abstractions. Hence also the easy deification of Ἁρμονία, *Fortuna* etc. *Timor, Minae* and *Cura* are all personified in Horace, *C.* 3.1.37ff., where their appearance constitutes the poet's warning to the *dominus . . . terrae fastidiosus: sed Timor et Minae / scandunt eodem quo dominus neque / decedit aerata triremi et / post equitem sedet atra Cura*. Fear is personified also in Virg. *A.* 9.719, *atrum . . . Timorem*, and Phobos son of Ares already appears in Homer and Hesiod (*Il.* 4.440, *Theog.* 934). *Timor* like *Cura* resides in the mind of the rich owner, the *Minae*, which are personified here perhaps for the first time, inspire that fear from without. So *Timor et Minae* is almost a hendiadys.

31.2. The personification of *Cura* itself is found elsewhere in Augustan poetry, e.g. Virg. *A.* 6.274, *ultrices . . . Curae*. However, the metaphorical animation of Anxiety already occurs in *Theognis* 729, Φροντίδες . . . πτερὰ ποικίλ' ἔχουσαι, which is echoed by Horace in *C.* 2.16.11, *Curas laqueata circum tecta uolantes.*[67] Later in the same ode (21–2) there is an interesting anticipation of the present passage: *scandit aeratas uitiosa nauis / Cura nec*

---

[67] Here, as usual, the commentary by Nisbet and Hubbard (1978) is illuminating.

turmas equitum relinquit, where *uitiosa* suggests both the diseased mental state and, within the trope itself, the corrosive effect on the metal.

31.3. The eerie presence of the trio is adumbrated in just a few descriptive details. The vigorous *scandunt* mocks *fastidiosus*, and this is emphasized by the repetition of *dominus*. More static images are presented in *neque decedit . . . et . . . sedet . . . .* Both *triremi* and *equitem* are usually taken to refer to the rich man's expensive recreations, sailing and horse-riding. This may well be true of *equitem*, though Horace is perhaps exploiting the ambiguity of the word to make the point that those in the top income bracket are as much at risk as cavalry officers. The nautical image seems more distinctly military: *triremes* were usually warships and *aerata* 'armoured' is a familiar epithet of *naues longae* (e.g. Caes. *Civ.* 2.3.1; cf. *ratem aeratam*, attributed to Naevius in Var. *L.* 7.23). The verb *decedere* has strong military connotations also, of retreat (Caes. *Civ.* 1.71), retirement from active service (Liv. 41.10.7) and even desertion (Cic. *Sen.* 73). *Cura* is continually on active service aboard expensive warships, whatever purposes they are being used for. Finally *atra*, in implicit visual contrast with *aerata*, yet invisible to the knight himself, suggests, as *nigra* would not, a baleful presence uninterrupted and unseen. *Timor, Minae* and *atra Cura* enclose the whole passage.

32.1 Of the other tropes of semantic transfer metonymy and synecdoche in particular merit attention here. Metonymy like metaphor plays an important role in the lexical history of a language, as for instance *ago, ciuitas, dies* and *res* all illustrate. It is most frequently seen in the shift from 'verbal action' to 'concrete effect' in the meaning of nouns like *comitium, legio, natura*, where the original meaning was displaced, and *gaudium, oratio, cultura*, where it was not. The semantic shift was particularly clear in the plural forms (as was the separate and less remarkable shift from generic or collective to specific or individual in *nix, frumentum, aes* etc.).

32.2. In literary usage the effects of this trope are less permanent, as in the examples cited by Cicero (*De or.* 3.167), *curia* for *senatus, campus* for *comitia, arma* and *tela* for *bellum, toga* for *pax*. This last example is attested in a notorious line from his own poetry, *cedant arma togae, concedat laurea linguae* (cited in *Off.* 1.77), with the combination of two very Roman metonymic images in *toga* and *laurea*[68]. The contents of Cicero's list illustrate once more the common property shared by poets and orators.

---

[68] The reading *linguae* is preserved in Quint. 11.1.24. The tradition of *De officiis* itself strongly favours *laudi*.

32.3. Metonymy, like metaphor, has many uses for a poet, whether he is writing in a high or low genre. In Horace's *Graecia barbariae lento conlisa duello* (*Epist.* 1.2.7) the opening words give a sense of depersonalized contestants that *Graeci* and *barbari* would not (cf. *Graecia* but *barbaris* in Cic. *Off.* 3.99). The already current use of *barbaria* in the sense of 'barbarity' adds an emotive element to the traditional interpretation of the war, whose epic status is marked by the archaic *duello*. In *Graecia capta ferum uictorem cepit et artis / intulit agresti Latio* (*Epist.* 2.1.156–7) the contrast is between geographical possession, which comes from military victory and cultural conquest, which is made more threatening and pervasive by the replacement of *Graeci* by the more impersonal *Graecia*. *Latio* for *Latinis* enhances the play on the two senses of *agrestis*, also an instance of metonymy.

32.4. One of the most frequent poetic metonymies is the substitution of divine names for the object or activity of which they were in traditional religion the patrons. Cicero (*De or.* 3.167) again instances *Mars* for *bellum*, *Ceres* for *fruges*, *Liber* for *uinum*, *Neptunus* for *mare*. A characteristic Ovidian example is *quis Veneris famulae conubia liber inire / . . . uelit?* (*A.* 2.7.21–2). The witty juxtaposition of *famulae* with the goddess' name, used metonymically though it is, is compounded by *conubia* and *liber*. For although Lucretius' *conubia ad Veneris partusque ferarum* (3.776), where the metonymy identifies Venus not with the one who inspires *amor* but with *amor* itself, offers precedent for the use of *conubium* for *concubitus*, the presence of *famula* and *liber* recalls that *conubium* in the strict sense was a legal impossibility between slave and freeborn. The adynaton would no doubt have struck Corinna as an irrelevance.

33.1. Synecdoche too is common to all registers. For instance the use of *caput* of one's person or personal status is well established in legal terminology and in prose generally, and need not be a calque on κάρα, κεφαλή. But poetry shows much bolder and more extensive use of the figure. Nautical terminology shows a remarkable diversity of synecdoche in poetry. Varro defines *ratis* as being used *ubi plures mali aut asseres iuncti aqua ducuntur* (*L.* 7.23). In the sense of 'raft' it is distinguished from *nauis* in Cic. *Ver.* 5.5, but Ennius already has it by metonymy in the latter sense in *ratibusque . . . fremebat/imber Neptuni* (*Ann.* 515 Sk); whence it passes to classical poetry, e.g. *pandas ratibus posuere carinas* (Virg. *G.* 2.445). Horace already has *carina* 'keel' by synecdoche for *nauis* in *C.* 1.35.8, *quicumque Bithyna lacessit / Carpathium pelagus carina*, where the Greek loan-word *pelagus* 'sea', first attested in Pacuvius and Lucilius, also contributes to the alliterative effect and even perhaps to the sense of geographical distance.

33.2. Another synecdoche is the use of *puppis* for *nauis* (cf. Quint. 8.6.20). This is already attested in Cat. 64.6, *uada salsa cita decurrere puppi*, which is also one of the earliest attestations of *uada* 'shallows', again a synecdoche for 'sea'. Virgil has *nautica pinus* (*E.* 4.38) for 'ship', where the direction of the trope is clarified by the epithet, as it is by the context in *quos . . . infesta ducebat in aequora pinu* (*A.* 10.205–6). In the next line *arbor* for 'oar' is similarly disambiguated: *centenaque arbore fluctum /* *uerberat adsurgens*. In *A.* 5.504 the reference to a mast is explicit: *sagitta . . .* *aduersi . . . infigitur arbore mali*. In Ov. *M.* 11.476 *arbore* is similarly disambiguated by the following *malo*; but Valerius Flaccus' *celsior arbore pontus* (1.496) no longer needs more than a general contextual support.

33.3. To revert to words used by trope for 'the sea': Cic. *Arat.* 67 seems to be the earliest attestation of *aequor* without explicit specification. There is a well-known ambiguity in Virgil's *omne tibi stratum silet aequor* (*E.* 9.57), and the context alone disambiguates *aequora* in *A.* 10.206. The need for specification was increased in *A.* 2.780, *uastum maris aequor arandum*, by the metaphoric use of *arare*, but it is less severe in *A.* 5.158, *longa sulcant uada salsa carina*, where a comparable metaphoric verb is combined with two unambiguously synecdochic nouns. The colour noun *caerulum* (<*cael-ul-*) is already used of 'the sea' by Cicero in *FPL* 29.3B, *nemo haec umquam est transuectus caerula cursu*. The rise of this rival metaphoric use partly explains Lucretius' wish to specify the original meaning in 1.1090, *et solis flammam per caeli caerula pasci*, echoing Enn. *Ann.* 48 Sk. When Silius writes *sulcarunt caerula puppes* (15.239) the tropic character of the statement is less striking inasmuch as all three of the constituents were already well established in their transferred meanings (see §29.8). It should be noted again (cf. §29.6) that all the words cited continued to be used in their literal sense in poetry as well as prose. Virgil could still write an Ennian portrait of Octavian, *cum patribus populoque, penatibus et magnis dis, / stans celsa in puppi* (*A.* 8.680), with *puppis* used in its original sense.

34.1. What has been said by a great critic about metaphor applies equally to all the tropes of semantic transfer that we have just been considering: 'the inimitable mark of the poet is his ability to control the realization of a metaphor to the precise degree appropriate in a given place'.[69] The

---

[69] F. R. Leavis (1948: 77).

creative mind that perceives the relevant similarity between dissimilars also creates the context within which that similarity is sufficiently clarified.

34.2. An important consequence of the various types of semantic transfer that we have been surveying was that poets had a large store of synonyms for many common words.[70] For *mare* we could add to the examples cited already *altum, fretum, gurges, pontus, profundum*; for *nauis* there are *prora, remus, trabs, uelum*. For *aqua* poets could use *latex, liquor, lympha, umor*; for *amor* there are *aestus, ardor, cura, furor, ignis* etc., for *amica* we find *cura, domina, era, lux, puella, uita*. Many of these are ordinary words, used in poetry sometimes with their ordinary prose meanings, sometimes with special poetic meanings, like *puppis* (§33.3). Such too are *cedere, mortalis, mucro, ponere* (for *deponere*). Alongside these instances of occasional poetic diction are those words which are virtually exclusive to poetry, such as *ensis, fari, letum, meare, olle, -que ... -que*, or unprefixed forms like *fessus, gradi, linquere*.

34.3. Last among semantic transfers comes the substitution of plural forms of nouns for singulars. τὸ ἓν πολλὰ ποιεῖν is recognized by Aristotle (*Rh.* 3.6.4) as a feature of poetic discourse, but there is no reason to think that the Latin usage is much indebted to Greek.[71] Some distinctions need to be made: first between plurals that generally have a semantic opposition to singulars, e.g. *thalami* v. *thalamus*, and those that do not, e.g. *nuptiae* (see §5.8); second between *thalami, thalamus* and *niues, nix* or *rationes, ratio* (see §32.1). Which leaves us with the difficult question of what the distinction between *thalami* and *thalamus* etc. actually was. There are various possibilities: an aggrandizement of the concept signified by the singular, the recognition of a plurality of components or adjuncts in the singular concept, an expressively heavier or lighter texture in the sound of the plural form. But confronted with a typical list like *aequora, astra, otia, regna, saecla*, no one would have much confidence in assigning meanings distinct from *aequor, astrum* etc. except in the relatively few instances in which the neuter plurals appear to be collectives. Two things are certain however: first that none of these plurals became permanent synonyms of their singulars (in contrast to vulg. *gaudia, folia* etc.), occurrences are occasional and selective; second that the trope provided metrically useful variants (see §§6.1, 11.3).

35.1. The poet's other major lexical tool is the creation of images and imagery, not only as a source of pleasure for the reader but also as an

---

[70] See Kroll (1924: 264–5), Leumann (1959: 155).
[71] On the poetic plural see Löfstedt (1942: 27–65, esp. 38ff.), Marouzeau (1962: 221–3).

integral part of the poetic argument itself.[72] Unlike tropes, which can acquire the status of poetic diction if they became part of the literary convention, imagery rarely depends on allusive vocabulary and requires no contextual support to clarify its meaning. The vividness and emotive power of Livy's description of the destruction of Alba (1.29) or of the Battle of Trasimene (22.4–6) show that imagery also has an important function in historiography[73] that again makes it *proxima poetis*.

35.2. Horace, as we saw in §31.1, often presents his imagery with remarkable brevity. Important here is the complementary distribution of contrasting descriptive details. Thus in *soluitur acris hiems* (*C.* 1.4.1) the verb implies the adjectives *dura* and *rigida*. Conversely *acris* implies *mitescit* not *soluitur*; cf. *frigora mitescunt Zephyri* (4.7.9). So what we get, elliptically presented, is s*oluitur et mitescit acris rigidaque hiems*.

35.3. The complementary distribution of epithets is well employed in *C.* 2.3.9–14, which begins with the contrast between the (dark green) *pinus ingens* and the (slender but thickly leaved) *alba ... populus*. The trees are then personified in forming a partnership to provide hospitality, *umbram hospitalem consociare amant*. Personification extends to the busy stream *lympha fugax*,[74] which *laborat ... trepidare*, so that what might have been a second component of the *locus amoenus* becomes instead a symbol of futile activity in a transitory world. The unease thus awakened is continued into the conventional symposiastic imagery, where the visual focus *flores amoenae rosae* is described ominously as *nimium breuis*, thus becoming another symbol of transitoriness, which links up with the closing image of *sororum fila trium atra*. The vocabulary of the two stanzas is rich and variegated and the imagery that it creates in effect constitutes the argument.

35.4. Almost the whole argument of *C.* 1.9 is conducted through a sequence of images, beginning with images of winter — visual in *candidum Soracte* and *siluae laborantes*, tactile in *gelu ... acuto*, and concluding with the spring season of human life, *dulcis amores* and *choreas, campus et areae, lenes ... sub noctem susurri* and *gratus puellae risus*, where the imagery is more nominalized and the epithets more subjective. The link between the real winter and the metaphoric spring is provided by *donec uirenti canities abest / morosa* (17–18), where *canities morosa* looks back to *candidum Soracte*, making it into a symbol of old age, while *uirenti*

---

[72] For the interrelationship between imagery and metaphor see Silk (1974) and also Fantham (1972), whose main concern is with Plautus, Terence and Cicero.

[73] Here, as always, the literary characteristics of historiography must be taken to include prose fiction. For imagery in literary dialogue and oratory see Fantham (1972: 115–75).

[74] For the 'disjunctiveness', as Postgate called it, exemplified in *laborat lympha fugax trepidare riuo* for *riuus lympha fugace trepidare laborat*, see Nisbet–Hubbard ad loc.

looks back to *siluae* that are however not *laborantes*, and forward to youth (cf. *uirentis . . . Chiae* in 4.13.6) that is not content with the sedentary pleasures of *focus* and *merum* (5 and 8). All this abundant imagery surrounds the central message of the ode, *quid sit futurum cras fuge quaerere et / quem Fors dierum cumque dabit lucro / adpone* (13–14), presented as an old-fashioned and prosaic exhortation, in which the only trope is a metaphor from accounting.

36.1. Similes are founded on images and so on the selection and deployment of lexical meanings. This is true even of brief examples, like the description of Pindar *monte decurrens uelut amnis, imbres / quem super notas aluere ripas*, which is followed by the metaphoric *feruet inmensusque ruit profundo / Pindarus ore* (*C.* 4.2.5–8; on which stanza see further §45.3). Horace describes himself *apis Matinae more modoque / grata carpentis thyma per laborem* (*ibid.* 27–9) in humble contrast to Pindar, *Dircaeum . . . cycnum* (25). This time the accessibility of the imagery is limited by the allusions. We need to know what *Matinae* and *Dircaeus* refer to, what the bee is doing in Tibur, and above all that Pindar used the bee comparison (e.g. *P.* 10.53–4) of his own conception of poetic composition, so that Horace is not after all as self-deprecatory as he appears.

36.2. Virgil's epic similes provide a kind of poetic commentary on the context in which they are set, and every specific part of the image tells. There is nothing comparable to what we sometimes find in Homeric similes, where a detail is included which, while it may bring the image into familiar focus for the hearer, does not always relate easily to the context and may even become bizarre if we attempt to relate it. A famous example is the end of the simile describing the slaying of Sarpedon, who falls like an oak ἠὲ πίτυς βλωθρή, τήν τ᾽οὔρεσι τέκτονες ἄνδρες / ἐξέταμον πελέκεσσι νεήκεσι νήιον εἶναι (*Il.* 16.483–4).

36.3. Virgil by contrast will sometimes sacrifice realism within the simile to gain a contextual point. Aeneas' reaction to his first sight of Dido (*A.* 1.496–7) is depicted in a simile intended to recall Hom. *Od.* 6.102–9.[75] But whereas Nausicaa seems to Odysseus like the maiden goddess Artemis at play with the nymphs, Dido is compared to the regal Diana coming in procession to one of her great cult-centres. Her mother is present in both similes. Homer's γέγηθε δέ τε φρένα Λητώ is very apt; Virgil's *Latonae tacitum pertemptant gaudia pectus* is passing strange. The image of the silent heart and the unsettling temptation must apply not to Latona within the simile but to Aeneas outside it.

---

[75] For an ancient view of the two similes see Valerius Probus *ap.* Gell. 9.9.12.

36.4. Imagery is important to Lucretius[76] not only for the relief it offers
to the austere doctrinal exposition. It is also appropriate that the exponent
of a materialist philosophy should appeal to the senses in order to instruct
his readers as well as to delight them and appeal to their emotions. This
skill shows itself especially in places where the rational argument becomes
a bit thin, though we cannot be sure whether the change in discourse was
calculated or unconscious. For instance in 2.308–32 the poet is expounding
the doctrine that though the atoms are constantly in motion — like the
motes in the sunbeam that helped him over a similar problem in 125–8 —
the objects formed from them appear at rest. *non est mirabile*, the poet
says, pre-empting the reader's reaction. *omnis enim longe nostris ab sen-
sibus infra / primorum natura iacet.* So the epistemological criterion of
sensation has to be rejected here, to be superseded not by *iniectus animi*
but by two elaborate and highly poetic analogies, summarized in 322 and
332, before we are moved rapidly on to the next topic. The two quasi-
similes have been deservedly lauded for their vivid concentrated imagery
and contrasting details — *collis* and *campus, lanigerae ... pecudes* and
magnae legiones, pabula laeta and *belli simulacra, herbae gemmantes rore
recenti, agni ... blande ... coruscant* and *aere renidescit tellus, reptant* and
circumuolitant. But the brilliance and familiarity (or rather familiarizing —
for how many of Lucretius' readers had looked down on two armies on
manoeuvre?) of the imagery beguile us into forgetting that this is analogy,
not proof. Atoms are like this, if they are like this. The *mellis dulcis
flauusque liquor* no longer serves to disguise the *absinthia taetra* (1.936–8):
it conceals its inefficacy. Similes are no mere ornaments.

SYNTAX

37.1. The meanings of individual words — their lexical stems and grammatical inflections — are fully articulated only in syntactic combinations,
and the repeated combinations in turn affect the meanings of words. The
syntax used by poets, including syntactic tropes, is therefore essential to
the definition of the poetic register. So too is the ordering of the words,
though in a highly inflected language this belongs not to syntax, as it does in
English, but to pragmatics and in particular stylistics. A few representative
phenomena will be discussed in the paragraphs that follow.

37.2. Among case uses the extension of direct object accusatives is
frequent. Cicero has *canere*, already old-fashioned in the sense of 'to sing',
with *clarorum uirorum laudes* (*Tusc.* 4.3) but not with *claros uiros*; yet

---

[76] See West (1969) for a detailed treatment of the subject.

Lucretius writes *cur... non alias alii quoque res cecinere poetae?* (5.326–7). Whence Horace extends to *Liberum, Musas Veneremque... canebat* (*C.* 1.32.9), Virgil to *arma uirumque cano*. The verb *ardere* is used of emotional states with the instrumental ablative specifying the emotion, e.g. *militibus... studio pugnae ardentibus* (Caes. *Civ.* 3.90.3), and in poetry also the object of love, e.g. *arsisse Bathyllo / Anacreonta* (Hor. *Epod.* 14.9). But Terence, who also writes *amore ardeo* (*Eun.* 72), already has a direct object in *hanc ardere coepit perdite* (*Ph.* 82). So Virgil's *ardebat Alexin* (*E.* 2.1) is not as innovative as it might seem. Quintilian (9.3.17) takes *Tyrrhenum nauigat aequor* (Virg. *A.* 1.67) as a Graecism. That the accusative need not be perlative, as we might surmise from, say, *me... nauigasse... per infesta latrociniis litora* (Sen. *Ben.* 7.15.1), is clear from the passive use in *etiamsi nauigari posset Oceanus* (Sen. *Suas.* 1.8).

37.3. The internal accusative function might be thought, on the basis of the equation of *dulce ridentem* (Cat. 51.5) with Sappho's γελαίσας ἰμέροεν, to owe something to Greek influence. But the adverbs *multum, parum* (<*paruom) and *dulcius* etc. together with 'cognate' usages like *noxiam noxit* from the Twelve Tables guarantee a native origin, even if, as elsewhere, Greek influence helped to maintain what might otherwise have been a non-productive or even obsolescent usage. An interesting interaction of external and internal uses is Virgil's *nec uox hominem sonat* (*A.* 1.328). For *humanum* with *sonat* would be internal; cf. *horrendum sonuere* (*A.* 9.732). However, *hominem* with *indicat* or *monstrat* would be external. The syntax here, as in *ardebat Alexin*, reflects a shift in the semantic orientation of the verb itself.

37.4. The pursuit of economy leads to a reduction of prepositional phrases. Most often this results in archaisms[77] like Virgil's *Italiam... Lauiniaque uenit / litora* (*A.* 1.2–3) and the even more antique *ibimus Afros* (*E.* 1.64), which is followed immediately by the incongruously epic *rapidum cretae ueniemus Oaxen*. Not surprisingly the ablative, being a syncretic case, offers divers examples. Thus from Propertius *uaga muscosis flumina fusa iugis* (2.19.30) where the ablative indicates separation, *multis decus artibus* (1.4.13) origin, *contactum nullis ante Cupidinibus* (1.1.1) agent, in fact an instance of dative-ablative indeterminacy, *illa meo carus donasset funere crinis* (1.17.21) location, and *medius docta cuspide Bacchus erit* (2.30.38) accompaniment. A remarkable haul, but although Propertius like Horace is notably bold in his case usage, each of the examples can be paralleled widely from other classical poets. The ablative of comparison is also employed more frequently and extended more boldly than in prose e.g. *turpior et saecli uiuere luxuria* (Prop. 1.16.12), and *inuidiaque maior*

---

[77] For the development of prepositional syntax in Latin see Coleman (1991).

urbis relinquam (Hor. *C.* 2.20.4–5), which clearly echoes Callimachus' κρέσσονα βασκανίης (*Ep.* 21.4).

37.5. A poetic rival to *ibit Afros* for *ibit ad Afros* is *ibit Afris*. The dative had always shared with the accusative the semantic function of allativity, the distinction being between subjective involvement, implying animatedness, and purely physical direction. Thus *Panthoiden iterum Orco / demissum* (Hor. *C.* 1.28.10–11), where the dative suggests that the obscure underworld deity, not the underworld itself, is being referred to; cf. the more physical *missos ad Orcum* (*C.* 3.4.75). Virgil's *it clamor caelo* (*A.* 5.451; cf. *tollitur in caelum clamor* in 12.462) indicates that Heaven, which in traditional culture was not after all an unpopulated region, is moved by the shout.

37.6. A number of distinctive uses of the genitive can be observed in poetic discourse. This had originally been the normal case of dependency with adjectives as with nouns, but was steadily encroached upon by the instrumental ablative. Phrases like *tempus edax rerum* (Ov. *M.* 15.234), *laeta laborum . . . Sidonia Dido* (Virg. *A.* 11.73–4; cf. *laetus Eois / Eurus equis* in 2.417), and *aeui maturus Acestes* (5.73; cf. *animo maturus et aeuo* in Ov. *M.* 8.617) are all conservative, if not archaizing.

37.7. Especially interesting is the famous *integer uitae scelerisque purus* (Hor. *C.* 1.22.1), where the two genitives chiastically juxtaposed have different semantic relations with the head adjectives of their grammatically parallel phrases. For whereas *integer uitae* implies *cui uita integra est*, s*celerisque purus* does not imply *cui scelus purum est*, and the alternative constructions are *integer uita* (instrumental) and *a scelere purus* (ablatival). Nothing anomalous here: genitives of reference need not always denote the same kind of reference. But the second phrase disambiguates the first, which taken by itself would more likely refer to physical health than moral goodness. Such clarification is an important function of double or multiple descriptive phrases (cf. the similar role of the Propertian similes in §28.3). Finally Virgil's *ereptae uirginis ira* (*A.* 2.413) is not as strange as it has sometimes been made out to be, since the genitive is the regular dependency case in the nominalization of all predicative complements, whatever their case; *ira* + genitive beside *irasci* + dative is paralleled in pairs like *inuidia, inuidere* and *usus, uti* beside *timor, timere*.

37.8. Some uses of the genitive are influenced by Greek. While *iustitiaene prius mirer belline laborum* (Virg. *A.* 11.126) can be placed with the genitive of reference that is found with *pudet, piget* etc., cf. *de impudentia singulari . . . sunt qui mirentur* (Cic. *Ver.* 2.1.6), this specific example is best seen as an extension of the native idiom under the influence of θαυμάζειν + genitive. Horace's *desine mollium / tandem querelarum* (*C.*2.9.17–18) is modelled on the ablatival uses of the Greek syncretic genitive, and may

have an *ad hominem* point, given Valgius' neoteric attachments.[78] The
same is also probable in *eripa te morae* from the Maecenas ode, *C.* 3.29.5;
cf. the ablatival phrase in *aegrum eripere de periculo* (Vitruv. 1.1.15).
However, a datival interpretation is just possible, with *morae* personified,
as if Cicero had written *huic me timori* rather than the more normal *hunc
mihi timorem eripe* (*Cat.* 1.18). Lastly *qua pauper aquae Daunus agrestium /
regnauit populorum* (Hor. *C.* 3.30.11–12), which begins with a straightforward genitive of reference. The genitive with *regnauit* could be partitive,
'some peoples', but it is more likely modelled on the Greek ablatival
genitive of comparison with verbs of ruling, a syntactic reflection of the
fusion of Italian and Greek in the final quatrain of the ode. What is clear
is that the Graecisms are no mere ornamental affectation.

38.1. In the Latin verb the middle voice is reflected in deponents like
loquor, utor and semi-deponents like *confido, gaudeo,* in none of which
does it have a distinctive meaning. A semantic distinction can however be
identified in certain uses of the passive of active verbs like *induor, lauor,
mutor, reuertor, uetor.* The co-existence of doublets like *arbitro/-or,
assentio/-or, comperio/-or* suggests that the loss of systematic distinction
was recent.

38.2. All this provided a platform, if an obsolescent one, from which
to launch a revival of the middle voice. At what date the revival began is
uncertain. The earliest instances[79] are from Plautus and Ennius: *cingitur.
certe expedit se* (*Am.* 308) and *indutum . . . pallam* (*Men.* 511–12) could be
native, though the absence from early prose — unless the isolated *togae
parte caput uelati* (Cato, *Orig.* 1.18) is genuine — and its rareness in
classical prose is then very strange. In Ennius' *succincti corda machaeris*
(*Ann.* 519 Sk) the presence of the Greek loan-word perhaps reduces the
probability that this is a mere Latin archaism,[80] while the transitive use, in
contrast to *cingitur* and to Ennius' own *succincti gladiis* (*Ann.* 426 Sk),
which is a normal passive, confirms that this is a middle. But thereafter
the construction is rare before the Augustans, e.g. Catullus' *non contecta
leui uelatum pectus amictu*, where the enclosing word order enacts the
meaning, and *lactentis uincta papillas* (64.64–5). More striking examples
appear in the *Eclogues* (see §38.3).

38.3. The area of the revival was very circumscribed. The overwhelming
majority of instances are in poetry. Livy's *uirgines longam indutae uestem*

---

[78] On which see Nisbet–Hubbard (1977: 135, 148).
[79] For a collection of examples see Kühner–Stegmann (1955:2.1.288–90).
[80] For the difficulties of classification here see Coleman (1975).

(27.37.13), a rare prose example, can be set beside Cicero's more typical *soccos quibus indutus esset* (*De or.* 3.127), no less clearly a passive. Moreover, the use was restricted both lexically and morphologically. Most of the examples are with verbs of covering and putting on or removing clothing and armour, e.g. *suras euincta cothurno* (Virg. *E.* 7.32), *inutile ferrum cingitur* (Virg. *A.* 2.510–1) and even Horace's alliterative *laeuo suspensi loculos tabulamque lacerto* (*S.* 1.6.74). Conspicuous among the exceptions are Ovid's *oculos in humum deiecta modestos* (*Am.* 3.6.67) and *suffunditur ora rubore* (*M.* 1.484), Virgil's *inflatum hesterno uenas, ut semper, Iaccho* (*E.* 6.15), where the Greek tone is reinforced by the metonymy chosen for *uino*, and *inscripti nomina regum... flores* (*E.* 3.106–7), with its allusion to Greek mythology, in which the middle use contrasts with the passive in Cicero's *sepulcrum inimico nomine inscriptum* (*Dom.* 100).

38.4 The examples cited have illustrated the morphological restriction. Most occurrences are in the perfect participle used in a descriptive rather than narrative sense. Latin had no perfect active participle except in the deponents, which in phrases like *talia clara uoce locutus* provide a syntactic model for many of the middle uses that have just been cited. There is a growing tendency to more frequent use of present tense finite forms. Ovid's *suffunditur* is already an extension from Virgil's *suffusa* (*A.* 1.228), Virgil's *loricam induitur*, coupled with a passive *fidoque accingitur ense* (*A.* 7.640), an extension from *indutus*. In *A.* 11.6 he writes *fulgentia induit arma* with a clear semantic distinction from the middle *induitur*.

38.5. Another construction, again poetic in occurrence, is syntactically parallel but semantically distinct. It is represented clearly in Lucretius' *percussi membra timore* (5.1223), where the participle must be understood not as a middle, as in *percussae pectora matres* (Virg. *A.* 11.877), but as a passive, with the accusative in its perlative sense, indicating the area within which a state or prolonged action occurs, a usage already found, it seems, in Enn. *Ann.* 310 Sk, *perculsi pectora Poeni* [81] and of course more familiar in the 'accusative of duration in space or time'. It is thus comparable to other poetic constructions like *tremit artus* (Lucr. 3.489) beside the more normal construction exemplified in *et corde et genibus tremit* (Hor. *C.* 1.23.8). The revival and extension of both accusative uses, assuming that they had native precedent, was clearly influenced by Greek, as are adnominal uses such as *cetera Graius* (Virg. *A.* 3.594) and *flaua comas* (Ov. *M.* 9.307). Sometimes analysis is uncertain. Thus *sensus deperditus*

[81] See also Skutsch's note on *fossari corpora telis* (583), where the text and context are less secure.

omnes (Prop. 1.3.11) may refer either to total loss (middle) of the senses or destruction (passive) over all the senses.

39.1. A number of uses of the infinitive are characteristic of the poetic register. In dependence on adjectives as in *celerem sequi* (Hor. *C.* 1.15.18) the infinitive is older than the gerundival constructions which replaced it in classical prose; cf. *auidus consul belli gerundi* (Sall. *Iug.* 35.3) with *auidi committere pugnam* (Ov. *M.* 5.75), and in the predicative complement *sum defessus quaerere* (Pl. *Epid.* 197) with *defessus sum ambulando* (Ter. *Ad.* 713). The infinitival construction is Indo-European and the infinitive had originally kept to the active form, being like all verbal nouns unmarked for voice, but adjustment is sometimes made for voice, as in *niueus uideri* (Hor. *C.* 4.2.59). A comparison between *felix et ponere uitem* (Virg. *G.* 1.284) and *felix uobis corrumpendis fuit* (Liv. 3.17.2) indicates the economical value to poets of the infinitive, which was used similarly but independently in Vulgar Latin.

39.2. In dependence on nouns the same two constructions were in rivalry already in Plautus, e.g. *tempus est subducere hinc me* (*As.* 912) but *tempust adeundi* (*Trin.* 432); *tantus amor casus cognoscere nostros* (Virg. *A.* 2.10) but *amor sceleratus habendi* (Ov. *M.* 1.131). In *pudor est quaedam coepisse priorem* (Ov. *Ars* 1.705) the adjective is in agreement with a non-existent subject, a situation that has fascinated generations of grammarians. Strictly speaking, only the gerundial construction is adnominal, 'the time of approaching exists', the infinitive is a datival complement, 'the time exists for approaching'. In the last example the infinitival phrase is a predicative complement, 'the shame is to begin'.

40.1. Greek influence also helped to re-establish the purely aspectual distinction between infinitives in the complements of certain verbs. Its native credentials are guaranteed by *neiquis eorum Bacanal habuise uelet* (*CIL* I²581) and *nequid emisse uellet* (Cato, *Agr.* 5.4). The revival in poetry clearly had something to do with the metrically useful trochaic ending, but a firm aspectual sense can be seen in Horace's *tendentes opaco / Pelion inposuisse Olympo* (*C.* 3.4.51–2) and Propertius' *ergo uelocem potuit domuisse puellam* (1.1.15), both in contexts rich in Greek mythological allusion. The occurrence of this usage at Vindolanda[82] illustrates once more the

---

[82] *cras quid uelis nos fecisse rogo domine praecipias, Tab. Vindol.* ii 505 in Bowman and Thomas (1996: 324) and p. 8 above.

possibility of correspondence between poetic and colloquial usage against literary prose (see §13.4).

40.2. In contrast to these usages, which became established as permanent additions to the poetic register, there are other Graecisms that remain extremely rare. The plain infinitive complement in *quo ire dixeram* (Pl. *Cap.* 194) and *quae conuenere... / fatetur transtulisse atque usum* (not *usus esse!*) *pro suis* (Ter. *An.* 13–14), may be native to Latin. But Catullus' *phaselus ille... ait fuisse nauium celerrimus* (4.1) is a specially motivated Greek intrusion, perhaps intended to characterize the old boat as an immigrant from the Greek-speaking East. Horace's *uxor inuicti Iouis esse nescis* (*C.* 3.27.73) addressed by Venus to Europa may also be intended to give localized Greek colour. This could apply to Androgeos in Virg. *A.* 2.377, *sensit medios delapsus in hostes,* and to Penelope in Prop. 2.9.7, *uisura et quamuis numquam speraret Vlixen.*

41.1. Another economically motivated preference is for participial syntax as an alternative to subordinate clauses. Here the morphological poverty of the Latin participial system and the predominantly adjectival function of the present participle in early Latin reduce the probability of native precedent. Catullus is the first poet to use participles extensively in his syntax (there are many in the narrative parts of 64; seven in lines 1–10 alone), at a time when they were little employed in prose. Cicero, significantly, has participial constructions more often in his poetry than in his prose. The Augustan poets followed Catullus' lead, and the usage then spread through Livy into the conventions of prose writing. All this confirms a Greek stimulus.

41.2. As in Greek, the syntactic conciseness is purchased at the cost of semantic precision. The distinction between a state described and action narrated is blurred, and the relation between subordinate constituent and principal clause, whether it is descriptive (viz. relative), temporal, conditional, causal or concessive, is left unspecified unless some clarifying adverb is attached to the participle, which reduces the gain in conciseness. In *diua quibus retinens in summis urbibus arces / ipsa leui fecit uolitantem flamine currum* (Cat. 64.8–9) the *uolitantem* phrase is descriptive but *retinens* could be taken temporally, like *aspirans* and *implorata* in 68.64–5.

41.3. Participles are much less prominent in the *Aeneid* than they are in the *Peleus and Thetis* and are deployed with more subtle diversity. They are an important ingredient in Horace's concentrated style, and the ambiguities mentioned above are exploited semantically by the poet. *C.* 4.7 is by his own standards very short on participles, but *decrescentia* (3) and *interitura* (10) are both impressive. The pentasyllabic present participle with its opening e-sounds evokes the more leisurely flow of the spring river and with *praetereunt* becomes, like the river in 3.29.33–41, symbolic of growth and decay and the relentless passage of time, which is also reiterated in *interitura*. No image this time: the participle draws on the unusual imagery of *uer proterit aestas*, to which it is an ominous appendage, whether we take it as descriptive, concessive or both. Sometimes the participles come in force, as in 3.2.6–9, *illum ex moenibus hosticis matrona bellantis tyranni prospiciens et adulta uirgo suspiret*, where the second is temporal, the first and third descriptive, and the compression achieved by them is important in focusing the image. The various expressive possibilities of the choice between participle and clause are explored to full effect by the Augustan poets and by their imperial successors, in prose as well as verse.

42.1. Syntactic dislocations of various kinds are widely used by the Latin poets. Hypallage is perhaps the most frequent. We have already noted *Tyrrhena regum progenies* (§28.5). Also from Horace is *obliuioso leuia Massico / ciboria exple* (*C.* 2.7.21–2), an easy transfer of an epithet that is itself rare and means simply 'full of forgetfulness'. Virgil's *saeuae memorem Iunonis ob iram* (*A.* 1.4), seems like a reciprocal transfer or enallage from the metrically parallel but phonetically inferior *saeuam memoris Iunonis ob iram*. The transfer gains semantically too: *saeua* becomes the characterizing epithet for Juno, and the wrath is given its specific motivation. A similar enallage occurs with comparable effect in the famous *ibant obscuri sola sub nocte* (*A.* 6.268). Hypallage is not unknown in prose, e.g. Cic. *Man.* 22, *eorum* (sc. *membrorum*) *collectio dispersa*; but it is primarily poetic.

42.2. More violent dislocations can be seen in Prop. 2.26.18, *qui, puto, Arioniam uexerat ante lyram*, where the grammatical form, in contrast to the prosaic *Ariona lyram ferentem*, makes Arion subordinate to his lyre, a witty conceit underlined by *puto*. The same quasi-satiric effect can be seen in 3.2.19, *Pyramidum sumptus ad sidera ducti*, a bizarre dislocation of the prosaic *Pyramides sumptuosae ad sidera ductae*, which would still retain the central alliteration and the hyperbolic *ad sidera*. Juvenal in *Sat.* 1.10–11 has *unde alius furtiuae deuehat aurum / pelliculae*, for the prosaic *alius pelliculam auream furtiue deuehat*. The casual *alius*, the choice of the diminutive *pelliculae*, made subordinate grammatically to *aurum*, which is thus highlighted, and the transfer of *furtiue* into the object phrase all conspire to reduce the heroic legend to an anonymous act of larceny. Such dislocations are the converse to hendiadys; but like it they are seldom mere word games.

42.3. Hendiadys itself, in replacing a head-plus-dependent noun phrase by a co-ordinate one, invites the reader to contemplate an object and its material component as distinct and equal items. In *qualem pateris libamus et auro* (*G.* 2.192) Virgil describes wine offered in sacrifice. The hendiadys highlights, as *pateris aureis* could not, the visual image of colour and wealth. In *clausae tenebris et carcere caeco* (*A.* 6.734) Virgil reinforces the disjunction by the alliterative link back across *tenebris* to *clausae*. The semantic extension of *caecus*, itself perhaps originally the result of hypallage, was as old as Accius, *nocte caeca* (*tr.* 32) and too widespread by now to be distinctive. Some alleged examples can be analysed more satisfactorily in other ways. In Remulus' taunt, *non pudet obsidione iterum ualloque teneri*? (*A.* 9.598), *ualloque* adds the physical object that accompanied the siege, and it is hard to envisage a unitary noun phrase that would convey this. Again in Horace's *oppida publico / sumptu iubentes et deorum / templa nouo decorare saxo* (*C.* 2.15.18–20) the two instrumental phrases have different semantic relations with the infinitive, which once again a single noun phrase of the head-plus-dependent type would not be able to represent.

42.4. Oxymoron perhaps belongs here also, since it breaches the conventions of syntactic collocation between lexical items. Again examples occur in prose, such as *absentes adsunt et egentes abundant*... (Cic. *Am.* 23), emphasizing the paradoxical character of friendship; but the figure is more characteristic of poetry. In Horace's *quid uelit et possit rerum concordia discors* (*Epist.* 1.12.19) the noun phrase aptly indicates the unity of disparates that was the goal of philosophical systems and by combining it with a verbal pair appropriate rather to an animate subject seems to suggest that this goal has an existence independent of its proponents. In Horace's famous description of Hypermestra as *splendide mendax* (*C.* 3.11.35) the contrast with her *impiae* sisters and *periurum parentem* underlines the moral dilemma, resolved in a way that may itself be liable to the charge of impious treachery but still ensured that she would be *in omne uirgo nobilis aeuom*. Sometimes an oxymoron, once created, comes to be exploited in prose as well as verse; cf. *cruda deo uiridisque senectus*, used of Charon in Virg. *A.* 6.304, with *senem sed mehercules uiridem animo et uigentem* (Sen. *Ep.* 66.1) and other imperial examples.

43.1. It is well known that Livy's prose style represents a distinct move towards poetic usage, especially in lexicon and syntax (see, e.g. §38.3). Conversely Augustan poetry introduces into its syntax something associated primarily with prose style, the extended complex sentence. Among numerous Virgilian examples[83] is *A.* 1.305–9: (1) *at pius Aeneas* (2) *per noctem plurima uoluens,* / (3) *ut primum lux alma data est* (1) *exire locosque / explorare nouos* (4) *quas uento accesserit oras,* / (5) *qui teneant* — (6) *nam inculta uidet* — (7) *hominesne feraene* / (1) *quaerere constituit sociisque* (8) *exacta* (1) *referre.*

43.2. There are eight constituents[84] in this narrative sentence, and the structure is quite elaborate. It is a pure period in that no terminal point is possible until the end; the principal clause (1) weaves through the sentence from the start to the finish: *at pius Aeneas exire ... explorare ... quaerere constituit sociisque ... referre.* The participial constituent (2), which is directly dependent on (1), is semantically a past imperfective participle ('having been turning over ...') a semantic distinction for which the finite verb system offers no exponent either ('when he had been turning over ...'). The group of indirect questions (4) (5) (7) is dependent not loosely on *locosque explorare nouos,* as it seems to be at first, but firmly on the delayed *quaerere.* It shows moreover an internal incoherence. For *qui teneant* (5) is effectively replaced by *hominesne feraene* (7) with *teneant* understood from the former. Since *nam* is not a subordinating conjunction, its constituent (6) must be treated as an aside. This incoherence aptly reflects the hero's bewilderment. The structural profile of the whole sentence can be represented thus:

It is very reminiscent of a prose period and even the word order is surprisingly prosaic. But what is remarkable is that the entire event from Aeneas' sleepless night to his report back to his men is reported in a single five-verse sentence, recalling in fact many of Livy's narrative periods.

43.3. Horace's Cleopatra ode (*C.* 1.37), consists of three sentences, each longer than its predecessor: 1–4, 2–12, 12–32. The last of these offers a sharp contrast to the Virgilian example. It is very complex but not strictly periodic, since numerous stopping points would have been possible — after *ab ignibus* (13), *Caesar* (16), *adurgens* (17), *columbas* (18), *Haemoniae* (20) and *fatale monstrum* (21), which is indeed taken by some editors to mark the end of a sentence; after *oras* (24), *seuero* (26), *serpentes* (27), *uenenum* (28), *ferocior* (29), *invidens* (30) and finally *triumpho* (32). The effect is of a long succession of narrative or descriptive details being added by way

---

[83] See Norden (1903: 377–90) for some aspects of Virgil's practice not covered here.
[84] For the method of analysis employed here see Coleman (1995).

of qualification to what has gone before, so that after the principal clause, comprising *sed minuit furorem... mentemque... redegit Caesar* (12–16), the focus of the sentence is moved steadily away via the predator–prey simile to the image of the noble queen — *generosius / perire quaerens nec muliebriter / expauit ensem* (21–3) — the final epic noun here like the epic simile in 17–20 adding heroic status to the events — *uoltu sereno... fortis... ferocior... non humilis mulier* (26–32). The radical shift of focus effected by this constant series of additions anticipates Tacitus. By contrast the continual addition of new material to the famous complex sentence in *C.* 4.2.5–24 (see § 36.1) has a cumulative effect after the initial principal clause (5–8). The choice of words in 1.31 is much more poetic than Virgil's, and the word order, though conditioned to a great extent by the metre, is highly effective, beginning with the emphatic predicate-subject order in 12–16. The use of complex structures may have been inspired by classical prose, but the poets exploited the innovation to various expressive effects.

44.1. Apostrophe, by replacing third person by second person narration, is a calculated intrusion by the poet into the impersonal context, in order to suggest his own emotional involvement and invite the reader to respond accordingly. It is especially appropriate to the more highly charged contexts of poetry. Thus Laodamia's desperation is highlighted by Catullus' direct address *in quo tibi tum casu pulcherrima Laodamia, / ereptum est uita dulcius atque anima / coniugium* (68.105–7). In Prop. 3.2.7–8, within a triad of mythological musicians, Polyphemus is highlighted for the erotic success of his *carmina* by a remarkable apostrophe: *quin etiam, Polypheme, fera Galatea sub Aetna / ad tua rorantis carmina flexit equos.* The ironic humour of this misinterpretation of the tale is compounded by the mock-heroic connotations of the concluding equestrian image.

44.2 The figure is of course not unknown to early epic e.g. already Hom. *Od.* 14.55, τὸν δ'ἀμειβόμενος προσέφης, Εὔμαιε συβῶτα, but Virgil uses it for various more emotive purposes, e.g. to elevate the Campanian chieftain in *A.* 7.733, *nec tu carminibus nostris indictus abibis, / Oebale,* preceding an explicit prosopographical account clearly significant for Italian legend and an Italian poet but now largely obscure. The most famous instance is of course the powerful and self-fulfilling promise, *Fortunati ambo! si quid mea carmina possunt...* (9.446–50), following the death of Nisus and Euryalus. Apostrophe is of course a familiar figure in oratory. Quintilian (9.2.38) cites examples from Cicero's speeches, including one based on personification, *uos iam, Albani tumuli atque luci, uos, inquam, imploro atque testor, uosque Albanorum obrutae arae* (*Mil.* 85). The difference between the two registers is chiefly one of frequency.

45.1. One of the most notable differences from prose is word order variation, in part metrically conditioned, though disrupted word orders are by no means unknown in literary prose e.g. *breuis a natura nobis uita data est* (Cic. *Phil.* 14.32). In a highly inflected language word order has no syntactic function, as it has in English, but it does have an important pragmatic role, adding emphasis to a word or phrase by distancing it from words with which it is grammatically linked, by juxtaposing it with words that are not grammatically connected but which help to define its meaning more specifically or by any major deviation from the patterns of ordinary prose writing, e.g. *uita breuis a natura nobis data est* or *fluctus uastos ad litora uoluunt*. In *uastos uoluunt ad litora fluctus* (Virg. *A.* 1.86) *uastos*, in alliteration with *uoluunt* with which it forms a menacing pair, is held in suspense till *fluctus* at the end. The wind-driven waves from all sides converge *ad litora*. In *aureus et foliis et lento uimine ramus* (6.137) epithet and noun are separated, with the colour image emphatically first and the noun coming as a revelation at the end. In *ingentes Rutulae spectabit caedis aceruos* (10.245) the definition of the appalling image awaits the two final nouns and the chiastic word order enclosing the verb enacts the vivid sense that its subject, the personified *crastina lux* (244), will be surrounded on all sides.

45.2. A couplet taken almost at random from Propertius illustrates the effects that variation from the prosaic order can contribute: *his tum blanditiis furtiua per antra puellae / oscula siluicolis empta dedere uiris* (3.13.33–4) v. *tum puellae oscula furtiua his blanditiis empta uiris siluicolis per antra dedere*. The hypallage of *furtiua*, placed in a metrically prominent position, in any case distances the latter phrase from prose. The reproach of *empta* is emphasized in the separation from its noun by the syntactically ambiguous *siluicolis* (with *empta* or *dedere?*) and in the oxymoronic juxtaposition with *dedere*. The lofty compound adjective itself is a witty reminder that the passage began with the Golden Age image of *felix agrestum quondam pacata iuuentus* (25).

45.3. The severe metrical constraints of the Horatian lyric metres clearly entailed distortions of the normal Latin word order, but the poet shows again and again an unparalleled skill in turning the necessities to relevant poetic effects. Take the river simile in 4.2.5–8: *monte decurrens uelut amnis, imbres / quem super notas aluere ripas, / feruet immensusque ruit profundo / Pindarus ore.* If we rewrite the stanza in a normal prosaic order, e.g. *Pindarus, uelut amnis monte decurrens, quem imbres super notas ripas aluere, feruet immensusque ore profundo ruit*, the contrast is very marked. It is worth noting incidentally that, as with most good poetry, rearrangement into a prose order leaves us with a very unprosaic piece of prose.

45.4. The noun *amnis* is attested predominantly in poetry, *ex* or *de montibus* would be more normal in prose (Livy has *amnis diuersis ex*

Alpibus decurrentes in 21.31.4), and the particular metaphoric use of *aluere* is not found in prose before Tacitus. But the order contributes to the poetic effect. The delaying of *uelut* gives the powerful initial image prominence before its reference is specified, and the preposing of *imbres* to its relative clause juxtaposes it emphatically with *amnis*. The fact that *feruet immensusque ruit* and *profundo* do not refer to *amnis* is held back till the last verse, where their metaphoric reference is at last made clear and the aptness of the simile confirmed. The only notable alliteration reinforces the link between *Pindarus* and *profundo*.

CONCLUSION

46.1. This long but far from exhaustive survey[85] can now be summarized and its argument brought together. An attempt has been made to describe and illustrate poetic diction, which in both the narrow and the wider sense (§1.1) essentially defines the poetic register of the language, that is to say the form of Latin in which poetic discourse was conducted. Literary prose, being more selectively rationalized, establishes a linguistic norm against which we can plot the characteristics of the poetic register as a series of deviations. The task of plotting ought to have led us to a body of exclusive criteria, but in practice the number of linguistic phenomena that are found exclusively in poetry is small, if far from negligible. This is perhaps not so surprising, given that no dividing line can be drawn between poetic and prose subjects. It is worth recalling for instance that Virgil wrote out a preliminary prose version of the *Aeneid* (Don. *Vita* 23) and that many manuscripts of Horace's odes offer titles for most of the poems that include standard rhetorical categories, such as *pragmatice* (1.1, 3.30), *paraenetice* (1.9, 4.7), *exprobratio* (1.25), *inuectio* (1.23). Not all of them are helpful, but the use of them is revealing.[86]

46.2. Nevertheless it is possible to point to linguistic usages that are more prominent in poetry and this is what I have done in §§3–45. The most fundamental distinguishing characteristic of Latin poetry is metrical form (§3–4). Of less importance at the phonetic level, since it is their frequency not their presence that is distinctive, are Greek sounds and Greek collocations of Latin sounds (§15). More infrequent are

---

[85] For a longer treatment of relevant phenomena see Hofmann–Szantyr (1965: 685–858).
[86] The rhetorical classifications of ancient poetry have been taken up, developed and modified by Cairns (1972). Some of his classes correspond with those in the Horatian manuscripts, e.g. *propemptice* (1.3), *hymnus* (1.21); many do not.

phonetic archaisms like *animāī* (§7–8) and innovations, which are virtually confined to words that are otherwise metrically intractable but never
distort the basic phonology of the language (§5–11): *metri gratia* is not
laissez-faire.

46.3. In the area of grammatical morphology archaic inflections are
sometimes retained (§12). This illustrates an important difference between
poetry and prose. Whereas literary prose was closely in touch with current
educated speech and archaism tended to be disapproved,[87] poetry was less
at the mercy of linguistic change. In a literate society the written poetry
that survived from the past was not only constantly accessible — this was
equally true of prose — but it also exercised a formative influence on the
work of individual poets, who consciously imitated it as a deliberate signal
of allegiance to a specific tradition.[88] This was quite distinct from the
largely unconscious and impersonal influence that past states of a language
must always have upon its present character. Literary works that acquired
a classic status within their genres obviously had the greatest influence
upon individual poets. This can at different periods be true also of prose
genres, as illustrated in the influence of Cicero on patristic writing from
Minucius Felix and Lactantius onwards,[89] or of The Authorized Version of
the English Bible on subsequent prose literature in English.

46.4. This timeless status of poetry applies even more to the lexicon,
where it not only signals adherence to a tradition but also extends the range
of synonyms available to the poet (§§21–3). Innovations were certainly
acceptable in this area, principally loan-words from Greek (§§27–8) and
the formation of compound words, scrupulously modelled on existing
patterns of Latin word formation even though their inspiration almost
invariably came from a particular Greek word (§26).

46.5. However, the two most important features of the poetic lexicon,
not only in Latin, do not need to depart from ordinary vocabulary. The
first is the use of semantic transference, as in metonymy (§32), synecdoche
(§33) and above all metaphor (§29–31). These are largely responsible for
the creation of poetic diction in the narrow sense (§34.2). The second is
imagery, which is often created out of very unpoetic vocabulary, not least in
similes (§§35–6). A word may have the status of poetic diction temporarily
conferred on it by the context of poetic discourse in which it is set, as for
instance the metaphoric *praesidium* of Maecenas in Hor. *C.* 1.1.1 or the
hyperbolic *centum clauibus* to characterize the miser against his wasteful

---

[87] For the rationalizing process by which classical prose usage was formed see Neumann
(1968).

[88] For comprehensive treatment of this important subject see Williams (1968), Thill (1979).

[89] The influence of the teachings of *Romani auctor eloquii* is pervasive in *De doctrina
Christiana*, though Augustine never names him there.

heir in the magnificent final stanza of *C.* 2.14. Other words become established as permanent elements of poetic diction by successive imitations of an original trope — *carina, fretum* etc. (§§3–34).

46.6. It is in syntax that the contrast with the rationalizing processes of prose is most striking. Both archaism and innovation are again at work here, and the placing of a given construction on the diachronic axis is often difficult. An archaic construction, purged from literary prose in favour of a more rational rival, may be identical with a vulgarism similarly rejected by literary prose (§39). The poetic and vulgar registers after all share a concern for concise and vivid expression which will end up in the same place, whether it is a preference for metaphor or for infinitival constructions. Finally while the introduction of complex sentence structure into poetry (§43) shows interaction with literary prose that is remote from vulgar usage, the various forms of syntactic dislocation (§42) and manipulation of word order (§45) mark off poetry from both vulgarism and prose literature.

46.7. The poetic register thus contained far more than poetic diction even in the wider sense of the term. A poet may, as we saw in §20.7–9, choose to confer the status of poetic diction on words that in other contexts of occurrence are thoroughly prosaic, simply by placing them in an appropriate setting. Thus the plain 'unpoetic' vocabulary of the famous *Wher'ere you walk* quatrain from Pope's *Pastorals,* 2.73–6, is charged with poetic power by the thoroughly traditional use of the trope known since Ruskin as the pathetic fallacy.[90] Conversely the poetic effect may depend precisely on the words retaining their prosaic connotations. Only the context of the poetic discourse itself can enable us to decide. For it is not just the presence of this or that linguistic item that is definitive, but rather the texture of a whole passage, formed from the accumulation of other ingredients summarized in these concluding paragraphs. This is why, in many of the examples cited to illustrate a particular feature of the poetic register in the course of this essay, other features of the context not relevant to the point immediately under discussion have been noted. Moreover, because the poetic register is not just a set of procedures for translating prose into verse and so embellishing an argument otherwise conceived, but a vehicle for deploying its own kind of argument, the reason why a particular feature or group of features is there has been constantly sought. For they always form an integral part of poetic discourse. This is why the definition of poetic diction in the narrow sense does not take us beyond a circumscribed and relatively small area of the lexicon; but the definition of the poetic

[90] The phonetic and syntactic composition of which is finely analysed by Nowottny (1962: 11–12).

register takes us into the entire concept of what a poem is and what it is created to do.[91]

[91] I am grateful to the two editors and to Professor H. D. Jocelyn, who have greatly improved this chapter by their learned and trenchant criticisms and by their corrections of downright errors, and would no doubt have improved it even more, if I had allowed them to do so.

WORD ORDER

Proceedings of the British Academy, **93**, 97–133

Nominative Personal Pronouns and Some Patterns of Speech in Republican and Augustan Poetry

J. N. ADAMS

Summary. A use of the nominative personal pronouns *ego* and *tu* is discussed. *Ego* and *tu* are not necessarily 'emphatic' or contrastive, but may be attached to emphatic, focused or 'preferential' terms which stand at the head of a clause. The function of the pronoun in such cases seems to be much the same as that of certain patterns of intonation in English. The pronoun highlights the emphatic term on which it hangs. Given its function, the usage certainly belonged to 'speech', which in this paper means 'educated speech'. The distribution of certain patterns (e.g. verb + *ego*: *credo ego* etc.) is discussed in republican and Augustan poetry. It is shown that Catullus (in hendecasyllables and elegiac verse) readily admits patterns which there is reason to believe were commonplace in speech, whereas the practice of Augustan poetry is more variable. Ovid in particular goes far beyond the norms of speech, both in displacing the unit focused term + *ego/tu* from initial position, and in developing complex forms of hyperbaton around the pronoun.

I. INTRODUCTION

THIS CHAPTER WILL BE about the use of the nominative personal pronouns *ego* and *tu*, but particularly *ego*. I will identify and discuss one of the factors determining the use of nominative pronouns in classical Latin, prose as well as verse.[1] A specific aim will be to explain the motivation and placement of *ego* in Catullus 16.1 ('pedicabo ego uos'), but I will be dealing not only with Catullus but also with Augustan poetry (elegy, Horace and Virgil). The use of nominative pronouns which will be identified here is not peculiar to poetry, or indeed to 'colloquial' Latin. It had a place in speech. I use the term 'speech' in a general sense in reference to educated speech of different degrees of formality; the term is intended to embrace in particular dialogue in the plays of Plautus and the oratory of Cicero. The chapter will examine the manner of the transfer to poetry of certain patterns of speech, and what that transfer has to tell us about the nature of poetic language in republican and Augustan Latin. The question arises to what extent these patterns were admitted, avoided, modified or extended by different poets.

The view is not uncommonly stated or implied that the nominative personal pronouns *ego* and *tu* are 'emphatic', or if used without emphasis are 'colloquial' or substandard in some way. Fordyce (1961: 149), for example, commenting on *legas tu* in (1),

(1)   Catull. 22.9   haec cum legas **tu**, bellus ille et urbanus
                     Suffenus unus caprimulgus aut fossor
                     rursus uidetur

suggested that *tu* may be no more than a 'metrical stopgap', i.e. it is apparently 'unemphatic', and must therefore lack proper motivation. Goold (1983) was moved to change *tu* to *tum* (*tum* g: *tu* V). Kroll too (1922) was bothered by nominative pronouns in Catullus which seem to be without emphasis. On Catull. 6.14, for example, he notes that an example of *tu* is unemphatic, 'wie oft in der Umgangssprache'.

A common type of emphasis expressed by *ego* and *tu* might be called 'contrastive emphasis', as in (2)–(3), where *ego* and *tu*, at the head of their cola, are in antithesis:

(2)   Cic. *Brut.* 151 de Seruio autem et **tu** probe dicis et **ego** dicam
                     quod sentio
(3)   Cic. *Phil.* 8.17 immo uero **ego** D. Bruto faueo, **tu** M. Antonio.

But in any classical text, and I do not refer only to 'colloquial' texts, it is easy to find examples of *ego* and *tu* which do not participate in obvious contrasts of this type. I mention here a few other conditions which seem to have been influential, up to a point, in motivating the use of *ego* in Cicero and Plautus. I do not claim to be exhaustive.

First, 'subjective' verbs, that is verbs signifying feelings, belief, sense

[1] See in general Marouzeau (1907), Hofmann–Szantyr (1965: 173–4, 400), Adams (1994*a*: 141–51).

perception etc. (e.g. *existimo, uolo, nolo, scio, credo*) are often used in association with *ego*, and *ego* does not necessarily have 'contrastive emphasis'. There are however variations in the frequency of the pronoun from verb to verb which are difficult to account for. *Existimo*, for example, is frequently accompanied by *ego*, but *credo* less commonly so (see below). And it is often difficult or impossible to see why *ego* is used with a particular verb in one passage but not in another. Presumably the strength or personal character of the feelings etc. which a speaker wishes to express is particularly sensitive to the context, and for that reason one and the same verb may sometimes have *ego*, sometimes not.

Secondly, threats, promises, statements of intent and the like, utterances which again have a subjectivity about them, often seem to generate the use of *ego*.[2] The verb is in the future tense (4)–(6):

(4) Plaut. *Amph.* 348 **ego** tibi istam hodie, sceleste, **comprimam** linguam

(5) Plaut. *Amph.* 556 iam quidem hercle **ego** tibi istam / scelestam, scelus, linguam **apscidam**

(6) Ter. *Heaut.* 730 **ego** pol istos **commouebo**.

In some of these passages *ego* is also juxtaposed with *tibi* or a demonstrative; *ego* is often alongside an oblique-case form of *tu* (see below, p. 108). The focus is on the future-tense verbs, and *ego* has no real contrastive emphasis of the type seen in (2)–(3), but collocations such as *ego tibi* may be reflections of the contrastive potential of *ego* and *tu*.

Thirdly, it has been plausibly suggested that a distinction should be made between conversational texts and narrative texts: 'in conversations *ego* (*nos*) and *tu* (*uos*) are either used to identify the speaker or addressee or to carry some form of "focal" ... information ... In narrative texts, however, the nominative forms of the first person pronoun are used to ndicate a change of "Topic"' (Pinkster (1987: 369)).

The factors motivating the use of the nominative pronoun *tu* will often have differed from those motivating the use of *ego*. *Ego* may occur in the statement of feelings, beliefs etc. held personally by the speaker, but *tu* implicates a person other than the speaker in the discourse. Whereas *ego* is found (e.g.) in threats, *tu* is often used when an order is given. A full account of the uses of the nominative personal pronouns would have to treat the functions of *ego* and *tu* separately. I am not attempting such a comprehensive account in this chapter.

A good deal of this chapter will be concerned with standard patterns.

---

[2] See Pinkster (1987: 369).

It will be suggested that there are structures which determine the use of *ego* and *tu*, regardless of their emphasis or pragmatic function.

II. STRUCTURES CONTAINING *EGO*

In subjective statements of the type defined above, or in contexts in which *ego* is motivated in some way by its pragmatic role, it may be placed at the start of its clause, as in (7):

> (7) Cic. *Pis.* 79 **ego** C. Caesarem non eadem de re publica sensisse quae me **scio**; sed tamen . . . .

It seems to be true of classical prose that if *ego* is expressed for some reason its normal tendency is to go to the head of its clause; it does not, for example, have a special liaison with the verb. One expects to find collocations of the type *ego scio* mainly in contexts in which *ego* is at the start of the clause.

But *ego* is often excluded from first place by what might be called 'preferential' terms of one sort or another,[3] that is terms which characteristically occupy the first place in their clause. If there is a preferential term at the start of the clause, *ego* may be placed second, immediately after that preferential term. I list some categories of words which often precede *ego* (or *tu*) at the start of a clause:

(i) Relatives, including the connective use of the relative, e.g.

> (8) Cic. *Q.fr.*1.2.16 **quibus** *ego* ita *credo* ut nihil de mea comparatione deminuam.

The use of the nominative pronoun here may, superficially at least, be explained from the subjective character of the verb *credo*, or perhaps even from an element of contrastive emphasis, but that may not be the whole story (see below). *Ego* has been debarred from the first position by *quibus*, which almost inevitably comes first. A comparison of (7) with (8) shows that it would not do to see in (8) the operation of Wackernagel's law, according to which pronouns and certain other clitics are said to occupy the second position in their clause.[4] There is no general rule of second-position placement at work in the two examples; it is the presence of a preferential term, *quibus*, which causes *ego* to be later than first in (8).

If the (connective) relative is adjectival, it may be split by *ego* from the noun in agreement:

---

[3] I take the term from Dover (1968: 20). Latin like Greek had a set of words which more often than not are at the head of the clause.
[4] See Wackernagel (1892); also Adams (1994*a*).

  (9)   Plaut. *Bacch.* 214 **quam** *ego* **fabulam** aeque ac me ipsum *amo*
 (10)   Plaut. *Men.* 903 **quem** *ego* **hominem**, si quidem uiuo, uita
        euoluam sua
 (11)   Cic. *Verr. a.pr.* 4 **quibus** *ego* **rebus** uehementissime *perturbor*
 (12)   Cic. *Verr. a.pr.*18 **quem** *ego* **hominem** honoris potius quam
        contumeliae causa nominatum *uolo*
 (13)   Cic. *Verr.* 4.140 **quas** *ego* **litteras** obsignandas publico signo
        deportandasque curaui
 (14)   Cic. *Att.* 8.16.1 **quem** *ego* **hominem** ἀπολιτικώτατον omnium
        iam ante *cognoram.*

The verbs in four of these examples express feelings and the like, and that
might have been at least one of the determinants of the use of *ego*. (10),
on the other hand, is a threat. Note the formulaic character of at least
some of the examples (those with *quem ego hominem*).

It is of some interest that the incomplete utterance of Neptune at Virg.
Aen. 1.135 takes the form *quos ego —*!

(ii) Another constituent which often precedes *ego* is the demonstrative
hic, which of course is interchangeable with the connective relative. In
(15),

  (15)   Cic. *Fam.* 11.20.1 **hoc** *ego* Labeonem *credo* illi rettulisse aut
         finxisse dictum

the verb (*credo*) is again subjective, and again, in (16)–(20), we see the
tendency for *ego* to split the demonstrative from a noun:

  (16)   Cic. *S. Rosc.* 47 nihil intersit utrum **hunc** *ego* **comicum**
         adulescentem an aliquem ex agro Veienti nominem
  (17)   Cic. *Diu. Caec.* 25 **huic** ego **homini** iam ante denuntio
  (18)   Cic. *Verr. a. pr.* 2 **huic** *ego* **causae**, iudices, cum summa
         uoluntate et exspectatione populi Romani actor accessi
  (19)   Cic. *Cat.* 3.17 **hunc** *ego* **hominem** tam acrem, tam audacem,
         tam paratum . . . nisi . . . compulissem
  (20)   Cic. *Verr.* 3.104 duarum mihi ciuitatum reliquos *feci* agros,
         iudices, fere optimos ac nobilissimos, Aetnensem et
         Leontinum. **horum** *ego* **agrorum** missos *faciam* quaestus
         trienni.

Hunc ego hominem in (19) should be compared with *quem ego hominem*.
In (20) *feci* in the first sentence is without *ego*, whereas *faciam* in the
second has an accompanying subject pronoun, and it is only in the second
that a demonstrative is present. Or could it be that the future tense
(expressing intent) is the determinant of *ego*? It is not immediately obvious
in some of the other examples what has motivated *ego*. Is it possible that
the pattern *hic ego* had formulaic status such that the semantic content
of the verb or of *ego* itself was not necessarily a determinant of its use?

(iii) *Ego* often follows interrogative words, particularly *quis*, e.g.

> (21)   Cic. *Verr* 1.75 **quid** *ego* nunc in altera actione Cn. Dolabellae
> spiritus, quid huius lacrimas et concursationes proferam ...?

The examples in (22) have a formulaic structure which recurs over a long period:[5]

> (22)   a   Ennius, *Ann.* 314 Skutsch **sed quid ego haec** memoro?
> b   Lucil. 1000 **sed quid ego haec** animo trepidanti dicta
>   profundo?
> c   Cic. *Mil.* 18 **sed quid ego illa** commemoro?
> d   Catull. 64.164 **sed quid ego** ignaris nequiquam conquerar
>   auris?
> e   Ovid, *Her.* 9.143 **sed quid ego haec** refero?
> f   Livy 8.32.5 **sed quid ego haec** interrogo?
> g   Livy 38.48.6 **sed quid ego haec** ita argumentor?

The verb is one of saying or the like, and the answer expected is that the speaker should not be saying what he is saying, or that it is being said in vain. *Sed* precedes *quid*, and *ego* is usually followed by a neuter demonstrative. Since this type of question implies a personal view on the part of the speaker which he attempts to impose on the hearer, the presence of *ego* may originally have been explicable from the subjectivity of the utterance. But it had surely become a mere manner of speaking, with the use of *ego* triggered as much by the interrogative *quid* and the collocation of words as by the semantic contribution which the pronoun might have to make.

If the interrogative is adjectival, it may in the usual way be separated from its noun by *ego*:

> (23)   Plaut. *Bacch.* 357 **quas** *ego* hic **turbas** dabo! (the exclamatory
> use of *quis*)
> (24)   Cic. *Att.* 1.16.1 **quas** *ego* **pugnas** et quantas strages edidi! (note
> the contextual similarity of this to the previous example)
> (25)   Cic. *Att.* 2.15.3 **quos** *ego* **homines** effugi cum in hos incidi?

In (24) it might be said that the boastful nature of the claim determines the use of *ego*; (23) is a threat.

For *tu* used in the same structure, see:

> (26)   Plaut. *Pseud.* 1195 **quem** *tu* **Pseudolum**, **quas** *tu* mihi praedicas
> **fabulas**?
> (27)   Cic. *Cat.* 1.13 **cui** tu **adulescentulo** ... non aut ad audaciam
> ferrum aut ad libidinem facem praetulisti?

(iv) A strongly focused term, whether e.g. a word in antithesis, or

---

[5] See Skutsch (1985: 363; also 493) on Enn. *Ann.* 314.

participating in a rhetorical anaphora, will often be placed at the head of a clause. If *ego* is expressed for some reason, it will be prevented from adopting first position by the focused term. In (28) *ego*, as often, is expressed as subject of *uidi* (see below, pp. 123–4), but the first position goes to *alios*, which is part of an extended anaphora; *ego* is attached to it:

> (28)   Cic. *Pis.* 21 **alios** *ego* uidi **uentos, alias** prospexi animo procellas, **aliis** impendentibus tempestatibus non cessi.

In (29)

> (29)   Cic. *Cat.* 3.26 **in animis** *ego* **uestris** omnis triumphos meos, omnia ornamenta honoris, monumenta gloriae, laudis insignia condi et conlocari *uolo*

Cicero has said that he wants no *concrete* memorial. It is enough for him to be retained in the citizens' *minds*. *Animis* is part of a loose contrast. The verb (*uolo*) is subjective. *Ego* has moved towards the start of the sentence, attaching itself to the antithetical term *animis* and separating thereby *animis* from *uestris*.

See further:

> (30)   Plaut. *Men.* 978 nam magis multo patior facilius **uerba. uerbera** *ego* odi.

Here the verb (*odi*) is a subjective one which elsewhere has *ego* expressed as its subject (see below, (97)–(99); *ego* is placed after one of a pair of overtly (alliterative) antithetical terms.

(v) Negatives are frequently at the head of a clause. *Ego*, motivated by one of the factors identified earlier, may move towards but be prevented from adopting first place: e.g.

> (31)   Plaut. *Pers.* 533 **numquam** *ego* te tam esse matulam credidi
> (32)   Cic. *Marc.* 8 **non** *ego* eum cum summis uiris comparo, sed simillimum deo iudico
> (33)   Cic. *Att.* 1.12.1 **nihil** *ego* illa impudentius, astutius, lentius uidi.

I summarize. *Ego*, if expressed, is often placed at the head of its clause. But it may be prevented from adopting that position if one of a variety of preferential terms normally placed first is present in the sentence: for example a relative, *hic*, an interrogative, a focused or rhetorical or antithetical term, a negative. In such sentences *ego* is constantly found attached to the preferential term. It is probably true to say that in prose if *ego* is not in first place in the clause, it will usually follow a preferential term. Many of the examples so far quoted show quasi-formulaic structures of one sort or another, e.g. *hunc ego hominem, sed quid ego haec*. The question arises whether in such cases *ego* is motivated only by its own 'emphatic' or 'subjective' or 'focal' character. Is it possible that certain types of preferential terms placed at the head of a sentence in effect attracted *ego*, or even generated its use if the verb was first person?

I ask this question partly because in some of the examples quoted so far it is difficult to see any other reason why *ego* should have been expressed, but particularly because there is evidence in Latin that certain preferential and focused terms attracted enclitics of other kinds.[6] Consider first (34):

> (34)   Cic. *Fam.* 13.73.2 sed mihi ita persuadeo (potest fieri ut fallar) //
>   eam rem **laudi** *tibi* // potius quam **uituperationi** fore.

The double lines mark off colon division. *Tibi*, the unemphatic enclitic oblique case pronoun, ought, by Wackernagel's law, to be in second position in its colon. Instead it is right at the end of the colon, attached to the antithetical term *laudi*, which stands in a contrast with *uituperationi*. *Tibi* has been attracted to the right by the antithetical term, and this is a common process in classical Latin. The antithetical or focused term exercises an attracting power over enclitics. Take again (35):

> (35)   Caes. *Gall.* 6.40.7 quorum non nulli **ex inferioribus** ordinibus
>   reliquarum legionum // uirtutis causa // **in superiores** *erant*
>   ordines huius legionis *traducti*.

Here a transfer from lower ranks (*ex inferioribus ordinibus*) to higher (*in superiores ordines*) is described. *Inferioribus* and *superiores* are antithetical. The auxiliary *erant*, which would usually follow *traducti*, has moved to the left and attached itself to one of the antithetical terms.

I would suggest that *ego* often behaves in a similar way to oblique case pronouns, and the copula or auxiliary, in that it seeks out focused or preferential terms and links itself to them, even in contexts in which it appears to have no particular emphasis itself and is apparently redundant. Consider (36)–(39):

> (36)   Plaut. *Aul.* 322 **coquom** *ego*, **non furem** rogo
> (37)   Plaut. *Aul.* 457 **coctum** *ego*, **non uapulatum**, dudum
>   conductus fui
> (38)   Cic. *Att.* 14.14.2 ita Brutos Cassiumque defendis quasi eos ego
>   reprehendam; quos satis laudare non possum. **rerum** *ego* uitia
>   collegi, **non hominum**
> (39)   Cic. *Verr.* 5.130 itaque ad me, iudices, hanc querimoniam
>   praeter ceteras Sicilia detulit; **lacrimis** *ego* huc, **non gloria**
>   inductus accessi.

---

[6] See Adams (1994*a*, 1994*b*).

In each case *ego* has moved towards the start of the sentence, but instead of reaching first position has been attached to antithetical terms, which stand in an 'A *non* B' structure. *Ego* seems usually to be semantically redundant. In (38), for example, the first sentence contains a contrast between Atticus, the subject of *defendis*, and Cicero, who refers to himself by means of the contrastive use of *ego*. But in the third sentence the primary contrast is between *rerum* and *hominum*. The main motivation of *ego* seems to be its tendency to occur as enclitic on certain categories of focused terms.

I wish to consider further the possibility that the use of *ego* may sometimes be determined not by its own emphatic or contrastive potential, but by its mechanical place in certain structures, in attachment to a limited range of focused or preferential terms. Two pieces of evidence are offered (*ego* used as subject of *credo*, and of *accuso*).

I take first *ego* used in conjunction with the verb *credo* (in the present tense, indicative). *Credo* might seem to be the archetypal subjective verb which would often be accompanied by *ego*. However, in Cicero, *credo* occurs 337 times, and *ego* is expressed with it only 6 times. The 6 examples are set out at (40):

(40) a *S. Rosc.* 1 **credo ego** uos, iudices, mirari quid sit quod . . .
      b *Dom.* 134 **quem ego** tamen credo
      c *Nat.* 3.14 **quibus ego** credo
      d *Att.* 1.16.12 **quod ego** non credo
      e *Q. fr.* 1.2.16 **quibus ego** ita credo
      f *Fam.* 11.20.1 **hoc ego** Labeonem credo illi rettulisse aut finxisse dictum.

There is evidence here that the use of *ego* is structurally determined. In four places (b — e) *ego* follows a connective relative, and in a fifth (f) it follows *hoc*. It seems to be the presence of the preferential term which generates the use of *ego*, in attachment to it.

Of particular note is (40a), which is the opening of the *Pro Roscio Amerino*. The same expression opens the *Stichus* of Plautus —

(41) Plaut. *Stich.* 1   **credo ego** miseram
                          fuisse Penelopam

— and is found elsewhere in speeches:

(42) C. Sempronius Gracchus frg. 34, p. 184 Malcovati **credo ego** inimicos meos hoc dicturum
(43) Livy 21.21.3 **credo ego** uos, inquit, socii . . .
(44) Livy 24.38.1 **credo ego** uos audisse, milites . . . .

I take it that the emphasis of (40a) is 'I IMAGINE, gentlemen, that you are surprised'. The focus is on *credo*. *Ego* is neither genuinely contrastive nor emphatic, but appears to be attached to a focal initial verb. It could not be argued that the order *ego credo* has been reversed to throw the verb into relief, because, as we have seen, *ego* is not necessarily expressed in combination with *credo* in Cicero. It would seem to be more accurate to say that the use of *ego* has been motivated by the presence of a focused term at the start of the sentence which Cicero wishes to highlight. Speeches of Cicero often have a first-person verb in the first sentence, but usually it is unaccompanied by *ego* or *nos*; it would not do therefore to suggest that the orator had a habit of expressing *ego* as a mannered speech opening to stress (e.g.) his personal involvement in or commitment to the case. At *S. Rosc.* 1 then it is both the presence of *ego*, and its placement, which have to be explained. Positioned thus, the pronoun virtually has a focusing role.

I move on to my second piece of evidence. At (45) Cicero poses a number of rhetorical questions, each introduced by *quis*:

> (45)   Cic. *Verr.* 4.104 pro di immortales! **quem** *ego* **hominem** accuso? quem legibus aut iudiciali iure persequor? de quo uos sententiam per tabellam feretis?

Ego does not seem to have any special emphasis. Could it be that its use has been determined by the verb *accuso*? There are 15 examples of *accuso* (first-person present indicative) in Cicero.[7] Only four times is *ego* expressed with it. There is a second case of the pronoun attached to an interrogative:

> (46)   Cic. *Verr.* 3.137 pro deum hominumque fidem, **quem** *ego* accuso?

The context is virtually identical to that of (45), and in both passages the emphasis seems to be on the interrogative: '*what sort of man is this* that I am accusing'.

In a third example *ego* begins a sentence, and may be intended to be emphatic *(Att.* 13.22.3). It is also subject of another, coordinated, verb *(libero)*. Finally, at *Sull.* 48 *ego* is contrastive:

> (47)   Cic. *Sull.* 48 'inimicum ego', inquis, 'accuso'. et amicum ego defendo meum.

There are then no grounds for thinking that the presence of *ego* is related to the nature of the verb *accuso*; in two places it is the interrogative *quis* which must surely have determined its use. Whereas the two questions of the form *quem . . . accuso?* both have *ego* attached to *quem*, in none of

---

[7] *S. Rosc.* 94, *Verr.* 3.16, 3.17, 3.187, 4.104, 5.166, *Planc.* 17, *Sull.* 48, *Att.* 3.15.4, 3.15.7, 4.16.1, 10.5.3, 13.22.3, 13.22.5, *Q.fr.* 2.2.1.

the places where *accuso* occurs *without ego* is it preceded by the interrogative.

Further evidence could be cited suggesting that *ego* is often expressed
because the structural conditions are right to motivate it, but the two cases
discussed above are enough for our purposes.

I summarize. The infrequency with which *ego* is expressed as subject
of (e.g.) *credo* shows that the subjectivity of the verb was not sufficient
cause in itself to determine the use of the pronoun. *Ego* seems to be
motivated by the presence of a restricted range of preferential terms —
that is, terms which habitually come at the head of their clause and to
which it might attach. I refer, in the case of *credo*, to the emphatic deictic
demonstrative *hic*, to the connective relative *qui* which is interchangeable
with *hic*, and to the miscellaneous category of focused initial terms placed
at the head of the clause, represented by initial *credo* at *S. Rosc.* 1. The
tendency which *ego* shows of linking itself to such preferential terms has
a parallel in the tendency which oblique case pronouns, and the copula
esse, also show of seeking out preferential terms as their host. What is
different about the nominative pronoun *ego*, as compared for example
with an oblique case form such as *mihi*, is that logically it is redundant. If
its use is related to the presence of a preferential term in the clause, then
one would have to say that the preferential term not only attracts it, but
in many cases even causes it to be expressed.

III. CATULLUS: VERB + *EGO/TU*

I turn now to Catullus. I will be arguing that Catullus falls constantly into
the patterns of speech, with a minimum of adaptation or innovation. I
begin with one type of attachment of *ego/tu* to preferential terms, that is
their attachment to emphatic or antithetical verbs, as in Cicero's expression
credo ego.[8] The nature of the phenomenon may be even more clearly
illustrated from (48)–(50):

> (48) Cic. *Caec.* 38 **reieci ego** te armatis hominibus, **non deieci**
> (49) Cic. *Scaur.* frg. (f) non enim tantum **admiratus sum ego** illum
>   uirum, sicut omnes, sed etiam praecipue **dilexi**

---

[8] There are 20+ examples of *ego* placed immediately behind a first-person verb in Cicero,
and 30+ examples of *tu* after a second-person verb. The structure is not particularly common,
but it was clearly available as a functional form of placement. Many of the examples of both
ego and *tu* so placed fit the pattern discussed here (e.g. in (48)–(50)), but the use of *tu* in
particular in a comprehensive account of pronoun placement would require a detailed
treatment.

(50)   Cic. *Verr.* 1.124 **das** possessionem ei qui non iurauit; concedo;
       praetorium est. **adimis tu** ei qui iurauit.

In (48) the argument turns on the question whether Caecina was
'ejected' (*deicere*) from a farm, or excluded, i.e. prevented from entering
it. Here Cicero's opponent is imagined as making the defence 'I *rejected*
you, I did not *eject* you'. There is an explicit antithesis between the two
verbs, or rather between their two prefixes, as Cicero in effect goes on to
observe: 'ut tantum facinus non in aequitate defensionis, sed *in una littera
latuisse* uideatur'. The structure is again 'A *non* B' (cf. (36)–(39)). Neither
ego nor *te* carries any discernible emphasis. The pronouns are, it is true,
in the familiar first-person/second-person pattern, but that is not sufficient
to cause *ego* to be used here; *te* is often subject of a first-person verb
without a juxtaposed *ego*.[9]
    In (49) two verbs are again in antithesis, with the second a deliberate
intensification of the first. There is a secondary contrast between *ego* and
omnes, but the main focus lies undoubtedly on the two verbs. In (50) there
is contrast of complete opposites, with *tu* attached to the second of the
pair. The presence of *tu* here can only be explained as a manifestation of
a usage whereby a nominative pronoun follows an antithetical or focused
verb at the start of its clause, and thereby, one assumes, sharpens the
focused character of that verb, much as if the emphasizing particle *quidem*
had been tacked on instead. Even if one were to maintain that in, say,
(49), *ego* is required because of contextual factors other than its focusing
function, it would still have to be allowed that its position is significant,
behind a markedly antithetical term.[10] Regular positioning of this kind in

---

[9] In reference to the collocation *ego te* a referee comments: 'the very regular way in which
[*ego*] is followed (or embraced) by an accusative (phrase) might suggest that what comes
after [it] may be just as relevant as what comes before. And the same could be true of
datives too.' I have collected every example of first-person verbs in the first 20 letters to
Atticus (as published in Shackleton Bailey's edition) which are accompanied either by the
direct object *te* or the indirect object *tibi*. In 21 cases *ego is not expressed at all.* Four times
where *ego* (or *nos*) *is* expressed, it is separated from *te/tibi*. And only once is *ego* followed
immediately by the second-person pronoun (*tibi*). These figures do not support the possibility
that the use of *ego* could be determined by the presence of a second-person pronominal
object. Where *ego* and *te/tibi* occur in juxtaposition, it must be assumed that *ego* is independently motivated. The figures given here from Cicero do not include those cases in which *te/
tibi* is in an embedded clause, and *ego* would have been in the matrix clause, had it been
expressed. If such cases had been included, the argument of this footnote would have
been further strengthened.

[10] Pinkster (1987) does not distinguish between those pronouns which precede the verb and
those which are placed after it. He quotes (1987: 372), for example, Petron. 74.15 'ego...
accipere potui. *scis tu* me non mentiri', with the comment: 'Fortunata is called as a witness
for the truth of Trimalchio's statements: "others may not know this, but *you* know it damned
well".' But what is the significance of the placement of *tu*? It is at least as likely that the

passages in which *ego* might have been motivated as well by the context opened the way for the pronoun to be given a focusing role in its own right.

At Catull. 22.9 (cited above (1)) *tu* can without difficulty be interpreted as linked to a focused verb. In the previous lines (5–8) the splendid, even luxurious, *appearance* of Suffenus' book of poems is described. But, says Catullus, when you READ them, the truth is revealed.[11] The contrast between superficial appearances and reality is implicitly rather than starkly expressed as in some of the examples discussed earlier.

The focusing usage of *ego* can be clearly seen in Catull. 14.4:

(51)   Catull. 14.4   nam quid **feci ego** quidue **sum locutus**,
                     cur me tot male perderes poetis?

'What have I *done* or what have I *said* that you should want to destroy me with so many poets?' Here there is a hackneyed antithesis between doing and saying, and *ego*, without real contrastive function itself, follows the first of the antithetical pair. For a comparable use of *ego*, cf.:

(52)   Plaut. *Capt.* 414 **feci ego** ita ut commemoras, et te meminisse
                     id gratum est mihi

'I DID do as you say' (expressing agreement with the previous speaker).[12]

---

focus is on *scis*: 'you KNOW that I am telling the truth'. See Marouzeau (1907: 27) on the difference between *ego scio* and *scio ego* in comedy: e.g. Plaut. *Pers.* 616–7 'quanquam ego serua sum, / scio ego officium meum' ('although I am a slave, I am WELL AWARE of my duty'), alongside Ter. *Hec.* 849–50 'X. nescio. Y. at *ego scio*' ('I don't know.' 'But *I* do'). Note too Plaut. *Bacch.* 202 'uide quaeso ne quis tractet illam indiligens; / scis tu ut confringi uas cito Samium solet', 'you KNOW how readily Samian ware breaks'. Similarly I cannot accept that at Petron. 111.12 ('*uis tu* reuiuiscere? *uis* discusso muliebri errore ... lucis commodis frui') the emphasis is on *tu*, as in Pinkster's paraphrase (1987: 372), 'Do *you* want to begin life afresh? In that case the body itself ... of your dead husband ought to persuade you.' In fact *uis tu* is a well-established idiom, expressing a strong exhortation = 'WON'T you, CAN'T you', with the emphasis most definitely on the modal nuance of the verb, not on *tu*. Cf. Livy 25.6.22 '*uis tu* mari, *uis* terra, *uis* acie, *uis* urbibus oppugnandis experiri uirtutem?', Hor. *Sat.* 2.6.92 '*uis tu* homines urbemque feris praeponere siluis?', Sen. *Dial.* 10.19.2 '*uis tu* relicto solo mente ad ista respicere'. The idiom was explained, with numerous other examples, by Bentley (1711: 327 on Hor. *Sat.* 2.6.92): note his remark, 'In illis omnibus τὸ VIS non interrogantis modo est ut VIN; sed orantis, hortantis, flagitantis, iubentis'. The Livian example above is particularly telling, as the repetition of *uis* shows that it is this, not *tu*, which is emphatic.

[11] Roland Mayer draws my attention to Tac. *Dial.* 3.3 *leges tu*, where *tu* may have a similar function. It has caused editors some problems.

[12] Often in Plautus a verb preceding *ego* is emphatic (see e.g. the examples cited in n. 10, with Marouzeau (1907)), but his usage is somewhat variable, perhaps partly because of the pressures applied by the metrical form of the text. With (52), compare *Bacch.* 410 '**feci ego** istaec itidem in adulescentia', where it is *ego* which is strongly emphatic. For some factors favouring this placement of emphatic *ego*, see below (116)–(120).

Perhaps the most interesting example of *ego* in this function is at Catull. 16.1, 14:

    (53)   Catull. 16.1, 14 pedicabo **ego** uos et irrumabo.

The word order adopted by Catullus is not haphazard. The structure is of a type which belonged to speech, but its determinants are complex. *Ego*, as often, is juxtaposed with a second-person pronoun, but that is not the main reason for its use. The utterance is a threat, and in threats, as we saw ((4)–(6)), *ego* is constantly expressed. *Ego* may go to or towards the start of the threatening utterance, but there can be no doubt that the real weight of any future-tense threat lies on the verb itself, or in this case on the pair of verbs, which are of increasing intensity. If translated into spoken English the line will inevitably have a falling intonation on the verbs, a sure sign of focus in the sense in which I use that term,[13] and there will be little or no stress on the pronouns. Because of the inherently focused character of threatening verbs, there is a tendency for the verb to be placed at the head of the clause with *ego* following. The structure occurs repeatedly in Plautus, and is also found in Terence:

    (54) a Plaut. *Amph.* 295 timet homo: **deludam ego** illum
          b Plaut. *Bacch.* 571   si pergis paruom mihi fidem arbitrarier,
                                  tollam ego ted in collum atque intro
                                    hinc auferam
          c Plaut. *Bacch.* 766 **uorsabo ego** illunc hodie, si uiuo, probe
          d Plaut. *Cist.* 367 **ludam ego** hunc
          e Plaut. *Most.* 1168 **interimam hercle ego** <te> si uiuo
          f Plaut. *Pseud.* 382 **exossabo ego** illum
          g Ter. *Eun.* 803 **diminuam ego** caput tuum hodie, nisi abis.

The object of the verb is usually a pronoun, but it need not be second-person. If the object pronoun is third- rather than first-person, then the utterance is strictly a statement of intention rather than a threat, but the intention is threatening. There is clearly a pattern of speech exemplified here. It is moreover in contexts of this type that the focusing use of *ego* might have developed. In this case *ego* is not motivated solely by its habit of following an antithetical or focused verb. It has its own motivation, in that a person making a threat may graphically refer to himself as the one who will carry the action out. But *ego* tends, in its attempt to reach the start of the utterance, to be blocked by the strong future-tense verb in the focal initial position. The next stage in the development of *ego* might have been the mechanical attachment of the pronoun to a focused term at the head of a clause, even when it was not independently motivated.

---

[13] On 'focus', see Adams (1994*a*: 121; 1994*b*: 18–19).

The practice of Plautus (see further above, (4)–(6)) suggests that a person making such a threat had the choice of either placing the pronoun in initial (or peninitial) position, or of giving priority to the verb. If we leave aside the possible influence of metrical factors in Plautus, we might suggest that the pattern chosen would depend on the speaker's subjective judgement whether in a particular context the focus of the threat should be placed on his personal participation in the act, or on the nature of the act itself.

IV. CATULLUS: (CONNECTIVE) RELATIVE + *EGO/TU*

It was seen earlier that a common pattern in prose is relative (including the connective use) + *ego/tu*, with the relative often separated from an associated term. The use of the pronoun may again originally have been inspired by its own emphasis or by the subjective nature of the verb, but it was suggested that the pattern became a mechanical one, with the preferential term itself causing the pronoun to be expressed. I begin with Catull. 23.22:

> (55)   Catull. 23.21–3   atque id durius est faba et lapillis;
> **quod tu si** manibus teras fricesque,
> **non umquam** digitum inquinare posses.

Kroll (1922: 45) correctly describes *tu* as unemphatic, and he adds a cross-reference to his note on 6.14, where another instance of unemphatic *tu*, as we saw (see p. 98), is accounted for as a colloquialism. That is far from satisfactory as an explanation of the use of the pronoun. Fordyce's note (1961: 154) is equally uninformative: 'for the rare addition of the unemphatic pronoun to a subjunctive of the indefinite second person, cf. . . .'. But *tu* is not an addition to *teras*; it is rather an attachment to the relative *quod*. Not only that, but there are structural parallels between this sentence and various sentences in Cicero. Note first (56):

> (56)   Cic. *Rab. perd.* 25 **quod tu si** audisses aut si per aetatem scire
> potuisses, **numquam** profecto istam imaginem . . . in rostra atque
> in contionem attulisses.

The connective relative has attracted *tu*, which in this context may be loosely contrastive, and there is then a conditional clause (with *si* following *tu* as in Catullus), followed by a main clause introduced by *numquam*, which may be compared with Catullus' *non umquam*. Catullus' use of *tu* reflects a mechanical attachment of *tu* to the connective relative originating

from structures of the type seen in (56), where *tu* is perhaps independently
motivated.

Similar again is (57), where again a *si*-clause follows connective relative
+ *tu*:

> (57) Cic. *Q. Rosc.* 42 **quem tu si** ex censu spectas, eques Romanus
>   est, si ex uita, homo clarissimus est, si ex fide, iudicem sumpsisti,
>   si ex ueritate, id quod scire potuit et debuit dixit.

Here *tu* seems to be without emphasis: the emphasis lies on a series of
contrasted terms which follow (*ex censu, ex uita*, etc.), and partly also on
quem, in that various persons are contrasted in the passage. *Quod tu si* is
found nowhere in Augustan poetry; Ovid, *Am.* 2.14.20 is not structurally
parallel.

Another 'unemphatic' instance of *tu* in Catullus (as noted by Kroll
(1922: 30)) is in (58):

> (58) Catull. 13.13 **quod tu cum** olfacies, deos rogabis,
>   totum ut te faciant, Fabulle, nasum.

For the structure here, cf. the following Ciceronian example:

> (59) Cic. *Flacc.* 51 **quem tu cum** ephebum Temni cognosses, . . .
>   semper nudum esse uoluisti.

With the examples of *tu* from Catullus quoted so far in this section
also belong those at 15.11 and 30.5.

I move on to a different pattern in Catullus, but one which again
displays *ego* linked to a connective relative. It was noted earlier that in
Cicero *ego* so placed may separate the relative from an associated term.
This pattern is found in (60):

> (60) Catull. 66.37 **quis** ego **pro factis** caelesti reddita coetu
>   pristina uota nouo munere dissoluo.

The preposition on which *quis factis* depends (*pro*) follows *ego*. For this
structure in Cicero, see (61):

> (61) a *Verr.* 1.103 **quibus** ego **in** rebus
>   b *Verr.* 5.72 **quorum** ego **de** acerbissima morte
>   c *Cluent.* 106 **quorum** ego **de** sententia
>   d *Sull.* 62 **cuius** ego **de** uirtute
>   e *Dom.* 144 **quorum** ego **a** templis
>   f *Har. resp.* 2 **cuius** ego **de** ecfrenato . . . furore.

I note in passing that *ego* in (61a) is undoubtedly emphatic. It must be
stressed again that *ego* (or *tu*) in the structures which I am identifying is
not necessarily unemphatic. I am suggesting rather that its original motiv-

ation was the carrying of some sort of emphasis or pragmatic function, and that it then became formulaic in certain structures, its emphasis no longer a necessary determinant of its use.

Also of note is the disjunction in the following example:

> (62)   Catull. 68.25 **cuius** ego **interitu** tota de mente fugaui / haec studia.

Here a genitive form of the relative is separated from the noun on which it depends, as in some of the Ciceronian examples in (61), and those in (63):

> (63)   a   *Cluent.* 194 **cuius** ego **furorem**
> b   *Cael.* 14 **cuius** ego **facinora**
> c   *Red. Sen.* 20 **cuius** ego **clientibus.**

Cuius ego is not found in elegy, Horace or Virgil, but note the following examples:

> (64)   Plaut. *Amph.* 141 **quoiius** ego fero **hanc imaginem**
> (65)   Lucr. 5.55 **cuius** ego ingressus **uestigia.**

The patterns discussed in this section cannot be dismissed as colloquial, even in those cases where *ego* and *tu* are manifestly unemphatic. Moreover the parallelism between Catullus and Cicero sometimes goes beyond the mere attachment of *ego/tu* to a (connective) relative; there is sometimes a more extensive structural similarity. Catullus has employed in verse some structures of speech.

I discuss in the next section the attachment of *ego/tu* to the demonstrative *hic*, particularly in the pattern *hunc ego hominem.*

V. CATULLUS: DEMONSTRATIVE + *EGO/TU*

In (66) *haec* is separated from *commoda* by *tu*, and again *tu* is noted by Kroll (1922: 45 on line 22) as unemphatic:

> (66)   Catull. 23.24 **haec** tu **commoda** tam beata, Furi, / noli *spernere.*

Haec tu commoda tam beata is followed by a vocative, a structure which can be seen in Cicero in the examples at (67):

> (67)   a   *Phil.* 8.28 **haec** tu **mandata**, L. Piso, et tu, L. Philippe ...
> b   *Mur.* 34 **hunc** tu **hostem**, Cato, *contemnis*
> c   *Verr.* 3.97 **hunc** tu in hac causa **testem**, Verres, habebis.

Catullus has again fallen into a pattern of wording which is rooted in the spoken language. Note also the similarity of the verb phrase in (66) with that in Cicero in (67b). In (67a) *tu* is contrastive, but it has lost that function in (66).

A clear-cut instance of a demonstrative, which is focused (antithetical), separated from the word in agreement is found in (68), where *haec* (*singula*) is antithetical with (*totum*) *illud*:

> (68)   Catull. 86.2   **haec** ego sic **singula** *confiteor.*
>   totum illud 'formosa' nego.

Compare the contrastive use of *hunc* (*ego*) in Cicero in (16). In (68) *ego* is unemphatic. In the previous line Catullus contrasts himself with others (*multis/mihi*), but in line 2 *ego* is no longer antithetical. (68) might be compared with the Plautine passage (69), which contains the same verb:

> (69)   Plaut. *Capt.* 296 **haec** tu **eadem** si *confiteri* uis.

In (69), however, *tu* is contrastive. I stress again the fact that *ego* and *tu* recur in our various patterns whether or not they are themselves 'emphatic'.

I quote in (70)–(71) two further examples from Catullus where the nominative pronoun, apparently unemphatic, hangs on the demonstrative, which in these cases is not separated from a noun:

> (70)   Catull. 56.6   deprendi modo pupulum puellae
>   trusantem; **hunc ego**, si placet Dionae,
>   protelo rigida mea cecidi
> (71)   Catull. 24.9 **hoc tu** quam lubet abice.

Note the position of the *si*-clause in (70). A clause is often inserted after an enclitic, thereby isolating the emphatic host term (in this case *hunc*) and its dependent enclitic.[14] For *hunc ego* in a similar context in Plautus (where a form of punishment is at issue), note:

> (72)   Plaut. *Pseud.* 447   hic mihi corrumpit filium, scelerum caput;
>   hic dux, hic illist paedagogus, **hunc ego**
>   cupio excruciari.

The combining of the demonstrative *hic* with *ego* or *tu* is common in elegy and Augustan poetry in general, but there are some subtle differences between the way in which Catullus uses the pattern and the way it is used by other poets, particularly Ovid. Catullan usage is directly relatable to that of Cicero. I return to Augustan poetry later.

---

[14] See Adams (1994*b*: 37 on (190)).

VI. CATULLUS: INTERROGATIVES + *EGO/TU*

It was pointed out earlier (see (21)–(27)) that interrogatives, particularly *quis*, often have *ego* or *tu* following. In this section I concentrate by way of illustration on just one interrogative, the old instrumental *qui*, which often means 'how?'. In (73) Catullus uses *qui* with *tu* following:

> (73) Catull. 67.37 qui tu **istaec**, ianua, nosti . . .?

The emphasis probably lies on *tu*, but perhaps on *istaec* as well. *Qui ego* and *qui tu* are particularly common in comedy. They presumably lingered on in speech, their fading currency in the literary language determined not by the disappearance of *ego/tu* from questions, but by the obsolescence of instrumental *qui*. But the instrumental use of *qui* lasted somewhat longer in the colloquial language than in literature, as a recent attestation in a letter at Vindolanda shows (*Tab. Vind.* II.234). In this case Catullus' usage can with justification be classified as colloquial.

Various observations may be made about (73). First, *qui tu* is followed by the demonstrative form *istaec*, with its deictic particle *-ce*. For *qui ego* in Plautus followed by the same demonstrative term, note the following:

> (74) a Plaut. *Men.* 786 qui ego **istuc**, mi pater, cauere possum?
> b Plaut. *Merc.* 627 qui ego **istuc** credam tibi?

There is a distinct possibility that the whole sequence *qui ego/tu istuc/ istaec* was a formulaic way of opening a question in colloquial speech. The augmented demonstratives *illic/istic* had a colloquial character. *Ego* is often associated with *istic* in Plautus, and not only in the structure which we see here:

> (75) a Plaut. *Amph.* 925 **ego istaec** feci uerba
> b Plaut. *Men.* 265 **ego istuc** cauebo
> c Plaut. *Merc.* 477 omnia **ego istaec** auscultaui.

Secondly, *istaec* in (73) is followed by a vocative. For the identical structure in Plautus, see (74a).

Thirdly, the verb in Catullus is a verb of knowing. Again the idiom can be paralleled in Plautus:

> (76) a Plaut. *Capt.* 629 qui tu **scis**?
> b Plaut. *Pers.* 716 qui ego nunc **scio** . . .?

It should now be clear that Mynors's text (1958) of Catull. 67.37 ((73) above) is incorrect: 'quid? tu istaec, ianua . . .' (*quid* V: *qui* Aldina).

In this section we have identified in Catullus a highly stereotyped pattern of phraseology, a pattern which can be paralleled in this case in

Plautus rather than in Cicero. As such it probably belonged to that colloquial register which is extensively represented in Latin comedy, but
which leaves its mark in Catullus as well. This is not the only structural
parallel that we have found between Plautus and Catullus; there was also
the form of the threat *pedicabo ego uos*.

This is not the only example in Catullus, as we will see in the next
section, of a nominative pronoun associated with an interrogative. I refer
finally in this section to (77), which has a formulaic structure already noted
in (22):

> (77)   Catull. 64.164 sed **quid ego** ignaris nequiquam **conquerar**
>   auris?

(77) should be compared with the Ciceronian example (78), where the
verb is much the same:

> (78)   *Cic. Imp. Pomp.* 33 nam **quid ego** Ostiense incommodum atque
>   illam labem atque ignominiam rei publicae **querar**?

Nam quid ego in (78) is, like *sed quid ego*, a formulaic opening. For *nam
quid ego*, see:

> (79)   a   Plaut. *Amph.* 41 **nam quid ego** memorem . . .
>   b   Cic. *Verr.* 1.129 **nam quid ego** de cotidiano sermone
>   querimoniaque populi Romani loquar?

VII. CATULLUS: *QUIN + EGO/TU*

I next consider another type of expression showing nominative pronouns
in association with an interrogative. *Quin* is the negated form of the
instrumental *qui*, and it too may be followed by *ego/tu*.

In the self-address in Catullus 76 *tu* is unemphatic, as Kroll (1922: 14)
noted (on 6.14):

> (80)   Catull. 76.11 **quin tu** animo offirmas atque istinc teque reducis?

Tu is metrically unnecessary, and indeed is omitted by Ovid in his imitation
of the line:

> (81)   Ovid *Met.* 9.745 **quin** animum firmas teque ipsa recolligis . . .?

Quin tu undoubtedly belonged to speech. It occurs 70 times in Plautus:
e.g.

> (82)   a   *Asin.* 659 **quin tu** labore liberas te . . .?
>   b   *Curc.* 240 **quin tu** aliquot dies / perdura
>   c   *Merc.* 942 **quin tu** istas omittis nugas . . .?

In this case the expression was admitted also by Cicero (8 times, scattered across all genres).[15] Its rather stereotyped character may be illustrated by (83a) alongside (83b):

> (83) a Plaut. *Curc.* 611 **quin tu is** in malam crucem . . .?
>
>   b Cic. *Phil.* 13.48 **quin tu abis** in malam pestem malumque cruciatum?

Note *is/abis* immediately after *tu*, and then the prepositional expression. There is only one example of *quin tu* in Augustan poetry:

> (84) Virg. *Ecl.* 2.71 **quin tu** aliquid saltem potius, quorum indiget usus,
>
>   uiminibus mollique paras detexere iunco?

It may have been obsolete by the first century AD. It is not found in Petronius or Martial, and there is only one example in Apuleius (*Apol.* 79).

VIII. CATULLUS: *NUMQUAM + EGO*

Negatives, as noted earlier (see (31)–(33)), are often placed at the head of their clause in Latin. Sometimes the negative seems to cause *ego* or *tu* to be expressed after it; that is, an unemphatic, redundant nominative pronoun follows the negative almost as a focusing particle.

At Catull. 65.10 *numquam* is loosely antithetical with *semper* in the next clause. Two clitics (*ego, te*) follow *numquam*, but only *te* is necessary to the sense:

> (85) Catull. 65.10 **numquam ego** te, uita frater amabilior,
>
>   aspiciam posthac? at certe semper amabo.

For *numquam ego*, see above (31).[16]

The combination *numquam ego* is not found in Propertius, Horace, Tibullus or Virgil. There is one example in Ovid:

> (86) Ovid, *AA* 3.519 **numquam ego** te, Andromache, . . . rogarem.

---

[15] *Rosc. Com.* 25, *Sull.* 25, *Pis.* 61, *Phil.* 13.48, *Rep.* 1.61, 6.14, *Fam.* 7.8.2, *Att.* 4.19.1.

[16] Cf. e.g. Plaut. *Cist.* 44, 53, *Mil.* 1202, *Most.* 214, Cic. *Cat.* 2.15, *Pis.* 99, *Lael.* 18. Note too Petron. 134.9 '**numquam tu** hominem tam infelicem uidisti' (quoted by Pinkster (1987: 372) with the comment 'the personal experience of Oenothea is compared with the dreadful reality'). But it is *numquam* which is emphatic.

IX. CATULLUS: SOME CONCLUSIONS

Some uses of *ego* and *tu* in Catullus can be readily related to uses of
nominative pronouns on the one hand in Plautus and on the other in
Cicero. Sometimes the pronoun might be classed as 'emphatic' by a
speaker of a modern language, sometimes as 'unemphatic', and I have
referred to the views of Kroll and Fordyce on individual cases. But Kroll
and Fordyce considered *ego* and *tu* in isolation, without reference to the
preferential terms, which, in the data considered here, commonly preceded
them. These preferential terms are one of the determinants of the use of
ego and *tu*. Those examples of *ego* and *tu* which, while following preferential terms, themselves appear to be 'emphatic', might partly at least have
been motivated by their own emphatic potential. But pronouns which do
not seem to be emphatic might have been determined by the formulaic
place which they had acquired in attachment to certain preferential terms.

It is a mistake, with Kroll, to classify allegedly 'unemphatic' nominative
pronouns as colloquial, because equally 'unemphatic' pronouns can be
found readily in Cicero following the same categories of preferential terms.
I have been able to identify certain colloquialisms in Catullus (the structure
of *pedicabo ego uos, qui + ego/tu*), but not on the grounds that the pronoun
in question was unemphatic. Certain collocations of words or structural
patterns in which a nominative pronoun is embedded can be paralleled in
Plautus but not Cicero, and these probably belonged to the colloquial
registers of the language. Other patterns on the other hand *can* be paralleled in Cicero (or in Cicero as well as Plautus), and these may reflect the
spoken language in a wider sense. The patterns of speech, both colloquial
and more formal, are definitely to be detected in Catullus.

The question arises to what extent these speech patterns are found in
elegy and other Augustan poetry. I make no attempt here to go through
all of the categories of uses of *ego* and *tu* discussed earlier. I restrict myself
to two phenomena (*a*) the attachment of *ego* to a focused verb, and (*b*)
patterns showing *ego/tu* after the demonstrative *hic*.

X. AUGUSTAN POETRY: VERBS + *EGO*

The only Augustan poet who falls into line, up to a point, with Catullus
and Cicero in the attachment of *ego* to verbs is Propertius. On the one
hand Propertius sometimes makes what might be called a debased use of
the pattern, in that *ego* may follow a verb which is not focused or emphatic
or at the head of its clause. On the other hand there is an element of the
mundane about Propertius' exploitation of the pattern. *Ego* tends to follow

verbs with which it is associated also in prose and earlier Latin, particularly certain subjective or modal verbs, and verbs in the future tense. There are 23 cases of verbs followed by *ego* in Propertius,[17] of which I discuss a selection.

I begin with (87):

> (87)   Prop. 2.25.36   at si saecla forent antiquis grata puellis,
> essem ego quod nunc tu: tempore **uincor ego**.

Ego early in the line is obviously contrastive with *tu* (on the structure, see below (116)–(117)). I have stressed throughout that, while *ego* may be unemphatic in this position and tacked on to a verb merely as a means of focusing the verb, there is no theoretical reason why it should not acquire from the context its full contrastive function. In the second half of the line in (87) *ego* is 'given' in the context, and not conspicuously emphatic. The focus would seem to be on *tempore* rather than *uincor*. *Ego* is displaced by the norms of prose, in that it does not follow a term which is either focal or in initial position, but is mechanically positioned after a verb which is in second position in the colon. This example seems to represent a loosening of the connection between speech patterns and poetic discourse which we were able to demonstrate for Catullus.

But this example must be contrasted with (88):

> (88)   Prop. 2.8.5   **possum ego** in alterius positam spectare lacerto?

Possum ego begins a question, the expected answer to which is 'no'. I would interpret the force as 'how CAN I look at her in another's arms', or 'CAN I look at her', but certainly not 'can *I* look at her . . .'. (89) is similar:

> (89)   Prop. 2.20.28   cum te tam multi peterent, tu me una petisti:
> **possum ego** naturae non meminisse tuae?

'How CAN I not remember your (kind) nature? [It is impossible].'

It is metrically convenient to have a disyllabic word (ending in *-m* or *-o*) at the start of a line followed by *ego*. But the collocation is no mere metrical convenience. It is good idiomatic Latin for *possum* when focused to be followed by unemphatic *ego*. The pattern is found in Cicero. Note e.g. (90), where Cicero deals with a problem of translation:

> (90)   Cic. *Fin.* 3.35 quas Graeci πάθη appellant — **poteram ego**
> uerbum ipsum interpretans morbos appellare, sed non
> conueniret ad omnia

---

[17] 1.10.15, 1.12.11, 1.13.14–15 (twice), 2.8.5, 2.18b.37, 2.20.28, 2.24c.41, 2.24c.42, 2.25.36 (twice), 2.28.44, 3.8.27, 3.17.21, 3.21.24, 3.25.7, 4.2.53, 4.5.61, 4.5.67, 4.7.36, 4.7.51, 4.7.70, 4.8.81.

'I COULD [translating literally] have called them *morbi*, but that term would not be suitable.' The contrast is between what is possible, and what is appropriate, with the nuance 'possibility' rather than the person of the subject focused. Cicero uses another tense of *possum* with *ego* in (91):

> (91)   Cic. *Verr.* 5.179 **potero** silere ... **potero** dissimulare ... **potero ego** hoc onus tantum aut in hoc iudicio deponere aut tacitus sustinere?

Potero is used three times. There must be an emphasis of sorts on the series of infinitives dependent on *potero*, but above all Cicero is stressing the *impossibility* of silence, etc. The force of the rhetoric might best be rendered into English: 'how CAN I be silent, etc.', or, in the third clause, 'will it be POSSIBLE for me either to lay aside this responsibility, or to support it while saying nothing?'

Example (92) is again a question, with the same answer implied as in (88), (89) and (91):

> (92)   Cic. *Red. sen.* 29 **possum ego** satis in Cn. Pompeium umquam gratus uideri?

It is comparable in all respects to the Propertian examples (88) and (89). Propertius then has used an established idiom which happens to fit well into the first foot of the line.[18]

Possum ego also begins a line in (93):

> (93)   Prop. 1.10.15   **possum ego** diuersos iterum coniungere amantes
> et dominae tardas **possum** aperire fores;
> et **possum** alterius curas sanare recentis.

The presence of *ego* is not required by the metre, though it does produce a dactyl at the start of the line. There is a rhetorically insistent repetition of *possum*, which arguably might have been sufficient motivation for the use of *ego*. In this case though there is a personal claim carried by *ego*, which has a certain emphasis. It might have been expected to precede *possum*, but metrical convenience has triumphed over pragmatically determined word order.

Note finally (94):

> (94)   Tib. 1.6.70   laudare nec ullam
> **possim ego**, quin oculos appetat illa meos.

Tibullus places *ego* after a verb only twice, and in this case we seem to have a mechanical, metrically convenient placement which cannot be

---

[18] For *possum* + *ego*, cf. also Pacuvius 236, Ter. *Eun.* 712.

attributed to the emphasis of *possim*. The emphasis seems to lie on *ullam* or *laudare*.

Credo ego, I pointed out earlier, was a collocation found in Plautus (cf. *Cas.* 234, *Epid.* 535) and sometimes in oratory. It may have been a hackneyed sentence or speech opening.[19] It never occurs in Virgil, Horace, Ovid or Tibullus, but note first the following Propertian passage:

> (95)   Prop. 2.24c.41–2   **credo ego** non paucos ista periisse figura,
> **credo ego** sed multos non habuisse fidem.

This order seems to be adopted when a firm opinion is expressed, without any contrastive emphasis on the pronoun:[20] 'I am SURE that, I IMAGINE that, I TRUST that'. In (96) the emphasis is clearly on *credam*:

> (96)   Prop. 2.18b.37   **credam ego** narranti, noli committere, famae

— 'I will *believe* rumour'. Again Propertius has used an established idiom with its expected implication.

Another subjective verb which not unexpectedly sometimes has *ego* as its subject is *odi*. Propertius has the expression *odi ego* in (97) in a context in which *odi* is obviously the focus, though *ego* may be independently motivated:

> (97)   Prop. 3.8.27   **odi ego** quos nunquam pungunt suspiria somnos:
> semper in irata pallidus esse uelim

'I HATE sleep which sighs never punctuate. I would always prefer to be pale in the presence of an angry woman.'

Again the expression may have been a commonplace one. Note (98):

> (98)   Plaut. *Capt.*325   **non ego** omnino lucrum omne esse utile
> homini existumo:
> **scio ego**, multos iam lucrum lutulentos
> homines reddidit;
> est etiam ubi profecto damnum praestet
> facere quam lucrum.
> **odi ego** aurum.

I have quoted the passage at length because it illustrates particularly well the function of *ego* which I have been discussing. The three verbs *existumo*, *scio* and *odi* are all verbs of the type which I have called 'subjective'. If the presence of *ego* is in part determined by that feature, it is nevertheless true that it is attached in each of the three lines to a focused preferential

---

[19] It may be significant that Cicero employed the collocation in one of his earliest speeches, and never thereafter; it is possible that it had become banal in oratory. See further Landgraf (1914: 14) ad loc.

[20] Cf. Marouzeau (1907: 28).

term: 'I do NOT think...', 'I am WELL AWARE', 'I HATE gold'. *Odi ego* is also found in Pacuvius:

> (99) Pacuvius 348 **odi ego** homines ignaua opera et philosopha
>   sententia.

Verbs of asserting or revealing often have *ego* as subject, in Propertius and in the language in general. I offer a few observations on the motivation of the pronoun before turning to Propertius.

The legal formula quoted by Gaius (100) displays the formulaic *hunc ego hominem*, but *ego* is not determined only by its place in the collocation of words:

> (100) Gaius *Inst.* 4.16 **hunc** ego **hominem** ex iure Quiritium meum
>   esse **aio**.

A strong assertion may reflect the personal conviction of the speaker, or an undertaking to which he is personally willing to be held, or new information which he is prepared to stand by, or is claiming as his own, etc. The marked personal commitment to the assertion inspires the use of *ego*. This can be seen from an example such as (101), where the speaker's claim is underlined by his invocation of the gods.

> (101) Plaut. *Men.* 990 per **ego** uobis deos atque homines **dico**.

To describe a pattern such as this as manifesting 'Wackernagel's law' would be to miss the point entirely. *Ego* is not unemphatic, as second-position pronouns are supposed to be according to the conventional understanding of Wackernagel's law. It is not in second position *qua* second position, but has rather been blocked from *first* position by *per*, which in such old formulae began its clause for some reason. If a writer chooses not to give *per* the initial position, then that place is freed for *ego*: e.g.

> (102) Plaut. *Amph.* 436 at ego per Mercurium iuro tibi ....

If there is no preferential term to debar it from first position, *ego*, as subject of a verb of asserting *sim.*, often begins its clause:

> (103) Ter. *Andr.* 375 X. quor simulat? Y. **ego dicam** tibi
> (104) Ter. *Phorm.* 837 **ego** me ire senibus Sunium / **dicam** ad
>   mercatum.

A future-tense form, expressing intent, may act as an additional trigger to the use of the pronoun here.

But in an assertion or revelation containing *ego* the focus may readily be interpreted as being on the verb, and such an interpretation may entail initial placement of the verb. Thus (105) and (106), in both of which the verb expresses a revelation ('I TELL you', 'I shall TELL you'):

(105) Plaut. *Epid.* 668 **dico ego** tibi iam, ut scias
(106) Mart. 10.41.4 quid, rogo, quid factum est? subiti quae causa doloris?
nil mihi respondes? **dicam ego**, praetor erat.

Into this class falls the following Propertian example:

(107) Prop. 3.17.21 **dicam ego** maternos Aetnaeo fulmine partus.

In this case the revelation is to take the form of poetic composition, but this is merely a contextually determined nuance. *Ego* is as often metrically unnecessary. Another verb of asserting in initial position is at (108):

(108) Prop. 4.7.51 **iuro ego** Fatorum nulli reuolubile carmen / ... si fallo

'I SWEAR by the song of the Fates which cannot be unravelled by anyone (that I was loyal) ... If I LIE ...' There is a contrast between asserting the truth on oath, and lying, and *iuro* is accordingly emphatic.

Not unlike (107) is a case of *scribam*:

(109) Prop. 2.28.44 pro quibus optatis sacro me carmine damno:
scribam ego 'per magnum est salua puella Iouem'.

In return for the survival of Cynthia Propertius undertakes to Jupiter to write a poem.

Another hackneyed collocation is *uidi ego*.[21] The fairly frequent use of *ego* as subject of *uidi*, whether placed before or after the verb, no doubt derives in part from the speaker's/writer's desire to stress that his own personal observation was involved. Sometimes indeed the appeal to the evidence of one's own senses is made even more explicit, as e.g. in (110), where the *-met* form of the pronoun occurs:

(110) a Ter. *Ad.* 329 **hisce oculis** egomet uidi
b Hor. *Sat.* 1.8.23 uidi ego**met**.

The order *uidi ego* originally must have conveyed a particular nuance, e.g. 'I DID see', 'such and such did not go UNNOTICED', as in (111):

(111) Cic. *Planc.* 76 et mihi lacrimulam Cispiani iudici obiectas. sic enim dixisti: '**uidi ego** tuam lacrimulam'

---

[21] For *uideo* (*uidi* etc.) + *ego* (or *tu*), see e.g. Plaut. *Cas.* 349, Accius 647, Titinius 18, Ter. *Heaut.* 563, Cic. *Sull.* 41, *Flacc.* 53, *Fam.* 1.9.22, Livy 1.39.3, 6.29.1, 7.34.4 etc.

'I SAW your little tear, it did not ESCAPE me.'[22] This same type of nuance is readily identifiable in Propertius:

> (112)   Prop. 1.13.13–15   haec non <sum>[23] rumore malo, non
> augure doctus;
>   **uidi ego**: me quaeso teste negare potes?
>   **uidi ego** te toto uinctum languescere collo.

There is a contrast, the force of which is roughly: 'I did not HEAR about these things, for example from rumour: I SAW them. I SAW you in his embrace.'

But *uidi ego* seems to have become a banal expression, particularly in poetry, the force of which in any context may be difficult to discern. There are some problematical examples of the phrase in Propertius (4.2.53, 4.5.61, 4.5.67), and numerous ones in Ovid (see below).

Very similar to *uidi ego* (and particularly the example in Cicero at (111)) is the expression *sensi ego* in the following passage:

> (113)   Prop. 4.7.36 **sensi ego**, cum insidiis pallida uina bibi.

Cynthia's ghost is the speaker. When she drank the poisoned wine, it did not escape her notice: 'I NOTICED, I was well AWARE, when I drank the poison.' The emphasis clearly lies on *sensi*,[24] though since the verb is one of perception, the pronoun may also have a secondary justification.

I draw attention to one further example of a focused initial verb in Propertius:

> (114)   Prop. 3.21.24 **scandam ego** Theseae bracchia longa uiae.

Propertius is announcing a plan to go abroad to Athens. Various stages of the journey and its culmination are set out. *Scandam* expresses one of these, and is loosely focused as expressing an intention.

I have not considered all the evidence from Propertius, but it should be clear that the functional postponement of *ego* is fairly common in his work, that his use of the pronoun can be paralleled both in Catullus and Cicero, and that he has a habit of using *ego* in hackneyed collocations. Notable among these is *credo ego*, an expression which Cicero used in the *Pro Roscio Amerino*, but thereafter apparently rejected. We have also seen in Propertius a case of mechanical placement of *ego* behind a verb

---

[22] See Marouzeau (1907: 29) on Plaut. *Cas.* 349. Note also Cic. *Sull.* 41 '**uidi ego** hoc, iudices, nisi . . . testatus essem, fore ut . . .', 'I REALIZED, gentlemen . . .'. Here the emphasis is on the fact of the realization, not on the person who made that realization.

[23] So Rossberg (*non* N: [*ego*] *non* A).

[24] Cf. Plaut. *Pers.* 534 and Marouzeau (1907: 29).

(87) in a context in which the order is difficult to explain as functional. What I have called the 'debased' use of *ego* is also found in Tibullus (94).

I turn now to other Augustan poets. *Ego* never follows a verb in Virgil.[25] In Tibullus and the *corpus Tibullianum* there are just two examples, one of which has been seen (94). Note also (115), where *ego* is contrastive (with *alias*):

> (115) [Tib.] 4.5.5 uror ego ante alias.

Ego can have contrastive emphasis in this position in classical prose (see also above, n. 12), but it is relatively rare. Consider (116):

> (116) Cic. *Sen.* 68 sensi **ego** in optimo filio, **tu** in exspectatis ad amplissimam dignitatem fratribus, Scipio, mortem omni aetati esse communem.

A double antithesis is developed here after the verb, between *ego* and *tu* on the one hand, and two prepositional expressions on the other. *Ego*, placed after the verb, may be the marked focus if a contrast is expressed with another pronoun. A pattern of this type seems to have been favoured if both pronouns were subject of the same verb. Cf.:

> (117) Prop. 2.35.36 **essem ego** quod nunc **tu** (= (87) above).

Here a determinant of the initial placement of *essem* may have been the mood of the verb.[26]

Slightly different again is the following:

> (118) Cic. *S. Rosc.* 60 adsedit; surrexi **ego**.

Surrexi stands in a contrast of opposites (with *adsedit*). But there is a secondary contrast, between the first- and second-person subjects of the two verbs, with *ego* marking the change of subject.[27] A verb participating in such an antithesis may be followed by a pronoun which itself is contrastive. Cf.:

> (119) Cic. *Verr.* 5.121 **laetaris** *tu* in *omnium* **gemitu.**

Laetaris is in contrast with *gemitu*, and *tu* with *omnium*. Similar to (118) is the following Propertian example:

> (120) Prop. 4.8.81 indixit legem: respondi **ego** 'legibus utar'.

---

[25] It is a curiosity, as Professor Powell points out to me, that Virgil happily places *equidem* after a verb, but not *ego* (e.g. *Aen.* 4.12 *credo equidem*; cf. 2.704, 3.315, 4.382 etc.). Collocations of the type *credo ego* may have had some sort of nuance (such as a banal oratorical flavour) which made them less than acceptable in high epic.

[26] See Adams (1994b: 60 (on (295)), 76).

[27] Change of 'Topic', in the terminology of Pinkster (1987: 369).

Respondi contrasts with *indixit*, and *ego* with the subject of *indixit*.

In Horace there are six examples of verb + *ego*:

> (121) a *Sat.* 2.1.74 quidquid **sum ego** quamuis / infra Lucili censum
> ingeniumque
> b *Sat.* 2.3.235 ut aprum / **cenem ego? tu** piscis hiberno ex
> aequore uerris, / segnis **ego**
> c *Sat.* 2.7.80 nam / siue uicarius est qui seruo paret, uti mos /
> uester ait, seu conseruus, **tibi** quid **sum ego?**
> d *Epist.* 1.16.32 nempe / uir bonus et prudens dici **delector
> ego ac tu**
> e *Epist.* 1.17.19 **scurror ego** ipse mihi, populo **tu**
> f *Odes* 3.5.21 arma . . . / derepta **uidi; uidi ego** ciuium /
> retorta tergo bracchia libero.

Five of these are in the *Satires* and *Epistles* and only one in the *Odes*, but, contrary to what one might be tempted to conclude, this distribution cannot be used to argue that in the *Satires* and *Epistles*, but not the *Odes*, Horace was influenced by the usage of speech. In all five cases *ego* is itself contrastive, usually with *tu*. A use of *ego* which in prose in this position was rare, has become the norm in Horace; examples *d* and *e* are of the pattern seen in (116) and (117). *Vidi ego* (*f*) is, as we saw, a hackneyed collocation, and it is in the *Odes*.

I turn finally to Ovid. There are just 24 examples of the phenomenon in the whole of Ovid's work, scattered across the various genres, and 13 of these consist of the expression *uidi ego*.[28] It does not seem meaningful to attempt to analyse *uidi ego* in Ovid in terms of focus; it is a metrically useful line opening. Given that there are so few examples (11) outside this formula,[29] it is obvious that Ovid has not exploited our enclitic pattern. Moreover it is not certain in any of these 11 examples that the verb is focused. In (122), for example, both *quartus* and *ego* are in antitheses with earlier terms:

> (122) Ovid *Her.* 16.330 quartus in exemplis **adnumerabor ego**.

Ego can usually be interpreted as emphatic in some sense in the other cases.

In Catullus' insubstantial corpus *ego* and *tu* do not often follow a verb, but when this placement does occur it is functional in the manner of prose and comedy. No poet of the Augustan period so faithfully represents this spoken usage. In Horace and Ovid *ego* tends to be emphatic when it

---

[28] *Am.* 1.2.11, 2.2.47, 2.12.25, 3.4.13, *AA* 3.487, *RA* 101, *Met.* 12.327, 15.262, *Trist.* 2.143, 3.4.37, 3.5.11, 5.8.11, *Pont.* 1.1.51.

[29] *Am.* 2.8.13, *Trist.* 3.11.25, *Her.* 3.90, 7.82, 16.330, 17.50, 17.122, 18.117, 21.54, *Met.* 2.570, 7.38.

comes after the verb. In Propertius and Tibullus we have what I describe as a debased postpositive use of *ego*. Propertius, however, admits a number of banal collocations verb + *ego*, and it is Propertius in this respect who is closest to Catullus.

XI. SOME DISJUNCTIONS

We saw in Section II some disjunctions, whereby a connective relative or *hic* was separated from a noun by *ego*, and such patterns were illustrated in Catullus. In the Catullan examples, with the minor exception of (123), the pronoun alone effects the separation:

> (123)   Catull. 86.2 **haec** ego sic **singula** confiteor.

In Augustan poetry the disjunction is often much longer, as for example in (124), where *hunc ego* begins the line, but *dolorem* does not come until the end of the line:

> (124)   Virg. *Aen.* 4.419 **hunc** *ego* si potui tantum sperare **dolorem.**

Since disjunctions and so-called 'enclosing' patterns of word-order are thought to be characteristic of Augustan poetry,[30] I consider in this section the nature and distribution in poetry of those separations of which the first element comprises relative or demonstrative + *ego* (*tu*). Though there are obvious differences between (123) and (124), the enclosing order of (124) is clearly related to the tendency which we have discussed for *ego* to link itself to demonstratives. The question arises whether cases such as (124) represent a poetic development of an old pattern.

I repeat that in Catullus, with the exception of (123), the pronoun is the only word which separates the deictic from the noun. In this respect there is again a close similarity between Catullan and prose usage. I offer some statistics from Cicero. In the Verrine orations (including *diu. Caec.*) there are 24 cases of relative/demonstrative + *ego* followed by a noun. In 22 of the 24 cases the noun is located immediately after *ego*. The two exceptions show an adverb (*maxime*) and a subordinator (*si*) as additional separating constituents:

> (125)   a   *Verr.* 2.183 **quod** ego *maxime* **genus** ...
>   b   *Verr.* 5.130 **hunc** ego *si* **metum** ... deiecero.

But while such limited separations are the norm in Ciceronian prose, the

---

[30] See Pearce (1966).

host of *ego* (i.e. the demonstrative or relative) from time to time is at a much greater remove from the associated noun. Consider first (126a):

(126) a Cic. *Tusc.* 5.64 **cuius** *ego* quaestor ignoratum ab
Syracusanis, cum esse omnino negarent, saeptum
undique et uestitum uepribus et dumetis *indagaui*
sepulchrum
b *Sest.* 13 **cuius** *ego* nuper in Macedonia *uidi* **uestigia**
c *Flacc.* 106 eam **quam** *ego* patri suo quondam pro salute
patriae *spoponderim* **dignitatem**
d *Att.* 8.4.1 **cuius** *ego* cum satis *cognossem* **mores**
e *Att.* 13.33a.1 **horum** *ego* uix *attigi* **paenulam**
f *De orat.* 2.174 sic **has** *ego* argumentorum *notaui* **notas**
g Livy 2.2.7 **hunc** *tu* . . . tua uolunate, L. Tarquini, *remoue*
metum.

Of note here (126a), apart from the length of the disjunction of *cuius* and *sepulchrum*, is the fact that *sepulchrum* is immediately after the verb, and that a second disjunction is embedded within the structure *cuius ego . . . sepulchrum*. I refer to the fact that the participial expression *saeptum . . . dumetis* is itself separated by the verb from *sepulchrum*. (126f) combines the same two features: *notaui* is in the penultimate position, and *argumentorum* is separated from *notas* by the verb. All of the examples in (126) have a verb in penultimate position. It is as if the verb announces the arrival of the noun which is to close the construction. That noun is usually focal.[31]

This is by no means the full extent of longer separations in Cicero. I have concentrated on a particular type. In Augustan poets when compared with Catullus there is a change in the balance between short and long separations. When *ego* takes part in a disjunction, it is more often hosted in poetry by *hic* than by *qui* (a reversal of the norm for prose), and the disjunction is long more often than short. Short disjunctions do of course occur, but I have noted only about 13 in Virgil, Horace and elegy.[32] To what extent are longer separations in poetry artificial or distinctively 'poetic'? Can they be related to prose usage?

I return to (124). It may be true that *hunc dolorem* frames the line, but in fact there is no great difference between this line and some of the

---

[31] A participant at the Symposium suggested that in (126a) there is a correspondence between structure and meaning, in that the sentence describes the discovery of the tomb of Archimedes, and *sepulchrum* comes right at the end of the sentence. That may be so, but Cicero was able to achieve this correspondence because the appropriate structure existed already, to be exploited in this way.

[32] Prop. 2.10.19, 3.8.17, Ovid, *Am.* 1.4.32, *AA* 3.178, *Her.* 17.91, 17.136, *Trist.* 4.4.21, 4.7.19, 5.5.28, *Pont.* 2.1.12, *Fast.* 3.486, *Met.* 9.475, Virg. *Aen.* 9.323.

separations which we have seen in Cicero. Note first that *dolorem* is object of a verb which immediately precedes it, as is the case in every one of the prose examples quoted in (126). Moreover the line opening *hunc ego si*, where *hunc* and *ego* syntactically belong *within* the *si*-clause, can be found in Cicero at (125b).

If there is a difference between (124) and the Ciceronian examples, it may lie in the place of the focus. In the examples in (126) the final noun often seems to be emphatic, whereas in (124) the focus seems rather to be on *sperare*. But there can be no doubt that the pattern represented in (124) had its origin in the spoken language, rather than in a contrived form of poetic diction.

In (124), as we saw, *hunc ego si* is followed by a verb. For this structure in verse, cf.:

> (127) Hor. *Epist.* 1.7.34 **hac** *ego* si *compellar* **imagine**.

I quote in (128) further examples from verse which have the opening *hic ego si*:

> (128) a Ovid *Her.* 18.27 **his ego si** uidi . . . / noctibus
> b *Pont.* 4.12.15 **his ego si** uitiis ausim corrumpere nomen.

I return to the structure showing a verb in penultimate position. In the examples cited in (126) the enclosing expression is object of the penultimate verb. In (127) it is an instrumental. In the poetic examples quoted in (129) an accusative is to be seen in f, but poets seem to have been prepared to exploit a wider range of cases in this position:

> (129) a Prop. 1.6.11 **his** *ego* non horam possum *durare* **querelis**
> b Ovid *Pont.* 3.6.9 **huic** *ego*, quam patior, nil possem *demere* **poenae**
> c Hor. *Epist.* 1.1.27 restat ut **his** *ego* me ipse regam solerque **elementis**
> d Ovid *Her.* 19.128 **hac** *ego laedor* **aqua**
> e Prop. 4.8.33 **his** *ego* constitui noctem lenire **uocatis**
> f Lucr. 3.316 **quorum** *ego* nunc nequeo caecas *exponere* **causas**.

I would draw particular attention to (129f). Here the initial constituent is a relative, as often in prose. It is in the genitive, as again is typical of prose (see e.g. (126b)). And within the wider disjunction *quorum . . . causas* there is a secondary disjunction *caecas . . . causas*, as in the Ciceronian example (126a).

The type of disjunction which we have been considering was clearly domiciled in both verse and prose, though poets may have extended the range of cases in which the enclosing noun phrase might stand. The verb seems to have had a role in indicating that the construction was about to end. For this type of clause-ending in clauses which do not have *ego* in second position, see (130):

> (130) a   Cic. *Brut.* 6 **hunc** autem ... *sustineret* **dolorem**
>   b   *Phil.* 12.9 **omnis** aequo animo belli *patitur* **iniurias**.

(130b) recalls Lucretius (129g) and Cicero (126f), in that there is a secondary disjunction of *belli* from *iniurias*.

Long disjunctions, or 'enclosing' word orders, have been the subject of some discussion. In this section I have dealt with just one type, that in which a demonstrative or relative attracts *ego* and is detached from an associated noun. In its simplest form, which is the predominating type in Cicero, *ego* alone is the disjoining element. This simple structure is represented a number of times in Catullus in examples which have structural parallels in Cicero, and which, we have suggested, are grounded in the patterns of real speech. The simple type in Augustan poetry is outnumbered by more complex disjunctions. But despite the greater *frequency* of these longer disjunctions in Augustan poetry as compared with Cicero or Catullus, the poetic examples can constantly be paralleled in structure in Cicero. I conclude that, even if poets may have developed complicated patterns of their own, a topic to which I will return in the next section, the basic structure rel./*hic* + *ego* + disjoined noun had its origin in real speech, at least of a formal kind. It should not be seen as an artificial invention of poetry, or as something inspired from outside Latin, but rather as a native Latin phenomenon.

XII. POETIC DEVELOPMENTS

I turn now to the exploitation of the structure *hic* + *ego* ... noun by Augustan poets. I take in turns various developments discernible particularly in Ovid.

(i) Usually the pair *hic ego* belongs syntactically in the same clause: that is, *ego* is subject of a verb with which the deictic is also associated, as its object for example or instrumental satellite. But it is not unusual, even in prose, for *hic* and *ego* to belong in different clauses. Thus in (131) *ego* belongs in the main clause as subject of *confiteor*, whereas *hisce* belongs in the dependent clause, as object of *uti*:

> (131)   Cic. *Planc.* 87 **hisce** ego **auxiliis** studentibus atque incitatis
>   uti me ... potuisse confiteor (= (*ego confiteor*) (*me hisce
>   auxiliis uti potuisse*)).

An extension of structures of this type can be seen in the Ovidian example (132):

> (132)   Ovid *AA* 3.178 crediderim nymphas **hac** ego **ueste** tegi (= (*ego crediderim*) (*nymphas hac ueste tegi*)).

But here the main verb *crediderim precedes* the dependent clause. *Ego* comes after the verb of which it is subject, and is in the wrong clause. It has tracked *hac* away from the start of the sentence well into the dependent clause. The position of *ego* is determined by that of its favoured host. A striking analogy for this placement of *ego* can be found later in the same book:

> (133)   Ovid *AA* 3.522 credere uix uideor, cum cogar credere partu, / **uos** ego cum uestris concubuisse uiris.

Here again the verb phrase *credere... uideor* precedes the dependent clause in the second line. *Ego* is even more clearly detached from the main verb and embedded in the dependent clause, because an intervening *cum*-clause separates the main verb from its dependent clause. *Ego* is not in this case attached to *hic*, but it has a preferential term before it, namely an instance of *uos* which is emphatic in the context. In a way (133) is less remarkable than (132). The dependent clause occupies the whole of the second line. If that whole line could be placed before *credere*, then we would have much the same structure as that of (131). The whole dependent clause, with *ego* in its characteristic second position behind a preferential term, has been postponed. In (132), on the other hand, *ego* is not second word in the dependent clause, but is well within that clause.
(ii) The examples (134)–(136) differ from (132)–(133) in that *ego* and *hic* are syntactically in the same clause.

> (134)   Ovid *Met.* 8.771 nympha **sub hoc** *ego* sum Cereri gratissima **ligno**
> (135)   Ovid *Trist.* 5.5.28 fieri quis posse putaret, / ut facerem in mediis **haec** ego **sacra** Getis
> (136)   Prop. 2.34.58 ut regnem mixtas inter conuiua puellas / **hoc** *ego*, quo tibi nunc eleuor, **ingenio**.

They resemble (e.g.) (132) in that *hic ego* is not at the start of the clause but well within it. What these examples show is the intimate connection between *hic* and the nominative pronoun, and Ovid's readiness to displace the pair. If one is postponed, so too is the other. (136) resembles (133) because the whole second line could in theory be moved *en bloc* to the initial position (after *ut*) and a normal position for *hoc ego* restored.
(iii) In (136) a relative clause stands between *hoc ego* and *ingenio*. For this pattern, which is characteristic of Ovid, see (137)–(138):

(137)   Ovid *Pont.* 3.6.9 **huic ego**, *quam patior*, nihil possem demere
poenae

(138)   Ovid *Pont.* 4.10.19 **hos ego**, *qui patriae faciant obliuia*, **sucos.**

(iv) Finally, in (139) we see as usual *hac ego* separated from a noun (*nocte*):

(139)   Ovid *AA* 2.138 **hac** ego sum *captis* **nocte** reuectus *equis.*

But within this disjunction there stands *captis*, which is itself disjoined
from *equis*. A double disjunction of this type is more complex than a prose
example such as (126a).

XIII. CONCLUSION

Any attempt to account for the use of the nominative pronouns *ego* and
tu exclusively in terms of an opposition 'emphatic' vs. 'unemphatic', with
the 'unemphatic' use perhaps 'colloquial', is misguided. There is undoubtedly an emphatic use of both pronouns, which is most readily detectable
when they are contrastive. But there are many cases of *ego* and *tu* in high
literature which cannot be described as emphatic in this sense. I have
suggested that certain structural conditions are among the determinants
which may generate the use of a nominative pronoun, regardless of
whether that pronoun in the context is emphatic or not. *Ego* and *tu* have
a tendency to attach themselves to certain preferential terms, that is terms
which habitually are placed at the head of a colon.

When a use of *ego* is independently motivated, as for example by its
contrastive emphasis, it will seek out the head of its clause. But if there is
a relative, an emphatic demonstrative, an interrogative, an antithetical
term or a negative present in the clause, *ego* may be excluded by these
preferential terms from the first position. It therefore goes to the second
place, in attachment to the preferential term. The types of terms which
most often precede *ego* are thus preferential terms. A relationship is
accordingly formed between preferential terms and *ego/tu*, such that the
pronoun may sometimes be generated merely by the presence of its preferential host. It is also possible that this attachment of *ego* (or *tu*) to
preferential terms was influenced by or related to a larger phenomenon,
whereby enclitics in general in Latin (e.g. the copula and oblique case
pronouns) tended to gravitate to preferential or focused terms (see
(34)–(35)).

Our nominative usage is represented in verse as well as prose. Various
nominative pronouns in Catullus which have caused commentators some
puzzlement and have even led to emendation can be explained as typical

manifestations of the phenomenon, and we have seen that Catullan usage is very close in some respects to Ciceronian.

Discussions of poetic language tend to concentrate on the one hand on high-style vocabulary avoided in prose, and on the other on the presence of colloquialisms in lower genres. The phenomena dealt with in this paper cannot be classified in these terms. Fraenkel demonstrated in his work on colon structure that verse often falls into the types of cola found in prose. We have seen that certain quite intricate forms of disjunction in poetry, whereby *hic* in particular, with *ego* attached, is separated from a noun in agreement, are not the inventions of poets but are based in the spoken, or rather, formal spoken language. This aspect of poetic discourse reflects the fact that verse was intended to be read aloud, and it could therefore not reject entirely the communicative processes of formal speech. The collocation *hic ego* readily triggers the expectation that a disjunction may follow, and a later verb in its turn creates the expectation that that disjunction is about to end. Some poets, notably Ovid of those considered here, were able to develop the complexity of such disjunctions beyond that normally found in prose, whereas Catullus adhered to the types of patterns which would readily have been heard in speech.

Note. I am grateful to Professors H. D. Jocelyn, R. G. M. Nisbet, J. G. F. Powell and M. Winterbottom for their very helpful comments on a version of this paper.

Proceedings of the British Academy, **93**, 135–154

The Word Order of Horace's *Odes*

R. G. M. NISBET

Summary. The intricate word order of Horace's *Odes* is brought about by the repeated separation of adjectives from their nouns. Sometimes adjectives and nouns are interlaced in a pattern attested in Hellenistic poets and developed by their Roman imitators. As a result the force of the adjective comes over more sharply, and the structure of the sentence is more tightly integrated. The word order of the *Odes* conveys subtle shades of meaning, especially when a word's place in the line is also considered: possessive adjectives and personal pronouns sometimes have more emphasis than is recognized. A few points are added about Horace's colometry: his Graecizing use of participial and similar clauses to extend a period, his partiality for prosaic ablative absolutes even at the end of a sentence, his transposition of words to a colon where they do not properly belong. But even his abnormalities follow a system, and though the mosaic is so artificial, he follows his own rules rigorously without showing any constraint.

Quis multa gracilis te puer in rosa
perfusus liquidis urget odoribus
   grato, Pyrrha, sub antro?
     cui flavam religas comam,
simplex munditiis? heu quotiens fidem   5
mutatosque deos flebit, et aspera
   nigris aequora ventis
     emirabitur insolens,
qui nunc te fruitur credulus aurea,
qui semper vacuam, semper amabilem   10
   sperat, nescius aurae
     fallacis. miseri quibus
intemptata nites. me tabula sacer
votiva paries indicat uvida
   suspendisse potenti   15
     vestimenta maris deo.

(Horace, Odes 1.5)

THE FAMILIARITY OF this poem disguises its oddity. The vocabulary is normal enough, sometimes even a little prosaic (*gracilis, emirabitur, vacuam* in a semi-legal sense, *vestimenta*); the constructions are straightforward; there is ambiguity indeed in the words that refer both to the girl and the sea, but none of the off-centre use of language that makes Virgil so elusive. Yet though the components are simple, the composition is intricate: we can say with more reason than Lucilius ever could 'quam lepide lexis compostae ut tesserulae omnes / arte pavimento atque emblemate vermiculato' (84–5 M.). A scrutiny of Horace's word order may explain something about the character of his lyrics; it also reveals shades of emphasis that have received regular attention only in H. D. Naylor's neglected commentary (1922). As situations recur, any study must deal with the *Odes* as a whole, but I shall revert from time to time to the ode to Pyrrha; when the composition of the individual poems is so carefully integrated, it is desirable as often as possible to look at the total context.

The distinctive word order of the *Odes* depends above all on the placing of adjectives, which Horace, like the other Roman poets of his time, uses far more freely than prose writers. Though his lines tend to be short, he averages about an attribute a line ('attributes' include not just adjectives but participles); and as a rule the nouns with attributes considerably outnumber those without. Of course particular circumstances may distort the statistics: when a noun has a dependent genitive, it is less likely to have an attribute as well; and when three parallel nouns are joined by connectives, one at most is likely to have an attribute (as at 2.4.21 'bracchia et voltum teretisque suras'). When an ode is elaborate and picturesque, the incidence goes up (with 22 attributes in the 16 lines of the ode to

Pyrrha), but it declines in an austere poem like 4.7 ('diffugere nives') or a boring poem like 4.8 ('donarem pateras'). All in all, Horace uses far more attributes than Greek poets even of the Hellenistic age, and it is not till we come to Nonnus that we find a comparable profusion (Wifstrand (1933: 80)).

A poet's adjectives, for the most part, are not simply objective (as in *ius civile*); so, though various factors may operate, they are usually placed before their nouns (Marouzeau (1922); Hofmann–Szantyr (1965: 406–7); Adams (1976: 89)). What is more, 40 per cent of Horace's adjectives are separated from their nouns (Stevens (1953: 202)); in the ode to Pyrrha this is always the case except for 12 *fallacis*, and even that is in a different line from 11 *aurae*. Hyperbaton was a familiar feature of literary prose that becomes more abundant in the imperial period (Hofmann–Szantyr (1965: 690–1); Adams (1971)); but the Roman poets of the first century BC use it much more freely than contemporary prose writers. To some extent they are following the patterns of their Hellenistic predecessors (Van Sickle (1968)), but they go much further. Part of the reason lies in their greater number of adjectives: that helps to explain why the *Aeneid* has less hyperbaton than the *Eclogues* or for that matter than Lucan (Caspari (1908: 80–93)). Other factors were the avoidance of homoeoteleuton (for which see now Shackleton Bailey (1994)) and the attraction of rhyme; for Greek poets were less averse to homoeoteleuton and less attracted by rhyme.

Horace in the *Odes* often interlaces adjectives and nouns in a double hyperbaton: thus in the poem to Pyrrha we find 1 'quis multa gracilis te puer in rosa', 6f. 'aspera / nigris aequora ventis', 9 'qui nunc te fruitur credulus aurea', 13f. 'tabula sacer / votiva paries indicat'. Various sorts of interlacing are attested in Plato (Denniston (1952: 54–5)) and in late Greek prose, but Latin prose is much more restrained. Norden collected some examples in the notable third appendix to his commentary on *Aeneid* VI (1957: 393–6), and others have been added (Goodyear on Tac. *Ann.* 1.10.1, Woodman on Vell. 2.100.1, Winterbottom (1977a and 1977b)); but prose parallels to the verse pattern are rare in the central period, at least when special cases are excluded (as when one of the attributes is a genuine participle). There is a striking early instance at *Rhet. Her.* 4.63 'aut (ut) aliquod fragile falsae choragium gloriae conparetur'; but as that comes from a quotation it may be the rendering of a Greek orator. At Cic. *Phil.* 2.66 we find 'maximus vini numerus fuit, permagnum optimi pondus argenti'; but here *permagnum* picks up *maximus*, and *optimi pondus argenti* can be regarded as a single unit (cf. Caes. *Gall.* 5.40.6 'multae praeustae sudes, magnus muralium pilorum numerus'). There is a more unusual instance at Plin. *N.H.* 10.3 'caeruleam roseis caudam pinnis distinguentibus'; but here the metrical *caeruleam roseis* may suggest the imitation of a poet or at least the manner of poetry.

For though so rare in classical Latin prose, this sort of interlacing is superabundant in the Roman poets of the first century BC and later. Norden attributed their predilection to the influence of rhetorical prose (cf. *Rhet. Her.* cited above); but in that case it is strange that the arrangement is not significantly attested in Cicero's speeches or the declamations in the elder Seneca (though note *Suas.* 3.1 'miseri cremata agricolae lugent semina'). It is better to look for poetical origins for a poetical phenomenon (Boldt (1884: 90–6); Caspari (1908: 86–90)). The interlacing of adjectives is attested in Greek poetry as early as Theognis 250 ἀγλαὰ Μουσάων δῶρα ἰοστεφάνων, and Pindar provides lyric examples, but they usually lack the symmetry characteristic of Roman poetry. Such symmetry appears occasionally in Hellenistic poetry (e.g. Call. *H.* 4.14'Ικαρίου πολλὴν ἀπομάσσεται ὕδατος ἄχνην, 6.9), and particularly in pentameters (ibid. 5.12 πάντα χαλινοφάγων ἀφρὸν ἀπὸ στομάτων, 5.34); but among extant poets it is not common till Nonnus (Wifstrand (1933: 139–40)), who is likely to have been influenced by Hellenistic rather than Roman prototypes. On the other hand interlacing appears abundantly in Catullus 62–68 (so also Cinna, *FLP* fr. 11), occasionally in Lucretius, more often in an innovating earlier poet, namely Cicero (Pearce (1966: 164–6 and 299–301)). As both hexameters and pentameters naturally fall into two sections, this favoured a balanced distribution of adjectives and nouns (Patzer (1955: 87–9); Conrad (1965)); and as Latin hexameters usually have their main caesura after the first syllable of the third foot (rather than after the trochee as in Greek), this made it easier to deploy adjectives before this caesura. As the interlaced pattern was already established in Horace's day, and was used by him both in the iambics and hexameters of the *Epodes* (2.15, 43, 47; 16.7, 33, 55), it is not surprising that he extended it to lyrics.

What then is the function of hyperbaton in the *Odes*? It is often pointed out that it adds 'emphasis' to the adjective (cf. Marouzeau (1922: 112–18); Fraenkel (1928: 162–8)), but some qualifications are desirable (Stevens (1953); Dover (1960: 32–4)). In the first place 'emphasis' in this context need not imply a raising or other modification of the voice: that might be superfluous in a language with a more flexible word order than English. In a complex sentence other factors may play a part, for instance rhythm in a prose writer (Quint. 8.6.62–7), metre in a poet. Sometimes there is a wish not so much to add emphasis to the adjective as to stow away less important words between the adjective and the noun. Hyperbaton also helps to bind the sentence into an integrated unit; this aspect is particularly important for Horace.

It should also be recognized that the Roman poets developed their own conventions about word order and took a delight in their own symmetrical patterns. Sometimes an adjective is brought forward not because its semantic significance is great by prosaic standards but to set it against some parallel or contrasting expression: for one of many instances see 1.3.10f. 'qui fragilem truci | commisit pelago ratem', where by a typical chiasmus the fragility of the boat is set against the savagery of the sea. Even when there is no parallelism or antithesis a poet may highlight an adjective in a way that would seem excessive in prose: to cite again the ode to Pyrrha, 2 'liquidis ... odoribus' underlines the paradox that smells can be liquid, 4 'flavam ... comam' plays on the name 'Pyrrha', which suggests auburn hair, 14ff. 'uvida ... vestimenta' underlines in a vivid way that Horace has suffered shipwreck himself. Even adjectives that are described as 'conventional' may have more life in them than emerges from the English translations: thus at 1.38.1 'Persicos odi puer apparatus' the adjective evokes a picture and expresses an emotion. So instead of denying any emphasis to such adjectives in Horace, we can sometimes say that he gives his adjectives more prominence than would be natural in prose.

We may go further. When an adjective is detached from its noun, 'the temporary isolation of each word makes its own peculiar imagery the more vivid' (T. F. Higham, cited by Leishman (1956: 85)). The ear is kept waiting for the corresponding noun, which often rhymes; this is a persistent feature of classical Roman poetry, notably in the 'golden lines' of Catullus and the pentameters of Ovid. Sometimes the noun may surprise the reader; thus at 1.5.6f. 'aspera | nigris aequora ventis' it is a paradox that flat *aequora* should be rough, and *ventis* is also more arresting than the expected word for water. But it is the hardest thing for moderns to take the words in the order that they come: Milton is thought to force the English language when he translates 1.5.9 'qui nunc te fruitur credulus aurea' by 'Who now enjoys thee credulous all gold', but he is representing precisely what he found in the Latin.

The complexity of the *Odes* is not uniform throughout but is influenced by the context. Erotic and sympotic odes may be particularly intricate to suit the sensuous subject-matter; see the first line and last stanza of the ode to Pyrrha (1.5), the last stanza of the ode to Thaliarchus (1.9.21ff.) 'nunc et latentis proditor intimo | gratus puellae risus ab angulo' (with triple interlacing), the closing couplet of the ode to Quinctius (2.11.23f.) 'maturet incomptum Lacaenae | more comae religata nodum' (where the intricacy of the word order makes a piquant contrast with the simplicity of the girl's hair). On the other hand the great political poems are often written more directly, in what Horace would have called a more 'masculine' style (cf. *Serm.* 1.10.16, 91; Pers. 6.4); there is nothing involuted about the end of the ode to Lollius (4.9.45ff.): 'non possidentem multa vocaveris |

recte beatum; rectius occupat | nomen beati qui deorum | muneribus sapienter uti, | duramque callet pauperiem pati, | peiusque leto flagitium timet . . . .'. Metre also plays a part: Sapphics give relatively little scope for complexity, and the *Carmen Saeculare*, which was meant to be sung, has a notably simple texture.

The word order of classical poetry is sometimes said to correspond to the situation described (Wilkinson (1963: 65–6)); thus at 1.5.1 'quis multa gracilis te puer in rosa' the girl and the boy are in the middle of the line surrounded by *multa rosa*, and in 3 'grato, Pyrrha, sub antro' *Pyrrha* is indeed enclosed by *grato antro*. This aspect of Horace's hyperbata is subsidiary at most, for it affects a very small proportion of the material; see for instance 1.3.21ff. 'nequiquam deus abscidit | prudens Oceano disso-ciabili | terras', where the artificial placing of *terras* suits a special explanation (I owe this suggestion to Dr S. J. Harrison), 4.3.14f. 'dignatur suboles inter amabilis | vatum ponere me choros'. By a more general phenomenon a vocative is enclosed by words appropriate to the person addressed: thus at 1.5.3 (cited above) the cave is welcome to Pyrrha, at 1.17.10 'utcumque dulci, Tyndari, fistula' Tyndaris may enjoy the pipe because she is herself a musician (Fraenkel), at 2.1.14 'et consulenti Pollio curiae' the republican Pollio is associated with the senate-house (it is pointless to add that he is inside it), at 3.29.3 'cum flore, Maecenas, rosarum', the roses suit the notorious sybarite.

It has been calculated that in 85 per cent of the hyperbata in the *Odes* there is an interval of only one or two words (Stevens (1953: 202)); just as in hexameters and pentameters, the incidence of two-word intervals is greater than in prose. Longer hyperbata in prose tend to be reserved for special cases, as with interrogatives, or adjectives of size or quantity, or where there is a particular degree of emphasis or floridity (Adams (1971: 13)). In poetry longer hyperbata are used more freely: see for instance 1.17.1f. 'velox amoenum saepe Lucretilem | mutat Lycaeo Faunus', where the postponement of the subject makes us wonder who is bounding in, while the chiastic order sets *Lucretilem* against *Lycaeo*. In other places a special point may be recognized, or missed: thus at 1.4.7f. 'alterno terram quatiunt pede, dum gravis Cyclopum | Volcanus ardens visit officinas' *gravis* underlines a contrast with the nimble feet of the Graces. At 2.14.5ff. 'non si trecenis, quotquot eunt dies, | amice, places inlacrimabilem | Plutona tauris . . .' the hyperbole justifies the unusual emphasis on *trecenis* (though numerals are sometimes separated even in comedy and prose). At 3.10.19f. 'non hoc semper erit liminis aut aquae | caelestis patiens latus' the emphatic *hoc* suggests 'whatever other people might put up with'. Occasionally a long hyperbaton recalls the grand style of Pindar: see 3.4.9ff. 'me fabulosae Vulture in Apulo | nutricis extra limina †Pulliae |

ludo fatigatumque somno | fronde nova puerum palumbes | texere', 4.4.7ff.
'vernique iam nimbis remotis | insolitos docuere nisus | venti paventem'.

One type of hyperbaton is too common to be noticed: when a genitive
depends on a noun that is qualified by an adjective, it is usually sandwiched
between them. When this word order is upset, the effect is often to
emphasize the genitive; Horace is particularly precise in his regard for
such nuances (Naylor (1922: xxiii and xxvi)). See 1.10.6 'Mercuri, facunde
nepos Atlantis': the balancing proper names frame the line (cf. 1.19.1
'mater saeva Cupidinum'). 1.13.1ff. 'cum tu, Lydia, Telephi | cervicem
roseam, cerea Telephi | laudas bracchia . . .': in this position the first *Telephi*
underlines Lydia's infatuation. 2.1.17 'iam nunc minaci murmure cornuum':
cornuum balances *litui* in the next line. 2.1.23f. 'et cuncta terrarum subacta
| praeter atrocem animum Catonis': the proper name marks the climax.
3.5.53f. 'quam si clientum longa negotia | diiudicata lite relinqueret':
clientum emphasizes the mundane business that usually concerned
Regulus. 3.28.1f. 'quid festo potius die | Neptuni faciam?': Naylor explains
'What better can I do on a *feast-day*, and that the feast-day of Neptune?'
4.7.19f. 'cuncta manus avidas fugient heredis, amico | quae dederis animo':
the alien heir is contrasted with Torquatus' own dear heart (with appropriate stress on *amico*). The same principle operates with the ablative at
3.4.37ff. 'vos Caesarem altum, militia simul | fessas cohortes abdidit
oppidis, | finire quaerentem labores | Pierio recreatis antro': here *militia*
is not sandwiched between *fessas* and *cohortes*, but stressed to produce a
balance with *labores* and a contrast with *Pierio*.

Little need be said about the position of genitives where no adjective
is present. Here classical Latin uses both possible orders, with a tendency
for the earlier position to add emphasis (Adams (1976: 73–82)). Horace
sometimes highlights such genitives in the same way that he highlights
adjectives: see for instance 1.2.9f. 'piscium et summa genus haesit ulmo |
nota quae sedes fuerat columbis' (where by a characteristic chiasmus the
fish are contrasted with the birds). There is an illuminating case at 1.1.6
'terrarum dominos evehit ad deos'; as Naylor points out, the emphasis
on *terrarum* confirms that the first two words refer to the victors rather
than the gods.

In classical Latin, adjectives derived from proper names regularly
follow their noun, as *forum Romanum, horti Sallustiani*. In the *Odes* these
adjectives often come first, sometimes with hyperbaton: thus in the opening
poem we find 10 'Libycis . . . areis', 12 'Attalicis condicionibus', 15 'Icariis
fluctibus', 28 'Marsus aper'. Horace prefers the livelier order because he
tends to treat such adjectives as ornamental and emotive rather than
factually descriptive (Marouzeau (1922: 28–32)). On the other hand when
an adjective describes a particular place, he often gives it its standard

position immediately after the noun: cf. 1.2.14 'litore Etrusco', 1.3.6 'finibus Atticis', 1.11.5f. 'mare | Tyrrhenum', 1.31.14 'aequor Atlanticum', 3.4.15 'saltusque Bantinos', 3.7.26 'gramine Martio'. Sometimes he reverses this tendency for particular reasons: cf. 1.1.13f. 'ut trabe Cypria | Myrtoum pavidus nauta secet mare' (another chiasmus), 3.5.56 'aut Lacedaemonium Tarentum' (at the end of the Regulus Ode *Lacedaemonium* is evocative rather than merely factual), 3.14.3f. 'Caesar Hispana repetit Penatis | victor ab ora' (*Hispana* underlines the analogy with Hercules). Of course other exceptions to the general tendency can be noted: thus the adjective is ornamental at 1.31.6 'non aurum aut ebur Indicum', 2.13.8 'venena Colcha', 2.18.3 'trabes Hymettiae' and particular at 2.1.16 'Delmatico... triumpho' (yet emphasis is appropriate), 3.12.7 'Tiberinis... undis'. When people are given a geographical epithet this often comes immediately before the name (1.15.22 'Pylium Nestora', 2.5.20 'Cnidiusve Gyges'); but this order is attested in Ciceronian prose (*Amic.* 88 'a Tarentino Archyta' with Seyffert–Müller's note).

I turn now to possessive adjectives, where Latin normally puts the possessive after the noun (*pater meus*); when this order is reversed the effect is to emphasize the possessive, especially when the two words are separated by hyperbaton (Marouzeau (1922: 137–44)). There are many instances in Horace of this kind of point, though the nuance is sometimes ignored. See 1.13.3f. 'vae meum | fervens difficili bile tumet iecur' (a contrast with 1 'tu, Lydia'), 1.15.7f. 'coniurata tuas rumpere nuptias | et regnum Priami vetus' (Paris is set against Priam, as Naylor says), 1.22.9f. 'namque me silva lupus in Sabina | dum meam canto Lalagen...' (*meam* is not predicative, as Naylor suggests, but 'my very own Lalage', picking up the emphatic *me*), 1.26.9f. 'nil sine te mei | possunt honores (*mei* is set against *te* as at 4.9.30), 2.6.6 'sit meae sedes utinam senectae' ('I' and 'you' are often contrasted in the ode to Septimius, as in the following ode to Pompeius), 2.8.21 'te suis matres metuunt iuvencis' (underlining the possessiveness of the mothers), 3.29.54f. 'et mea | virtute me involvo' (a man's own *virtus* is contrasted with external possessions), 4.1.33f. 'sed cur heu, Ligurine, cur | manat rara meas lacrima per genas?' (correcting 29 '*me* nec femina nec puer'), 4.6.35f. 'Lesbium servate pedem meique | pollicis ictum' (Horace's thumb balances Sappho's metre), 4.10.2 'insperata tuae cum veniet poena superbiae' (the penalty is least expected by Ligurinus). There is a more difficult case at 3.4.69f. 'testis mearum centi-manus Gyges | sententiarum', where the emphasis on the trisyllabic *mearum* has seemed excessive to some editors; but the transmitted text is protected by Pindar, fr. 169.3f., where after saying that the violent are punished he adds τεκμαίρομαι | ἔργοισιν Ἡρακλέος. Perhaps Horace is saying with the self-assertion of a *vates* 'That's what *I* think, and Gyges proves it.'

Possessive adjectives that follow their nouns and are separated by hyperbaton sometimes have more emphasis than is realized, particularly when they occur at the end of a line; in the same way at the end of an elegiac pentameter the characteristic *meo*, *tuo*, etc. often have point. The situation is fairly clear at 1.16.15f. 'desectam et insani leonis | vim stomacho adposuisse *nostro*' (where the emphatic *nostro* is contrasted with *leonis*), 2.1.34ff. 'quod mare Dauniae | non decoloravere caedes? | quae caret ora cruore *nostro*? (where *nostro* balances *Dauniae*). Sometimes there is a contrast between the first and second personal pronouns: 2.13.10f. 'agro qui statuit *meo* | te, triste lignum', 2.17.1 'cur *me* querelis exanimas *tuis*?' (followed by 2ff. 'nec dis amicum est nec *mihi te* prius | obire, Maecenas, *mearum* | grande decus columenque rerum. | a, *te meae* si partem animae rapit, | maturior vis, quid moror alteram?', 3.13.13ff. 'fies nobilium *tu* quoque fontium, | *me* dicente cavis impositam ilicem | saxis, unde loquaces | lymphae desiliunt *tuae*' (*tuae*, the last word of the poem, continues the 'Du-Stil' of this hymnal address, and is also contrasted with *me* at the beginning of line 14). In view of Horace's liking for point, I also see emphasis in passages where some would deny it: 1.3.8 'et serves animae dimidium *meae*' ('I have entrusted *you*, the ship, with half of *my* life'), 1.7.20f. 'seu densa tenebit | Tiburis umbra *tui*' (Plancus came from Tibur), 3.4.65 'vis consili expers mole ruit *sua*' ('collapses from its own bulk'), 3.19.28 '*me* lentus Glycerae torret amor *meae*'. There is a puzzle at 2.7.18ff. 'longaque fessum militia latus | depone sub lauru mea, nec | parce cadis tibi destinatis'; here *mea* seems to make a contrast with *tibi*, for though it follows immediately on *lauru* it comes at the end of its clause and at a very unusual position in the line.

After possessive adjectives I come to personal pronouns, where the distinction is familiar between emphatic *me*, the equivalent of Greek ἐμέ, and weak *me*, the equivalent of enclitic με; on the same principle Milton spelt 'mee' when the pronoun was emphatic and 'me' when it was weak. In his famous article Wackernagel (1892) discussed the tendency of weak pronouns to occupy the second place in the colon, but the case should not be overstated; J. N. Adams (1994a) has shown that a weak pronoun sometimes nestles in the lee of a significant word, what he calls the 'focused host', even when this is not the first word in the colon. In the more informal registers the pronoun may come even at the end of the colon; thus Adams (1994a: 108) cites Varro, *Rust.* 1.2.2 'nos uti expectaremus se, reliquit qui rogaret', 1.2.7 'simul aspicit me, . . .'. When we turn to Horace as to the other Roman poets, it is not always obvious whether a pronoun is weak or emphatic; but I believe that we should be readier to recognize emphasis than editors sometimes are, particularly when the pronoun comes at the end of the line.

Thus at 3.9.1 'donec gratus eram tibi', I regard *tibi* as emphatic: the
amoebaean ode to Lydia repeatedly underlines personal pronouns. 3.13.6f.
'nam gelidos inficiet tibi | rubro sanguine rivos'; an emphatic *tibi* suits the
hymnal aspect of the ode to Bandusia (cf. 9f. 'te ... tu'). 3.16.33ff.
'quamquam nec Calabrae mella ferunt apes, | nec Laestrygonia Bacchus
in amphora | languescit mihi, nec pinguia Gallicis | crescunt vellera
pascuis'; here weak *mihi* at the very end of the second colon seems too
inert for the *Odes* (contrast Varro cited above), and I should rather place
it in the emphatic position at the beginning of the following colon (positing
an influence by the ἀπὸ κοινοῦ principle on its two predecessors); for the
same emphasis cf. line 27 'occultare *meis* dicerer horreis' and in a similar
context 2.18.1f. 'non ebur neque aureum | *mea* renidet in domo lacunar',
probably also 2.18.7f. 'nec Laconicas *mihi* | trahunt honestae purpuras
clientae'. 3.29.1 'Tyrrhena regum progenies, tibi ...'; the pronoun is
emphatic after the long vocative, which forms an independent colon (cf. 4
'pressa *tuis* balanus capillis'). 4.3.13ff. 'Romae principis urbium | dignatur
suboles inter amabilis | vatum ponere me choros'; here *ponere* does not
seem significant enough to act as 'focused host', so I regard *me* as emphatic,
balancing *vatum*. Contrast 4.15.1f. 'Phoebus volentem proelia me loqui |
victas et urbis increpuit lyra'; here Naylor again regards the delayed
pronoun as emphatic, but this time *proelia* is important enough to be
regarded as the 'focused host'.

When *mihi, tibi, sibi* come after the main caesura in a Sapphic hendecasyllable, they may be either weak or emphatic according to circumstances.
For weak instances (following a 'focused host') see 2.2.13 'crescit indulgens
sibi dirus hydrops', 2.4.1 'ne sit ancillae tibi amor pudori', 3.11.38f. 'surge,
ne longus tibi somnus unde | non times detur', 3.14.13f. 'hic dies vere mihi
festus atras | exiget curas', 3.27.45f. 'si quis infamem mihi nunc iuvencum
| dedat iratae'. But at other times I regard the pronoun as emphatic,
sometimes against the general opinion. See 1.20.5ff. 'ut paterni | fluminis
ripae simul et iocosa | redderet laudes tibi Vaticani | montis imago' (the
emphatic pronoun is natural in a panegyric, as also above at 2ff. 'Graeca
quod *ego ipse* testa | conditum levi, datus in theatro | cum *tibi* plausus'),
2.6.13f. 'ille terrarum mihi praeter omnis | angulus ridet' (cf. 6 'sit *meae*
sedes utinam senectae'), 2.8.17 'adde quod pubes tibi crescit omnis' (cf. 21
'*te* suis matres metuunt iuvencis'), 3.8.19 'Medus infestus sibi luctuosis |
dissidet armis' (*sibi* is to be taken with *luctuosis* and *dissidet*, but not with
infestus), 3.11.15f. 'cessit immanis tibi blandienti | ianitor aulae' (following
the hymnal *tu potes* at the beginning of the stanza), 3.18.14 'spargit agrestis
tibi silva frondes' (again hymnal, like 10 above 'cum *tibi* Nonae redeunt
Decembres'), 4.11.17f. 'iure sollemnis mihi sanctiorque | paene natali

proprio' (*mihi* like *proprio* underlines Horace's respect for Maecenas' birthday).

When the pronoun follows the central diaeresis in the Asclepiad line, I suggest that it is usually emphatic and perhaps always so. At 1.15.23ff. 'urgent impavidi te Salaminius | Teucer, te Sthenelus sciens | pugnae' the first *te* is emphatic (as the second clearly is) to underline the concentration of the Greeks on Paris. At 1.23.1 'vitas inuleo me similis, Chloe' it is generally assumed that *me* is weak, stowed away as it is between *inuleo* and *similis*, but the meaning is perhaps rather 'you avoid *me*' or even 'do you avoid *me*?'; in the last stanza (1.23.9f.) Horace proceeds 'atqui non ego te tigris ut aspera | Gaetulusve leo frangere persequor' ('after all, *I'm* not pursuing you like a tiger . . .'). At 4.1.7f. Horace says to Venus 'abi | quo blandae iuvenum te revocant preces'; here *te* may be the emphatic pronoun familiar from hymns. The case is clearer at 4.13.9ff. 'importunus enim transvolat aridas | quercus, et refugit te quia luridi | dentes, te quia rugae | turpant et capitis nives'; here the position of 11 *te* at the beginning of its clause shows that 10 *te* in the middle of the Asclepiad line is also emphatic. There is a more problematic instance at 1.19.1f. 'mater saeva Cupidinum | Thebanaeque iubet me Semelae puer | et lasciva Licentia | finitis animum reddere amoribus'; here most readers will regard *me* as weak (as at 5 'urit me Glycerae nitor'), but at 9 'in me tota ruens Venus' *me* is undoubtedly emphatic. To return to the ode to Pyrrha, a similar situation arises in the first line (1.5.1) 'quis multa gracilis te puer in rosa . . .'; here *te* seems usually to be regarded as weak, but perhaps the meaning is 'What mere boy presses a voluptuous person like *you*?' (with a contrast first between *multa* and *gracilis* and then between *te* and *puer*).

When the pronoun is first word in the line it cannot be enclitic, any more than μϵ can begin a line of Greek verse. Consider the ode to Postumus, 2.14.21ff. 'linquenda tellus et domus et placens | uxor, neque harum quas colis arborum | te praeter invisas cupressos | ulla brevem dominum sequetur'; here *te* must be emphatic, perhaps balancing *uxor*, which also derives point from its place in the line. 4.1.38ff. 'iam volucrem sequor | te per gramina Martii | Campi, te per aquas, dure, volubilis'; the position of *te* at the beginning of one line and another clause underlines Horace's obsession. 4.5.31f. 'hinc ad vina redit laetus et alteris | te mensis adhibet deum'; here *te*, in spite of its position between *alteris* and *mensis*, has the emphasis common in panegyrics as in prayers (note also the following line 'te multa prece, te prosequitur mero'). There is a striking instance at 1.8.1ff., where the commentaries offer no comment: 'Lydia, dic per omnis | te deos oro, Sybarin cur properes amando | perdere'. If this had been prose we should all have assumed that *te* was weak, hidden away between *omnis* and *deos*; but that leaves us with weak *te* at the beginning of the

line, where με would be intolerable in Greek. It seems that *te* is more
insistent than is sometimes realized; *te oro* is a common word order.

It is already clear that metre has an effect on Horace's word order, not
because it imposes abnormalities (as is too often implied), but because
certain positions in the line tend to suit particular elements. The word at
the beginning of a self-contained line often agrees with the word at the
end; this can sometimes produce an epigrammatic effect, as at 2.16.30
'longa Tithonum minuit senectus'. Such lines are attested in Greek and
are familiar in Latin from the time of Cicero and Catullus (Norden (1957:
391); Conrad (1965: 225–9); Pearce (1966: 162–6); Van Sickle (1968: 500));
they are notably common in the *Odes*, where it has been calculated that
247 lines (one in fourteen) are thus bound into a single colon (Stevens
(1953: 203)). The word before the caesura often agrees with the word at
the end of the line, and the word after the caesura often agrees with the
word at the beginning (cf. 3.3.5 'dux inquieti turbidus Hadriae'); for other
standard distributions see Drexler (1967: 126–34). A word in one line is
sometimes picked up by a corresponding word at the same place in a
following line (for such 'vertical responsion' cf. Boldt (1884: 82–3); Stevens
(1953: 203–4); Conrad (1965: 252–3)). See for example 1.1.9f. 'illum si
proprio condidit *horreo* | quidquid de *Libycis* verritur *areis*', and for longer
intervals 2.14.5ff., 4.4.7ff.; for a less obvious instance one may cite the
balancing adjectives at 1.22.5ff. 'sive per Syrtis iter *aestuosas*, | sive facturus
per *inhospitalem* | Caucasum, vel quae loca *fabulosus* | lambit Hydaspes'.

The last word in the line may or may not be significant. One in three
of the hyperbata in the *Odes* crosses verse boundaries (Stevens (1953:
203)), compared with one in seven in the *Aeneid*; when an adjective in
such circumstances comes at the end of the line, its position may reinforce
the emphasis imposed by the hyperbaton itself (as at 2.10.6ff. 'tutus caret
obsoleti | sordibus tecti, caret *invidenda* | sobrius aula'). On the other hand
the last word may be a mere connective like *et* or *neque*; for an extreme
instance of the former cf. 2.6.1ff. 'Septimi, Gadis aditure mecum et |
Cantabrum indoctum iuga ferre nostra et | barbaras Syrtes', where the
repeated enjambment may be meant to suggest persistent scurrying. For
other weak line-endings cf. such passages as 1.5.12f. 'miseri quibus | in-
temptata nites' (so 4.4.18), 3.7.14f. 'nimis | casto Bellerophontae'.

When the first word in the line is followed by a pause (not always
marked by punctuation in modern texts), it often has particular significance
(just as in hexameters); thus we find in the ode to Pyrrha 1.5.10ff. 'qui
semper vacuam, semper amabilem | sperat, nescius aurae | fallacis', where
sperat and *fallacis* are given an extra edge by their position. The slight
emphasis may easily be missed: cf. 1.9.17f. 'donec virenti canities abest |
morosa', 2.2.19ff. 'populumque falsis | dedocet uti | vocibus' ('empty

words', as Naylor suggests), 2.11.21f. 'quis devium scortum eliciet domo |
Lyden?' (the climax, with *devium scortum* in apposition, cf. 3.7.4f.), 2.16.9ff.
'non enim gazae neque consularis | summovet lictor miseros tumultus |
mentis' (the tumult of the mind is contrasted with the tumult of the streets,
and *mentis* derives emphasis from its place in the line as well as its place
outside *miseros tumultus*; cf. 2.13.7f. 'nocturno cruore | hospitis'), 2.16.21f.
'scandit aeratas vitiosa navis | cura' (the climax comes at the end of the
clause and the beginning of the line), 3.2.5f. 'vitamque sub divo et trepidis
agat | in rebus' ('in action', as Naylor says), 3.10.16f. 'supplicibus tuis |
parcas' (the key word of the supplication), 3.17.6f. 'qui Formiarum moenia
dicitur | princeps . . .' (the founder was particularly important, cf. 1.3.12
'*primus*' in the same position). When a first word followed by a pause
seems over-emphasized, it may prove to be contrasted with another word
in the context: see 1.3.21ff. 'nequiquam deus abscidit | prudens *Oceano*
dissociabili | *terras*, si tamen impiae | non tangenda rates transiliunt *vada*',
2.1.1ff. 'motum ex Metello consule civicum | . . . (7) *tractas*, et *incedis* per
ignes' (handling is balanced by walking), 2.3.9ff. 'quo pinus ingens albaque
populus | umbram hospitalem consociare amant | *ramis*? quid obliquo
laborat | lympha fugax trepidare *rivo*?' (the pause after *ramis* need not be
strong, a fact obscured by the modern question-mark), 3.10.5ff. 'audis quo
strepitu ianua, quo nemus | inter pulchra satum tecta remugiat | *ventis*, et
positas ut glaciet *nives* | puro numine Iuppiter?', 4.1.38ff. 'iam volucrem
sequor | te per gramina Martii | *Campi*, te per *aquas*, dure, volubilis'. But
not every word in this prominent position has point; see for instance
2.9.1ff. 'at non ter aevo functus amabilem | ploravit omnis Antilochum
senex | annos, nec . . .' (where Naylor notes the oddity), 2.10.13ff. 'sperat
infestis, metuit secundis | alteram sortem bene praeparatum | pectus',
4.13.9f. 'importunus enim transvolat aridas | quercus' (for further material
see Drexler (1967: 128)).

Sometimes a different effect may be recognized. Consider 1.11.7f. 'dum
loquimur, fugerit invida | aetas: carpe diem, quam minimum credula
postero': not only does the emphatic *aetas* balance *diem*, but the enjamb-
ment seems to underline the speed of time (note also 5f. 'mare |
Tyrrhenum'). There are a number of similar enjambments in the poem to
the ship (1.14), perhaps suggesting that things are out of control: see 2f.
'fortiter occupa | portum', 6ff. 'ac sine funibus | vix durare carinae | possint
imperiosius | aequor', perhaps 14f. 'nil pictis timidus navita puppibus |
fidit' (though there the contrast between *pictis* and *fidit* may be more
significant). In 3.19 (on the celebration for Murena) the combination of
enjambments and short sentences may suit a party that is livening up: see
10f. 'da, puer, auguris | Murenae' (with emphasis on the proper name),

14f. 'ternos ter cyathos attonitus petet | vates', 21f. 'parcentis ego dexteras | odi: sparge rosas'.

Sometimes the enjambment is so strange that the text has been doubted. Such a case arises at 2.18.29ff. 'nulla certior tamen | rapacis Orci fine destinata | aula divitem manet | erum. quid ultra tendis?'; here the position of *erum* before the pause seems intolerable, and I have proposed joining the word to the following sentence ('why do you strain proprietorship farther?'). Or consider 3.6.9ff. 'iam bis Monaeses et Pacori manus | non auspicatos contudit impetus | nostros, et adiecisse praedam | torquibus exiguis renidet'. Here *nostros* before the pause seems too emphatic, seeing that *impetus* is already qualified by *non auspicatos*; Bentley proposed *nostrorum* with *impetus* (it would be better with *praedam*), Shackleton Bailey considered *nostratem* or *Romanam*, I have tried *praeclaram*, which if it was corrupted to *praedam* would have caused rewriting. Some editors have felt difficulty at 4.11.4f. 'est hederae vis | multa, qua crines religata fulges': *multa* seems very emphatic in its isolated position at the beginning of the stanza. But here the adjective may be pointed, balancing 2 *'plenus* Albani cadus'; for other instances of an isolated *multus* at the beginning of a line cf. 2.16.17f. 'quid *brevi* fortes iaculamur aevo | *multa*' (a contrast), 3.17.10, 4.9.26.

This leads to the controversy about 3.6.25ff. 'motus doceri gaudet Ionicos | matura virgo et fingitur artibus | *iam nunc* et incestos amores | de tenero meditatur ungui'. Here editors disagree about whether to take *iam nunc* with the preceding or the following clause; this is linked to the problem about *de tenero ungui*, which is explained as either 'from earliest infancy' or 'with every fibre of her being'. I take it that the former is correct; this alone suits *meditatur* ('practises' or 'rehearses'), which itself balances *doceri* and *fingitur*. If that is so, *iam nunc* must be taken with *fingitur artibus* and followed by a comma; now each clause includes an indication of time (*matura*, *iam nunc*, and finally the hyperbole of *de tenero ungui*). This is not the only place where Horace emphasizes an adverb by placing it at the beginning of a line and end of a colon: see 1.34.5ff. 'namque Diespiter | igni corusco nubila dividens | plerumque . . .', 2.9.4 'usque', 2.20.9ff. 'iam iam residunt *cruribus* asperae | pelles, et album mutor in alitem | *superne* . . .'. But though an adverb may come at the end of a colon, it is less natural at the end of a sentence; here the movement of formal Latin differs from Greek.

This leads one to ask what part of speech most often ends a sentence in the *Odes*. In prose of the first century BC there is still a considerable tendency to end with the verb: thus in a sample of Caesar 84 per cent of verbs come at the end of the main clause, and though the proportion declines in the imperial period, even in a sample of Seneca the figure is

58 per cent (Linde (1923: 154–5)). In Horace, on the other hand, the last word is most often a noun, and a verb ends only a quarter of the sentences (Stevens (1953: 202)). This is partly a consequence of the greater use of adjectives than in prose and the higher incidence of hyperbaton; by an increasingly common word order a verb is often interposed between the adjective and noun (Adams (1971)). In rhetorical Latin there is some reluctance to let an isolated noun dangle at the end; but when the noun is supported by an adjective and the verb interposed, the sentence is clearly incomplete till the noun falls into place.

Horace sometimes places an adjective at the end of a sentence, usually with hyperbaton; this reversal of the normal tendency gives it particular point (see also above on possessives). Such adjectives may be contrasted with earlier words, sometimes with chiasmus: see 2.1.5ff. '*nondum expiatis* uncta cruoribus, | *periculosae* plenum opus aleae | tractas, et incedis per ignes | suppositos cineri *doloso*', 2.8.15f. 'semper *ardentis* acuens sagittas | cote *cruenta*', 3.3.72 '*magna* modis tenuare *parvis*', 3.6.35f. '*ingentem* cecidit | Antiochum Hannibalemque *dirum*', 3.15.6 'et stellis *nebulam* spargere *candidis*'. Or the adjective may be important even where there is no antithesis: cf. 1.9.24 'aut digito male pertinaci' (where the last word has the force of *resistenti*), 2.3.15f. 'dum res et aetas et sororum | fila trium patiuntur atra' (but there may be a contrast with 14 *rosae*), 3.2.31f. 'raro antecedentem scelestum | deseruit pede Poena claudo', 3.6.7f. 'di multa neglecti dederunt | Hesperiae mala luctuosae', 3.24.44 'virtutisque viam deserit arduae'. There is an unusual case at 4.4.3f. 'expertus fidelem | Iuppiter in Ganymede flavo', where an ornamental adjective with no particular emphasis immediately follows its noun at the end of the sentence and the stanza. Here the word order seems to give a conventionally 'poetical' effect, like the relaxed closure of Catullus 64 'nec se contingi patiuntur lumine claro' or the mock-neoteric cadence of Juvenal's ninth satire, 'quae Siculos cantus effugit remige surdo'.

In considering word order, questions about colometry are sometimes relevant, though in the case of poets they seldom attract attention (Quint. 11.3.36–8, Serv. *Aen.* 1.1, (Norden (1957: 376–90))). A descriptive clause may be separated from the vocative to which it belongs (as sometimes in Pindar); cf. 3.29.1ff. 'Tyrrhena regum progenies, ... | ... 3 Maecenas', and in a hymnal context 3.21.1ff. 'o nata mecum consule Manlio, | ... 4 pia testa'. There is a controversial passage at 1.12.19ff. 'proximos illi tamen occupabit | Pallas honores. | proeliis audax, neque te silebo | Liber'; here in another hymnal context I am now inclined to take 'proeliis audax' not with *Pallas* but with *Liber* (note the weapons associated with Diana and Phoebus later in the same stanza). A different question arises at 3.14.1ff. 'Herculis ritu, modo dictus, o plebs, | morte venalem petiisse laurum, |

Caesar Hispana repetit Penatis | victor ab ora'. Against the commentators I take *Herculis ritu* not with *petiisse* but with *repetit*; Augustus was recently thought to have sought the bay-wreath at the cost of his life, but the resemblance to Hercules lies not in this but in his triumphant return from Spain. A short clause like *Herculis ritu* can be an independent colon, and need not cohere closely with what immediately follows.

Horace sometimes develops a sentence by means of a participial clause, in a manner more characteristic of Greek than of standard Latin; or sometimes the appended clause depends on an adjective where Greek would have supplied the participle of the verb 'to be'. Thus in the ode to Pyrrha we find 2 'perfusus liquidis... odoribus' (too compressed for Cicero), 5 'simplex munditiis', 10f. 'nescius aurae | fallacis' (appendages more characteristic of Tacitus than of republican Latin). I add a selection of many other instances; just as in prose, editors do not always use punctuation to indicate colometry, preferring to follow irrelevant modern conventions. 1.29.7ff. 'puer quis ex aula capillis | ad cyathum statuetur unctis, | doctus sagittas tendere Sericas | arcu paterno?' 1.33.14ff. 'grata detinuit compede Myrtale, | libertina fretis acrior Hadriae, | curvantis Calabros sinus' (where many wrongly punctuate after *libertina* rather than *Myrtale*). 1.36.18ff. 'nec Damalis novo | divelletur adultero, | lascivis hederis ambitiosior' (a comparative may link an independent colon as at 1.18.16 'arcanique Fides prodiga, perlucidior vitro', 2.14.28). 1.37.25ff. 'ausa et iacentem visere regiam | vultu sereno, fortis et asperas | tractare serpentis, ut atrum | corpore combiberet venenum, | deliberata morte ferocior, | saevis Liburnis scilicet invidens | privata deduci superbo, | non humilis mulier, triumpho' (the accumulation of appositions is remarkable even for Horace). 3.6.31f. 'seu navis Hispanae magister, | dedecorum pretiosus emptor' (here the sentence is developed by a noun in apposition). 4.9.49ff. 'duramque callet pauperiem pati, | peiusque leto flagitium timet, | non ille pro caris amicis, | aut patria timidus perire'. 4.14.17ff. 'spectandus in certamine Martio, | devota morti pectora liberae | quantis fatigaret ruinis, | indomitas prope qualis undas | exercet Auster, Pleiadum choro | scindente nubes, impiger hostium | vexare turmas, et trementem | mittere equum medios per ignis' (another triumphant period).

Horace in the *Odes* shows a partiality for ablative absolutes that is unusual in a poet: the construction helps his desire for brevity, and if it suggests the language of historians and official discourse, that gives no cause for surprise. Sometimes he separates his ablative with the subject of the sentence or other elements (Naylor (1922: 23)); cf. 1.10.14 'Ilio dives Priamus relicto', 2.7.27f. 'recepto | dulce mihi furere est amico', or with an interlaced word order 1.16.27f. 'fias recantatis amica | opprobriis', 3.16.39f. 'contracto melius parva cupidine | vectigalia porrigam'. In these places the components are short enough to be accommodated in a single colon; so there is no more difficulty in splitting the ablative than there would be with an ablative of quality. Such hyperbaton is rare in early Latin (cf. Plaut. *Stich.* 602f. 'non me quidem | faciet auctore', with emphasis on *me*), and though Cicero has no difficulty about interposing a connective or an adverb, he does not normally do so with more significant elements (*Sest.* 11 'quibus hic litteris lectis' is an exception, but *hic* slips in very easily). On the other hand the subject is freely interposed in Caesar and particularly Livy (Hofmann–Szantyr (1965: 402)). Here again we find that Horace's practice has more affinities with historiography than with oratory or poetry.

Horace's ablative absolute often comes after the main verb, sometimes at the very end of the sentence, even when it describes an antecedent action. See for instance 2.7.9f. 'tecum Philippos et celerem fugam | sensi, relicta non bene parmula . . .', 3.1.33f. 'contracta pisces aequora sentiunt, | iactis in altum molibus', 3.3.17f. 'gratum elocuta consiliantibus | Iunone divis', 3.3.52, 3.3.65f., 3.5.2ff. 'praesens divus habebitur | Augustus, adiectis Britannis | imperio gravibusque Persis' (such 'officialese' suits the Roman Odes), 3.5.12 'incolumi Iove et urbe Roma', 3.6.27f. 'cui donet impermissa raptim | gaudia luminibus remotis' (an austere description of an erotic situation), 3.14.14ff. 'ego nec tumultum | nec mori per vim metuam, tenente | Caesare terras', 4.5.27 'incolumi Caesare'. Such postponement of the ablative absolute is found occasionally in early Latin (Plaut. *Amph.* 998 'vobis inspectantibus') and Cicero's letters (*Q.F.* 1.4.2 'infidelibus amicis, plurimis invidis'), but is untypical of his speeches, where he is working towards a climax. On the other hand the ablative absolute often follows the main statement both in Livy and Tacitus, though even in the historians it is relatively rare at the very end of the sentence.

I turn now to places where by a procedure common in Greek and Latin poetry the elements of two cola are intertwined. For a simple instance see once again the ode to Pyrrha, 1.5.1f. 'quis multa gracilis te puer in rosa | perfusus liquidis urget odoribus?'; here the main verb is included within the participial clause, as at 1.21.13ff. 'hic bellum lacrimosum, hic miseram famem | . . . vestra motus aget prece'. For a somewhat different trajection see 3.27.18f. 'ego quid sit ater | Hadriae novi sinus', where *novi* is inserted in the indirect question that depends on it; cf. Soph. *O.T.* 1251 χὤπως μὲν ἐκ τῶνδ᾽ οὐκέτ᾽ οἶδ᾽ ἀπόλλυται, Theoc. 16.16f. πόθεν οἴσεται ἀθρεῖ | ἄρ-γυρον, Boldt (1884: 130–59). There is a more unusual case at 1.22.17f. 'pone me pigris ubi nulla campis | arbor aestiva recreatur aura'; here the effect is to throw greater emphasis on *nulla*. See also 3.14.21f. 'dic et argutae properet Neaerae | murreum nodo cohibere crinem'; far from being hidden away, *properet* is emphasized by its unusual position and underlines the poet's impatience. At first sight we assume that *properet* means 'hurry to come' (cf. 2.11.23 *maturet*), so the infinitive *cohibere* comes as a surprise; there is something to be said for Muretus' *cohibente*, which gives a more straightforward word order.

I come now to other sorts of dislocation, beginning with the ἀπὸ κοινοῦ construction, where an element common to two parallel clauses is postponed till the second clause (Leo (1896)); the figure is common in Greek and Latin poetry, and though it may have originated as a metrical convenience, Horace must have felt it as an elegant poeticism that served the interests of balance and economy. To turn first to the ode to Pyrrha, we find 'heu quotiens fidem | mutatosque deos flebit' (1.5.5f.); here some editors interpret *fidem* as *perfidiam*, but it suits Horace better to understand *fidem mutatam*. For other examples of the construction see for instance 2.7.23ff. 'quis udo | deproperare apio coronas | curatve myrto?', 3.1.12 'moribus hic meliorque fama', 3.4.19 'lauroque conlataque myrto', 3.11.6 'divitum mensis et amica templis', perhaps 4.2.41f. 'concines laetosque dies et urbis | publicum ludum' (where Naylor explains the unexpected prominence of *urbis* by taking it with *dies* as well as with *ludum*). For an unusual repetition of the figure see the last three stanzas of the Alcaic ode to Bacchus, 2.19.23f. 'leonis | unguibus horribilisque mala' (where *horribilisque* is Bochart's plausible conjecture for *horribilique*), 28 'pacis eras mediusque belli', 32 'ore pedes tetigitque crura'. Perhaps Horace is using a construction that he regarded as typical of Greek hymns; in similar contexts note 1.30.5f. (to Venus) 'fervidus tecum puer et solutis | Gratiae zonis properentque Nymphae', 3.21.18 (the parodic hymn to the wine-jar) 'viresque et addis cornua pauperi'.

For a common kind of ἀπὸ κοινοῦ construction cf. 3.25.2 'quae nemora aut quos agor in specus'; here by a figure common in Greek and Latin poetry a preposition is attached to the second of two nouns to which it applies. For more complex cases see 1.27.11f. 'quo beatus | vulnere, qua pereat sagitta', where by a familiar elegance the common elements (*beatus* and *pereat*) are distributed between the two clauses; so also 2.8.3f. 'dente si *nigro* fieres vel *uno* | turpior ungui', 2.15.18ff. 'oppida *publico* | *sumptu* iubentes et deorum | templa *novo decorare saxo*'. There is a controversial passage at 3.12.8f. 'eques ipso melior Bellerophonte neque pugno | neque segni pede victus', where some take *segni* with *pugno* as well as with *pede*; I have suggested elsewhere (1995: 263–4, 434) that the adjective conceals a proper name, say *Cycni*, that again has to be taken with both ablatives.

I turn now to a few places where there is a more unusual dislocation. Consider 1.23.11f. 'tandem desine matrem | tempestiva sequi viro', where *tempestiva viro* is interrupted by the intrusive *sequi*. The metre is not a significant factor (for Horace could have written *tempestiva viro sequi*); in fact the artificial hyperbaton emphasizes *viro* and sets it against *matrem*. A similar case may be suspected at the end of the ode to Pyrrha, 1.5.14ff. 'uvida suspendisse potenti | vestimenta maris deo'; normally *maris* would come immediately after *potenti*, on which it depends, but its dislocation gives it unusual emphasis. This might support Quinn's idea that there is a pun on Neptune who rules the sea and Venus who rules the male; it is desirable that the ambiguity of the ode should be sustained to the end, and Horace makes a similar pun at *Serm.* 2.8.14f. 'procedit fuscus Hydaspes | Caecuba vina ferens, Alcon Chium maris expers'.

There is a stranger instance of a displaced genitive at 1.35.5ff. (the ode to Fortune): 'te pauper ambit sollicita prece | ruris colonus, te dominam aequoris | quicumque Bithyna lacessit | Carpathium pelagus carina'. Here *ruris* must be taken not with *colonus*, where it is otiose, but with *dominam*, where it is needed to balance *aequoris*. The emphasis on *pauper* might suggest a contrast with the merchant, but it is particularly difficult to give *ruris* the necessary emphasis when it interrupts the sequence of *pauper* and *colonus*. For these reasons I have sometimes been tempted to read 'te ruris ambit sollicita prece | pauper colonus, te dominam aequoris...'. The long hyperbaton would put great weight on *ruris*, which combines with *aequoris* to show the extent of Fortune's power (a kind of polar expression common in hymns); any contrast between the poor man and the rich man is much less significant in this context.

In discussing this last passage Housman said that 'every Roman child felt in the marrow of his bones that *ruris* depended on *dominam*' (*CR* 16 (1902) 445 = Diggle and Goodyear (1972: ii. 581)). That is an implausible assertion, even allowing for characteristic hyperbole: not just in this exceptional case but in general the word order of the *Odes* must have seemed strange to the uninitiated, and it is not surprising that the first reactions were disappointing (*Epist.* 1.19.35ff.). It is often remarked that in late antiquity the literary language was very different from spoken Latin, but the same was true to some extent of the Augustan poets, especially of one so original as Horace in the *Odes*. The formal organization of their verse is indeed remarkable, but it is unprofitable to look for explanations in the national character. Roman poetry was not an indigenous growth, and when it peaked it was very dependent on Hellenistic models, where the divorce from living Greek was greater than in the classical period.

All the same, Horace achieves such regularity in his self-imposed rules that they begin to seem inevitable. Far from cramping his style, they are an inseparable part of it. He achieves his effects not by flowery colouring but by balance and antithesis, precision and intensity, concentration and cohesion. The words interact as in a miniature physical system, the adjectives may seem conventional but their placing makes them tell, the interlocking produced by the hyperbata helps to bolt the monument together. Nothing could be more unlike the triteness and triviality of the usual English translations.

GREEK INFLUENCE AND
TECHNICAL VOCABULARIES

Proceedings of the British Academy, **93**, 157–182

Grecism

R. G. MAYER

Summary. The purpose of this review is first, to establish so far as is possible, by collecting for the first time all the evidence, how the reader of Latin poetry in antiquity understood the varied oddities of syntax borrowed more or less directly from the Greek language. These usages were classified under the term *figura Graeca*. The second purpose is to show how modern scholars, when reluctant to follow antiquity in this issue, treat syntactical grecisms, and then to compare their approach with that of the Romans themselves. From time to time modern philologists either ignore or seek an alternative to the ancient explanations. They have created evolutionary models which rely heavily on the modern concept of grammatical analogy (which gives rise to the term 'partial grecism') and on the bilingualism of Romans. I will urge that we should up to a point try to respect ancient opinion, because at bottom it was developed out of the Romans' own feel for propriety in their language. A sense was instilled in Roman readers by their teachers of the difference between poetic syntax and what was in normal use, either spoken or written. One of the means of differentiation was the use of the term *figura Graeca*. Modern attempts to find analogies for unusual syntax within Latin rather than pure grecisms in effect dilute the exoticism which the Romans found in the syntax they believed to be entirely borrowed.

LUCRETIUS NOTORIOUSLY COMPLAINED of dearth in his native language, (1.832, 3.260 *patrii sermonis egestas*).[1] What as a philosopher he probably missed most was an established technical terminology. But perhaps as a poet too, with his eye upon his Greek models, he will have regretted the

[1] He did so, however, in the first passage in a way that rather drew attention to the richness of the Latin vocabulary, at least in words denoting everyday activities like speaking.

sheer ductility of the Greek language, its more flexible word order, its delight in compound words and coinages, its varied syntax. The Latin he used was altogether less malleable, and one of the tasks which the Roman poets of his and later generations clearly set themselves was the improvement of the language in point of suppleness. One device they employed now goes by the generic name of grecism (spelling of the word varies). There are several distinct species of grecism; I will briefly mention a few which will not detain us, though they have a bearing on the issue of borrowing as a whole. We shall focus upon the most complex of the manifestations of the usage, the syntactical borrowings.

First come the lexical grecisms, borrowed Greek words. In some cases, the reason for the loan is clear: Lucretius called the famous wooden horse of Troy *durateus* at 1.476, because that was the word Homer had used at *Od.* 8.493, 512, and so he evoked the epic tradition with a word that the native *ligneus*, used at 4.1153 and 6.1059, could not have done (Bailey (1949: ad loc.) says the use is gratuitous, a failure of imagination (cf. Sedley p. 239)). It would be interesting to know why Virgil chose but once at *E.* 10.52 to use *spelaea*; Servius, who notes many such lexical grecisms in Virgil, remarks: *Graece ait pro speluncis*. As a verbal experiment it failed to catch on, though it was picked up by that industrious magpie, the author of the *Ciris* at 467. Some borrowed words can prove to be well worth remark; *gyros*, for instance, which is rare enough in Greek, was adopted by Romans, because *circu(m)itio* and many of the oblique cases of *circulus* were unsuitable to the dactylic hexameter. What is remarkable is that the Romans, especially the poets, worked this loan-word very hard and gave it a range of meanings apparently unknown to Greek (we may compare the articles on the word in the *OLD* and in LSJ). But verbal grecisms had to be deployed with discretion; Dr Sedley discusses in this collection Lucretius' scruples on this point. Horace, it may also be noted, did not approve of the mixture of Greek words in the Latin context of the satires of Lucilius (*S.* 1.10.20–30), evidence of the growth of purism, *Latinitas*, among some writers. This has a bearing upon syntactical borrowings.

The next type of grecism to be noticed is the morphological. Greek inflections of proper names deserve careful attention, because poets had varying practices in their use of Greek terminations. Horace, as Bentley pointed out in his note on *Epode* 17.17, affected a transmarine elegance in his lyrics, but prefered native terminations as stylistically appropriate in his iambic and hexameter poems. In the post-Augustan poets there was a tendency to favour Greek inflections for proper names over the Latin (though here we have to reckon with problems of transmission). Statius provides abundant evidence of this fashion.

A third type, less usually recognized in discussions, deserves to be included in this brief overview, namely grecisms of word order. Greek poets departed from the spoken norm in the placement of conjunctions and prepositions, and the Romans most under their influence introduced the practice into their poems. The postponement of co-ordinating conjunctions is always recognized as a borrowed practice, e.g. by Kroll (1922) on Catull. 51.9 *lingua sed torpet* and 64.93 *funditus atque imis exarsit tota medullis* (cf. Pfeiffer on Callim. 260.55), by Norden in his commentary on *Aen.* VI, p. 402 and by Harrison on *A.* 10.372–3 *fidite ne pedibus.*[2] But there are refinements upon this practice, seen for instance in the anastrophe of the comparative particles *ut* and *ceu.* Greek allows this with ὥς but we do not find it in Latin before Horace, and then remarkably in a satire, a genre often reckoned to be closer in style to spoken Latin: *S.* 1.3.89 *captiuus ut.* When it occurs in Virgil, as at *A.* 2.355 *lupi ceu,* Servius sorts out the unusual word order for his readers. Wackernagel (1926: i.11) reckoned that Virgil imitated Greek, λύκοι ὥς. Perhaps the most characteristically Greek word order to have been adopted was the anastrophe of a monosyllabic prepostition, which was followed by a genitive dependent on the transposed noun; this artificial word order is even found in the *Annals* of Tacitus, a point to bear in mind, for as we shall see, historical prose was felt to be entitled to the sort of grecism which this essay will chiefly be concerned with.[3] Euripides is fond of this word order, and the first to use it in Latin is that great experimenter Cicero (*Arat.* 201 *parte ex Aquilonis*).[4] The usage is extended by Lucretius at 3.49 *conspectu ex hominum,* 1088 *tempore de mortis*[5] and 6.1265 *silanos ad aquarum* (there is even *viam per* in the previous line[6]). Virgil is apparently rather restrained in his use of the licence: *E.* 8.59 *aerii specula de montis,* *G.* 4.333 *thalamo sub fluminis alti* (we are in the narrative portion of the book, the Aristaeus epyllion), *A.* 7.234 *fata per Aeneae.* So much then for some features of Latin poetic style that are reckoned to be owed to imitation of the Greeks.

We will from now on focus upon the more difficult avenue of grecizing, syntactical borrowing; this type from time to time entails lexical loan-shifts (called calques) as well. (But the syntactical grecisms that appear to be

---

[2] See K–G ii.179 note 1.

[3] See Hofmann–Szantyr (1965: 216), where Greek influence is acknowledged, and Nipperdey–Andresen on Tac. *Ann.* 3.72. There is a still useful list of Tacitean grecisms in Boetticher (1830: C-CII). Cf. p. 266 below.

[4] See Platnauer on *IT* 1460 and add Bond on *HF* 527; for *ex* see *TLL* v.2.1130.56. For another of his verbal experiments see footnote 36.

[5] This collocation is unnoticed by Gudeman in *TLL* v.1.42.75–6, but cf. ibid. 52.17.

[6] For that see Bailey (1949: i.107), but he does not specifically note the kind to which attention has just been drawn, and anyway regards the practice as due chiefly to metrical convenience. This is important, for Bailey was inclined to minimize the poet's debt to Greek style. It is odd that Catullus appears not to have adopted the practice.

due to direct translation of a Greek model, such as we find at *G.* 3.232 *irasci in cornua*, derived from Eur. *Ba.* 742, will not here concern us.) The origin of the Roman notion of syntactical grecism cannot now be recovered. We may speculate that it developed in the line-by-line exposition (*praelectio*) of contemporary poetic texts by *grammatici* like Q. Caecilius Epirota, who first expounded Virgil and the 'new poets' in the early principate, according to Suetonius (*Gram.* 16.3, with Kaster's commentary). However that may be, a form of doctrine appears at its earliest in Quintilian, who drew attention to syntactical grecism in his general discussion of *figurae* (*Inst.* 9.3.17). We notice at once a characteristic approach to the phenomenon: the Romans dealt with it as a part of rhetoric, and so a feature of style. This should not surprise. Latin grammarians leaned heavily upon the Greeks for their categories, and obviously Greek grammar had no concept of 'grecism', i.e. borrowing of syntactical practice from a different language, to pass on to them. Moreover, grammarians before Apollonius Dyscolus spent most of their time describing and accounting for accidence; their analysis of syntax was, compared to ours, limited, and they largely handed it over to the rhetoricians, who described it as grammatical figures or as virtues and vices of style.[7] It was therefore the rhetoricians who accommodated these imported syntactical practices within their own category of grammatical *figurae*. The poet whose works provide the most examples is Virgil, not only because of his range, but because we have an invaluable (though often neglected) guide to his practice in the commentary of Servius. We cannot know just how extensive or independent Servius' own knowledge, and that above all of his successors, was in this department. Much of their information was traditional, and presumably went back to the earliest commentaries, composed when a knowledge of Greek literature was more secure. Even very late grammarians and rhetoricians who refer to grecism are clearly trotting out standard examples; they may themselves have been comparatively ignorant of Greek and its influence, but their snippets of traditional learning seem well founded. My approach in this essay will be historical, starting with the Romans themselves and concentrating on Servius above all. I want first to present the ways in which they came to terms with the apparent irregularities they noticed in poetic usage and how they described and drew attention to them.

---

[7] There is a brief discussion by A. Gudeman, art. 'Grammatik', *RE* vii.1806.18–51; for a fuller account see Baratin (1989) and Atherton (1996: 256–7).

ROMANS ON *FIGURA GRAECA*

We start with Quintilian. It is striking that when he introduced the vast topic of figures of speech he first exemplified their historical development by the use of the cases, for instance with verbs like *incumbere* or with adjectives like *plenus* (*Inst.* 9.3.1). This indicates the keen sense the élite Romans had of what was correct or at least permissible where two words were to be joined together. There was a flexible norm, which might alter over time, but a serious departure from it could only be justified as a figurative usage (otherwise it was condemned as a solecism). The usage of the cases provided the clearest examples, so far as Quintilian was concerned. He then proceeded to what we now call grecism (*Inst.* 9.3.17): *ex Graeco uero tralata uel Sallusti plurima, quale est: [uulgus] 'amat fieri', uel Horati, nam id maxime probat: 'nec ciceris nec longae inuidit auenae', uel Vergili: 'Tyrrhenum nauigat aequor', et iam uulgatam actis quoque: 'saucius pectus'.*[8] Three writers, Sallust, Horace and Virgil, provide his examples. All are classics (they of course reappear in the tenth book in his list of authors whose style is to be studied for imitation) but none, it is significant to observe, was an orator. At once Quintilian's reader, who was studying to be an orator, ought to have been on his guard, for the usage of historians and poets might not always be available to those who meant to follow what Horace had called the *norma loquendi*. For, as the later grammarian Fortunatianus said, in answer to his own question *'aliena uerba quae sunt?'*: *'quae non sunt oratori accommodata, sed historico aut poetae'.*[9] Among the Romans themselves grecism was seen as a feature of style in the more highly wrought literary forms, history and poetry, which were implicitly ranged together against the norm established for formal oratorical Latin.

Let us now look at Quintilian's examples of grecism. First and very briefly, the Sallustian usage: *amat fieri* is as much a lexical as a syntactical grecism, since the sense of *amat* here ('is accustomed') is not native, but a loan-shift from Greek;[10] it was that new sense which facilitated the novel syntax.

Now for Horace. Quintilian, who was later to describe him as *uarius figuris et uerbis felicissime audax* (*Inst.* 10.1.96), assured us that Horace

---

[8] The passage referred to in Sallust may be from a now lost part of the *Histories*, though it is sometimes regarded as a mis-recollection of *Iug.* 34.1 (*uulgus* was deleted by Radermacher; others emend it); the others are *S.* 2.6.83–4, *A.* 1.67 and 12.5 (though the phrase also occurs in Tibull. 1.6.49).

[9] *Ars rhetorica* iii.4–5 in Halm (1863: 123). For *aliena uerba* see *TLL* i.1578.63ff., esp. 79–80.

[10] Coleman (1977: 106); *TLL* i.1956.35–59.

was specially keen on syntactical grecisms, yet he contented himself with
only the one example. It is remarkably from the *Sermones*, which, generically considered, might have been thought to stick close to spoken Latin
norms.[11] To Quintilian however the syntax of *nec ciceris nec longae inuidit
auenae* was totally strange, unidiomatic, and yet it could be accounted for
straightforwardly as a borrowing from Greek. Nowhere else in classical
Latin is *inuideo* used with the genitive and so it has every appearance
here of an experiment on Horace's part, one which failed to take even in
poetry. That is why Quintilian chose so striking an example: he had begun
his section on *figurae* with the observation that in older Latin Romans
said *hanc rem inuidere*, whereas in his own day everybody said *hac re
inuidere*. So Horace's genitive with this verb stuck in his mind as a freak.
We might have expected, in the light of what he said of Horace's fondness
for grecisms, to find numerous references to them in what remains of the
Horatian scholia, but it is only Porfyrio who has two explicit statements
on the figure, in his notes on *C.* 2.6.15–16 *uiridique certat | baca Venafro*,
where he observes: *Graeca figura dictum est 'illi certat' pro 'cum illo certat'*
(a usage to be discussed in more detail below, pp. 167–8) and 2.9.17 *desine
querelarum: Graeca elocutione figuratum est. alioquin nos 'desine queri'
dicimus*. The dearth in these scholia is probably due to their scrappy
transmission. But sometimes Horace's scholiast does not specify that the
'figured' syntax is owed to the Greek. All that Porfyrio said about *C.*
3.30.11–12 *agrestium | regnauit populorum* was: *adnotanda elocutio per
genetiuum figurata*. A figure to be sure, but not to him precisely a grecism
(if his full note has come down to us). Servius, however, discussing *A.*
11.126, is more explicit: *figura Graeca 'miror illius rei' et 'regno illius rei',
ut Τενέδοιό τε ἶφι ἀνάσσεις* [*Il.* 1.38]: *inde Horatius ait 'et qua pauper aquae
Daunus agrestium | regnauit populorum' pro agrestibus populis* (his quo-
tation of a snippet of Homer which illustrates Greek usage, and the MS
transmission of this text will both be discussed below, pp. 166–7 and 170).
So the grecism was explicitly acknowledged, at least by some.

   We turn now to Quintilian's citations from Virgil. His first, *A.* 1.67, is
more remarkable than it may appear to us at first sight, and it therefore
requires some discussion. Quintilian perhaps chose *nauigat aequor* design-
edly, because in his first book (1.5.38) when he came to illustrate solecisms
he used as one of his examples the phrase *ambulo uiam*, his point there
being that normal Latin usage required a preposition before the noun
indicating 'ground covered' with a verb of movement (internal objects are

---

[11] But cf. the observation on p. 159 above about borrowed word order.

of course related but different).[12] According to that doctrine then Virgil's use of *nauigo* without a preposition before *aequor* ought to have seemed a solecism. A defence was needed for the poet's usage, and the one that Quintilian chose was that of a grammatical figure borrowed from the Greek; he might also have chosen to regard it as an ellipse, an explanation often found in the Virgilian scholia on other passages.[13] But here, Servius concurs with him, noting: *figura Graeca est; nos enim dicimus 'per aequor nauigat'*. With this he compares the use of *iuro* at *A.* 12.197.[14] It may also be noted that 'Julius Rufinianus' also lists this usage of *nauigo* and of *iuro* (though he has in mind *A.* 6.351 *maria aspera iuro*) among his few instances of grecism.[15] But the intricacies of the explanation of *inauigat aequor* have not been exhausted.

One of the MS of Servius, called by Thilo D, regularly adds further explanatory matter, and on *A.* 1.67 it appends a Greek phrase: τὴν θάλασσαν πλέει (a practice of which more notice will be taken later). This obviously confirms the reader's conviction that the Latin syntax is borrowed. But that little Greek phrase crops up again in the Verona scholia on *E.* 6.2 *habitare casas*, where once more the accusative object was felt to need defence. The full note runs thus: *antiqua consuetudine, sicut: centum urbes habitant magnas* [= *A.* 3.106], *ut Graeci dicunt* πλέει τὴν θάλασσαν *et alibi Vergilius: caua trabe currimus aequor pro 'super aequor currere'* [= *A.* 3.191]. The situation with *currere* was felt to be the same as with *nauigare*, and indeed on *A.* 3.191 the DServius commentary cross-referenced to *A.* 1.67. In both cases a preposition would have been the norm in prose, but the poet's practice is felt to be borrowed from the Greek. At the same time the Verona scholiast adds as a possible explanation archaism (*antiqua consuetudo*). We shall meet this alternative again.

Now for Quintilian's second Virgilian example, *saucius pectus*. Here an adjective, rather than a verb, 'governs' the accusative case of a noun which

---

[12] We should not expect to find many instances of *ambulo* in the poets, since the verb is colloquial, and anyway metrically unwieldy; nonetheless at *F.* 1.122 Ovid wrote *libera perpetuas ambulat illa uias*.

[13] Virgil frequently omitted a preposition where prose would employ it, e.g. at *A.* 1.2 *Italiam . . . uenit*. This omission is noted by Servius (*detraxit*) at *A.* 1.52 *Aeoliam uenit* and at *A.* 11.683 *agminibus totis*, cf. the note of DServius on *A.* 9. 598 where he glosses the simple accusative with *ad Italiam*. Mühmelt (1965: 111) drew attention to similar notes in the Homeric scholia which he believed served as Servius' models both for the grammatical issue and its explanation.

[14] Ovid picks up the figure at *Her.* 16.321 *iurabo . . . numina*.

[15] *De schematis lexeos* in Halm (1863: 56.13–14). It is interesting that 'Rufinianus' spoke of these two passages as instances where the preposition had been removed (*praepositione detracta*), perhaps thus echoing an alternative scholiastic explanation such as we find elsewhere in Servius himself, see n. 13 above.

specifies or limits its scope (in this case the adjective may be thought to have verbal sense, 'wounded', not that Quintilian observes this). Servius in his comment on *A.* 12.5 does not mention Greek practice, but glosses the expression with a turn of phrase that he regularly uses in his commentary to explain this sort of accusative: *saucium pectus habens*; he went on to observe: *et bene alia uerba interposuit, quia 'saucius pectus' et sonabat asperrime et imperitis poterat soloecismus uideri.* He thus shows that he was dealing with a grammatical figure, for it is often a short step between a legitimate figure and an unacceptable solecism. The student is warned.

This particular usage and the scholiasts' form of words to expound it deserve more notice. The 'figure' was first introduced by Virgil at *G.* 2.131 *faciem . . . simillima lauro* (where there is no comment from antiquity). It then occurs twice in *A.* 1, where Servius does have notes. On 320 *nuda genu* he is explicit: *nudum genu habens, ut si dicas 'bonus animum'. et est Graeca figura, sed non ea quam diximus fieri per participium praeteriti temporis et casum accusativum; haec enim per nomen* ['adjective'] *fit, quamuis ad unam significationem recurrant.* (He cross-references back to this note at 1.328 *uox hominem sonat*, where he also says: *Graeca figura est.*) This phrase, *nuda genu*, became a standard example of the usage;[16] Diomedes (*GLK* i.440.21–2) also used it to illustrate what he calls 'hellenismos': *ibi enim nudum genu habens debuit dicere. sed seruiens schemati* (NB = *figurae*) *quod appellatur hellenismos . . .* (a word rarely used in antiquity to refer to the *Graeca figura*).[17] The note Servius composed on *A.* 1.320 *nuda genu* is crucial to our understanding of how this grecism struck a Roman reader. The best way he could think of to demonstrate its outlandishness was to compose a piece of dog-Latin, *bonus animum*, a construction unknown to good usage, which, as Dr Horsfall pointed out in discussion, was precisely the point at issue.[18] The same 'figured' usage of the accusative is found a second time at *A.* 1.589 *os umerosque deo*

[16] On the very difficult *A.* 2.273 *traiectus lora* Servius says: *traiecta lora habens; ut nuda genu* adds DServius. This particularly troublesome passage is discussed by Mariner (1963); Professor José-Luis Perez Vidal kindly brought this article to my notice. *nuda genu* was used as an example of a *figura λέξεως* by 'Fortunatianus' (Halm 1863: 126.25–6), but he did not specify grecism.

[17] For the origins of the term ἑλληνισμός see Lohmann (1915: 1) and Dionisotti (1995: 45–58). It is also found in Donatus' comment on Ter. *And.* 543 *ne me obsecra* for *ne obsecres*; Donatus remarks upon the common usage only here (see McGlynn (1963: 389) s.v. *ne*). Where did he get this notion? Can he mean that Terence is translating Menander? Even if so, the usage cannot have escaped his notice, so common is it (eighty examples in comedy alone according to K–S i.202–3). Prose avoids it however, so perhaps by Donatus' time it seemed a poeticism. Cf. Servius on *A.* 6.95 and 7.202, where he rewords *ne* + imperative to *ne* + subjunctive (he ignores *E.* 2.17); he nowhere calls it a grecism. See Penney, p.253, in this volume.

[18] See *TLL* ii.2097.71–2098.41.

similis, where again Servius says: *est Graeca figura, ut diximus supra* (he simply notes the presence of a figure at *A*. 4.559). Similar notes on this sort of accusative are found on *A*. 5.285 *Cressa genus*, where Servius identifies the syntax as *Graeca figura*, with a cross-reference to 8.114 *qui genus?* Finally, DServius notes on *A*. 12.25 *non genus indecores* that it is an *elocutio figurata de Graeco*.[19] The feeling of antiquity is clear: such an accusative is to be accounted for as foreign idiom.

Let us return now to Quintilian. His examples of grecism were few, and chiefly concerned the use of cases; the phenomenon sheltered under the broad umbrella of *figura*. It is worth looking at some of the other 'figures' he drew attention to, because, though he did not class them as grecisms, some later commentators did. For example, Quintilian noticed Persius 1.9–10 *nostrum istud uiuere triste | aspexi*, but only saw in it a figure: *cum infinito uerbo usus est pro appellatione: nostram enim uitam uult intellegi*.[20] But the scholiast to Persius specifies that it is a *figura Graeca*. This ought to be correct, so far as ancient doctrine was concerned, since the use of the infinitive as a noun that might be in the accusative case was felt by Roman grammarians to be borrowed from Greek; so Servius and Sergius on Donatus call it a *graeca elocutio*.[21]

Another related figure Quintilian found in Virgil, *A*. 5.248 *magnum dat ferre talentum*, of which he said: *utimur et uerbo pro participio: 'magnum dat ferre talentum', tamquam ferendum* (*Inst*. 9.3.9).[22] Whether or not he defined more precisely the sort of figure is not clear, thanks to a lacuna in the transmission; he clearly did not include it among grecisms. It is, however, plain what sense he attached to the construction: the infinitive is epexegetic, and replaces another form of the verb, e.g. gerundive.

---

[19] When the usage is encountered in Horace, however, Porfyrio merely notes it as a figure. On *C*. 1.21.12 *Apollinem umerum insignem* he says: *per figuram haec eloquutio intelligenda . . . hoc est umerum insignem habentem ut laeta comam* (probably = *A*. 7.60 *sacra comam*) *dicitur a Vergilio et multa similia*. The failure to call it specifically a grecism may be due either to accident or to the commentator's refusal to go into detail about origins.

[20] *Inst*. 9.3.9; but if his text is here correctly transmitted his memory betrayed him since the infinitive phrase is *not* the object of the verb *aspexi* but of a preceding *ad*. This does not alter his argument.

[21] See *GLK* iv.411.24–5 and 502.32; the issue is discussed by Wölfflin (1886). Persius is especially fond of this use of the infinitive as a noun, but 1.9–10 is the sole example of its use after a preposition. 'Julius Rufinianus' (Halm 1863: 58.10) drew attention to 1.122 *hoc ridere meum* as a *figura per eclogam uerborum* in a section which groups together a number of non-native usages of the infinitive.

[22] It is, however, odd that Quintilian says *utimur* since this is not true of usage in general, as Servius pointed out; the infinitive with *dare* is only found in prose in Vitr. 7.10.4 (cf. *TLL* v.1.1688.59–1690.29) and remained poetic syntax (albeit widespread there: first in Lucr. 6.1227). See now for a general discussion Domínguez Domínguez and Martín Rodríguez (1993).

Other students of the language defined this usage as a grecism, for instance the grammarian Pompeius, who in explaining that the verb had no case in Latin noted none the less that it appeared to be in the accusative when it followed *do*. He insisted that this usage was not Latin but an *elocutio Graeca*; under this head he included the common expression *da bibere*, and compared Ter. *And*. 484 (*GLK* v.213.12–15). Now this little expression came to be usual in accounts of the 'abnormal' syntax of *do*. All such syntax, Pompeius assures us, is acceptable in poets, but quite foreign to everyday usage.

For Servius too the infinitive with *do* was borrowed from Greek; he said in his own note on *A*. 5.248: *Graecum est duo uerba coniungere, ut paulo post* (= 262 *donat habere uiro*), *sed hoc datur poetis*. The construction he clearly felt to be exceptional, and earlier in his commentary he had set out the doctrine a bit more fully, on *A*. 1.318: *unde 'da bibere' usus inuenit, quod facere non debemus, ne duo uerba iungamus nisi in poemate*. He thus made a point of offering a considerable number of notes on it as it occurred throughout the *Aeneid*.[23]

After Quintilian there is a single notice in Aulus Gellius, who drew attention to a use of the passive of *exigo* in a speech of Metellus Numidicus and in a play of Caecilius which he felt was a *Graeca figura* (*Noctes Atticae* 15.14).[24] This is most curious since an oration and a comedy are not, given the opinion of Quintilian, the genres in which we would expect to find abnormalities. None the less it shows that the strategy of tracing some abnormalities in Latin syntax to a deliberate (because 'figured') borrowing from Greek is part of the exegetic tradition well before we reach our extant scholiasts. To them we may now turn in earnest.

Servius provides our most abundant information for Virgilian grecisms, and some of his notes have already been referred to. (Others, which do not call for detailed comment, are gathered into an appendix.) Here let us consider some of the devices he had for drawing attention to grecisms, especially to their 'Greekness'. As we have already seen above, he (or at any rate some of his MSS) sometimes offered a similar Greek expression, either as pure illustration, or as a sort of paraphrase of the Latin. Among the illustrations are these: on *E*. 5.1 *boni inflare: Graecum est ἱκανός λέγειν* (DServius);[25] on *A*. 8.127 *cui . . . precari* the Servian scholia offered three

---

[23] E.g. at 1.319 *dederatque comam diffundere uentis* where he glosses: *ut diffunderetur: Graeca autem figura est. sic alibi* (5.248) *et* (1.79); there are similar notes on 10.235, 701, 12.97 and 211.

[24] For Gellius' use of Greek syntactical practice to justify some constructions in Latin see Holford-Strevens (1988: 137).

[25] See Page ad loc. and cf. *TLL* ii.2098.33–41 (where Servius is quoted quite differently from Thilo's ed.)

explanations, one archaism, another hyperbaton and yet a third runs: *est Graecum, ut* εὔχεο Ἀπόλλωνι (= *Il.* 4.101). Similar is the note on *A.* 10.698 *Latagum occupat os: est Graeca figura, in Homero frequens,* which went on to explain: *ut si dicas* ἔκρουσεν Ἀχιλλέα τὸν πόδα, *id est Achillem percussit pedem pro percussit Achillis pedem*[26] (he made up his Greek phrase, for κρούω is not found in epic). On *A.* 11.383–4 *timoris argue* Servius said: *est de Graeco: nam ita dicunt* κατηγορῶ σε φόνου, and at *A.* 12.649 *indignus auorum* he noted the use of the genitive as a *Graeca figura* and explained: *nam nos 'indignus illa re' dicimus, contra Graeci* ἀνάξιος στεφάνου, *id est indignus coronae.*[27]

Translations (more or less) of the Virgilian original into Greek are found in the Servian scholia on *A.* 1.440 *cernitur ulli: et est Graecum* οὐδενὶ ὁρώμενος, *A.* 1.465 *multa gemens: Graecum est* πολλὰ στενάζων (DServius).[28] At *A.* 3.426 *prima hominis facies* Servius took *prima* as neuter plural: *est Graeca figura* τὰ πρῶτα ἄνθρωπος; his opinion is not shared by modern commentators but that does not affect his observation. We find more translations at *A.* 6.341 *quis deorum: 'quis deus' debuit dicere sed graece dixit* τίς θεῶν (= *Il.* 1.8, 18.182),[29] *A.* 8.217 *una boum: Graeca figura,* μία τῶν βοῶν,[30] and at *A.* 8.676 *cernere erat* Servius after again specifying *Graeca figura,* translates: ὁρᾶν ἔνεστι.[31] A few more examples of paraphrase into Greek or citation of Greek syntactical practice will be mentioned below, but it is time now to consider how the scholiasts handled a general topic in Latin syntax which they often faced in their poets.

Most verbs of fighting or contending took the dative in Greek, and in Latin usually a prepositional construction (K–S i.319). One of the first to depart from the native usage was Catullus at 62.64 *noli pugnare duobus.* We have no scholia on Catullus, but when we find the same construction in Virgil, at *A.* 4.38 *pugnabis amori,* we can turn to Servius, who says: *est Graecum 'pugno tibi', nam nos 'pugno tecum' dicimus.*[32] The same view is

---

[26] See Landgraf (1898: 215) and Müller (1908: 131). There is a similar construction at *A.* 12.273–6 *unum... transadigit costas,* but Servius only noted on 273: *figurate dixit pro unius.*

[27] The usage is picked up by Val. Flac. 8.38 and Silius 8.383; cf. *TLL* vii.1.1190.32–9.

[28] So far as the adverbial use of the plural neuter adjective is concerned we may compare Servius on *A.* 11.471 *multaque se incusat: multa pro multum, Graeca figura* (cf. DServius on 12.402). See Löfstedt (1933: 412), Wölfflin (1885: 98), *TLL* viii.1617.41–50 (Virgilian examples omitted!). Cf. Hor. *Ep.* 5.74 *o multa fleturum caput.*

[29] *OLD* 1 only cites this example, then Apul. *Met.* 1.25. Commentators and grammars are strangely silent.

[30] The usage is also classed as *figura Graeca* by 'Julius Rufinianus' (Halm 1863: 56.12). See Clausen on *E.* 6.65 *una sororum.*

[31] He missed both *G.* 4.447, on which Bourgeois (1940: 85) astutely noted that it is a Greek who is speaking, and *A.* 6.596.

[32] Cf. *A.* 11.600–1 *sonipes... pugnat habenis,* and Hor. *S.* 1.2.73 *pugnantia... istis* (again in the satires, where we might not have expected abnormality).

found in 'Julius Rufinianus'; this passage from the *Aeneid* is the second in his brief list of instances of *figura Graeca*.[33] Such syntax is frequently adopted for other verbs of fighting as well, e.g. *certo*, by Horace and Virgil, but when their ancient commentators come to describe the usage they are not always consistent in their terminology. By various means they none the less drew attention to the oddity of the syntax; Servius on *A.* 1.493 *uiris concurrere* says that it is a *Graeca figura*, but no specific detail is given (see Thilo's note), nor does he always say that the dative so used is a loan from the Greeks.[34] What needs to be stressed here is that sometimes we can only get the full picture of the ancient opinion by combining scraps of information from various sources. Thus in his note to Horace, *S.* 2.5.19 Pseudo-Acro says: *certans datiuo casui iungitur* with an appeal to the same usage in Virgil at *E.* 8.55 *certent et cycnis ululae* (where there is no Servian note) and 5.8 *tibi certat* (where Servius says unspecifically *usurpatum est; nam hodie 'certo tecum' dicimus*). This latter line is of the first importance, because it provides Porfyrio with a reference point; on Horace, *Ep.* 11.18 he says: *imparibus autem certare per datiuum casum figuratum est* and cross-references to Virgil, *E.* 5.8 *tibi certat*. This is surprising since he might have been expected to refer to his own note on *C.* 2.6.15–16 (quoted above on p. 162), one of only two explicit references to the *Graeca figura* in the whole of the Horatian scholiastic tradition. In fact, only one writer explicitly places *E.* 5.8 among examples of *figura Graeca*, the late (but not for that reason untrustworthy) 'Julius Rufinianus' (see n. 33). We must then be alert to the unspecific use of terms like *figura*, *figuratum*, *figurate* or *usurpatum*, as well as to paraphrases into Greek and to cross-references to a standard example of a particular usage.

When for instance we turn to Priscian's grammar, we find him remark on Virg. *G.* 3.53 *crurum tenus: (praepositio) apud nos duobus solis praeponitur, id est accusatiuo et ablatiuo, nisi ἑλληνισμῶι utatur auctoritas, ut Vergilius in III Georgicon genetiuo est usus secundum Graecos pro ablatiuo.*[35] This view is endorsed by Servius on *A.* 3.427 *pube tenus*, but without specific note of Greek usage, and by DServius on *A.* 10.210 *laterum tenus*,[36]

---

[33] *De schematis lexeos*, in Halm (1863: 56.9–14).

[34] He has, for instance, no note on *G.* 2.99 *cui non certauerit ulla*, but on *G.* 2.138 *laudibus Italiae certent* he says: *figurate: nam 'certo tecum' dicimus*. See also *G.* 2.96 *cellis contende Falernis*, to which there is a false reference in *TLL* iv.667.55–61; the correct reference appears ibid. 670.20–6. The syntax is not found in prose until Plin. *Ep.* 8.8.4.

[35] 14.14 = *GLK* iii.32.11; cf. 18.262, 279 = *GLK* iii.343.13–18 *secundum Graecos dixit*. For 'hellenismos' see n. 17. It is telling that Mynors has no note on the usage, Thomas notes it without attempting to account for Virgil's practice.

[36] Harrison ad loc. does not mention the possibility of grecism in the usage, nor does Austin on Virg. *A.* 1.737 or 2.553 (where he does suggest metrical convenience). The usage is first found in poetry in Cic. *Arat.* 324 (83), in prose in a letter of Caelius (*Fam.* 8.1.2).

where there is a cross reference to the *Georgics* passage and, more significantly, a translation into Greek, ἄχρι τῶν πλευρῶν, one of the scholiasts'
ways of indicating grecism.

Another grammarian who draws attention to Virgilian grecism is Diomedes (*GLK* i.312.20). In discussing the cases used with *diues* he says that
the genitive is Greek, for πλούσιος or ἀφνειός are so used with genitive or
dative (e.g. *Od.* 1.165); from Virgil he cites *A.* 9.26 *diues equum, diues
pictai uestis et auri*. Servius there simply notes that it is used figuratively
with the genitive (Virgil in fact has the genitive often, not that he spurns
the normal Latin ablative).

Let us conclude this trawl through the scholiasts and grammarians of
antiquity with a remaining notice of our figure that calls for special discussion. The author of the *Adnotationes super Lucanum* regarded *felix
esse mori* at 4.520 as *secundum Graecam elocutionem*. This passage,
however, clearly gave other ancient students pause. For Priscian regarded
it as the normal Latin use of the infinitive as an accusative object.[37] If we
had more and fuller scholia on poets other than Virgil we would surely
find a wider range of observations upon the usage than have survived.

To close this account of the attitude to syntactical grecism in antiquity
we may notice a different sort of evidence which reinforces the conclusion
that grecisms were felt to be exotics: in our MSS they are sometimes
normalized out of existence. Scholiasts too betray the practice. This is
found for instance at Virg. *A.* 9.789 *excedere pugnae* and 10.441 *tempus
desistere pugnae*. In the former case the Medicean MS and in the latter
the codex Romanus offer the uariant *pugna*, as well they might since the
construction with the genitive is unnecessary metrically, and the normal
ablative was found at *A.* 1.37. At *A.* 10.154 *libera fati* Servius knew the
reading *fatis*; again the syntax was not metrically generated, and the normal
ablative was to be found at *G.* 3.194.[38] A yet more taxing use of the
genitive is found at *A.* 11.126 *iustitiaene prius mirer, belline laborum*. Here
the MSS give variant readings, and Donatus appears to have read *iustitiam*
and *laborem*, which metrically and syntactically are unexceptionable: Virgil
could have written them. But Servius saved the syntax and the text, not
only here but in the passage of Horace referred to above (p. 162): *figura
Graeca 'miror illius rei'*; he derived the construction from θαυμάζειν, and
was supported by Priscian, who said: *illi* [Attici] εὐδαιμονίζω σοῦ τόδε καὶ
εὐδαιμονίζω σε τοῦδε. *nostri quoque auctores hanc saepissime* [!] *imitati sunt*

---

[37] The reference in the *Adnotationes super Lucanum* will be found between 4.536 and 4.537
in Endt's edition. For Priscian see 18.260 (= *GLK* iii.342.8–10) and cf. *TLL* iii.767.77–80.
[38] This < ἐλεύθερος, and is picked up by Horace at *AP* 212 (see Brink ad loc. and *TLL* vii
2.1288.29–35, but also Hofmann–Szantyr (1965: 78)).

figuram, and went on to refer to this very line from the *Aeneid*.[39] Horace's MS tradition also provides an example of normalization at *C.* 3.30.13, the passage referred to by Servius in the note just quoted (and on p. 162 above). *agrestium regnauit populorum* appears as *agrestium regnator populorum* in our oldest MSS. This reading used to be found even in early printed editions, but though it produces locally normal syntax, it ruins the run of the sentence. These more or less clumsy attempts to foist a normal expression upon the transmitted text suggest dismay in the face of the unusual.

We may now take stock. The Romans themselves created a more or less homogeneous category by treating certain syntactical abnormalities as 'figures of speech'. This indicates that they regarded the phenomenon as fundamentally ornamental, but it had also to be deliberate. For whilst ordinary speakers of a language use *figurae*, they do so unconsciously. Those who speak and write formally, on the other hand, are expected to choose every detail, especially when using figures, for a figure used unawares is a solecism (so Quintilian reiterates, *Inst.* 1.5.53 and 9.3.2, and cf. Sen. *Ep.* 95.9). This *figura* Quintilian classed among the 'grammatical' ones because it changed normal syntactical practice (*loquendi rationem nouat, Inst.* 9.3.2). It differed somewhat from the others in this group in that Quintilian appears to have felt that it belonged especially to historical prose and to poetry generally; it was less suitable to oratory. That would indicate a sense that this particular figure was exotic. Now figures need some justification, and, leaving authority, antiquity and usage to one side, that justification may be found in giving a reason (*Inst.* 9.3.3). The simplest reason for *this* figure is provided by the epithet *Graeca*. All sorts of deviations from the syntactical norm were thus swept into the single basket called *Graeca figura*, and no further attempt was made to account for the usage. So much was already owed, especially by the poets, to Greek literary practice that it sufficed to point to a model in the foreign idiom. Later commentators sometimes underscored this exoticism by reference to what the Romans actually said (*dicimus*), or by a fullish grammatical account of normal Latin syntax, or by translation into or quotation from Greek, or even, once, by the formation of a bit of dog-Latin (*bonus animum*) to warn the reader of the 'foreignness' of the expression. The ancient reader, trained in rhetorical doctrine and the poetical exegesis of the *grammatici*, was ready to pigeon-hole certain abnormalities of syntax as *figurae* modelled upon the Greek. We may now turn to the much more sophisticated views of modern philologists.

---

[39] 18.219 = (*GLK* iii.316.13–15); cf. 17.102 = *GLK* iii.163.1–5.

THE MODERN POSITION

Nowadays when we want to know about grecism, we turn to grammars and to special studies, particularly those of Brenous (1895), Löfstedt (1933) and, for Virgil, the special studies of Lohmann (1915) and of Görler (1985). We now also have a critical survey of the whole topic by Coleman (1977). Despite differences over details, we encounter in them a measure of unanimity about the approaches to be taken. There lies behind all of them a considerable amount of theorizing about the genesis of the phenomenon and a desire to categorize the manifold instances. At the end of his essay on the Greek influence on Latin syntax Coleman (1977: 147), for instance, concluded that 'grecism must be recognized not as a sharply differentiated monolithic category but as a spectrum comprising greater or lesser degrees of abnormality'. (The contemporary model reflects at some remove the first work dedicated to grecism, Vechner (1610). Vechner's approach too was largely theoretical, and he relied only occasionally on ancient comment.) The modern taxonomists have carefully laid out the systematic beds in which our exotics bloom. Some are seen as direct transplants, full-scale grecisms, for instance the 'accusativus Graecus' (or some of its manifestations at any rate). Others are treated as hybrids, created either by developing a peculiar, but still native growth, or by a foreign graft upon a Latin stock; these latter are called 'partial grecisms' (a concept owed to Löfstedt (1933: 410) and (1959: 93)). In either case it is apparently assumed that the process works by analogy. It is with this concept of analogy that I want to deal first.

ANALOGY

Many modern philologists explain the origin of unusual syntactical usages by a process of analogy to some related feature of the language. This approach looks at first sight plausible, but its applicability to grecism is less clear cut. Of course, within the Latin language we can detect analogy at work on syntax. But even then we expect a measure of difference between what ordinary Romans said, and what the poets chose to write. For example, Professor Adams draws attention to *adiuto* used exceptionally with the dative in the speech of a freedwoman in Petronius (62.11) and in a letter of Claudius Terentianus. Latin-speakers of little sophistication obviously borrowed the syntax from intransitive verbs of helping for one which was normally transitive. Such a practice was no doubt common, but also largely unconscious. We would, however, not assume that Ovid was as unaware of what he was doing when he wrote at *Met.* 8.215 *damnosasque erudit artis* ('Daedalus *taught* Icarus the devilish skills'). He could have used the metrically equivalent *edocet*, and produced normal syntax, but preferred something unusual. It must be stressed that the poet's analogical procedure was deliberate and that the newly minted syntax of *edoceo* never became current (in the way that *adiuto* with the dative appears to have been colloquial); it remained purely artificial and cropped up again only in later poets, who of course imitated Ovid as a master of the language (Val. Flac. 2.50 and Stat. *Theb.* 10.507). Let us now look at some of the grecisms attributed in modern studies to analogical development within Latin. We will begin with the passages referred to by Quintilian, and then notice some others.

ANALOGY WITHIN LATIN

1(i) On the Horatian example in Quintilian (cf. p. 161): Coleman (1977: 137), noting the low genre, urged that the homely context — the fable of the mice — suggested that the genitive with *inuideo* could be seen as an extension of the native use of *dare* or *sumere* + genitive, which is especially characteristic of colloquial Latin. He was aware of Quintilian's view, but he did not comment upon it, either to accept it or reject it. This evenhandedness leaves us to follow the ancient or the modern account *ad libitum*. But we surely end up with a different view of Horace's verbal mastery if we decide either that he wrenched the language into an unexampled direction, or gently nudged it along a line which it was anyway pursuing.

Horace's great modern commentator Paul Lejay, however, was more decisive. Albeit in his note ad loc. he quoted Quintilian, yet he denied that the genitive with *inuideo* was a grecism; he saw in it rather a recovery of an older usage of the genitive with words meaning fullness or privation. This approach somewhat mitigates the freakishness of the syntax, its experimental quality, by an appeal to allegedly similar, but normal usages, particularly in the older language. What the modern philologist failed to reckon with, however, was the difficulty that any Roman had in recovering older practice reliably. One example will suffice to illustrate their help-lessness.

As was noted at the outset, Quintilian exemplified the concept of *figura* by drawing attention to the use of cases with *plenus* (*Inst.* 9.3.1), and he clearly believed that the genitive was alone found in older authors, down to Cicero, and that the use of the ablative had developed in his own day. We, however, can check in a moment a comprehensive grammar (e.g. K–S i.386) or dictionary or authoritative commentary to learn that the ablative is certainly found, albeit rarely, in late republican prose writers, Cicero and Caesar included. Ancient discussions of usage were bedevilled by the lack of comprehensive information retrieval systems. We need to bear this in mind when we detect archaism at work; we must ask what chance the Roman had of securing the information we command so readily. We have seen (p. 167 above) that the Servian scholia offered archaism as an alternative explanation of *precor* governing the dative, so the strategy adopted by modern philology was up to a point available to an ancient commentator, but his difficulties in deploying it were considerable (that particular defence was misconceived: old Latin *precor* + dative meant 'pray for').

1(ii)   Horace's use of *regno* (cf. p. 162) has prompted debate among philologists, adjudicated by Löfstedt (1933: 416). He was disinclined to follow those who looked for motivation for the usage in analogy, e.g. with *potior*. He followed most others in the view that this is a pure grecism, < βασιλεύω. Neither he nor more recently Coleman (1977: 141–2) cited the opinion of Servius, but they might well have started with him.

2   On one Virgilian example in Quintilian (cf. p. 161) everyone agrees that *saucius pectus* is a pure grecism. Brenous (1895) failed to draw attention to Quintilian or Servius in discussing *nauigat aequor* (Lohmann, however, did (1915: 22)). When we turn to an eminent contemporary student of Virgil's syntax, Woldemar Görler (1982: 71), we find a different approach. He began his valuable discussion of 'displacements' in Virgilian syntax with this very line, but chose not to notice Quintilian's use of it to illustrate grecism[40] and, albeit admitting that *Od.* 3.71 πλεῖθ᾽ ὑγρὰ κέλευθα was perhaps a model, he was at one time disinclined to agree with Servius that this is a 'real' grecism. It may be urged, however, that we are not here trying to establish a matter of fact. We cannot know by what mental process a poet came to choose an abnormal form of expression or how he would have defended his practice, but we can establish how his readers did so on his behalf. Servius and Quintilian knew that Virgil's usage was strange because it is not what 'we [Romans] say'; to account for this (since solecism in a classic writer was unthinkable) they explained it as a figurative form of writing, and they looked to Greek for a model. Görler, on the other hand, sees it as another instance of the transitivization of intransitive verbs (which is indeed a phenomenon of Augustan verse). But this leaves explanation at half-cock. We still wonder why the poets should have taken it upon themselves to treat the native verbs in this way.

3   *do* + infinitive (cf. pp. 165–6). Some philologists look for a native Latin idiom that might prepare the ground for the extended usage of the

---

[40] Later (1985: 267) he did so, though it is not clear if this in any way altered his earlier argument.

poets, and our grammars find it in *da bibere*, which is claimed to be purely Latin and is seen as providing the springboard (so, e.g. Hofmann–Szantyr (1965: 345)). On the other hand, Heraeus (1937: 195–6 n. 3.) reckoned that the view of the Roman grammarians themselves that *da bibere* was a grecism was not without merit, and he drew attention to what Servius said on *A.* 1.319.[41] Coleman (1977: 135) too refers with approval to his doctrine.

4   Verbs of fighting + dative (cf. pp. 167–8 above): Lohmann (1915: 53), who as usual noted earlier Latin usage that to his mind paved the way to Virgil's own, none the less ignored Porfyrio and Servius. Similarly in his commentary on *E.* 5.8 *tibi certat* Coleman betrayed the modern preference for explanation by analogy, for he drew attention to the syntax of *resisto*, which normally governs the dative. He also fairly acknowledged that *tibi certat* might be a grecism.[42] More reductive and indeed circular is the note of Wendell Clausen, who in his recent commentary on the *Eclogues* (Oxford, 1994) did not draw attention to Greek usage at all, but appealed to analogy with *contendo* at Lucretius 3.5–6 and to *pugno* at Catullus 62.64. Yet these verbs only take the dative in Latin as a grecism! His additional reference to Kühner–Stegmann's grammar goes some way to alerting the industrious reader to the borrowed syntax, but his note showed no interest in the phenomenon, and only put back a generation the basic question why Virgil should have altered the native syntax. The 'analogous' syntax which Clausen cited is itself abnormal and needs an explanation.

Ronconi (1971: 158) sought to diminish the audacity of Catullus 62.64 *noli pugnare duobus* by appealing to vaguely similar uses of the dative in Plautus.[43] His blind spot was *parti pris*. He decided in advance that grecism was inappropriate to a less formal genre like the wedding song, and so he resolved to dilute any apparent examples. But as we have seen, this particular syntax is found in the colloquial satires of Horace at 1.2.73 and the 'humble' pastorals of Virgil.

5   *diues* + genitive (cf. p. 169 above). Görler (1985: 266) refers to Diomedes (without comment) but also looks for analogy in the syntax of *plenus*. We are here given alternative explanations, but it should be noted that the concept of analogy employed here had not been formulated in antiquity; it was not an available account (though paradoxically this does not mean that they did not use it unconsciously). This will be discussed further below.

---

[41] Servius none the less presents his information somewhat glibly; he knew that a number of verbs take a complementary infinitive in prose.

[42] But later Coleman (1977: 138) cited Servian doctrine and revised his statement on the passage in the *Eclogues*.

[43] *Bacch.* 967, *Trin.* 838 (cf. Brenous (1895: 146)).

6 *indignus* + genitive (cf. p. 167 above). Wölfflin (1882: 114), followed by Lohmann (1915: 46), would have none of Servius' explanation, because *dignus* already took the genitive in Latin and so in their opinion this usage must be produced by analogy. They never thought, however, that Servius might have been ignorant of the usage, since it occurs very rarely (K–S i.398–9), and not at all in educated writing.

7 A larger problem with the modern analogical model should be remarked. Any claim that analogy was the agent or catalyst of syntactical borrowing needs scrutinizing. Let us consider for instance the treatment of *A.* 2.10 *sed si tantus amor casus cognoscere nostros.* Of the syntax of *amor* and the infinitive Servius said: *cognoscendorum casuum et Graeca figura est.* The construction first appears here; more instances are listed, but without comment or reference to Servius, in *TLL* ii.1969.83–1970.8.[44] Austin ad loc. fails to notice Servius, and explains: 'the infinitive is used as if a verb of desiring had preceded'. He offers what he regards as similar constructions, e.g. *est lubido* as the equivalent of *libet*, and *pudor est* of *pudet*. He concludes: 'no doubt this helped towards a natural [NB] development of the construction'. He was, however, too astute a Latinist to say that this case was devised as if *amo* itself had preceded. For the construction of *amo* with the infinitive was not native to Latin but borrowed, hence his vague reference to '*a* verb of desiring'. It is of course quite different with *studium* + infinitive at *G.* 1.21 *studium quibus arua tueri*, because *studeo* naturally takes the infinitive in Latin, and the expression is no more than a periphrasis, the equivalet of *qui student* (a form of the verb which cannot appear in hexameters unless the poet is prepared not to lengthen the necessary short vowel before st). This holds for a number of his examples: they are substantival periphrases for common verbal constructions, which is not true of the case at issue, *amor* + infinitive. So the analogical model is here insufficiently cogent. Servius seems correct in identifying this instance as a grecism, for ἔρως was constructed with the infinitive; to him there was nothing 'natural' about it, it was best accounted for as a figure and borrowed from Greek. This example demonstrates the ease with which a modern philologist appeals to analogy, but analysis of the process shows up weak links in the chain of argument.

---

[44] Hofmann–Szantyr (1965: 351) do not refer to this example nor to Servius, but classify *amor habet* + infin. at *A.* 12.282 as an instance of not so much the noun, as the whole idea which it represents as governing an infinitive.

PARTIAL GRECISM

Modern philology generally assents to the view that the construction of *nuda genu* (*A.* 1.320) is not native, and the practice is identified as the 'accusativus Graecus'. The assent, however, is sometimes qualified, and refinements of this analysis should now be considered.

Löfstedt (1959: 94) called this phenomenon a 'partial grecism', because he saw it as an extension of native Latin syntax, a view shared by Palmer, who reckoned that here 'Greek stimulated a native Latin usage' (1954: 289). In discussing Horace's use of the genitive with *inuideo* Löfstedt (1933: 416–7) referred to Quintilian's use of the expression as an instance of grecism, but he nevertheless preferred to regard it as only 'partial', since he reckoned that it recovered an older, partitive usage of the case; he is followed by the *Thesaurus*, vii.2.195.16.[45] This may be a fair description of the process that went on in the writer's unconscious (something about which we can only speculate), but the distinction between whole and partial grecisms was clearly unavailable to native readers like Quintilian and Servius (and so presumably to the poets themselves); to them this syntax was unmitigatedly foreign in feel. Servius, to be more precise, drew attention to the formal difference from a more widespread (but still poetic) use of the accusative with the past participle passive,[46] which he still noted on 1.228 *oculos suffusa nitentes* simply as a figure. Löfstedt's attempt to refine analysis betrays the historical approach of the modern philologist and raises the question of the role of such analysis in the assessment of the phenomenon.[47] It also raises a further problem: the philologists who employ the notion of syntactical analogy do not explain how it came into operation across a linguistic divide. Analogy, whether unconscious or deliberate, may operate easily enough *within* a language. But how is it

---

[45] But one of Löfstedt's examples of this old, unusual partitive genitive, Enn. *Ann.* 235 V., was impugned by O. Skutsch in *Studia Enniana* (London, 1968), 95 (and he has maintained his opinion in his n. on *Ann.* 270 Sk.).

[46] His note on *A.* 1.320 concluded: *quamuis ad unam significationem recurrant* 'they come to the same thing'. What this means is shown in his glosses, for he regularly paraphrases both expressions with *habens*, e.g. on 1.228 *nitidos oculos lacrimis perfusos habens*. So one usage is clearly Greek to him, the other simply figurative, and no attempt is made to trace its origins. On the other hand when we reach 12.5 Servius glosses, as we have seen, in the usual way: *saucium pectus habens* but DServius adds: *ut 'nudatosque umeros oleo perfusa nitescit'* [= *A.* 5.135], which rather overrides the distinction set up on 1.228. The blurred distinction is followed by Lactantius on Statius; cf. his notes on *Th.* 2.506 *erecta genas: erectas genas habens* and on 4.365 *ora deformis: deformia ora habens*.

[47] For analysis of aspects of the usage and a general bibliography on the 'accusatiuus graecus' see Harrison on *Aen.* 10, pp. 290–1. It is worth pointing out that Landgraf (1898: 209) is mistaken when he gives as the earliest occurrence Plautus, *Pseud.* 785: *qui* is ablative there and *manus* nominative.

supposed to work *across* languages? It seems to be accounted for by the bilingualism of the Romans, or at any rate some of them. This issue must be briefly — and inexpertly — noticed here.

BILINGUALISM

Both Brenous (1895) and Coleman (1977) provide at the outset of their discussions theoretical expositions of how linguistic borrowings take place in societies. Brenous offered over forty pages of introduction on the progress of linguistic exchange in the European vernaculars before he turned to the application of his theory to Latin (1895: 45). He drew attention to the tendency to bilingualism in Roman education and to the cultural cross-fertilization in much of Italy, which even prompted some Romans to write in Greek. The most important section of his introduction is the last, in which he set out his system for analysing the phenomena, at the same time answering possible objections to his method (1895: 58–81, résumé: 77–81). Coleman's approach is more schematic but at bottom no different; he discusses first the principles of linguistic interaction and then applies them to Latin (1977: 101–4).

Since Brenous's time there have been many studies of the phenomenon of bilingualism among speakers of modern vernaculars.[48] One conclusion seems to have commanded until recently general assent, and it checks a too ready assumption that syntactical interference whether generated by analogy or otherwise occurs. Susan Romaine (1995: 64) noted that, compared to borrowings of vocabulary, 'syntax has often been thought to be the least easily diffused aspect of language'. If this observation holds good it has a particular bearing upon our study of syntactical, rather than lexical, grecism. But Romaine goes on to draw attention to evidence which might weaken the common view. The work of C. Myers-Scotton (1993) presents an alternative model, which is avowedly speculative.[49] It would be impertinence in me to pronounce upon the success of her hypotheses. But even granting that the view that syntactical interference between languages spoken by bilinguals is more common than has been allowed, the convertibility of the hypothesis to the sort of Latin we are here concerned with is questionable. It is remarkable that studies of bilingualism focus upon speech or conversation, not formal writing. Moreover the speakers whose practice is recorded and analysed are often children or those with little

---

[48] Professor Adams's considerable advice has much improved this discussion.

[49] Myers-Scotton (1993: 208, 228), esp. ch. 7 'Codeswitching and Deep Grammatical Borrowing'.

education (Myers-Scotton studied pidgin and creole, and an East African spoken language, Ma). We should also bear in mind the comparatively straightforward syntax of modern vernaculars. There is on the other hand evidence to confirm the commonly held view referred to by Romaine. P. Gardner-Chloros (1991: 153–4) noted the skill with which bilinguals generally manage to avoid syntactical conflict in conversation and to preserve the syntax appropriate to one language or the other; she also analysed several conversations, and noted that in spite of their frequency 'cases where switching leads to syntactic infelicities', i.e. interference, remained rare. For all these reasons we should be disinclined to attribute syntactical grecism in the Latin poets to the fact that élite Romans were bilinguals. When they came to write their language (as opposed to speaking it) they could easily check interference from Greek; grecisms are not found in the speeches of Cicero, for instance, and Quintilian, as we noted earlier, hints that they will be avoided in oratory. Moreover, if such syntactical interference was common at lower levels of society, the élite would be the more determined to avoid it, especially since they insisted upon purity of Latin (*Latinitas*), and regarded solecisms as stylistic blemishes.

If bilingualism by itself cannot facilitate the use of an analogical model to explain syntactical interference among élite speakers and writers, we are left with a fundamental problem: how does linguistic analogy produce syntactical interference *across* languages? The only answer is that it does not of itself. There must still be in formal, written language the element of deliberation. A Roman poet consciously departed from the norm, and knew that his practice would be scrutinized or even mocked if a reader failed to see any justification; recall Numitorius' parody of a usage in Virgil's *Eclogues* recorded by Suetonius in his life of the poet, section 43: *Dic mihi, Damoeta: 'cuium pecus' anne Latinum?* A writer had to be ready and able to justify his procedure. Now this brings us to a final problem with the modern use of the term analogy.

The Romans too had the term *analogia*, but used it to explain morphological, not syntactical, practice. They had no terms in use (to my knowledge) which would serve to explain our concept of 'syntactical analogy'. It may be that the closest ancient students of Latin came to it was simple comparison. For an example, let us return to the use of *tenus* with a genitive (discussed on pp. 168–9 above). Servius on *G.* 3.53 referred — perhaps in paraphrase — to the view of Modestus:[50] *tenus pro fine ut Sallustius 'fine inguinum ingrediuntur mare'*. Does *pro* here imply something more than simple substitution or comparison? Is it what modern

---

[50] He may have been Iulius Modestus, the freedman of Hyginus, who lived under Tiberius; see *RE* x.1.680–1.

grammars mean by 'analogy'? Hofmann–Szantyr (1965: 268) (following the more hesitant Wackernagel (1928: ii.164)) say that the genitive with *tenus* 'folgt dem von *fini*'. This is a matter for further investigation, but my belief is that the Romans lacked the concept altogether. How they explained analogical practice in their own language (for it surely occurred, as we have seen) is a mystery. But if a grammarian or rhetorician, whose business it was to account for the language of the poets and historians, could not expound a principle of grammatical analogy similar to ours, then it is not too much to assume that the poets who generated the syntax were no more likely to think in our terms of what they were doing. Certainly, once the explanation provided by *figura Graeca* was available, it will have sufficed all who needed to explain or justify poetic practice, including the poets themselves.

It is time to draw the threads together and offer a conclusion. The modern approach to grecism is largely historical and grammatical. We appeal to linguistic processes founded on analogy, without establishing how they might operate between the syntaxes of different languages. In effect we also diminish the deliberately artistic effect sought by poets in their use of language. When we turn to antiquity we find a rhetorical description, *Graeca figura*, which falls within the grammatical category (according to Quintilian). *figura* indicates that we are dealing with a departure from the norm of the spoken and written language, one which serves above all as an ornament of style. The usages grouped under this head are comprehensive, the syntax of nouns, verbs and adjectives being all ranged together under it. *Graeca* too pulls its weight and provides an aetiology of the figure; it draws attention, as our grammatical terminology rarely does, to the origin of the ornament, imitation of the Greek. This hints at a satisfactory account of how poets actually work, for it suggests something conscious, which our appeal to analogy or to the partial grecism does not. Latin poets knew and admired the Greek language and literature; some may even have believed with Varro that Latin was a dialect of Greek and that in borrowing from the older language they were recovering their birthright. But even without endorsing that extreme position, it is demonstrable that the Roman poet, bred in the tradition of *imitatio*, kept his eye on Greek for his themes and literary forms; the use of his native language was also influenced by the admired literary culture of Greece. The Romans themselves did not refine upon their understanding of syntactical imitation and look for analogies closer to home. The *Graeca figura* always remained an exotic, so much so that sometimes it was removed by normalization from the text. I would not urge that we reformulate or abandon all that has been said in accounting for aberrant syntax in the poets. But we ought to resensitize ourselves to the artistry that lies behind the use of grecism. Our grammatical categories somewhat deaden our response; they suggest gradual, even unconscious development, rather than deliberate poetic invention. Analogy cannot account for a poet's mastering of his medium. We need to bear constantly in mind the sense the ancient readers had about those aspects of poetic manipulation of the language which produced a sort of 'Sondersprach'. Grecism was an important element in the process.

Modern analyses fall short in their failure to draw sustained attention to the doctrine of antiquity on grecism. The doctrine is after all Roman in origin and it ought to be our first business to understand what Romans thought constituted the phenomenon. The modern philologist may well decide that the Roman approach is incomplete or even deeply flawed. We might compare the Romans' understanding of etymology. Their bogus etymologies cannot compare with the altogether more securely founded knowledge of the modern day. But, however faulty the etymologies of antiquity may prove to be, it is undeniable that many ancient poets believed them to be true, and indulged themselves in word play founded upon the erroneous doctrine. For example, the second-century BC writer of the epitaph with the famous word-play in its second line, *hic est sepulcrum hau pulcrum pulcrai feminae* (*ILS* 8403, *CIL* i².1211, vi.15346 add. p. 3517, *CE* 52), probably did not know that the 'se' of *sepulcrum* was not a prefix, nor that it could not be derived from the long vowel in *sed*, used in compounds like *segrego*, *secerno*, etc. But if we insist on the true etymology, we will never appreciate his punning *figura etymolgica*. Nor will we grasp why Cicero styled the hare, *lepus*, at *Arat.* 121 *leuipes*, unless we know the (false) etymology.[51] Appreciation of the sometimes misconceived learning of antiquity, and its application to poetic composition does not necessarily entail the overthrow or rejection of what modern research has achieved. We must face the fact that what we know (or believe) was not available to the Roman poet or to his readers. What they thought was true (however false it appears to us) has its own historical validity. We need to bifocalize our knowledge, and create within ourselves a dual sensibility in order to appreciate some aspects of ancient poetry.

---

[51] See Colson on Quint. *Inst.* 1.6.33.

APPENDIX I

In this appendix are collected together the remaining references in the scholiasts to grecism.

(i) *A.* 1.41 *Aiacis Oilei.* Servius feels this is a grecism (<*Il.* 2.527), *Il.* 2.527), but it seems to be common: K–S i.414.

(ii) *A.* 1.669 *nota tibi.* Servius calls it a *Graeca figura* and refers to Ter. *Eun.* 288, where Donatus, after observing *mira pro mirum*, repays the compliment by referring to Virgil. See Austin ad loc. and Löfstedt (1942: 63ff.); it is not noticed by Lohmann (1915) or Görler (1985: 270).

(iii) *A.* 3.594 *cetera Graius.* Servius: *sane . . . Graeca locutio est*, a view approved by Wölfflin (1885: 90; he notes on 93 that this is the first time it is used with a noun). The usage is not uncommon, and appears first in Sallust, then the historians; see Williams ad loc. and Austin on *A.* 4.558.

(iv) *A.* 4.35, 10.67 *esto.* Servius regards it as a grecism when used as an 'adverbium concedentis'.

(v) *A.* 6.313 *primi transmittere.* Servius: *ut primi transmitterent, figura Graeca est.*

(vi) On *iuro* Servius holds two views: the simple accusative at *A.* 6.351 *maria aspera iuro* (cf. 6.324) he regarded as a *Graeca figura* in his note on 1.67, but as an archaism in his note to *A.* 12.197. (Cf. his note on *A.* 8.127 *cui . . . precari* discussed on pp. 166–7 above.) The latter account is plausible, see K–S i.264, and ii.633.

(vii) *A.* 8.676 *cernere erat.* Servius specifies *Graeca figura*; Görler (1985: 271) is aware of the view of Servius, but denies that the usage is primarily a grecism; Wölfflin (1885: 135–6), however, agrees with the ancient view. Cf. Lohmann (1915: 83), K–S i. 669d, Hofmann–Szantyr (1965: 349), *OLD* 9. This is another instance of a calque generating a new construction, cf. *amare* = φιλεῖν in Sallust (p. 161 above).

(viii) *A.* 11.416 *fortunatusque laborum.* Servius: *sicut* {11.73 *laeta laborum*} *et est Graecum.* The use is picked up by St. *Th.* 1.638.

APPENDIX II

In this appendix are brought together some observations of Servius' which seem to be contradictory or mistaken or confused, but none the less illustrate a readiness to see a poetic usage as an imitation of the Greek.

(i) Servius says on *A.* 2.247 *non umquam* that a double negative such as is found at Ter. *Hau.* 63 is employed *Graeco more.* He does not call it a *figura.* It appears, however, to be native to both tongues (K–S i.827–8, Roby §2246).

(ii)   On A. 3.501 Servius tries to justify the reading *Hesperia* by taking it closely with *Dardanus* as if it = Ἑσπερόθεν: *nam Graece dixit, et est de loco aduerbium*. This destroys the run of the passage entirely and is not to be countenanced. Once again, however, he does not call it a figure; when he uses the adverb *Graece*, he usually means that the poet is borrowing the word directly from the other language.

(iii)   On A. 12.680 *furere furorem* Servius says *figura antiqua ut 'serui-tutem seruit', 'dolet dolorem'* (that is to say, he regards it as an archaism) but on A. 2.53 *cauae . . . cauernae* he notices the *figura etymologica* as a *Graeca figura* and compares *uitam uiuere* or *mortem mori* (the latter an unexpectedly biblical phrase, cf. *TLL* viii.1493.25–32). The etymological figure was perhaps less common in Latin than in Greek, but was hardly borrowed. Servius' note on A. 12.680 therefore seems to be more judicious and finds support from Quintilian, *Inst.* 7.3.26. See Lohmann (1915: 25–7), Görler (1985: 276).

(iv)   What is DServius explaining on A. 12.568 *ni frenum accipere et uicti parere fatentur: et quidam hunc uersum per figuram Graecam dictum tradunt* ὁμολογοῦσιν μέλλειν λαβεῖν? Is it the meaning of *fateor* 'consent' (*OLD* 3) or the tense of the infinitive (or these combined; see Fordyce on A. 7.433 *parere fatetur*)?

Proceedings of the British Academy, **93**, 183–225

The Language of Poetry and the Language of Science: The Latin Poets and 'Medical Latin'

D. R. LANGSLOW

Summary. This paper is intended as a pilot study of the relations between literary, especially poetic, language and technical/special languages in Latin. After an introductory description (**I**) of some existing work on this subject in Greek literature, it offers (**II**) some general observations on the use of technical vocabulary in Latin poetry, both *sensu proprio* and in metaphor, drawing examples for the most part from the field of medicine. It is suggested that the literary use and avoidance of technical vocabulary of different kinds may be a useful critical tool for characterizing poems, poets, genres, traditions. The general hypothesis is developed that in a live metaphor drawn from a technical activity the vocabulary used will usually be authentic, current *uocabula propria*. This would allow a live literary metaphor to serve as linguistic evidence for ordinary technical vocabulary of the period; conversely, attention to known special vocabulary can sharpen appreciation of poetic imagery, even unearth unsuspected metaphors. In the last part (**III**), from a series of examples of the metaphorical use by Latin poets of medical vocabulary, I suggest some possible results, of sociolinguistic and historical interest, of making systematic comparison between literary and technical texts.[1]

[1] I should like to thank Professor Adams and Professor Mayer for their invitation to contribute to this Symposium. This paper profited from discussion both at the Symposium itself and at a meeting of the North-East Classical Research Seminar (NECROS) in Newcastle-upon-Tyne in May, 1996. For information and comments, and for help of various sorts, I am indebted and grateful particularly to K.-D. Fischer, R. K. Gibson, S. J. Harrison, A. Kerkhecker, V. Langholf, A. K. Langslow, R. C. T. Parker, J. H. W. Penney and M. D. Reeve.

I. GREEK POETRY AND SCIENCE

(1) Homer

I BEGIN WITH the Greeks in general because their literature gives some well-known examples of the sorts of contact that may occur between poetry and science; and with Homer in particular both because Homeric language appears to have been of long-lasting relevance in the Greek medical tradition and because, if there may be a trace of poetic colour or even of an analogous tradition in Latin medical literature, then this Homerizing tradition in Greek medical prose deserves to be borne in mind as a possible model.

In the final chapter of *Homerische Wörter* (1950: 308–15), Manu Leumann observed a number of words which occur in the Greek record only — or almost exclusively — in Homer and the Hippocratic corpus. These include both 'homerische Wörter', in Leumann's special sense,[2] such as καταπρηνής[3] 'with the palm down', and other items of Homeric vocabulary, such as the notorious λίπ' [ἐλαίῳ][4] or the temporal conjunction ἦμος used for specifying the time of day, especially sunrise or sunset.[5] Leumann's other examples include: ἄρμενον 'fitted' (Homer) — 'tool' (Hippocrates), γυιόω 'make lame' (Hom.) — 'weaken, reduce' (Hp.), ἐνδυκέως 'carefully' (Hom.) — 'continually' (Hp.), ἰχώρ 'gods' blood' (Hom.) — 'a serous discharge' (Hp.), ὠτειλή 'wound' (Hom.) — 'scar, cicatrization' (Hp.), and a further nineteen words of which he is prepared to venture the same account.

Leumann was in no doubt that these (near-)exclusive agreements in vocabulary reflected a conscious use of epic language by writers of medical prose. He suggested that the Hippocratic writers may have used Homeric words not purely on stylistic grounds but also because of the need to

---

A near-final draft was read by J. N. Adams, D. M. Bain, G. O. Hutchinson, R. G. Mayer and G. D. Williams and has benefited greatly from their perceptive and learned criticism. I should like publicly to thank them for the generous gift of their time and care, and to exonerate them from any responsibility for what follows.

[2] That is, a new word or a new meaning which arises within the bardic tradition by reinterpretation of an earlier form or forms.

[3] Supposedly from κατά in tmesis + adjacent πρηνής. See Leumann (1950: 77–9). So, e.g., *Il.* 16.792 [Ares strikes Patroclus] χειρὶ καταπρηνεῖ. Cf. Hp. *Fract.* 2, 40 [= 3.418, 546 Littré]; *Off.* 4 [= 3.286L] καταπρηνής 'with the palm down'.

[4] *Il.* 10.577, al. ἀλείψασθαι λίπ' ἐλαίῳ, *Od.* 3.466, al. ἔχρισεν λίπ' ἐλαίῳ Cf. Hp. *Mul.* 2.150 [= 8.326L] μύρῳ ... ἀλειφέσθω λίπα, *Mul.* 1.35 [= 8.84L] χρίεσθαι λίπα (apparently adverbial), *Mul.* 2.133 [= 8.288L] χρίσμα δὲ λίπα ἔστω (cf. 145, 147 [= 8.322, 324L]; apparently an indeclinable adjective).

[5] *Il.* 1.475, al. ἦμος δ' ἠέλιος κατέδυ. Cf. Hp. *Mul.* 1.23 [= 8.62L] ἦμος ἥλιος δύνῃ, *Prorrh.* 2.4 [= 9.14L] ἦμος ἠέλιος νεωστὶ καταλάμπει.

supply vocabulary for the new technical language of medicine, 'das Ausdrücksbedürfnis einer neu aufkommenden Fachsprache' (1950: 315).

Leumann himself admitted that all these words are difficult and certainly they seem to be of variable quality as evidence of a relation of dependence of Hippocrates on Homer. 'Homerische Wörter' proper (see n. 2) are probably the best witnesses on this side, but some other individual words — perhaps most famously ἰχώρ (Jouanna and Demont (1981)) — have been challenged as being of no value at all for such an inference. And already in 1957 more general doubts were voiced by C. J. Ruijgh (1957: 85–6), who raised the question whether the 'traits épiques' in Hippocrates (and Herodotus, too; cf. Leumann (1950: 303–8)) should not be explained rather as 'réminiscences de la poésie dactylique', that is, as deriving not directly from Homer but from an intermediate didactic source in epic verse, such as that of the Χίρωνος ὑποθῆκαι, or Καθαρμοί of the Περὶ φύσιος of Empedocles.[6] Indeed, an instance of lexical borrowing by medicine from poetry had been proposed earlier (E. Schwyzer in Deichgräber (1935: 95)) on the basis of an agreement between Hippocrates and Empedocles in the use of the verb ἀΐσσω (ἀΐσσομαι) of the orientation of body parts.[7]

(2) Tragedy

A Leumann-type view of poetic words in technical prose has been taken also of exclusive lexical agreements between Hippocratic writings and Athenian tragedy. Examples include: ἀλέξημα 'defence' and 'remedy', ἀνθέω 'to flower' and 'to become acute', οὐκ ἀτρεμαῖοι and πλάνοι 'deranged, disturbed', πλημμυρίς 'flood tide' and 'congestion of fluid'; some non-

---

[6] On which see Schmid–Stählin (1929: 287–8, 318–9). Contrast van Brock's view (1961: 103–4 n. 8): 'je crois que les "traits épiques" de la langue médicale sont tout simplement des homérismes'. Deichgräber's important chapter (1971: 19–29) on Homer, Hippocrates and Aretaeus modifies and refines but essentially upholds Leumann's position (cf. (4) below).

[7] Emp. B 29.1D–K. Hp. Carn. 5.3 [= 8.590L], Epid. 2.4.1 [= 5.122L]. Cf. also Hes. Th. 150 and Il. 23.627f. Ancient associations of Empedocles with Homeric language and medicine include: D.L. 8.57 (Aristotle says that καὶ Ὁμηρικὸς ὁ Ἐμπεδοκλῆς καὶ δεινὸς περὶ τὴν φράσιν γέγονεν), 8.77 (he wrote an ἰατρικὸς λόγος in 600 hexameters); Gal. 10.6 Kühn (De methodo medendi 1.1; he is one of 'the doctors from Italy'). The Suda (Hsch. Mil.) characterizes Empedocles as ... φιλόσοφος φυσικὸς καὶ ἐποποιός but notes also that he wrote ἰατρικὰ καταλογάδην. Cf. also Arist. Po. 1447b16–18 (Homer and Empedocles have nothing in common except their metre). Bollack (1965–69: I.277ff.) is important on Empedocles and Homeric language and technique; note especially p. 283: 'Les éléments de son art [Empedocles'] proviennent de l'atelier des rhapsodes', and ibid. n. 5: 'Empédocle emploie, et crée sans doute souvent, des mots homériques dans l'acception que M. Leumann a donnée à ce terme'. See now, on Empedocles and Homer, Kingsley (1995: 42ff., 52f.). I owe the last reference to D. M. Bain.

technical vocabulary with the same distribution has also been noticed, such as: δνοφερός 'dark, murky', παραμπέχεσθαι 'to use a cloak of words' and ἐκ νυκτῶν 'after nightfall'. (For references, further examples and discussion see Lanata (1968).)

In such cases it has been inferred by some scholars that the writers of the relatively young scientific prose were borrowing expressive means from literary genres of more solid tradition (Lanata (1968: 30)). This is akin to Leumann's account (quoted above) of Homeric words in Hippocrates as serving both lexical need and stylistic ambition. The approach is in general complementary — if in the case of some words contradictory! — to earlier accounts of the use of technical terminology by the tragedians, which set up a relation of dependence running the other way (notably Dumortier (1935); Miller (1944; cf. 1945); Collinge (1962)). Others again (such as Page (1936), reviewing Dumortier (1935) and Jouanna (1970) reviewing Lanata (1968)[8]) have argued more or less forcefully that there is no relation of dependence either way, that poets and medical writers are drawing their words from the common language. The few generally acknowledged significant instances of agreement between technical vocabulary and tragedy, such as ἔμμοτος of a special kind of plug-dressing (A. *Ch.* 471; see Garvie (1986) ad loc. and on lines 185–6), σπασμός 'convulsion' (S. *Tr.* 805, 1082; see Easterling (1982: Index, *s.v.* 'medical language')) or μεγαλόσπλαγχνος 'with enlarged abdomen' (E. *Med.* 109 metaph.) imply that special and technical languages lend to rather than borrow from the language of tragedy.[9]

(3) Hellenistic Poetry

From Alexandria two centuries later, a third set of supposed contacts between science and (non-didactic) poetry has caught and held scholars' attention: this is 'the employment in poetry of science more as we understand the word nowadays, especially medicine' as part of the Alexandrian 'appeal to scientific and scholarly knowledge for realistic effect' (Zanker (1987: 113)).[10] It is suggested, for example, that the four-layered shield (as opposed to the seven-layered Homeric original at *Il.* 7.220, *al.*) to which

---

[8] Cf. *mutatis mutandis* the published discussions of Scherer (1963), esp. pp. 108–10 and of Dover (1963), esp. pp. 213–14. I owe this reference to Professor Bain.

[9] Although we do not know the *uox propria*, μονορρύθμους δόμους at A. *Supp.* 961 may be a precise, unmetaphorical designation of a type of terraced housing under construction in the Piraeus at the time. See Rösler (1989). I owe this reference to A. Kerkhecker.

[10] Cf. Zanker (1987: 124–7) for a descriptive summary, with further examples and references, and, for an instance involving astronomy, Hutchinson (1988: 221, n. 13).

Callimachus compares the Cyclops' eye in the hymn to Artemis (*Dian.* 53) is an allusion to the recent discovery, perhaps by Herophilus, of a fourth layer to the membranes of the human eye. Likewise the position in which Leto gives birth to Apollo and Artemis in Callimachus' hymn to Delos (*Del.* 206–11) is different from that described in the Homeric hymn to Apollo (*h.Ap.* 117–18) and may reflect contemporary obstetrics, again perhaps Herophilean.[11]

Apollonius of Rhodes is held to have achieved contemporary scientific colouring in some descriptive passages of the *Argonautica* by his anatomical precision and by his use of particular words and images. Passages such as the description of the effects of love on Medea's nerves (see Hunter (1989: ad loc.):

> A.R. 3.762–3   [sc. τεῖρ' ὀδύνη] ἀμφί τ' ἀραιὰς
> ἶνας καὶ κεφαλῆς ὑπὸ νείατον ἰνίον ἄχρις,

and of the death of Mopsos from the snake-bite (4.1521–31, including κερκίς 'tibia bone' and ἄφασσεν 'palpated') have been said to reflect knowledge of contemporary science and to presuppose not mere use of a medical glossary but 'eingehende Lektüre eines Spezialwerkes' (Erbse 1953: 190).

(4) Aretaeus

Finally — to end for present purposes in the early imperial period — it seems that a Homerizing tradition established itself in later Greek medical prose. If true, this will have been partly because medicine was closely linked with philology from Hellenistic times to late antiquity (see Wellmann (1931: 1, 58–62, 85) on Erotian; Brock (1961: 206, n. 1), with further literature), partly because of observed Homerisms in Hippocrates. This tradition is exceptionally well represented in Aretaeus of Cappadocia (first century AD: see Kudlien (1963)). He appeals to Homer as an authority (*SD* 1.5.2 [= 39,21 Hude] τέκμαρ δὲ Ὅμηρος); several times he works phrases or lines from the *Iliad* into his text (*SD* 2.13.2, 15 [= 85,24–8, 89,4–5H], *CA* 2.3.14 and 2.9.1 [= 129,15 and 138,25–6H]);[12] and frequently he uses further instances of Homeric vocabulary, such as ἄλκαρ 'remedy', ἠδέ

---

[11] On the uncertainty of the ascription of either of these doctrines to Herophilus, see von Staden (1989: 160–1 and 394–5), with further references.

[12] As other examples of Homer citations, Brock notes (1961: 104, n. 4) that Hp. *Art.* 8 [= 4.98L] includes an unknown line of Homer: ὡς δ' ὁπότ' ἀσπάσιον ἔαρ ἤλυθε βουσὶν ἑλιξιν, and that Galen quotes Hom. *Il.* 22.107 at *in Hp. Epid. 6 comm.* 4.10 (p. 203 Wenkebach). On these and other striking examples see Deichgräber (1971: 21ff.).

'and',[13] τηκεδών in the sense 'consumption', ἔμμεναι 'to be', and even ζωγρέω
in the sense 'restore, refresh', a 'homerisches Wort' not mentioned by
Leumann ((1950); see Janni (1967)) and features such as tmesis and
apocope (e.g. ἀμβολή), in his generally hyper-Ionic prose. (See Ruijgh
(1957: 85); Brock (1961: 103–4, 144, 198 ff.); Deichgräber (1971: 19–29).)

I shall say no more on Greek literature now, although I believe that
all of the issues alluded to in this introduction deserve renewed attention,
some work of synthesis and a general reassessment. The purpose of this
brief survey is to make clear that there is reason to believe that in the
Greek world at least from the fifth century BC there was a lively two-way
relationship between the language of poetry and the language of science,
and in particular a Homerizing tradition, direct or indirect, in medical
prose. The title of this paper, then, makes obvious sense for Greek literature; what of Latin?

II. SCIENTIFIC AND SPECIAL VOCABULARY IN LATIN POETRY

At first sight the presence in poetry of scientific and, more generally,
technical and special vocabulary is a promising topic for Latinists, too. It
is common to find in modern commentaries on the Latin poets references
to, say, 'the language of medicine' or 'the language of the law' as the
source of this word or that usage. Consider just two medical examples, to
which we shall have cause to return more than once: first, R. D. Brown's
comment on Lucretius' image of love as a disease:

> Lucr. 4.1068–72   ulcus enim uiuescit et inueterascit alendo
> inque dies gliscit furor atque aerumna grauescit,
> si non prima nouis conturbes uulnera plagis
> uulgiuagaque uagus uenere ante recentia cures
> aut alio possis animi traducere motus:

[With nourishment the festering sore quickens and grows chronic. Day by
day the frenzy heightens and the grief deepens. Your only remedy is to
lance the first wound with new incisions; to treat it in its early stages with
promiscuous attachments; to guide the motions of your mind into some
other channel, (transl. R. Latham, slightly modified).]

'for sheer concentration of imagery and intensity of language the passage
has few rivals among other ancient versions of the love-sickness theme; . . .
the -*sco* verbs of 1068f. . . . are probably chosen to mimic the drily accurate

---

[13] ἠδέ and ἄλκαρ are in Galen's *Hippocratic Glosses* (19.75.7 and 19.102.8K). I am grateful to
Professor Bain for this information. In using these words, then, Aretaeus may have been
following Hippocrates rather than Homer directly.

style of medical discourse' (Brown (1987: 209, 210)); and, second, Paolo Fedeli's note on these lines of Propertius:

> Prop. 1.1.25-7   aut uos, qui sero lapsum reuocatis, amici,
> quaerite non sani pectoris auxilia.
> fortiter et ferrum saeuos patiemur et ignes:

'AVXILIA: nel senso di *remedia* si tratta di un termine del linguaggio medico . . .; d'altronde anche *ferrum* ed *ignis* al v. 27 sono vocaboli del linguaggio medico' (Fedeli (1980: 83)).

While such isolated ascriptions are common in modern commentaries, it is much rarer to find a developed general account of poets' attitudes to, and use of, technical and special language;[14] it is rarer still to find in discussions of Latin special and technical languages any account at all of their occurrence in (non-didactic) poetic texts.[15] I offer now under these two headings some provisional observations and working hypotheses, in the belief that the use and avoidance by poets of special vocabulary may have much to teach us both about the poet and his work and about the terminology of the special subject or technical discipline in question.

(5) The use and avoidance of technical vocabulary *sensu proprio*

It is well known that some subjects are simply not admitted to high poetry. A good example is human anatomy in Virgil. Note the striking conclusions of J. N. Adams (1980b: 59): 'Virgil's men are anatomically shadowy. . . . They are without genitals and buttocks, and largely without internal organs. The nose is unmentionable, as is the hip and skin. In some cases the technical term for the body part seems to have been unpoetic (*coxa, nasus*). Certain areas, whatever the terminology available, were not considered fit to mention.'

Even if a subject is deemed acceptable, its proper vocabulary may not be admitted to a literary work. This applies to many subjects, including anatomy, pathology and parts of therapeutics, which concern us especially today, and particularly, though not only, to serious poetry. Even

---

[14] Mayer (1994) is one recent exception: see esp. pp. 17–18, 19–20 and Index, *s.vv.* 'legal terminology', 'medical analogy / terminology', 'technical terminology avoided'.

[15] The work of I. Mazzini on medicine in Latin poetry is an important exception, even though his concern is with medical *ideas*, rather than language. See Mazzini (1988) on Lucilius, Lucretius, Catullus and Horace; (1991a) on Horace; (1992a) on Plautus; and (1990) on the pathology of love, in Alfonso *et al.* (1990), to which Dr R. K. Gibson drew my attention. Note also Migliorini (1990) on medical terminology in Persius. Dr G. D. Williams alerted me to Menière (1858), a still useful collection of medical passages in Latin poetry from Ennius to Martial, though with little on the form of expression.

here, however, technical and special words are to be found *sensu proprio*, and I begin by mentioning some of the factors which favour their admission.

In an acceptable subject area, especially formally striking words may be admitted *sensu proprio*. Consider the following examples of special words, three from Propertius[16] and three from Lucan:

Prop. 3.12.12   ferreus aurato neu *cataphractus* equo [*scil.* laetetur tua caede]
Prop. 3.14.8   et patitur [*scil.* femina] duro uulnera *pancratio*[17]
Prop. 3.22.27   at non squamoso labuntur uentre *cerastae*[18]
Luc. 1.426   et docilis rector monstrati Belga *couinni*[19]
Luc. 3.222   nondum flumineas Memphis contexere *biblos*[20]
Luc. 10.318   excepere tuos [*scil.* lapsus, Nile,] et praecipites *cataractae*.

These instances illustrate well the fondness of special vocabulary for the end — more rarely the beginning — of the line;[21] the admission of the tetrasyllables at line-end (*pancratio* and *cataractae*) seems further to highlight the specialness of the vocabulary.[22] The examples from Lucan are from among those called 'technical terms' by Bramble (1982*b*: 541–42). Ideally, I think, one would draw a distinction between technical terms, which belong to a τέχνη, special words belonging to the language of a group, such as soldiers' language, and more or less isolated exotic words denoting items of foreign culture. Of the examples above, I suppose that *pancratium* (e.g.) is in principle a technical term of sport, while *cataracta* is an exotic word for a foreign object, but my remarks about form and line placement apply to all these words equally and, in their contexts, they all share a further artistic function, that of evoking a picture of an exotic world[23] rather than of a technical discipline. In other cases technical vocabulary may be used to evoke the associated special activity or field

---

[16] See Fedeli (1985: ad locc.); Tränkle (1960: 113, 122).

[17] Very rare in our Latin record, and only here in verse, but probably a familiar word given its metaphorical use already at Var. *Men.* 519.

[18] Recalling Virg. *G.* 2.153–4 'nec rapit immensos orbis per humum neque tanto | squameus in spiram tractu se colligit *anguis*', but bringing with *cerastae* a more exotic flavour. Lucan (9.716) and Statius (*Theb.* 11.65) follow suit, both at line-end, the latter with a Greek ending (*cerasten*).

[19] Possibly recalling Virg. *G.* 3.204 '*Belgica* uel molli melius feret *esseda* collo', but with a more exotic edge.

[20] Said to be the only occurrence of the word in Latin literature, but note the attractive proposal of R. G. M. Nisbet (1978: 96–7) to read *nouae bibli* at Catul. 22.6.

[21] In Prop. 3.14 evocative special words close also lines 1 (*palaestrae*), 2 (*gymnasii*), 6 (*trochi*) and 7 (*metas*); line 11 begins with *gyrum*.

[22] I owe this observation to G. O. Hutchinson.

[23] Compare D. N. Sedley's remarks in this volume, pp. 238–44, on Lucretius' use of Greek words in non-philosophical contexts for exotic authenticity. Professor Petersmann makes a similar observation on the effect of special vocabulary in Lucilius, in this volume, p. 301.

of knowledge. This is often so especially in didactic poetry. So, for instance, the exotic names of the examples chosen by Lucretius of strong-smelling substances are intended to suggest to the audience not their far-off place of origin but the stock-in-trade of the local *pharmacopola*:

> Lucr. 4.123–5   praeterea quaecumque suo de corpore odorem
> expirant acrem, *panaces absinthia* taetra
> *habrotoni*que graues et tristia *centaurea* . . .

Genre, too, is clearly highly relevant to the admission of technical vocabulary. The more conversational genres — comedy, satire and epigram — show apparently in their lower registers no constraints on the admission *sensu proprio* of banal technical vocabulary that is not to be found in epic (or, usually, in lyric or elegy), such as that relating to disease and its treatment; indeed, such vocabulary seems here to be actually cultivated for its vivid 'lowness'. A wonderful example from Martial illustrates also the points I was making about form by occupying the whole of the first half of the hexameter:

> Mart. 10.56.5   *enterocelarum* fertur Podalirius Hermes.

But, formal fireworks apart, in the first book of *Sermones*, Horace can make (apparently[24]):

> Hor. *S.* 1.5.30–1hic oculis ego nigra meis collyria lippus
> illinere.

a straightforward statement about his treatment of his perennial eye-disease, using 'ordinary' special vocabulary in its primary sense; both the theme and its vocabulary were unthinkable in Latin epic.

The relevance of genre to the admissibility of technical vocabulary is seen most clearly in the use for the same object of different referring-expressions in different types of poetry. A well-known case is that of *hippomanes*, the name of '(1) one or more medicinal herbs (Theocr. 2.48); (2) a small black growth on the forehead of a newborn foal, which is normally eaten by the mare (Arist. *h.a.* 6.22, 577a9 and 8.24, 605a2); (3) a thin fluid that runs from the sexual organs of the mare in these circumstances (6.18, 572a20)' (Mynors 1990: 225). Virgil admits the word, in sense (3), in the *Georgics*:

> Virg. *G.* 3.280–3   hic demum *hippomanes* uero quod nomine dicunt
> pastores, lentum destillat ab inguine uirus,

---

[24] Beware the common metaphorical use of *lippitudo* in satire to denote intemperance and debauchery (e.g. Hor. *S.* 1.3.25, Pers. 2.72, 5.77: cf. Bramble (1974: 35ff.)); not that I see any point to so understanding it here.

> *hippomanes*, quod saepe malae legere nouercae
> miscueruntque herbas et non innoxia uerba,

but avoids it, in senses (1) and (2),[25] in the *Aeneid*:

> Virg. *A.* 4.513–16   . . . quaeruntur . . .
> pubentes herbae nigri cum lacte ueneni;
> quaeritur et nascentis equi de fronte reuulsus
> et matri praereptus amor.

Naturally the subject matter of didactic poetry will have obliged the poet more often to confront special and technical vocabulary *sensu proprio* and to decide whether to use it or to allude to it. Ultimately, however, the taste of the individual poet was a more important factor than the genre of his composition, so that, to take an extreme case, Lucan's epic admits many more names of species of snake than does Virgil's didactic passage on reptilian pests in *G.* 3. 414–39. Virgil introduces in the second line of this section some colour from special vocabulary, again at the end of the line:

> Virg. *G.* 3.414–15   Disce et odoratam stabulis accendere cedrum
> galbaneoque agitare grauis nidore *chelydros*.

but he uses no other exotic snake-name in this catalogue[26] and avoids, for example, Nicander's *chersydrus* (*Ther.* 359 ff.), preferring a paraphrase in line 425:

> Virg. *G.* 3.425   ille malus Calabris in saltibus anguis.

Virgil proceeds in a similar way in his section on diseases: he announces the subject, gives early on some authentic technical colour but subsequently avoids medical terms:

> Virg. *G.* 3.440–1   Morborum quoque te causas et signa docebo.
> turpis ouis *temptat scabies*.

The contrast with Lucan could hardly be stronger. Lucan shows no restraint at all in his remarkable catalogue of African snakes in Book 9.700–33. Seventeen exotic, jewel-like names form a serpentine pattern through 28 verses. Two names are Latin (720 *natrix, iaculus*), fifteen Greek; three have appeared in earlier Latin poetry (*aspis, cerastes, chelydrus*[27]); four have appeared in earlier Latin prose (*dipsas, draco, haemorrhois, natrix*);

---

[25] *Pace* Ernout (1956: 13, n. 2) who sees sense (3) at *A.* 4.515–6. Cf. Sharrock (1994: 72–3). Ovid avoids the word in sense (3) at *Med.* 38 *nocens uirus amantis equae*.

[26] Compare, in tragedy, Seneca's avoidance of snake-names in the 'catalogue' at *Med.* 681–705. I owe this reference to Dr Hutchinson.

[27] The last only in poets and Celsus 5.27.8; Celsus deals with the treatment of snakebite in 5.27.3–10.

ten occur first in Lucan.[28] Virgil is typically restrained, even in a didactic poem; Lucan is characteristically unrestrained, especially for a writer of epic.[29] Lucan returns momentarily to didactic mode a hundred lines later, when the snakes catalogued at 700ff. are taking it in turns to fall on the Roman captains in good Homeric fashion. Paulus falls prey to the species which kills without poison by hurling itself spearlike through its victim, picking up a didactic gloss and etymology on its way:[30]

Luc. 9.823   torsit et inmisit — iaculum uocat Africa — serpens.

Another general factor affecting the use of technical vocabulary *sensu proprio* was allusion. I distinguish two types: first — and I have to be tentative here — that in which a Latin author imitates a Greek model. Rarely a technical anatomical or disease term is used apparently *sensu proprio* in high poetry. In such cases the usage is likely to be essentially literary, rather than technical. So, for example, when Virgil uses *stomachus* of the oesophagus:

Virg. *A.* 9.698–700   uolat Itala cornus
                                    ... *stomacho*que infixa sub altum
                                    pectus abit,

he is probably conscious not of Latin technical prose usage (Cels. 4.1.3, *al.*; André (1991: 76, 131)) but rather of Homeric usage, as, for example, in:

Il. 17.47–8   ... κατὰ στομάχοιο θέμεθλα
                            νύξ[ε].

A similarly striking use of a body-part term in epic is that of *musculus* 'muscle' by Lucan describing the death of Sabellus from the bite of the snake called *seps*:

Luc. 9.771–2   ... femorum quoque *musculus* omnis
                           liquitur.

Again, there are plausible literary models in Homer (e.g. *Il.* 16.315, 324) and Apollonius Rhodius. Indeed, the Greek μυών 'muscle' occurs in Apollonius' account of the snakebite that kills Mopsos:

---

[28] Three are not in Plin. *Nat.*: *ammodytes, chelydrus, parias*; three are not in Nic. *Ther.*: *ammodytes, parias, prester*. Presumably Nicander was modified by Aemilius Macer (cf. the end of (9) below), Lucan's direct source at this point; see the *commenta Bernensia* on Luc. 9.701.

[29] On the question of genre and the contacts between epic and didactic poetry, with reference to Lucan's Catalogue of Snakes, see Lausberg (1990). I owe this reference to Dr Hutchinson.

[30] I shall say no more here about the formal conventions of didactic poetry and technical prose (the gloss, the programme, the etymology, the paragraphing, the forms of address to the reader, the list of physical requirements in the successful practitioner of the art, etc.); on these see Hollis (1977: xvii–xix *et passim*; Index, *s.v.* 'didactic tradition').

A.R. 4.1519–21   ... αὐτὰρ ὁ [the snake] μέσσην
κερκίδα καὶ μυῶνα ...
σάρκα δακὼν ἐχάραξεν.

It is perhaps worth adding, however, that *musculus* 'muscle' occurs only here in Latin verse and is not found in prose before Celsus, who wrote only a generation or so before Lucan. It is inviting to speculate that Lucan at this point in his borrowed desert sequence (Hutchinson (1988: 353)) is imitating Apollonius not only in making reference to this part of the body but also in using a word with contemporary scientific flavour; the effect of Lucan's *musculus* would then be comparable to that supposed for Apollonius' κερκίς. A similar view may be taken of other Latin poetry.[31] The general hypothesis — of a Roman version of Alexandrian scientific realism in Latin poetry — may deserve further attention and may yield an important qualification to the general rule that technical vocabulary *sensu proprio* is avoided in high poetry.

The second, much clearer, type of allusion is when a special word admitted by an admired predecessor could be echoed by being copied,[32] especially in the same position in the line,[33] and perhaps accompanied by another special word from the same lexical field. So, for example, the line-opening *hippomanes* is the clearest of the echoes of Virgil G. 3.280–3 (quoted above) in these lines of Tibullus and Propertius:

> Tib. 2.4.58   *hippomanes* cupidae stillat ab inguine equae,
> Prop. 4.5.17–18   et in me
> *hippomanes* fetae semina legit equae.

Similarly, given its gender, number and place in the line, *elleboros* in Columella's continuation of the *Georgics* is surely consciously evoking his model and inspiration: compare

> Col. 10.17   sed negat [sŏlum] *elleboros*, et noxia carpasa succo
> with   Virg. G. 3.451   scillamque *elleboros*que grauis nigrumque bitumen;

and note that elsewhere Columella prefers the Latin synonym *ueratrum* (6.32.2, 6.38.3, 7.13.2). Again, given the rarity of the word in Latin litera-

---

[31] E.g. the simile of the panting stag in: Hor. *Carm.* 1.15.31 '[quem tu, ceruus uti] *sublimi* fugies mollis *anhelitu*', where *sublimis anhelitus* corresponds to the Gk μετέωρον πνεῦμα (or ἆσθμα), the medical expression for shallow, panting breath, and may be a deliberate medical touch, perhaps comparable in effect with Apollonius' neuro-physiological description of Medea in love (3.762–3, quoted in (3) above). See Nisbet and Hubbard (1970) on Hor. *Carm.* 1.15.31.

[32] Or alluded to by the context and the use of another special word from the same lexical field. I am thinking of, for example, Luc. 1.426 or Prop. 3.22.27: see above, nn. 18, 19.

[33] On the snake *chelydrus*, for example, note Mynors (1990: 244): 'V[irgil] bequeathed the word to numerous successors, who gratefully use it to end their hexameters'.

ture, it is tempting to believe that *centaurea* 'knapweed' signals that Lucretius' strong-smelling substances:

> Lucr. 4.124–5   panaces absinthia taetra
> habrotonique graues et tristia *centaurea*

are being echoed by Virgil in a different context:

> Virg. *G.* 4.270   Cecropiumque thymum et graue olentia *centaurea*;

and that both passages are intended to be heard in Lucan's description of the snake-repellent mixed by the Psylli[34] to protect the Roman camp in Book 9:

> Luc. 9.918   et *panacea* potens et Thessala *centaurea*,

a passage which contains a potent mixture of eleven exotic ingredient names in six lines.

In general, then, especially in one of the 'higher' genres, a poet's use of special/technical vocabulary *sensu proprio* will serve one or more of at least three purposes: (a) to display his learning and simultaneously to evoke an exotic, far-off world (or a special activity closer to home); (b) to share his enjoyment of the sound of the special word, this receiving formal expression in the predilection of items of special vocabulary for the end, or beginning, of the line; (c) to recall the work of a revered predecessor by the use of a striking special word. Special vocabulary *sensu proprio* is avoided in high poetry if either its form or its meaning is held to be banal or otherwise unsuitable; in particular cases the tastes of the poet were of greater consequence than the genre of his work for the means of expression.

On the other hand, if a technical object is to be mentioned but its proper name is formally or otherwise inappropriate, it is referred to by means of a paraphrase: the term and its meaning remain instantly recognizable but the everyday name of the banal object is avoided. H. D. Jocelyn (1969*a*) has commented on a few examples in Ennius' tragedies, such as *prolato aere* (*scen.* 2 Jocelyn [= 16V], for *scuto proiecto*), *me huic locabas nuptiis* (*scen.* 127J, for *nuptam locabas*) and *sub armis* (*scen.* 232J [= 262V], for *(in) armis*).[35] No different in terms of linguistic intent are those to be found in Horace, *Epistles 1*,[36] such as *ciuica iura* (*Ep.* 1.3.23, for *ius ciuile*), *curule... ebur* (*Ep.* 1.6.53–4, for *sella curulis*) and *consulta patrum* (*Ep.* 1.16.41, for *senatus consulta*); in Propertius, e.g. *praetexti... amictūs*

---

[34] Cf. Cels. 5.27.3B–C; Plin. *Nat.* 7.14–15.

[35] With reference to legal matters, however, Ennius appears generally to use the proper terms; see Jocelyn (1969*a*: Index, *s.v.* 'legal language').

[36] Usefully collected by R. G. Mayer (1994: Index, *s.v.* 'technical terminology avoided').

(3.15.3, for *toga praetexta*) and *arma... de ducibus... recepta* (4.10.2, for *spolia opima*); or in Juvenal, such as *caeduntur... mariscae* (2.13, for *secantur ficus*), *uectetur* (4.6, for *gestetur*) and *torret quarta dies* (9.17, for *male habet quartana febris*).

Lucan's practice in respect of disease names is especially instructive.[37] He avoids these Greek words altogether, in striking contrast with his admission of Greek names of species of snakes and of the exotic plants and minerals used in the snake-repellent (9.700–33 and 916–21: see above). Even some common Latin disease words are paraphrased by Lucan, presumably to heighten the effect of the expression. So, for example, he avoids *rabiosus* (or *rabidus*), writing instead:

> Luc. 6.671   spuma canum *quibus unda timori est*,

unda timori, juxtaposed and so ordered, presumably intended to recall ὑδρο-φοβ-. He avoids even the old Latin phrasal term *ignis sacer*, although both Lucretius and Virgil employ it in their respective accounts of the plague. Lucan uses a paraphrase for this skin condition in his plague passage but so orders the words as to give a clear signal of the intended, 'underlying', form, notwithstanding the syntax of the noun phrases:

> Luc. 6.96–7   *ignea ... sacro* feruida morbo
>   pestis.

This very avoidance of ordinary terms for the banal subject of disease afforded an opportunity for poetic effect and inventiveness. Virgil clearly intends *melancholia* to be understood as the root of Heracles' madness in:

> Virg. *A.* 8.219–20   hic uero Alcides furiis exarserat *atro*
>   *felle* dolor.

The juxtaposition and order of *atro felle* are close to the Greek term; the choice of Latin words[38] and the enjambement keep the banal special vocabulary at the appropriate distance from epic narrative.[39]

Two Ovidian couplets illustrate 'low' and 'high' lexical tactics in successive lines, the pentameter being strikingly more high-flown than its hexameter, the first on gout and rabies:

---

[37] And appears to constitute an exception to Braund's (1992*b*: xlvi) generalization about Lucan's admission of technical terms avoided by other epic poets.

[38] On *ater*, see André (1949: 387): 'terme spécifiquement épique', but cf. p. 220 below; on *fel* vs. *bilis*, Nisbet–Hubbard (1970: 172) *ad* Hor. *Carm.* 1.13.4.

[39] So, too, perhaps, *G.* 3.497 *sues... angit* for ὑάγχη, a form of angina.

> Ov. *Pont.* 1.3.23–4   tollere nodosam nescit medicina *podagram*[40]
> nec *formidatis* auxiliatur *aquis*,[41]

the second a stricture against the use of *lana sucida* (wool with its natural grease):

> Ov. *Ars* 3.213–14   *oesypa* quid redolent, quamuis mittatur Athenis
> demptus ab immundo *uellere sucus* ouis.

Although in a humbler genre, perhaps in an Alexandrian mode, Ovid departs completely from the form of the Greek term *hydropici* in:

> Ov. *Fast.* 1.215   sic *quibus intumuit suffusa uenter ab unda.*

Perhaps because he is taking the patient's point of view, Horace alludes to the same disease by means of another of its symptoms, avoiding its name, in the Letter to Florus:

> Hor. *Ep.* 2.2.146–7   si tibi nulla sitim finiret copia lymphae,
> narrares medicis,

lymphae for 'water' heightening the non-technical allusiveness of the patient's self-observation. We shall see (in (**6**) below) the Horatian passages in which this disease is given its proper Greek name. These last four examples illustrate also how the verse epistle — possibly elegy as a whole — partakes of the lexical conventions of more and less exalted forms (cf. Axelson (1945: 26, 143)).

The absence from epic — and usually lyric and elegy, too — of Greek names of diseases can result only partly, if at all, from avoidance of Greek *tout court*, since we have already, in this brief survey, seen numerous examples of Greek technical polysyllables. Poets' avoidance of the words *melancholia, hydrops, hydrophobus* and the like, in their primary meaning, reflects above all their tendency to paraphrase mundane vocabulary.

In the extreme case, of course, mundane special vocabulary is suppressed altogether, even if the semantic field is central to the topic of the poem. A good example of this is Propertius' poem about Cynthia's illness (2.28), in which there is no word for disease and Cynthia's condition has

---

[40] Cf. Lucian, *Trag.* (*Podagra*) 143 ἦν οὔτε Παιὰν φαρμάκοις νικᾶν σθένει. The word seems to be very rare in verse: Tib. 1.9.73, probably following Catul. 71.2, 6; Virg. *G.* 3.299 of animals and 'softened' by being in the plural, and satire (Hor. *S.* 1.9.32, Juv. 13.96). It is several times avoided in prose (e.g. Cic. *Fam.* 6.19.2, *Brut.* 130 *dolores pedum*, Plin. *Ep.* 1.12.4 *pedum dolor*). This, and Lucian's choice of theme for his paratragedy, indicates the intrinsic 'lowness' of the condition and its proper name. I owe this observation to Dr Hutchinson.
[41] Surely to be understood as hydrophobia, rather than as dropsy, the elements of the Greek compound being rendered as at Plin. *Nat.* 28.84 'si *aqua* potusque *formidetur* a morsu canis'. Cf. Scholte (1933: ad loc.).

to be inferred from oblique hints in *affectae* (line 1), *pericula*[42] (15, 46) and *saucia* (31).[43] The absence in Propertius of words to do with disease when disease is the theme is a natural corollary of the constant metaphorical use of disease words when the subject is love. This observation brings us to consider next the use of special vocabulary in metaphor in Latin poetry.

(6) Technical vocabulary in metaphor

It is above all in metaphorical usage that special and technical vocabulary is to be found in Latin poetry (with the qualified exceptions of didactic and the conversational genres). If, in the use of a technical word in its primary meaning, the poet is aiming in part to impress his audience through sound, in a metaphor he wants to affect his listeners with meaning, with a striking comparison of a target domain with a source domain. The poet here naturally uses normal vocabulary (*uocabula propria*) in order to depict the source domain as clearly and directly as possible; for the image to succeed, to engage rather than alienate the audience, the source domain must be familiar and authentic, both in content and in form.[44]

Accordingly, from Lucretius' straightforward use of authentic Greek terms in his simile of the apothecary's composition:

> Lucr. 2.847–9   sicut *amaracini* blandum *stactae*que liquorem
> et *nardi* florem, nectar qui naribus halat,
> cum facere instituas, . . .

I infer not, with W. Goethe, that the poet was a doctor, nor, with T. P. Wiseman (1974: 19–22), that he was a *pharmacopola* (although these are of course not to be excluded) but that his audience were sufficiently familiar with the substances and their names for the comparison to be illuminating rather than the reverse.

In order to gain an impression of the *reverse* effect, we may contrast, for instance, T. S. Eliot's 'suggestive analogy' for his theory of the depersonalization of the poet: 'I therefore invite you to consider, as a suggestive analogy, the action which takes place when a bit of finely filiated platinum

---

[42] Admittedly, *periculum* is occasionally found meaning roughly 'illness' (e.g. Plin. *Nat.* 23.48; perhaps Cels. 7.26.5H. 5.26.1C.) but I do not believe that it is to be so taken here.

[43] The same is true, I think, of Ov. *Am.* 2.13.1 and 2.14.3–5, where he is speaking of an abortion.

[44] D. N. Sedley notes (below, p. 237, n. 28) that Lucretius, while rejecting *harmonia* as a philosophical term, admits it at 4.1248 'where he may feel that his need for the musical metaphor leaves him no option'. Lyne (1989: *passim*, esp. e.g. 165–8) gives excellent illustration from the *Aeneid* of the power of words proper to what he calls 'business prose' when used metaphorically to evoke their source domain for poetic effect.

is introduced into a chamber containing oxygen and sulphur dioxide' (Eliot (1932 [1917]: 17)). This analogy is suggestive only to those with some knowledge of chemistry. Indeed, Eliot proceeds to explain it in detail before applying it to his theory of poetry; presumably he did not expect his average reader to find it helpful without further explanation. On the other hand, given the required amount of shared knowledge of the source domain, between author and reader, the analogy stands only to gain in strength from the writer's use of ordinary technical language and his avoidance of literary, or layman's, paraphrase. Any banality or 'lowness' attaching to certain types of special vocabulary used *sensu proprio* is nullified by artful semantics. As Gregory Hutchinson puts it in a slightly different context (1988: 227), '[s]uch [*scil.* 'low'] material in similes, as in metaphors, has a very different resonance from such material when it is the direct subject of discourse'.

It is for these reasons, I suggest, that we find special vocabulary in poetic imagery, and that we can infer that it is vocabulary of some currency in the source domain. So it follows that, for example, *hydrops* (Gk ὕδρωψ 'dropsy; sufferer from dropsy') owes its famous appearance in Horace, *Odes 2*, to the fact that it is used metaphorically, for avarice (and, perhaps, the avaricious man[45]):

> Hor. *Carm.* 2.2.13–16   crescit indulgens sibi dirus *hydrops*
> nec sitim pellit, nisi causa morbi
> fugerit uenis et aquosus albo
> corpore languor.

The same account may perhaps be given of *hydropicus* in another of Horace's warnings against over-indulgence:

> Hor. *Ep.* 1.2.33–4   . . . atqui
> si sanus noles curres *hydropicus*.

The occurrence of these words tells us further that they had at least equal currency with the Latin expression, which is Celsus' only term for dropsy, *aqua inter cutem*.

It would go well beyond the scope of this essay to attempt any kind of systematic discussion of Latin poetic imagery based on special and technical vocabulary; I would, however, offer at this stage three general observations of a provisional nature.

First, it is clear that disease is both common and versatile as a source domain for metaphor — versatile in the sense that it is regularly applied to

---

[45] The sufferer can properly be the subject of *pellit*, with an abrupt change of subject as, for example, at Cels. 3.15.6. Or we may accept Peerlkamp's *pellas*; see Nisbet and Hubbard (1978: ad loc.).

several target domains, notably vice[46] and love[47] but also literary style[48]. This versatility may be taken to indicate that — not surprisingly — disease was a familiar subject with a familiar vocabulary. This is in keeping with poets' general avoidance, noted in (5) above, of disease words *sensu proprio*.

Second, given a versatile source domain, such as disease, and the poet's need to explore various metaphorical approaches to central themes (target domains), such as love, metaphors may come to interact in fruitful and suggestive ways. One such instance, centred on the theme of love, and involving the metaphors of disease, medical treatment and soldiery, may have caught Ovid's attention. I have in mind simply that the whole conception of the *Ars amatoria* and, especially, the *Remedia amoris* seems inspired by the metaphorical accounts of love as a disease (cf. Pinotti (1988: 16)) and of medicines as soldiers in the battle with illness.[49] It is as if in these poems Ovid is offering an *ars medicinae* of a new order for the treatment of love, the poet being no longer a soldier in the service of love but the dispenser of remedies — rational remedies in which magic no longer plays a part[50] — which will join battle with love.

[46] Especially in satire, continuing a tradition going back to Plato by way of the diatribe and Cynic and Stoic philosophy. See Bramble (1974: 35, nn. 2, 3) with numerous examples, including, e.g., Hor. *Ep.* 1.1.33 '*feruet* auaritia . . . pectus, . . . (35) laudis amore *tumes*'. A possible unnoticed medical instance at Hor. *C.* 3.24.48–9 'aurum et *inutile* | summi materiem mali'?

[47] Note e.g. Prop. 1.1.26–7 (quoted at the beginning of (II) above), 2.14.19 hoc sensi *prodesse* magis', 3.24.18 '*uulnera*que ad sanum nunc *coiere* mea' and Ov. *Met.* 1.523–4 'ei mihi quod nullis amor est sanabilis herbis | nec prosunt domino quae prosunt omnibus artes' [Apollo is speaking]. This image, too, has a long tradition in both Greek (cf. S. *Tr.* 445, 491) and Latin (cf. Enn. *scen.* 254 'Medea animo aegro, amore saeuo saucia'). For collections and discussion of the countless examples, both Greek and Latin, and further references, see e.g. Svennung (1945), La Penna (1951), Flury (1968), Müller (1980), Mazzini (1990). Note that Lanata (1966) proposes the converse account — the drawing of terms of pathology from poetic love language — of the Hippocratic use of πῦρ, ἄση, ἀνίη, words already in Sappho of the torments of love.

[48] Note in verse e.g. Catul. 44, and Pers. 1.76–8 'uenosus liber Acci . . . uerrucosa . . . Antiopa', with Migliorini (1990: 61–5), and see Bramble (1974: 36–7).

[49] For the wars between disease and medicine, note e.g. Man. 2.902 '*bella*que morborum caecis pugnantia telis'; Cels. 6.6.31A 'si uero scabri oculi sunt, . . . potest *militare*: id quod habet' . . . (Löfstedt (1990), *contra* Flury (1990)). Diseases have *impetus* (*TLL* VII 1.604.79ff., 608.36ff.), they *occupant* (*TLL* IX 2.386.29ff.), they *temptant*; the doctor must fight (Cels. 3.12.2, 6.6.37A *pugnandum est*), a disease is *expugnandus* (Cels. 3.15.4; *TLL* V 2.1811.30ff.); medicine may be defeated (Cels. 3.27.4A; 5.26.1C *uicta* [ars]) or the disease may be (Cels. 3.22.8 *euincitur morbus*; *TLL* V 2.1042.77ff.).

[50] Note Ovid's three express rejections of magic, at *Ars* 2.99–107, *Rem.* 249–90 and *Med.* 35–42. Sharrock (1994: 50ff.) argues brilliantly that the first two of these passages at any rate should not be taken at face value, since there are features of the language of magic in the language that Ovid uses to denounce magic. Cf., however, Wilhelm (1925: 158–9) on Ovid as *medicus aeger* in *Pont.* 1.3, and Pinotti (1988: 15–24) on properly medical, especially empirical, aspects of the *Rem.*

Third, many of the more prominent metaphors which recur in Latin poetry appear early in Roman literature; most are to be found already in classical or Hellenistic Greek literature (see nn. 46, 47), whence they were perhaps imitated in the first place. Some, of course, notably those of the *foedus amoris* and the *militia amoris*, received a peculiarly Roman development; (see Reitzenstein (1912); Spies (1930); Paludan (1941); Benediktson (1977: 347)). In order, however, to keep an old metaphor alive, a poet must introduce new elements from its domain, so that we find, for example, fresh figurative use of legal terminology in the parody of a humiliating peace-settlement that Propertius puts into Cynthia's mouth:

> Prop. 4.8.74   accipe quae nostrae *formula legis* erit

and at the end of Cornelia's speech from the grave (4.11) before the imaginary court (lines 19–22):

> Prop. 4.11.99   *causa perorata est,*

or, again, of soldiers' jargon in Ovid:

> Ov. *Ars* 1.131–2   Romule, militibus scisti dare *commoda* solus!
>   haec mihi si dederis *commoda*, miles ero,

technical and special language unparalleled in poetry (cf. Fedeli (1965), Hollis (1977) ad locc.).

Tentatively to summarize so far: (i) technical vocabulary *sensu proprio* is avoided by the Latin poets — with the obvious but qualified exceptions of writers of didactic and satire — if its subject does not fit the aesthetics of the poem or of the poet, or if it is formally uninteresting; (ii) if reference is made to the thing whose *uox propria* is avoided, it is by means of a paraphrase, the form of which is more or less reminiscent of the ordinary expression; (iii) conversely, quite ordinary items of special vocabulary are the norm in metaphor.

These general statements, based on a limited amount of close reading, are at this stage no more than working hypotheses. They may appear obvious and uninteresting, but they merit systematic testing since they will apply in varying degrees to various texts, poets, genres, traditions and hence promise to yield a critical tool (in principle quantitative) not only to Latin poetry but to literary language generally. On the one hand, further study of the admission to literary texts of technical vocabulary *sensu proprio* will bring out formal and thematic aspects of the aesthetics of individual poets and poems; on the other hand, an increased sensitivity to the existence of special uses of apparently ordinary words may in the best case, according to the prediction in (iii) above, sharpen and enrich our reading of imagery — even uncover unsuspected metaphors — in well-known texts.[51] Conversely, in lexicography, literary use of technical vocabulary, especially in metaphor, may prove to be a valuable supplementary source of information on the ordinary words in current (educated) use relating to various special and technical activities. In the final section of this paper I should like to illustrate with reference to medicine this last general prediction of the relevance of poetic imagery to special lexicography. This section, no less than **(I)** and **(II)**, offers merely a few examples of the phenomena discussed, examples drawn from only a small sample of the relevant texts in verse and prose.

III. THE LATIN POETS AND MEDICAL LATIN

Study of medical vocabulary in the poets[52] has, I believe, a contribution to make in return to our knowledge of the history of Latin medical discourse. It follows from the generalizations of **(5)** and **(6)** above that consistent use of a particular item of medical vocabulary in poetic imagery implies that the word was current and familiar in its ordinary, non-metaphorical medical sense. There are three immediate and important consequences of this inference, which bear on the history of medical Latin and more generally on republican Roman social, literary and intellectual history. These concern: (i) the date of the widespread diffusion at Rome of Greek and Latin medical terms; (ii) the relationship between the language of technical Latin medical prose and educated colloquial usage in medical matters, in the late Republic and early Empire; (iii) the question of the date of origin — indeed, of the very existence — of specialist discourse on medicine in Latin. I deal with each in turn in **(7)**, **(8)** and **(9)** below.

(7) The figurative use of medical vocabulary in Plautus

A first, and very simple, implication of the transferred use of medical words in Latin verse is that there was at Rome a high degree of familiarity with Greek and Latin medical vocabulary from an earlier date than is often supposed.

---

[51] A possible minor example: *caruisse* 'to be *cured of*' at Hor. *Ep.* 1.1.42; cf. Cels. 2.15.1, 3.21.6, Larg. 38, 122.

[52] And, to be sure, in non-medical prose also, above all in Cicero and Seneca. While the bibliography on medicine in Seneca is considerable, little has been done on Cicero; for references see Mazzini (1988: 50, n. 7; 1991*a*: 101, n. 8). A useful collection of other special vocabulary in Seneca's letters is in Summers (1910: xlii–xlix). I owe this reference to G. D. Williams.

It is striking that a number of medical expressions make their first appearance in Plautus, or other early republican verse, used figuratively as well as literally. Greek γλαύκωμα 'cataract'[53] appears first in Plautus in a phrase meaning something like 'pull the wool over his eyes', declining as a first-declension noun and with Latin -ū- for Greek -ω-:

> Pl. *Mil.* 147–9   ei nos facetis fabricis et doctis dolis
> *glaucumam* ob oculos obiciemus eumque ita
> faciemus ut quod uiderit ne uiderit.[54]

Similarly, *stomachus* is found first meaning 'annoyance, vexation' and *stacta* standing for the bouquet of wine, or a lovely woman:

> Pl. *As.* 422–3   quin centiens eadem imperem atque ogganniam,
> itaque iam hercle
> clamore ac *stomacho* non queo labori suppeditare.
> Pl. *Cur.* 101–2   tu mihi *stacta*, tu cinnamum, tu rosa,
> tu crocinum et casia es, tu telinum.
> Pl. *Mos.* 309   cum *stacta* accubo.

Plautus attests also humorous *Latin* medical expressions, implying a certain currency to the terms *sensu proprio* at an earlier date. So, *lippitudo* 'inflammation or watering of the eyes' occurs already in Plautus not only in its primary sense but also used figuratively to mean the opposite of *oculus* 'darling':

> Pl. *Poen.* 393–4   huiius amica mammeata, mea inimica et maleuola,
> oculus huiius, *lippitudo* mea, mel huiius, fel meum,

showing, incidentally, a use that is not attested for its Greek equivalent ὀφθαλμία.[55]

While this is a strikingly early instance of the figurative use of a disease-name, I admit freely that *lippitudo* is hardly a technical term of the sort that presupposes a public familiarity with any form of medicine or medical language; it was quite probably an ancient homely word for a common

---

[53] On the history of the meaning of γλαύκωμα see Marganne (1993: 101). I owe this reference to Professor Bain.

[54] I owe this reference to Professor Adams.

[55] While ὀφθαλμός has a use similar to that of Latin *oculus* ('a person or thing as precious as the eye'), the only attested metaphorical use of the disease term ὀφθαλμία and derivatives has to do with coveting, so ὀφθαλμιάω at Hyp. *Fr.* 258, Plb. 1.7.2, 2.17.3, 31.21.1.

Other examples of relatively early figurative use of medical terms include: Lucil. 764M '*aquam* te in animo habere *intercutem*' (*sensu proprio* at Pl. *Men.* 891); Laber. *com.* 1 'quid est ius iurandum? *emplastrum* aeris alieni' (*sensu proprio* at Cato *Agr.* 39.2); Lucr. 4.528–9 'praeterea radit uox fauces saepe facitque | *asperiora* foras gradiens *arteria* clamor' (playing on the name of the trachea); Cael. *Fam.* 8.14.4 (50 BC) 'persuasum est ei [Appio censori] censuram lomentum aut *nitrum* esse'.

affliction. There may be a more telling example of this type of humorous medical Latin in the diagnosis performed by Palinurus in *Curculio*:

Pl. *Cur.* 236–40 PA. sed quid tibi est? CAPPADOX lien enicat, renes dolent,
pulmones distrahuntur, cruciatur iecur,
radices cordis pereunt, hirae omnes dolent.
PA. tum te igitur *morbus* agitat *hepatiarius*.
(240)   CA. facile est miserum inridere.

If the text is right, the reaction of Cappadox ('It's easy to mock the afflicted.') and the fact that this disease term occurs only here make it likely that *morbus hepatiarius* is a comic nonce-formation.[56] Such expressions depend for their comic effect on familiarity with established types, so that *morbus hepatiarius* might be taken to suggest two things: one is the audience's familiarity with Latin phrasal lexemes of the type *morbus articularis, morbus comitialis, morbus regius*, etc.; the other is the currency of Greek ἧπαρ 'the liver', or ἡπάτια 'liver (as a dish)' (Lucil. 310M), the latter a more suitable base for a comic formation.[57]

Accounts of medical Latin — or of the reception by Latin writers of Greek medical words — generally begin with Cato's *De agricultura* (*c.* 160 BC)[58] but the presence of these words with transferred meaning already around 200 BC presupposes close familiarity with the primary meaning of the words and hence argues strongly for a much earlier establishment and widespread diffusion of medical words at Rome (contrast Rawson (1985: 170)). How long does it take for a borrowed technical term to become usable in a play in a transferred or metaphorical sense? Did a mass of Greek medical terms, whether or not introduced by practising medical men, become current in Plautus' middle age, in the period in which Rome acquired her first Greek public doctor, Archagathus, in 219 BC (Hem. *Hist.* 26, Plin. *Nat.* 29.12)? Or had they been current already for generations,

---

[56] Acidalius, followed by several others, put line 244 CA. *lien dierectust.* PA. *ambula. id lieni optumumst.* after 239 so that the *inrisio* of line 240 consists not in the diagnosis but in the suggested cure. See Thierfelder (1955).

[57] Late in the day, I find that Thierfelder (1955) has taken exactly this view of this passage; he gives a good summary history of the textual criticism. It should be noted, however, that Mazzini (1992a: 90–2) takes the symptoms, the diagnosis and the term *morbus hepatiarius* quite seriously, as corresponding to the Greek πάθος ἡπατικόν; similarly (1992a: 93) he sees *solstitialis morbus* (*Trin.* 544) as Plautus' serious version of Gk σειρίασις 'sunstroke'. Questions of this kind are clearly important for our appreciation of Plautine humour and realism, and of his treatment of his Greek models. I hope I may be forgiven for not pursuing them here on the grounds that their resolution will not affect the main point of this section, namely what Mazzini (1992a: 103) calls 'la retrodatazione della prima attestazione ... di una serie di conoscenze, convinzioni, tecniche e istituzioni mediche'.

[58] See, for example, Ilberg (1907); De Meo (1983: 224ff.); Weis (1992).

since the official installation of the cult of Asclepius in Rome in 293 BC, the third year of a destructive plague (Livy 10.47.6–7) — or still earlier (Nutton (1993: 57f.))?

In general, the transferred or metaphorical use of any item of special vocabulary is good evidence of its familiarity in its primary sense and gives to the lexicographer and the historian a reliable *terminus ante quem* for the coming to currency of objects and ideas, and their names.

(8) Disagreements in the choice of medical words between poetry and medical prose

As we have seen, there is in one way and another a good deal of medical vocabulary in Latin poetry, generally, one notes, with consistent use of particular words. There are numerous agreements between the medical vocabulary of Latin poetry — especially in metaphorical usage — and that of the nearest thing we have to contemporary technical prose (Celsus, *De medicina*[59] and Scribonius Largus, *Compositiones*[60]). There are also some disagreements, which raise an interesting question. Here are a few examples.

aegrotus 'ill; (as noun) one who is ill' occurs alongside *aeger* '*id.*' in comedy,[61] epigram (Catul. 97.12), satire (Pers. 3.83) and in prose, including Cicero (who, however, prefers *aeger* by 41:15). *aegrotus* would appear to be an ordinary everyday medical word[62] but it is avoided by Celsus and Scribonius, and by high poetry (with the sole exception of Accius *trag.* 71), in favour of *aeger*.

lippus 'having watery or inflamed eyes; (as noun) one so afflicted' is common in comedy, satire and epigram (e.g. Mart. 6.39.11, 6.78.2), although rare in prose (once in Vitruvius, 8.4.1) until Petronius (28.4, *al.*) and the

---

[59] Text: Marx (1915); Mudry (1982) of the preface; Contino (1988) of book 8. Introduction: Jocelyn (1986); Contino (1988: 13–50).

[60] Text: Sconocchia (1983). Introduction: Sconocchia (1993).

[61] In Plautus *aegrotus* is confined to *senarii*, *aeger* to long lines, a distribution that conforms well with Löfstedt's (1933–42: II 305ff.) stylistic characterization of the language proper to the different verse forms. I owe this observation to Professor Bain. It may also be significant that of the eight occurrences of *aeger* in Plautus and Terence, six of the seven that mean straightforwardly 'physically unwell' are fem. (Pl. *Truc.* 464, 475, 500, Ter. *Hec.* 188, 256, 341); at Pl. *Epid.* 129 it is used of the mind; the sole exception is Ter. *Eun.* 236, where the surrounding words also appear to be unusual.

[62] It is used in ordinary down-to-earth medical contexts e.g. at Pl. *Cap.* 190, *Men.* 884, *Cur.* 61 and Cic. *Div.* 2.13, 133, 145, *Att.* 6.1.2; and metaphorically e.g. at Pl. *Trin.* 76, Ter. *An.* 193, 559, *Hau.* 100.

Elder Pliny (28.130, *al.*). It is avoided by Celsus and Scribonius, who use only *lippio, -īre*[63] and *lippiens* (as adjective or noun).[64]

The loan-word *podager*[65] and the Latin derivative *podagrosus*[66] '(one) suffering from gout' are found in Plautus, Ennius, Lucilius and Horace, used either literally or metaphorically.[67] Neither of these words is to be found in medical prose, where the only word for '(one) suffering from gout' is *podagricus* (ποδαγρικός).[68]

Now, as I noted above, the converse of my hypothesis that *uoces propriae* are usual in metaphor implies that the lexicographer has an unnoticed tool at hand for determining the register and currency of a large number of words. To spell this out in more concrete terms, any dictionary of a special or technical language should take very seriously the vocabulary used in literary texts in metaphors drawn from the special field in question. On the face of it the words just listed constitute serious counter-examples to this principle: surely one will prefer to follow medical prose rather than a figurative use in poetry in determining the vocabulary of medical Latin, as a technical idiom? It is curious that the very existence of such a technical variety of Latin is either denied (e.g. by André (1987: 29–31)) or baldly asserted without argument (e.g. by Mazzini (1991*b*)) by those specialists working in this field; I return to this question in **(9)** below. Those who deny its existence have no reason for confining themselves to medical prose and excluding the numerous medical expressions to be found in non-technical literary texts; those who would believe — against, I think, the majority view — that there was a characterizable medical variety of Latin spoken or written by those with specialist knowledge of the field are missing an important opportunity to illustrate this idiom with reference to these disagreements in the choice of medical words between figurative use in literature and medical prose.

[63] *lippīre* is found first used metaphorically at Pl. *Cur.* 318 'lippiunt fauces fame'; cf. Cic. *Att.* 7.14.1 (*sensu proprio*). On the 'medical' and 'psychiatric' denominatives in *-īre*, see Mignot (1969: esp. 71–2) and Leumann (1977: 556).

[64] *lippientes* and *aegri* may be proper also to official army language under the Empire. The former appears on a strength report at Vindolanda (II 154, 22. Bowman, Thomas and Adams 1994: 90–8). I owe this reference to Professor Adams. Lists of men unfit for service through illness are headed by the word *aegri*, not *aegroti*, both at Vindolanda (*ibid.*) and frequently at Bu Njem (Marichal 1992: 84–8).

[65] From ποδαγρός with the regular Latin treatment of word-final *-ros* or *-ris* after a consonant.

[66] The formation of a derivative with a native suffix on the stem of a foreign word is indicative of the complete integration of that stem into the borrowing language. Cf. Biville (1989: 37).

[67] *podager* at Enn. *sat.* 64V (fig.?), Hor. *Ep.* 1.2.52 (lit.); *podagrosus* at Pl. *Poen.* 532 (fig.), *Mer.* 595, Lucil. 331M (lit.). On the interpretation of the Ennius line (*numquam poetor nisi [si] podager*), see Schäublin (1988: n.12) and Naiditch (1988); I owe these references to Professor M. D. Reeve. See also Grilli (1978).

[68] *podagricus* is read also at Laber. *com.* 6 but entirely without context.

Let a fourth example, of a partial disagreement between poetry and medical prose, suggest an alternative account of *aegrotus, lippus, podager/podagrosus*. The verb *coīre* is used in elegy and elsewhere of the closing of metaphorical wounds (e.g. Prop. 3.24.18; Ov. *Tr.* 4.4.41, 5.2.9; *Pont.* 1.3.87, 1.6.24; cf. Hor. *Ep.* 1.3.32; Petr. 113.8). I am bound by my general hypothesis about the nature of vocabulary used in metaphor to regard this as an 'authentic', natural, medical expression for this context, and indeed this use of the verb is found (once) in Scribonius (121, p. 64,4 Sconocchia). Celsus, on the other hand, does not attest it, using instead for the first time in our record the simplex *glutinō, -āre* (and derivatives) which takes the medicament as subject and the wound as object. The disagreement between Celsus and Scribonius reminds us of the (probably universal) existence of variation within technical terminologies (cf. Langslow (1989: 39–40)); that between the medical writers and the elegists of a particular type of this variation, namely that between ordinary educated but lay medical usage and specialist idiom (cf. Adams (1995*b*: 663); Langslow (1989: 38–9)), or what I am about to argue is the elevated style of literary medical prose. Such variation may be recorded by Celsus in cases such as:

> Cels. 8.1.15   a ceruice duo lata ossa utrimque ad scapulas tendunt: nostri *scutula operta*, omoplatas Graeci nominant.

This is the only occurrence in the Latin record of *scutula operta* 'the shoulder-blades'. It belongs, I suggest, to the educated, colloquial language, much like English *shoulder-blade* (vs. technical English *scapula*). Celsus' own term is the phrasal lexeme *latum scapularum os*, which he uses nine times (5.26.10, 8.1.16, *al.*). Analogously, *aegrotus ~ aeger, coire ~ glutinari, lippus ~ lippiens, podager/podagrosus ~ podagricus* could be regarded as four more isoglosses that will have contributed to characterizing different types of Latin medical discourse, which we could tentatively label 'lay–colloquial–informal' and 'specialist–elevated–formal', respectively.

In general, then, in reconstructing non-specialist educated usage on special and technical subjects, we should not assume as a matter of course that 'technical' prose is our best witness; we should consider equally — and sometimes even prefer — the vocabulary of literary texts, especially when it is used metaphorically.

(9) Lucretius 4.1068 ff. and the beginnings of Latin medical discourse

The hypothesis developed above that *uocabula propria* are poets' first choice in metaphors is fully in keeping with commentators' ascriptions of the vocabulary of poetic imagery to, for example, 'il linguaggio medico' (Fedeli 1980: 83) or 'the drily accurate style of medical discourse' (Brown

1987: 210). I should like to dwell a moment longer on these two comments in order to explore the assumptions underlying them and to consider the meaning of the phrase 'medical language' applied to Latin. 'Medical Latin', it seems to me, can mean either (i) Latin words and expressions used (no matter by whom) to denote or discuss medical matters, including parts of the body, disease and its treatment, both theoretical and practical, and so on; or (ii) Latin words and expressions, used to denote or discuss these same medical matters, *that are characteristic of a group, or groups, of Latin-speakers/writers with specialist medical knowledge.*[69] We could say that (i) is the weak sense and (ii) the strong sense of the phrase 'medical Latin'. (i) could amount to no more than isolated laymen's words for generally-known parts of the body, diseases and types of therapy in the absence of Latin-speaking doctors, in a world, say, in which all medical specialists spoke and wrote only in Greek among themselves and in contact with Latin-speaking patients improvised each a different sort of Latin. (ii) does not require the assumption that there was a group of doctors who had Latin as their first language or that Latin was used extensively, or at all, *within* the medical profession, but it does require that doctors spoke to, or wrote for, educated laymen in a characteristic style of Latin, with its own linguistic stamp.

How, then, do Brown and Fedeli mean us to understand 'medical discourse', 'linguaggio medico'? Fedeli's 'linguaggio medico' could perfectly well have the weak sense, (i) above. I doubt, however, that this is the intended sense — if, that is, this question was considered at all — since 'linguaggio medico' enjoys apparently equal status, in the indices and discussion elsewhere in his commentaries on Propertius, with clear cases of special language in the strong sense (sense (ii) above), such as 'linguaggio forense, giuridico, militare, politico, sacrale'. On the other hand, in Brown's comments on the medical language in Lucretius' metaphor, I think that there can be no doubt that sense (ii), 'medical Latin' in the strong sense, is intended.

Now, I do not wish ultimately to disagree with Brown's — or Fedeli's — ascription of the poet's figurative vocabulary to medical Latin in the strong sense. What I miss, particularly in Brown's discussion, is any attempt to substantiate the implications of this strong claim, or rather any acknowledgement of the fact that it *is* a strong and controversial claim; this is so at any period of Roman history — at least until the later Empire[70] — and

---

[69] For this strong characterization of technical languages as autonomous varieties, see, in general, Sager *et al.* (1980: 63–5) and, with reference to medical Latin, Mazzini (1991*b*: 175 and n. 1).

[70] Some would say even then, and even in a single area, Africa, where several medical texts were produced in the fourth and fifth centuries; see Adams (1995*b*: 648).

all the more so before the composition of the *De rerum natura*, in, we suppose, the 50s BC.

There is, to be sure, good reason to suppose that the Latin poets, like most of their educated contemporaries, were both interested in and well informed about Greek medical theory and practice.[71] Lucretius' inclusion of Hippocratic, alongside Thucydidean, material in his account of the plague at the end of the poem, is the clearest and longest textual instance of such contacts and interests in the republican period; it gives us, incidentally, our oldest Latin version of a piece of Hippocrates.[72] Elsewhere, in Books 3 and 1, Lucretius appears to have been inspired by the Hippocratic *De flatibus*.[73] There are probable echoes of, or allusions to, doctrines of Asclepiades and Themison in Lucretius and Virgil respectively; these have to be argued for rather more carefully and cautiously.[74] Then there are the numerous references to medical concepts and language above all in Horace (Mazzini (1988: 69; 1991a)), and also in Ovid (Pinotti (1988: 15–24)). Horace, for one, will have been personally acquainted with the leading medical men of his day, including Augustus' physician Antonius Musa, who is named at *Ep.* 1.15.3 and probably alluded to at *Ep.* 1.3.26 (*frigida fomenta*: see Mayer (1994: ad locc.).

To all this we may add circumstantial indications that medicine generally is rising in status as a profession in the last generation of the Republic: witness Cicero's statement (*De off.* 1.151) that medicine and architecture were suitable careers for free men, and Caesar's inclusion of doctors in his offer of citizenship to those teachers of the liberal arts living in Rome (Suet. *Iul.* 42). Even if, therefore, the passages purporting to show the intellectual interests of the Augustan poets are purely literary imitations without bearing on the real world,[75] there is sufficient evidence of interest in Greek medicine for us to regard Varro's inclusion of medicine in his *Disciplinae* in the 30s BC as *following* the mood of the times, with its broad intellectual interests, rather than as trend setting.

But it remains doubtful whether the substance of the last two paragraphs amounts to evidence for the existence of medical Latin in the

[71] For more generous illustration and bibliography, see Mazzini (1988: 46–9).
[72] Compare: Lucr. 6.1193–5 'compressae nares, nasi (ῥίς) primoris acumen | tenue, cauati oculi, caua tempora, frigida pellis (δέρμα) duraque' with: Hp. *Prog.* 2 [= 2.114L] ῥὶς ὀξεῖα, ὀφθαλμοὶ κοῖλοι, κρόταφοι ξυμπεπτωκότες, ... καὶ τὸ δέρμα τὸ περὶ τὸ μέτωπον σκληρόν τε καὶ περιτεταμένον καὶ καρφαλέον ἐόν (cf. *Coac.* 2.209 [= 5.630L]); and also with: Cels. 2.6.1 'nares acutae, conlapsa tempora, oculi concaui, ... cutis circa frontem dura et intenta'.
[73] See Phillips (1984), with references to earlier literature.
[74] See Pigeaud (1980) and (1982), and the excellent summary in Pigeaud (1988). I owe the last reference to Dr S. J. Harrison.
[75] I mean above all: Virg. *G.* 2.477–81 (praise of Lucretius), *A.* 1.742–6 (the song of Iopas; cf. A.R. 1.496ff.), Prop. 3.5.23–46, Hor. *Ep.* 1.12.14–18 and Ov. *Met.* 15.66–71.

strong sense in the first half of the first century BC. Notwithstanding the extant medical sections of Varro, *De re rustica*,[76] and reliable testimonies to a *De medicina* by Varro and pharmacological works in Latin by Pompeius Lenaeus, C. Valgius Rufus and Aemilius Macer (Plin. *Nat.* 25.4–5; Ov. *Tr.* 4.10.43–4) — even with allowance made for exaggeration in the Elder Pliny's famous remark on the language of medicine in his day,[77] the easier assumption has been, and remains, that any distinctive medical idiom in first-century Rome was a form of Greek.[78]

As things stand, then, the existence of Brown's Latin medical discourse in the age of Lucretius looks on general grounds decidedly doubtful. Perhaps its strongest available support so far is the aesthetic point (related to the general hypothesis developed above about the use of *uocabula propria* in metaphor) that Lucretius' image is so much more effective if its peculiar language puts his hearers in mind of the way that medical men of their acquaintance speak and/or write. Failing this, we must read Lucretius' metaphor as no more than medical Latin in the weak sense, and the striking accumulation of *-sco* verbs[79] (four in two lines) as having some other (less pointed?) effect, such as reminiscence (or parody?) of epic or tragedy.

(10) Medical vocabulary in Lucretius

Brown's belief in Latin medical discourse rests by implication on the lexical agreements between Lucretius, in the metaphor of love and elsewhere, and medical prose, above all Celsus. His commentary brings out very well the status as ordinary medical expressions of many of the words of 4.1068–71: *ulcus, inueterascit, in dies, furor, grauescit* (but add Cels. 6.6.29!), *uulnera, recentia curare*, as well as the *-sco* verbs of 1068–9. In these lines more might be made certainly of *plagae* 'surgical incisions' (41× in Celsus, e.g. 3.21.12, 4.7.3, 7.2.6); probably of *conturbare* (in medical contexts at e.g. Cic. *Tusc.* 3.15, 4.30; Larg. 19, 20; Sen. *Dial.* 12.5.3); possibly of *gliscit*, which occurs in a medical expression in Plautus (*Cap.* 558 *gliscit rabies*) and

---

[76] Varro distinguishes (*R.* 2.1.21) two sorts of veterinary and human medicine: 'scientiae genera duo, ut in homine, unum ad quae adhibendi medici, alterum quae ipse etiam pastor diligens mederi possit'. This view is in contrast with that of Cato, whose medical recipes were to be administered by the *pater familias*. For this reason I exclude Cato at this point; but see the end of **(10)** below on the phraseology of medical recipes, which appears to have remained constant from the time of Plautus until late antiquity.

[77] Plin. *Nat.* 29.17; note especially: 'immo uero auctoritas aliter quam Graece eam tractantibus etiam apud inperitos expertesque linguae non est, ac minus credunt quae ad salutem suam pertinent, si intellegunt'.

[78] See e.g. Rawson (1985: 178, 182); André (1987: 29–30).

[79] On which see **(11)** *(i)* below.

which Lucretius uses in another medical metaphor (3.480 *clamor, singultus, iurgia gliscunt*, the 'symptoms' of drunkenness; cf. 1.474). In general, however, Lucretius' medical vocabulary, *sensu proprio* or metaphorical, coincides with that of medical prose (particularly but not only Celsus) in many passages in the poem, notably in the description of the Athenian plague with which the poem ends (6.1138–286) — but there are many other places, too.[80] Here are some examples of Lucretius' medical words and phrases.

ardor 'high temperature of the human body' (3.477, 4.1098): cf. Cic. *FPL* 34.33, Cels., Larg., Plin. *Nat.* and later medical writers *saepe*, Sen.(?) *Her. O.* 1278. The phrase *nimius ardor* occurs at Lucr. 6.1163 and Cels. 1.8.3, 3.7.2D, 4.12.4, 5.28.11D (*TLL* II. 490.60 ff.).

decedere 'to remit', of a fever (2.34): cf. Cic. *Att.* 7.2.2, Nep. *Att.* 22.3, Hor. *Ep.* 2.2.152 (metaph.), Cels. 3.3.4, 3.4.17, 3.5.10, *al.* (*TLL* V. 1.122.43 ff.).

capitis dolor 'headache' (6.784, 1202): cf. Lucil. 1277M, Hor. *S.* 2.3.29, Ov. *Am.* 1.8.73, *al.*, Cels. *saepe*, and later medical writers (*TLL* V. 1.1839.56 ff.).

feruor 'a feverish heat within the body' (6.656, 1145): cf. Var. *Men.* 33, Hor. *S.* 2.1.25 (metaph.), Cels. 2.7.28, 3.3.4, 3.6.7, 4.13.6, Larg. 158, Col. 6.12.1, Sen. *Dial.* 2.9.1, Plin. *Nat.* 15.19, *al.* and later medical writers (*TLL* VI. 1.601.1 ff.).

male habere 'to cause physical distress to' (3.826 metaph.): cf. Pac. *trag.* 277 (of old age), Ter. *An.* 436, Cels. 1.5.1. 2.1.14, 18, *al.* (21x of a disease distressing the patient or a body part), Apul. *Fl.* 23 (used by a doctor), etc. (*TLL* VI. 3.2440.31 ff.).

laborare 'to be ill' (1.849, 2.970, 3.176, 507, 733): cf. Var. *R.* 2.1.21, Vitr. 1.4.12, Cic. *Att.* 5.8.1, 7.2.2, Cels. *pr.* 56, 67, 1.8.1, 2.8.16, *al.* (*TLL* VII. 2.806.53 ff.).

lethargus (ληθαργός) 'lethargy' (3.465, 829): cf. Hor. *S.* 2.3.145 (in a medical context); Cels. 2.1.21, 3.18.14, 15, 3.20.1, Plin. *Nat.* 32.116, *al.* (*TLL* VII. 2.1187.17 ff.). Lucretius and Celsus agree in avoiding the old Latin term *ueternus*, although the doctor uses it at Pl. *Men.* 891 and Horace of himself at *Ep.* 1.8.10 (cf. Cato, *orat.* 81 Sblendorio Cugusi (simile), Ter. *Eun.* 688, Catul. 17.24, Virg. *G.* 1.124 and Probus ad loc.: *ueternum grauem somnum uolunt intellegi . . . quem medici lethargum uocant). ueternus ciui-tatem occupans* is a well-attested medical image of the body politic (Cael. *Fam.* 8.6.4, Cic. *Fam.* 2.13.3, Sen. *Ep.* 82.19, 88.19, *al.*); perhaps *ueternus*

---

[80] Mazzini (1988: 54–5) lists, with references to the poem, the numerous items of medical theory and practice of which Lucretius shows knowledge, though it is not Mazzini's purpose to comment on the vocabulary used.

~ *lethargus* is another isogloss dividing lay from specialist usage (cf. **(8)** above): this would give a good account of Horace's use of *lethargus* in the medical context at *S.* 2.3.145, but *ueternus* at *Ep.* 1.8.10, where the point of view is very much that of the patient or of his friends.

partes extremae (corporis) 'the extremities' (6.947): cf. Cels. 2.4.4, 2.7.12, 4.21.1, *al.* (*TLL* V. 2.2000.25 ff.).

partes genitales 'the genitals' (4.1044, 6.1206): cf. Val. Max. 7.7.6, *al.* Col. 6.26.2. (cf. 6.36.2 *genitalia loca*), Cels. 4.1.11 (*genitale* neut. sg. noun), Garg. Mart. *med.* 5, etc. (Cf. *TLL* VI. 2.1814.1 ff. and Adams (1982*a*: 57–8).)

profluuium sanguinis 'a flux of blood, haemorrhage' (6.1205): cf. Cels. 2.7.2, 28, 4.11.4, 5.22.6, *al.*, Col. 6.26.3.

sacer ignis one or more forms of erysipelas (6.660, 1167): cf. Virg. *G.* 3.566; Cels. 5.22.7, 5.24.4, 5.28.4ACD; Plin. *Nat.* 26.121, *al.*

signa mortis 'indications of impending death' (6.1182): cf. Cels. 2.6.6, 9, 14.

singultus 'hiccough' (3.480): cf. Cels. 2.7.17, *al.*, Larg. 191, Plin. *Nat.* 20.87, etc. The phrase *singultus frequens* is found at Cels. 2.7.17, 3.24.2 and Lucr. 6.1160. In the latter it denotes the convulsive catching of the breath of the dying, a use closer to the other meaning of the word, 'sobbing' (Cic. *Planc.* 76, Catul. 64.131, Hor. *C.* 3.27.74, etc.). When was this word first used for the humble hiccough? In Greek, λύζω shows a similar pattern of use: 'sob' in verse, 'hiccough' in (medical) prose.

temptare 'to attack', of disease or similar (3.147, 5.346, 6.1104): cf. Hor. *Carm.* 1.16.23 (in a medical image), Cels. (6×, 2.8.10, 3.21.4, *al.*), Larg. (7×, 89, 101, 161, *al.*).

uenus 'sexual intercourse', in humans or animals (4.1235, 1276, *al.*): cf. Virg. *G.* 4.199, Livy (4×: 4× *concubitus*), Cels. (14×: 2× *concubitus*: 2× *coitus*), Sen. (2× in prose: 9× *concubitus/concumbo*; 17× in verse:[81] 2× *concubitus*), Col. (11×, 6.24.2, etc.), Plin. *Nat.* (*c.* 60×, 20.146, etc.), Tac. *Ger.* 20.4*, Cael. Aur. (see Ernout (1956)). Cicero does not use *uenus* for 'sex' but rather, on the rare occasions when he has to, *concubitus* (*Rep.* 4.4, *N.D.* 1.42) and *concumbo* (*Fat.* 30, *Inv.* 1.44, 73, 74, 75). Adams (1982*a*: 189) characterizes *uenus* as 'one of the standard neutral nouns of the educated language for sexual intercourse' and gives the following summary of its distribution: '*uenus* is common from Lucr. onwards, in writers who deal with sexual activity in a technical and neutral tone'. One might add that it is common also in the poets[82] and raise the question whether both

---

[81] Although here the word generally means sexual love, sexual desire.

[82] The other examples in the *OLD* s.v. 4. are poetic, save Apul. *Met.* 1.9, 5.10, which are doubtful, and Ulp. *Dig.* 48.5.24 (mid-second century), which is different in that it uses the phrase *res ueneris*.

poetic and technical uses derive from a Lucretian innovation; whether they reflect a different innovator and, if so, whether technical or poetic; or whether they reflect independent innovations.

ueratrum 'hellebore' (4.640–1): cf. Cato, *Agr.* 114,1, 115,1, 2, Cels. 2.6.7, *et saepe*, Larg. 10, 99; Col. 6.32.2, 6.38.3 (where the word is ascribed to *rustici*), 7.13.2. Lucretius, Celsus and Scribonius agree in avoiding *elleborus*, although this Greek loan-word is common, especially in medical contexts, real and metaphorical, from Plautus on (e.g. Pl. *Men.* 913, Cato *Agr.* 157.12, Catul. 99.14, Virg. *G.* 3.451 (plur.), Hor. *S.* 2.3.82, Col. 10.17 (plur., imitating Virgil), Mart. 9.94.6).

This set of sixteen words and phrases gives some illustration of what we may regard as standard Latin medical expressions which occur already in Lucretius. They may be used to support a case for the existence of Latin medical discourse contemporary with Lucretius which the poet's audience would have 'heard' in the intense language of his medical metaphor. This is based on the assumption, no more (but see below), that these agreements between Lucretius and medical prose depend on a common source, that is at least one well-known Latin medical work (or course of lectures?[83]) that was composed before Lucretius wrote his poem and that influenced the vocabulary of medical discourse to the first century AD and beyond. A second possible interpretation of these lexical agreements is that there is a relation of dependence of Latin medical prose on the language of Lucretius, that a post-Lucretian composer of the first literary Latin medical text, as distinct from recipes — Varro, say, or Pompeius Lenaeus or C. Valgius Rufus — was influenced by Lucretius' choice and creation of high-sounding (Ennian) vocabulary for treating a new scientific subject in Latin (cf. Gigon (1978: 171)), and so borrowed from Lucretius in order to give a particular colour and status to his new medical prose. An obvious consequence of this is that these agreements are no evidence for pre-Lucretian medical Latin in the strong sense; any medical variety to which they were proper was post-Lucretian and could not have been imitated in the metaphor at 4.1068ff. The third available view of this first set of lexical agreements is the easiest of all: they are quite insignificant; they are all ordinary words from the language of everyday; agreements between Lucretius and Celsus which look like departures from normal usage (e.g. *lethargus, uenus, ueratrum*) are accidental results of our fragmentary record of republican Latin.

---

[83] Professor Adams raises the interesting question whether Latin medical expressions and terminology could have been disseminated in a consistent form in lectures forming part of an *encyclios disciplina*. Vitruvius (1.1.12–18, 6.pr.4) had an education of this sort, certainly including some medical theory, which surfaces frequently in his treatise.

As circumstantial evidence in favour of Brown's (implied) view of a common source of the above agreements between Lucretius and (especially) Celsus may be cited some typically telling observations in J. N. Adams's latest book (1995*b*) on Latin veterinary terminology. Adams writes (1995*b*: 642): 'The language of doctors could be parodied as early as the time of Plautus.' The parodies which he discusses (pp. 608, 637, 638) are three: (a) several features of the following line[s]:

> Pl. *Mer.* 139[–40]   CH. resinam ex melle Aegyptiam uorato, saluom feceris.
> AC. at edepol tu calidam picem bibito, aegritudo apscesserit.

I add line 140 because this is really a double parody, Charinus mimicking contemporary medical phraseology, Acanthio parodying Charinus. Adams draws attention to the medical use of *ex* 'dipped in', the (medical) *-to* imperative, the prediction, in a future tense, of successful cure after the prescription; (b) the use by the doctor of *aliquis* in conjunction with a numeral at:

> Pl. *Men.* 950   elleborum potabis faxo *aliquos uiginti* dies;[84]

(c) the emphatic *figura etymologica* in the same medical context:

> Pl. *Men.* [895–] 897   SENEX magna cum *cura* ego illum *curari* uolo.
> MEDICUS quin suspirabo plus sescenta in dies:
> ita ego eum cum *cura* magna *curabo* tibi.[85]

It may be objected that neither (b) nor (c) is strictly medical, as (b) appears to be a general colloquial use of *aliquis* (Hofmann and Szantyr (1965: 211)), and since (c) is found in a variety of special and technical contexts, from *Lex XII* 12.2 *noxiamue noxit* and Enn. *Ann.* 77V *curantes magna cum cura* on (see Hofmann and Szantyr (1965: 124–5, 791); Jocelyn (1969*a*: 173) and cf. Haffter (1934: 10–43) and below, n. 103). But, even setting these for the sake of argument aside, we still have in (a) an undeniable instance of the phraseology of medical recipes which will recur constantly in medical and veterinary treatises and which requires the assumption of a tradition of (at least) medical recipe literature[86] dating

---

[84] For parallels see Adams (1995*b*: 637 and n. 602); he compares in particular Cato, *Agr.* 156.1 and Pelag. 146.1.

[85] For parallels see Adams (1995*b*: 504 and n. 170).

[86] Adams (1995*b*: 639) prefers this 'medical' phraseology to be characteristic of *written* treatises rather than of the speech of practising *medici* (or *ueterinarii*). This implies that these Plautine parodies of doctors (like other humour in Plautus) suppose a literate audience. It is relevant to the last point that Varro and his interlocutors in the *Res rusticae* expect both

from the age of Plautus or earlier. This tradition is, of course, well attested already in parts of Cato, *De agricultura* (above, n. 76); Adams adduces several other parallels of construction and phraseology between Cato and Pelagonius (summarized at 1995*b*: 636–8), which 'underline the conservatism of the didactic (particularly recipe-) style over many centuries' (1995*b*: 637). Is this, then, another side of the medical discourse which Lucretius mimics? It is tempting to answer, 'Yes'. Admittedly, Celsus happens to exhibit rather few of the features of the recipe style characterized by Adams,[87] nor are any of them, to my knowledge, to be found in Lucretius. But, given so little material on which to base a reconstruction of any medical Latin in the strong sense, should we not be content with hard evidence for one type of Latin medical discourse older than Lucretius? In reality, both general considerations and surviving material in both Greek and Latin make it not merely plausible but overwhelmingly likely that there would have been from the beginning several quite different types of medical texts and utterances, the style varying with the content, the background of the author and the intended audience or readership.[88] Given this, as well as the theme of our Symposium, and the title of my chapter, I venture an exploratory coda.

(11) Further lexical colour in medical prose?

Studies of Latin technical prose have repeatedly drawn attention to two contrasting stylistic tendencies: conservatism and colloquialism (see De Meo (1983: *passim*), on individual technical languages). Both emerge in Adams's account of the language of Pelagonius and of medical recipe phraseology; both are characteristic of Celsus.[89] A third lexical colour — poeticism — has been observed by some in technical prose, both ancient

---

magistri pecoris and humble *pastores* to be literate and to carry with them written records (*commentarii*) of the symptoms and treatment of animals' diseases. See Adams (1995*b*: 72–8). How formal and how consistent was the Latin of these *commentarii*?

[87] I know of no examples in Celsus of the use of *aliquis* + numeral, of the *figura etymologica* or of the future-tense prediction of successful cure mentioned above; in particular, Celsus avoids religiously the -*to* imperative.

[88] On this stylistic variety, see Adams (1995*b*: 642–6, 653–5, 662–8). In veterinary terminology, in particular, Adams, summarizing (1995*b*: 668), distinguishes (i) terms of *pastores* or *rustici*, (ii) terms of specialist *ueterinarii*, (iii) 'terms with a "learned" flavour introduced to veterinary discourse by educated laymen with stylistic pretensions, (iv) inactive (non-current) terms crudely transferred or calqued from Greek'. Much the same variety will have existed in the sphere of human medicine.

[89] Conservatism: in vocabulary, see n. 97 below on *atra bilis* and *aqua inter cutem*; in syntax, note Celsus' use of gerund + accusative object at 1.3.8 and 7.26.5C: see Löfstedt (1990: 60), Hofmann and Szantyr (1965: 372–3) and J. H. W. Penney in this volume, pp. 259–60. On the question of colloquialism in Celsus, see most recently Önnerfors (1993: 243ff.).

and modern: L. Guilbert (1965: 70) and J. Dubois (1966: 104) have seen it in the modern French language of aviation; L. Callebat (1982: 704–7) has noted splashes of it in Vitruvius. I am not aware of any modern attribution of poetic colouring to Latin medical prose but I have been struck by a number of lexical agreements between Celsus and high poetry, including but in some instances possibly going beyond Lucretius. The very idea of such agreements brings with it a sense of *déjà vu*, and some foreboding: F. Marx thought to see lexical agreements between Celsus and Ovid sufficient to postulate influence of the poet upon the encyclopaedist (1915: xvi, xcvii, cviii, Index *s.v. Ouidii imitatio*), an idea which was to be thrown out rudely — if rightly — by Önnerfors (1993: 238–9) in a recent volume of *ANRW*. The agreements that I am about to illustrate are different in kind and will, I hope, merit further attention.

(i) Word formation

I have tried to show elsewhere (Langslow (1991: 118–20[90])) that already in Celsus' medical terminology certain suffixes stand out by their frequency in the text and by clustering in well-defined lexical or semantic fields; I say 'already' because this is a feature of modern scientific language; (see, for example, Sager *et al.* (1980: 257–64) and Fluck (1980: 84–5).) Several of these formations seem to have been favoured also by Lucretius and more generally by old high Latin poetry, in particular, nouns in *-(it)iēs*, *-iei* (fem.), *-or*, *-ōris* (masc.), *-us*, *-ūs* (masc.) and 'inchoative' verbs in *-scō*, *-scere*.

I begin with the last, the *-scō* verbs supposedly characteristic of pre-Lucretian Latin medical discourse. This productive formation (see Mignot (1969: 145–228)) is common in Celsus; he uses more than forty different verbs with this suffix, a good number of which are found earlier in high poetry, such as *albescere*, *grauescere*, *inueterascere*, *mollescere*, *nigrescere*, *ommutescere*, *spissescere*. This type is especially favoured by Lucretius (106 verbs, according to Swanson (1962: 38–9, 130–3)) and is frequent also in early epic and tragedy; with reference to the last Jocelyn (1969a: 198) remarks that these verbs 'probably had a poetic tone. Such forms are comparatively rare in the fragments of Ennius' tragedies but pullulate in those of his *Annales* and the rest of republican tragedy.'

Jocelyn (1969a: 199) has a similar comment on masculine abstract nouns in *-us*, *-ūs*: these 'were much affected by more elevated genres of archaic poetry; Ploen [1882] counted 63 in 1,940 verses of tragedy, and

---

[90] See now on this aspect of veterinary and medical Latin Adams (1995b: 519–68, esp. 519–20, 566–8; cf. 653), who states some doubts and reservations.

only 125 in 30,000 lines of comedy'. This is one of the formations singled out by Bailey (1947: 135) in his *Prolegomena* on the style of Lucretius; Swanson (1962: 8) lists 121 such forms used by Lucretius, including a dozen hapax (e.g. 4.1242 *adhaesus*). The preference of high poetry for *-us*, *-ūs* over *-io*, *-iōnis* (fem.) is due largely to metrical considerations; and yet *-us* is generally held to have been of higher style than *-io* (Hofmann and Szantyr (1965: 743)). Celsus attests more medical words in *-io* than in *-us* (58: 37) and yet the proportion of the latter is, I suggest, strikingly high for a prose work on a technical subject, higher, I think, than that to be found in Vitruvius or in Cicero's philosophical terminology (though this is, I confess, an impression only, based on the examples and discussion in Lebreton (1901), Poncelet (1957), Callebat (1974)). They are used especially to name natural bodily functions (e.g. *spiritus* 'breathing', *pulsus* 'the pulse', *conceptus* 'conception', *usus* 'a bodily function') including the five senses (*sensus: uisus, auditus, tactus, gustus, odoratus*). Celsus has a small group of concrete nouns in *-cessus* (*abscessus* 'abscess', *excessus* 'protuberance', *processus* 'process', *recessus* 'recess'), of which only the last is attested in the given concrete sense before Celsus, *recessus* having been used, perhaps significantly, chiefly by poets (e.g. Virg. *A.* 8.193 of a cave, cf. Ov. *Met.* 11.592 *et saepe*).

Several studies of masculine nouns in *-or*, *-ōris* have served in comp-lementary fashion to indicate their semantic homogeneity. Instances of the type down to the time of Cicero have been most recently characterized by Untermann (1977: 334–5) as 'Empfindungen, die als temporäre Eigen-schaften eines Menschen (übertragen auch jedes anderen belebten oder unbelebten Individuums) auftreten und durch Sinnesorgane wahrge-nommen werden'. Such a formation lent itself ideally to the service of medical writers in describing the look, the feel, the temperature, and other symptoms of a patient's condition. In the medical vocabulary of Celsus I have counted 28 examples of this formation which name signs and symp-toms of disease; these include very common words, such as *dolor, rubor, tremor*, etc. and some much rarer, e.g. *liuor, marcor, pallor, sopor* 'le synonyme poétique de *somnus*' (Ernout 1957a: 45), *stridor* (see **(11)** *(iii)* below), etc.[91] After Cicero it is principally in medical writers that new forms are found. As to the stylistic register of the formation, in a note on Ennius' tragedies, Jocelyn (1969a: 195) comments 'abstract formations in *-or* tended generally to have a lofty tone; Ploen [1882] counted 26 in 1,940 verses of tragedy and only 35 in 30,000 of comedy'. The formation is favoured by high poetry, tragedy and epic (Ernout 1957a: 53), especially

---

[91] The forms *fluor* 'a flux' and *marcor* 'apathy, languor' appear first in Celsus; he is the first to use *rubor, sopor* and *tepor* of the human body and disease.

by Lucretius, who attests 48 such nouns (Swanson (1962: 53–4)), nearly half of those known, including rare forms such as *amaror, leuor, stringor*, and *aegror, angor, luror, pallores* (plur.), the last four in medical contexts.

The use of formations in *-itiēs*, finally, is striking even before the end of the Republic, above all in prose, because by then the productive suffix was very definitely *-itia* and even in old Latin new first-declension forms were competing with and replacing old *-(it)iē*-stems (Hofmann and Szantyr (1965: 744 (g)); Leumann (1977: 285, 296)). Celsus attests the following pathological terms in his medical vocabulary: *caries, macies, materies, pernicies, sanies, scabies*; and *durities, mollities, nigrities*; the type may remain marginally productive in medical terminology, *cantabries* and *uermicies*, for example, appearing late. Forms in *-ies* are absent from Plautus, Terence and Cato (Swanson (1962: 53)); those in *-ities* are hardly to be found in classical prose but are commoner in poetry, especially in Virgil, metrical considerations again playing a part in hexameter poets. Lucretius attests some striking examples, including *amicities, durities, notities* (for Epicurean πρόληψις), and *spurcities* 'dirt, impurity' (6.977).

(ii) Accumulation of rhyming derivatives

As I noted, the suffixes mentioned in the last paragraph are characteristic not only of Celsus and Lucretius but also of high Latin poetry more generally. A nice indication of this is the accumulation in *parodies* of epic and tragedy of rhyming derivatives in just these suffixes.[92] The repeated suffix was clearly seen as typical of the target of the parody, as for example in:

Lucil. 599–601M	hic cruciatur fame
	frig*or*e, inluu*ie*, inbaln*itie*, inperfund*itie*,
	incuria,[93]
or Pl. *Rud.* 215	alg*or*, err*or*, pau*or* me omnia tenent,
or Pl. *Capt.* 133–4	ego qui tuo maer*or*e maceror
	mace*sc*o, consene*sc*o et tabe*sc*o miser.[94]

---

[92] An analogous phenomenon in Greek literature is Aristophanes' use of the suffix -κός to parody the 'new learning': see Peppler (1910).

[93] Parodying Pac. *trag.* 9 (*Antiopa*), according to Char. *GLK* 1.101.20f.

[94] Note in this connection Jocelyn's words (1969a: 198): 'Ploen [1882] counted 85 inchoative formations in comedy but it would be wrong to think that many came from ordinary Roman speech. 64 of them occur only in Plautus' plays and many of these nowhere else in Latin. Very often a paratragic tone is plainly detectable in the context of utterance.' Lucretius' 'uiue*sc*it ... inuetera*sc*it ... gli*sc*it ... graue*sc*it' (4.1068–9) is surely itself a parody of some sort: is it of tragic / epic diction, or of medical discourse?

Accumulation, though less concentrated, of rhyming derivatives is found also in serious poetry. Note, for example:

Enn. *scen.* 151–3V	caelum nite*s*cere, arbores fronde*s*cere,
	uites laetificae pampinis pube*s*cere,
	rami bacarum ubertate incurue*s*cere,
Pac. *trag.* 294	sed nescioquidnam est, animus mi horre*s*cit, et
	gli*s*cit gaudium.
Fur. Ant. *FPL* 3	incre*s*cunt animi, uīre*s*cit uolnere uirtus
Pac. *trag.* 274–5	corpusque meum tali
	maer*ore*, err*ore*, mac*ore* senet,
Acc. *trag.* 349	persuasit maer*or*, anxitudo, err*or*, dol*or*,
Virg. *A.* 5.5	duri magno sed am*ore* dol*ore*s

and, with another formation:

Enn. *scen.* 97–9V	haec omnia uidi inflamm*ari*,
	Priamo ui uitam euit*ari*,
	Iouis aram sanguine turp*ari*;

Ernout (1957*a*: 53) pointed to Virgil's frequent use of -*or* derivatives in a strongly archaizing passage in the *Aeneid* (7.458–66).[95]

In Celsus, too, it is not only in the number of such derivatives in a list of his vocabulary that he shows his predilection for these formations; he shows also a fondness for accumulating rhyming formations in twos or threes. Notice, for example:

Cels. pr. 24	[vivisection shows of the internal body parts] dur*itie*m, molli-*tie*m, leu*ore*m, conta*ctu*m, proce*ssu*s deinde singulorum et rece*ssu*s.

and the famous summary of the symptoms of inflammation:

Cels. 3.10.3	notae uero inflammationis sunt quattuor: rub*or* et tum*or* cum cal*ore* et dol*ore*.

Sometimes a sentence will be marked not by a rhyming pair but by the close association of two or more of these suffixes, as for instance:

Cels. 3.24.2	totum corpus cum pall*ore* quodam inalbe*s*cit
Cels. 4.7.1	lingua faucesque cum rub*ore* intume*s*cunt

---

[95] The similar, though quite separate, phenomenon of homeoteleuton, in Shackleton Bailey's (1994) sense of the term, is also significantly more common in pre-neoteric Latin verse. Its high incidence in the *Aeneid* (four times as high as in *Ecl.* and *G.*) may reflect, according to Shackleton Bailey (1994: 100), Virgil's desire, even if unconscious, to imitate Ennius and eschew neoteric practice in his epic.

Cels. 6.6.29   [oculi] cum dolo*r*e quodam graue*s*cunt et noctu praegraui
               pituita inhaere*s*cunt.[96]

(iii) Vocabulary

Finally, I mention briefly below a few examples of other items of Celsus'
vocabulary, medical and non-medical — apart from the suffixal formations
touched on above — which may possibly have had a poetic ring to them.

It was noted in **(8)** above that *aegrotus*, although common in prose and
the less exalted forms of poetry, and though apparently the ordinary
doctor's word for '(one who is) ill' in Plautus and Cicero, is avoided by
epic poetry, including Lucretius, and by Celsus and Scribonius Largus.

The colour term *ater* 'black' — 'terme spécifiquement épique', according
to André (1949: 387) (cf. p. 196 above) — is preserved in medical prose not
only in the old phrasal term *atra bilis*,[97] but also in descriptive phrases such
as *sanguini atro similis* (Cels. 2.8.43; cf. 3.25.1, 5.26.20E). *ater* used of blood
occurs most famously at Enn. *scen.* 363V *tabo, sanie et sanguine atro*, a line
that appears to have been imitated in later epic poetry.[98] I acknowledge,
however, that *ater* may not in itself have been poetic, but rather 'affective',
denoting black in a sinister or unpleasant sense, evoking 'ce que la couleur
noire peut avoir d'impressionnant, de triste, de lugubre' (Marouzeau 1962:
166; cf. 1949*b*: 67 f.), so that it could have been used naturally and quite
independently in epic poetry and medical prose.[99]

effundere is common in Celsus in the sense 'to let out (a liquid)' (25
times). Once, rather strikingly, it is used to mean 'to let (a body part) fall
back' (7.7.4A *ut in gremium eius [medici] caput resupinus effundat [aeger]*).
This use appears to be unparalleled in prose, although it is quite common
in poetry, beginning with Lucretius (3.113; cf. *TLL* V.2.221.51 ff.).

Likewise, the intransitive use of *repetere* (= *redire*), which is found
several times in Celsus (2.1.6, 2.8.23, 3.22.3, *al.*) and Scribonius (56, 122)
(cf. Önnerfors (1963: 164 n. 33)), can be paralleled only in poetry (*Culex*
105, Virg. *A.* 7.241).

---

[96] With this pattern compare the humorous (pseudo-medical?) line in Cael. *Fam.* 8.6.4 'si
Parthi uos nihil calfaciunt, nos hic frigo*r*e frige*s*cimus'; cf. Haffter (1934: 33).

[97] Celsus' term for μελαγχολία, *atra bilis* is already in Pl. *Am.* 727, Cato, *Agr.* 157,7. It and
aqua inter cutem 'dropsy' are nice instances of Celsus' lexical archaism. In the latter note
the 'undoing' by Celsus of the compound adjective *intercus*, made to acc. *intercutem*, gen.
intercutis, etc. arising by hypostasis. The age of this formation may be reflected in its use of
the preposition *inter* 'under' (?), parallels with which are not easy to find; Leumann (1977:
403) explains it as from *inter cutem et carnem*, but quotes no supporting examples.

[98] Note e.g. Virg. *A.* 8.487. For *ater sanguis* of the dead, cf. Virg. *A.* 3.28, 33, 622, *G.* 3.221,
507.

[99] I owe this observation to Professor Adams.

mortifer(us) 'deadly, fatal' is common in poetry, including elegy, from Ennius on; in poetry it is used to qualify a wide range of nouns. In prose it is less common[100] and its distribution and uses are striking. Nearly all prose occurrences are of wounds, diseases and their symptoms, injuries and poison, including snakebite: they are, in a word, medical. These contexts account for all occurrences in Cicero (10×), Hirtius (1×), Nepos (1×), Livy (4×), Valerius Maximus (2×), Ammianus Marcellinus (2×), as well as those in technical prose, where the word is most common (more than ten times in Celsus and the elder Pliny; three times in Columella, twice in Vitruvius and once in Scribonius Largus). It may be that its restricted use in prose reflects an archaic, even poetic, medical usage (*TLL* VIII. 1517.72 ff.).

praesens[101] 'effective' (of a remedy; with comparative and superlative), later 'immediate, swift in effect' (of trauma or remedy), is found first in Virgil's *Georgics* (2.127, 3.452) and is then common in technical prose (including Celsus, Columella and Pliny and later medical and veterinary writers). Semantically, it seems to be a step away from the use of the word with *deus, numina* and the like to mean 'present so as to bring aid' (cf. Ter. *Ph.* 345, Virg. *G.* 1.10 *uos, agrestum praesentia numina, Fauni, A.* 9.404 *tu dea tu praesens nostro succurre labori*, even Larg. *epist. dedic.* 1 [*quosdam*] *medicamento... dato, protinus uelut praesenti numine omni dolore... liberasse aegrum*, etc. and *TLL* X. 2.843.64 ff.). Pascucci (1961: 47) implies that Virgil invented the medical use and bequeathed it to later technical writers. But Virgil seems to allude to the medical use in Juno's speech to Iuturna:

> Virg. *A.* 12.152   tu pro germano si quid *praesentius* audes[102]

and, if this is right, it is more likely that the medical use of this 'religious word' (Nisbet–Hubbard 1970: *ad* Hor. *C.* 1.35.2) was already established. Of course, religious is not at all the same as poetic and, notwithstanding the allusion in Virgil, *praesens* may be an instance of an entirely different lexical source of medical Latin.[103]

stridor, which Celsus uses of the grinding of teeth (2.7.25 *insolitus dentium stridor*; cf. 2.6.5), is said to be a poetic word (Fedeli 1985: *ad* Prop. 3.7.47–8), and certainly the vast majority of its occurrences are in poetry

---

[100] As are compounds in *-fer* generally: see Arens (1950: esp. 243) and Bader (1962: 107–11).

[101] See Pascucci (1961) and *TLL* X.2.843.64ff., 844.51ff. and 849.42ff.

[102] Notice another medical image in this speech at line 158, in the words *conceptumque excute foedus* (*excutere* 'to cause a miscarriage' Ov. *Ep.* 11.42, *Fast.* 1.624, Cels. 2.7.16, Larg. *epist. dedic.* 5).

[103] Emphatic *figurae etymologicae* like *cura curare* (above, p. 214) may also according to Haffter (1934: 33n.) originate in 'feierliche Sakral- oder Gesetzessprache'; Haffter sees them, however, as proper mainly to 'hohe Dichterdiktion' (1934: 33 n. 43).

(Accius, Virgil, Tibullus, Ovid), though it is not unknown in prose (Cic. *Agr.* 2.70 of the tribune Rullus, *Tusc.* 5.116 of a saw, Vitr. 2.4.1 of a type of earth).[104]

(12) Possible accounts and conclusion

In principle, any linguistic feature shared by poetry and prose can arise in one of three ways: (a) by common inheritance from a single source, such as the ordinary language of everyday, or (b) through borrowing by one linguistic variety of features proper to the other, that is either (i) by poetry from prose or (ii) by prose from poetry. This set of possible accounts faces the Hellenist pondering agreements in vocabulary between Homer and Hippocrates or Hippocrates and tragedy; it faces us now if we are minded to consider the features shared by Celsus and high poetry set out in **(11)**. Let us take the options one by one.

On the first view — (a) common inheritance from a single source — we shall regard the above agreements as coincidental and insignificant; we shall deny any relation of dependence between Celsus*[105] and Latin epic. We shall say that *-sco* verbs, for example, are indeed common in epic and medical prose but as a result of independent exploitations of an inherited formation present in ordinary Latin in the pre-literary period.

Clearly this is the easiest position to take. It is of course akin in its motivating scepticism to the view taken on the Greek side that, say, Hippocrates and Euripides are simply using common (Ionic) words which happen to be otherwise unknown to us, so that certain lexical agreements are no indication of a relation of dependence, nor of any significance for Greek lexicography or literary history. On the Latin side, this account need not be quite so negative, since we know some Latin prose from the period separating Celsus from Lucretius (or Ennius) and it does not share the lexical features under discussion. In other words, even if we take up position (a) above, we are left with some non-trivial differences between Celsus and other literary Latin prose, and furthermore with the inference that one could use (in the first century AD) a number of Latin words and suffixes favoured by high poetry without sounding like a poet.[106]

---

[104] Like *singultus* or Gk λυγ- 'sob; hiccough', this medical use of what may have been felt to be a poetic word is reminiscent of the Greek use of the root βρυχ- (βρυγμός, βρύχειν) of grinding the teeth.

[105] Celsus* means 'Celsus or any Latin source of Celsus'.

[106] H. D. Jocelyn (1986: 330, n. 132) appears to take this view by suggesting in a note on *durities* that, given its distribution before Celsus (Lucr. 4.268, Catul. 66.50, Var. *R.* 1.55.1, Vitr. 2.9.7) the tone of the word was 'grandiosely archaic for poets, soberly archaic for writers on technical subjects'.

The second view — (b) (i) medical vocabulary in poetry — is ruled out by the fact that the shared items under consideration are not medical expressions, with the exception of *aegrotus/aeger*, which, though medical, conveys an ordinary everyday notion.

The third account, however — (b) (ii) poetic vocabulary in medical prose — is available. On this view, the words which occur only in Celsus and the poets would be flashes of poetic colour worked deliberately by Celsus* into medical discourse (just like those observed by L. Callebat (1982: 704–7) in Vitruvius).[107] And yet even this account does not easily yield an argument in favour of a pre-Lucretian Latin medical idiom, since very few of these poetic flashes have echoes that are demonstrably older than Lucretius; they may simply be further examples of Lucretian influence on Celsus* — one possible interpretation of Lucretius' medical vocabulary, aired in **(10)** above — and, as such, offer no support for R. D. Brown's explanation of the language of Lucretius' medical metaphor since any Latin medical discourse to which they are proper would be post-Lucretian.

Only a very strong version of this third account would allow these lexical agreements to yield support for Brown's reading of Lucretius; I mean a strong version something like this: the agreements between Celsus* and old high Latin poetry are dim reflections of the idiom of at least one famous example of a Latin medical discourse, spoken or written in Latin tinged with grandiose poetic language. The purpose of this lexical colour would have been to appeal to conservative taste, to confer high status on the subject and by echoing Ennius, the Roman Homer, to imitate the Homerizing tradition in Greek medical prose. This Latin medical discourse — composed perhaps by Varro[108] or Pompeius Lenaeus,[109] or by

---

[107] And we could add to the examples in **(11)** *(iii)* the snake *chelydrus* (above, n. 27).

[108] Varro (116–27 BC) is a likely suspect, above all because he devoted the eighth book of his *Disciplinae* to the subject of medicine. Although he is never mentioned by Celsus (anyway, Celsus, like modern encyclopaedias, gives very few references to his sources), he seems to allude to a contemporary scientific theory of contagion (*R.* 1.12.2; Lehmann (1982)) and he distinguishes (*R.* 2.1.21) the type of medicine requiring the help of a professional from that which the *pater familias* can take care of in the manner dealt with by Cato (see n. 76). He has at least one, later standard, translation of a Greek medical expression (*Men.* 447A *aluum subducere* for κοιλίαν ὑπάγειν, here in a *double entendre*). As for contacts with epic, it is to be noted that Varro quotes Ennius on points of terminology and usage (e.g. in *Disciplinae* Bk 5 [arithmetic], *apud* Gel. 10.1 on *quarto* vs. *quartum*, 3.14 on *dimidium* vs. *dimidiatum*. Note also *R.* 1.48.2 '[gluma "husk"] apud Ennium solum scriptum scio esse'; and 1.4.1 'eius principia sunt eadem, quae mundi esse Ennius scribit, aqua, terra, anima et sol').

[109] A second strong candidate, as a putative Ennianizing Latin source of Celsus*, is Pompeius Lenaeus, a freedman of Pompey, born about 100–90 BC. Lenaeus was the translator of Mithridates' medical library and, as far as Pliny knew (*Nat.* 25.5), he was the first man to write on pharmacology in Latin. Lenaeus was known also as a *grammaticus* and as an authority on early Latin literature. (See Suet. *Gram.* 15 and Kaster (1995: ad loc.).) He will

any of the πολὺ φῦλον of scholars who flooded into Rome from Greece from the middle of the second century BC (Plb. 31.24.6–7; Kaster (1995: 62)) — could have been older than Lucretius' poem and it could have been the language of this discourse that Lucretius' audience heard in the metaphor of love as a disease at 4.1068ff.

While the weaker version of (b) (ii) may deserve some consideration and further investigation, the weight of the reconstruction involved in the strong version in the last paragraph cannot reasonably be borne by the shared features so far identified (in **(11)** above) which may plausibly have echoes older than Lucretius: *ater sanguis, mortifer(us), praesens, stridor* and the suffixes and their accumulation, above all the *-sco* verbs which Lucretius uses in superabundance at 4.1068–9, our point of departure (in **(9)** above).

An idle thought: although the two sets of *comparanda* are very different, there is a certain similarity between the caution just expressed in provisionally preferring Lucretius over Ennius as the source of possible epicisms in literary medical Latin and (e.g.) Ruijgh's ascription, in **(1)** above, of epicisms in Hippocrates to the influence of the imagined idiom of the medical parts of Empedocles rather than directly to that of Homer.[110]

Much of the argument of the last part of this paper **(III)** stems from the seemingly innocuous claim that Lucretius mimics in a metaphor the style of contemporary doctors' Latin. This claim seems right in literary terms — i.e. it gives the metaphor more point, and is in keeping with the general hypothesis (in **(6)** above) that a poet (indeed, any user of a language) will use in a metaphor language proper to the metaphor's source-domain. It is also lexically well founded — i.e. the key words of the medical metaphor are found in later medical contexts, above all in Celsus — but it runs against the historian's view of medicine as an exclusively Greek-speaking profession in republican and imperial Rome. On the historical side — at first sight difficult — it may be observed that already Plautus can parody doctors' language and that there are testimonies in our sources to Latin medical texts that may have been around before Lucretius published his poem; one may conclude simply at this point, then, that it may have been their style that Lucretius' metaphor parodied. However, the simple-seeming lexical agreements between Lucretius and Celsus hold out the prospect, whatever account one gives of them, of

have been fully bilingual and equally learned in Greek and Latin literature. As an academic with philological and medical interests, he was certainly aware of the Greek tradition of medical prose and its Homerizing lexical strand. Is it unthinkable that the first literary Latin medical work should have been modelled on the post-Hippocratic tradition in the Greek world by incorporating lexical colouring from the Latin Homer?

[110] On Empedocles as Lucretius' literary model see Sedley (1989).

deriving more from Lucretius than evidence for medical Latin. To be sure, the establishment of a link between the medical vocabulary of Lucretius and Celsus* would be of significance for more than the history of medicine; but the lexical agreements between Celsus and Lucretius go beyond the medical metaphor and even beyond medical vocabulary *sensu proprio* to include non-medical items of high-poetic diction; a few other items of Celsus' vocabulary, not found in Lucretius, appear to be proper to Latin poetry and may be deliberate splashes of poetic colour in medical prose. The possibility that Celsus' vocabulary and Lucretius' metaphor give us the dim reflection of an archaizing, even Ennianizing, Latin medical text in circulation in Rome before the end of the 50s BC remains theoretical only, even if a persuasive reading of Lucretius implies something of the sort.

I am acutely aware that this paper yields more questions than answers, and, perhaps worse, that there are yet more questions that it fails to raise. I hope, however, that some of these questions regarding contacts between the language of poetry and the language of science may help to reawaken interest in the Greek themes with which I opened **(I)**; that these Greek paradigm-cases together with the working hypotheses developed in **(II)** may provoke some reaction among Latinists; and that the illustrative case-studies in **(III)** are not perceived simply as an overlong and ultimately indecisive commentary on three lines of Lucretius — their intention has been to indicate some general possibilities and problems for sociolinguistics in a corpus-language, and to suggest some of the results that may stand to be gained from systematic comparative study of literary and technical texts.

Proceedings of the British Academy, **93**, 227–246

Lucretius' Use and Avoidance of Greek

DAVID SEDLEY

Summary. Lucretius uses highly technical Greek Epicurean sources, but his strategy is to replace technical terms with complementary sets of metaphors and images. Above all, he never merely transliterates a Greek philosophical term, unless for the exceptional purpose of keeping the corresponding concept at arm's length. His aim is to make Epicureanism thoroughly at home in a Roman cultural context. In the first half of the present chapter, this policy is illustrated with examples such as his vocabulary for visual 'images' in book 4 (where, thanks to the accidental survival of two successive versions of the book's programme of topics, his methods can be observed in action). The second half of the chapter examines the ways in which he does nevertheless introduce numerous Greek loan-words into his vocabulary, arguing that this is done in order to build up contexts which convey an exotic and alien Greek world.

Why does Lucretius combine these two antithetical policies towards the Greek language? He is drawing a cultural map in which the Roman and the Greek are widely separated, but in which Epicureanism can, uniquely, cross that divide, and thus prove its true universality.

IN A FAMOUS MANIFESTO (1.136–45), Lucretius laments the linguistic struggle that he faces: 'Nor do I fail to appreciate that it is difficult to illuminate in Latin verse the dark discoveries of the Greeks, especially because much use must be made of new words, given the poverty of our language and the newness of the subject matter.' In the first half of the chapter, I shall be considering how he handles this task of Latinizing the technicalities of Epicurean philosophy. In the second half I shall turn to his own poetic use of Greek loan-words and idioms. The two practices will come out looking antithetical to each other, and at the end I shall suggest how we are meant to interpret this antithesis.

A central theme will be Lucretius' avoidance of technical terms. By 'technical term' I intend a single word or phrase, either especially coined or adapted from existing usage and earmarked by the author as his standard and more or less invariable way of designating a specific item or concept within a discipline. Its sense must be recognizably different from, or at least recognizably more precise than, any distinct sense that the same term may bear in ordinary usage. While medicine and mathematics were disciplines which had long possessed technical vocabularies, philosophy had been slow to catch up, acquiring little technical terminology before Aristotle. Nevertheless, Hellenistic philosophies had become thoroughly technical in their terminology, and Epicureanism, despite its (misplaced) reputation as an ordinary-language philosophy, was very nearly as jargon-ridden as Stoicism. It could in fact plausibly be maintained that the atomistic tradition from which Epicureanism emerged had, in the hands of its fifth-century exponents, itself pioneered the creation of a philosophical technical vocabulary.

The Latinization of technical Greek, at least in rhetorical treatises, was a familiar practice by the mid first century BC, when Lucretius wrote. But from Cicero's letters one may get the impression that when educated Romans were locked in philosophical discussion they preferred simply to pepper their Latin prose with the authentic Greek terms. It was not until more than a decade after Lucretius' death that Cicero composed his principal philosophical works, in which the Latin philosophical vocabulary was largely forged.

A full-scale study of Cicero's handling of this task is, as far as I know, yet to be written.[1] Among many things it might help teach us is just what is distinctive about Lucretius' own near-contemporary efforts to accommodate Epicureanism within the Latin language. For the present, let Cicero speak for himself as he reflects on the task of Latinization, in a characteristic exchange between speakers from the first book of the *Academica* (1.24–6):

> ' ... But the combination of the two they called "body" and, as one might put it, "quality". You *will* permit us occasionally to use unknown words when dealing with unfamiliar subject matter, just as is done by the Greeks, who have been dealing with these subjects for a long time.' 'We will,' replied Atticus. 'In fact it will even be permissible for you to use Greek words when you want, if you happen to find no Latin ones available.' 'Thanks, but I'll do

---

[1] However, I have not yet been able to consult Hartung (1970).

my best to speak in Latin, except that I'll use words like "philosophy", "rhetoric", "physics" or "dialectic" — words which along with many others are now habitually used as Latin ones. I have therefore named "qualities" the things which the Greeks call ποιότητες, a word which among the Greeks is itself not an everyday one but belongs to the philosophers. The same applies in many cases. None of the dialecticians' words are from public language: they use their own. And that is a common feature of virtually all disciplines: for new things either new names must be created, or metaphors must be drawn from other fields. If that is the practice of the Greeks, who have already been engaged in these things for so many centuries, how much more should it be allowed to us, who are now trying to deal with these things for the first time.' 'Actually, Varro,' I said, 'it looks as if you will deserve well of your fellow countrymen, if you are going to enrich them not only with facts, as you have done, but also with words.' 'On your instigation then,' he said, 'we will venture to use new words if it becomes necessary.'

Two features deserve particular attention. First, the simple transliteration of Greek words was, as the speaker Varro acknowledges, a familiar and accepted practice, albeit confined largely to the names of the disciplines themselves, such as 'dialectic' and 'rhetoric'. Second, Cicero presents his colleagues as considering it highly commendable when discussing philosophy in Latin to coin the necessary technical jargon, if possible on the analogy of the Greek original, as in the proffered example of *qualitas* for Greek ποιότης.

In both respects Lucretius offers a stark contrast. Take the names of disciplines once more. The *De Rerum Natura* is a poem about physics, what Lucretius' own contemporaries were calling *physica*, yet nowhere in it can that term or its cognates be found. Does Lucretius then have no name for the physical science he is practising? One clear case in which he does is at 1.148, where the proper Epicurean justification for the study of physics is given: ignorant and superstitious fears are to be dispelled by *naturae species ratioque.* The phrase captures quite closely Epicurus' preferred term for physics, φυσιολογία, with *naturae* and *ratio* picking up its constituents φύσις and λόγος respectively. But in Lucretius' rendition it has lost all terminological technicality, and become a subtly descriptive formula for the poem's theme. Read actively, *naturae species ratioque* no doubt denotes the rational philosophical procedure of 'looking at nature and reasoning about it'. But at the same time the Latin permits and even encourages the additional reading, 'the appearance and rationale of nature': such a rendition emphasizes the power of nature herself to confront us with the truth — a motif which Lucretius will be turning to good use in the poem. No strand in this web of connotations goes beyond the potential significance of the one Greek word φυσιολογία.

Similarly with individual technical terms within his chosen discipline,

Lucretius' constant practice is to render Greek technicality neither with Latin technicality nor with mere transliteration, but with a range of his own metaphors. Take the case of 'atoms'. Of the earlier Latin prose writers on Epicureanism, we know only that Amafinius had rendered the term *corpuscula*,[2] although Lucilius' reference to 'atomus... Epicuri' (753 Marx) shows that simple transliteration had long been another available expedient. Cicero, for his part, actually shows a strong preference for this transliterated form, with occasional resort to *corpuscula*[3] or to his own probable coinage *individua*, 'indivisibles'. None of these is ideal. Transliteration of a term from within a discipline — as distinct from the name of the discipline itself — is a rare resort for Cicero, and savours of defeat. *Corpuscula* captures the minuteness of the atoms but not their all-important indivisibility. And *individua* suffers in Cicero's philosophical prose from having to stand in for too many different Greek originals: he had already, in his paraphrase of Plato's *Timaeus* (21, 25, 27), used it to represent ἀμέριστος, ἀμερής and ἄσχιστος, all terms with importantly different technical connotations both from each other and from 'atom'.

Lucretius, characteristically, introduces his own set of terms for atoms in the proem to book 1, 54–61, more than 400 lines before his first proof of their existence: *rerum primordia, materies, genitalia corpora, semina rerum, corpora prima*. Unlike *corpuscula*, all these concentrate not on the smallness of atoms but on their role as the primitive starting points from which other entities are built up. In introducing them, he places the chief emphasis on their dynamic generative powers, already indicated in the procreative implications of *materies* (a derivative of *mater*), *genitalia* and *semina*. These implications he then exploits in his first set of arguments, those against generation *ex nihilo*, in the course of which he seeks to persuade us that the biological regularities which are evident at the macroscopic level depend on fixed *materies* or *semina* at the microscopic level. The metrically convenient transliteration *atomi* never so much as puts in an appearance. But *corpuscula* does crop up as an occasional variant in later books, especially where their generative powers are not at issue.[4] So does *elementa*, 'letters', a convenient equivalent for στοιχεῖα ('elements' but also more specifically 'letters'), which helps to reinforce Lucretius' favoured analogy between atomic rearrangement and alphabetic ana-

---

[2] Cicero, *Ac.* 1.6.
[3] *ND* 1.66–7, 2.94, *Ac.* 1.6, *Tusc.* 1.22.
[4] 2.153, 529, 4.199, 899, 6.1063. At 4.899 it is specifically their smallness that he wishes to emphasize with the diminutive.

grams.[5] Hence it tends to occur in contexts where the *ordering* of atoms is in focus.[6]

A similar but more cautious metaphorical diversification of a single original Greek term is illustrated in book 4 by Lucretius' range of renditions for εἴδωλα, the thin films of atoms which stream off bodies and cause vision. Lucilius, once again, had simply transliterated the word as *idola* (753 Marx). Cicero and his Epicurean correspondent Cassius, discussing the topic in 45 BC,[7] agreed to be appalled at the Roman Epicurean Catius for his translation of εἴδωλα as *spectra*. *Spectrum* is otherwise unattested in Latin before the seventeenth century (when it seems to mean 'appearance' or 'aspect'). It probably represents Catius' attempt to invent an off-the-peg jargon for Latin Epicureanism. I have no idea what connotations it conveyed to a Roman ear, but Cicero and Cassius seem to have found them comic.

Lucretius, at any rate, is considerably more subtle. He conveys εἴδωλον with a range of words which collectively capture the idea, already present in the Greek, of a painted or sculpted image preserving the surface features of its subject. His most regular term for this is *simulacrum*, but he also commonly uses *imago*, with the occasional further variants *effigies* and *figura*. (All four renditions were to enjoy at least some success with later Latin writers on Epicureanism).[8]

By an extraordinary stroke of luck, the text of book 4 preserves side by side Lucretius' earlier and later versions of the introductory lines in which his range of terms is sketched.[9] In the earlier version (45–53), the existence of εἴδωλα is first broached with the words

> nunc agere incipiam tibi, quod vementer ad has res
> attinet, esse ea quae rerum simulacra vocamus,
> *quae quasi membranae vel cortex nominatandast,*
> quod speciem ac formam similem gerit eius imago
> cuiuscumque cluet de corpore fusa vagari. (4.49–53)

> I shall now begin to deal with what is closely relevant to this: that there are that which we call images of things, which are to be

---

[5] 1.196–8, 907–14, 2.688–94, 1013–22.

[6] E.g. 1.827, 2.393, 463, 4.941, 6.1009.

[7] *Fam.* 15.16.1, 19.1.

[8] *Simulacrum*, Vitruvius 6.2.3, Gellius 5.16.3; *imago*, Cicero, e.g. *ND* 1.114, and often; *effigies*, Cicero, *ND* 1.110; *figura*, Seneca, *NQ* 1.5.1, Quintilian, *Inst.* 10.2.15.

[9] 45–53 represent an early phase when our book 4 was to follow book 2, thus retaining the order of material established in Epicurus' *On nature*. 26–44 were substituted when our book 3 had been placed in between. These lines also announce a new central function for book 4, to dispel belief in ghosts, although at his death Lucretius had clearly not yet reshaped the book along such lines.

termed 'like membranes or bark', because the image bears a shape
and form similar to those of whatever thing's body we say it has been
shed from and travelled.

He thereby recruits, in addition to the family of artistic metaphors, the
biological vocabulary of 'membranes' and 'bark' as helping to convey
the difficult idea of these ultra-fine detachable surface-layers of bodies.
In the event, neither of the biological terms is brought into play in this
role anywhere in book 4.[10] And that must be why, when for other reasons
he came to rewrite the proem, Lucretius edited them out, limiting his
vocabulary for εἴδωλα exclusively to the iconic imagery.[11]

In the rewritten passage (26–44) the existence of εἴδωλα is broached in
language which starts out identical to the first version, but then departs
significantly from it:

> nunc agere incipiam tibi, quod vementer ad has res
> attinet, esse ea quae rerum simulacra vocamus,
> quae quasi membranae *summo de corpore rerum*
> *dereptae volitant ultroque citroque per auras* . . . (4.29–32)

> I shall now begin to deal with what is closely relevant to this: that
> there are what we call images of things, which, like membranes
> snatched from the outermost part of things' bodies, fly hither and
> thither through the air . . .

'Membranes' here is no longer part of the designated vocabulary for
εἴδωλα, but forms instead the basis of an extended simile, designed
to convey one specific aspect, the detachability and volatility of these
atomic films. As for the other biological term 'bark', a clumsily in-
apposite name for a light and volatile surface layer of atoms, this has
now been deleted. It does however put in an appearance at the end
of the rewritten passage, in the company of the preferred sculptural
imagery:

> dico igitur rerum effigias tenuisque figuras
> mittier ab rebus *summo de cortice eorum.*

> I say, therefore, that things' effigies and tenuous figures are
> despatched from them off their outermost bark.

Like J. Godwin, the recent editor of book 4, I see no justification for the

---

[10] On *cortex*, see below. *Membranae* occurs once, at 4.95, but only in the descriptive phrase
'tenuis summi membrana coloris', where it is not left to fend for itself.
[11] *Effigiae* and *figurae* are in fact used only twice and three times respectively in the remainder
of the book. *Imago* (most commonly singular, for metrical reasons) is used some seventeen
times. Curiously, it does not occur in the revised version of the proem.

standard emendation of *cortice* to *corpore*.[12] Lucretius has in his revised version rightly seen that 'bark' most appropriately conveys the idea of the stable outer part of an object, *from* which the εἴδωλα flow.

It might seem pointless to wonder what motivated Lucretius' original abortive attempt to introduce the pair of biological terms. But as it happens the question can be answered with a surprising degree of confidence. Alexander of Aphrodisias,[13] in attacking the Epicurean theory of vision by *simulacra*, asks why, if *simulacra* are as volatile as the proponents assert they are, windy conditions are not sufficient to prevent our seeing things. In describing the images' volatility, he quotes the actual words of the theory's proponents: ἐκ φλοιωδῶν καὶ ὑμενωδῶν ὥς φασιν, '[consisting][14] "of bark-like and membrane-like" stuffs, as they put it.' Once we place this Greek phrase alongside Lucretius 4.51, it becomes scarcely deniable that he has quite simply *translated* it. His 'quae quasi membranae vel cortex nominatandast' announces that 'membrane-like' and 'bark-like' are appropriate descriptions to use of the *simulacra*. Although there is evidence that the Epicureans did sometimes also call the visual images 'barks' or 'membranes',[15] it seems clear that on this occasion Lucretius' *quasi* is added in order to capture the adjectival force of the -ώδης termination: not membranes and barks, but membrane-like and bark-like. The conclusion must be that Lucretius was ready in principle simply to draw his imagery from the technical terminology of Greek Epicurean prose, but that such borrowings only survived into subsequent drafts if they could prove their independent worth in the context of Latin poetic imagery. In this particular case, while the sculptural imagery survived, the biological imagery failed the test and was edited out.

This privileged glimpse of Lucretius at work on refining his own vocabulary reveals something about his motivation. Rather than follow Catius in supplying a Latin technical term for εἴδωλα, he seeks to embody the notion in a set of metaphors which will complement each other in focusing on the cardinal feature of εἴδωλα, their power to preserve a

---

[12] Godwin (1986: 94–5). Bailey's comment ad loc. that *cortice* cannot be right because *cortex* designates for Lucretius the εἴδωλον, overlooks the point that that was only in the now discarded version of the proem.

[13] *De anima mantissa* 135.24–6, εἰ δέ ἐστιν εὔκολος αὐτῶν ἡ κίνησις ἐκ φλοιωδῶν καὶ ὑμενωδῶν ὥς φασιν, καὶ πᾶσα ῥοπὴ ἱκανὴ παρασῦραι αὐτά, ἔδει μὴ ὁρᾶν τοὺς κατὰ τὸν ἄνεμον βλέποντας. For discussion of the passage, see Avotins (1980).

[14] See Avotins (1980: 438 n. 40) for discussion as to whether a participle such as πεποιημένων has fallen out here. Given the Lucretian parallel, I am at least confident that the phrase describes the composition of the *simulacra* themselves, not (a possibility considered sympathetically by Avotins) some external agent which moves them.

[15] For ὕμενες see Diogenes of Oenoanda fr. 10 V 3 Smith; φλοίους is one available MS reading at Plutarch, *Non posse* 1106A.

portrait-like resemblance to the object emitting them, even over a considerable distance travelled. Their detachability and volatility will be conveyed in other ways, by both simile and argument,[16] without being allowed to dilute or obfuscate the dominant metaphor of portraiture.

To those familiar with Cicero's philosophical works it may seem that there is nothing unique about Lucretius' search for a mutually complementary set of terms corresponding to a single Greek term. A similar-looking process can be glimpsed in Cicero's own forging of a philosophical vocabulary, where he often introduces a Greek term with a whole bevy of Latin equivalents. The Stoic term for infallible cognition, κατάληψις, literally 'grasping', provides a good illustration. Its use in rhetorical theory may have earned it Latinization at an earlier date, since already in his youthful *De inventione* Cicero uses *perceptio* in a way probably intended to correspond to κατάληψιν.[17] Yet still in the second book of the *Academica* his spokesman Lucullus can be found tinkering with the rendition of it, and listing a range of alternatives: ' ... "cognitio" aut "perceptio" aut (si verbum e verbo volumus) "comprehensio", quam κατάληψιν illi vocant ...' (*Ac.* 2.17, cf. 18, 31).

Normally in Cicero this little fanfare would herald the first introduction of a term. But we are already here in the second book of the *Academica*, and it is certain that κατάληψις had already featured in book 1.[18] What Cicero in fact turns out on closer inspection to be doing here is not creating but *enlarging* his stock of Latin terms for it, adding *comprehensio* to the terms *perceptio* and *cognitio* which he had been using up to now (in the *Academica*, that is, and also in the *De finibus*, composed contemporaneously with it.) And one can see why. Both *perceptio* and *cognitio* were too widely and loosely used within the ordinary Latin cognitive vocabulary to capture the very special flavour of Stoic κατάληψις, whereas *comprehensio* and its cognates were barely yet familiar in a cognitive sense, so that the usage could still retain a suitably technical ring.[19]

Curiously enough Cicero too, just like Lucretius in book 4, can here be watched in the act of refining his vocabulary. Our version of book 2 comes from the *Academica priora*, Cicero's first edition. In his revised edition, the *Academica posteriora*, from which part of book 1 survives, *comprehensio* is heralded as the single correct translation right from the start (*Ac.* 1.41): ' "When that impression was discerned in its own right, Zeno called it *comprehendibile*. Will you accept this?" "Yes," he replied.

[16] 4.54–216.
[17] *Inv.* 1.9, 36.
[18] *Ac.* 2.28 indicates that Hortensius had already used it in book 1.
[19] For the various cognate forms of *comprehensio* in Cicero, see Lévy (1992).

"How else *could* you express καταληπτόν?" "But when it had already been received and endorsed, he called it *comprehensio*, like things grasped with the hand." '

This exclusive use of *comprehensio* for κατάληψις seems thereafter to become canonical in what survives of the revised book 1, and was undoubtedly continued in the lost books 2–4 of the revised version. It enables Cicero to let it stand in contrast, as a term of art, with the less technical 'knowledge' vocabulary — *scire, cognoscere* and *percipere* — which in the ensuing chapters he puts into the mouths of pre-Stoic philosophers.[20]

Consequently, it would be quite misleading to assimilate the practices of Lucretius and Cicero when each sets about establishing a group of alternative or complementary Latin terms for a single Greek original. Cicero does it only as a step towards what will, if all goes well,[21] prove to be their eventual whittling down to a single technical term. For Lucretius, on the other hand, the range of alternative terms is no stopgap or compromise, but is intrinsically desirable. By means of it, he seeks to capture the Greek original, not by substituting a Latin technical term for a Greek one, but by keeping in play a whole set of mutually complementary metaphors. The policy is one not of finding a technical terminology, but of avoiding one. And in pursuing it Lucretius is doing no more than observing the rules of his genre, the hexameter poem on physics. The proper comparison to make is not with Cicero, but with Empedocles, whom Lucretius reveres as the founder of his genre.[22] Empedocles has no technical vocabulary for the six primary entities in his physics — the four elements plus the two powers Love and Strife — but deploys for each a varied set of metaphors and allegorical names: thus the element water is represented not only by the word 'water' (ὕδωρ), but also by 'rain' (ὄμβρος), 'sea' (θάλασσα, πόντος) and 'Nestis', probably a Sicilian cult name for Persephone. Lucretius too, it should be remembered, explicitly retains the right to deploy divine names allegorically, such as 'Neptune' for 'sea' (2.655–60) — another implicit declaration of allegiance to his genre and its founder.

I do not mean to deny that any word in Lucretius ever has a technical sense assigned to it, although interestingly enough the most prominent cases are ones where the Greek original *lacked* such a term. (I am thinking here of *coniunctum* for 'permanent property' at 1.449ff.,[23] and the *animus/*

---

[20] See e.g. 1.44

[21] Hence *Fin.* 3.15, where Cato remarks 'equidem soleo etiam, quod uno Graeci, *si aliter non possum*, idem pluribus verbis exponere'. On this passage, cf. Powell (1995a: 292–4).

[22] I argue this in Sedley (1989).

[23] That *coniunctum* does not, as commonly supposed, translate the single Greek word συμβεβηκός is argued in Long and Sedley (1987: §7), and more fully in Sedley (1988). As for *eventum* in the same passage, it is introduced as already a familiar Latin usage (458).

anima distinction set out in book 3.) But what we have already seen, the conversion of Greek technicality into Latin metaphor, is a far more pervasive feature of his poetry. One very satisfying case, which was first detected by Myles Burnyeat,[24] is Lucretius' rendition at 4.472 of the exclusively Epicurean technical term for a thesis which 'refutes itself', περικάτω τρέπεται. Scepticism, the claim to know nothing, is dismissed as self-refuting, but Lucretius conveys the dry technicality of περικάτω τρέπεται with a picture of the sceptic as an acrobat or contortionist: 'If someone thinks that nothing is known, he doesn't even know whether *that* can be known, since he admits that he knows nothing. I therefore decline to argue my case against this person who *has stood with his own head pressed into his footprints*': 'qui capite ipse suo in statuit vestigia sese'. The sceptic's confusion is reinforced in the last line with the Lucretian device which David West has christened 'syntactical onomatopoeia': intellectual contortion is symbolized by contorted grammar, with the proper order *statuit in* reversed in defiance of basic syntax. (I see no advantage in emending *suo* to *sua*, with most editors since Lachmann. That merely substitutes one grammatical inversion — *sua in* for *in sua* — for another. Anyone who objects that the grammatical inversion is too harsh for Lucretius to have perpetrated should consider the example in my next paragraph.)

I am inclined to see a similar story as underlying a nearby passage, 4.832–3. Lucretius rejects another topsy-turvy piece of thinking — the teleologist's mistake of supposing that, because a human bodily part serves a function, that function must have been conceived prior to the part's coming to exist. In Lucretius' view, a thing must already exist before any thoughts about its function can even be entertained. Teleology is back-to-front reasoning; or, as he puts it, 'All such explanations which they offer are back to front, due to distorted reasoning': 'cetera de genere hoc inter quaecumque pretantur | omnia perversa praepostera sunt ratione'. What was in his Greek original? My guess is that what he found there was a description of teleological reasoning as διάστροφος, 'distorted'. This term, which translates literally into Lucretius' word *perversa*, is one which, according to Sextus Empiricus,[25] Epicurus used for opinion which imposes a distorted construal on primary empirical data. But once again Lucretius has backed up the accusation with syntactical onomatopoeia. The distortion is attributed to 'back-to-front' (*praepostera*) thinking, which in turn is conveyed by the reversal of linguistic elements contained in the tmesis in *inter quaecumque pretantur*. Tmesis is a common Lucretian device (one

[24] Burnyeat (1978).
[25] S.E. *M* 7.209; for the authenticity of the Epicurean terminology in *M* 7.206–10, see Sedley (1992: 44–55), and cf. Gigante (1981: 118–48).

rarely if ever used without a specific point), but this is one of only two tmeses in which the bare verb stem, left exposed by separation from its prefix, is not a Latin word at all.[26] The teleological reversal cannot be contemplated, Lucretius' message runs: it produces nonsense.

In all these Lucretian strategies for the conversion of Greek technicality into Latin imagery, one invariable rule is observed: never transliterate the Greek term. There are, in fact, only two significant breaches of that rule,[27] and they both speak eloquently in its favour. A leading contender for the title of Lucretius' worst line is 1.830: 'Now let us also take a look at Anaxagoras' *homoiomereia* ["nunc et Anaxagorae scrutemur homoeo-merian", 830] — as the Greeks call it, but which the poverty of our native language prevents us from saying in our own tongue' (1.830–2). The ungainliness conveys a point about the unacceptable consequences of resorting to mere transliteration of the Greek. Anaxagoras' word is glaringly not at home in the Latin language; and that in turn foreshadows the fact, which Lucretius satirically develops in the sequel, that the concept underlying it is equally unwelcome.

This link between the alienness of a word and the alienness of the concept it expresses is virtually explicit in the other passage where bare transliteration is resorted to. Early in book 3 the old Greek theory that soul is a harmony or attunement of the bodily elements is dismissed (3.98–135). In Lucretius' discussion of it the Greek word ἁρμονία is simply transliterated, not translated. This is not in itself surprising, since ἁρμονία is as resistant to rendition into Latin as it is into English. Even Cicero, in his paraphrase of Plato's *Timaeus* (27), while attempting the translation *concentio* for ἁρμονία, is sufficiently uneasy about it to take the step, uncharacteristic in this work, of supplying the Greek word too. Elsewhere Cicero's own preference with regard to *harmonia* is for simply transliterating it.[28] But more is at stake for Lucretius: the word's undisguised alienness to the Latin language is symptomatic of the concept's irrelevance:

> So, since the nature of mind and spirit has been found to be part of man, give back the name of *harmonia*, whether it was brought down to the musicians from high Helicon, or whether they themselves drew it from some other source and transferred it to what previously lacked a name of its own. Whatever it is, let them keep it. (3.130–5)

---

[26] For the other, see the brilliant article of Hinds (1987).

[27] I do not count *prester* (6.424), which although in a way technical is not a philosophically controversial term.

[28] E.g. *Rep.* 2.69, *Tusc.* 1.41. Even Lucretius himself once outside book 3 uses the transliterated *harmoniae*: at 4.1248, where he may feel that his need for the musical metaphor leaves him no option.

An alien concept deserves an alien name. By the same token, Lucretius' habitual practice has made clear, philosophically welcome concepts must make themselves at home in the language too.

Now I come to the great Lucretian anomaly. Although Lucretius studiously avoids using transliterated Greek *terminology*, his whole poem is nevertheless knee-deep in Greek loan words.

These Greek words have been usefully catalogued by Bailey,[29] who concludes (a) that in some cases Lucretius' hand was forced by the unavailability of a suitable Latin word; but also (b) that in others, where a perfectly good Latin word was at his disposal, he was using Greek out of sheer 'caprice'; and (c) that in one extreme case, 4.1160–9, where sixteen Greek words occur in the space of ten lines, it was impossible to resist the conclusion that Lucretius is translating a Greek original.

It is hard to think of a more implausible set of explanations. With regard to (a), what we have already seen of Lucretius' handling of philosophical terminology should put us on our guard against ever assuming too readily that he has been forced to resort to Greek by the lack of a Latin word.[30] As for (c), Bailey's explanation implies a very poor opinion of Lucretius' skills as a translator, and one totally negated by a passage like 3.18–22, where we know that Lucretius is following a Greek original, the Homeric description of Olympus.[31] But in the remainder of this chapter I want to concentrate on (b), the kind of cases where Bailey thought the intrusion of Greek merely gratuitous. It seems to me that there are remarkably few genuine cases that fit this description.

Most of the Greek words attributed by Bailey to Lucretian 'caprice' do not occur in isolation. They tend to turn up in droves. And again and again this concentration of Greek words in a passage is exploited for a specific effect — to conjure up for the readers a Greek or an otherwise exotic context. When Greece joined the European Common Market, one British newspaper celebrated with a competition for the reader's poem with the largest number of Greek-derived words. This is pretty much what Lucretius is up to too: when he uses a whole convoy of Greek words, he is usually quite simply trying to make us think of Greece.

'Greek words' here should be interpreted broadly. It naturally includes Greek proper names as well as common nouns and adjectives. Moreover,

[29] Bailey (1947: i. 138–9).

[30] However, see n. 28 above on *harmoniae* at 4.1248, and n. 27 on *prester* at 6.424.

[31] *Od.* 6.42–6. See the notes on Lucretius ad loc. in Kenney (1971), and notice especially *innubilus* (21) for the Homeric ἀνέφελος, an apparent Lucretian coinage designed to capture the special flavour of the original, but decidedly not a transliteration.

it can be extended to include Greek linguistic idioms, such as the formation of compound adjectives, not native to the Latin language. These points are well illustrated by 1.464–82, the wonderful description of the Trojan war. In the space of five lines, 473–7, we have not only six Greek names, but also the quasi-Greek compound adjective *Graiugenarum*:

> ... numquam Tyndaridis forma conflatus amore
> ignis, Alexandri Phrygio sub pectore gliscens,
> clara accendisset saevi certamina belli,
> nec clam durateus Troianis Pergama partu
> inflammasset equos nocturno Graiugenarum.

> ... never would that flame kindled deep in Alexander's Phrygian
> heart and fanned with love through the beauty of Tyndareus'
> daughter have ignited the shining battles of savage war, nor would
> that wooden horse by giving birth to its Grecian offspring at dead
> of night have set fire to the Trojans' Pergama.

Especially telling is the authentic Homeric adjective *durateus* used of the 'Wooden' Horse (where, as Bailey ruefully points out, there was the perfectly good Latin word *ligneus* available). And in this already Greek context it is legitimate to regard the archaic Latin nominative *equos*, with its Greek-like termination, as yet another linguistic detail contributing to the same cumulative effect. (It should therefore not, with the majority of editors, be normalized to *equus*.)[32]

The argumentative context of this description is Lucretius' discussion of the metaphysical problem how facts about the past maintain their present existence: what is there in existence now for them to be properties of? It therefore serves his purposes to present his example, the Trojan war, as a remote one. The epic ring of the Greek helps locate it in a context far removed from present-day Rome. This brings me to a general observation: that the creation of a Greek context tends, in Lucretius' hands, to emphasize the remote and the exotic.

Bailey's list of gratuitous Greek imports includes *scaphiis*, 'basins', at 6.1046. The word was a common enough one in Latin by Lucretius' day to pass unnoticed. Nevertheless, since it occurs here in a Greek context, flanked by Greek proper names, it does deserve consideration. It occurs in the course of a long and involved discussion of the magnet, and at this point Lucretius is describing the phenomenon of magnetic repulsion:

---

[32] As Jim Adams points out to me, the retention of the old *-os* termination is not particularly unusual in a noun whose stem ends in *-u* (to avoid the collocation *uu*). Nevertheless, it may be judged to acquire a Hellenizing significance when contained, as here, within a broader Hellenizing context.

> exultare etiam Samothracia ferrea vidi
> et ramenta simul ferri furere intus ahenis
> in scaphiis, lapis hic Magnes cum subditus esset. (6.1044-6)

> I have even seen Samothracian iron objects dance, and iron filings
> all simultaneously go crazy in bronze basins (*scaphiis*), when this
> Magnesian stone was placed underneath.

What are these Samothracian *ferrea*? Iron rings, the editors usually say.
But I doubt it. There were rings called 'Samothracian', but they seem to
have been a combination of iron and gold: on one report, gold rings with
an iron 'head'; on another account, iron rings plated or decorated
with gold.[33] It seems unlikely that either of these is meant. The neuter
ferrea cannot easily imply the masculine complement *anuli* or *anelli*.[34]
Besides, someone displaying the powers of a magnet would not be likely
to use objects containing gold as well as iron, since the weight of the gold
would reduce their responsiveness to the magnetism. Finally, both types
of ring clearly had a predominantly gold exterior, and would not very
naturally be known as 'iron' rings. (It would only be if you wanted to
cause offence that you would be likely to refer to someone's gold-plated
ring as their 'iron ring'.)

Ferrea must mean just what it appears to mean, namely 'iron objects'.
But why, then, are they called 'Samothracian'? There is only one plausible
answer: Lucretius is describing a display he once witnessed *in Samothrace*,
and 'Samothracia ferrea' means 'the ironware of Samothrace'. The natural
magnet or lodestone, variously called the Magnesian stone and the Heracleian stone, was as the names suggest predominantly associated with
Magnesia or Heracleia, whether the Heracleia in Lydia or the one in
Pontus. But according to one variant tradition the magnet was first found
in Samothrace, and was named after the city of Heracleia on that island.[35]
If there had actually been a Heracleia in Samothrace, this association of
the Heracleian stone with the island might have been dismissed as a simple
error of geography, the confusion of one Heracleia with another. But since
Samothracian Heracleia seems to be a fiction, a better explanation for the
origin of this variant tradition must be that lodestones were indeed found
on Samothrace, and that this led to a misconception regarding the location
of the Heracleia in question. The Lucretian passage, if I have interpreted
it correctly, now stands in strong confirmation of that hypothesis. This use

---

[33] For the evidence, see Lewis (1959: T 30, T 213).
[34] For similar doubts, see Godwin (1991: ad loc.).
[35] *Etymologicum Magnum*, s.v. Μαγνῆτις = Lewis (1959: T 20).

of a first-person eye-witness account is a rarity in Lucretius,[36] and confirms
that, exceptionally, he is recounting to us an exhibition of the powers of
the magnet which he had seen when himself in Samothrace — whether
from a vendor, or in a religious ritual, or in other circumstances is impossible to guess.

But how likely is it that he had been to this particular island? A picture
of Lucretius the seasoned Aegean tourist does not carry conviction, and
should become still less plausible when we proceed to explore his wary
attitude to things Greek. Nor is Lucretius, of all people, very likely to
have gone on a religious pilgrimage to the celebrated Kabiric mysteries
held there.[37] However, there is no obligation to see this visit as motivated
by either tourism or religious zeal. Samothrace, lying just off the coast of
Thrace, was a natural point of anchorage for anyone on a sea voyage
between Europe and Asia. *Acts of the Apostles* 16.11 describes how St
Paul put in there for the night when sailing from the Troad to Macedonia,[38]
and Ovid changed ships there on his way to exile in Tomi (*Tristia* 1.
10.19–22). Any Roman sent on a tour of duty to an Asian province might
well stop off there on the outward or homeward journey. One plausible
such journey might be — but here I am entering the realms of fantasy —
a tour of duty to Bithynia, where Lucretius' patron Memmius was pro-
praetor in 57 BC.

At all events, the use of the Greek word *scaphiis* at 6.1046 can now
hardly be called gratuitous. It is part of the window-dressing for Lucretius'
brief excursion into an exotic world — his report of tricks with magnets
in Greek bronze vessels, witnessed in person on this remote Aegean island.

Nor are the remote and the exotic by any means always viewed with
sympathy or approval. In book 4, for example (1123–30, 1160–9), Greek
vocabulary piles up to describe the absurd luxuries and euphemistic epithets which deluded lovers, blinded to the realities of life, bestow on the
objects of their affections. (These lines, incidentally, feature prominently
in Bailey's list of gratuitously introduced Greek words, and include the
ones which he thought must be translated from a Greek original.) And
book 2 has another build-up of Greek words and names in the frenetic

---

[36] Another case is 4.577, recalling his own experience of multiple echoes. Given how sparing
he is with them, I would take these autopsy claims seriously. When he has not witnessed
something in person, Lucretius is ready to admit it: cf. his indication at 1.727 that he has
never been to Sicily.

[37] There is reason to think that some Romans did go to Samothrace for the mysteries, possibly
including one with Epicurean links. See Bloch (1940: esp. n. 18).

[38] Although Samothrace was said to be ill-provided with harbours (Pliny, *NH* 4.12.73), it
certainly had at least one (Livy 45.6.3).

description of the worship of Cybele (600–43),[39] a cult whose theological implications we are immediately urged to shun. Just as they are culturally remote,[40] so too they are, as Lucretius puts it (2.645), 'far removed from true reasoning'.

This shunning of the exotic can be felt in the important ethical proem to book 2, at lines 20–61. The simple idyllic Epicurean lifestyle is eulogized in pure pastoral Latin. Greek words and formations creep in only when Lucretius is describing the pointless luxuries with which it stands in contrast (*lampadas igniferas* and *citharae* in 24–8, where 24–5 themselves recall the well known Homeric description of Phaeacian opulence at *Odyssey* 7.100–2).

One less hostile use of Greek is book 3's quasi-heroic parade of the great men who, for all their greatness, proved mortal (3.1024–44) — *Scipiadas* (note the Greek termination), the companions of the *Heliconiades*, i.e. the poets, including Homer, who out of all of them was the one who won the *sceptra* (1038), Democritus, and even Epicurus — whose actual Greek name appears nowhere but here in the entire poem. What is evoked this time is not alienness or remoteness, but the larger than life heroism of Homeric (as well as Ennian) epic, in a parade of the dead also reminiscent of the Homeric *Nekuia*.[41]

Homer's own canonisation in this list does reflect a recognition on Lucretius' part of Greek superiority in both music and poetry. This emerges from the key Greek terms and forms which highlight his own celebrated poetic manifesto at 1.921–50: his poetic ambitions have struck his heart with a *thyrsus* (1.923), inspiring him to expound his philosophy 'with sweet-talking Pierian song' (*suaviloquenti | carmine Pierio*, 1.945–6). We should perhaps also detect an implicit contrast of Roman and Greek noises at 2.410–13:

> ne tu forte putes serrae stridentis acerbum
> horrorem constare elementis levibus aeque
> *ac musaea mele, per chordas organici quae*
> mobilibus digitis expergefacta figurant.

> So you must not think that the harsh grating of a shrieking saw
> consists of elements as smooth as those constituting the musical

---

[39] As well as the Greek proper names in the passage, note *tympana* and *cymbala* (618), *chorea* (635), and the compound adjectives at 601, 619, 627 and 632.
[40] This is emphasized by Lucretius' specific indications (600, 629) that he is giving us a *Greek* portrayal of Cybele.
[41] 1025 is Ennian (see fr. 137 Skutsch), followed immediately by the Iliadic line 1026 (cf. *Il.* 21.107). The thematic link with the *Nekuia* is already set up by the preceding lines, 980–1012, on myths of torture in Hades. For the dense series of further echoes of Greek literature in this passage, see Segal (1990: esp. 177–8).

melodies which the instrumentalists with nimble fingers arouse and
form on their strings.

The almost pure Greek third line contrasts with the pure Latin which
precedes. Where Greece has given us sublime music, Rome's more characteristic noise is the shrieking sawblades of a workshop.[42]
    Sudden switches of vocabulary have this power to transport us instantly
to and fro between the Greek and the Roman worlds. They can be used
not only to praise Greek superiority, and to marginalize what Lucretius
shuns as alien, but also, on the contrary, to universalize a concept. In book
5 (1028–90), Lucretius argues for the natural origin of language partly by
appeal to the way that all animals alike from infancy instinctively know
their innate powers:

> cornua nata prius vitulo quam frontibus extent,
> illis iratus petit atque infestus inurget;
> *at catuli pantherarum scymnique leonum*
> unguibus ac pedibus iam tum morsuque repugnant
> vix etiam cum sunt dentes unguesque creati. (5.1034–8)

> The calf angrily butts and charges with his incipient horns before
> they have even protruded from his forehead. Panther whelps and
> lion cubs already fight with claws, paws and biting at an age when
> their teeth and claws have barely appeared.

Scymni (1036), the Greek *vox propria* for lion cubs, occurs in Latin literature only here. Bailey objected to it on the ground that there was a
perfectly good Latin word for cubs available, *catuli*, and one which Lucretius could hardly have overlooked since he uses it in the very same line!
But this once again misses the point. The butting calf, a familiar sight in
the Italian countryside, is described in pure Latin. The young panthers
and lions, on the other hand, those exotic inhabitants of the eastern
Mediterranean and beyond, belong to another world. The switch to that
other world is made instantaneously with the consecutive Greek-derived
words *pantherarum scymnique* in line 1036. Lucretius neatly gets across the
point that this instinctive use of innate powers is the same the whole world
over, even though the nature of the powers themselves may vary from
region to region. Likewise, he is arguing, human beings the world over
naturally express themselves in language, even though the actual sounds
produced differ according to region.
    It is worth looking out for a comparable universality in the account of
disease with which the whole poem closes (6.1090–1286). Initially, Lucre-

---

[42] Cf. 2.500–6, Lucretius' catalogue of qualitative extremes, where Graecisms indicate the
exotic character of the finest dyes (500–1) and of the most sublime music (505).

tius emphasizes how widely diseases differ from one region of the world
to another (6.1103–18). The diversity is brought home mainly by the
deployment of geographical names, although the exotic character of
the Egyptian elephantiasis disease is further emphasized by its Greek
name, *elephas* (1114). When Lucretius turns to his long closing description
of the Athenian plague, however, there is no attempt to bring out its
exotic character by the use of Greek, despite the ready availability of
suitable vocabulary in the Thucydides text which he is following.[43] I do
not intend here to speculate about Lucretius' purpose in closing with the
plague passage. I shall simply observe that the linguistic pattern I have
described confirms that its lessons, whatever they are, are meant to be
universal ones.

I hope that these examples have succeeded in demonstrating the wide-
ranging evocative powers of strategically placed Greek names, idioms and
loan words in Lucretius' poem. If I am right, something unexpected has
emerged. Despite the proclaimed Greek origins of both his poetic medium
and its message, Lucretius is very far from being a philhellene or Hellen-
izer. Although the Greeks are acknowledged to outshine the Romans both
artistically and philosophically, Greekness for him frequently symbolizes
the culturally remote, the morally dangerous and the philosophically
obscure. Seen in this light, the wholesale Latinization of Greek philosophical terminology which I discussed in the first half of this paper will
need careful interpretation. We can now see that Lucretius' concern is not
the philosophical spoon-feeding of disadvantaged Roman readers linguistically incapable of savouring the Epicurean gospels in their original Greek.
On the contrary, his readers' familiarity with the Greek language, as with
Greek literature, is assumed from the outset, and is systematically
exploited. Nor on the other hand is he transporting his Roman readers to
Athens. He is importing to Rome from Athens its single most precious
product, which, as the proem to book 6 eloquently declares, is Epicurus'
philosophy.

It is certainly no part of his strategy to play down Epicurus' Greekness.
Right from the proem to book 1, Epicurus has been labelled the great
Greek discoverer ('primum Graius homo . . .', 1.66).[44] And in the proem
to book 3 not only is Epicurus hailed as the 'glory of the Greek race' ('o
Graiae gentis decus', 3.3), but his Greekness is brought out with the

---

[43] For Lucretius' use of medical vocabulary, see D. Langslow's paper in this volume.
[44] As Farrell (1991: 34–5, n. 17) points out, 'Graius homo' echoes Ennius' application of the
same phrase to Pyrrhus, thus implicitly bracketing Epicurus and Pyrrhus as formidable Greek
invaders of Italy.

very linguistic device that I have beeen documenting. Lucretius professes himself Epicurus' imitator, not his rival:

> quid enim contendat hirundo
> cycnis, aut quidnam tremulis facere artubus haedi
> consimile in cursu possint et fortis equi vis. (3.6–8)

> For how should a swallow compete with swans, or what would kids, with their trembling limbs, be able to do in a race to compare with the powerful strength of a horse?

The familiar pattern emerges once again. Lucretius is the swallow, or the kid, described in his own langage, Latin. Epicurus is the swan, or the horse. The swan is so named in Greek: the Greek *cycnus* became common enough in Latin, but this may well be its earliest occurrence;[45] and at all events, the native Latin word *olor* was available to Lucretius as an alternative. Even the dative form of *cycnis* imports a further Graecism, the indigenous Latin construction after verbs of contending being *cum* plus ablative.[46] What is more, *fortis equi vis*, although Latin, honours the horse with the Greek idiom, familiar from epic, whereby a hero is periphrastically called not 'x' but 'the (mighty) strength of x', e.g. *Iliad* 23.720 κρατερὴ . . . ἲς 'Οδυσῆος (where ἲς is cognate with Lucretius' *vis*).[47]

So at this crucial juncture Lucretius is not only emphasizing Epicurus' Greekness, but even acknowledging that the Romans are, philosophically, the poor relations. The question 'How can a Lucretius compete with an Epicurus?' turns out to carry the subtext 'How can a Roman philosopher compete with a Greek philosopher?'

What are we to make of these contradictions? Lucretius considers Greek culture artistically and philosophically superior, and yet at the same time deeply alien. He floods his poem with Greek words, but religiously avoids them in the course of doctrinal exposition. Let me close with a suggested explanation of these anomalies. Epicurus is a Greek, a voice from an alien culture to which Lucretius has no interest in acclimatizing himself or his reader. Lucretius' mapping-out of the Greek and the Roman, effected by his strategic interweaving of Greek and Latin vocabulary, is a constant reminder of the gulf that divides the two worlds. But although Epicurus' world is alien, his philosophy is not. It directly addresses the universal moral needs of mankind, and to that extent it transcends all

---

[45] See André (1967: 65).

[46] I am grateful to Roland Mayer for pointing this out to me. He illuminatingly compares the device of using a Greek nominative-plus-infinitive construction at Catullus 4.1–2, where the purported speaker is designated by a Greek noun, *phaselus*.

[47] This Graecism is noted by Kenney (1971: ad loc.), and I owe to David West the further point that ἲς, rather than βία, is the Greek form directly echoed by Lucretius.

cultural barriers. Lucretius, we have seen, is constantly emphasizing the barriers. It is precisely by drawing attention to the cultural divide between the Greek and the Roman, while making Epicurean philosophy nevertheless thoroughly at home in his own native language, that he proves to us its true universality.[48]

[48] My thanks to audiences at the Oxford Philological Society, at the British Academy Colloquium 'The language of Latin poetry', at the University of Leiden, and at St Petersburg for helpful discussion, and, for additional comments, to David West, Ted Kenney, Michael Reeve, Jim Adams, Roland Mayer, Voula Tsouna, David Langslow, Mieke Koenen and Han Baltussen. An enlarged version of the paper appears as Chapter 2 of my book *Lucretius and the Transformation of Greek Wisdom* (Cambridge, 1998), and I am grateful to Cambridge University Press for permission to print it here.

SYNTAX

Proceedings of the British Academy, **93**, 249–268

Archaism and Innovation in Latin Poetic Syntax

J. H. W. PENNEY

Summary. A number of syntactic patterns that are familiar features of classical Latin poetry show divergences from the norms of formal prose, and in many instances it has been claimed that an archaic pattern has been preserved or adopted and has become part of the distinctively poetic language. This chapter presents a selection of these patterns and examines some of the problems associated with their classification as archaisms, and the question of their poetic resonance. It may at times be hard to establish whether a pattern is genuinely archaic; some early Latin patterns recur not only in poetry but as features of everyday language; archaisms may have been perceived as such by the poets and used for deliberate effect, but within the tradition they may equally have become mere 'poeticisms'; archaic patterns may have come to be used in innovatory ways; they may have been retained, or even re-introduced, under the influence of Greek, in which case their antique associations may no longer have been felt; an archaic-looking pattern may have arisen simply from developments within the language of poetry. There is no simple opposition between archaism and innovation: rather the innovatory tendencies of Latin poetic language extend to the manipulation of archaisms for literary effect.

MATTHEW ARNOLD'S POETIC version of the Tristan legend naturally includes references to places connected with the story, amongst them King Mark's seat in Cornwall; but unfamiliar British place names can be hazardous, and Arnold was unlucky enough to fall into the trap of supposing a natural pronunciation to be the correct one. The result was unfortunate:

> When the feast was loud and the laughter shrill
> In the banquet-hall of Tyntagil

— unfortunate because the place-name is in fact to be stressed on the second syllable, and in a later edition Arnold amended his poem to restore the rhythm:

> When the feast was gay and the laughter loud
> In Tyntagel's palace proud
>
> (*Tristram and Iseult* II 114–15).

Part of the solution in this instance was to introduce an inversion of the normal adjective–noun sequence, a feature at once archaic and poetic, and one can see here a clear example of its metrical convenience, and contribution to the rhyme-scheme. When the same phenomenon is found, say, in III 1 *In King Marc's chapel, in Tyntagel old*, one naturally suspects a similar history, and this is borne out in part, since the preceding edition had *At Tyntagil, in King Marc's chapel old*: here, however, the postposed adjective is already present, and indeed there are several other such instances in the poem. It is clear that for Arnold this inversion of the adjective–noun sequence was a standard poetic device, since it is found in other poems too;[1] it can only be a matter for speculation whether the occurrences in *Tristram and Iseult* might in part be accounted for by some subconscious notion that the syntagm was, as an archaism, particularly apt for the early medieval setting.

This English example may serve to introduce a discussion of archaic syntactic patterns in Latin poetry, which can be regarded in much the same light. Archaisms may have some attraction because of their metrical possibilities: the infinitive of purpose, for instance, may generate a convenient dactyl. It is, however, their resonance as archaisms, or at least as traditional poetic features, that will chiefly encourage their use. The distinction between deliberate selection of an archaic pattern because of its antiquity and its adoption simply in imitation of forerunners must be borne in mind,[2] but naturally there is always the possibility that a poet intends a combination of the two.

In this chapter, I shall review some familiar syntactic features of Latin poetic language to illustrate the variety of ways in which archaisms are used, but also to note the difficulty, in some instances, of determining

---

[1] A quick count gave the following figures: sixteen instances in *Tristram and Iseult* as against one in *Sohrab and Rustum*, a poem of similar length, but eight in *Thyrsis*, and four in *The Scholar Gipsy*, both considerably shorter poems; the crucial factor accounting for the difference seems to be not that *Sohrab and Rustum* is an epic poem, but that it is unrhymed.

[2] Cf. the remarks of Leumann (1959: 142ff.) on archaisms and Ennianisms, and the distinction between direct and indirect archaisms made in Hofmann–Szantyr (1965: 768f.).

whether an archaism is truly in question, and to point, in others, to the fact that an archaic syntactic pattern may be used in a new way. The classification of archaisms is a more complex matter than it may at first appear.

How conscious Roman poets were that a syntactic pattern was archaic rather than simply part of an established poetic language is often difficult to determine, but the isolation of some examples of archaism must point to deliberate selection for effect: for instance,

urbem quam statuo vestra est   (Virg. *Aen.* 1.573).

This is an instance of so-called *attractio inversa*, which may be seen as a continuation of an inherited Indo-European pattern for restrictive relatives with the head incorporated into the relative clause.[3] The pattern is well attested in early Latin: cf. Terence, *Eun.* 653 *eunuchum quem dedisti nobis, quas turbas dedit!;* Cato, *Or.* fr. 3,2 *agrum quem vir habet tollitur;* id., *de agr.* 51 *ab arbore abs terra pulli qui nascentur, eos in terram deprimito,* and is even extended, though rarely, to appositive clauses, cf. Plautus, *Am.* 1009 *Naucratem quem convenire volui in navi non erat.* It is, however,

[3] On Indo-European relative clauses, see Lehmann (1984) and Hettrich (1988: 467ff.); on Latin developments Lehmann (1979). A distinction is sometimes made between a relative clause with embedded nucleus (i.e. what might traditionally be taken to be the antecedent is incorporated into the relative clause and takes its case from that) and *attractio inversa*, where it is assumed that the antecedent is extracted from the main clause and fronted, with attraction to the case of the relative pronoun: so there would be a difference between the two sentences from Cato cited in the main text, with *ab arbore abs terra pulli qui nascentur, eos* ... as an example of an embedded nucleus, and *agrum quem vir habet, tollitur* as an example of *attractio inversa*; I follow Hettrich (1988: 505 fn.53) in regarding the distinction as unnecessary in such instances — he would accept *attractio inversa* where a demonstrative precedes the fronted nucleus, as in Plautus, *Capt.* 110ff. ... *istos captivos duos heri quos emi* ... *is indito catenas.* There are numerous Hittite and Vedic Sanskrit parallels for a relative clause with an embedded nucleus, and it seems a secure reconstruction for Indo-European. It is then quite straightforward to suppose that an embedded nucleus might be fronted for emphasis, as seems clearly to be the case in the following Oscan example (Ve. 11): **v. aadirans v.** (name in nom. sg.) **eítiuvam** ('money', acc. sg.) **paam** (rel. pronoun, acc. sg. fem.) **vereiiaí púmpaiianaí** ('to the Pompeian *vereia*', dat. sg.) ... **deded** ('gave', 3sg.), **eísak eítiuvad** ('with that money', abl. sg.) ...; one may note here that the name of the donor has been placed first, and that 'money', in the accusative as the object of **deded**, has also been positioned before the relative pronoun that agrees with it, and that 'money' is repeated in the main clause in what is there the appropriate case. This pattern, with the nucleus appearing both in the relative clause and the main clause, can be paralleled in Hittite and Vedic Sanskrit, and has been claimed as a feature of Indo-European 'high' style; cf. Watkins (1995: 541), who would derive the Virgilian sentence from a similar construction, with deletion of *urbs* from the main clause, and fronting of accusative *urbem* in the relative clause round the relative pronoun (ibid. fn.2).

apparently found nowhere else in classical poetry or prose, and it seems a safe conclusion that the stately archaism is deliberately selected to emphasize the solemn pronouncement.[4] If the poetic tradition has played any part here, it can only be through some specific allusion to an earlier work that escapes us — and seems to have escaped ancient commentators too.[5]

It has been claimed that another example of the deliberate use of an archaism for effect is to be recognized in Propertius' statement of intent to strive for the grand manner:[6]

> sumite vires,
> Pierides: magni nunc erit oris opus   (Prop. 2.10.11f.).

For the genitive rather than the usual ablative after *opus est* an early Latin parallel is provided by Lucilius 294 *nummi opus atque assis*; further instances from classical Latin are regularly cited, two from Livy (22.51.3 *ad consilium pensandum temporis opus esse* and 23.21.5 *in stipendium quanti argenti opus fuit*) and one from Quintilian (12.3.8 *lectionis opus est*). In some of these examples, including the line of Propertius, one might argue that the meaning is essentially 'it is a matter of . . .' rather than 'there is a need for . . .', and see this as evidence for the original nature of the construction, with a genitive that would later have been largely replaced by the ablative under the influence of *usus est*;[7] this would accord the usage some antiquity, but would perhaps not suffice to show that its tone for Propertius was specifically archaic. Conversely, it has also been maintained that it is the ablative that is in fact original, a relic of the Indo-European instrumental, and the poorly attested genitive due to the analogy of *egeo*;[8] there need then be no presumption of great antiquity, but this would not necessarily exclude the possibility that Propertius had adopted

---

[4] See the excellent note of Austin (1971) ad loc., with further refs.

[5] Servius remarks on this passage: *hoc schema de antiquioribus sumptum possumus accipere*; he cites parallels but no source for the Virgilian line. (I am grateful to Professor Roland Mayer for advice in connection with Servius' comments here and elsewhere.)

[6] Cf. Tränkle (1960: 48): 'Der feierlich gehobene Klang liegt offensichtlich in der Absicht des Dichters'.

[7] See Wackernagel (1926: 65); for an original genitive also Hofmann–Szantyr (1965: 123). In the passage from Propertius, as Professor Jonathan Powell reminds me, it would be quite possible to give *opus* a more definite meaning as 'the work [that I am about to compose]': so various translators and commentators, cf. Rothstein (1966) 'es wird eine Arbeit sein, die ein *magnum os* erfordert', Paganelli (1961) 'cette oeuvre demande une voix puissante', as against e.g. Goold (1990) 'a loftier tone will now be needed'. A preference for this latter interpretation might be justified by appealing to the other attestations of *opus* + genitive, which, few though they are, seem to establish this as a Latin syntagm.

[8] For an original ablative, Lindsay (1907: 33), Hofmann–Szantyr (1965: 83), and more cautiously Ernout–Thomas (1953: 92).

as a perceived archaism a usage encountered in older texts.[9] Whatever may be the truth of the matter (and the paucity of attestations must be an obstacle to any very confident assessment of the resonance of the genitive construction), the example may serve to alert us to the possibility that not all 'archaisms' are necessarily archaic.

Alternatively, a genuinely archaic pattern may be used in a way that constitutes an innovation. A case in point, as Hélène Vairel-Carron has convincingly shown,[10] is the use of *ne* + present imperative for negative commands. In early Latin this syntagm has an inhibitive meaning, effectively 'stop doing...'; some clear instances are: Plautus, *Stich.* 20 *ne lacruma, soror*, said by a man comforting his disconsolate sister; id., *Pers.* 227 *ne me attrecta*, not so much 'don't touch me!' as 'get your hands off me!'; id., *Am.* 1109f. — *eí mihi! / — ne pave*, an expression of fear followed by an admonition to be of good courage; Terence, *And.* 868 *ah ne saevi tanto opere*, an attempt to calm someone down. There is a contrast with other constructions (e.g. *ne* + subjunctive) that have a more general prohibitive function, including reference forward in time. *Ne* + imperative is adopted by Virgil (and after him becomes general poetic currency); it may be used with the same inhibitive sense as in early Latin, so:

> ne dubita, nam vera vides   (Virg., *Aen.* 3.316);
> ne saevi, magna sacerdos   (Virg., *Aen.* 6.544);

but it is clear that it can also function as a prohibitive with future reference, cf.

> foliis tantum ne carmina manda   (Virg. *Aen.* 6.74);
> tu ne cede malis, sed contra audentior ito   (Virg. *Aen.* 6.95);

and that the use of the pattern has been expanded, so that there is no longer a contrast as in earlier times, and direct equation between the usage of Virgil and Plautus is not possible. The antiquity of the expression is remarked by Servius (on *Aen.* 6.544) but not its innovatory applications.

A more straightforward case of continuity might perhaps be sought in the infinitive of purpose, current in early Latin after verbs of motion,[11] e.g. Plautus, *Bacch.* 354 *senex in Ephesum ibit aurum arcessere*; id., ibid. 631 *militis parasitus modo venerat aurum petere hinc*; id., *Pseud.* 642 *reddere hoc, non perdere eru' me misit*. In classical prose, a single instance is cited from Varro (*R.R.* 2.1.1), but there are frequent occurrences in poetry:

---

[9] Note the suggestion of Tränkle (1960: 48) that the example in Livy 22.51.3 is 'vielleicht aus einem Annalisten'.

[10] 1975: 183ff., esp. 312f.

[11] See Bennett (1910: 418f.); Hofmann–Szantyr (1965: 344f.).

> nec dulces occurrent oscula nati / praeripere   (Lucr. 3.895f.);
> non ... Libycos populare penates / venimus   (Virg. *Aen.* 1.527f.);
> processerat ... / quaerere aquam   (Prop. 1.20.23f.);
> omne cum Proteus pecus egit altos / visere montes   (Hor. *Carm.* 1.2.7f.).

By extension the infinitive of purpose comes to follow verbs that express not only motion but also impulsion:

> quaerere terras agimur   (Virg. *Aen.* 3.4);
> ardor agit nova quaerere tecta   (Virg. *Aen.* 7.393);
> quiscumque virum perquirere silvis / egit amor   (Val. Fl. 3.684f.).

This particular use of the infinitive is adopted by the historians: so in Livy, for instance, the infinitive occurs after *impellere* and *subigere*.[12] Tacitus uses the infinitive after these, but also after an unusually wide range of other verbs and expressions (*certare, accingi, agitare, hortari, cura est,* etc.);[13] this suggests, given his general avoidance of the everyday, an artificial literary extension of usage, in which connection it is probably significant that he seems not to use the infinitive after ordinary verbs of motion, the pattern so familiar from early Latin and the poetic language (and conceivably current in the spoken language — see below).

The infinitive of purpose is notably more successful than its competitor after verbs of motion, the supine in *-tum* (the old accusative form of a verbal noun), which occurs with some frequency in early Latin, e.g.:

> ob portum obvagulatum ito   (*XII Tab.*)
> de nocte qui abiit piscatum ad mare   (Pl. *Rud.* 898);
> neque te derisum advenio ...   (Pl. *Trin.* 844);
> nunc hinc parasitum in Cariam misi meum
> petitum argentum a meo sodali mutuom   (Pl. *Curc.* 67f.);

but it turns out to be remarkably rare in classical poetry,[14] though there are a few instances, e.g.:

> vastatum finis iverat Assyrios   (Catullus 66.12);
> non ego ... / ... Grais servitum matribus ibo   (Virg. *Aen.* 2.785f.);[15]

---

[12] See Riemann (1885: 281ff.).

[13] For the usage of Tacitus, see Draeger (1882: 59f.).

[14] See Kühner–Stegmann (1955: I 723f.); for early examples see Bennett (1910: 453ff.)

[15] I am not convinced by the contention of Austin (1964) ad loc. that the supine is to be regarded as a feature of familiar language in early Latin and so here marks the ordinary everyday tone of the conversation between Creusa and Aeneas. It is true that one finds *cubitum ire* in general use (Cato, Cicero, Suetonius, etc., and cf. Horace, *Serm.* 1.5.48 *lusum it Maecenas, dormitum ego Vergiliusque*)) and that there are some obviously popular expressions such as *cacatum ire* (*CIL* IV 5242; cf. also C. Titius, *orat.* 2 *iudex testes poscit, ipsus it minctum*) but this simple pattern consisting just of *ire* + supine may best be regarded as a set idiomatic type; as an indication that freer use of the supine was a feature of colloquial

> vidimus flavum Tiberim . . . ire deiectum monumenta regis   (Hor.
> *Carm.* 1.2.13ff.).

One may note in these examples the apparent restriction to use after
forms of *ire*,[16] although there is a further remarkably bold use of the supine
by Virgil:

> si fortuna permittitis uti,
> quaesitum Aenean et moenia Pallantea, . . .   (*Aen.* 9. 240f.),

on which Wackernagel (1926: 278f.) justly observes that the poet has
chosen the more *altertümlich* expression in preference to a more usual *ut*-
clause or *ad* + gerundive.

In preferring the infinitive to the supine to express purpose after verbs
of motion, poetry may agree perhaps with everyday language: direct evidence to this effect is lacking for the classical period, and the argument
would rest on an assumption that the infinitive of purpose that appears in
late Latin (and survives everywhere in Romance, while the supine is hardly
continued at all) continues the early Latin construction that was avoided
in classical prose but persisted in the spoken language. This is beyond
demonstration, and separate developments at various periods cannot be
ruled out: the influence of Greek has been invoked[17] — certainly a plausible suggestion for classical poetry, and quite probably a factor in late Latin
developments. The question then arises as to whether it is appropriate after
all to speak of the perpetuation of an archaism: some qualification is surely
needed, if the old usage has had to be reinforced by external influence.[18]

The use of the infinitive with the verb 'give' seems to show a similar
blend of inheritance and Greek influence. There is a well-established early
Latin imperatival expression *da bibere*:[19]

> bibere da usque plenis cantharis   (Pl. *Pers.* 821);
> meridie bibere dato   (Cato, *de agr.* 89);

but some of the uses of the infinitive with *do* in classical poetry, as in:

> argenti magnum dat ferre talentum   (Virg. *Aen.* 5.248),

Latin, one might be tempted to cite Petronius 71.8 *ne in monumentum meum populus
cacatum currat*, with a different verb of motion, but this is clearly just an elaboration
of *cacatum ire* and offers no independent testimony. Certainly no colloquial tone is obviously
detectable in *Aen.* 4.117f. *venatum Aeneas unaque miserrima Dido / in nemus ire parant*; and
Tacitus shows no tendency to avoid the construction, cf. Draeger (1882: 88f.).
[16] This is predominantly the case with Tacitus too, though note *miserant . . . oratum* (*Ann.*
14.25).
[17] Cf. Kühner–Stegmann (1955: I 680).
[18] On the question of the revival of obsolescent Latin syntactic patterns under the influence
of Greek, see Coleman (1975).
[19] See Bennett (1910: 418f).

seem to have as much to do with Greek models (δῶκε δ' ἄγειν) as early Latin,[20] and particularly so in examples such as:

> dederatque comam diffundere ventis   (Virg. *Aen.* 1.319);
> praebuit ipsa rapi   (Ovid *Her.* 5.132);
> tristitiam et metus / tradam protervis in mare Creticum / portare ventis   (Hor. *Carm.* 1.26.1ff.).

Further 'Greek' usages can be seen in connection with the granting of prayers by the gods:

> tu das epulis accumbere divum   (Virg. *Aen.* 1.79);
> da flammam evadere classi   (Virg. *Aen.* 5.689);
> da ... Latio considere Teucros   (Virg. *Aen.* 6.66f.);
> nova da mihi cernere litora ponti / telluremque novam   (Lucan 1.693f.).

Here one thinks naturally of Greek δός + infinitive in prayers,[21] and the extension to addressing humans in a polite formula:

> da iungere dextram   (Virg. *Aen.* 6.697);
> date tangere vultus   (Val. Fl. 4.634);
> da iungere dona, da Scythicas sociare domos   (Val. Fl. 5.515f.);

or to impersonal uses of *do*:

> sed non ante datur telluris opaca subire / ... quam ...   (Virg. *Aen.* 6.140f.);
> nullaque datur considere terra   (Val. Fl. 4.511);
> verum inter medias dabitur si currere cautes   (Val. Fl. 4.587);

follows naturally enough. Greek influence here is hardly to be denied, and indeed it was noted by the ancients: Servius on *Aen.* 1.319 states: *graeca autem figura est*, and even adds that this usage is the source of *da bibere*. This last conclusion is unnecessary, but one may well have doubts about simply reversing the derivation and allowing that development of the early Latin figure was responsible for all occurrences of *do* + infinitive in poetic language.[22]

The antiquity of *da bibere* may be accepted, but there has been some division of opinion as to whether the infinitive is to be taken as equivalent to an object noun, and so parallel to *da aquam*, or (more plausibly) as related to the infinitive of purpose, and perhaps, if one accepts a parallel with Cato, *de agr.* 5.3 *satui semen dare*, providing evidence for the origin

---

[20] Cf. Williams (1960) ad loc.; Ernout–Thomas (1953: 286f.).
[21] Cf. Norden (1903) on *Aen.* 6.66f.
[22] Despite Hofmann–Szantyr (1965: 345); cf. p. 174 above.

of the Latin -*re* infinitive in a dative case-form.[23] An argument for the infinitive of purpose is seen in the existence of an alternative construction with a 'final' subjunctive:

> tum vos date bibat tibicini   (Pl. *Stich.* 757);
> dato bubus bibant omnibus   (Cato *de agr.* 73);

which is not confined to the verb *bibere,* cf.

> vin aquam? — si frustulenta est, da, opsecro hercle, absorbeam
> (Pl. *Curc.* 313).

This type of construction, with a dependent subjunctive but no subordinating conjunction, is found after several verbs in early Latin, in competition with *ut* clauses, and can be readily explained as arising from original parataxis:[24] This is well attested in the case of imperative forms of *sino*:[25]

> postea amurca spargito bene sinitoque combibat   (Cato *de agr.* 91);
> noli sis tu illic aduorsari, sine amet, sine quod lubet id faciat . . .
> (Pl. *Cas.* 204ff.);
> sinite abeam, si possum, uiua a uobis   (Pl. *Mil.* 1084).

The plain subjunctive after the imperative of *sino* recurs in classical poetry (and Livy), cf.

> sinite instaurata revisam / proelia   (Virg. *Aen.* 2.669);
> sine pascet durus aretque   (Hor. *Ep.* 1.16.70);
> dem sinite amplexus   (Val. Fl. 4.635).

With some verbs instances are rarer, as, for instance, with *decet*:

> decet animo aequo nunc stent   (Pl. *Poen.* 21f.).

---

[23] Cf. Blümel (1979: 89 with 80 fn.9), and earlier Ernout–Thomas (1953: 260). See also Kühner–Stegmann (1955: I 681); Bennett (1910: 418f.).

[24] Cf. Kühner–Stegmann (1955: II 227ff.); the truly paratactic stage, with two separate clauses (as opposed to subordination with no subordinating conjunction), may lie a long way back, cf. Bennett (1910: 245). It seems clear that use of the subjunctive alone, without *ut*, was quite normal in colloquial Latin following *rogo* (standardly at Vindolanda), *volo* and *opto* (see Adams (1995a: 117f.)); it may be no accident that the examples seem to show first-person forms of these verbs, so that they can be seen as simply reinforcing a jussive subjunctive or subjunctive expressing a wish, and this will also fit the occurrence of the pattern with the imperatives of *sino, facio, dico,* etc. — even *scribe dentur mi* in a Vindolanda letter (343.16f.) is merely a variant of this. More striking is the unusual example in the same letter of the plain subjunctive following a third-person verb, *desiderabat coria ei adsignarem* (343.31f.), on which see Bowman *et al.* (1990).

[25] Bennett (1910: 234f.) notes only two instances of non-imperatival forms of *sino* with a substantive clause in early Latin: Ter. *Hec.* 590f. *neque sinam ut qui nobis, mater, male dictum velit, mea pertinacia esse dicat factum* (the only instance in early Latin of *sino* with a following *ut*-clause, readily accounted for by the complex structure of the sentence, with the subject of *dicat* given by a relative clause); Plautus *Miles* 54 *sivi viverent.*

This is probably the only good Plautine example,[26] and the usage is not continued later, but it is almost certainly old given the Umbrian parallel construction seen in **façia tiçit** 'faciat decet' (*Tab. Ig.* II 17). By the same token then, Umbrian *deitu etaians* 'dicito eant' (*Tab. Ig.* VIb 64), where the subjunctive represents a transformation of the imperative of direct speech as seen in *deitu etato iiouinur* 'dicito -"itote, Iguvini"' (ibid. 63), provides support for the antiquity of *dico* + subjunctive in Latin, e.g. Plautus, *Stich.* 624 *dixi equidem in carcerem ires.*[27] This continues later, but in everyday language as well as poetry, though not in formal prose:

> dices igitur vel amico tuo Suettio . . . vel Labeoni nostro paulum
> proferant auctionem   (Cic. *Att.* 13.12.4);
> dic corpus properet fluviali spargere lympha . . .   (Virg. *Aen.* 4.635);
> dic Ama[. . .] Antonino acc[i]piat . . .   (*O.Max.* 254).[28]

Given this distribution, the status of the construction must be uncertain: old, it certainly is, but surely too familiar in the spoken language to be perceived as archaic.

A similar problem arises over the use of the subjunctive after forms of *facio*: this is frequent in early Latin after the imperative,[29] and this usage recurs in Cicero's letters and in everyday language as well as in classical poetry, with *fac* functioning almost as a sort of imperative particle:[30]

> opera omnia mature conficias face   (Cato *de agr.* 5.7);
> fac fidele sis fidelis   (Pl. *Capt.* 439);
> in medium turbae fac memor agmen eas   (Ovid *Am.* 1.4.56);
> fac (denarios) mi mittas   (*Tab.Vind.*: II 343.26).

In early Latin the plain subjunctive is found after other forms of *facio* also, but in only a few of the instances are these second- or third-person forms, e.g:

> nunc haec res me facit festinem   (Titinius 98 (Davault));
> labeam bifariam faciat habeant   (Cato *de agr.* 20.2);

---

[26] There are uncertainties over the text of *Most.* 72f. The example from the *Poenulus* comes in a passage that is full of jussive subjunctives, but that need not detract from its evidential value.

[27] Bennett (1910: 212f.) notes only 3 instances of *dico* + subjunctive in early Latin, as against 21 with an *ut*-clause.

[28] See Bülow-Jacobsen *et al.* (1994: 34), text no.4; this is an ostrakon of the second century AD from the Red Sea region. (I am grateful to Professor J. N. Adams for drawing my attention to this example.) It will be noted that the subjunctive follows an imperative form, which may be parallel to the tendency to preserve the subjunctive after *fac*, see below.

[29] For figures, see Bennett (1910: 224f.).

[30] Cf. Hofmann–Szantyr (1965: 530f.); see also *TLL* VI i.105.1ff. for one or two examples even from more formal prose.

> paupertas fecit ridiculus forem   (Pl. *Stich.* 177);

and the normal pattern here, persisting into the classical period, would seem to be a clause introduced by *ut*.[31] The plain subjunctive, however, predominates in early Latin after a first-person form, as, for instance, the archaic future *faxo*:[32]

> ervom tibi aliquis cras faxo ad villam adferat   (Pl. *Most.* 65);
> ego faxo dicat me in diebus pauculis / crudum virum esse   (Pl. *Truc.* 644f.).

The form *faxo* is rare in classical and later Latin, but the usage with a following subjunctive makes the occasional appearance in verse,[33] e.g.:

> haud sibi cum Danais rem faxo et pube Pelasga / esse ferant (*v.l.* putent)   (Virg. *Aen.* 9.154f.).

Morphologically and syntactically this might well be accounted archaic, but it might be more appropriate to think in terms of archaic elements surviving in a set idiom that was part of the living language, as the occurrence in Petronius 95.3 *faxo sciatis* might suggest,[34] without necessarily having archaic connotations for speakers. One may, however, suspect that the adoption of *faxo* + subjunctive by later poets is more self-conscious:

> iam foedera faxo / Haemonii petat ipse viri metuatque morari   (Val. Fl. 7.177f.);
> te tamen hac ... formidine faxo / iam tua silva ferat   (Val. Fl. 4.191f.);

the Virgilian echoes (*ego foedera faxo / firma manu* (*Aen.* 12.316f.)) and the relentless alliteration combine to suggest that here we have to do not so much with archaism as a resounding epicism.

A progression to mere imitation can be observed also in connection with another rare construction, the use of the impersonal gerundive with a direct object.[35] It occurs only once in Plautus:

> hercle opinor mi advenienti hac noctu agitandumst vigilias   (Pl. *Trin.* 869),

with isolated instances in other early writers, e.g.

---

[31] See the examples given by Bennett (1910: 227).

[32] After *faxo*, according to Bennett (1910: 225ff.), a plain subjunctive occurs eighteen times, as against solitary *faxo ut scias* (Plautus, *Asin.* 897).

[33] Cf. also Ovid, *Met.* 3.271, 12.594; Seneca, *Med.* 905 has (unusually) 2nd sg. subj. *faxis*.

[34] Similarly Apuleius *Met.* 1.25 *faxo scias*; etc.

[35] The examples are collected by Risch (1984: 186ff.). For Blümel (1979: 85f.) this is 'die historisch älteste Konstruktionsweise' for the gerund(ive), but more convincing is the argument of Hettrich (1990: 14ff.) that it is an innovation.

> optandum uxorem, quae non vereatur viri   (Afranius *com.* 99R).

It occurs a number of times in Varro, who is much given to employing archaisms, it is found ten times in Lucretius, e.g.

> aeternas quoniam poenas in morte timendumst   (Lucr. 1.111),

and it is once used by Cicero, with what seems to be deliberately archaising effect, to establish the character of the speaker:

> ... viam ... quam nobis quoque ingrediundum sit   (Cic. *Cato* 6).[36]

An archaic tone is therefore probably to be recognized in the single Virgilian instance:

> ... alia arma Latinis
> quaerenda, aut pacem Troiano ab rege petendum   (*Aen.* 11.229f.),

which is manifestly the inspiration for the later use of the construction in Silius Italicus:

> nunc pacem orandum, nunc improba ...
> arma reponenda et bellum exitiale cavendum
> auctor ego   (11.559ff.).[37]

Several of the features so far mentioned have in common that they make for a denser texture to the sentence, without explicit markers of subordination. Some such factor no doubt encouraged also the tendency to prefer simple case-forms to prepositional phrases, which is such a notable feature of Latin poetic language — including, for instance, a preference for a plain ablative in place of *in* + ablative. This is noted as an archaism by Servius on *Aen.* 11.686 *silvis te, Tyrrhene, feras agitare putasti?*, where he remarks, no doubt correctly, that *silvis* is *pro 'in silvis'*

---

[36] See Powell (1988: 114) ad loc. Professor Powell has also noted (private communication) that in *Cato* 42, two of the manuscripts read *notandum putavi libidinem*, where again the archaism would suit the speaker, and adoption of this reading might be seriously considered — the generally preferred *notandam* might well be an instance of the regularization that has perhaps removed a number of instances of the less familiar gerund (cf. the next note).

[37] The readings in both these passages require discussion. In *Aen.* 11.230, *petendum* is a correction in one of the ancient capital manuscripts, and was read by Servius and other ancient grammarians (see the *apparatus criticus* in Geymonat (1973)); it has been generally accepted in preference to the *petendam* of the tradition, no doubt rightly, given that the standard gerundive construction is the more likely interloper. In the *Punica* passage, *orandum* rests only on the reading of the lost Cologne manuscript reported by Modius, though the Virgilian parallel is persuasive support (see the *apparatus criticus* in Delz (1987)), and this is a particularly striking illustration of the danger posed to unfamiliar syntactic patterns by widespread regularization in the manuscripts. Other interesting archaic features may in this way have been totally obliterated.

et est archaismos. There is an ablative *campis* with a slightly different sense, 'across the fields', in the well-known half-line *Aen.* 4.404 *it nigrum campis agmen*, borrowed from Ennius: here one may well suppose that the listener or reader is expected to recognize the loan and to appreciate the humorous adaptation to a description of ants of a verse originally relating to elephants, so that any connotations of archaism will be a secondary matter. Such instances would, however, add to the variety of functions of the case-forms, and the deceptively similar *it tectis Argoa manus* of Valerius Flaccus (3.3), where the Argonauts are in fact leaving the palace and the ablative has the value 'from', suggests that poets enjoyed playing with the ambiguities of the simple ablative form.

It is worth considering in more detail two ways of using a case-form to express direction. From Indo-European, Latin will have inherited an accusative of direction (which accounts, *inter alia*, for the use of the supine in *-tum* after verbs of motion); this is continued in the use of the simple accusative with names of towns, but in early Latin a freer use is found, in that names of countries can also appear with a simple accusative and no preposition (in competition with *in* or *ad* + acc.)

> partim errant, nequinont Graeciam redire   (Liv. Andr. *Od.* 14);
> parasitum misi nudiusquartus Cariam   (Pl. *Curc.* 206).[38]

This is picked up by the later poets, who use the simple accusative for countries, e.g.

> ibitis Italiam   (Virg. *Aen.* 3.254),

or equivalent expressions:

> Italiam fato profugus Laviniaque venit / litora   (Virg. *Aen.* 1.2f.);
> quo regnum Italiae Libycas averteret oras   (Virg. *Aen.* 4.106);

and more generally for expressions of place:

> ea ... loca cum venere volantes   (Lucr. 6.742);
> devenere locos ubi ...   (Virg. *Aen.* 1.365);[39]
> speluncam Dido dux et Troianus eandem / devenient   (Virg. *Aen.* 4.124f.).

This extension to common nouns (other than *domum*) is essentially a

---

[38] It is now generally accepted that there is no reason to suppose that Plautus believed Caria to be the name of a town. Lindsay (1907: 25 fn. k) argues that Plautus simply does not follow the strict rules of classical Latin, but Wackernagel (1928: 223ff.) points out that the rules apply in Old Latin to Italian placenames but that there is fluctuation in the use of prepositions with towns as well as countries with non-native names, suggesting that usage was simply less well established for these.

[39] Servius ad loc. remarks: *'ad' minus est*, without further comment.

feature of poetry, and once again it is a question of innovatory use of an archaic pattern.

More complex is the dative of direction, where Greek influence has often been recognized and as often disclaimed.[40] In early Latin we find a construction that seems to be native, and where indeed a dative of goal is barely distinguishable from an indirect object (particularly if there is any suggestion of personification of 'death' or 'sleep'):

> Quiris leto datus   (Festus 245M);
> quattuor viros sopori se dedisse autumat   (Pl. *Am.* 306);
> ibo ad medicum atque ibi me toxico morti dabo   (Pl. *Merc.* 472);
> ob sutelas tuas te morti misero   (Pl. *Capt.* 692).

A natural extension of this usage can be seen in classical poetry:

> multos Danaum demittimus Orco   (Virg. *Aen.* 2.398);
> corpora non leto missa trecenta forent   (Ovid *Fast.* 2.664);
> si quis casus puerum egerit Orco   (Hor. *Serm.* 2.5.49);

yet at the same time echoes have been perceived of Homeric Ἄιδι προίαψεν. Another fairly straightforward use of the dative might be seen in the notion of stretching out one's hands in imploration to the gods:

> quas (manus) pro vobis diis immortalibus tendere consuevit   (Cic. *Font.* 48),

by extension to the all-powerful Romans:

> quae paulo ante Romanis de muro manus tendebant   (Caes. *B.G.* 7.48.3),

and to heaven in general:

> Anchises ... / ... caelo palmas cum voce tetendit   (Virg. *Aen.* 2.688f.).

In the last case there is the possibility of a shift in interpretation from person to place, which results in:

> it clamor caelo   (Virg. *Aen.* 5.451),

where the sense is rather 'sky', and so to other terms, yielding the poetic dative of direction, e.g.

> pelago Danaum ... dona / praecipitare iubent   (Virg. *Aen.* 2.36f.).

There may even be an example of the usage with a proper name in:

[40] Greek influence is admitted by Kühner–Stegmann (1955: II 320), Hofmann–Szantyr (1965: 100f.); but Leumann (1959: 146) firmly denies that this is a Graecism.

tum Cilicum liquere solum Cyproque citatas / immisere rates
(Lucan 8.456f.).[41]

These could be seen as purely analogical Latin developments, or one might accept that there was reinforcement from Greek. A further factor may well have been the increasing degree of competition in many contexts between the dative and *ad* + accusative (compare, for instance, with *morti dabo*, etc. cited above, Plautus *Capt.* 1019 *ego hunc ob furtum ad carnuficem dabo*, or the variation between *Capt.* 360 *quae ad patrem vis nuntiari* and 400 *numquid aliud vis patri nuntiari?*): this could provide a basis for artificial extension of the use of the dative.[42] At all events, in the poetic dative of direction, something new has arisen that involves more than simply the maintenance of an archaism.

These instances of case-syntax seem to reflect, as was previously noted, a preference for avoiding prepositions: this can no doubt be associated with reaction to the general tendency of Latin, which — as the Romance languages abundantly show — was towards increasing use of prepositional phrases rather than simple cases. But is avoidance of the new to be counted as a penchant for archaism?

Prepositions are also involved in my final examples, which concern word order.[43] It seems that in classical Latin, indeed from Plautus on, an attributive genitive normally followed the governing noun, though it might precede it to mark antithesis or for other stylistic reasons.[44] These patterns are maintained when there is a preposition governing the head, so that in the classical period one would normally find, say, *per finis Sequanorum* but marked *in Allobrogum finis* and residual set phrases like *de senatus consulto*; the preposition will normally come first. An inspection of

---

[41] Professor J. N. Adams has drawn my attention to the fact that in imperial Latin the ablative in *-o* came largely to replace the locative in *-i* in place names of the second declension (e.g. *Londinio* for *Londini*), and that just as directional forms in *-ae* of the first declension (e.g. *Alexandrie* (= *-ae*) 'to Alexandria') are most plausibly to be taken as locatives rather than datives of direction, so directional forms in *-o* (2nd decl.) are more likely to be locatival ablatives (see Adams (1995a: 108ff.)). This might allow an alternative explanation of Lucan's *Cypro*, but one that is probably not to be projected back onto the Virgilian examples of the dative of direction.

[42] See Löfstedt (1942: 187ff.); more briefly Ernout–Thomas (1953: 69f.).

[43] Strictly speaking, variations in word order that are not grammatically significant would be classified as stylistic rather than syntactic features, but there is some advantage in linking them in the present context, when the same issues of apparent innovation within poetic language are in question.

[44] See Adams (1976: 73ff.). The validity of his contention that in an earlier period the genitive normally preceded the governing noun (cf. *senatus consultum, Marci filius*, etc.), except in special cases (*paterfamilias, tribunus militum*, names of temples such as *aedes Bellonae*, etc.), cannot be discussed here, though I am inclined to accept it.

examples in the *Aeneid* and in Lucan,[45] to see what orders occur and with
what frequency, yields the results tabulated below. The first set of figures
(with percentages adjusted to the nearest half per cent) includes instances
where adjectives are present that do not disrupt the basic pattern, and
instances of discontinuity, discussed later. The abbreviations used are:
P[reposition], S[ubstantive], [Attributive] G[enitive], A[djective in agreement with the Substantive = As, or with the Genitive = Ag].
The basic patterns are:

		Aeneid	Lucan
G—P—S	*(reginae ad limina)*	42.5%	24.0%
P—G—S	*(in Eurotae ripis)*	10.0%	20.5%
P—S—G	*(ad sidera caeli)*	30.0%	33.0%

One must also allow for some patterns where the positioning of an adjective can create a semblance of ambiguity (e.g. in *nigri cum lacte veneni*
the order of the main constituents is P—S—G, but the case of the preceding
adjective can give an initial impression of a pattern G—P—S); the figures
for these are:

G—P—Ag—S	*(rupis ab Illyricae scopulis)*		
P—As—G—S	*(ex alto delubri culmine)*	15.5%	20.0%
Ag—P—S—G	*(nigri cum lacte veneni)*		
P—Ag—S—G	*(in duri certamina Martis)*		

and it can be seen that these make up a hefty part of the instances. (The
rare pattern, S—P—G and its variants, discussed below, accounts for the
remainder percentages.)

The G—P—S pattern is strikingly frequent in Virgil in comparison
with the usual marked variant P—G—S, while even the 'standard' P—S—
G has only a medium frequency. The G—P—S pattern is very rare in
prose: in Book I of Caesar's *De bello Gallico*, for instance, amongst
numerous instances of the other two patterns (*in finis Vocontiorum, in
Santonum finis*), G—P—S is found only once in *quorum per finis* (28.1),
where the usual fronting of the relative pronoun is responsible for the
different order.[46] Nor does the pattern seem to be a regular feature of
early Latin — there is no example in the *Captivi* of Plautus, nor in the

---

[45] The choice of Lucan for comparison is motivated simply by a desire to see how closely
the Virgilian pattern was followed by a later epic poet. It would be interesting to have a
more comprehensive set of figures, especially those for other Augustan poets.
[46] Note the other prose examples given by Marouzeau (1949: 60).

Rudens (despite frequent occurrences in this play of *in fanum Veneris* and *in Veneris fanum*, and similarly with other prepositions, there is not a single instance of *Veneris in fanum* or the like); it is, however, found in Ennius, cf. *Ann.* 260V. (Skutsch 222) *sulpureas posuit spiramina Naris ad undas; Satur.* 41V. (from the *Hedyphagetica*) *Nestoris ad patriam hic capitur magnusque bonusque*, where it already occupies the two positions within the hexameter that are its preferred sites in classical poetry.

Given this distribution, it hardly looks as though the G—P—S pattern can be reckoned as an archaism. It is interesting to note that in Umbrian, which retains a number of postpositions as bound forms, the normal order is S—P + G, cf. **vuku-kum kureties** 'ad lucum Coredii' (*Tab. Ig.* Ib4), etc.,[47] with the genitive preceding S—P only when it is a pronominal form, e.g. *erer nomne-per* 'pro eius nomine' (*Tab. Ig.* VIa34).[48] This seems to afford a parallel to Latin prose usage, and surely suggests that a more general use of G—P—S is a poetic innovation, perhaps associated with the development of hexameter verse and imitation of Greek (cf. Homeric patterns of the type οὔρεος ἐν κορυφῇς (*Il.* 2.456)), although adaptation of the Latin pattern As—P—S (*magnis de rebus*) with replacement of the adjective by an attributive genitive might have played a part. A further phenomenon may point to one of the reasons for its usefulness: if we take the simple cases of three-word groups, and look at the frequency of discontinuities, we find (with number of occurrences):

> G—P—S: G <> P—S *(Libyae vertuntur ad oras)*
> *Aen.* 39: 18; Lucan 17: 8.

In as many as one third of the examples, the genitive is actually separated from the rest of the prepositional phrase: there are instances already in Lucretius (e.g. 5.707 *quantum solis secedit ab orbi*). This provides a way of breaking up the phrase, comparable to the separation of adjective and noun, without disrupting the association of the preposition and the noun it governs.

This cannot be said of another pattern of discontinuity, P—G <> S, of which there are instances from Lucretius on; in the earlier examples, the

---

[47] There are a number of good examples in the description of the city boundaries of Iguvium given in *Tab. Ig.* VIa12–14, e.g. *presoliaf-e nurpier, tettom-e miletinar, randem-e rufrer*, all showing a noun in the accusative governed by postposition *-e* 'to' and a following genitive; unfortunately the meaning of most of the words is obscure.

[48] Adams (1976: 3) cites *erer nomne-per* as showing that in Umbrian a genitive normally preceded its head, but the immediate juxtaposition of *erer* (masc.) *nomne-per* and *erar* (fem.) *nomne-per*, referring back to the Fisian mountain and the city of Iguvium respectively, suggests that the pronouns are fronted for contrast.

inserted element seems most commonly to be a single word, some form of the verb:

> in equi conscendere costas   (Lucr. 5.1297);
> in luminis erigit oras   (Lucr. 5.1455);
> sub luminis edidit oras   (Virg. *Aen.* 7.660);
> ad Hesperiae venturos litora   (Virg. *Aen.* 3.186).

This persists later, as in:

> et prior in Nili pervenit litora Caesar   (Lucan 8.641),

but now further elements, e.g. the object of the verb, may also intervene, as in

> in Magni viventem ponite castris   (Lucan 6.233),

or instead of a verb, another noun:

> conlapsaque flebat iniquae / in Veneris Medea sinus   (Val. Fl. 7.251f.).

This pattern sets up a considerable tension by leaving the preposition before the genitive, which it cannot possibly govern. In another pattern that produces this result without discontinuity, S—P—G, one might be tempted to see a simple inversion of S and P, so:

> cava per calamorum   (Lucr. 5.1382);
> corpus in Aeacidae   (Virg. *Aen.* 6.58);
> litus harenosum ad Libyae   (Virg. *Aen.* 4.257);
> Hyperboreae plaustrum glaciale sub Ursae   (Lucan 5.23).

It seems likely, however, that this pattern (if it is not simply modelled on Greek 'anastrophe' of prepositions) is based on the type S—P—As (*rebus in arduis*), where the preposition is inserted between the noun and the adjective that agrees with it, a poetic variant of the more frequent type As—P—S (*magnis de rebus*).[49] The curious thing about this S—P—G pattern is that it reproduces the one that seems to be normal in Umbrian, where postpositions are involved (see above on **vuku-kum kureties**, etc.). Since it is widely believed that Latin also originally had postpositions, and still shows traces of them in forms such as *mecum*, etc., it looks as though, paradoxically, Latin has created as a poetic feature a sequence that might be supposed to be very archaic indeed. This is quite a new hazard to be reckoned with in the quest for archaisms.

There is the possibility of discontinuity with this pattern too, S <> P—G, and the result is something startlingly new, and thereby no doubt

---

[49] See Marouzeau (1949: 57ff.) and p. 159 above.

poetically arresting, with the preposition stranded before a genitive, far
from the noun it governs:

> metasque dati pervenit ad aevi   (Virg. *Aen.* 10.472),

the only instance I have noted in the *Aeneid*, but echoed by Lucan:

> Cambyses longi populos pervenit ad aevi   (Lucan 10.280),

in a nice instance of variation. There are further examples from several
poets:[50]

> magni speciem glomeravit in orbis   (Ovid *Met.* 1.35);
> dum vada tendis ad Hebri   (Ovid *Her.* 2.15);
> patriae sedes remeamus in urbis   (Lucan 1.690);
> ipsius aspectu pereant in velleris   (Val. Fl. 7.551).

This can no doubt be seen as part of the general trend towards the
adoption by poets of word orders that result in the wilful separation of
elements that naturally go together; this seems quite foreign to archaic
Latin, and nowhere else, perhaps, can the innovatory tendencies of Latin
poetic syntax be quite so clearly seen.

In this paper, I have naturally not attempted to cover all possible syntactic
features that might be classified as archaic (let alone those that involve
some form of innovation), but rather to give some idea of the problems
inherent in any such classification: the need to know whether something
is truly archaic, or perceived as such; whether its use is to be explained by
that fact, or whether it was just felt to be a 'poeticism'; whether the poetic
use is the same as the archaic use, or shows adaptation and development;
whether changes, or indeed retentions, can be accounted for purely within
Latin, or whether Greek influence is to be recognized (I have ignored
here Graecisms pure and simple, like the accusative of respect); or whether
we may at times have been duped into thinking that something is an
archaism whereas it has in fact arisen through a process of change that
has come full circle.

It may be remarked, in cautionary conclusion, that Latin poetic language, with its fondness for parataxis and unmarked subordination arising
from it, and its use of plain case-forms rather than prepositional phrases,
shows a remarkable similarity to the syntactic patterns reconstructed for
the Indo-European parent language; but this should not be taken to imply
continuity. Very little of what might be reconstructed as Indo-European

---

[50] For a useful collection of examples from Ovid onwards, see Eich (1925).

poetics seems to have survived the development, from the third century BC, of an essentially innovative literary language at Rome under the heavy influence of Greek,[51] and there is no reason to suppose that poets had access to a remoter poetic past, except in so far as features of it were preserved in religious or legal usages, and the connotations of these were not necessarily archaic rather than technical. The interplay between archaism and innovation surveyed above is concerned with a relatively small span of time, and with the reaction within the poetic tradition both to the usages of the early Latin authors and to trends in the development of the language as a whole. The 'Indo-European look' of certain characteristics of Latin poetic syntax illustrates only that apparent archaism may in fact result from rampant innovation.

[51] Cf. Watkins (1995: 62).

Proceedings of the British Academy, **93**, 269–286

Rowing Strokes: Tentative Considerations on 'Shifting' Objects in Virgil and Elsewhere

WOLDEMAR GÖRLER

Summary. To denote the activity of rowing in Latin prose, as a rule a single specific verb is used: *remigare*. In poetry, more general verbs (*pellere* and its compounds) governing appropriate syntactical objects are preferred. Mostly it is the ship that is 'impelled', but the same may be said of the oars, of the sea (it is 'struck' by the oars, 'displaced' or else — by optical illusion — 'shoveled by'), and even of the rowers' breast (which is 'impelled' = struck by the oars' handles in heavy rowing). All such phrases, being more copious than the specific verb, come near to an effect of alienation; this is most obvious where one of the less conventional objects is chosen.

The objects employed may be classified as follows: oar = (immediate) 'tool', ship = 'vehicle' (indirect 'tool'), sea = 'field of action'. An analogous set occurs with analogous activities, e.g. ploughing and horse-riding: what is 'pressed' (*premere*) is the handle of the plough or the plough or the land ploughed; the horseman 'tosses' (*quatere*) the bridle, the horse or the land stamped on. The potential syntactical objects 'shift' from the 'tool' at hand to the more remote 'area' where the action is going on; again it is by using a less familiar type of object that we are invited to see things anew. But it is also brought home to us that all parts involved are factually and causally linked, so an all-embracing picture emerges.

The verbs discussed (*pellere*, *premere*, *quatere*, etc.) are notoriously poor in semantic content. In poetry this is a clear inconvenience (and indeed visual vividness is due to the nouns only). But Virgil and others often turn it into an advantage.

Functional and colourless verbs may serve as a common
denominator of a variety of activities and thus convey a general
message. In *Aen.* 8.3 *impellere* (*arma*) and *concutere* (*equos*)
both carry the idea of violent motion; not incidentally, the verbs
are virtually interchanged. A more elaborate example of what
effects may be brought about by functional verbs interplaying
is Numanus' speech *Aen.* 9.603–20 (general idea: the hardness
of the old Latins). None the less there is full graphic force in
all details. It is largely by 'shifting' and varying the objects
in the way hinted at that the same wording can convey both a
colourful description and a symbolic sense.

I REALIZE THE above title sounds rather enigmatic. This is not due to
eccentricity nor to the wish to attract attention. The title simply explains
from where I started. Quite accidentally I happened to notice that the
activity of rowing can be described in Latin by a range of significantly
different modes of expression. When 'rowing strokes' are mentioned in
English, there is, I take it, general agreement as to what is actually 'struck':
it is clearly the water. Not so in Latin. The apposite verb is 'pellere' or its
compound 'impellere'. They have basically two meanings, not always neatly
distinguished: (a) 'to beat', 'to strike'; (b) 'to set in motion'. Hence it is
not really surprising that, when applied to rowing, '(im)pellere' may have
various objects: the oars are 'set in motion', so is the boat, and it is the
sea that is 'struck' or 'beaten'; a fourth type of object is rather unexpected;
in heavy rowing the rower's breast is 'struck' by the handle of the oar.

It seemed that such a range of object types might be a more general
syntactical scheme; and indeed a largely analogous spectrum of direct
objects is to be found with some other verbs. Apparently the phenomenon
has not been noticed so far, and it is the primary aim of this chapter to
draw attention to it. In default of an established or a more fitting term it
has seemed justifiable to call it a syntactical 'shift'. A further aim is to
give the reader some idea of what semantic and poetic effects may be
brought about by the scheme. But note the qualification in the subtitle:
the following reflections and interpretations are preliminary and indeed
tentative. They should not by any means be considered a chapter of a
definitive syntax of Latin poetical diction; they are just meant to give
a first impulse and to stimulate further discussion.

I

Let us look first at '(im)pellere' and rowing in detail. Here and in the following section completeness is aimed at as to the basic verbs in question.[1] It has proved helpful to consider synonyms as well. So quite a bit of lexical information has been collected, which is hardly conducive to easy reading. But a fairly general view seemed necessary to make it clear that the shifts we are dealing with are the exception rather than the rule, and also to find out whether our scheme is a specific feature of poetry at all.

1. The oars are 'set in motion'. As far as I can see the only example is Virgil, *Aen.* 4.594 (Dido addressing her men, when she has realized Aeneas and the Trojans are about to leave) 'ferte citi flammas, date tela, impellite remos!'[2] In Vitruvius 10.3.6 'remi ... cum manibus impelluntur et reducuntur ...' 'impellere' clearly has the restricted technical sense of moving the oars backward (outside the water), whereas the 'pull' driving the boat ahead is expressed by 'reducere'. There are several more or less synonymous verbs: Ovid, *Met.* 1.294, *Pont.* 1.5.40 'ducere remos'; Virgil, *Aen.* 8.689f., Ovid, *Met.* 11.461f. 'reducere remos' (see above on Vitruvius 10.3.6), *Trist.* 4.1.9 'referre remos' (compare Zwierlein (1986: 145), Hillen (1989: 227) on Seneca, *Med.* 366f.), Seneca, *Ag.* 437f. 'adducti remi', cf. *Aen.* 5.141 'adductis ... lacertis'; Ovid, *Am.* 3.8.43 'remum demittere', Silius 14.359 'remos mergere', (Livy 36.44.8 in a different sense: to stabilize the ship); Seneca, *Oed.* 540 'movere remos' (see Hillen 1989: 265), Manilius 4.284 'remos agitare' (cf. *Aen.* 5.211 'agmen remorum'); Valerius Flaccus 1.340 'remum concutere' (see also below pp. 280 on 'shaking' a ship, on 'shaking' horses pp. 281).[3]

---

[1] In addition to the dictionaries (including *TLL* and the PHI CD-ROM data bank) de Saint-Denis (1935) has proved most helpful; see also Jal (1861), Segebade (1895), Mohler (1948), Bonjour (1984), Gianfrotta (1987).

[2] With the deverbative nouns 'pulsus' (Cic. *De or.* 1.153 'impetu pulsuque remorum', Laberius frg. 53 Ribbeck (67 Bonaria) 'palmularum pulsus') and 'impulsus/-io' (Vitr. 10.3.6 '[remi] impulsu vehementi protrudunt ... navem'; Cassianus, *Conl.* 6.14.1 'remorum impulsione' (cf. Ov. *Met.* 3.662 'remorum in verbere'); Sidonius, *Epist.* 2.2.17 'impulsu') it cannot be decided whether the sense is that the oars are (passively) 'struck' or that the oars (actively) 'strike' the sea. Other verbs: Virg. *Aen.* 5.136 'intentaque bracchia remis' (just before starting the race), Silius 14.358 'tonsis aptare lacertos'.

[3] Some verbs emphasize the specific two-time rhythm of rowing (see n. 2 on Vitr. 10.3.6): Virg. *Aen.* 5.15, 8.108, 10.294 'incumbere remis' (after Homeric ἐμβαλέειν, *Od.* 9.489), *Aen.* 5.198 'procumbunt' (cf. *Aen.* 3.668 'proni'; note the charioteer's analogous posture *Georg.* 3.103, *Aen.* 5.147) = 'bend forward to the oars', clearly in moving the oars back outside the water. When 'drawing' (pulling) the oars the rowers 'rise' backwards: Virg. *Aen.* 3.207, 3.560, 5.189 'remis insurgere', *Aen.* 10.299 'consurgere tonsis' (*Aen.* 5.120 'terno consurgunt ordine

2. It is also the boat that is 'set in motion' or 'impelled': *Aen.* 5.119f. (the ship Chimaera) 'triplici pubes quam Dardana versu / impellunt'; Propertius 3.21.11 'propellite in aequora navem' (by rowing); Ovid, *Epist.* 3.153 'impellere remige classem'; *Met.* 8.102f. 'classis retinacula solvi / iussit et aeratas impelli [recc., edd.: *impleri* codd.] remige puppes'; Lucan 3.527 'impulsae tonsis tremuere carinae'; Silius 1.568 'ite citi, remis velisque impellite puppim' (modelled after *Aen.* 4.594?); metaphorically Cicero, *Tusc.* 4.9 '[orationem] dialecticorum remis propellere'. For 'navem [etc.] propellere' see further Ovid, *Epist.* 21.41f., *Trist.* 1.10.33, Lucan 3.1, 5.430f., Valerius Flaccus 1.494. Presumably it is just by chance that the simplex 'pellere' is nowhere found in this sense. Other verbs: Virgil, *Aen.* 5.116 'velocem Mnestheus agit acri remige Pristim', Ovid, *Epist.* 12.7f. (~*Met.* 4.706f.) 'iuvenalibus acta lacertis ... arbor' (the Argo), Livy 33.30.6 (~45.35.3) '[regiam navem] sedecim versus remorum agebant' (cf. 24.34.7), Lucan 3.535f. 'puppis / verberibus senis agitur', Florus 1.18.35 'classis ... remis quasi habenis agebatur'; Varro *Men.* frg. 49 Bücheler, Astbury (Nonius p. 533) 'nautae remivagam movent celocem', Virgil, *Aen.* 5.280 'tali remigio navis se tarda movebat', 10.195 'ingentem remis Centaurum promovet', Ovid, *Epist.* 13.101 'remoque move veloque carinam'; Vitruvius 10.3.6 '[remi] impulsu vehementi protrudunt ... navem'; Caesar, *B. G.* 3.14.6 'navigio remis incitato'; Valerius Flaccus 2.429 'iam remi rapuere ratem'; Virgil, *Georg.* 1.201f. 'qui adverso vix flumine lembum / remigiis subigit'.[4]

3. The grammatical object of 'pellere/impellere/propellere/pulsare' is the sea: Ennius, *Ann.* 377 Skutsch 'caeruleum spumat sale conferta rate

---

remi' may well have this meaning, 'remi' standing for 'remiges', but is generally assumed to mean 'there are three rows of oars, one above the other'), Val. Flac. 1.450 'insurgit transtris et remo Nerea versat', 2.13 'vela legunt, remis insurgitur'. The final phase of this backward move is meant in Enn. *Ann.* 218 Sk. 'poste recumbite', 219 'pone petunt', and in Luc. 3.543 'in transtra cadunt' (pace Maurenbrecher, *TLL* s.v. *cado* col. 22. 12f.). In Virg. *Aen.* 3.384 'lentandus remus in unda', the physical resistance of the water is stressed: the oars will be 'bent' (and therefore rowing will be 'slow': a play on the ambiguity of 'lentus'); similarly Catul. 64.183 'lentos incurvans gurgite remos' (cf. *Ciris* 461; Ov. *Trist.* 4.1.9), Sen. *Ag.* 437f. 'properat iuventus omnis adductos simul / lentare remos' (cf. Virg. *Aen.* 7.28 'in lento luctantur marmore tonsae', 8.89 'remo ut luctamen abesset').

[4] At times the rowers' activity is described as 'lifting' the ship: Virg. *Aen.* 10.294f. 'validis incumbite remis; / tollite, ferte rates', Luc. 3.526f. 'remige classis / tollitur', Val. Flac. 1.340 'ratem ... tollere remo', cf. Silius 14.379f. 'exsurgens ictibus alnus / caerula ... findit.' *Aen.* 10.207f. 'it gravis Aulestes centenaque arbore fluctum / verberat adsurgens' deserves special attention: 'adsurgens' goes with (king) Aulestes, but he clearly does not row himself, so his ship must be meant (on this type of ambiguity see Hahn (1958: 249–52); Harrison (1991: ad loc.)). Virgil makes us see the rowers' drawing up when pulling and the ship being 'lifted', carrying its captain, as one single move. For an analogous 'rising' of chariots see *Georg.* 3.108f. (modelled after Hom. *Il.* 23.368f.).

pulsum'; Cicero, *Acad.* frg. in Nonius p. 162 'eius (maris) unda, cum est pulsa remis, purpurascit'; Catullus 64.58 'iuvenis fugiens pellit vada remis'; Virgil, *Georg.* 1.254 'infidum remis impellere marmor'; Tibullus 2.5.33f. 'ire solebat / ... pulsa [abl.] per vada linter aqua'; Propertius 3.22.11 'propellas remige Phasim', 4.2.8 'remorum auditos per vada pulsa sonos'; Ovid, *Met.* 3.657 'impellit properantibus aequora remis'; *Trist.* 4.1.10 'pulsa bracchia iactat [varia lectio: pulsat] aqua'; *Pont.* 3.1.1 'aequor ... pulsatum remige'; *Pont.* 4.10.33 'remus iter pulsis ... fecerat undis'; Lucan 2.702 (not explicitly about rowing) 'impulsum rostris sonuit mare' (cf. Petronius 89 v. 34 'pulsumque marmor abiete'); *Octavia* 315 'resonant remis pulsata freta'; Isidorus, *Orig.* 19.2.7 'palmula est extrema latitudo remi ... qua mare impellitur'.[5]

As may be seen from more specific synonyms three different meanings should be distinguished:

(a)   To 'beat' the sea, to 'churn it up'. This is a means and an effect of rowing, not however its purpose proper[6]. This meaning clearly prevails in Ennius, *Ann.* 377, Cicero, *Acad.* frg., Lucan 2.702 and *Octavia* 315, where attention is drawn to the visible and audible effects of rowing. Synonyms are 'quatere/percutere', 'ferire', 'verberare', 'icere', 'verrere'; more general: 'agere', 'sollicitare', see e.g. Silius 13.241f. 'tonsae / percussere fretum'; Virgil, *Aen.* 3.290 = 5.778 'feriunt mare'; *Aen.* 10.207f. (the ship) 'Aulestes centena ... arbore fluctum / verberat'; Ovid, *Met.* 3.662 'remorum in verbere perstant'; Lucan 3.535f. 'puppis / verberibus senis agitur'; Silius 11.490 'centeno fractus spumabat verbere pontus'; 14.360f. 'verberibus torsere fretum, salis icta frequenti / albescit pulsu facies' (cf. [Ovid], *Epist.* 18.23 'dare verbera ponto', of swimming, cf. Statius, *Silv.* 1.3.73f. 'natatu / plaudit aquas'); 'ictus' = 'rowing stroke': Virgil, *Aen.* 5.198, Ovid, *Am.* 3.6.3, *Met.* 11.463; Silius 6.361, 13.243, 14.379; Valerius Max. 3.2.10; Pliny the Younger, *Paneg.* 82.1; Ennius, *Ann.* 377 Skutsch

[5] See further Ov. *Epist.* 3.65 'canescant aequora remis'; Silius 14.360f. 'salis icta frequenti / albescit pulsu facies'; Sidonius, *Epist.* 2.2.17 'spumoso canescit impulsu'. In Tac. *Ann.* 2.23.2 'aequor mille navium remis strepere aut velis impelli' the second verb may be understood 'in common' of both rowing and sailing. Goodyear (1981: ad loc.) expresses his doubts as to the soundness of the textual transmission, as others have done before him: ' ... a freakish expression ... I am much inclined to print *inpleri* or to obelize'. Sen. *Ag.* 161 'maria pigro fixa languore impulit' is different: Iphigenia has 'released' the sea's standstill in an abstract sense. There are remarkable 'hypallagai' (syntactical inversions) in Luc. 9.319f. 'remis actum mare [nom.] propulit omne / classis onus [acc.]' instead of 'remi classis onus per mare [or mari] propulerunt', and in Ov. *Met.* 6.512 'admotum ... fretum remis' (see Bömer (1969: ad loc.), Görler (1982: 78)).

[6] Note that 'verberare' can also mean futile 'beating' of the air ('sawing the air') and fluttering: Virg. *Aen.* 5.377 (the boxer Dares) 'verberat ictibus auras', *Aen.* 10.892f. (a wounded horse) 'tollit se ... et calcibus auras / verberat', *Aen.* 11.756 (an eagle attacking a snake) 'simul aethera verberat alis'.

'verrunt... mare'; Virgil, *Georg.* 3.201 'aequora verrens' (not explicitly about rowing), *Aen.* 3.208 = 4.583 'caerula verrunt' (in *Aen.* 5.141 'adductis spumant freta versa lacertis' and *Aen.* 10.208 'spumant vada marmore verso' the past participles are more likely to be derived from 'vertere'); Lucan 9.319 'remis actum mare'; Valerius Flaccus 2.77 'remis agitur mare'; Virgil, *Georg.* 2.503 'sollicitant... remis freta' (on the moral undertone see below p. 284 n. 23). In Lucan 1.370f. (Caesar's soldier) 'Oceani tumidas remo compescuit undas, / fregit et... Rhenum' the meaning comes near to 'subjugation'. With some verbs the idea of 'turning up' prevails, and thus the image of 'ploughing' is evoked: 'vertere', 'versare', 'convellere', 'fodere', 'torquere', 'eruere', 'subigere': Virgil, *Aen.* 3.668 'vertimus... aequora remis'; 5.141 'spumant freta versa'; 10.208 'spumant vada marmore verso' (but the past participles may be derived from 'verrere' see above); 5.119f. (the ship Chimaera) 'triplici pubes quam Dardana versu / impellunt'[7]; 5.143, 8.690 'convulsum remis... aequor' (imitated *Anthologia Latina* 388[a] = 384 Shackleton Bailey 15); Silius 14.359 'fodit aequora remis'; Catullus 64.13 'torta... remigio... unda'; Ovid, *Fast.* 5.644 'remis... torsit aquas' (cf. Virgil, *Aen.* 3.208 = 4.583 'torquent spumas'); Silius 14.360 'verberibus torsere fretum'; Ovid, *Epist.* 5.54 'remis eruta... aqua'; *Am.* 3.8.43 'freta... eruta remo'; Valerius Flaccus 1.471 'pontum remo subigit'. The image of ploughing is even more obvious when the sea is said to be 'furrowed' (not so much, of course, by the oars as by the boat rowed); typical verbs are 'sulcare', 'scindere', '(in)findere', 'secare': Ovid, *Met.* 4.706f. (the sea-monster) 'velut navis... / sulcat aquas, iuvenum... acta lacertis'; Silius 14.379f. 'alnus / caerula nigranti findit spumantia sulco'; Ovid, *Met.* 11.463 'ictu scindunt freta'; *Ars* 2.671 'mare remigiis findere'; *Fast.* 3.586 'findite remigio... aquas'; [Ovid], *Epist.* 18.146 (Leander) 'findam corpore (aquas)'; Virgil, *Aen.* 5.142 (the rowers) 'infindunt pariter sulcos'; Valerius Flaccus 1.688f. 'pinus / infindit... salum' (not on rowing); Virgil, *Aen.* 5.218f. (on rowing) 'secat... [the ship] Pristis / aequora'.

(b) To 'displace' the water. This technical meaning seems dominant in Ovid, *Am.* 2.11.5 'ne quis remo freta... moveret' (but see below), *Pont.* 4.10.33 'remus iter pulsis... fecerat undis', Lucan 5.448f. 'classes... tonsis / aequora moturae'. A more specific verb is 'dimovere'; in the extant texts it is used only with reference to swimming (which may be due to chance): [Ovid] (on Leander) *Epist.* 18.80 'dimotae corpore... aquae', 19.48 'lentaque dimotis bracchia iactat aquis', *Met.* 4.708 (the sea-monster threatening Andromeda) 'fera dimotis impulsu pectoris undis [sulcat aquas]'; compare Tibullus 1.4.12 'placidam niveo pectore pellit aquam',

---

[7] 'Versus' = action of 'turning', it is often taken to mean 'tier of oars', but here the primary meaning clearly prevails; cf. Val. Flac. 1.450: 'versare' = to row.

[Tib.] 3.5.30 'pellitur unda manu'; Ausonius, *Mos.* 344 'flumen pepulisse natatu'.

(c)   In some instances the idea may be that by rowing the sea is 'set in motion' (the second basic meaning of 'pellere/impellere'). This sounds like a paradox, but when there is no land in view to serve precisely as a fixed base this may be a credible subjective impression. 'Impellere marmor' (Virgil, *Georg.* 1.254) may well point to the relativity of the ship's movement[8]; likewise, when rowing against the wind, one may wonder whether the ship is actually moved or whether the sea is 'shovelled' by the boat.[9] See further Ovid, *Am.* 2.11.5 'ne quis remo freta longa moveret' (i.e. the sea in all its width, not just the stretch beaten by the oars), *Met.* 3.657 'impellit properantibus aequora remis'.

4.   The fourth type of object is rather unexpected: Ennius, *Ann.* 218 Skutsch 'poste recumbite vestraque pectora pellite tonsis', Lucan 3.543 'remis pectora pulsant'.[10] At first sight, it sounds odd that the rowers should 'strike' or indeed 'shake' their own breasts. But it is a realistic feature; in the 'pull', the oars are in fact 'drawn' towards the breast: Ennius, *Ann.* 219 Skutsch (not necessarily the same context as 218) 'referunt ad pectora tonsas', Ovid, *Met.* 11.461f. 'reducunt / ... ad fortia pectora remos', *Trist.* 4.1.9 'refert ... ad pectora remos', Silius 13.241 'revocatae ad pectora tonsae', and when 'pulled' forcefully they will touch the chest.[11] Of course, 'pectora pellere' is hyperbolic, a symbol for fast

---

[8] This is, however, hardly true of the alleged Homeric model Il. 7.5f. ἐλάτῃσι/πόντον ἐλαύνοντες. David West has suggested in the discussion and in subsequent correspondence 'marmor' in *Georg.* 1.254 might have connotations of marble proper, smoothness, colour, above all rigidity: 'It seems to hint at the perversity of man in daring to attempt to set "*infidum marmor*" in motion.' Virgil does indeed in some passages stress the unnatural character of navigation (see below p. 284 n. 23). But 'to set marble in motion by rowing' amounts to an outright adynaton, and one may wonder whether this fits in with the context.

[9] See Lucr. 4.389f. '... fugere ad puppim colles campique videntur,/ quos agimus praeter navem ...'. Tränkle (1960: 84f.) may well be right on Prop. 3.22.11: 'propellas remige Phasim', 'das Schiff erscheint stehend und das Wasser fortgestoßen'; Fedeli (1985: ad loc.) thinks of the water 'displaced'. It is tempting to assume an analogous notion of relativity in Catul. 61.14 'pelle humum pedibus': could not the dancer give the impression of actually 'pushing' the soil under his feet? See further Ov. *Met.* 4.711f. (Perseus) 'pedibus tellure repulsa / arduus in nubes abiit', 6.512 'admotum ... fretum remis [see note 5] tellusque repulsa est', 2.786 'inpressa tellurem reppulit hasta'.

[10] Possibly an echo of Ennius, G. B. Conte (1970: 135), but see O. Skutsch ad *Ann.* 218. Compare Val. Flac. 1.369 'percusso pectore tonsa', Silius 11.489f. 'adductis percussa ad pectora tonsis'.

[11] In a paper of 1982 (Würzburger Jahrbücher für die Altertumswissenschaft, Neue Folge 8, p. 77 n. 25) I had quoted with modified approval G. Maurach (1975: 480) who had taken 'pectora pellite tonsis' to be a 'Figur der Umkehrung'. Otto Skutsch, in a letter of 25 Feb. 1983, protested: '... eines verstehe ich nicht: was soll denn poste recumbite vestraque

rowing (just as 'churning up the sea' may be indicative of the rowers' effort, see above p. 274).

It is worthwhile to try a systematic (and, for that matter, somewhat pedantic) classification. Rowing, as opposed to running, for example, is a complex procedure. Motion is brought about indirectly. First a 'tool' (the oar) is moved (object type 1). Thereby the 'vehicle', an 'indirect tool', is set in motion along with the rower (type 2). Type 3 may be called 'field of action'. This label is no more than a stop-gap expedient, as three different aspects are meant. In rowing, the sea is the place where the operation is going on and which is traversed by rowing. The sea is also affected by the rowers' activity; it is 'beaten' by the oars; sometimes the second meaning of 'pellere' seems to prevail and the idea is that the sea is 'set in motion'. These aspects cannot always be kept apart, so a general term has been chosen. Object type 4 may be described as 'parts affected secondarily' (one might also say κατὰ συμβεβηκός); it is in no sense a purpose of rowing that the rowers' breasts be beaten. 'Beating' the breast is a secondary or side-effect. But being a highly typical side-effect it may stand symbolically for rowing itself.

II

Looking at this classification, analogous cases come to mind, for instance ploughing and horse-riding; further candidates are flying[12] and charioteering[13].

---

pectora pellite tonsis fuer eine Figur sein? Ein alter Ruderknecht wie ich weiss, dass man sich hintenueberlegt und dann die Stange an die Brust zieht. Ich habe Maurach nicht zur Hand und kann mir nicht denken, was er will; nur scheint mir sicher zu sein, dass er nie in einem richtigen Ruderboot gesessen hat (Vergnuegungskaehne zaehlen nicht mit).' In a seastorm, the oars may 'fall uselessly onto the breast' (Stat. *Theb.* 5.375 'remi ... cadunt in pectus inanes') or, worse, break and then strike ('percutere' in a more literal sense) the chest (Val. Flac. 3.477 'percussit ... deceptum fragmine pectus').

[12] See e.g. Catul. 66.53 (Zephyrus?) 'impellens nutantibus aera pinnis' (cf. Virg. *Georg.* 1.254 'remis impellere marmor'). Flying is frequently compared to rowing: Aesch. *Ag.* 52 πτερύγων ἐρετμοῖσιν ἐρεσσόμενοι, Lucr. 6.743 (birds approaching Lake Avernus) 'remigi oblitae pennarum vela remittunt', Virg. *Aen.* 1.301, 6.19 'remigium alarum'. For details see Luck-Huyse (1996: 205–9, 213–15).

[13] Typically, 'flectere' is used with the reins (e.g. Virg. *Aen.* 12.471, Ov. *Met.* 2.169 (Bömer: ad loc. 'habena i.q. currus'), Val. Flac. 5.436), with the horse (e.g. Virg. *Aen.* 1.156, 9.606, 10.577; Ov. *Pont.* 2.9.58 'colla ... velocis flectere doctus equi'), with the 'vehicle' (e.g. Ov. *Met.* 10.447 'plaustrum'), and with a 'field of action' (Ov. *Ars* 2.428 'iter'); cf. Cic. *Fin.* 5.49 (translation from Homer) 'quin puppim flectis', Virg. *Aen.* 5.28 'flecte viam velis'. There is a remarkable sentence with 'regere' in Virg. *Aen.* 12.624: 'currumque et equos et lora regebat' — a 'vehicle', a 'secondary tool' (if the horses may thus be called), and an 'immediate tool' governed by one and the same verb. See now Dingel (1997) on *Aen.* 9.402,606,590,776.

Ploughing: what is 'pressed' ('premere') is (1) the handle, a 'direct tool': Ovid, *Fast.* 4.825 '[Romulus] premens stivam designat moenia sulco'; compare *Met.* 8.218 'stiva . . . innixus arator'; (2) the plough, 'indirect tool' or 'vehicle' as it were: Lucretius 5.209 'terram pressis proscindere aratris', Virgil, *Georg.* 2.203 'presso . . . sub vomere', 2.356 'presso . . . vomere' (*Georg.* 1.45 'depresso . . . aratro') etc.; (3) the 'field of action': Virgil, *Aen.* 10.78 (Juno, denouncing the Trojan's hostile behaviour) 'arva aliena iugo premere atque avertere praedas'. This is my only example for this type of object[14], and I am aware it is a disputed case. It has been argued that 'iugo premere' should not be taken in the literal sense (e.g. by Eva Baer, *TLL* s.v. *iugum* 641.26f. classifying the passage under the heading 'in imagine et translate, praevalente vi subigendi', and by Harrison (1991: ad loc.)). In fact, the Trojans had not had much opportunity for ploughing so far (excepting the 'sulcus primigenius' mentioned in *Aen.* 7.157). But Juno clearly overstates her case (as Aeneas does in *Aen.* 8.118); note also that she, to an extent, echoes, with reversed premises, the boasts of Numanus (*Aen.* 9.608, 612f., see also below p. 285) '[iuventus] . . . aut rastris terram domat aut quatit oppida bello . . . semperque recentis / comportare iuvat praedas et vivere rapto'; thereby, she (and the poet, we may surmise) counterbalances the conception of the Trojans being effeminate. Moreover, 'iugum', to the best of my knowledge, is not used elsewhere in Virgil in the alleged metaphorical sense (for 'iugum' = plough see *Ecl.* 2.66, 4.41). So there is good reason to keep to the plain literal sense: 'the Trojans plough other people's soil'.

Horse-riding: the relevant verb is 'quatere'. It is (1) the reins that are 'shaken' (a 'tool'), (2) the horse (a sort of 'indirect tool' or 'vehicle'), and (3) the field stamped on (for details see below p. 280).

There seem to be no strictly analogous instances of object type 4: parts affected as a side-effect, neither with 'premere' nor with 'quatere'. But Virgil, *Georg.* 1.43–6 may well be compared: 'vere novo . . . depresso incipiat iam tum mihi taurus aratro / ingemere et sulco attritus splendescere vomer'. Virgil would hardly have been satisfied with a farmer who made his oxen groan for nothing and who had simply polished his plough in a furrow suited to this end. But both the groans of the draught-cattle and the shine of the share are easily understood as a symbol, and a highly

---

[14] In *Aen.* 10.295f. a furrow ('sulcus') is 'effected' object of 'premere': 'inimicam findite rostris / hanc terram sulcumque sibi premat ipsa carina' (modelled after or imitated by an unknown poet, quoted Isid. *Orig.* 1.37.3 = Morel/Büchner inc. 35 'pontum pinus arat, sulcum premit alta carina'). This is a peculiar case. Ships are often said to 'furrow' the sea, but here a real furrow is in mind, to be drawn in the enemy's soil. There is a strong connotation of violence, and by the conflation of images the reader is reminded that both seafaring and agriculture are original sins (see also below p. 284).

graphic picture of heavy ploughing emerges. Just so, in Horace *Epod.* 1.26, a 'good number of oxen put to shining ploughs' symbolizes assiduous tilling. *Georg.* 2.211 'rudis enituit impulso vomere campus' reads like an 'inversion' of 1.45f. 'incipiat ... / ... sulco attritus splendescere vomer'. In fact, the friction is mutual and fresh (wet) clods do shine; there is a common notion of freshness and brightness, brought about by hard work.[15]

The semantic and syntactical findings are basically the same; one given verb may govern a variety of objects which may be classified as in the case of rowing.

	1 (immediate) 'tool'	2 'vehicle' ('indirect tool')	3 'field of action'	4 'parts affected secondarily'
Rowing *(im)pellere*	oar	boat	sea	the rowers' breast
Ploughing *premere*	handle (*stiva*)	plough	land ploughed	(the oxen, the ploughshare)
Horse-riding *quatere,* *concutere,* *quassare*	bridle, reins	horse (see below p. 281)	(battle-) field, hostile towns	(see below p. 281)

Presently, some typical passages will be examined in detail. But let us begin with a general consideration. What happens in making either the oars or the ship or the sea syntactical objects of '(im)pellere' may be called a shift. 'Shifting objects' are a well known phenomenon; quite a few Latin verbs take different types of direct objects, i.e. in the accusative case. Most prominently, a group of verbs denoting some sort of adding or detracting (as the grammarians put it) may govern both the movable thing added or detracted, and the unmoved, i.e. the person or thing to which the movable is given or from which it is taken away: 'murum oppido circumdo', 'oppidum muro circumdo'. At first sight, our examples, too, may seem to belong to this same group, as the oars, being the smaller and more movable thing, appear both as direct object and as the instrument. But our type of shifting is different. That is most obvious in the passive forms: 'donatur' has not the same meaning in 'liber donatur' and in 'amicus donatur'. In the first case it means: 'the book is moved from one possessor to another'; in the second 'the friend is enriched by a gift'; in the city-wall example 'circumdatur' means either 'is built' or 'is walled in'. Not so in our examples. Be it the oar or the boat or the sea, 'impellitur' means 'is

---

[15] On other connotations of 'terere' see below p. 285.

beaten', 'is pushed or impelled' throughout; the handle of the plough ('stiva'), the plough itself, the field are all 'pressed down'; the bridle, the horse, the battlefield are 'shaken' or 'battered'. In all these instances the objects are acted upon the same way, there is no change in meaning. In the grammatical sense they are all direct external objects. The 'shifting' occurs in that the handle, both of the oar and of the plough, and the bridle are literally in the hand(s) of the acting subject, whereas the sea 'is impelled' and the battlefield 'is shaken' indirectly. It is a shift from nearness to distance. And that is why the latter expressions are suited to metaphorical use as well, — and some of our examples have, indeed, been read as such (see above p. 277, below p. 285). On the other hand, when what is physically near functions as syntactical object, the description, as a rule, seems more vivid and graphic.

III

But let us not rashly generalize. The respective currency of the single modes of expression has to be taken into account as well. Some of the verb-object phrases we have looked at are frequent and widespread, nay stereotypes. These, evidently, like familiar and thus faded metaphors are of small interest; they are inconspicuous and with them hardly any graphic quality is felt. It is when the poet has 'shifted' to a less familiar object that interesting effects may be brought about.

The most common syntactical object of 'pellere' is the ship: 'to set' or 'to keep the ship in motion'. To 'impel the oars' and to 'impel the sea' are unusual, and so the procedure of rowing, familiar to most readers, is alienated; it is brought to our attention that the oars have to be moved first, and laboriously so, to get a ship into motion. In *Aen.* 4.594 (see above p. 271) this contrasts with 'citi' in the same verse, and thus we come to realize that Dido's men have little chance to catch up with Aeneas and the Trojans. In *Georg.* 1.254 'remis impellere marmor', as has been remarked, the direction seems inverted: it is not the ship that is 'impelled' across the sea, but the sea by the ship, 'impelled' by the oars. There may be a connotation of moral reproach: seafaring comes near to a reversal of nature (see below p. 284). But it carries also much visual quality. Primarily, it is the ocean the poet makes us see, and the oars 'pushing it aside' or even 'setting it in motion'. But indirectly — and quite irresistibly — the rowers and their efforts are 'viewed' as well.

Here a typical feature of the shifts in hand may be noticed. All parts involved in rowing (the rower, the oars, the ship, the sea) are factually and causally linked; hence whatever part functions as the syntactical object, the description will still, as a rule, work up to an all-embracing picture. To be sure, the actual stress may vary greatly, there are shades and nuances, and indeed it is the essential function of our phenomenon to shift the point of view. In *Aeneid* 4.594 all attention is focused on the rowers' immediate task, to 'move the oars'; in *Georgics* 1.254, on the other hand, the act of rowing is seen as if from a distance, at the widest angle possible and in a very general sense, 'mankind challenging the sea', as it were. But no aspect of the activity in question has ever totally faded out.

That is also why in Ennius, *Ann.* 218 Skutsch the 'parts affected secondarily' (object type 4) can carry particular expressive weight; the coxswain's command 'pectora pellite tonsis' should be read as 'try your best', and we get a full picture of hard rowing. A more complex example of a symbolic side-effect is *Aeneid* 5.197–200 ' . . . olli certamine summo / procumbunt: vastis tremit ictibus aerea puppis / . . . tum creber anhelitus artus / aridaque ora quatit . . .'. Obviously, the 'trembling' of the ship is brought about by the 'vasti ictus', i.e. by the rowers' efforts. Yet it is not their primary goal to make the ship tremble. It is by a sort of repercussion that the ship quivers and rocks. What follows is no less telling. The rowers are 'shaken' by their own accelerated breath. It goes without saying that the rhythm coincides with the 'vasti ictus' (compare Lucan 3.527f. 'impulsae tonsis tremuere carinae / crebraque sublimes convellunt verbera puppes'; Valerius Flaccus 1.340 'concusso . . . ratem . . . tollere remo'; Silius 14.379 'anhelatis exsurgens ictibus alnus'). In the poet's eyes, all this is basically the same: various aspects of one homogeneous, concerted operation, a true symphony of tossing and rocking, preceded and indeed prompted by an analogous symphony from the spectators' part (*Aen.* 5.148–50). The Trojans' 'plausus fremitusque' makes the groves resound; it is then 'spread rolling' along the 'sheltered shores'; even the surrounding hills re-echo the cheering.

As to horse-riding, 'quatere' and its cognates often govern the reins ('lora', 'habenae') as their syntactical object: Virgil, *Aen.* 5.146f. 'immissis aurigae undantia lora / concussere iugis', 6.100f. (metaphorically, Apollo 'breaking in' his priestess) 'frena furenti / concutit', Ovid, *Am.* 2.16.50 ' . . . per admissas *concute lora iubas*' (note the hypallage: what is to be 'set loose' ('admittere') is clearly the reins ('lora'), not the horse's mane), Seneca, *Phaedra* 1006 'acer . . . habenis lora permissis quatit' (see Hillen (1989: 107)), Silius 16.439 'quatiuntur inania lora', 17.541 'largas Poenus quatit asper habenas', Statius, *Theb.* 10.218 'quassat habenas'.

Elsewhere it is the field that is 'shaken', i.e. stamped on: Ennius, *Ann.* 242 Skutsch 'totam quatit ungula terram' (compare 263, 431), Virgil, *Aen.* 8.595 'it clamor, et agmine facto / quadripedante putrem sonitu quatit ungula campum'. Here, it is primarily physical noise and vibrations that are depicted, albeit with hostile undertones. In the following passages the connotation of 'upsetting' and 'overthrowing' prevails, but it is still strongly supported by the basic (physical) component: Lucretius 2.329f. 'circumvolitant equites mediosque repente / transmittunt valido quatientes impete campos', Virgil, *Aen.* 11.511–13 'Aeneas ... / exploratores ... / praemisit, quaterent campos', 9.608 'quatit oppida bello' (see below p. 285 for the context)[16]. Both are picturesque but also rather familiar poetical expressions, and so comparable to faded metaphors. Now Virgil, in three instances, applies 'quatere'/'concutere' to the horse: *Georg.* 3.132 (the horse-breeders) 'saepe etiam cursu quatiunt et sole fatigant [sc. equos]'; *Aen.* 8.3 '[Turnus] ut ... acris concussit equos ...'; *Aen.* 12.337–40 'equos alacer media inter proelia Turnus / fumantis sudore quatit, miserabile caesis / hostibus insultans: spargit rapida ungula rores / sanguineos mixtaque cruor calcatur harena'. In a way, the horse is the 'vehicle', so these passages may rightly figure in column 2 in our table. On the other hand, it is clearly not the rider's primary goal to 'shake' his horse (just as the rowers do not primarily labour to hit their breasts nor to make their boat tremble). The rider's true aim is to set the horse in motion; 'shaking' the horse is a side effect of fast riding. And if so, our texts might bette come under column 4. But no clear-cut decision is asked for. The horse's rocking is brought about by the fast movement; there cannot be one without the other. The poet, typically, has given preference to the expression which carries the stronger visual impact. The unusual and presumably newly coined verb-object phrase makes us realize that horse-riding is all shaking and tossing: the reins, the bridle, the horse, all are moved simultaneously and rhythmically, the horseman no less, and it is in the same rhythm that the soil is beaten, covered, in *Aen.* 12.337ff., with enemies slain in the battle. The details are gruesome, and they are forced upon us in full visual strength. This may be seen with 'insultans': the verb is frequently used in the extenuated metaphorical sense of 'taunting' — here, inescapably, the grim literal meaning comes to mind first.

   To sum up: 'shifting' from a familiar to a less common syntactical object, without, of course, changing the general sense, is an effective

---

[16] It is not by horses but by his ships that Caesar has 'shattered' the hostile coastline of Epirus in 48 BC (Luc. 5.489 'percussi medias alieni iuris harenas', a passage strongly reminiscent of Virg. *Aen.* 10.295 'inimicam findite rostris / ... terram', see n. 14). Heyne points to a rather wild variation in Claud. 15.491: 'quassatis cupio tellurem figere rostris', the land is to be 'speared', as it were, by the shattering 'rostra'. In Stat. *Theb.* 5.409f. the sea and towns are shattered by turns: 'quatiunt inpulsibus illi / nunc freta nunc muros'. The general idea is hostility and violence, throughout; see below p. 283 for the manifold connotational links between the verbs we are dealing with ('pellere', 'premere', 'quatere' etc.).

stylistic device. Like a fresh metaphor, it makes us see things anew; so it may contribute a notable degree of precision and impact to a poetical text. It is a special case of what we are now accustomed to call 'effect of alienation'.

IV

But that is not yet the whole story. There is some sort of paradox in the technique we are discussing. The effects just mentioned, i.e. precision and pictorial vividness, cannot be brought about by the verbs. 'Pellere', 'premere', 'quatere' etc. are all remarkably poor in semantic content. Necessarily so: verbs more specific and graphic govern, as a rule, a limited range of objects, and vice versa: if a verb admits of a great number of objects, it is of necessity colourless and of a general character. This is clearly an inconvenience, but Virgil has turned it into an advantage — and this brings us to another feature of his art. He makes the more general and colourless verbs serve a specific poetic purpose. Being applicable to a variety of fields, they may function as a sort of common denominator and thus express a general idea. First, a short example (Virgil, *Aen.* 8.3): '[Turnus] ut ... acris concussit equos utque impulit arma ...'. Fordyce (1977: ad loc.) paraphrases: 'threw his mettlesome horses into violent motion', and takes 'impulit arma' to mean 'struck his shield with his spear'. This is probably correct, but none the less the wording is peculiar. If just fragments of the line had been preserved, the two verbs plus the two objects, and we were free to assign them, it is a safe bet that many would give the horses to 'impellere' and the weapons to 'concutere'.[17] True, it is not an outright syntactical exchange as in *Aeneid* 6.847f.: 'excudent alii spirantia mollius aera / ... vivos ducent de marmore vultus ...'. This is a notorious case: 'excudere' fits the marble, 'ducere' only and exclusively the bronze.[18] Here, 'concutere equos' may be explained as a 'shifted object'. It has been noted that 'concutere equos' gives a lively impression of horse-riding when seen within the range of 'quatere habenas, iubam, terram' etc.; there are also some vague parallels for 'impellere

---

[17] See e.g. Silius 2.71 'cornipedem impellere', 7.697 'equum impellere'; Ov. *Met.* 1.143 (War personified) 'crepitantia concutit arma', 7.130 'concutit arma', 12.468 'arma ... concussit'. Virg. has 'quatere/quassare hastam' etc., but the meaning is different: to 'brandish' a spear, an axe, a firebrand or the like *Aen.* 9.521f., 10.762, 11.656, 11.767, 12.442.

[18] See Bömer (1952, 1965, 1967); a more general discussion of the phenomenon may be found in Görler (1985: 276); to the examples quoted there add Lucr. 2.1161f. 'conterimus ... boves et viris agricolarum,/ conficimus ferrum ...'.

arma'.[19] But it is still true that Virgil's first readers will have been puzzled just as we are.

Virgil must have been aware of this, and it may be taken for granted that he has not unreasonably preferred the verb-object relations as they stand. In fact he did not twist his language:[20] Both verbs are general in semantic content; so they can serve as a link. What Virgil, exchanging the objects, wants us to see is the common denominator which may be paraphrased as 'to set in violent and threatening motion'.

The phenomenon is widespread. It may have been noticed that the three verbs from which we started are not limited to the specific activities indicated in the above chart (p. 278); on the contrary, they are next to interchangeable: Turnus 'impels' horses, not oars or a boat, boats are 'shaken' no less than horses and the battlefields stamped on, and there is no need to prove that many things can be 'pressed' other than the plough and its handle. Indeed, there is a common denominator for 'impellere', 'quatere' and 'premere'. It is physical force and violence.

A highly telling example of what effects may be brought about by general verbs co-operating and interplaying is the speech of Numanus Regulus, Turnus' brother-in-law, praising the Old Latins' toughness and roughness (*Aen.* 9.603–20):

> durum a stirpe genus, natos ad flumina primum
> deferimus saevoque gelu duramus et undis;
> 605   venatu invigilant pueri silvasque fatigant,
> flectere ludus equos et spicula tendere cornu.
> At patiens operum parvoque adsueta iuventus
> aut rastris terram domat aut quatit oppida bello.
> omne aevum ferro teritur, versaque iuvencum
> 610   terga fatigamus hasta, nec tarda senectus
> debilitat viris animi mutatque vigorem:
> canitiem galea premimus, semperque recentis
> comportare iuvat praedas et vivere rapto.
> . . .

---

[19] *Aen.* 8.528f. 'arma . . . vident pulsa tonare'. Luc. 7.16 'quaecumque fugax Sertorius impulit arma', may be modelled after *Aen.* 8.3 (*TLL* s.v. *impello* col. 537.84), and seems of more abstract character. Virg. *Aen.* 12.856 'nervo impulsa . . . sagitta', Ov. *Met.* 11.325 'nervo sagittam (impulit)', and Silius 1.318 'impulsa levi torquetur lancea nodo' are different: to 'launch' an arrow or a spear. Claud. *Rapt. Pros.* 1.210 'impellere ensem' seems fairly unique.
[20] Generally speaking, a poet is bound to comply with the rules of his language; to use de Saussure's well-known opposition, whatever he says ('parole') must conform to the linguistic system ('langue') employed. But there are degrees. An author may, deliberately, prefer a very rare or obsolete way of expression; he may also actualize what had been just a potentiality, so far, latent in the 'langue' and unnoticed, and in doing so, he (and his eventual followers) may gradually contribute to minor changes within the 'langue'.

620   . . . sinite arma viris et cedite ferro.'[21]

The leitmotif of vv. 603–13 is hardness; 'iron', taken up most impress-
ively at the very end of Numanus' speech,[22] stands out as an obvious
symbol. There can be no doubt that allusion is made to the Age of Iron
in contrast to the Golden Age of the past. Agriculture and war, the two
basic activities Numanus boasts about are peculiar features of 'Jupiter's
Age' and had not been practised before mankind had been made worse
by iron: Virgil, *Georg.* 1.125 'ante Iovem nulli subigebant arva coloni';
Ovid, *Met.* 1.141–4 'iamque nocens ferrum . . . / prodierat; prodit bellum . . .
vivitur ex rapto' (compare *Aen.* 9.613). But it would be rash to gather
from the speaker's hateful tone and from his exaggerations that Virgil
himself disapproves unequivocally of the way of living praised by Numanus
(see *Aen.* 7.749 on Ufens). From *Georg.* 1.125–46 (and other passages) it
emerges that he, in fact, gives a dignity of its own to the laborious life in
the Age of Iron; agriculture, navigation, and warfare are not just original
sins as they appear in Ovid, *Met.* 1.121–44. None the less, what the human
race has been compelled to invent and to do under Jupiter's reign relates,
largely, to violence and force. Typically, in Numanus' list, warfare and
agriculture are put closely together and indeed interwoven (609–11); note
that the (iron!) 'hasta' serves both purposes.[23]

Again, the leading idea, hardness and violence, is conveyed by verbs
of general and interchangeable character, and indeed some of them seem
to have been interchanged. Strictly speaking, it is not the arrows that are
'bent' but the bow ('tendere', v. 606); 'flectere' fits the bow ('cornu', v.
606) no less than the horses (v. 606); 'domare terram' is a bold metaphor.
Again, if the rest had been lost and we had but a list of verbs and nouns

[21] For details see the comprehensive interpretations of Schweizer (1967: 14–22), Horsfall
(1971), and Dingel (1997: ad loc.).

[22] Most commentators and translators take 'cedite ferro' to mean 'renounce iron' (Hardie
1994: ad loc.), 'ferro' being ablative of separation. This is perfectly possible, but slightly
pleonastic after 'sinite arma viris'; so 'yield to iron' should at least be considered (R. A.
Schröder in his translation of 1952 ' . . . weichet dem Eisen'; see Dingel (1997: ad loc.)).

[23] See also Thomas (1988) on *Georg.* 1.160 and 174. Elsewhere ploughing is equated to
'wounding the earth' by 'cutting in furrows' (e.g. *Ecl.* 4.31–3 'priscae vestigia fraudis . . . quae
iubeant . . . telluri infindere sulcos'). Numanus does not (nor could he) boast of seafaring,
the third original sin; but it is frequently described by Virg. as 'furrowing the sea' (e.g. *Aen.*
5.142 'infindunt sulcos', 158 'longa sulcant vada salsa carina', ~ 10.197; on *Aen.* 10.295f. see
n. 18) and thus closely approached ploughing and its connotations. *Georg.* 1.50–2 (about
ploughing) is almost ambiguous: 'ac prius ignotum ferro quam scindimus aequor [here: the
soil], / ventos [!] et varium caeli praediscere morem / cura sit.' Navigation in general is
sometimes thought of as 'violating' and 'inverting' nature: *Georg.* 1.136 'tunc [in the Iron
Age] alnos primum fluvii sensere cavatas', 2.503 'sollicitant alii remis freta caeca' (on *Georg.*
1.254 'remis impellere marmor' see n. 8); see further Hor. *Odes* 1.3.21–4; Tib. 1.3.37f.; Ov.
Met. 1.132–4.

we might easily have given the horses to 'domare'. We have just noticed
that 'quatere' is typically said of horses and horse-riding. Now it is towns
that are 'shaken' ('quatere', remember: boats are rocked by the rough sea,
oars are shaken, the Argonauts 'shatter by their strokes' now the sea, now
city-walls).[24] 'Fatigare' governs two very different objects: 605 'silvas', 609f.
'iuvencum terga', and so functions as a link, the idea being: 'we never get
tired, neither by hunting in the woods nor by ploughing — it is "the others"
who get tired by our activity'.[25] 'Premere', typically used of ploughing, in
Numanus' speech (v. 612) governs 'canitiem'.

Here it becomes imperative to ask a question put off so far. Are we
to read 'canitiem galea premimus' as a literal description, i.e. are we to
imagine a helmet pressed upon a white-haired head, or are we to understand metaphorically: 'Old age cannot harm us, as we simply go on
fighting'? Similarly in v. 609 'omne aevum ferro teritur': does Virgil want
us to understand 'Latins of all ages are in steady physical contact with
iron', 'rub with iron', or is the meaning rather: 'All life is passed [a well
attested sense of "terere"] under hard conditions'?[26] It has also been
suggested that 'oppida quatere bello' (v. 608) is just a metaphor, 'to worry,
to disquiet the enemies' towns'; similarily Aen. 10.78 'arva aliena iugo
premere', adduced above p. 277 as an example for a 'shift' from 'tool' to
'field of action', has been read as 'suggesting not so much the literal yoke
of ploughing as the metaphorical one of oppression'.[27]

True, in no case can a metaphorical meaning be ruled out, nor should
it be. If our common-denominator hypothesis is correct, there is indeed a
metaphorical and general meaning in the passages discussed. And it can
hardly be denied that symbolic sections of the kind may add up to what
is sometimes called the poet's message. But it would be silly to conclude
that the verses just cited should be read as abstract metaphors only; even
more than that, it would be disastrous for our understanding of Virgil. It
is a gross error to make this an either/or decision — it is possible,
indeed essential to appreciate both, the full vivid graphic force of a
description and the more abstract idea behind it. If there is any doubt,
the literal sense and the live description should be seen first and in all
details.

---

[24] Georg. 3.132 (the horse-breeders) 'saepe etiam cursu quatiunt' (the horses); Aen. 9.91
'cursu quassatae [naves]'; Val. Flac. 1.340 'concusso . . . remo'; Stat. Theb. 5.409f. (the
Argonauts) 'quatiunt impulsibus illi / nunc freta nunc muros'.

[25] Aen. 8.94 'olli remigio noctemque diemque fatigant' is even bolder; cf. Aen. 7.582 'Martem
fatigant' and Fordyce (1977: ad loc.).

[26] Looking at Georg. 4.114 'ipse labore manum duro terat' it is fairly clear that 'ferro teritur'
is physical rubbing as well.

[27] Harrison (1991: ad loc.); in the reprint (1997) the literal meaning is given equal weight.

'Shifting objects' as hinted at may help to explain how and why the same wording can convey both a colourful description and a symbolic sense.

Let us finally ask whether we have really dealt with a specific feature of poetical art, rather than with a general syntactical scheme common to both poetry and prose. In this regard, first of all, the relative figures of the lexical material presented in sections I and II speak for themselves. Prose authors have been taken into account as well as poets, but the number of examples from prose has turned out to be almost negligible; rowing, ploughing, horse-riding etc. are not normally expressed in prose by a general verb governing a specific object. This should not come as a surprise. To mention rowing by calling it 'moving the oars' or 'moving a ship by oars' and to call ploughing 'pressing the plough' is not the most obvious and easiest way to do so; there are specific verbs which serve the purpose better: 'remigare', 'arare', 'equitare'. Consequently, whenever a verb-object phrase of the type we are looking at occurs in prose readers tend to be struck as if by something unfamiliar, and attention is drawn to the mechanism and to the details of the procedure, e.g. in Caesar, *B. G.* 3.14.6 'navigio remis incitato' (a skilful artifice in a naval battle) and in Vitruvius 10.3.6 (see above p. 271). This, as is manifest from the above lists, does not happen very often. Prose tends to be plain and straightforward.

Nearly all our examples have been found in poetry, more precisely in epic, i.e. in narrative texts. The latter restriction will be largely due to the semantic fields of the activities and verbs considered, and the picture may change with further research. That it is poetical texts is not due to chance. Far be it from us to attempt a definition of what are 'the' specific features of poetry. But it can hardly be disputed that graphic vividness, subtle focusing, changing perspectives from significant details to all-embracing tableaus are to be included, as well as a certain ambiguity and messages conveyed indirectly and by symbols. And if so, it should be clear from the above sections III and IV that the 'shifts' we have pointed to are very much in their right place in poetical texts.[28]

---

[28] I have greatly profited from the discussion after the talk and from subsequent criticism by the editors and anonymous referees; to Nicholas Horsfall and to the editors I am also indebted for emending my English in this chapter.

STYLISTIC AND GENERIC VARIATION

Proceedings of the British Academy, **93**, 289–310

The Language of Early Roman Satire: Its Function and Characteristics

HUBERT PETERSMANN

Albrecht Dihle septuagenario quinto votis optimis

Summary. The topic of this paper is the satirical language of Ennius and Lucilius. After a brief account of the characteristic qualities of *satura*, there is an analysis of the linguistic variety adopted by Ennius in the scanty remains of his satirical work. He appears to have avoided the use of Greek and of obscenity, and parodied the high style of the *Annales*. His linguistic register displays colloquial and elevated style and even a medley of these expressions within textual units. Ennius wrote for the educated social class and their requirements were kept in mind. He occasionally used language to mock ridiculous traits of human behaviour in general, but not for personal invective. Lucilius on the other hand, whilst continuing the strong parodistic use of language, is more open to the use of Greek, but he always has some special point to make; it is not there for show or because he cannot find a Latin equivalent. In general he was conservative in his linguistic views. It was one of his main literary intentions to reproduce colloquial speech, subordinating the various levels of language to his poetic intentions in his *Saturae*, because he experienced language as a social phenomenon. Lucilius is one of the greatest artists of the Latin language.

BEFORE STARTING WITH the topic of my chapter some preliminary remarks might be necessary in order to avoid any misunderstandings: whenever in the following article we speak of 'Satire' — or use the Latin expression *satura* — we do not mean the ancient stage performances which were given this title,[1] but the literary genre which Quintilian, *Inst.* 10.1.93 proudly declares to be a Roman invention: *satura quidem tota nostra est.*

The word *satura* originally denoted a play or a poem whose characteristics seem to have been not only a mélange of metre, rhythm, structure and contents, but also a variety of language and style. Lucilius, however, was the first Roman poet to introduce further typical elements into this kind of poetry, which henceforth were regarded as its main characteristics, namely, mockery and invective, both personal and general, concerning various topics, to an extent which had been unusual in Latin literature up to his time. Thus, from Lucilius onwards, the word *satura* received its new meaning (as we understand it today), and it is for this reason that Lucilius was regarded by the ancient literary critics as the inventor of satirical poetry — not, however, of the *satura* as a sort of medley literature on the whole, for which Diomedes *GLK* I 485 (drawing amongst others on Varro) refers to Pacuvius and Ennius. But was Ennius really the *auctor* of this kind of literature, as has been supposed? I am rather sceptical about it.

Festus p. 306.25 L quotes a verse from Naevius' poetry, which he calls *satura* (frg. 61 *FPL* = p. 3 C): *quianam Saturnium populum pepulisti.* The Saturnian metre makes it probable that this verse was not part of a dramatic play. Consequently, *satura* seems to denote here the same literary genre which was cultivated by Ennius. We do not have the slightest idea of the context of this Naevian verse. It is only evident that it is a Saturnian line showing alliteration, a common feature of archaic Roman poetry. The linguistic level of this line seems to be solemn. *quianam* in the sense of *cur* obviously belonged to epic style: it occurs elsewhere in Enn. *Ann.* frg. 127 V[2] (= 121 Sk = 525 W) and 259 V[2] (= 246 Sk = 228 W), in Virg. *Aen.* 5.13, 10.6 and perhaps in Stat. *Ach.* 1.498 also. In Naevius' *Satura* it is probably a god or a king who was asked this question. There is, however, no indication that Naevius himself called this kind of literature *satura.* The same holds true for *Satura* or *Saturae* as a title of Ennius' medley poetry.

In investigating the fragments of the Ennian *Saturae,* we do not detect a satiric tendency in the Lucilian manner, but some of his lines suggest that Ennius parodied the metre and language of his own elevated poetry (Jocelyn 1972: 1026). In any case, he proves a master in handling the appropriate metre, style and language. It is obvious that he was acquainted with Greek literature and scholarship. According to the demands of Aristotle, *Rhet.* 3.7.1ff. (= 1408.10ff.), he knew exactly when to make use of

[1] Cf. Livy's report (7.2.7) on the origin of Roman dramatic plays called *saturae*; *Satura* is also the title of a *fabula togata* of Atta (frg. 12 R[3]) and one of Pomponius' Atellanae (frg. 163–6 R[3]), which obviously had an analogon in Epicharmus' Ὀρύα or Ὀροία 'The Sausage' (frg. 108 *CGF* = 122 *FCG*).

specific linguistic varieties. He was fully aware that the linguistic level of an utterance had to be in accordance with the speaker and the person addressed as well as with the subject matter and the literary intention he had in mind. It is quite natural that in antiquity the style and language of literature always depended on the author's aim, whether he merely wanted to describe or to instruct, to parody, to amuse or to do all these simultaneously. Therefore, tragedy and epic are generally solemn in style, whereas the *satura* as a kind of literary medley could draw on many more registers of Latin speech, as Jocelyn (1977: 136f.) has rightly observed in his subtle analysis of Ennius' *Sat.* frg. 6–8 V^2 (= 6–8 W = 11–12 C): 'Any personage, human or divine, might range in his discourse up to the highest poeticism or down to the lowest contemporary vulgarism. It would be possible to plot without great difficulty the general stylistic differences between the utterances of personages of different status in an extant *satura* but quite another matter to identify the status of the speaker of a fragment lacking a secure context.'

Nevertheless, even the few fragments of Ennian *Saturae* give us the impression that the author displayed a wide range of different stylistic levels and linguistic varieties depending on the speaker's situation, mood, social rank and background as well as on his geographical origin. But what holds good for Ennius' *Saturae* is also a characteristic of some other minor poems of this author. It has been well observed by Gratwick (1982: 159) that the tone and contents on the whole are so similar to those of the *Saturae* that some of them transmitted under individual titles could be regarded as parts of them. This is especially true of the two minor works entitled *Scipio* and *Euhemeros*.

Since in this respect we cannot be sure, I shall not concentrate on this question. Furthermore, I shall exclude from my discussion the Aesopic fable of 'The Crested Lark and its Chicks', *Sat.* frg. 21–58 V^2 (= pp. 388f. W = 17 C), not following Courtney ((1993: 13ff.) on frg. 17 with text, annotations and further recent literature on the whole passage), since the transmitted text might be a paraphrase of Gellius 2.29.3ff. (Coffey 1989: 28), except for the proverbial end, which has retained its original metrical form composed in *uersus quadrati* (Scholz (1986b: 48f.)).

This is also the metre of another fable written by Ennius: the story of 'The Piper and the Fish', where in frg. 65 V^2 (= 20 W = 21 C) the expression *quondam* indicates the beginning of the tale: *subulo quondam marinas propter astabat plagas*. The tone of this line is obviously colloquial. Varro, *L.L.* 7.35 and Festus p. 402.2ff. L, who quote this Ennian verse because of *subulo*, give evidence that the word is of Etruscan provenance. The question here is: was *subulo* in Ennius' times still regarded as a foreign

word or had it already been integrated into Latin? As this is the only
passage in Latin in which the word *subulo* 'flautist' occurs, and since
Ennius could just as well have used the more common *tibicen*, it seems
probable that the poet deliberately introduced this foreign word here in
order to evoke a scene in Etruria or an Etruscan person now living amongst
Romans. With the exception of Greek words and the Praenestinian *tongent*
in a fragment of the *Sota* (= *var.* 28 V² = 3 C = 4 W), this is the only
expression from a different language which occurs in the *Saturae* and the
other minor poems of Ennius.[2]

It is perhaps remarkable that in this kind of Ennian literature even the
use of Greek is very restricted. This, however, does not happen by chance:
it reflects the general linguistic trend of a certain kind of educated member
of the upper class of Roman society in the second century BC who, to a
high degree, tried to avoid Greek in their speech. This was the attitude of
the Scipiones, to whom Terence was attached, and it was praised by the
adherents of *sermo purus* in subsequent periods as well: cf. Cic. *Off.* 1.111
*sermone eo debemus uti qui innatus est nobis, ne ut quidam Graeca uerba
inculcantes iure optimo rideamur* and *Tusc.* 1.15 *scis enim me Graece loqui
in Latino sermone non plus solere quam in Graeco Latine.*

Now we may ask, which were considered the characteristics of good
Latin? The *Auctor ad Herennium* 4.17 gives the following answer: *Latinitas
est quae sermonem purum conseruat ab omni uitio remotum*, and Diomedes
GLK I 439.15f., quoting Varro's definition, says: *Latinitas est incorrupte
loquendi obseruatio secundum Romanam linguam*, or, in the words of
Quintilian, *Inst.* 6.3.107, it is the urbane language of Rome, *in qua nihil
absonum, nihil agreste, nihil inconditum, nihil peregrinum neque sensu
neque uerbis neque ore gestuue possit deprendi, ut non tam sit in singulis
dictis quam in toto colore dicendi, qualis apud Graecos* ἀττικισμὸς *ille
reddens Athenarum proprium saporem.*

In examining the linguistic level of the fragments of Ennius' *Saturae*,
Scipio and *Euhemerus*, we can see that in the former there is no Greek at
all, except for technical terms, and in *Euhemerus* the poet, whenever he
introduces a god with his Greek name, also gives the Latin equivalent: cf.
frg. 78 V² (= 31f. W) *Pluto Latine est Dis pater, alii Orcum uocant*, and frg.
139 V² (= 131–3 W) *inque sepulcro eius est inscriptum antiquis litteris
Graecis ZAN KRONOY, id est Latine Iuppiter Saturni.*

In *Sat.* frg. 3f., 10f. and 66 V² (= 3f., 10f. and 24 W = 9, 13 and 22 C),
owing to the subject matter or to the parodic intention, the style is very
elevated. In frg. 3f. V² (= 3f. W = 9 C) someone contemplating the sky

---

[2] On the etymology of *subulo* and *tongent* see Walde–Hofmann (1930–56: 620f. and 690) and
Ernout–Meillet (1959: 622 and 695).

says: *contemplor | inde loci liquidas pilatasque aetheris oras*. The words *inde loci* are interesting. According to Hofmann–Szantyr (1965: 53) the partitive *loci* after local or temporal adverbs usually belongs to colloquial speech: it is quite often used by Plautus and Terence. For later times Hofmann–Szantyr mainly refer to Cicero's letters, Sallust and Vitruvius. The occurrence of this kind of structure in Enn. *Ann.* 22 V² (= 19 Sk = 21 W) *constitit inde loci propter sos dia dearum*, *Ann.* 530 V² (= 544 Sk = 488 W) *inde loci lituus sonitus effudit acutos*, Lucretius (5.437, 741,791), Cic. *Arat.* 327 and *interea loci* in Pacuv. frg. 76 R³ (= 82 W) clearly demonstrates, however, that this kind of partitive was not primarily colloquial, but an archaic construction belonging to solemn style, and as such, since popular language is often conservative, it had survived into later times. Other examples of elevated style can be found in Enn. *Sat.* frg. 10f. V² (= 10f. W = 13 C), where someone says: *testes sunt | Lati campi quos gerit Africa terra politos*. I cannot agree with Scholz's opinion (1986b: 47) that these lines probably do not refer to a speech of P. Cornelius Scipio Africanus Maior delivered against the *tribunus pl.* M. Naevius in 187 BC. On the contrary, the words *Africa terra* might indicate that this assumption is not too far fetched: they seem to be a reference to Scipio's *terra Africa* (cf. *ORF* frg. 3, pp. 8–9), which was the regular word order of this phrase, and which Ennius might have changed intentionally to suit an elevated poetic style. Apart from our passage, the expression *Africa terra* occurs also in Enn. *Ann.* frg. 310 V² (= 309 Sk with commentary p. 487) and Virg. *Aen.* 4.37, where it also seems to allude to Scipio Africanus (cf. *TLL* I. 1256.54; in prose cf. *Bell. Afr.* 26.3). The difference between *Africa terra* and *terra Africa* is not a semantic but a grammatical one. In its poetic form *Africa* is an adjective, whereas in the regular word order — cf. *terra Africa* (*ORF* frg. 4.3.9), *terra Italia* (Varro, *R.R.* 1.9.1, Liv. 25.7.4 and 30.32.6), *terra Gallia* (Caes. *Gal.* 1.30.3) or *terra Etruria* (Liv. 29.5.6)³ — *Africa* is a postponed noun. In both forms, however, the poetic and the prosaic, the word *Africa* is not applied to the Roman province Africa (to which the adjective *Africanus* refers⁴), but is used to denote Africa in its function as a country, as in the above quoted passage of Ennius' *Satires*. There the poet also mentions Africa's *Lati* or *Magni campi* — Polybius 14.8.2 calls them Μεγάλα πεδία, where according to Livy 30.8.3 the Romans fought the Carthaginians in 203 BC. The poet speaks of these fields as *politi*, which was obviously an agricultural term: cf. Non. 66.18 (quoting besides these Ennian lines also Enn. *Ann.* 319 V² = 300 Sk (*rastros dente*

---

³ Cf. more examples also from Old Latin in Kühner–Stegmann (1955: II 568).
⁴ Therefore, *Africanus* is used as an agnomen for the two Scipiones, and from Cicero's epoch onwards this adjective occurs also in connection with *bellum, legiones* etc. (cf. *OLD* s.v.).

†*fabres capsit causa poliendi* | *agri*)) on the word *politiones*: *agrorum cultus diligentes, ut polita omnia dicimus exculta et ad nitorem deducta. gerere* in the sense of 'to produce', 'to have', can also be found in epic poetry of later times: cf. Ov. *Met.* 2.15 (in the description of a picture) *terra uiros urbesque gerit siluasque ferasque* | *fluminaque et nymphas* (cf. *OLD* s.v. *gero* 2a). The question in this context is: does Ennius parody his own *Annales* here too? Jocelyn (1977: 131ff.) thinks that he did so in *Sat.* frg. 3f. V² (= 3f. W = 9 C), quoted above. The epic traits of our fragment seem to point towards a similar conclusion.

A parody of an epic work could also be assumed in *Sat.* frg. 66 V² (= 24 W = 22 C): *propter stagna ubi lanigerum genus piscibus pascit.* Here someone is feeding sheep, called *lanigerum genus.* That reminds us of the elevated expressions in the *Annales* for birds, *genus pennis condecoratum* frg. 10 V² (= 8 Sk = 10 W) and *genus altiuolantum* frg. 81. V² (= 76 Sk = 85 W). But what does *piscibus* mean in this context? There seems to be a pun on the sense of *pisces*, with which *pascit* alliterates. Perhaps Ennius, in a jocular way, uses the word *piscis* here in the same sense as *raniculus*, which, as a translation of the Greek botanical term βατράχιον, could denote a kind of wild flower, i.e. the buttercup (cf. Plin. *N. H.* 25.175). The word *stagna* seems to support this interpretation, which Warmington in his commentary on this line proposed. According to Courtney, however, this verse could also be taken as part of a description of a θαυμάσιον. In this case it would not be surprising if sheep were to eat animals instead of plants.

There are many more lines of the *Saturae* where Ennius uses puns: cf. e.g. frg. 64 V² (= 21 W = 20 C): *numquam poetor nisi si podager.* The verb *poetor*, which apart from this passage occurs only in late Latin, and there in its active form, was perhaps a witty invention of Ennius himself. (It would be interesting to know whether it was the poet himself to whom these words refer.)

Sat. frg. 6f. V² (= 6f. W = 11 C), however, certainly deals with the poet Ennius himself. A drinking companion appears to address him as one who toasts with flaming verses drawn from his very marrow: *Enni poeta, salue, qui mortalibus* | *uersus propinas flammeos medullitus.* Here we have a mixture of elevated and humble styles, as has been pointed out by Jocelyn (1977: 131ff.): *mortalis* and *flammeus* belong to the former register, while *propinare* and *medullitus*, found also in comedy (e.g. Plaut. *Most.* 243, *Truc.* 439, *As.* 772, *Curc.* 359, *Stich.* 425 etc.), were obviously lower in tone.

Sat. frg. 12f. V² (= 12f. W = 14 C) belongs to the same comic register: *neque <ille> triste quaeritat sinapi* | *neque caepe maestum.* The stylistic level of this passage, where someone is said to try to get mustard and onions, is colloquial: *sinapi* and *caepe* are words found in comedy,[5] where food and meals play an important role. *tristis* in the sense of *amarus* evidently reflects archaic style: Macrobius 6.5.5, who quotes Virg. *Geo.* 1.75 *tristisque lupini* (on which see Mynors (1990: 17)) and our Ennian passage, obviously admired this usage, saying: *tristis pro amaro translatio decens est.* Consequently, *tristis* in the sense of *amarus* was not only felt as an archaic but also as a refined word. It is used by Lucr. 4.634 (*triste et amarum*) as well as by Ov. *Pont.* 3.1.23, and as archaic features are often characteristic of rural life, one must not wonder that the expression occurs also in Virgil's *Georgics* (cf. besides 1.75, 2.126 and 3.448).

As for *maestus* in this fragment, we know that it is usually associated with grief, sorrow, distress and gloom (cf. *OLD* s.v.); here it amusingly refers to the smell of onions, which causes tears. In connection with 'odour' this adjective occurs also once in late antiquity: cf. Drac. *Romul.* 9.11 *non docuit quia maestus odor quia putre cadauer | aera tellurem uentos animasque grauabit* (cf. *TLL* VIII. 49.52ff.). In the Ennian passage *maestus* shows that the poet not only plays with the meanings of words (cf. *tristis* referring to the taste and *maestus* to the smell), but also with their sounds (cf. the reiterated -*ae*- in *quaeritat, caepe, maestum*).

Comic tone is also to be felt in *Sat.* frg. 14–19 V² (= 17–19 W = 15 C) where Ennius introduces a parasite. Here this comic figure is said to devour like a wolf the goods of an angry patron:

> quippe sine cura laetus lautus cum aduenis
> infestis malis expedito bracchio,
> alacer celsus, lupino expectans impetu,
> mox alterius abligurris cum bona,
> quid censes domino[s] esse animi? pro diuum fidem,
> ille tristis est dum cibum seruat, tu ridens uoras.

Here the words *abligurris* and *uoras* exactly suit the mood of a hungry wolf. *abligurrio* is a rare word (*TLL* 1. 106.6ff.); its base-form is *ligurrio*, which in Plaut. *Capt.* 84 is also said of a parasite who compares his life with a hunting dog eagerly consuming what belongs to the hunters. The compound *abligurrire* is used in the same way (cf. Non. 195.24f. L: *ligurrire: degustare, unde abligurrire, multa auide consumere*, *CGL* IV 201.42 and V 531.10, where *abligurrire* is rendered as *deuorare*). Until the imperial period, besides in Ennius, *abligurrio* is only found in Ter. *Eun.* 235 *patria qui abligurriat bona.* Nevertheless, this is evidence enough to suppose that in our passage, too, *abligurrire* is the right verb (the cod. Vat. has *obligurias*, the Ricc. Oxon. *ablinias*, the vetus codex of Pithou *ablingas*). Vahlen and

---

[5] For *caepe* see Naev. com. 18 R³, for *sinapi* Plaut. *Ps.* 817 and *Truc.* 315.

Warmington have adopted the reading of the cod. Leid. *mox cum alterius abligurias bona*. Courtney, however, for metrical reasons has convincingly altered the text to *mox alterius abligurris cum bona*. In addition to Courtney's arguments one can state that the spelling of the word with *-rr-* (cf. also *ligurriant* in Plaut. *Capt.* 84) must be right because it imitates the noise the wolf makes when fearing that his quarry might be taken away by somebody else. This word exactly fits the tone of this passage, in which *uoras* as a technical term for 'swallow' (cf. Adams (1995*b*: 608–10)) also suits the context.

Ennius' mastery in depicting the atmosphere of real life by means of language is also obvious in frg. 5 V² (= 5 W = 10 C), where the enormous resistance of people to a decision imposed upon them is not only expressed by five heavy trochaics, but also by the prefixes *re-* and *ob-*: *restitant, obcurrunt, obstant, obstrigillant, obagitant*. (It is remarkable that *obagito* cannot be found elsewhere in Latin literature.)

Surveying the characteristics and function of the language of the scanty fragments of Ennius' *Saturae*, we can see, according to their pragmatic dimension, a large range of varieties. The linguistic register displays: (a) colloquial speech; (b) the elevated style reflecting epic and tragic language; (c) a medley of colloquial and elevated expressions even within textual units.

On the whole, Ennius seems to have written his *Saturae* for the educated social class of contemporary Roman society, mainly represented by the Scipiones. It was their requirements in respect of language and style that Ennius had in mind when composing his *Saturae*. Therefore, Ennius shied away from any obscene words, so far as we can see. (Among his minor works it is only in the *Sota* that an indecent expression occurs. But this might be an exception, since it is the Ennian version of a coarse poem composed by Sotades, an Alexandrian author, after whom a certain kind of verse often dealing with obscene themes was named.) We can say that Ennius occasionally uses language as a means of mocking and parodying ridiculous traits of human behaviour in general, but not, however, for personal invective. (In fact attacks against persons of higher social standing would not have been possible for Ennius, who was not himself a native Roman citizen. In frg. 63 V² (= 22 W = 19 C) he attributes this mild attitude to his gentle nature, saying: *meum non est, ac si me canis memorderit.*)

His successor Lucilius, however, would not merely retaliate, but also attack and criticize in a personal and often very fierce way. He evidently could do so, because he was a Roman citizen,[6] although he was not born in the capital. This new attitude which Lucilius introduced into his medley literature was so unusual as well as stimulating that henceforth *satura* became the term for a *carmen maledicum*, as Varro called it. But this was not the only function of Lucilius' *Saturae*, or rather *Sermones* as he himself seems to have named his invective poetry. Sometimes it serves as a means of recalling remarkable occurences in his life, or to express his own personal opinion on certain events. Many of his satires were spontaneous. Therefore, the style and language of his poetry very often seem to be non-reflective. He also used to write a large amount of verse within a short time. Varro (*apud* Gell. 6.14) considered Lucilius a representative of *gracilitas*: the characteristics of this style are *uenustas* and *subtilitas* (Leo (1913: 230 and 425)). Horace, however, regarded Lucilius' style and language as contrary to what was expected of educated Romans. He was, therefore, one of his most severe critics. In his opinion, his predecessor was obviously too unrestricted and vulgar in language. And he also failed to satisfy that demand for pure and clear Latin which was explicitly expressed by Cicero, *De orat.* 1.144: *pure et Latine loquamur, deinde ut plane et dilucide.* As a result, Horace at *Sat.* 1.4.11 calls Lucilius *lutulentus, garrulus,* and at *Sat.* 1.10.50 *piger scribendi ferre laborem.*

There seems to have been general agreement, however, that Lucilius was not only a witty, but also a learned author. Furthermore, Cicero at *De orat.* 2.25 informs us that Lucilius used to say that what he wrote was intended neither for the *doctissimi* nor for the *indoctissimi*: *C. Lucilius, homo doctus et perurbanus, dicere solebat ea quae scriberet neque se ab indoctissimis neque a doctissimis legi uelle, quod alteri nihil intellegerent, alteri plus fortasse quam ipse.*

It was due to his frankness and wit that Lucilius was highly appreciated by many learned Romans of later times, who preferred him even to Horace, as Quintilian, *Inst.* 10.1.93f. states.

Cicero at *Fin.* 1.7 records that Lucilius himself had said in a jocular way that, as he was afraid of the judgement of the Scipiones, he was writing for the people of the southern provinces. He said this on purpose since he was born in that part of Italy. From this statement we can also deduce that Lucilius did not conform to the demands of the Scipiones concerning the usage of the Latin language. As was mentioned above, the Scipiones and other *literati* of this period insisted that the *sermo purus Latinus* should not contain any Greek. In Horace's opinion, however, Lucilius did not observe this requirement at all. Therefore, Horace at *Sat.*

---

[6] This is rightly deduced from Vell. 2.9.4, according to whom Lucilius served as *eques* in the army of his friend Scipio Aemilianus: cf. Hanslik (1969: 257).

1.10.20ff. ridicules the linguistic mixture in Lucilius' *Satires* and those people who admired this technique. Yet Horace's criticism is evidently prejudiced. Lucilius in general did *not* assent to an indiscriminate use of Greek words in Latin. He looked disapprovingly on this custom when there was no need to use Greek words. This was obviously the case when good Latin expressions were unnecessarily replaced with Greek equivalents, which became more and more the vogue. In frg. 15 M (= 15f. W) Lucilius ridicules this custom perhaps by making somebody use the Greek word σεμνῶς in a passage where this same person seems to criticize exactly this habit: *porro* clinopodas lychnos*que, ut diximus* σεμνῶς| *ante*[7] pedes lecti *atque* lucernas. Possibly, Lucilius in this passage mocks the use of *clinopodae* and *lychni* in Ennius' *Annales*.[8]

Another example where Lucilius ridicules not only the unnecessary but in some way also the inappropriate use of the Greek language is frg. 88–94 M (= 87–93 W). In this passage the Roman praetor Scaevola reveals his scorn for the magistrate Albucius, whose Graecomania he had publicly mocked in Athens by addressing him officially in Greek. This seems to be even more ridiculous, since Latin until late aniquity was considered the official language of the Roman Empire, even in its eastern parts,[9] although it was never rigorously practised,[10] and in everyday life often only played a marginal role.

---

[7] All the manuscripts of Macr. *Saturn.* 6.4.18 quoting these words transmit *ante*. Since the meaning of *ante* is very close to that of the Greek ἀντί, there is no need to alter this form as Warmington following Mueller did.

[8] *clinopous* does not occur elsewhere in Latin literature; for *lychnus* cf. Enn. *Ann.* frg. 323 V² (= 311 Sk); for *lucerna* in Lucilius, cf. frg. 146 M (= 148 W) and frg. 681 M (= 638 W).

[9] Cf. Val. Max. 2.2.2 *magistratus uero prisci quantopere suam populique Romani maiestatem retinentes se gesserint hinc cognosci potest, quod inter cetera obtinendae grauitatis indicia illud quoque magna cum perseuerantia custodiebant, ne Graecis umquam nisi Latine responsa darent. quin etiam ipsos linguae uolubilitate, qua plurimum ualent, excussa per interpretem loqui cogebant non in urbe tantum nostra, sed etiam in Graecia et Asia, quo scilicet Latinae uocis honos per omnes gentes uenerabilior diffunderetur,* Liv. 45.29.3 *Paulus Latine quae senatui quae sibi ex consilii sententia uisa essent pronuntiauit. ea Cn. Octauius praetor — nam et ipse aderat — interpretata sermone Graeco referebat,* Gai. *Inst.* 2.281 *legata Graece scripta non ualent,* Iustin. *Dig.* 42.1.48 *decreta a praetoribus Latine interponi debent.* Latin was also the language of the Roman army: cf. Suet. *Tib.* 71 *sermone Graeco, quamquam alias promptus et facilis, non tamen usquequaque usus est: abstinuitque maxime in senatu . . . militem quoque, Graece testimonium interrogatum, nisi Latine respondere uetuit,* and the Latin commands in Ps.-Maur. *Strategicon* on which see Reichenkron (1961: 18ff.), Lot (1946: 203ff.), Dagron (1969: 23ff.) and Petersmann (1992: 223ff.); one must not forget in this context also the Latin acclamations as testimonies of the official function of the Latin language in Byzantium: see Petersmann (1992: 228ff.) on Constant. VII Porphyrogenn. *De caerimon. aulae Byz.* 1.83f. [74f.], II 169ff. ed. Vogt.

[10] Cf. Kaimio (1979: 94ff.); concerning Egypt cf. especially Bagnall (1993: 231f.).

In other respects, however, Lucilius does not refrain from mixing up Greek with Latin. This was especially the case in letters, since they were regarded as a form of written conversation (cf. Dem. *Eloc.* 225f. and Sen. *Ep.* 75.1). Therefore their language and style on the whole were expected to be colloquial, as Cicero *Fam.* 9.21.1, after inserting in his Latin text a Greek expression (*qua re nihil tibi opus est illud a Trabea, sed potius ἀπότευγμα meum*), says: *uerum tamen quid tibi ego uideor in epistulis? nonne plebeio sermone agere tecum? . . . epistulas cotidianis uerbis texere solemus.*[11]

This intermixing of Latin with Greek had a long tradition from Plautine comedy onwards. Lucilius makes use of this technique[12] in frg. 181–8 M (= 186–93 W):

> ut perisse uelis, quem uisere nolueris cum
> debueris. Hoc 'nolueris' et 'debueris' te
> si minus delectat, quod atechnon et Isocration
> lerodesque simul totum ac symmiraciodes:
> non operam perdo, si tu hic.

This is Leo's (1906: 845f. = 1960: 230f.) convincing emendation of the text,[13] which I have adopted with the exception of *Isocration* (= Housman (1907: 150 = 1972: 687), while Leo (1906: 845f. = 1960: 230f.) writes *Isocratium hoc*; others, following the MSS more closely, prefer *Eissocratium hoc* (Ch. I p. 150, frg. 1) or *Eisocration* (W), and Marshall (1968: II 550) in his Oxford edition of Gellius (18.8.2) writes *Eisocratium est*. The fragment is part of a letter which Gell. 18.8.2 quotes because of the ridiculous use of the homeoteleuta *nolueris* and *debueris*. It is addressed to a friend whom he reproaches for not having visited him when he was ill. In a witty way Lucilius not only composed this letter in the *uersus heroicus* but also introduced into it rhetorical sound effects which Isocrates had already inappropriately used in his correspondence.[14] The poet is aware that this

---

[11] This statement corresponds with the general rules of epistolography theories: cf. also Dem. *Eloc.* 223ff. and Peter (1901: 21ff.).

[12] On Graecisms of diction in Lucilius cf. Mariotti (1960: 50ff.); in general cf. Leumann (1977: 258, § 249 and 453ff., § 365) and Hofmann–Szantyr (1965: 37f.* and 80*).

[13] M. reads v. 2f. in this fragment: *si minus delectat (quod atechnon) et Eissocratium hoc / lerodesque simul totum ac si miraciodes,* W. *si minus delectat, quod atechnon et Eisocration / lerodesque simul totum ac sit meiraciodes,* and Ch. (with Marshall (1968: II 550) *si minus delectat quod ἄτεχνον et Eissocratium hoc / ληρῶδεςque simul totum ac συμμειρακιῶδες.* For a general interpretation of the whole fragment cf. also Fiske (1920: 432f.), Puelma Piwonka (1949: 21–4), and Housman (1907: 149–51).

[14] Cf. Cic. *De orat.* 3.141 . . . *ipse* (= sc. Isocrates) *suas disputationes a causis forensibus et ciuilibus ad inanem sermonis elegantiam transtulisset . . .* For more on Isocrates' epistolary

is against the rules of art (*atechnon*),[15] all rubbish (*lerodes*) and altogether childish (*symmiraciodes*),[16] but says that he will not care about that and will write as Isocrates did, although his friend belongs to the opponents of this kind of style.

Here Lucilius not only mocks the homeoteleuta but also the usage of Greek words. Since they have retained their original inflection they can be interpreted as ridiculous manifestations of 'code switching' for which there is a lot of evidence in Lucilius' *Satires* (Marx (1904: I 156–8)). Cf. e.g. frg. 24f. M (= 28–9 W): *ut contendere possem | Thestiados Ledae atque Ixiones alochoeo*. The last two words of this passage are a *cento* taken from the end of Homer, *Il.* 14.317, just as frg. 230 M (= 267 W) is part of *Il.* 20.443: <*nil*> *ut discrepet ac* τὸν δ' ἐξέπραξεν Ἀπόλλων | *fiat*. In frg. 462f. M (= 491–2W) even a whole line is taken from Homer (*Od.* 11. 491):

> non paucis malle ac sapientibus esse probatum
> ἢ πᾶσιν νεκύεσσι καταφθιμένοισιν ἀνάσσειν;

Furthermore, there are often single Greek terms and phrases, mainly of technical, scientific or literary nature, which have been integrated into the Latin text, probably being spelled in Latin,[17] but retaining, under certain circumstances, their Greek morphological inflection. The problem is difficult, and in many cases it becomes even more complicated by the doubtful transmission of the text. Housman (1907: 150 = 1972: 687) had already brilliantly observed that it was Lucilius' practice to give Greek adjectives the Greek inflection (cf. apart from Housman's examples *Atticon, dissyllabon, empleuron, cacosyntheton, calliplocamon, callispyron, pareutacton, poeticon*, also *aigilipoe* and *pareutactoe*) and to reserve the Latin ending for substantives (e.g. *exodium, zetematium, cobium, schedium*). According to this practice Lucilius also declined the masculine *o*-stems and the feminine *a*-stems: cf. nom. sing. *echinus, atomus, cyathus*, dat. *gymnasio*, acc. *ephebum*, nom. pl. *hippocampi, oenophori, moechocinaedi, androgyni*, acc. pl. *cinaedos, lychnos* and *propola, naumachiam, maltam*, etc. In the third declension Lucilius used in the genitive sing. the Latin ending (e.g. *aetheris*), but in the acc. the Greek one (*euphona*). In the gen. plur. of nouns, however, Lucilius made an exception. In this

---

style, especially concerning the use of homeoteleuta, with testimonies and further bibliography see Marx (1905: II 79f.), comm. ad loc., Leo (1906: 845f. = 1960: 230f.), Kroll (1913: 47) on Cic. *Or.* 37f. and Radermacher (1951: 153ff.).

[15] Cf. Leo (1906: 845f. = 1960: 230f.).

[16] The connection of *miraciodes* with *sym* is a hapax legomenon. It may be a witty word formation by Lucilius himself, in analogy to e.g. σύμπλεως, συμπλήρης etc. Cf. Leo (1906: 845 = 1960: 230).

[17] On the Latin spelling of Greek words in Lucilius cf. Marx (1905: II 10, 79, 114, 203).

case the inflection is also Greek:[18] cf. e.g. frg. 1100 M (= 397 W): *adde soloecismon genera atque uocabula centum.*

Most examples of the huge number of Greek expressions which Lucilius introduced were probably still regarded by his contemporaries as foreign technical words. At least in two cases, however, it seems strange that Lucilius gives two adjectives the Greek inflection, although in his time they might have been fully integrated already into the Latin language: cf. *Atticon* and *poeticon.* One reason for this practice, however, might be due to metrical convenience, as e.g. in frg. 1199 M (= 1259 W): *lecti omnes; Atticon hoc est* and frg. 495 M (= 542 W): *scit poeticon esse, uidet tunica et toga quid sit.*

Many of these terms had become firmly established in Latin and were used until the end of antiquity; very often, however, attempts were made to replace them with Latin equivalents. Cf. e.g. *zetematium* (frg. 650 M = 675 W) for which Lucilius did not yet have a Latin equivalent: *siquod uerbum inusitatum aut zetematium offenderam.* Here the diminutive *zetematium,* whose base-word has a parallel in *CIL* IV 1877f. and VI 28239.2, is a philological term denoting a pedantic grammatical problem. Cicero *De orat* 1.102 substituted this Greek expression with the Latin word *quaestiuncula.*

Another illustrative example is frg. 753 M (= 820 W), where Lucilius speaks of Epicurus' *eidola atque atomus,* which in Lucretius' *De rerum natura* became *principia* and *primordia.*

Lucilius, furthermore, does not hesitate to use Greek terms in order to create a specific Greek atmosphere, and he tries to achieve this by special stylistic means. For that reason in his description of his journey to Sicily (frg. 110–13 M = 102–5 W) he calls the steep mountains of Setia *aigilipoe,* comparing them with the highest Greek mountains, Aetna and Athos. It is not by chance that their transmitted epithet is *aigilipoe,* not *aigilipes* as Marx (with Francken) conjectured, since according to the testimony of Hesychius, besides the regular αἰγίλιψ (Hom. *Il.* 9.15, Aesch. *Suppl.* 794, Lyc. 1325), there also existed αἰγίλιπος, which probably was a form of South Italian Greek (cf. LSJ s.v.).

On the other hand, there is a total absence of Greek expressions where the subject-matter is entirely Roman. Consequently, no Greek word can be found in the verbose Lucilian definition of the concept and nature of Roman *uirtus* in frg. 1326–38 M (= 1196–208 W):

> uirtus, Albine, est, pretium persoluere uerum,
> quis in uersamur, quis uiuimus rebus, potesse,

---

[18] And this continued to be the practice in later times too: cf. the genitive in book titles like *Petronii libri Satyricon* etc.

uirtus est, homini scire id quod quaeque habeat res,
uirtus, scire, homini rectum, utile quid sit, honestum,
quae bona, quae mala item, quid inutile, turpe, inhonestum
uirtus quaerendae finem re scire modumque,
uirtus diuitiis pretium persoluere posse,
uirtus id dare quod re ipsa debetur honori,
hostem esse atque inimicum hominum morumque malorum,
contra defensorem hominum morumque bonorum,
hos magni facere, his bene uelle, his uiuere amicum,
commoda praeterea patriai prima putare,
deinde parentum, tertia iam postremaque nostra.

This passage evidently reminds us of the numerous reflections on typical Roman moral concepts which are to be found in Ennius and Pacuvius. Here the diction is marked by archaic traits: cf. e.g. Ennius' description of a true friend in *Ann.* frg. 234–52 V² (= 268–86 Sk), his reflections on *otium* and *negotium* in the tragedy *Iphigenia* (frg. 234–41 V² = 195–202 J) or his thoughts on the goddess Fortuna, who, as Warminton puts it, 'on a sudden casts down the highest mortal from the height of his sway, to become the lowliest thrall' (frg. 398–400 V² = 313–15 J).

Lucilius, however, is not only interested in moral questions, but he makes use of his poetry also in order to join in the discussion about literary and linguistic problems of his mother tongue. This is already apparent in his earliest satires (cf. e.g. the above mentioned frg. 650 M = 675 W), but it becomes more and more evident in book IX, which was written later than books XXVI–XXX.

In this book IX Lucilius deals with numerous philological aspects of the Latin language. One of them is orthography, so e.g. the graphematic reproduction of long vowels which according to Quintilian, *Inst.* 1.7.14 had an old tradition (*usque ad Accium et ultra*) and was common in Oscan (Leumann (1977: 12f.)). Lucilius, however, disapproved of it: cf. frg. 350–5 M (= 368–72 W):

'a' primum est, hinc incipiam, et quae nomina ab hoc sunt,
deinde —
'aa' primum longa, 'a' breuis syllaba; nos tamen unum
hoc faciemus et uno eodemque ut dicimus pacto
scribemus pacem: placide; Ianum, aridum: acetum,
Ἄρες Ἄρες Graeci ut faciunt.

In frg. 362f. M (= 375f. W) the poet proposes the spelling *i-* in the genitive singular of *-io* stems, since by his time the spelling *-ei* had come into fashion, and subsequently Varro (frg. 252 *GRF*) recommended the spelling *-ii* (Leumann (1977: 424f.)). In frg. 356f. M (= 373f. W) Lucilius prefers the older form *feruĕre* to *feruēre*, but he does not seem to have a dogmatic opinion concerning this matter: *feruĕre, ne longum. uero: hoc lectoribus tradam.*

In general one can say that Lucilius was conservative in his linguistic views. If there were two reasonable linguistic options, he preferred the older standard form, but he explicitly mocked solecisms.

In frg. 1215–17 M (= 398–400 W) he offers two examples, namely the colloquial confusion of *apud* and *ad* and *intro* and *intus*:

> nam ueluti *intro* aliud longe esse atque *intus* uidemus,
> sic <item> *apud te* aliud longe est, neque idem ualet *ad te*:
> *intro* nos uocat, at sese tenet *intus*.[19]

Most essential to Lucilius was the common *usus* (Hor. *Ars* 71f. and Quint. *Inst.* 1.6.43) or *consuetudo* (Cic. *Or.* 159) in language. Perhaps this is the reason why our poet has eleven instances of an *ablatiuus qualitatis*, which in common language prevailed until the end of the republican period, whereas there is no example of a *genetiuus qualitatis* to be found in his satires (cf. Marx (1904: I 160), Index gramm.) and Hofmann–Szantyr (1965: 68 and 118)). Lucilius was neither a purist like the Scipiones nor did he approve of the linguistic innovations which the Scipiones proposed as analogists. Therefore, he rejected forms like *pertisum* instead of *pertaesum*, and *rederguisse* instead of *redarguisse*, which according to Festus p. 334. 28ff. L. Scipio Africanus is said to have used (cf. also Cic. *Or.* 159: *quidam pertisum etiam uolunt, quod eadem consuetudo non probauit*). In frg. 963f. M (= 983f. W) Lucilius obviously addresses Scipio:

> quo facetior uideare et scire plus quam ceteri
> pertisum hominem, non pertaesum, dicere humanum genus.

In additon, there is another example which clearly demonstrates that Lucilius did not agree with Scipio's recommendation to use a generalized form *ue-* instead of *uo-* in the paradeigma of *uertere*, as Quintilian, *Inst.* 1.7.25 says: *quid dicam uortices et uorsus ceteraque ad eundem modum, quae primus Scipio Africanus in e litteram secundam uertisse dicitur?* Krenkel's view (see his commentary on frg. 349 K = 357 M = 374 W) that the form *uortere* is older than *uertere* is incorrect. The fact is that the present tense of this verb initially always was *uertere*, whereas the forms of the past tense were *uorti* and *uorsus*. This is due to the Indo-European apophony, which can still be observed in the corresponding German present form *werden*, in the past tense *wurde, ge-worden,* and in Umbrian present tense *couertu* and Ppp. *trahuorfi* (cf. Leumann (1977: 48)). Unfortunately, in Old Latin inscriptions there are no present forms of *uertere*,

---

[19] Cf. also Quint. *Inst.* 1.5.50 *intus et intro sum soloecismi sunt* and Hofmann–Szantyr (1965: 277) and Svennung (1935: 388f.).

whereas there are perfect forms such as *CIL* I² 586.4 *aduortit* and SC Bacch. *aruorsum*. We can observe that in this matter, too, Lucilius' linguistic attitude is conservative: he uses the stem *uert-* in the present forms (frg. 139 M = 132 W *uertitur*, 899 M = 858 W *auertat*, 745 M = 838 W *uertenti*) whereas *uort-* occurs in the forms of the past tense: frg. 988 M = 1082 W *uorsus*, 1197 M = 1188 W *uorsum*.[20]

It was one of Lucilius' main literary intentions to reproduce colloquial speech in most parts of his *Saturae*, which he himself frg. 1039 M (= 1039 W) probably called *ludus ac sermones* (the latter expression appears also in frg. 1015 M = 1085 W). This kind of speech is often very informal and ignores linguistic regulations. As has been mentioned already, it is sometimes very conservative in phonetics and morphology as well as in syntax. Therefore the occurrence of archaisms is not surprising. Numerous examples of them can be found in Lucilius' *Saturae*. In most cases, however, when they do occur, owing to the fragmentary character of Lucilius' poetry, we are not able to say whether they are intentionally introduced to characterize or to make fun of a particular kind of person or to parody another author. Cf. e.g. frg. 328f. M (= 357f. W) where someone mentions a glutton whose name is *Cerco*:

> quid ergo, si ostrea Cerco
> cognorit fluuium limum ac caenum sapere ipsum?

Unfortunately, we do not know who the speaker of these words is. To my mind, however, it is certain, that it cannot be the poet himself. The language of the passage is individualized by such odd traits, which for the linguistically well-trained poet Lucilius are inconceivable in this context. Therefore the speaker seems to have been a person of lower social standing. Perhaps he was a slave, a cook or a parasite, who in Roman comedy often are characterized by traits of vulgar Latin (cf. Petersmann (1995*b*: 128 n. 12)). He could also have been a freedman like Trimalchio or one of his uneducated friends in Petronius' *Satyrica*, whose *sermo vulgaris* is sometimes so archaic in tone that these characters are given a ridiculous dignity (Petersmann (1995*a*: 533–47)).

Anyway, the above-quoted passage is a good example of the language of this kind of person: cf. the form of the genitive plural of the *o-* stems ending in *-um*, which is certainly an archaism. Leumann (1977: 428) declares: 'Literarisch ist *-um* bis in spätere Zeiten nur erhalten in festgeprägten Wendungen oder in Sachgruppen, zumeist von Personenbezeichnungen: *pro deum fidem* und *deum virtute, praefectus* und *centuria fabrum*.'

---

[20] On the pres. forms *vort-* in the text of Plautus which seem to have been introduced by grammarians of a later period cf. Leumann (1977: 48).

In older times, however, the usage was much wider, but it was confined mainly to tragedy and epic: cf. Enn. *Ann.* 246f. V² (= 281f. Sk = 222f. W)) *uerbum paucum* instead of *uerborum paucorum.* Consequently, *fluuium* for *fluuiorum* in the context of everyday life here must have sounded funny. The same applies also to the hypercorrect neuter accusative form *ostrea,* which is used here instead of the feminine *ostreas.* One would have expected the latter form, since this noun is a loan-word taken over from the Greek neuter ὀστρέον long before Lucilius' time. In Latin it had changed its gender (via the neuter plural) to feminine *ostrea*: cf. e.g. Plaut. *Rud.* 297 *echinos, lopadas, ostreas* and Lucilius frg. 132 M (= 126 W) *ostrea nulla fuit, non purpura, nulla peloris.* Therefore in the context of our fragment as well as in frg. 1201 M (= 1222 W) *luna alit ostrea et implet echinos...* the nom. and acc. plur. *ostrea* is a hypercorrect form which was intended to create the same amusing effect as *fluuium.*

Linguistic mockery is also obvious in a series of other words: *collus* (frg. 268 M = 316 W and frg. 703 M = 780 W), *forus* (frg. 146 M = 148 W) etc. Mariotti (1960: 102f.) provides more examples but does not mention *utria* in frg. 1104 M (= 1212 W) instead of *utres.* This form is very interesting. It occurs again in late Latin (e.g. Arnob. *Adu. Nat.* 1.59 R), which demonstrates how long some substandard words continued to be alive. Often they still exist in the Romance idioms. The word *demagis,* meaning 'furthermore' is such an example: Lucilius frg. 527–9 M (= 544–6 W) gives the only literary evidence of this adverb in entire Latinity. As an expression of the popular language it was taken to the Iberian peninsula by Roman colonists and has survived only there: cf. Spanish *demás,* Portuguese *demais,* etc. (*REW³*: no. 2546 and Tovar (1969: 1022ff.) and already Marx (1909: 437)).

Another very illustrative example of this kind is the verb *uannere* 'to winnow' (from *uannus* (= 'the winnow for fodder or cereals'), whose first attestation is found in Col. 2.20.4), which apart from Lucilius does not occur elsewhere in Latin literature, but has survived as a technical term in idioms of the Romance area (*REW³* no. 9141f. s.v. *uannere* and **uannitare*). In both Lucilian passages where the word occurs it is applied to sexual intercourse (Adams 1982a: 153): frg. 278 M (= 302 W) *hunc molere, illam autem ut frumentum uannere lumbis* and 330 M (= 361 W) *crisabit ut si frumentum clunibus uannat.*

rostrum is another remarkable word, on which Adams (1982b: 103) comments much more accurately than Tovar (1969: 1024): 'lit. "beak" (e.g. Plin. *Nat.* 8.97) or "snout" (e.g. Plin. *Nat.* 8.121) of an animal or bird, was applied to the human anatomy in colloquial Latin, as Nonius noted (p. 729 L)'. Nonius quotes from Plautus, Novius, Lucilius and Varro's Mennipean Satires, to which Petron. 75.10 has to be added. Originally *rostrum* could be used to denote either the human mouth or face, or both together like the English slang word 'mug' or the vulgar German 'Schnauze', 'Fresse'. Lucilius uses the word three times in this sense (frg. 210 M = 233 W, 336 M = 362f. W and 1121 M = 1184 W). In Varro, *Men.* 419 and Petron. 75.10 the word apparently refers to the human face, in which sense it has survived in the Iberian peninsula, whereas the meaning 'mouth' (already attested in Plaut. *Men.* 89) can be found in Old Romanian (*REW*[3] no. 7386). And it is Lucilius, not Cicero, as Walde–Hofmann (1930–56: 439 s.v. *rodo*) state, who gives the first literary evidence for the meaning of the plural *rostra* as 'a speaker's stand'.[21] Cf. frg. 261 M (= 273 W): *haec, inquam, rudet ex rostris atque heiulabit...*

In frg. 557 M (= 590 W) *rugosi passique senes* the word *passi* must not be translated with Warmington as 'shockheaded', but as 'having become wrinkled, dry': cf. Non. 11.28 *passum est proprie* rugosum *uel* siccum... *unde et uua* passa *dicta est quod sit rugis implicata*. The word is used mainly in connection with plants (especially of dried grapes). Therefore in most cases (cf. *TLL* X. 200.23ff.) the adjective occurs as an epithet of *uua* or in metaphorical expressions where somebody's appearance is compared with dry and wrinkled grapes: cf. e.g. *Priap.* 32.1 *uuis aridior puella rugosis*, Claud. 18.111 *passa facies rugosior uua*. According to this image in Lucilius *passus* is applied to old men who look like wrinkled grapes.

A testimony of popular usage is also the plural *ligna* in frg. 131 M (= 125 W) *si dent hi ligna, uidete*, on which Charisius *GLK* I 72.6, quoting the Lucilian fragment, comments: *lignum singulariter dici semper debet in multitudine*. This nom./acc. form *ligna* is also the basis of Ital. *legna*, Span. *leña*, Port. *lenha*, Log. *linna* etc. (cf. *REW*[3] no. 5034) denoting firewood, just as e.g. *gaudia* instead of *gaudium* (cf. frg. 98f. M = 94f. W) became the basis of Ital. *gioia*, Span. *joya*, French *joie* etc. (cf. *REW*[3] no. 3705).

No less interesting is the way in which Lucilius uses diminutives. It has been often stated that in familiar or vulgar speech diminutives are sometimes employed where elevated speech normally would have used the base-forms. But this is only partly right. Adams in a most illuminating chapter of his recent book on *Pelagonius and Latin Veterinary Terminology in the Roman Empire* (1995b: 543ff.) has demonstrated the inadequacy of the general term 'vulgarism', for in such contexts many diminutives are not used in a colloquial or vulgar manner, but are chosen deliberately with a special meaning as technical terms: cf. e. g. *auricula* in Lucilius frg. 266 M

---

[21] Cf. also the other two testimonies of the word in pre-Ciceronian times: *CIL* I.583.36 (= lex rep. a. 123/122 BC) *iudices... omnes pro rostreis in forum [uorsus iouranto]* and Varro, *L.L.* 6.91 *collegam roges ut comitia edicat de rostris.*

(= 298 W):[22] *ne auriculam obsidat caries, ne uermiculi qui.* In this passage, as in the veterinary treatises of later periods, *auricula* is not a mere substitute for the base-form *auris* but is used technically for the inner ear, just as in the same fragment *uermiculi* is not simply said of worms in general but of a special kind of worms affecting the ear (cf. in addition to Adams (1995*b*: 560), on *uermiculus* Cels. 6.7.5 *ubi uero uermes orti sunt, si iuxta sunt, protrahendi oriculario specillo sunt . . . cauendumque ne postea nascantur,* and more in Marx (1905: II 100f., commentary ad loc.)). The same holds good also for *pellicula* in frg. 534–6 M (= 559–61 W):

> 'ibat forte aries,' inquit, 'iam quod genus, quantis
> testibus! uix uno filo hosce haerere putares,
> pellicula extrema exaptum pendere onus ingens.'

Here *pellicula* seems to have a special connection to the skin of the ram's belly (cf. the localizing adjective *extrema*). In Pelagon. 3.6.1 the same word is applied to the skin of the chicken's *uenter* (Adams (1995*b*: 544)). Lucilius, furthermore, gives evidence that this manner of using diminutives in a technical sense is not restricted to veterinary contexts but is to be found elsewhere too: cf. frg. 1143 (= catal. p. 420 W) *corolla*, which is not only the diminutive of *corona*, but according to Isid. *Et.* 19.30.1, who quotes this word, it has a special meaning: *corona insigne uictoriae siue regii honoris signum . . . haec a Lucilio corolla, ab Homero* στεφάνη *dicta est.*

There might be one Lucilian passage in which a real diminutive occurs instead of the base form. It is *muliercula* in frg. 565–7 M (= 592–3 W):

> peniculamento uero reprehendere noli,
> ut pueri infantes faciunt, mulierculam honestam.

Marx (1904: I 162, Index gramm.) thinks that in this fragment the diminutive *mulierculam* is used *metri causa*. If his interpretation is right (which is doubtful since the tone of *muliercula* might be affectionate), we could also explain the shorter form *guberna* instead of *gubernacula* in frg. 578 M (= 622 W). In this fragment a seaman gives the following command: *proras despoliate et detundete guberna.* Here *guberna* is not an artificial form as Marx, Krenkel (frg. 579) and Charpin (XX frg. 5) in their editions of Lucilius believe. I cannot see any reason, however, why a seaman in ordinary speech should have imitated epic style. Therefore, we should rather assume that *gubernum* instead of *gubernaculum* was a colloquial form. This can be proved by the fact that the word signifying *helm* in Old Italian is also *governo*, in Old French *gouver* and in the language of Provence it is *governe* (cf. *REW³*: no. 3905).

---

[22] I am very grateful to Professor J. N. Adams for his highly illustrative remarks on this word in a letter to me.

Another colloquial element seems to occur in the above-mentioned command, frg. 578 M (= 622 W): cf. the form *detundete*, which Marx conjectured *metri causa* for the transmitted *detundite*, whose meaning here is 'dismantle'. It is not clear, however, whether *detundete* replaces *detundite* (from *de* + *tundere* as Charpin thinks) or *detondete* (from *de* + *tondere*), in which case *detundete* might be explained as a rustic form instead of *detondete* (cf. Marx (1905: II 215 ad loc.)).

It is beyond doubt that Lucilius enjoyed ridiculing rustic or dialect speech: see e.g. frg. 1130 M (= 232 W) where Lucilius mocks the monophthongized pronunciation of *e* instead of *ai* used by one of his opponents. This was probably the designated *praetor urbanus* C. Caecilius Metellus Caprarius who by his way of speaking Latin would turn out to be a *praetor rusticus*: *Cecilius pretor ne rusticus fiat*.

Lucilius, who was born at Suessa Aurunca in Campania, obviously had some knowledge of Oscan-Umbrian dialects. According to Strabo 5.3.6. (= C 233) his birthplace was a Roman colony that was close to the Oscan-speaking territory (Leo (1967: 406)). The influence of this idiom on Latin is evident in frg. 1318 M (= 1237 W) where someone says: *uasa quoque omnino redimit non sollo, dupundii*. Festus 384.29f. L comments on *sollo*: *Osce dicitur id quod nos* totum *uocamus*. Mras (1927/28: 79f.) regarded the ending *-o* in *sollo* as the exact Oscan morpheme of the accusative neuter plural corresponding to Latin *-a*. Vetter (1953: 374), on the other hand, assumed a compound *sollodupundi* as e.g. in frg. 1058 M (= 1048 W) *moechocinaedi*.

In another passage (frg. 1249 M = 1209 W) the poet mocks the verb *pipas*: '<*quare me insidiis*> *petis, pipas? da.*' '*Libet*' <*inquit*>. The verb *pipare* obviously is of rural origin (cf. Varro, *Men.* 3 B *gallina pipat*). It is an onomatopoetic word. In the above fragment it has the meaning of 'to bewail in a shrill voice': cf. Festus in *CGL* IV p. xviii where the word is quoted and interpreted thus: pipatio *est clamor plorantis acerba uoce*, and Paul. Fest. p. 235.11 L pipatio *clamor plorantis lingua Oscorum* testifies that word formations with *pip-* in this sense have also parallels in other Italic idioms.

Even more evident is the rural tone of frg. 581 M (= 623 W), which is documented by the dialect pronunciation of *abiit* as *abzet*, and where I as well as Charpin (XXII frg. 5) have adopted the punctuation of Terzaghi (= frg. 617): *primum Pacilius: tesorophylax, pater, abzet*. Glossaries (cf. Marx (1905: II 216)) explicitly comment on *abzet: extincta est uel mortua*. The word *abzet* has a parallel in a Pelignian inscription which says of a priestess: *afded = abiit* 'she passed away' (*CE* 17.6 and Vetter (1953: no. 213)). Moreover, the name *Pacilius* recalls the Oscan name *Paakul*, but above all the pronunciation *tesorophylax* instead of *thesaurophylax* suggests a kind of artificial rustic Latin. Charpin (1979: II 266) following Mariotti (1960: 97) remarks on this Lucilian fragment: 'La langue de ce fragment est très composite; il semble que Lucilius ait voulu créer une atmosphère non romaine, plutôt que restituer un dialecte donné.'

To my mind, Lucilius here and in some other passages also tried to individualize persons of lower social standing by the same lingusitic methods which later on were used by Petronius in his portrayal of Trimalchio and the other freedmen (Petersmann (1995a: 533–47)). This is evident, above all, in the field of lexicography: here Lucilius, for the sake of ridicule, sometimes introduces more or less Latinized expressions which the *sermo plebeius* had taken over not only from Greek-speaking territory but also from other peregrine regions, such as the Celtic word *bulga* (frg. 244–6 M = 279–81 W), the Syrian *mamphula* (frg. 1251 M = 1056 W), the Etruscan *mantisa* (frg. 1208 M = 1225 W), the Umbrian *gumia* (frg. 1066 M = 1029 W and frg. 1237 M = 203 W), and *carissa* (frg. 1129 M = catal. W p. 419), whose linguistic provenance is completely uncertain.[23]

It is quite natural that different ethnic groups mingling with each other as they did in Italy also left traces of their original idioms in Latin. As a result the standard Latin language, whose ideal was the *sermo purus* of the capital Rome, became more and more corrupted. This was already the opinion of Lucilius himself, who in frg. 1242f. M (= 1255 W) ridicules someone because of his or her wrong pronunciation by imitating it with the words *ore corupto* instead of *ore corrupto*.

The *os corruptum* is one of the main targets of criticism not only of the authors of the classical period — Cicero, *Brut.* 258 speaks of the foreign population of contemporary Rome *inquinate loquentes* — but also of the grammarians of later times: cf. e.g. apart from *CE* 1012.2, above all Quintilian, *Inst.* 1.1.13 and 1.5.55f. In the latter passage, where Quintilian talks about the *oris plurima uitia in peregrinum sonum corrupti et sermonis*, he informs us that Lucilius satirically ridiculed a certain Vettius for speaking Latin like the inhabitants of Praeneste (frg. 1322 M = 1138–41 W). And it is this idiom which already in Plautus' comedies was an object of mockery (cf. *Truc.* 691 and *Trin.* 609).

Thus Lucilius proves to be one of the greatest artists of the Latin language. There cannot be any doubt that Lucilius in his satires not only continued what Ennius had started to do in his *Saturae*, but also tried to surpass his predecessor in many ways: first of all by introducing personal ridicule and harsh invective, and secondly by subordinating the various levels of language to his poetic intentions. His skill in characterizing

---

[23] On the etymology of these words see the relevant articles in Walde–Hofmann (1930–56), and Ernout–Meillet (1959) s.vv.

persons by an individual style and marking situations by an appropriate choice of words was already acknowledged by Fronto p. 57.3 v.d.H. (ed. Teubn.): *in uerbis cuiusque artis ac negotii propriis*. Lucilius uses language as a means of satiric mockery in order to excite laughter as well as to instruct. He is not only a master of parody when imitating Latin epic, tragic and comic style,[24] but he is also fully acquainted with the representatives of the various genres of Greek literature (cf. Marx (1904: I 100) and Coffey (1989: 41ff. and 54ff.)). Above all, Lucilius is a brilliant artist in reproducing the different varieties of the Latin language in all its nuances from the refined heights down to its vulgar and obscene depths (Coffey (1989: 51)).

As a Roman citizen, Lucilius' own linguistic model obviously was that type of language which Aristophanes too regarded as ideal: a $\delta\iota\acute{\alpha}\lambda\epsilon\kappa\tau o\varsigma$ $\mu\acute{\epsilon}\sigma\eta$ of the city, which was neither sophisticated nor vulgar nor rustic in tone (frg. 706 *PCG* III 2, p. 362). Therefore, Lucilius disapproved of the analogical and artificial manipulation of language by the Scipiones, and he also mocked dialect traits which he himself at times introduced in order to individualize his characters. But he also rejected the typical *Graecomania* of certain groups of Roman society. On the whole, one can state with Puelma Piwonka (1949: 28) that Lucilius experienced language as a social phenomenon. And he did so to a degree matched by no poet before him nor by any of the subsequent verse satirists, Horace, Persius and Juvenal. It was Petronius who, to a certain extent, not only imitated the function Lucilius attributed to language and style, but also continued to develop this technique of early Roman satire as a literary creation *sui generis*.

Note. I should like to express my sincere thanks to Professors J. N. Adams and R. Mayer for their helpful suggestions and corrections.

---

[24] Cf. Marx (1904: I 100), *index auctorum*, quoting from Ennius, Plautus, Terence, Caecilius, Pacuvius, and Coffey (1989: 41ff. and 52ff.) on Accius; on Afranius cf. Krenkel frg. 1106 = 1029 M (= 1074 W).

Proceedings of the British Academy, **93**, 311–334

Stylistic Registers in Juvenal

J. G. F. POWELL

Summary. Juvenal is commonly said to have adopted the 'grand' or 'high' style. In this paper it is argued that statements to this effect are misleading. Over-schematic contrasts between Juvenal and Horace are deprecated, in favour of a recognition of the satiric qualities of both writers. It is contended that Juvenal's references to contemporary or earlier epic, important as they are, are all in the nature of parody, and that a proper appreciation of the difference in style between Silver Latin epic and Juvenal's satire would obviate an over-serious view of Juvenal. Some passages in Juvenal that are commonly alleged to be programmatic statements about his own style are then discussed, with the aim of showing that they do not constitute a proclamation that he will adopt the 'grand' style, or indeed any style foreign to the genre of satire. An attempt is then made to define some of the different things that are meant by 'style', and to distinguish in particular the concept of 'register' from other ingredients of literary style. Against the background of Axelson's work on stylistic register in Latin poetry, it is argued that Juvenal's style is not 'grand' in terms of stylistic register, except when he is parodying epic, and that his passages of epic parody generally include some clear stylistic incongruity which reveals the ironical purpose behind them.

IT IS COMMONLY STATED that Juvenal adopted the 'high' or 'grand' style; indeed, it is sometimes presupposed as a fact, and explanations are looked for.[1] But before one attempts to explain a phenomenon, one ought to

---

[1] The first major scholarly treatment of this question is apparently that of Scott (1927); see also Anderson (1961), Kenney (1963), and Bramble (1974: 164–73). In (I think) my second

make sure that one has defined and observed it correctly. One should first ask what the high style is (and indeed whether it is one thing or several), and then what precise use Juvenal is alleged to have made of it, before the statement can even be tested against the evidence of the text. I shall argue that, at least in its simple form as just stated, the proposition that Juvenal adopted the high style is misleading. The quest for stylistic categories which are not merely legitimate (whether in ancient or modern terms), but also helpful in enabling us to read the text of Juvenal in an enlightened and appreciative way, is not by any means an easy one. While I have certainly encountered people (particularly young cynics in the late 1980s and '90s) who appreciate the tone of Juvenal's satires with immediate and genuine gusto, without ever having worried much about precise definitions of stylistic features, it is equally certain that the imposition of inappropriate categories will impede reception and stifle understanding. So I think the attempt to be rather more precise about these things is worth while.

This matter of high style is not the only mismatch between my own experience of Juvenal and what I read in some of the secondary literature about him, but it is one of the most persistent. I am seriously quite puzzled as to how any competent Latinist could read even a single satire of Juvenal all the way through, except just possibly the Tenth, and come out thinking that this author is a consistent practitioner of the high or grand style; and yet that is what people say. For an explanation of this, I am tempted to look for factors outside the text. Juvenal does, indeed, occupy a rather peculiar position within the twentieth-century canon of Latin authors. He is the only classical verse writer after Ovid who is generally accorded the first rank, and whose works figure largely in school and undergraduate syllabuses, at least in this country (these observations may be Anglocentric). Hence he tends to be accorded the reverence due to a *premier cru* classic, while the serious poetry of his time is neglected. The modest expansion in recent years of specialist interest in Silver Age epic and tragedy has not substantially affected the position, because those who deal seriously in Silver epic are often not the same as those who work on Juvenal. It is relatively uncommon for Juvenal to be seen in proper perspective within his period. The genuine high style in Silver Latin poetry is to be found in Seneca, Lucan and Statius. The style of Juvenal seems to

term as an Oxford undergraduate, John Bramble set me to write an essay on 'Juvenal's reasons for adopting the high style'. This paper may be said to represent the mature growth from a seed of puzzlement sown in that tutorial. I am grateful to Professor Susanna Morton Braund for comments on a late draft of this paper. Even later, Professor Braund's edition of *Satires* 1–5 (Braund (1996)) came to hand, and it was possible to take it into account in the final stage of revision: see especially the comments at the very end of this paper.

me far different from this and impossible to mistake for it; but that is clearly not how it has seemed to others.

The waters may be muddied by the fact that both Lucan and Statius cultivate striking verbal effects, and both show tendencies towards a bitterly ironical tone: features which may seem to bring them closer to satire in general and to Juvenal in particular. But in the end I would wish to maintain a firm distinction, though with all due sense of the inadequacy and slipperiness of the categories: Lucan and Statius are basically serious, though not by any means always solemn; Juvenal is basically comic, though not necessarily always frivolous. Indeed, given that contemporary epic did contain passages of ironical denunciation, there would be no reason why Juvenal should not parody those along with the rest. In such a case the reader would indeed be faced with a difficult task in determining the tone, if it were not for the fact that Juvenal usually sooner or later undercuts the dramatic pose.

Genre and literary tradition are universally acknowledged to be important for the study of any Roman author; and while Juvenal's relations with other authors of his period may receive insufficient attention, his work is very commonly treated as part of an organic tradition of Roman satire, and the relations between his work and that of Lucilius, Horace and Persius are often studied in detail. While a study of this aspect is indeed necessary for a proper appreciation of Juvenal, this approach has its dangers too. Perhaps paradoxically, it may lead to an exaggerated view of the differences between these four authors, while the generic similarities may be taken for granted.

On a first inspection, it may well seem that Juvenal has little in common with the pedestrian Horace of the *Satires* and *Epistles*; he can easily seem 'high' by comparison. But the similarities between Horace's hexameter style and Juvenal's, and the markedly satirical and un-epic qualities of the latter, can easily be underplayed.

Take in particular the question of metrical technique. 'The central fact about the verse technique of Juvenal,' says Courtney, 'is that it is very different from that used by Horace in his Satires.'[2] But let us look at Courtney's own very useful statistics. We are told, for example, that Juvenal has about 130 monosyllabic line-endings, 'much the same proportion as Horace', as against the far more sparing use of this feature in Virgil and its almost complete absence from Silver epic. As for polysyllabic endings, 'Horace Satires has 43 such cases, much the same proportion as Juvenal'.

---

[2] Courtney (1980: 49). On the metrical technique of Horace see Nilsson (1952), from whom the selection of diagnostic features is taken. Braund (1996: 29–30) deals with metre along roughly the same lines as Courtney.

(In this case the Virgilian proportion seems to be comparable.) Courtney gives us a scale of frequency of elision, in which it appears that Juvenal is more sparing with elision than Horace in the *Satires* (though we are not told how much more); but Virgil in the *Aeneid* uses more elision and Ovid in the *Metamorphoses* less than either. With the facts as they are, it is very difficult to know what stylistic interpretation to put on the statistics for elision, but certainly the difference between Juvenal and Horace does not seem to stand out. The details given on enjambment are also ambiguously significant. The statistic for *atque* ending a line (two in Virgil, four in Juvenal, 29 in Horace) may merely indicate a Horatian idiosyncrasy. *Et* at line-end, absent from Virgil, is said to occur six times in Juvenal, 12 in Horace; Courtney comments that Juvenal 'stands far behind Horace'; in fact he is just as different from Virgil as from Horace, and it could indeed be argued that the difference between the presence of a feature and its complete absence may be more significant than the difference between twelve occurrences and six. On the other hand, Juvenal takes more liberties than Horace in his use of monosyllabic prepositions at line-end and of relative pronouns in the same position; the former do not occur at all in Horace, of the latter Juvenal has 34 as against 15 in Horace ('a significantly higher proportion' according to Courtney).

Juvenal has fewer pauses at 'unusual' places in the line than Horace, but at the same time significantly more than Virgil. Although on first impression Juvenal may seem more regular than Horace, every now and again he produces a line-ending which clearly signals that we are in the world of satire and not in that of epic. *Nescis | quem tua simplicitas risum vulgo moveat, cum | exigis . . .* (13.35) is as odd as anything in Horace, if not odder (doubtless the dislocation of rhythm suits the meaning); Horace can provide no parallel for 3.273 *ad cenam si | intestatus eas* (the word order highlights *ad cenam*; the unusual rhythm may serve to reinforce this, and the combination of enjambment with hiatus in *si | intestatus* presumably suggests a more deliberate enunciation than would be normal). In two respects, Juvenal makes use of distinctively poetic features which are not used by Horace: hiatus within the line, and spondaic line-endings. Courtney's discussion shows sufficiently that the great majority of these are used for special effect and have a clear nuance of parody.

From all this, it is really not clear why the differences between Juvenal's metrical practice and Horace's should be treated as the 'central fact', while the similarities between them are laid on one side. It is a question of emphasis, and there is one fact that needs emphasizing more than any stylistic differences between Juvenal and Horace: the fact that they are both satirists, and that they both do some things (metrically and otherwise) that on the whole only satirists do.

The 'satiric tradition' was never self-contained and self-perpetuating. Braund (1992a: 3–4) has aptly characterized it as 'parasitic'; it was so both in relation to the established classics (the same for us as for Juvenal: mostly Virgil, Horace and Ovid) and in relation to the latest poetic fashions. From the earliest times, satire borrowed the metre of epic and, to some extent, its ways of forcing language into metre: potentially an act of parody in itself; cf. Braund (1996: 21 and 24), who however stops short of admitting that it is parody, and calls it 'counterpoint' instead. Everyone agrees that at least some of Juvenal's references to epic are in the nature of parody (see e.g. Highet (1951: 375ff.); Marache (1964: 476); Cèbe (1966: 320ff.); Townend (1973: 154ff.). Some have distinguished two different purposes for this: ridicule of a commonplace and unworthy object by dignifying it in elevated language, or ridicule of the conventions and mannerisms of epic itself (Lelièvre (1958); Romano (1979)). This is all very fine. But not everyone has been prepared to go the whole way and to say, as I would be inclined to, that every reference to epic in Juvenal is parodic. Part of the problem is that the word 'parody' is used in different ways. The word παρῳδία no doubt originally referred to direct parodic imitation of an identifiable passage of some more serious author (there are plenty of well-known examples, including some in Juvenal) and some modern writers seem to confine it to this sense; but we need a word for more general 'sending up' of epic or tragic diction, and there seems to be no objection in modern usage to employing 'parody' in this wider sense as well.

On the other hand, if all that is meant by Juvenal's supposed high style is precisely this tendency to indulge in epic parody (in this wider sense), then the categories are misleading. Epic parody does not constitute the high style. In any case, Juvenal's satires are not full-blown epic parodies; not even the main narrative of Satire 4 comes into this category, for however much of Statius' *De Bello Germanico* lies behind this satire, the style never remains in the realm of high epic for more than a few lines at a time.[3] In general, Juvenal's epic parody typically comes in fairly short

---

[3] The narrative begins with parody of an epic scene-setting, lines 37–46. From 46 *quis enim* to 56 *ne pereat* is virtually pure prose (though there are doubtless one or two parodic touches; e.g. the singular for plural *multo delatore* may be one such). Then the style rises again to the level of epic, from 56 *iam letifero* to the end of the fisherman's speech *ipse capi voluit* (69), though we shall note the pointedly incongruous *obsonia* at line 64. Sustained imitation of high epic style is largely abandoned thereafter. Isolated epic mannerisms are employed, but usually in a ludicrous fashion (107 *Montani venter*, 108 the grandiose hyperbaton *matutino . . . amomo* immediately deflated by *quantum vix redolent duo funera*, 109–10 *saevior . . . aperire*, a type of brachylogy brought into poetic usage by Horace and much beloved by the Silver poets; and so on); and there are a number of phrases which strike this reader at least as very clearly prosaic or conversational in tone (e.g. 78 *anne aliud tum praefecti?*, 98 *unde fit ut malim fraterculus esse gigantis*, 106 *et tamen improbior saturam scribente cinaedo*, 128–9 *hoc defuit unum Fabricio . . .*).

bursts (I mean, of course, what would appear to be short bursts to one reading, or listening, at normal speed), and is cast into relief by the contrast with the surrounding style, which is very much not that of epic.

Even so, some have asserted that Juvenal adopted the epic manner, or something less well defined called the grand style, not for purposes of parody but with a serious poetic or at least rhetorical and moralizing aim (Scott (1927); Bramble (1974); (1982*a*)). We are told that the Roman vices attacked by Juvenal had reached epic proportions and therefore demanded epic treatment. Or Juvenal is alleged to have aimed to supplant a supposedly played-out epic tradition from its privileged place in the hierarchy of genres (Anderson (1962: 284); Braund (1992*a*: 43); (1996: 22–3)). Such diagnoses, based as they presumably are on an interpretation of Juvenal's own words in Satire 1, must be regarded with caution. In the first place, clearly, Juvenal's programmatic statements, such as they are, are themselves part of the satire and must be taken in that spirit. In the second place, it is not clear that these interpretations accurately represent what Juvenal's words actually claim about his own work. In the first paragraph of Satire 1, and then again in lines 52–4, he does, indeed, ridicule contemporary epic writers as a rhetorical foil for his own writing, but he says nothing directly about transferring their style into satire, nor about any comparison between the material of satire and that of epic, nor about supplanting epic from its position. All these ideas have been imported by interpreters; but there was no need to do this, if only the essentially facetious tone of Juvenal's apologia had been recognized. All that is actually said is (to paraphrase) 'Everyone else is at the writing game: comedy, elegy, tragedy, epic — the lot. (15) Why shouldn't I have a go as well? (19) But I have decided that my field will be satire. Why? (30) Because it's difficult not to write satire with Rome as it is. (51) The iniquities of modern Rome are worthy of Horace's pen. Would you prefer me to write about the deeds of Hercules? (79) I may be no poet but my indignation will see me through. There has been material for satire since the world began, but never more than now . . .'. Explicitly Juvenal claims only to follow Lucilius and Horace; epic is no more than the rejected alternative. Of course, this might have been the prelude to a consistently epic-style narrative of contemporary Roman misdeeds, but what follows in the first satire, and in most of the others with the obvious exception of the fourth, is not even narrative, but argumentative conversational discourse — in fact *sermo*.

The foregoing remarks have been preliminary to my main purpose in this paper, which is to enquire into the ways in which a detailed study of Juvenal's language might help to resolve this question of his seriousness or, as I would contend, absence of seriousness. But first, it is necessary to

clear away a possible objection. Has not Juvenal himself told us that he
will adopt the grand style? Many have thought so. In particular, attention
has been drawn to a famous passage near the end of Satire 6, one of
the three most commonly quoted allegedly programmatic statements in
Juvenal.[4]

Juvenal has alleged that mothers, in contemporary Rome, poison their
children. He turns aside from the narration to counteract possible disbelief
on the part of the audience, in the following words:

> Fingimus haec, altum Satura[5] sumente cothurnum,
> scilicet, et finem egressi legemque priorum
> grande Sophocleo carmen bacchamur hiatu
> montibus ignotum Rutulis caeloque Latino?
> Nos utinam vani . . .

The interpreters take this to be a proclamation about style.[6] But this is
surely not right. It is about the credibility of the subject-matter. Juvenal
says (to paraphrase): 'I suppose you think I'm making this up? I suppose
you think this is the stuff of Greek tragedy, not satire? I suppose you
think I'm overstepping the limits of the genre and giving you a grand
Sophoclean performance, unknown in Italy? I only wish you were right . . .'
The crucial word is the ironical *scilicet*, which qualifies the whole sentence,
and is immediately countered by *nos utinam vani* 'I only wish my words
had no substance'. The implication, then, to spell it out phrase by phrase,
is that Juvenal is *not* making it up; this is *not* the stuff of Greek tragedy;
he is *not* overstepping the limits of the genre; he is *not* giving a grand
Sophoclean performance unknown in Italy; he is *not* 'vanus', but is telling
the plain truth. To take these words as asserting that Juvenal *is* overstep-

---

[4] The others are 1.85–6 and 1.170–1. The former, the famous passage containing the word
farrago, I have myself discussed (Powell (1987)) and hope to have shown that it is not as
directly programmatic as it is usually supposed to be. The latter is Juvenal's claim to attack
the dead: *experiar quid concedatur in illos quorum Flaminia tegitur cinis atque Latina.*
Contrary to the usual belief, this claim, genuine enough in itself (especially if taken with
reference to the dead Domitian in satire 4), is neither exclusive nor exhaustive. There is in
fact some evidence for living victims, or at any rate the evidence is not all unambiguously
for dead ones; see Highet (1954: 291–2), Ferguson (1987). The dogma that Juvenal flogs only
dead horses, like some other dogmas attacked in this paper, has had an adverse effect on
criticism and appreciation of the satires, and it is refreshing to realize that, in its extreme
form, it is not justified by the evidence.

[5] The capital *S* is deliberate; it is a personification.

[6] Scott (1927: 6); Bramble (1974: 165; 1982: 598); cf. also Anderson (1962: 152), Rudd
(1986: 107–9), Morford (1972). Smith (1989: 811–23) rightly sees the problem with these
interpretations. If he had been more radical in refuting them, this part of my paper would
have been rendered unnecessary.

ping the limits of the genre and *is* adopting a tragic style, is clean contrary to the rhetoric of the passage.

A similar rhetorical move occurs in Satire 4 when Juvenal calls upon the Muse to narrate the story of Domitian's council: *non est cantandum, res vera agitur.* 'No need to sing: this is what happened in real life.' The proclamation, if proclamation it is, is that this will be the plain truth told in plain unadorned narrative. Now, of course, this disclaimer is immediately followed by a Tale of a Turbot which obviously *isn't* true, or at least is not the plain unvarnished truth, and is told (at least initially) in what the densest reader could see to be a sustained parody of epic style. That is a comic incongruity, and something of the same sort is also going on in this passage of the sixth satire.

Here, Juvenal's rejection of tragic invention and fable is immediately followed by a direct parody, not actually of tragic style, but of tragic content. Apparently in order to underline the claim that this is the plain truth, Juvenal makes Pontia, who was, it seems, a real murderess[7], not merely confess but shout her confession (6.638): *sed clamat Pontia 'feci, | confiteor, puerisque meis aconita paravi, | quae deprensa patent; facinus tamen ipsa peregi'.* It is not realistic to suppose that murderesses commonly spoke to that effect. Her brazen unrepentance is being exaggerated, but there is more than that. Murderesses *do* sometimes speak to that effect in tragedy; for example, Medea at the climax of Seneca's play of that name, though for all we know Juvenal may have had in mind some even closer parallel in a play now lost to us. The fateful word *feci* is there, twice (990–1); in fact, Medea shows a twinge of remorse, but not so Pontia. Further, at a stage of the action when Medea has disposed of one son but has not yet started on the second, Jason, wishing to be put out of his suspense, says to her *Iam **perage** coeptum **facinus*** (Juvenal: ***facinus*** tamen *ipsa **peregi***). Again: Juvenal[8], incredulous, asks Pontia whether she really poisoned two sons at one meal; to which she is made to reply (6.642): *septem, si septem forte fuissent.* Compare, for the content, Seneca, *Medea* 1010–1, *ut duos perimam, tamen | nimium est dolori numerus angustus meo.* At this point Juvenal gives in and says he will believe the tragedians

---

[7] She is mentioned as such by Martial; references in Courtney (1980: ad loc.).

[8] I make no apology for using the name 'Juvenal' to refer to the person who speaks in the satires, even when that person happens to be conducting an imaginary dialogue with some other character. It was always the tradition of Roman satire that the satirist represented himself as speaking *in propria persona*, whether in monologue or in dialogue. The modern use of the rather ill-defined literary-critical term 'persona' carries a danger of obscuring this fact (cf. Braund (1996: 2)). It can, doubtless, be useful for pointing out the distinction between the writer's literary self-portrayal and his ordinary 'off-stage' personality; of course, in Juvenal's case we know virtually nothing about the latter.

after all. One would have thought that the humour of this imaginary interchange was hardly mistakeable, black though it is; and the *fingimus haec?* lines are there to heighten it, just as *res vera agitur* heightens the humour of the tall story in Satire 4.

From the stylistic point of view, indeed, there is a considerable contrast between Juvenal's Pontia and her counterpart in genuine tragedy. Seneca's Medea speaks with interlaced hyperbaton; Pontia speaks ordinary Latin. Her words, despite the possible verbal reminiscence of Seneca (containing only the merest hint of tragic diction), are not above the stylistic level of everyday prose. But they are reminiscent of Medea in tone and subject-matter, and in terms of content Pontia makes the kind of speech that could be made only in tragedy, not in real life. The incongruity between the content (high tragic horror) and the style (everyday and nonchalant) is part of the satirical effect. Juvenal has told us that we are not in the world of tragedy, and that things like this now happen in ordinary life. He has reinforced the idea by a deliberate use of ordinary, uncoloured language. Anything further from a wholesale adoption of tragic style would be difficult to imagine. Yet people still talk of Juvenal overstepping the limits of the genre.

The advocates of altitude also base part of their case on the imagery used by Juvenal in Satire 1 to describe his writing, which, as John Bramble rightly pointed out, is of a kind often used by serious poets to describe their own poetry. At the beginning Juvenal refers to Lucilius, the founder of the genre, using a chariot-driving image (1.19): *cur tamen hoc potius libeat decurrere campo | per quem magnus equos Auruncae flexit alumnus* ... In summing up at the end of the satire, he states that in the present age vice has reached its highest point, and apparently addresses himself (1.149) in the words *utere velis, totos pande sinus.* And in the concluding dialogue with the cautious interlocutor, satire is envisaged as a battle (not unnaturally, since it involves attacking people). Lucilius, as if with drawn sword, roars in the heat of his anger (1.165): *ense velut stricto quotiens Lucilius ardens | infremuit*; and Juvenal is to consider well before he goes into the fray (1.168): *tecum prius ergo voluta | haec animo ante tubas: galeatum sero duelli | paenitet.* Chariots, sails, battles: not only are these images common in poetry (and high oratory), but the language here is also poetic: *equos flexit,* the paraphrase *magnus Auruncae alumnus, ense stricto,* even the archaic *duelli.* The trouble is that the stylistic register of this language is altogether above the normal level in Juvenal's satires. *Ensis* and *duellum* are nowhere else used by him. If these images are really meant to raise expectations about the kind of style that we are in future to expect from Juvenal, those expectations are doomed to disappointment. The truth is, rather, that this particular context of talking about his own work has inspired Juvenal to parody the style in which serious poets generally talk about *their* own work. If this is the case, it should not necessarily be taken to have any wider implications. The content of the passages is programmatic, but there is no prima-facie reason to suppose that their style also is.

Furthermore, since in the first and third passages the grandiose language is linked in each case with the mention of Lucilius, one may possibly suspect some particular influence from that quarter. It has been held that Juvenal in the first satire misrepresented Lucilius and made him out to be much more like Juvenal himself than he actually was (Bramble (1974), developing a suggestion of Anderson (1961)). I do not think we have sufficient evidence on which to convict Juvenal of this. What we do know is that there was plenty of epic parody in Lucilius, and Professor Petersmann has reminded us that epic and tragic parody was a vital ingredient in Latin satire from the earliest times. There was, at any rate, nothing particularly original in Juvenal's pervasive use of this technique. Juvenal is often said to have deviated from the gentler and more urbane standard set by Horace, but it could just as well be argued that Horace was the deviant, and that Juvenal's style was a true reversion to the Lucilian model; or, alternatively, that both Juvenal and Horace were equally like Lucilius, but imitated different aspects of his writing. Such judgements on literary history should be made, if at all, only with great caution, given that we do not possess all the relevant texts.

This leaves the second passage, a mere five words: *utere velis, totos pande sinus*. A grand image, certainly, but surely a hackneyed one in the literary circles of the time, as we may see, for example, from comparison with a Pliny letter often quoted in this context (8.4.5 *immitte rudentes, pande vela, ac si quando alias, toto ingenio vehere*), noting in particular Pliny's self-conscious parenthesis '*cur enim non ego quoque poetice cum poeta?*', which immediately follows, but tends to be left out by commentators on Juvenal who quote the passage. Given that even Pliny could not use this well-worn image without a certain irony, it stretches the imagination to believe that Juvenal's use of the same image, in a satirical context, is not also ironical. The satirist's hoisting of sails is at most a facetious mimicry of the orator's or poet's. Kenney (1962: 33) says of this passage: '... these phrases are rhetorical claptrap, and are obviously meant to be read as such' (cf. Smith (1989: 814 and note 6)).

In sum, Juvenal has not told us in advance what style we are to expect from him; and the only way to find out more about Juvenal's style is to look and see. But what, in this context, is 'style'? This question may seem Socratic, but it is, I think, capable of a more analytical answer than has sometimes been provided. I apologize in advance for the rather general and theoretical nature of what follows next, but I think it is necessary in the interests of clarity. Inevitably, also, I shall be going over points already made by other contributors to this volume.

There are at least five different things that can be referred to by the word 'style' (this analysis is not, of course, meant to be exhaustive). First, there is the bread and butter of rhetoric: tricks of sentence construction such as tricolon, anaphora, asyndeton and the rest; figures of speech or thought such as similes and metaphors; and forms of argument such as *exempla, praeteritio* or *anticipatio.* The occurrence of these in Juvenal has been usefully documented, principally in the dissertation of De Decker (1913) entitled *Juvenalis Declamans,* in Courtney's introduction (Courtney (1980)) and in Braund (1996: 19–21 and 27–9). De Decker's treatment, still often cited, needs to be used with caution. He does not distinguish sufficiently between generalized rhetorical features and specifically declamatory ones, i.e. those that belong to the specialized environment of the rhetorical schools.[9] These schools, it should be noticed, are treated by Juvenal with profound disrespect, and the tendency to see them as the key to his work (apart from their general educational influence on first-century Roman culture) seems to me to be yet another scholarly illusion. De Decker is also prone to criticize Juvenal for tasteless hyperbole, in passages where one would have thought the exaggeration was clearly made deliberately for satirical effect (see e.g. his discussions of 10.190ff., 15.51ff.).

It is a mistake to suppose that rhetorical vehemence and the use of rhetorical figures in itself constitutes the grand style. At the very least, grand rhetorical style should be distinguished from grand poetic style. The former is natural in prose; the idea that it can be transferred unchanged into verse is not without its problems. The attempt to manipulate anaphora, asyndeton, accumulation and the rest in verse can sometimes result in a clearly prosaic effect. Simple examples of this may be found on occasions when Juvenal's sentences (deliberately for comic effect) outrun the metre, as in 2.145ff. *et Capitolinis generosior et Marcellis | et Catuli Paulique minoribus et Fabiis et | omnibus ad podium spectantibus, his licet ipsum | admoveas cuius tunc munere retia misit.* Rhetorical figures may be found in conjunction with features of vocabulary or content that would naturally

[9] Nor is it always clear, in these discussions, whether we are to think merely of habits of speech and thought which Juvenal caught from his rhetorical training and put to good use in satire (habits whose presence nobody doubts), or of a more systematic and conscious use of rhetorical modes. Braund (1996: 19) certainly implies the latter: 'Satire 6, for example, gains from being read as a *progymnasma*'. 'Gains' in what way? What marks would this essentially irreverent composition have got from a real rhetorical teacher? At the most — to risk labouring the point once more — it might gain from being read as a *parody* of the sort of things that were said in such exercises.

be associated with low style, as for example in the *accumulatio* of 3.31–3
quis facile est aedem conducere flumina portus, | *siccandam eluviem, por-*
tandum ad busta càdaver, | *et praebere caput domina venale sub hasta.*
Processing sewage and carrying corpses are not dignified activities, and
the latter is described in the brutally concrete terms *portandum cadaver*
rather than e.g. *ducendum funus.* One should allow above all for an element
of self-mockery in Juvenal's rhetoric.

In the second category of style I would include together what may be
called texture (simplicity and complexity, and so forth) and tempo (rapidity
or retardation of argument or narrative) and any other features that have
to do with the broader structure of a piece of writing. Thirdly, there is
what we more specifically mean when we talk of the style of a particular
author; the peculiarities in vocabulary or phrasing favoured or avoided by
an individual, the sort of thing that makes attributions possible on the
basis of stylometric analysis; what we might call the author's thumbprint.
These two features have no necessary correlation with the categories of
'high' or 'low'.

Fourthly, there is the question of what may be called tone: the way an
author treats his envisaged audience. In this context we may talk of a
serious or flippant style, a moralizing or didactic style, or whatever. The
attempt to judge the tone (or, in this sense, the style) of a piece of writing
is very closely related to the attempt to judge the intention behind it. For
that reason it is often very difficult, at least where other evidence for the
intention is lacking (and, as some of our friends in the profession never
tire of pointing out, this is quite frequently the case). It is possible entirely
to mistake the tone of a piece of writing. A competent author should be
able to avoid this kind of problem in the short term, but no author,
however careful, can ensure that the tone of his work will not be misjudged
at some time or other in the next couple of millennia. Comic and satirical
writers are particularly prone to misunderstanding of this sort, since they
often presuppose a large shared background in their readership and the
ability to pick up signals of considerable subtlety. A modern example that
occurs to me often in this context is Chekhov, who I believe is generally
regarded in Russia as a great comic writer, although his humour does not
come over at all well in English translation. Of course, in the case of
Juvenal, there are no native readers left to ask, so we have to argue from
our own experience and try to back up our view with evidence; but there
must once have been a right answer to the question, and there may yet
be one more plausible than its rivals.

Fifthly, and here we come to my central point, there is what is sometimes by traditional critics called diction or stylistic level, and by linguists,
register.

Stylistic register has two characteristics that mark it off from some of the other features normally thought to belong to style. To speak in broad general terms, it is public, not individual; it belongs to the linguistic code shared by the community, and there are fairly circumscribed limits to the extent to which any individual writer or speaker can interfere with it. I illustrated this with a class of students by giving them the following four English sentences: (1) Orestes killed his mother; (2) Orestes committed matricide; (3) Orestes slew her that bore him; (4) Orestes did in his mum. There was absolutely no disagreement as to how those four sentences should be described in terms of their stylistic register. While the set of registers available in a given linguistic community at a particular time may be different from what is available in another, nevertheless some kind of public definition of registers is possible, even across cultural boundaries, and even though the actual manipulation of register within a speech-community is in most cases largely unconscious.

The second characteristic, doubtless a corollary of the first, is that the register of words can to some extent be measured objectively by looking at the kinds of texts in which they occur. Some of the difficulties inherent in this procedure have been pointed out by Professor Robert Coleman. To his remarks I shall add merely that negative tests are a good deal easier to apply than positive ones. Comparative statistics are often difficult to evaluate, but if a word is entirely absent from a particular author or genre, it is easier to draw conclusions.

The fundamental work on register in Latin poetry is, of course, B. Axelson's *Unpoetische Wörter* (1945). This deals with only one part of the subject, albeit perhaps the most important part: that concerned with vocabulary. However, syntax, word order and sentence construction are also relevant. In English, for example, the phrase *twiched his mantle blue* contains both a poetic item of vocabulary (mantle) and a poetic feature of word order (postposition of adjective). Anyone going into Marks and Spencer's and asking for a 'coat blue' would be looked at in a strange way.[10] In Latin, the most obvious feature of poetic register as regards word order is persistent hyperbaton of noun and adjective (see Pearce (1966), who however does not deal with post-Augustan poetry). One of the things I would like to see done by way of research in this field is to determine a hierarchy of register for different types of hyperbaton. It might seem, for example, that an emphatic adjective separated from its noun by a main

---

[10] But not e.g. in the army, where, in official references to clothing or equipment, the logical principle that *genus* comes before *differentia* overrides natural English word order, giving rise to items such as 'socks thick woollen'. On poetic word orders, cf. also J. H. W. Penney's chapter in this volume, pp. 263–8.

verb, as in *bonos habemus consules*, is quite ordinary and prosaic, while the interlaced hyperbaton of *saevae memorem Iunonis ob iram* is distinctively poetic (in classical Latin: medieval prose writers imitate it indiscriminately); but for cases between these extremes, things are not so clear.

A full study of Juvenal's use of hyperbaton remains to be done.[11] But I note that in the first fifty lines of Satire 1 he has 26 hyperbata, as against 20 in the first fifty lines of the *Aeneid* (in the latter I have not counted three of the trivial type adjective+preposition+noun, as in *una cum gente*), and 17 in the first fifty lines of the first book of Horace's satires. This might make him seem more 'poetic' than Virgil; but Juvenal pales beside Statius, who has about 36 in the first fifty lines of the *Thebaid* (all these figures are approximate and rely on certain arbitrary assumptions about what constitutes a hyperbaton). Again it must be stressed: the true point of comparison for Juvenal's 'epic' style is the epic that was being written in his own lifetime. As for complex hyperbata, Virgil has only *saevae memorem Iunonis ob iram* in the fifty-line passage, while Juvenal has 1.20 *magnus equos Auruncae flexit alumnus*, 32 *causidici nova cum veniat lectica Mathonis*, and 38 *optima summi | nunc via processus*. We should probably not count 8 *Aeoliis vicinum rupibus antrum* and 13 *assiduo ruptae lectore columnae* in quite the same category, since these can be divided clearly into a noun, *antrum* or *columnae*, qualified by an adjectival phrase *Aeoliis vicinum rupibus* or *assiduo ruptae lectore*, whereas a true interlaced hyperbaton cannot be divided into smaller sense-units. Even without these, however, Juvenal clearly outdoes Virgil. But so does the pedestrian Horace, who has S.1.1.28 *gravem duro terram qui vertit aratro*, 29–30 *nautaeque per omne | audaces mare qui currunt*, and (perhaps) 45 *milia frumenti tua triverit area centum*. A larger sample might reveal a clearer pattern, but this modest excursion is enough to show the potential difficulties of such an approach.

Any language is bound to contain a large number of words and constructions that are virtually neutral as regards register. This applies to *Orestes killed his mother* as opposed to the other three ways of saying this. The use of such words is not, in itself, a clear indicator of stylistic level. One can draw significant conclusions only if such words are largely avoided (e.g. in favour of poetic, official or slang equivalents), or if a text is entirely composed of them. Further, register is not the same as literary or generic convention. In a literary culture there may be special conventions about what one can and cannot say in particular sorts of literature. For example,

---

[11] Braund (1996: 27) lists examples of a special case of hyperbaton, the so-called 'golden line'.

problems were apparently experienced in translating *Othello* into French in the eighteenth century, because the conventions of the time did not allow the mention of a *handkerchief* in formal dramatic style. Commentators sometimes seem to think that when Juvenal mentions hoes and mattocks and the like (3.309–11, 11.89, 15.165ff.) he is evoking the poetic world of the *Georgics*: in fact he is pulling us down to earth much more sharply than we might at first suppose. These words (*ligo, marra, sarculum*) are treated with circumspection in dignified writing; Virgil avoids them, even in the *Georgics*, and allows only the evidently more decorous *rastrum*, while Tacitus' periphrasis for them at *Annals* 1.65 is notorious (though Goodyear (1972: 343) rightly points out the occurrence of *ligones* without apology in *Annals* 3.27; the stylistic nuance in any given passage is a matter for delicate judgement). For us, maybe, mattocks and scythes are poetic in themselves because they conjure up an age romantically simpler than our own: this fact is irrelevant and should be dismissed from the mind. If the occurrence of these plebeian words were not enough, it could also be noted that 3.310 contains a highly unepic line ending *ut timeas ne*; 15.165, on the other hand, juxtaposes the hoes with high epic parody, *ast, ferrum letale, incude nefanda*.

Axelson was not primarily interested in Juvenal, and often inexplicably leaves out our author when he gives statistics for all the others in his list. However, he provides some details which are significant. He notes, for example, Juvenal's free use of diminutives, certainly a prosaic feature, and, following Friedländer, he observes Juvenal's use of prosaic turns of phrase such as *quod cum ita sit* (found also in elegy, but not, of course, in epic). Regarding single items of vocabulary, Axelson notes for example *iumentum, vas* (*vasis*), *vehemens*, used by Juvenal and to some extent elsewhere in the 'lower' verse genres, but entirely absent from high poetry. The general picture, which would doubtless be confirmed by further research, is clear: Juvenal belongs firmly on the lower slopes of Helicon, along with the *Satires* and *Epistles* of Horace and with elegy, and does not share the fastidiousness of the epic poets when it comes to avoiding prosaic words.

Indeed, it appears to me that much of Juvenal's vocabulary, and more of his sentence-construction than is often supposed, is simply neutral for register, and that this makes the moments of epic parody all the more effective by contrast. It is difficult to illustrate stylistic neutrality by example. On this central issue I wish I could refer to a paper of which a summary appeared in *REL* 42 (1964) 57–9, but which does not seem ever to have been published *in extenso*. The author, P. Schmid, referred to Juvenal's 'sévérité du style et langue moderne' and observed that he 'se tient également à distance du purisme livresque et du maniérisme littéraire', referring on the one hand to his occasional use of everyday or colloquial words (common of course to all the satirists) and on the other to the contrast between Juvenal and his contemporary Tacitus. This is surely right and refreshing.

Juvenal does also use distinctively poetic words, although on the whole sparingly; I have already noticed that *ensis* and *duellum* occur only once each, in a special kind of context, and it would be an insensitive reader who did not see mockery in Juvenal's use of the archaic form *induperator* at 4.29. But more generally, an author as fond of irony and parody as Juvenal raises a particular problem for such lexicographical studies. One may be able, without too much trouble, to recognize the stylistic register of a particular word or construction used by him. But the tone in which he uses it may still escape one. How is one to detect irony or parody when it is there, or to be sure that one is not also detecting it when it is not there? One relatively recent study of Juvenal (Romano (1979)) vouchsafes the statistic that of 171 lines in the first satire, 109 have ironical content. I do not aim to quantify as precisely as this, but rather to establish rational grounds on which one can argue for the presence of irony.

Theoretically, there may not be any difference, on the surface and on paper, between a sentence meant 'straight' and one meant ironically. But on the other hand, there may be. One of Juvenal's commonest tricks is to introduce a mismatch of register, either between one word and another in the same passage, or between sentence structure or verse structure and vocabulary, or an incongruity between the content and the level of language used to express it. The commentators have noticed plenty of individual instances of this type of thing, but it seems to me that it is an even more pervasive feature of Juvenal's style than most people have realized, and that a full recognition of it would simply preclude an over-serious interpretation of his writing.

For example, Courtney (1980: 45) refers to the juxtaposition in 4.28–9 of the 'grand' *induperator* with the low words *gluttio* and *ructo*, but comments on this merely as an illustration of the 'wide range' of Juvenal's diction. This comment, with all respect, is beside the point. *Induperator* is not merely grand but, in this context, absurdly archaic: too archaic for Virgil, let alone the Silver poets. The absurdity is increased all the more by the guzzling and belching. Scott (1927) draws attention to a number of such cases, particularly 3.118, the periphrastic reference to Pegasus as *Gorgoneus . . . caballus* (he is *Gorgoneus equus* in Ovid and Statius), while Schmid (1964) notices 5.23 *serraca Bootae*. Similarly, Wiesen (1989) draws attention to 15.66: 'one word, the homely *coxam*, is the key to the irony'. To multiply examples would be tedious, but a cumulative picture begins to emerge. The point is that incongruities of this sort are incompatible with the grand style in any simple sense of that phrase. The whole point of the grand style is that it has to be sustained. The slightest bathos or incongruity, even if unintentional, will ruin it. Where incongruity is deliberately sought, as it clearly is by Juvenal (unless he did these things in his sleep), it is surely no longer appropriate to talk of grand style.

Some passages, indeed, appear to shift about so quickly from the everyday world to the world of epic and back again that the unwary reader might get an impression of a chaotic mixture of stylistic levels, over which the author may seem to have lost control. In these cases too, however, it would be more charitable to assume that Juvenal is being deliberately facetious. Take for example, almost at random, a passage like 3.257–67, the description of the man killed in the street by the collapse of a cartload of marble:[12]

> nam si procubuit qui saxa Ligustica portat
> axis, et eversum fudit super agmina montem,
> quid superest de corporibus? quis membra, quis ossa
> invenit? obtritum vulgi perit omne cadaver
> more animae. domus interea secura patellas
> iam lavat et bucca foculum excitat et sonat unctis
> striglibus et pleno componit lintea guto;
> haec inter pueros varie properantur; at ille
> iam sedet in ripa taetrumque novicius horret
> porthmea, nec sperat caenosi gurgitis alnum
> infelix, nec habet quem porrigat ore trientem.

In line 257 nothing is poetic except the postponement of *axis* until after the relative clause, but the following phrase *eversum fudit super agmina montem* produces an epic effect, not because the words in themselves are particularly poetic but because of the metaphorical hyperbole: the load of marble has become an upturned mountain (Harrison (1960: 99–101) observes that translators persistently miss this) and the crowds in the streets have become marching columns. Then some rhetorical questions, agitated in manner, but simple and prosaic in style: what is left of the bodies? Who can find limbs or bones? The next sentence, however, brings us into the world of Lucan and Statius. The rhythm of line 260 recalls Lucan 4.787 *compressum turba stetit omne cadaver*, while the content goes one better than Statius *Theb.* 6.884–5 (quoted by Braund (1996: ad loc.)), *penitus fractum obtritumque cadaver | indignantem animam propriis non reddidit astris*. In Statius the soul of the miner as well as his body is trapped

---

[12] Braund (1989*a*: 35) also discusses this passage — a fact which I had forgotten until she kindly pointed it out, at a late stage in the preparation of this paper for publication — and makes a number of the same points, but there is enough difference between her discussion and mine to justify letting the latter stand.

under the rock. This makes fairly dangerous play with the high Platonic doctrine of the soul's return to the stars, and may be thought already to hover on the edge of the grotesque; but Juvenal, assuming the common-sense view of the complete disappearance of the soul, implies that no trace remains even of the body. It is difficult not to assume that this is deliber-ately ludicrous.

Meanwhile, at home the servants, all unknowing, are getting ready for the victims of the accident to return. Of course epic also has its domestic scenes, but the point here is the vocabulary, which is strikingly homely and unpoetic: *patellas* (diminutive), *bucca* (not *ore*!), *foculum* (diminutive), *striglibus* (note the colloquial syncopated form), *lintea*, *guto*. Such everyday words often survived in Romance: *patella* = *poêle*, *bucca* = *bouche*. *Strigles*, so spelt, and *gutus* occur together in a graffito from Herculaneum (see Della Corte (1958: 271, no. 388, with facsimile in Tav. 3, facing pp. 264–5)). It is uncharitable to Juvenal to suppose that his *striglibus* is no more than a distortion for the sake of the metre, as apparently does Braund (1996: 219): it is a genuine colloquial form.[13] Doubtless without it he could not have mentioned strigils at all, but in that case he would not have mentioned them. This passage, then, is full of prosaic, colloquial language; yet the use of *domus* as the collective designation of the house's inhabitants is on a higher level; and the homely oilflask is drawn into a poetic hyperbaton, *pleno . . . guto*. The next line, *haec inter pueros varie properantur*, is impec-cably dignified, and the poetic, perhaps specifically Virgilian twist in *at ille*, with the sudden shift of scene to the banks of the Styx, has been well noticed by the critics (Jenkyns (1982: 191)). One is prepared for some real pathos in the description of the unburied ghost, but the expectation is defeated to some extent by the utterly prosaic word *novicius* ('tiro', or even 'greenhorn'). And does any serious Latin poet use *triens*?

The discussion by Scott just mentioned contains, in addition to many correctly identified examples of epic parody, a section entitled 'serious imitations of epic'. The latter section is, indeed, much shorter than the former, but I think I should spend a little time on it. I must confess that I find it a little difficult to see why some of the passages included in it are classified as 'serious', since Scott herself seems to admit that there is a

---

[13] As a syncopation of the correct form *strigilibus*, it would be highly irregular. The syllable that has been lost is actually the accented syllable, while syncope regularly affects only unaccented syllables. If syncopation of (short) accented syllables were generally permissible in verse, poets would have had no difficulty in accommodating e.g. *facilius* or *pepulerat* to dactylic verse by turning them into **faclius* or **peplerat*; but they do no such thing. The only plausible explanation of *striglibus* is that it is remodelled on the stem of the regularly syncopated *striglem* (etc.). There are parallels for this process in sub-standard Latin, e.g. the form *virdia* for *viridia*, attested in an Egyptian ostracon (Cavenaile (1958: no. 304)).

nuance of parody about them. But in others too it seems to me that there is often an incongruity of the type I have mentioned, of a type to disqualify the passage from being a genuinely serious poetic imitation. For example, Scott quotes in this category the list of deities and divine attributes in 13.78–83, by which the perjurer is alleged to swear:

> per Solis radios Tarpeiaque fulmina iurat
> et Martis frameam et Cirrhaei spicula vatis,
> per calamos venatricis pharetramque puellae,
> perque tuum, pater Aegaei Neptune, tridentem,
> addit et Herculeos arcus hastamque Minervae,
> quidquid habent telorum armamentaria caeli.

But even if one passes over the possible disrespect to Mars involved in investing him with a Germanic barbarian's spear (*framea*: perhaps 'assegai' would be a rough near-modern equivalent) and to Diana in calling her *venatrix **puella*** (cf. 4.36 *prosit mihi vos dixisse puellas*), the whole dignified effect is destroyed by the bathos of the final line *quidquid habent telorum armamentaria caeli*. Of course, if we translate this as 'celestial armoury' or something equally poetic, we miss the point entirely. This is, I think, the only occurrence of *armamentarium* in classical Latin verse of any sort. We would be nearer the stylistic mark if we talked of celestial ironmongery. Many passages in Juvenal are like this: for several lines he appears to be talking in a serious poetic vein, leading us up the garden path, only to end in an abruptly deflationary punch-line (cf. Martyn (1979) for a collection of such passages; cf. also the surprise effects listed by Braund (1996: 26 and 27)). To stop quoting before you get to that point is a sure way to encourage radical misunderstanding.

In some instances the similarity to serious poetry is merely in subject matter, not in style (3.309–11 cf. Virg. *Georg.* 1.505–8; 15.127, on Egypt, cf. *Georg.* 4.287–9; 10.265 cf. *Aen.* 3.1; 267 cf. *Aen.* 2.509–10; 328–9 cf. *Aen.* 5.5–6; etc.); such instances are clearly no help for our present purpose. Sometimes any serious effect is ruined (deliberately, of course) by a ridiculous and whimsical twist given to a familiar *topos*: for example, Scott quotes in her 'serious' category 12.57–9 *i nunc et ventis animam committe, dolato | confisus ligno, digitis a morte remotus | quattuor aut septem, si sit latissima, taedae*; but what genuine poet talking about the dangers of seamanship would speculate about whether you were four or seven inches removed from death? 13.100 is quoted as being similar to *Iliad* 4.160: the gods' anger is slow but sure. In the right context such a sentiment could be taken quite seriously, but this is not the right context. Juvenal's line is actually a reversal of the Homeric sentiment, expressed in an extremely prosaic style for good measure (the locution *ut sit . . . tamen certe* would

hardly be suitable in epic): 'well, suppose the gods' anger *is* great, you
have to admit it's slow'; and let us not leave out the next two lines either:
'so if they really take the trouble to punish all wrongdoers, they'll surely
take a long time to get round to me'. That such a passage should be
included in a catalogue of 'serious imitations of epic' is all but incredible.

I think I could do much the same as this for all the items in Scott's
list, but I shall not labour the point. All I shall say is that if anyone can
find a sustained, serious imitation of epic anywhere in Juvenal, without
some incongruity or bathos or parody, I shall be very interested to hear
of it.

After all this, some may be tempted to ask me whether I think Juvenal
is ever serious at all. To this I reply that I think there are some passages
in which he approaches a sort of seriousness, and that they are almost all
of one kind: more or less nostalgic expressions of an ideal of moral virtue
and simplicity, sometimes in generalized quasi-philosophical terms, as in
10.356ff., but more usually associated with the distant past or the remoter
parts of the Italian countryside, as in parts of Satire 3; other such passages
are 8.98, 11.77–98, 12.83ff. Even in these passages, however, there is often
some incongruity or mockery which may be taken to undermine any
serious message.[14] It may easily be supposed that the sacred sausages at
the end of the tenth satire cast their frivolous shadow over the moralistic
message, and that the reference to *captatio* in 12.95 has a similar effect.
Further, it should be noticed that Juvenal, in the earlier satires at least,
rarely gives vent to such sentiments in his own person; indeed, one of the
most effective passages of this sort is put in the mouth of the pervert
Naevolus at the end of Satire 9, a consideration which must have, if
anything, an even more unsettling effect on the reader than the revelation
in Horace's second *Epode* that the praise of country life was spoken by a
speculator on the Roman stock exchange. In any case, the style of these
passages is (I submit) never high or grand in any normally accepted sense;
they tend rather to be marked by a clear abandonment of the style of epic
or rhetorical parody, doubtless accompanied in recitation by a straight-
ening of the features and a quietening of the voice. The occasions on
which Juvenal leads us to think that he is letting down the satirical mask
to reveal a plain honest Roman or homespun philosopher underneath do,
indeed, add greatly to the effect. Without them, the otherwise continually
mocking and denunciatory tone might seem forced; but these passages

---

[14] Cf. Wiesen (1989: 710): 'The past is almost never represented by Juvenal in other than
ironic and ridiculing terms.' Yet at the same time, the past and the countryside in Juvenal
function largely as rhetorical foils to the present and the city, and the denunciation of the
latter depends on the idealization of the former. This would not be so effective if the treatment
of the past were to be seen as entirely ironic.

throw the rest into relief. They are the times at which Juvenal comes closest to his predecessor Horace, and retreats furthest of all from anything resembling the grand style. Critics tend to talk of loftiness and sublimity in these contexts; but if there is sublimity, it is the special kind that comes from simplicity, the kind that Longinus found in Sappho and the Book of Genesis. It has nothing at all to do with the *genus grande dicendi*.

To conclude. A satirical writer can suffer no worse fate at the hands of posterity than to be taken too seriously. Persius has suffered in this way: his Stoic moralising has been exaggerated out of proportion and his subtly whimsical, ironical tone often entirely missed; he has been quite unjustly branded as obscure and humourless, and consequently remains largely unread, except by a few specialists. Juvenal is read, indeed, and often with enjoyment. But he has been regarded as something of a problem case; few Latin authors can have been more systematically damned with faint praise or praised more for the wrong reasons.[15] I am fairly sure that failure to understand the subtleties of his manipulation of the stylistic registers of Latin has been one of the major obstacles to his appreciation. At the end of his much-cited, not so much bewildering as bewildered essay entitled 'Is Juvenal a Classic?', H. A. Mason (1963) pointed the way to the next step after clearing away the misleading views of Juvenal as a moralist or social historian, which was, according to him, 'to appreciate Juvenal as a supreme manipulator of the Latin language'. Exactly so; and I am only too conscious that I have been able to do little more in this paper than put forward a manifesto. In order to work out in full the practical implications of what I have said, having first divested oneself of prejudices about the grand style and related matters, one would need to subject the text as a whole to a detailed line-by-line scrutiny, with close attention to context, and without forgetting the larger-scale effects achieved by manipulation of register, tone and tempo over whole sentences and paragraphs. Many of the stylistic effects could be brought out most clearly by a simple translation, if the translation could only be got right; 'ironmongery' for *armamentaria*, for instance, would speak for itself.

It is possible that those of a modernistic turn of mind will tell me that my way of attempting to understand Juvenal, with reference to known or ascertainable facts about the language he used, is no more than one 'reading' out of many and that I have no right to present it as though I believed it to be in any sense correct or demonstrable. For the present

---

[15] Over the last few years there have been some voices raised in protest against literal and humourless views of Juvenal: see Marache (1964), de St-Denis (1965: 224–36), Martyn (1979), Wiesen (1989). I commend these articles to the attention of anyone still unconvinced by my arguments.

I leave aside the complex and obscure philosophical issues that lie behind this often rather muddled kind of thinking. I reply merely by means of a parallel, which I know to be imperfect, because modern satirical journalism is not as concentrated a literary brew as Roman satire. Nevertheless, let us suppose that in the fortieth century AD, if there are still literate human beings alive at that time, someone gets hold of a copy of *Private Eye* and categorises it as a serious treatise on morals and politics or as an exercise in the mechanical deployment of rhetorical figures on set themes. That person may get great pleasure and even academic credit from doing so, but he or she will be wrong.

After the delivery of a version of the above paper at the British Academy Symposium, I had many very positive reactions from members of the audience. Some simply expressed agreement. A few, however, felt that despite everything I had said, it was still true (and less misleading than the contrary) to say that Juvenal used the grand style. I think that the difference between us is partly a matter of definition, and partly a matter of literary judgement and taste.

First, as regards the definition, it could be urged against me that I have defined the grand style in such a way as to exclude Juvenal from it, and that therefore my argument is ultimately circular. I would claim that I have simply tried to define what I think the grand style is, partly on the basis of the ancient concept of the *genus grande dicendi* and partly on the basis of observable differences of stylistic register among Latin authors. I believe that this category, in rough terms, is one which Juvenal himself would have recognized, and one into which the objects of much of Juvenal's literary parody clearly fall. Juvenal very often imitates the grand style by way of parody, ridicule and deflation; this is universally agreed; but as I said above, I cannot find any passage in which he appears to me to be using it 'straight'.

Regarding the question of taste, the case for grandeur may perhaps be put like this. In the first place, Juvenal parodies the grand style (whether epic, tragic or rhetorical) so much and so consistently that the parody in itself develops a sort of grandeur. In the second place, there is a grandeur in the scale, structure and overall rhetorical conception of the satires, for which the word 'panoramic' is not inappropriate; this, of course, reaches its highest point in the sixth satire.

This latter point has a great deal in it, but it has little to do with style in the sense we have been talking about. On the former point, I repeat that Juvenal's parody of the high style most often works by contrast and incongruity, and that even a relatively long passage of epic style, sustained over a dozen lines or so, can be punctured by a single prosaic or colloquial word at the end. It is very easy to miss these effects, and if one does miss them, one has no reason not to believe that Juvenal's style is often simply that of epic. Many of us first met Juvenal at an early stage of our Latin studies, when we had not yet been trained to respond accurately to differences of stylistic register in Latin, and it is not easy to displace the impressions received at that stage. Perhaps, too, we are influenced by the views of earlier ages. The eighteenth century saw Juvenal as grand and dignified and translated him accordingly. Dr Johnson did not have the opportunity to benefit from Axelson's researches. I do of course admit that Juvenal has a certain dignity of style. He does not use obscenities in the way that, say, Martial does; though Juvenal's references to obscene doings in decorous language (conveniently listed by Braund (1996: 26)) are often much more striking than Martial's cheap vulgarisms. But decorum is one thing, and grandeur is another. The former can exist without the latter.

Last of all, a few words are called for in connection with the reassertion of Juvenal's grandeur by his latest editor. Braund (1996: 17) states: 'Juvenal writes in "the grand style". His adoption of the grand style — which is continually punctured or debased — seems to be an innovation within the genre . . .'. But as I have argued, if it is continually punctured or debased it is not the grand style in any simple sense, since the effect of the genuine grand style depends precisely on not being punctured. It is interesting to look at Braund's list of examples of the grand style (p. 26). Out of the first five satires (nearly a thousand lines), twenty-nine passages are listed. Braund suggests that the list is not exhaustive, but it would not be easy to find many more. Of these, fourteen are accounted for by the explicit epic parody of Satire 4, and a further four by the programmatic passages of Satire 1 discussed above. This leaves eleven. Four of these are single words: 1.100 *Troiugenas* and 2.154 *Scipiadae* (both in very clearly parodic contexts), and the word *proceres* in two passages (2.121, 3.213) apart from two instances of the same word in Satire 4, already counted. This is Juvenal's standard term for lords or nobles. In fact, if one looks at the usage of *proceres* in general, it does not seem by any means to be confined to high poetry; it is doubtless a dignified word, but it is not uncommon in prose, and it has the advantage that (unlike *nobiles* or *principes* or *optimates* — though *primores* would have done well enough) its nominative plural will fit into dactylic verse. Then, in 5.49, there is a double -*que* (the lightest of epic touches, in the context of a rich patron's indigestion). 1.52–3 is included in the list, though I do not see why, since it seems merely to contain allusions to epic titles and subject matter rather than any particular hint of epic style. 1.81–4 burlesques the Deucalion and Pyrrha myth. 1.88–9 is a description of gambling in what are claimed to be epic terms; the style is more rhetorical than poetic, though perhaps slightly like Lucan. 5.78–9 is a clearly parodic description of a *salutator* drenched with rain on a wet spring morning, and finally we have 5.93 and 5.100, slightly poetic-sounding local descriptions of the provenance of mullets and lampreys. I think I can safely rest my case.

Proceedings of the British Academy, **93**, 335–375

The Arrangement and the Language of Catullus' so-called *polymetra* with Special Reference to the Sequence 10–11–12

H. D. JOCELYN

Summary. It is contended that the order of the first 61 of the items transmitted under the name of 'Catullus Veronensis' shows signs of a conscious design, whether by the author or by some editor, that item 61 should be placed with its predecessors rather than with the seven 'long' poems which follow, that the widely used term 'polymetrum' is a thoroughly confusing misnomer, that metrical pattern requires the division of the 61 items into three distinct groups — ἐπιγράμματα in 'Phalaecian' verse, ἴαμβοι, and μέλη — and, most importantly, that even where they take up apparently similar themes the μέλη distinguish themselves in verbal style markedly from the 'Phalaecian' ἐπιγράμματα and only a little less markedly from the ἴαμβοι. In order to illustrate this last point the lyric item 11 is compared in systematic detail with the two 'Phalaecian' epigrams which precede and follow it in the transmitted collection. Discussion of each feature of items 10, 11 and 12 centres on its relationship with what third- and second-century BC poets might have written and with what first-century speakers of Latin might have said. The character of our record of the Latin of the two centuries following 240 BC makes a degree of tentativeness inevitable.

The three groups of the 61 items in question take us to a linguistic world distant from that of items 62–68. This is not, however, the world of the Latin used in ordinary conversation by members of the Italian élite in the middle of the first century

BC. It is a highly artificial world with its own quite distinct
internal boundaries.

I. THE THREE METRICAL TYPES PRESENT IN ITEMS 1–61 OF
THE *LIBER CATULLI VERONENSIS*

THE LANGUAGE OF the first sixty items of the collection transmitted through
the Middle Ages as the *liber Catulli Veronensis* has often been treated as
a unity to be contrasted with the language of all the others, or with that
of the next eight, or with that of the final sixty. The purpose of this paper
is to deplore such treatments and to suggest that at least two distinct kinds
of language, if not three, were perceptible to a first-century BC reader or
hearer of the sixty items in question.

The term 'polymetra' has been used of them since the last decade of
the nineteenth century[1] and enjoys at present almost universal acceptance.[2]
It has a learned ring about it but is in reality a nonsense. If the sixty be
treated as a group, the group could be described as 'polymetrical', but no
individual item could be called a πολύμετρον/*polymetrum* in any known
ancient sense.[3] The term is worse than a nonsense, in so far as it encourages
the neglect of significant differences between the items. The application
of other apparently ancient terms, like *nugae*, to the sixty is equally perni-
cious in its effect. So too the use of terms like 'lyrics', which wander
between an ancient and a modern sense.[4]

Items 11, 17, 30, 34, 51 group themselves together metrically against 4,
8, 22, 25, 29, 31, 37, 39, 44, 52, 59, 60 and, in my opinion, against those in
sets of the so-called 'Phalaecian' verse. Item 61 ought not to be separated
from 11, 17, 30, 34, 51 and put with the hexameters of 62 and 64, the
galliambics of 63 and the elegiac distichs of 65, 66, 67, 68 simply on
the grounds that it is a 'long poem'. Such a distinction would have made
no sense at all to men of the first century BC. There were many μέλη as

[1] Cf. Reitzenstein (1893: 103 n. 1).
[2] Cf. Svennung (1945: 21), Tränkle (1967a: 206), Ross (1969: 1), the heading of the second
chapter of Wiseman (1969: 7–16), the heading of chapter 2.4 of Lyne (1980: 42–52), Syndikus
(1984: 69), E.A. Schmidt (1985: 29), the heading of the fifth chapter of Newman (1990:
138–203), Gaisser (1993: 4). Some, e.g. Goold (1983), avoid the term but not its influence.
[3] For the term see Dionys. Hal. *Comp.* 26, Athenaeus 13.608e. The Latin record has only the
unexplained title *Polymetra* attributed to Laevius in Priscian, *Gramm.* II 258.12.
[4] Catullus uses *nugae* in a tone of mock modesty at 1.4. Schuster (1948: 2365–6), Ronconi
(1939: 18 = 1953: 26 = 1971: 28; 1940a: 8 = 1953: 114 = 1971: 94; 1940b: 142–4 = 1953: 194–7 =
1971: 174–7) and Heusch (1954: 14–20) may serve to illustrate the modern philological use
of the word. Goold (1974) and (1983) resurrects nineteenth-century talk of 'lyrics'.

long as, or longer than, this one among those attributed to the canonical exponents of the genre.

Item 51 adapted the substance of a famous μέλος by Sappho and employed the same metrical pattern. This is also the pattern of 11. The pattern of 34 was one we know to have been used by Anacreon, and there is no reason to suppose that the closely related pattern of 61 did not occur in some μέλος now lost. About the patterns of 17[5] and 30[6] we need be only slightly less certain.

Items 4, 29, 52 deployed a pattern used by Archilochus for iambic poetry; 8, 22, 31, 37, 39, 44, 59, 60 one used by Hipponax for poems thought to belong to the same genre; 25 had likewise a pattern closely associated with Hipponax.[7] It is certainly legitimate to wonder about the differences which the ancients perceived between these three patterns, as about those between the five patterns of lyric verse. For the purpose, however, of the present enquiry I leave such problems aside.

A form of the 'Phalaecian' verse (xx-⌣⌣-⌣-⌣--) had been an element of certain lyric stanzas composed by Sappho, but continuous runs of the verse were perhaps first composed by the fourth-century poet who gave the verse his name.[8] Some ancient metricians analysed the hendecasyllabic verse in the same ways as they analysed the so-called 'Sapphic', 'Glyconic' and 'Pherecratean' verses used in the stanzas of items 11, 17, 30, 34, 51, 61.[9] Their particular ways of analysis are no longer fashionable, but the new ways[10] still lead scholars quite willing to keep 4, 8, 22, 25, 29, 31, 37, 39, 44, 52, 59, 60 metrically apart from 11, 17, 30, 34, 51, 61, to refuse to separate off the pieces in stichically arranged 'Phalaecian' verses. Martial included imitations of these in books of so-called *epigrammata*. Since, however, the ἐπιγράμματα in elegiac distichs which form the third part of the *liber Catulli Veronensis* have their own peculiar stylistic features, I shall call the pieces in 'Phalaecian' hendecasyllables Phalaecian epigrams.

---

[5] Hephaestion, pp. 33–4 Consbruch, cites three successive 'Priapeans' by Anacreon. Horace does not use the system in his *carmina*, but neither does he that of 34 nor that of 61.

[6] What Hephaestion says about Sappho's third book and the 'Sapphic' 16-syllable verse (pp. 34, 63) is not entirely clear. Horace has three *carmina* of the shape of 30 (1.11, 18; 4.10).

[7] On the 'Hipponactean' tetrameter see Hephaestion, p. 16, Schol. Aristoph. *Pl.* 253.

[8] See *A.P.* 13.6. Cf. 5.309 (Diophanes), 6.193 (Statyllius Flaccus), 7.390 (Antipater of Thessalonice), 9.110 (Alpheius), 598 (Theocritus).

[9] For 'antispasts' see Hephaestion, p. 33; for derivation from other lengths see Caesius Bassus, *GLK* VI 258–63, 'Apthonius', *GLK* VI 118, 148, Diomedes, *GLK* I 509, Terentianus Maurus, *GLK* VI 401 (vv. 2539–68).

[10] Hermann (1816: 369; cf. 1796: 214–17, 288–9) analysed the verse as consisting of a 'basis' plus a 'logaoedic' sequence of a dactyl and three trochees. So too, effectively, Christ (1879: 537–9). Wilamowitz (1921: 105, 137–53, 251) came to regard it as a 'Glyconic' verse extended by ⌣ - -; cf. Münscher (1921: 73–7), Vollmer (1923: 15), Schuster (1948: 2395–6), Mette (1956: 35–6), West (1982: 151, 198).

Catullus himself could talk of *hendecasyllabi*, but this chapter is not meant to be a poem.

The question of how Catullus and his ancient audiences heard a poem consisting of 'Phalaecian' verses as compared with, say, item 11 or item 34 has, I think, to be kept separate from the one of how a lyric poet of old Greece related a 'Phalaecian' verse to the other units with which he or she constructed a particular stanza. We know that in Greek-speaking communities from at least the fourth century BC on a sequence of 'Phalae-cian' verses seemed to have so little of a musical character as to be capable of use for a public inscription[11] and that there were theorists in Catullus' day who analysed the verse as if it were more closely related to the catalectic ionic trimeter (or 'Galliambic') — the verse of item 63 — than to the 'Sapphic', the 'Glyconic' or the 'Pherecratean'.[12] Theorists of the first century AD thought that Catullus himself accepted such an analysis,[13] and there were even those who blamed him for failing on occasion to keep the first two elements of the verse long and for thus 'roughening' or 'hardening' the ionic rhythm.[14] It is remarkable in fact how many pieces do keep the elements in question long and how relatively rare the alleged licence is in the pieces which permit it.[15] Items 34 and 61 on the other hand positively prefer 'Glyconic' and 'Pherecratean' verses beginning with a trochee and even admit the iambus.[16] The running together of adjacent words is avoided rather less in items 1, 2, 2b, 3, 5, 6, 7, 9, 10, 12, 13, 14, 14b, 15, 16, 21, 23, 24, 26, 27, 28, 32, 33, 35, 36, 38, 40, 41, 42, 43, 45, 46, 47, 48, 49, 50, 53, 54, 55, 56, 57, 58, 58b than it is in the indisputable μέλη.[17] Words of more than three syllables, which seemed to Roman connoisseurs of rhythm to have a 'soft' character,[18] terminate with great frequency the

---

[11] See the poems cited in n. 8 together with two actually preserved on stone, *SEG* 39 (1989), 1334 (between 230 and 220 BC (drawn to my attention by M. D. Reeve)), and no. 1978.17–22 (third or second century BC) in W. Peek's *Griechische Vers-Inschriften*.

[12] See Varro *ap.* Caes. Bass. *GLK* VI 261.18–19.

[13] See Quint. *Inst.* 1.8.6. Cf. 9.4.6 on the effeminate ethos of 'Sotadeans', 'Galliambics' and certain oratorical rhythms.

[14] See Plin. *Nat.* praef. 1, Plin. *Epist.* 1.16.5.

[15] Item 1 has five verses out of 10 with the licence; 3 one out of 18; 7 two out of 12; 10 one out of 34; 27 three out of 7; 32 five out of 11; 35 six out of 18; 36 five out of 20; 38 four out of eight; 40 four out of eight; 41 five out of eight; 42 eleven out of 24; 45 eight out of 26; 47 one out of seven; 49 four out of seven; 50 one out of 21; 53 one out of five; 54 two out of seven; 58 one out of 5. Of the 70 cases *in toto* 39 have an iamb, 31 a trochee.

[16] I count 24 cases of the spondee, 225 of the trochee, two of the iamb. 61.99 would have a pyrrhic if *probra* were syllabified in the normal Latin way.

[17] Neither group shows quite so strongly the aversion manifest in item 64 and the elegies (65–8) against the elision of a long final vowel before an initial short.

[18] See Quint. *Inst.* 9.4.63–6.

verses of these pieces.[19] It is relatively seldom on the other hand that such words terminate lyric systems.[20] The two short syllables which usually come fourth and fifth in the 'Phalaecian' verse are replaced with one long syllable in thirteen of the 22 verses of item 55 and in two of the ten of item 58b. They are rarely divided between words,[21] whereas the pair of short syllables in the allegedly related 'Sapphics', 'Adonians', 'Priapeans', 'Asclepiadeans', 'Glyconics' and 'Pherecrateans' suffers no such restriction.[22]

The springs of the modern view of the 'lyrical' character of Catullus' 'Phalaecian' verses lie, I suspect, in the efforts of sixteenth-century vernacular poets to exploit the Latin poet's work for their own ends and in the prestige which these poets won among later practitioners and readers. By concentrating on ancient Greek poetry theoreticians of classical metre have unwittingly encouraged the view.[23] Close observation of the first-century BC Latin poet's actual practice seems to me to undermine it totally. Quintilian was well aware of certain thematic relationships between lyric poetry, elegy and Phalaecian epigram. Nevertheless he thought it worth maintaining a formal distinction of the three genres.[24]

When consideration of the layout of the *liber Catulli Veronensis* began in the middle of the last century it was quickly observed that the group of eight relatively long items was flanked by groups of shorter items of more or less equal size.[25] Emil Baehrens thought he could detect a verbal style shared by the middle items, one quite different from the style common to the opening sixty.[26] Robinson Ellis wrote with less clarity but in English rather than in Latin and with much greater long-term influence. Statements like 'the diction of Catullus ... seems indeed, if we confine ourselves to the lyrics [Ellis appears to include item 61 with 1–60], to be an exact

---

[19] Cutt (1936: 7–14) counts 138 such polysyllables in 502 verses. There are on the other hand only three genuinely monosyllabic terminations (5.5, 7.7, 24.7; those at 10.31, 13.1, 50.20 and 55.13 are parts of word-groups).

[20] I note 17.3 *rediuiuis*, 6 *suscipiantur*, 30.1 *sodalibus*, 2 *amiculi*, 61.5 *Hymenaee* (also as part of the same ritual cry at vv. 40, 50, 60, 118, 138, 143, 148, 153, 158, 163, 168, 173, 178, 183), 30 *Aganippe*, 86 *uenientem*, 193 *remorare*, 208 *ingenerari*, 223 *Penelopeo*.

[21] Cf. Meyer (1889: 208–27 (215)), Cutt (1936: 15–27). It is only in the antepenultimate element of the 'Galliambic' that a pyrrhic sequence is divided between words, and then not often.

[22] I count 45 cases in 552 verses, i.e. one in thirteen. Where the $\mu\acute{\epsilon}\lambda\eta$ are concerned the ratio varies between one in three and one in five.

[23] Wilamowitz changed his mind about the character of the old Greek 'Phalaecian' between 1898 and 1921. He stressed the gulf between the way Catullus thought of the verse and the way Sappho and others did.

[24] *Inst.* 1.8.6.

[25] See particularly Brunér (1863: 601–11), Westphal (1867: 1–24).

[26] (1885: 40–9). Contrast the dissertation of Hupe (1871), who treats the language of all the transmitted items as a unity.

illustration of Wordsworth's paradox, that the language of poetry does not essentially differ from the language of prose. There is an utter absence in it of anything strained, far-fetched, or artificial: the thought clothes itself without effort in the required words, and is passionate, jocose, or homely, as it were spontaneously'[27] had a particular appeal to the British.

Much ink has flowed in efforts to establish a conscious design in the order of items 1–60. The relationship between the themes still dominates the discussion.[28] It has, however, been usefully observed that the ἴαμβοι in the metres of Archilochus and Hipponax distribute themselves at fairly regular intervals: 41 verses (four poems) precede item 4; 42 (three poems) item 8; 198 (eleven poems) item 22; 37 (two poems) item 25; 27 (three poems) item 29; 12 (one poem) item 31; 81 (five poems) item 37; 8 (one poem) item 39; 48 (four poems) item 44; 94 (seven poems) item 52; 66 (seven poems) items 59 and 60.[29] I should like to go on from my demonstration that Catullus distinguished his μέλη metrically from poems in 'Phalaecian' verses to point out that the μέλη distribute themselves in an even more regular manner among the other items: 174 verses (eleven poems) before item 11; 90 (six poems) before item 17; 135 (nine poems) before item 30; 33 (three poems) before item 34; 234 (sixteen poems) before item 51; 80 (ten poems) before 61. The themes of the Phalaecian epigrams have more in common overall with those of the ἴαμβοι than they do with those of the μέλη.

A problem which haunts all theories alleging a deliberate arrangement in an ancient book of poems is that of how an ancient reader would have recognized the arrangement alleged. Proponents of a thematic arrangement of items 1 — 60 or 1 — 61 of the *liber Catulli Veronensis* may answer as they please. A formal arrangement would, however, without doubt have been more easily recognizable. Some ancient editions of lyric poems alerted the user to changes of metre by means of the asterisk.[30] There is no evidence for the existence of an ancient ancestor of the text of the *liber Catulli Veronensis* equipped with a set of critical signs, but the possibility cannot be ruled out. At all events the first-century reader of a group of poems like those in question would have been expected to understand

---

[27] (1876: xxii = 1889: xxix). Cf. Simpson (1879: 180) 'the simplicity and naturalness of his language, ... in great contrast to the later artificial Latin style ... His words seem to have fallen of themselves into metre without leaving their natural order and would make good prose — if they were not poetry. His language, in the epigrams, lyrics, and elegies is little removed from ordinary speech ...' (enthusiastically endorsed by Goold (1983: 7)).

[28] The bracing scepticism of B. Schmidt (1914) still has its value.

[29] See Heck (1950: 33–7, 61–5), Mette (1956: 35–6), Weinreich (1959: 84–90; 1960: 163–70).

[30] See Hephaestion, p. 74 (on the use of the asterisk in the Alexandrian editions of Sappho, Anacreon and Alcaeus).

something of metrical structures. His sense of the natural rhythms of his own language and his experience of listening to priests intoning prayers at public rituals and to orators speaking in the law-courts and at popular assemblies, to say nothing of actors performing comedy and tragedy at the great yearly festivals, would have taught him things now hard to recover. It may be noted that the recurrent metrical unit of five of the μέλη (11, 17, 34, 51, 61) ends like the dactylic hexameter introduced into Latin by Ennius for epic narrative, i.e. in the sequence – ˇ ˇ – –. This sequence orators avoided at rhythmically prominent points in their discourse.[31] The sixth μέλος (30) consists of units ending in – ˇ ˇ – ˇ –, a sequence which orators admitted, although not all that often.[32] Eight of the ἴαμβοι (8, 22, 31, 37, 39, 44, 59, 60) end their verses on the other hand in – ˇ – – –, the most popular clausular sequence in oratory, and three (4, 29, 52) in – ˇ – ˇ –, a sequence tolerated by the orators. The twelfth ἴαμβος (25) and the Phalaecian pieces end their verses in – ˇ – ˇ – –, the so-called 'ithyphallic'. This sequence formed the second colon of the 'Saturnian' verse in which Naevius' still often read account of the first Carthaginian War was set.[33] Orators avoided it even more carefully than they avoided – ˇ ˇ – –.[34] Catullus' affectation of polysyllabic final words both in the Phalaecian pieces and in item 25 would have been in part to escape the taint of the rude structure of the 'Saturnian', the second colon of which usually had a break of words after the second or third element.

Those who posit a deliberate thematic arrangement of the poems in question seem all to make Catullus himself responsible. Critics have found it easy to uncover a degree of incoherence hard to credit in an author with a conscious plan. Against the two formal distributions for which I am arguing it will doubtless be objected that they are insufficiently symmetrical to be thought more than an accident. If, however, a design is present, a scholarly editor aware of the generic distinctions of verse writing would seem at least as likely as the poet to be responsible.

II. THE THREE POETIC USES OF LATIN IN ITEMS 1–61

If the rhythms of the μέλη take them away from oratory, other aspects of their verbal style are likely to have brought them into the vicinity. The

---

[31] And particularly in the form – ˇ | – – – and – ˇ ˇ | – –; see Shipley (1911: 410–18).

[32] See Fraenkel (1968: 196–7).

[33] See Cic. *Brut.* 75–6, Hor. *Epist.* 2.1.53–4.

[34] Cicero's hendecasyllable at *Verr.* 2.3.43 — *successit tibi Lucius Metellus* — long brought ridicule upon him (see Mart. Cap. 5.517 *incurrit etiam in hendecasyllabi phalaecii petulantiam*).

singer and the orator could not avoid a certain formality in addressing their respective publics. What Cicero has to say at *Orat.* 183–4 about the music-accompanied verse of the lyric poets and the spoken *senarii* of the comedians is instructive not only about the character of comic verse but also about the distance which men of Catullus' time perceived between ordinary conversation (*sermo*) and a style of utterance (*oratio*) employed by both the orator and the lyric poet.[35]

An examination which I have made of items 11, 17, 30, 34, 51 and 61 seems to show a set of stylemes which, in conjunction with their metrical patterns, mark them off as a group from both the ἴαμβοι and the Phalaecian epigrams. I have also examined the eleven Phalaecian epigrams (items 10, 12, 16, 21, 28, 32, 33, 35, 49, 50, 53) and the three ἴαμβοι (29, 31, 52) which flank the μέλη in the transmitted collection. In practically every member of the three groups I find words and phrases requiring a pronunciation different from that of everyday, morphemes obsolescent except in certain special registers of the language, like the religious or the legal, or preserved only in the epic and tragic poetry of the third and second centuries, syntagms which had become rare in the everyday language or which were consciously modelled on features of Greek poetic syntax, orderings of clauses, phrases and words unimaginable in first-century BC speech, words and uses of words taken from the higher genres of the poetry of the third and second centuries or newly created within the modules offered by the older poets. A number of these phenomena mass strikingly and significantly in the μέλη. The ἴαμβοι carry more than do the Phalaecian epigrams. Nevertheless it must not be forgotten how few of the last-mentioned class are entirely without one or more of them. The often praised 'naturalness' of the 'diction' of items 1–60, 'the utter absence in it of anything strained, far-fetched, or artificial' is a myth, even if the field of 'diction' is limited, as it often is, to the lexicon.

The distinctive features which have emerged from my examination of the six μέλη concern the lexicon rather more than phonology, morphology or syntax. Nevertheless it seems worthwhile to report at some length the less distinctive features, if only to indicate problems. Sentence structure and the order in which words are placed within the sentence constituents show themselves to be almost as important as the lexicon. The nine Phalaecian epigrams and the three ἴαμβοι prove more remarkable for what they admit than for what they avoid. The variety of their stylemes reflects the variety of their themes.

The choice of words and phrases and their ordering must be, of course, to some extent a function of the different sets of metrical rules applied in

---

[35] Cf. Dionys. Hal. *De im.* 2.2, p. 20 Usener, Quint. *Inst.* 10.1.63 (on the lyric poet Alcaeus).

the three classes. But to some extent only. Theme and mood were important determinants of this choice as they were of that of the particular form of verse. A poet of Catullus' talent was never simply in the position of having to choose between one word and another in a particular part of a verse with the other words of his planned statement already fixed in their eventual pattern. It would thus be unhelpful to point out in connection with the use of *ocelle* at 31.2, for example, that the rules followed by Catullus in composing choliambic verses precluded *ocule* at the beginning and, indeed, everywhere else.

The selection of Catullus' pieces traditionally presented to school children in the company of Cicero's orations, Virgil's *Aeneid*, Horace's *Odes* and Livy's history leaves a superficial impression of straightforwardness, easiness and 'naturalness' which even the well-read find hard to shake off. Nevertheless the positive phenomena which occupy my attention have for the most part been often observed. All I have done is to marshal them in a way which illustrates my general thesis. It has, on the other hand, been less often observed how far the μέλη avoided those words, idioms and syntactical constructions of ordinary discourse which appeared to lack the dignity appropriate to a more formal mode of utterance and how much more receptive the ἴαμβοι and the Phalaecian epigrams were in this regard. I should not, however, wish to talk of 'unpoetic' words or the like. The difficulties inherent in such language have encouraged the idle to neglect the excellent observations made by Bertil Axelson[36] and to leave untrodden the paths he opened up. It was not only the poets who were choosy about what could be used of ordinary Latin speech. Orators too pursued a policy of selectivity.[37] As did those who endeavoured to write on technical themes. A doctor could not describe in a book the sexual parts in the way most of his patients did.[38] It was especially, it seems to me, in the avoidance of certain features of the ordinary language that Catullus differentiated his μέλη from their companions.

Several scholars convinced of the stylistic unity of items 1–60 have presented accounts, occasionally in statistical terms, of the phenomena which appear to them to mark these items off as a group from 61–116,

---

[36] (1945). The criticisms made by Ernout (1947: 55–70) cut deeper than those made by Williams (1968: 743–50). Bömer (1957), Müller (1975: 293–4) and Watson (1985) obtain useful results from the method.

[37] Theophrastus coupled poetry and oratory as preferring dignified words to the commonplace (Ammon. *Aristot. interpr.* Comm. Aristot. Graeca IV 5, pp. 65–6 Busse). For the orator and selectivity see Anon. rhet. *Herenn.* 4.17, Cic. *De orat.* 3.149–70, *Orat.* 79–80; for the poet Hor. *Ars* 46–59, *Epist.* 2.2.109–25.

[38] See Jocelyn (1986: 312–16).

from 61–68, or from 69–116.[39] In seeking to mark off items 11, 17, 30, 34, 51 from those which intervene I should not want to follow an exactly similar method. General statistics about any group of poems give little help in seizing the character of a particular member of the group. They can also be gravely misleading where poems of the kind here in question are concerned. Catullus made use of an unusually wide range of linguistic possibilities and often sought to an unusual degree after novelty of expression. Two features of the Phalaecian epigrams reduce, if they do not completely nullify, the value of statistics in discussing them. The first — shared with the classicizing ἴαμβοι — is a tendency to cast references to heroic saga, ancient history, non-Roman religious cult and exotic geography in language akin to that of the μέλη, language which makes them stand out from the body of the poem in which they are made. The second is a manner of ornamenting the distinctive rhythm of the second half of the verse with a variety of equally distinctive phonetic, morphological and lexical stylemes, some of which also occur in the μέλη and help to give these items their special character.[40]

Nothing separates the language common to the μέλη and the Phalaecian epigrams from what we can imagine to have been ordinary mid-first-century BC upper-class urban Latin to the extent that the language of a late fifth-century tragedy differed from that of Athens' leading citizens. No Catullan μέλος differs from a piece in 'Phalaecian' verses to the extent that the songs of a tragic chorus differed from the actors' speeches and dialogues. One may say, if one likes, that Rome never had a special poetic language with generic subdivisions of the kind Greece had. If, however, account is taken of the way in which certain subsidiary themes of the Phalaecian epigrams attracted both linguistic archaism and linguistic novelty and of some of the ways in which Catullus ornamented the concluding ithyphallic rhythm of the verse, the statistical preponderance of archaizing and neological phenomena in the μέλη takes on a considerable significance. Some of the difficulties of global statistics nevertheless remain. Furthermore, it is not so much in the choice of particular words as in the ways in which they are employed and ordered that the special character of each μέλος manifests itself. Where the choice of words and their ordering are concerned, what the composer of a μέλος has avoided often seems more significant than what he has decided to do. Here the isolation of

---

[39] See Baehrens (1885: 45–9), Schulze (1920: 47–72), Svennung (1945: 19–34, 47–50), Schuster (1948: 2383–92), Ross (1969: *passim*), Évrard-Gillis (1976: *passim*). Contrast B. Schmidt (1887: LXXX–LXXXVII). An observation by La Penna (1956a: 293) indicates how awkward items 34, 51 and 76 are for the conventional division.
[40] See Jocelyn (1995: 63–82).

countable phenomena becomes difficult and the value of any summation questionable.

There is only space in this volume to set out the results of my linguistic comparison of the μέλος item 11 with the Phalaecian epigrams which flank it. The results for the other sequences[41] point, however, it can be said, in the same direction.

III. THE LYRIC ITEM 11 AND ITS 'PHALAECIAN' COMPANIONS

Whether, as the metrical structure might suggest, item 11 had some well-known particular Greek μέλος as its model we cannot tell. Certainly, ancient readers would have assigned it to the genre of lyric poetry. Martial wrote no epigram in 'Sapphic' stanzas. The poem refers to a situation of the poet's life dateable to late 55 BC or soon afterwards,[42] a situation which, according to himself, he took very seriously. About the status of Furius and Aurelius, the poet's attitude to them, and the tone of his address there has been much unfruitful dispute.[43] Many suppose that Catullus has been in Rome for sometime pursuing an affair with the unnamed woman. It could be, however, that he is about to return. An acquaintance of long standing would expect to receive a message,[44] although not one of the sort that Catullus actually sends. Roman gentlemen in any case regularly terminated relationships of some length and depth in a formal way.[45] It would not have been unseemly or buffoonish to ask two friends[46] to take a message to the woman, however lightly or seriously he had regarded the relationship with her.[47] The faithlessness she had displayed certainly affected Catullus more than the embarrassing request of Varus' friend reported in item 10 or the theft by Asinius complained of in item 12. We should also note how much of item 11 relates to future possibilities as well

[41] I plan to publish accounts of these results elsewhere.

[42] All the great foreign adventures of 55 seem to be alluded to, from Gabinius' activities in Egypt to Crassus' expedition against the Parthians.

[43] Ronconi (1940*b*: 142–4 = 1953: 194–7 = 1971: 174–7 and Traina (1975: 254–6) find, as did Haupt (1841: 24 = 1875: 97), an element of parody in vv. 1–14; Évrard-Gillis (1976: 189–90) does not.

[44] Cf. Cic. *Att.* 4.10.2, Catull. 9.5.

[45] Cf. Tac. *Ann.* 2.70.2, Suet. *Cal.* 3.3, Gaius, *Inst.* 3.151.

[46] Even although slaves or freedmen normally carried such messages (cf. Ter. *Hec.* 314, Cic. *Att.* 10.4.7; 16.5, *Rep.* 1.18, *Ac.* 1.1). In so far as they 'accompany' Catullus on a journey Furius and Aurelius must be of slightly lower status (cf. Hor. *Serm.* 1.6.101–3, *Epist.* 1.7.75–6). Curtius Nicias was a man lower in status than either C. Memmius or Pompey's wife (Suet. *Gramm.* 14.1).

[47] Mayer (1983: 297–8) makes too much of the analogy of the form of Roman divorce procedure alluded to at Cic. *De orat.* 1.183.

as how surrealistically the woman's present activity is described. The other lyric items are likewise all — even item 51 — angled more to the future than to the past.

a. 11.17–20 and 58.4–5

It is the fifth stanza which has caused even those scholars who would allow a special status to items 34 and 51 to set item 11 in both substance and style with the ἴαμβοι and the Phalaecian epigrams.[48] Some philologists have talked of 'obscenity',[49] and some translators have ransacked the lowest registers of English in search of imagined equivalents.[50] Many have noted a similarity between the stanza and the final two 'Phalaecian' verses of item 58. A close comparison reveals on the other hand considerable and highly significant differences. It should be helpful to elucidate these differences before placing item 11 as a whole against its immediate neighbours.

Whether item 58 has Lesbia merely masturbating the descendants of Remus[51] or copulating fully with them,[52] we have to do with an activity of the real world pursued in degrading circumstances (in quadriuiis et angiportis) and represented by a crudely vivid agricultural image (glubit).[53] The noun quadriuium is absent from the rest of the record of Republican and early imperial literature.[54] The metrical shape of angiportum would have excluded it from epic but not from tragedy; nevertheless the tragedians seem to have avoided it.[55] The verb glubere and its compounds never appear in epic or tragic poetry, or even in oratory. The locution was a sordid one, whether Catullus took it from ordinary discourse or invented it himself. What is said in item 58 and how it is said fit with other passages of 'Phalaecian' verse[56] and with nothing in the μέλη.

---

[48] E.g. Ronconi (1940b: 144 = 1953: 174 = 1971: 176).

[49] Cf. Cairns (1972: 80, 216–17), Lateiner (1977: 26).

[50] Two US professors of literature, Myers and Ormsby (1970), have ' . . . she screws with all and never slows her pace, but busts their balls'. Goold (1983) and Lee (1990) display more sense of anatomy and a better appreciation of the tone of the Latin with ' . . . she holds in her embraces, loving none truly but again and again rupturing the loins of them all' and ' . . . hugging she holds, loving none truly but again and again rupturing all's groins' respectively. See also Wiseman (1979: 11).

[51] Jocelyn (1979: 89–90).

[52] O. Skutsch (1980: 21). Tränkle (1981: 245–8) has argued in favour of the view of Parthenius and others that Catullus refers to Lesbia's monetary exactions.

[53] See Cato, Agr. 33.5, Varro, Rust. 1.48.2. Butchers and tanners took up the verb (see Paul. Fest. p. 87 Lindsay, s.v. gluma, Lyd. Mag. 1.12). The sexual use (cf. Auson 71.1) is less likely to have developed from theirs.

[54] Significantly, its next appearance in the record is at Juv. 1.63–4.

[55] Horace has it once in his μέλη, in a very harshly worded passage (Carm. 1.25.9–10).

[56] E.g. with 6.13–14; 16.1–2; 21.7–8; 12–13; 32.7–8; 41.1–2; 47.3–4.

11.17–20 presents the woman's promiscuity in no realistic way. One female cannot embrace three hundred males simultaneously. Commentators mislead when they cite 9.2, 12.10 and 48.3. Catullus had in fact an epic number in mind, the three hundred Spartans who died at Thermopylae, for example, or the three hundred Fabii who died at the Cremera.[57] The participial phrase *nullum amans uere sed identidem omnium ilia rumpens* contrasts a lack of sexual arousal on the part of the *puella* with the congested state of the organs of the *moechi*. We need only compare passages like Martial 11.81.2 in the first case[58] and Catullus 32.10–11 in the second[59] to realize how reticently Catullus is writing at 11.19–20. The woman's state could have been put in starkly physical terms. It is, however, the psychic aspect which is alluded to by *nullum amans uere*. Likewise *identidem omnium ilia rumpens* diverts attention from the external to the internal organs of her male lovers. The account of the woman's promiscuity fits with that of the cuckolded husband's impotence in item 17, that of the poet's own lust at 51.9–10 and the allusions to past and future sexual activity in item 61 (51–5, 97–148, 164–73, 199–205, 225–8). The verb *rumpere* seems to be at home in all kinds of literature. *ile* is admittedly one of many words relating to the internal or external human anatomy which do not occur in the remains of oratory. It could not, however, be classified as an obscenity. Celsus admitted it freely to his elegant account of the art of medicine.[60] One might even deduce from Virg. *Aen.* 7.499, 9.415, 10.777–8 that with *ilia rumpens* Catullus was adapting some passage of older epic poetry.

The use of the word *moechus* at 11.17 does form a link with the verbal style of the Phalaecian epigrams (cf. 42.3; 11; 12; 19; 20). It and *moecha* are words avoided in epic and tragic poetry, in oratory and in history.[61] No large conclusions need, however, be drawn. The fastidious Horace admits *moechus* to a μέλος (*Carm.* 1.25.9) as does Catullus himself to an

---

[57] On the Spartan three hundred see Hdt. 7.202; on the Fabii Diodor. 11.53.6 (306 according to other accounts). The island of Ilva sent three hundred warriors to join Aeneas' forces (Virg. *Aen.* 10.173–4). Where lyric poetry is concerned, Horace has three hundred oxen sacrificed to Pluto (*Carm.* 2.14.5–7) and three hundred chains loaded on the over-amorous Pirithous (3.4.79–80).

[58] Cf. Ov. *Ars* 2.685–6. For the state of the fully aroused female see Aristoph. *Equ.* 1285, *Pax* 885, Ov. *Her.* 15.134, Mart. 11.16.7–8, Juv. 6.64, 10.321–2. For the desirability of mutual arousal see Plaut. *Pseud.* 1259–61, Catull. 45.19–20, Sulpicia, [Tib.] 3.11.13–16.

[59] Cf. for male tumescence Eurip. *Cycl.* 327–8, Aristoph. *Lys.* 980–1013, Hor. *Serm.* 1.2.116–18, Martial 11.16.5, *Priap.* 23.3–6, 33.5–6.

[60] 2.7.4 *et al.*

[61] Catullus has *adultera* at 61.98. It is odd that, while adultery is a frequent theme of oratory and history, *adulter* occurs frequently in Cicero and Sallust but *adultera* not at all. Livy has neither.

elegy (68.103) and Propertius to a poem of the same genre (4.5.44). *cum suis uiuat ualeatque moechis* quite lacks the crudity of *nunc in quadriuiis et angiportis glubit magnanimi Remi nepotes*. After the words employed hitherto the vulgar borrowing from Greek causes surprise, but it would have very effectively underscored the difference between the poet's feelings towards the woman and those towards Furius and Aurelius without destroying the lyric tone of the whole piece.

b. 11.21–4 and 58.2–3

It would also be worth setting the elaborate simile constructed in the final strophe of item 11 against the comparative statement at 58.2–3. The latter goes in form with several in the Phalaecian epigrams (3.5; 14.1; 23.12–14, 19, 21; 27.3–4; 35.16–17; 38.7–8; 48.5–6) and in the ἴαμβοι (22.14; 25.1–4; 39.16). The μέλη on the other hand have only the two in 17.15–16. The extended simile of 11.21–4 has many companions in the μέλη (17.12–13, 18–19, 20, 25–6; 61.16–20, 21–5, 33–5, 87–9, 102–5, 186–8, 219–23) and four in the ἴαμβοι (8.5; 25.12–13; 29.8; 37.12). In the Phalaecian epigrams on the other hand there can be found only two highly intellectualizing instances, at 2b.1–3, where reference is made to the heroic world, and at 7.3–9, where it is a question of parts of the contemporary world distant from Rome.[62] The tone of the simile of 11.21–4 can also be felt by contrasting a vulgar expression of the same idea: *tam perit quam extrema faba*.[63] The type of simile had its original home in epic narrative[64] and the more expansive kinds of lyric poetry.[65] It was usually the warrior struck by a weapon or missile who fell like part of a growing plant. Here it was the lover deprived of the will to live by the flight of his loved one.[66] One might, if one pleases, detect irony, as in vv. 1–16. But there can be no doubt about the essentially lyric stamp the use of such a simile puts on the item.

Item 11 may now be treated as a whole and the details of the extra-metrical ways in which it differs from the Phalaecian epigrams which flank it in the tradition considered.

---

[62] See Jocelyn (1995: 63–71).

[63] Cited by Fest. p. 496 Lindsay ('in prouerbio est').

[64] Cf. Hom. *Il.* 8.306–8 (Gorgythion dies), 11.67–71 (Trojans and Achaeans are slain), Catull. 64.353–5 (Trojans will be slain), Virg. *Aen.* 9.435–7 (Euryalus dies).

[65] Cf. Stesich. *Suppl. Lyr. Gr.* 15 col. ii 14–17 (Geryon dies).

[66] *meum . . . amorem* in v. 21 must be interpreted as the equivalent of *me . . . amantem*. The loved one was often addressed as *mea uita* (Plaut. *Cas.* 135 *et al.*) and the parted, betrayed or abandoned lover often complained that he no longer wished to live (cf. Plaut. *Merc.* 471–3).

c. Item 11: Phonetic Features

Two kinds of purely phonetic repetition accompany the repeated rhythms
of item 11: alliteration of successive initial phonemes and assonance of
neighbouring syllables. There is only one case of the termination of successive grammatically related words with the same long vowel or
diphthong.

The μέλη tend to favour alliteration (6.1 cases per hundred words in
11; 4.3 per cent in 17; 4.2 per cent in 30; 5.0 per cent in 34; 6.8 per cent
in 61) and to spread the figure evenly. The Phalaecian epigrams have on
the whole much less (1.6 per cent in 10 and 3.4 per cent in 12; 0.0 per cent
in 1, 2b, 3; 2.9 per cent in 5; 3.5 per cent in 6; 0.0 per cent in 9, 13; 4.5 per
cent in 15; 1.2 per cent in 21) and aim the figure at particular targets.
Nevertheless the ratio can drop as low as to 1.4 per cent in a μέλος (51)
and rise as high as to 7.7 per cent in an epigram (2; 5.2 per cent in 7; 4.5
per cent in 15; 6.3 per cent in 16). We cannot therefore make too much
of the 1.6 per cent–6.1 per cent–3.4 per cent sequence in items 10–11–12.

It is difficult to define assonance in a way which facilitates comparative
measurement of its incidence. However the figure is defined or measured,
differences between individual members of a genre seem as great as they
are between the genres themselves. I note therefore only that neither item
10 nor item 12 has much that is comparable with 11.3–4 *longe resonante
Eoa tunditur unda* or 13–14 *omnia haec quaecumque feret uoluntas caelitum*
or 18 *complexa tenet trecentos*.

It has been noticed that where grammatically related words are concerned homoeoteleuton involving a long vowel or diphthong is freely
allowed by Catullus in the Phalaecian epigrams but avoided in the epic
items 62 and 64 and in the elegies 65–69.[67] In the μέλη he seems to me to
have been equally shy, with only one case in item 11 (15), none in item
17, one in item 30 (10), none in items 34 and 51, one in item 61 (100).
Much more significant than the one case in item 11 (15 *meae puellae*) are
the six occasions when hyperbaton prevents it (2, 3–4, 6–7, 10, 17, 21)
and the two when obsolescent conjunctions stand in the way (6, 11–12). I
note by the way that the emotionally charged *meae puellae* occurs four
times in the epigrams (2.1; 3.3, 4, 17 (cf. 36.21)) and that those genres and
authors hostile to homoeoteleuton of noun and attribute are more relaxed
where the latter is a pronominal adjective.

The repetition of whole words and whole phrases has of course a

---

[67] Shackleton Bailey counts 54 cases in the Phalaecian epigrams (1992: 69). On the epic and
elegiac pieces see the same scholar (1994: 7–9, 16–18).

semantic as well as a phonetic aspect. The two genres differ in their own ways both of exploiting and avoiding such repetition.

In item 11 there is a striking case of the figure anaphora (2–12 *siue... siue... seu... siue... siue*). This figure appears as well in all the other μέλη, in some of them a number of times (17.17–18, 21; 30.2–3; 34.13–20; 51.1–2, 13–15; 61.46–9, 51–9, 110–11). Many Phalaecian epigrams do not on the other hand have it at all. Where it does appear in this genre it tends to be of the unremarkable character of *neque... nec* (10.9–10; 21).

Item 11 presents no example of the multiple repetition of a single thematic word like that of *pons* in item 17, of *fides* and related words and of *factum* in 30, of *bonus* in 61, and none of the repetition of a thematic statement like that of *quendam de tuo uolo ponte ire praecipitem* in item 17 (8–9; 23) and none of the incantatory repetitions of item 61 (*o Hymenaee Hymen, o Hymen Hymenaee* at vv. 4–5, 39–40, 49–50, 59–60, 117–18, 137–8, 142–3, 147–8, 152–3, 157–8, 162–3, 167–8, 172–3, 177–8, 181–2; *quis huic deo compararier ausit?* at vv. 64–5, 69–70, 74–5; *uiden ut faces splendidas quatiunt comas* at vv. 77–8, 94–5; *abit dies, prodeas noua nupta* at vv. 90–1, (96), 105–11, 112–13; *concubine nuces da* at vv. 128, 133). Such repetitions as item 10 presents (e.g. 20 *parare*, 30 *parauit*, 32 *pararim*) look on the other hand to be without semantic or rhetorical purpose, the result of an artful artlessness.

In the epic item 64 Catullus followed the model of Ennius' *Annales* in only occasionally putting words together in such a way that the final vowel of one ran into the initial vowel of the next.[68] This inevitably helped to make the sound of a piece of epic poetry very different from that of a story narrated in the ordinary language.[69] Catullus was not as hostile to synaloephe in either item 11 or its two companions (12.4 per cent; 12.6 per cent; 13.9 per cent ≠ 4.4 per cent in 64). Nevertheless, to judge by what went on in comedy, he did not try to ape the freedom of the ordinary language. The amount of synaloephe in the Phalaecian epigrams is not significantly greater than that in the μέλος. On the other hand one notes in item 11 *Furi et* (1) and *prati ultimi* (22–3) and no synaloephe at all of a monosyllable, in item 10 *sane illepidum* (4), *octo homines* (20), *quaeso inquit* (25) and two cases of synaloephe of a monosyllable (7, 28), and in item 12, *belle uteris* (2), *ioco atque* (2), *te inepte* (4), *quare aut* (10) and *exspecta aut* (11).

The paradosis of vv. 11–12 of item 11 — often emended in consequence[70] — requires the assumption of a hiatus difficult to parallel in other

---

[68] See Vollmer (1923: 20–1), Soubiran (1966: 600–3), O. Skutsch (1985: 52–3).
[69] See Cic. *Orat.* 152.
[70] Most recently by McKie (1984: 74–8): *horribiles uitro ultimosque Britannos.*

verse of the time, to say nothing of a very peculiar tricolon: *Caesaris uisens monimenta magni, Gallicum Rhenum, horribilesque ultimosque Britannos.* The hiatus between the directly quoted *mane* of 10.27 and *inquii* (Scaliger: *me inquit*) may on the other hand be justified by supposing a pause in delivery.

The prosody of words in classical Latin verse is remarkable for its regularity. Whether ordinary speech was ever as regular may be doubted. The verse of the third and second centuries shows a large amount of oscillation. Catullus was clearly out to reduce the amount. The metrical pattern of item 11 demanded two fairly clear artificialities. Others may be hidden by our ignorance of the facts of ordinary first-century BC speech.

How far in Catullus' time upper-class urban speakers of Latin always gave full value to a final sibilant is uncertain. Nowhere in the μέλη, the ἴαμβοι or the Phalaecian epigrams does anything like *tu dabi' supplicium* (116.8) appear. For Catullus the poet the sibilant regularly made position (e.g. at 11.7, 10, 22). That does not necessarily mean it did for Catullus the Roman gentleman.

It is very likely that in making *siue* a trochee in vv. 7 and 9 Catullus diverged from the normal pronunciation of his time.[71] About iambic *meae* in v. 15, *suis* in v. 17 and *meum* in v. 21 and cretic *illius* in v. 22 one cannot be sure.[72] The prosodical treatment of the pronominal adjective in comedy and its spelling in private letters of the first and second centuries AD indicate at least an oscillating pronunciation in the ordinary language, while the behaviour of both the old comedians and the first-century BC poets suggests that various measurements were possible of the relatively uncommon and apparently anomalous genitive of the deictic pronoun.

The other lyric items show equally little certain variation from the norm. Iambic *tibi* at 17.5; 51.13; 61.149 and 151 very probably had an

---

[71] A word beginning in a consonant was regularly preceded by monosyllabic *seu* in comedy (at Plaut. *Amph.* 69, 70, 71, as elsewhere) and tragedy. Lucretius has trochaic *siue* ten times (1.861 *et al.*) in his hexameters.

[72] It is unlikely that ordinary speakers were clearer about the prosody of the pronominal adjective than they had been in the previous century or were to be in following centuries (for *ma = mea* see Tab. Vindol. 292b. back 2–3, Pap. Michig. 8.471.34, Adams (1995a: 120)). As for cretic/dactyl *illius*, this form is also found at 3.8, 10.31 (Phalaecian epigrams), at 61.219 (μέλος), 64.348 (epic), 66.85, 68.44 (elegies). The molossic form (see *GLK* IV 233, 234) occurs only at 67.23. Lucretius on the other hand has the molossus 13 times, the cretic/dactyl only four. How much observation of the facts lies in the doctrine of the grammarians (*GLK* IV 233, 234) that the classical writers of prose always used the molossic form is hard to say.

archaic sound.[73] About dactylic *totius* (17.10) and *illius* (61.219) and trochaic *iste* (17.21), *ille* (51.1 and 2), and *ipse* (61.57)[74] uncertainty must prevail.

It may be chance that nowhere in item 11 does Catullus diverge from the practice of contemporary speakers of Latin in syllabifying words and word-groups involving the conjunction of a so-called 'mute' and 'liquid' or any of the collocations [sp], [st], [sk], [fr], [fl]. 17.6 has *sac-ra*, 17.24 *po-te s-to-li-dum*, 34.19 *ag-ri-co-lae*, 61.23 *Ha-mad-ry-a-des*.[75] Less a matter of chance would be the relatively large number of instances of the Graecizing syllabification in the ἴαμβοι (4.6, 7, 9; 22.7, 10, 12; 25.7; 29.4, 22; 31.8; 39.11; 44.18) and the relatively small number in the Phalaecian epigrams (3.11, 13; 28.15; 36.15; 55.2; 58.4), most of which occur in the ithyphallic close.

d. Item 11: Morphology and Syntax

In morphology item 11 could not be said to diverge much from ordinary Latin speech, something which is also true of other lyric items. There is nothing in item 11 or in 17 or in 51 as archaic as the *forent* of 30.8, the *deposiuit* of 34.8, the *sonantum* of 34.12, the *citarier* of 61.42, the *compararier* of 61.65, 75 the *ausit* of 61.65, 75, the *nitier* of 61.68. The Greek termination of *Arabas* (v. 5)[76] has parallels not only elsewhere in lyric poetry (61.30 *Aganippe* and 187 *parthenice*), in epic (64.15 *Nereides*; 35 *Tempe*; 53 *Thesea*; 85 *Minoa*) and in elegy (66.46 *Athon*; 48 *Chalybon*; 67 *Booten*; 68.116 *Hebe*) but also in iambic poetry (4.7 *Cycladas*; 9 *Propontida*; 13 *Amastri*) and even in Phalaecian epigram (36.13 *Ancona*; 14 *Amathunta*; 45.1 *Acmen*; 10 *Acme*; 58b.1–3 *Cretum . . . Ladas . . . Perseus*). The Arabs were known to the Romans at this time perhaps only through Greek literature.

The syntax of item 11 has aspects both of archaism and of modernizing

---

[73] As in the Phalaecian epigrams at 32.6 and 50.16 (≠ 1.3, 8; 13.2; 14.7, 9, 16; 15.1; 23.5, 15, 19; 35.16; 38.6; 40.3; 49.4). The iambic measurement was already relatively uncommon in comedy (c. 8 examples in Plautus' *Pseudolus* against c. 25 of the pyrrhic). Lucretius has it as an iambus 11 times, as a pyrrhic 52 times. Ancient students of prose thought it always had the value of a pyrrhic (*GLK* IV 232).

[74] Catullus has the dactylic form also at 37.9. The only genitive form recorded for comedy is *toti* (fem.) at Afran. 325. Lucretius has the dactylic form 17 times, the molossic 4 times. On *illius* see above, n. 72. The Phalaecian epigrams have trochaic *ille* (6.9; 47.4; 57.8; 58b.1) and *ipse* (55.9). In about 28 instances out of 173 in Plautine comedy *ille* can only be given the value of a long monosyllable. *iste* has been treated similarly at Plaut. *Persa* 520; *ipse* similarly at Plaut. *Asin.* 714, *Bacch.* 1160, *Epid.* 47, Ter. *Hec.* 560. Lucretius has trochaic *ille* and trochaic *ipse* often.

[75] The syllabification of *probra* in 61.99 must remain uncertain. See above, n. 16.

[76] Contrast Plaut. *Curc.* 443. The manuscripts have *Arabas*, however, at Cic. *Fam.* 8.10.2.

artificiality. The local use of the conjunction *ut* (v. 3) recurs at 17.10 and elsewhere in recorded Latin only in translations of Aratus' ἧχι (*Phaen.* 231: Cic. *Arat.* 2, Germ. 233) and in Manilius' *Astronomica* (2.273). The local use of ἵνα in epic and lyric texts would have been Catullus' model. The only clear cases of such Graecism in the other lyric items are 51.5 *dulce ridentem* (≠ Sappho's ἆδυ φωνείσας), 61.7 *suaue olentis*, 61.212 *dulce rideat*. The plural, or perhaps rather collective, use of *unda* (v. 4) was related to uses of the singular form in the ordinary language but had its immediate source in the practice of the old poets.[77] The phenomenon occurs twice in item 17 (13,19) and pullulates in item 61 (3–4, 9–10, 51, 54–5, 56–9, 108, 155, 161, 199, 202–3, 213). It appears three times in the ἴαμβοι (37.20; 39.20; 44.15) and seven times in the Phalaecian epigrams 6.17; 14.22; 23.21; 35.15; 43.2; 56.2; 58b.4). The singular — or perhaps again one should say collective — use of the plural *aequora* (v. 8) likewise came from old poetry.[78] The phenomenon occurs five times in item 61 (14, 28, 103, 110, 224) but not at all in the ἴαμβοι. The only clear case in the Phalaecian epigrams (apart from the affectionate uses of *mei amores* and *meae deliciae*) is at 35.15. The use of an accusative object with the participle in -*nt*- at vv. 10–12 and 19–20 occurs in other lyric items (17.20; 30.7–8; 34.17–18; 61.9–10, 12–13, 17, 26, 33, 54, 80, 99, 154, 211–12). In the previous century it had been largely restricted to the higher genres.[79] Orators contemporary with Catullus used it, but restrainedly. It occurs once in the ἴαμβοι (59.4), ten times in the Phalaecian epigrams (9.6–7, 8; 21.7; 35.3–4, 9–10; 45.1–2, 10; 50.4, 6; 53.4), with what tone it is hard to say. There are no grounds for calling *nec . . . respectet* (v. 21) either archaic or colloquial.

The other obsolescent syntagms detectable in the lyric items are few and open to doubt: the adjectival use of the ethnic noun *Ligus* at 17.9; the jussive use of the second person singular of the subjunctive at 34.21 and 24 and 61.91, 96, 106, 113 (refrain);[80] the use of the perfect subjunctive after *non . . . periculum est ne* at 61.83–6;[81] the use of *in* and the ablative

---

[77] Cf. Enn. *Ann.* 302.

[78] Cf. Enn. *Praet.* 4, *Ann.* 505 (hence Lucret. 1.8, 3.1002).

[79] Plautine comedy has only five instances of the present participle with an accusative complement (*Aul.* 8, *Merc.* 57, *Mil.* 204–5, *Persa* 253, *Rud.* 695; the last two in paratragic address to deities). The remains of Ennius' *Annales* on the other hand have a comparatively large number of instances, as does Catullus' epic item 64.

[80] 8.1 and 32.7 and a number of passages of Cicero's correspondence (*Att.* 1.17.11, 4.19.2, 10.15.4) show that it still had some life in the ordinary language. Oratory avoided it (see, however, Cic. *Verr.* II 3.37).

[81] Contrast Plaut. *Asin.* 388, *Pseud.* 289, Cic. *Sest.* 52, *De orat.* 2.69, *Rep.* 1.37, *Tusc.* 5.118, Pollio *ap.* Cic. *Fam.* 10.31.2. Interpreters and translators refer Catullus' *uiderit* to the past. This makes little sense.

with *deditus* at 61.97–8;[82] the use of the supine with *ire* at 61.146;[83] the use of *ne* with the present imperative at 61.193;[84] the volitive use of the third person perfect subjunctive *iuuerit* at 61.196.[85]

e. Item 11: Sentence-Structure and Word-Order

The considerable length of the two periods which form item 11 (of 66 and 38 words respectively) is to be paralleled at 17.1–7 (49 words), 14–20 (48); 34.5–16 (40); 61.1–15 (51), in the ἴαμβοι at 25.1–8 (49); 44.1–9 (55), and in the Phalaecian epigrams at 2.1–10 (51); 7.3–12 (48); 15.2–10 (49); 24.1–6 (36); 45.1–7 (36). Comparatively speaking the number of such periods in the epigrams is rare. The constituents of the periods never overrun strophe boundaries in this item, item 30, item 34, item 51 or item 61. They rarely overrun in item 17. So called 'enjambement' is on the other hand extremely common in the ἴαμβοι and the Phalaecian epigrams. The periods of item 11 do not have the complexity of high oratory, but they lack the parentheses and the inconcinnity that appear to have marked periods of such length in ordinary speech, except perhaps for the collocation *haec quaecumque* (*haec quacumque* Nisbet) at v. 13. Noteworthy is the nominal phrase *comites Catulli* at 11.1.[86] Likewise the number of extended participial phrases (3 *longe resonante*; 10 *Caesaris uisens monimenta magni*; 14 *temptare simul parati*; 19–20 *nullum amans uere, sed identidem omnium ilia rumpens*).

The order of words constituting the phrases and clauses of item 11 varies quite markedly from what can be deduced about the patterns of everyday first-century speech.

Whereas the orators and the historians maintained the ancient position of the accusative complement of the verb, ordinary users of the language had for some time tended more and more to have such a complement follow, at least where principal clauses were concerned.[87] Catullus has two cases of the accusative preceding a finite transitive verb and none of the opposite order in item 11; five and one respectively in 17; three and one in 30; two and none in 34; four and none in 51; thirty-two and fourteen in

---

[82] ≠ Plaut. *Mil.* 567, Cic. *Cael.* 12 *et al.* The parallels at Lucret. 3.647 (≠ Cic. *Fam.* 15.4.16 *et al.*) and 4.815 suggest that it was no new locution.

[83] Cicero has it in only a few set expressions (*cubitum, sessum ire*).

[84] Frequent in Plautus, much less so in Terence, rare in first-century BC and first-century AD prose (Liv. 3.2.9 (reported speech), Sen. *Contr.* 1.2.5 (often challenged by critics), Sen. *Dial.* 2.19.4).

[85] Cf. the prayer *quod di omen auerterint* at Cic. *Phil.* 12.14 (≠ *Flacc.* 104, *Phil.* 3.35, 13.7; 41, 14.26).

[86] Servius interprets *comitum* at Virg. *Aen.* 11.94 as 'comitantium'.

[87] See Adams (1976: 70–99).

61. It is not easy to suggest a reason for the last set of figures. I note that there was an especially strong tendency in the ordinary language for an injunctive verb to precede its object and that ten of the fourteen preposed verbs of item 61 are injunctive.[88]

The ordering of the noun and various types of attribute was already in the early second century undergoing a process of change. Ennius' *Annales* exploited the potentialities of the situation much more than his stage tragedies did. 331 cases of noun and attribute of every type have been counted in the fragments of the old hexameter poem: in 150 the noun precedes, in 181 the attribute; in the latter 181 cases the attribute is disjoined 63 times.[89] In the first 21 verses of Catullus' epic item 64 I count 25 cases of noun and attribute of every type: in three the noun precedes, in 22 the attribute; in the latter 22 cases the attribute is disjoined 19 times.[90] The difference is quite striking and not to be attributed to any change in the ordinary language between Ennius' time and Catullus'. Removal of the type of adjective which had continued in the second and first centuries normally to precede the noun would not significantly affect the statistics. A conscious policy appears to be at work.[91]

Item 11 is remarkable for the small number of nouns it carries without any attribute at all. Of its 24 attributes five follow and 19 precede. Only one of the five following is disjoined (10 *magni*), and this is an adjective which in the ordinary language normally preceded its noun. The disjunction gave it an emotionally heavy emphasis. Five of the nine immediately preceding (6 *sagittiferos*; 11 *Gallicum*; 15 *meae*; 22 *illius*; 22–3 *prati ultimi*) would in the ordinary languge as a rule have followed. Six of the ten preceding at a distance (3 *Eoa*; 7 *septemgeminus*; 10 *Caesaris*; 17 *suis*; 21 *meum*; 23 *praetereunte*) would normally have followed. They thus received an emphasis greater than that given the other four. One could give an account of each case in terms of the liberties the ordinary language allowed, but the impression left by the sheer number of licences which Catullus granted himself in item 11 remains. Items 17, 34, 51 and 61 behave similarly in regard to the position of the attribute; item 30 stands slightly apart. There are clear signs here of the operation by Catullus of a special stylistic agenda for lyric poetry.

---

[88] It is more significant for the tone of item 61 that sixteen injunctives follow the object.
[89] See O. Skutsch (1985: 67). Where the noun precedes, the attribute is disjoined no more than about fifteen times.
[90] Where an attribute follows a noun (vv. 3, 6, 18) it does so immediately.
[91] The history of so-called 'hyperbaton' in Latin as a whole with proper attention to the various kinds of prose and the non-literary material is yet to be written. See, however, Adams (1971: 1–16).

The splitting of the passive periphrasis *tactus est* in vv. 23–4 appears to be unique in the μέλη (contrast 34.23; 61.194), the ἴαμβοι (contrast 22.20; 29.16, 17; 39.2), and the Phalaecian epigrams (contrast 1.5; 3.3; 10.3; 26.2; 28.13; 36.4; 38.5; 58b.9–10). The epic item 64 has one case (v. 147: contrast vv. 6, 79, 268, 304); the elegies three (66.61; 67.9; 68.15; contrast 66.27 (bis), 29, 34; 67.26; 68.39, 80, 106, 125, 154); the elegiac epigrams six (87.2, 4; 99.13; 100.5–6; 102.4; 110.3; contrast 76.8; 83.6; 95.2; 99.7; 101.8; 102.1; 116.5). Contemporary oratory occasionally split the periphrasis in order to emphasize a contrast between the participle in question and another or to assist in the focusing of another element of the whole phrase.[92] At 11.23–4 Catullus appears to be enforcing some unspoken contrast between the *aratrum* and the *flos*.

Related in some degree to this phenomenon is the inversion and separation of participle and auxiliary, of which there are two cases in the μέλη: at 17.14 *cui cum sit uiridissimo nupta flore puella* auxiliary *sit* appears to attach itself to the emphasized pair of subordinators *cui cum*; at 34.21–2 *sis quocumque tibi placet sancta nomine* the volitive character of the phrase drives *sis* to the initial position. The former has parallels in oratory,[93] the latter none. Since, however, the orators avoided the positive use of the second person subjunctive in wishes and exhortations[94] this is not surprising. There are no cases at all in the Phalaecian epigrams of a preposed auxiliary helping to focus another constituent of the colon, but a scatter is to be found in the ἴαμβοι, the epic item 64, the elegies and the elegiac epigrams.[95] It could of course be argued that *sancta* at 34.21–2 is an adjective rather than part of a synthetic perfect passive verb. In that case there are parallels for the position of *sis* in the elegies (68.155) and the elegiac epigrams (100.8).[96]

The incorporation within the relative clause in 11.7–8 of its head *aequora* reflects to some extent an archaic practice still occasionally followed by orators but, it would seem, abandoned by the ordinary language.[97] The only near-parallels in Catullus' entire work are in the elegiac item 68

---

[92] See Adams (1994b: 34–43).

[93] See Adams (1994b: 34–40, 44–53).

[94] See above n. 80.

[95] See, where the ἴαμβοι are concerned, 37.13 (44.17 without separation); where item 64 is concerned, vv. 220, 396 (187 without separation); where the elegies are concerned, 67.6; 68.22, 59, 94, 130, 158; where the elegiac epigrams are concerned, 71.4; 75.1 (84.3 and 108.4 without separation).

[96] See further Cic. *Ad Q. fr.* 1.3.10 *sis fortis* (≠ *Fam.* 16.9.4 *cautus sis*), Prop. 1.1.32 *sitis et . . . pares*.

[97] Cf. for such incorporation Plaut. *Amph.* 7, *Cas.* 975, *Curc.* 433, *Epid.* 472–3, *Men.* 707, *Mil.* 73–4, *Most.* 505, Ter. *Andr.* 3, 26, 39, 681, *Eun.* 19–20, 449–50.

(vv. 147–8 as restored in the 1473 edition, 153–4).[98] One can only guess at what effect the poet aimed with such an order.

The placing of *ut* (v. 3) and *postquam* (v. 23) in the second position of their respective clauses had copious precedent in both the higher and the lower genres of older poetry.[99] First-century BC writers of formal prose felt able to position these and other subordinators after a word or group of words which required emphasis. Cicero's private correspondence shows a similar degree of liberty.[100] This liberty survived a long time in the ordinary language but was eventually curtailed in formal prose. It is arguable that the process of curtailment was already under way at some levels in the first century, if not already in the second. Catullus affected the freer order in his other μέλη,[101] and about as much in the epic item 64,[102] the elegies,[103] the elegiac epigrams,[104] and the ἴαμβοι.[105] I say this taking account of the

---

[98] Not, however, 64.207–9.

[99] Cf. Enn. *Trag.* 249, 300, 322 (*ut* ≠ 72, 263, 353, 383), *Ann.* 155, 461, 491, 578 (*postquam* ≠ 63, 137, 143, 225). The same positionings of *ut* and *postquam* can be found in Plautus' comedies; both subordinators normally, however, head their clauses (I count in the first 300 verses of the *Pseudolus* 24 cases of *ut* in the first position, ten of it later; the six cases of *postquam* in the whole script are all in the first position).

[100] It has been estimated from relatively small samples that Cicero postpones the subordinator in his orations between 15 and 20 times in a hundred; Caesar's practice is similar.

[101] Cf. for *ut* 17.10, 26; 30.12; 34. 9, 23; 61.149, 164 (contrast 11.21; 61.34, 41, 77, 204); for *uelut* 61.21, 102, 187 (contrast 11.22; 17.18); for relative *qui* 51.5; 61.29, 62, 139, (contrast 11.17, 22; 17.1; 30.12; 34.7; 51.3; 61.3, 23, 37, 71, 107, 110, 144, 151, 197, 202); for *cum* 17.14. There is no instance of *si* in the second or a later position (contrast 17.20, 24; 30.11; 61.92).

[102] Cf. for *ut* vv. 61, 138, 226, 236, 293, 402 (contrast vv. 117–23 (five cases), 230, 231, 233, 241); *uelut* occurs only at the beginning of a phrase or clause (105, 353, 369); for relative *qui* postponed cf. vv. 30, 48, 56, 71, 73, 95, 157, 216, 322 (contrast vv. 26, 66, 87, 96, 119, 142, 161, 165, 193, 196, 209, 219, 229, 254, 260, 272, 280–3, 284, 286, 296, 317, 325, 330, 340, 358, 359, 369); for *cum* vv. 80, 212, 388 (contrast vv. 4, 101, 237, 243, 305, 344, 350, 363, 392); for *si* v. 228 (contrast v. 158). I note v. 202 *has postquam* . . . and omit a number of subordinators which occur sporadically in item 64 and elsewhere.

[103] Cf. for *ut* 66.3; 68.3, 73, 84, 115 (contrast 65.19; 66.4, 5; 67.16; 68.130; *uelut* occurs at the beginning of a clause at 68.63); for relative *qui* 65.7; 66.1, 17, 79, 83; 67.21, 33, 47; 68.131, 159 (contrast 65.21; 66.2, 9, 11, 14, 27, 28, 43, 49, 68, 84; 67.3, 5, 9, 28, 30, 38, 45; 68.5, 15, 18, 24, 31, 59, 78, 91, 96, 111, 113, 118, 121, 126, 128, 133, 148, 153, 160); for *cum* cf. 66.89; 68.16, 75 (contrast 66.45, 45–6, 47, 52; 67.4; 68.8, 32, 53, 59, 61); for *si* cf. 68.40 (contrast 66.35, 73; 68.31, 86, 147).

[104] Cf. for *ut/uti* 72.4; 76.21, 23; 78.4, 90.5; 116.2 (contrast 72.3; 75.3; 89.5; 99.13; 101.3; 109.3, 5); for relative *qui* 70.3; 73.6; 82.3; 88.3; 101.7; 104.2; 106.1; 115.4 (contrast 69.5; 71.3; 73.5; 74.5; 76.9, 21; 78.1; 78b.1; 79.1; 81.2, 5; 86.5; 88.1; 89.1; 91.6; 98.2; 102.2; 110.8; 114.2); for *cum* 80.3 (contrast 76.2; 80.3; 84.4, 10; 100.7); for *si* 75.4; 82.1 (contrast 69.3; 70.2; 71.1, 2; 74.2; 75.3; 76.1, 16, 17 (bis), 19; 82.1; 83.3; 84.1; 88.8; 90.4; 96.1; 98.3, 5; 102.1; 103.3; 107.1; 108.1).

[105] Cf. for relative *qui* 22.21; 37.19; 44.8; 59.2 (contrast 4.1; 8.2, 7, 10; 22.1, 12, 19; 25.6, 8; 29.3–4, 19; 31.11; 37.11, 39.14, 20; 44.2, 3, 21); for *cum* 8.6; 22.9, 16; 39.5 (contrast 4.23; 8.4, 14; 25.5; 31.8; 39.3; 44.21; 59.4). Neither *ut* (contrast 22.5; 29.8, 13; 39.13, 20; 60.4) nor *uelut* (contrast 25.12) nor *si* (contrast 22.13; 39.2, 4, 10; 44.18) is displaced.

relatively small number of subordinate clauses in the μέλη. In the Phalaecian epigrams, on the other hand, the subordinator tended rather more to
be placed at the head of its clause.[106] It is hard to judge the import of this
tendency. Possibly excessive use of the liberty conflicted with the down-
to-earth tone normally sought in the epigrams. The position of *litus* at 11.3
stressed the idea, perhaps already stressed by the separation of *extremos*
from its noun, that India lay at the eastern edge of the northern landmass.
That of *praetereunte* at 11.23 brought out further the contrast being suggested between the plant and the plough. There was, it is clear, nothing
understated about the general style of lyric poetry.

f. Item 11: Vocabulary

The vocabulary chosen for item 11 would have marked it in both a positive
and a negative way; especially for a reader who came to it after item
10 and was immediately to proceed to item 12.

The absence of any particular word can hardly be significant in such a
short piece as item 11. Nevertheless it would be worth observing that the
class of enclitics and the like is represented only by -*ue* (vv. 5, 6), -*que* (vv.
11, 12, 17) and *est* (v. 24), that *penetrabit* (v. 2), *gradietur* (v. 9), *uiuat*
ualeatque (v. 17), *tenet* (v. 18), and *respectet* (v. 21) have no pronominal
subject and that *haec* is used rather than *ea* at v. 13 and *illius* rather than
eius at v. 22. The only forms of *is* which occur in the other μέλη are *id* at
17.22 and *eum* at 17.23.[107] Thirteen of the 114 words which compose the
item would have been perceptibly obsolescent in the ordinary language or
unknown except to those conversant with the higher genres of the poetry
of the previous two centuries, or quite new and decipherable only through
acquaintance with the modules of the established poetic language: these
are *resonante* (v. 3),[108] *Eoa* (v. 3),[109] -*ue* (vv. 5, 6),[110] *sagittiferos* (v. 6),[111]

---

[106] See below nn. 160, 161, 162.

[107] I have not been able to find another example of the conjunction of *hic* and *quicumque*
(≠ *is*: Cic. *Att.* 7.7.7, 8.11b.1, *Fam.* 13.6.1, *Orat.* 123, 237, *Tusc.* 5.33, *Off.* 3.20). On the
difficulty see Nisbet (1978: 94–5 = 1995: 79–80). *illi* appears rather than *ei* at 61.169; *illius*
rather than *eius* at 61.219.

[108] ≠ *sonante*. Old tragedy has *resonere/resonare* 5 times, *sonere/sonare* 8; comedy has the
former only once (Plaut. *Pseud.* 702 (paratragedy)), the latter 7 times.

[109] ≠ *orientali. Eous*, a borrowing from Greek poetry with an obviously Greek sound, occurs
here first in the record and thereafter largely in verse.

[110] The old disjunctive was already giving way to *aut* and *uel* in second-century comedy (only
14 times in Plautus, 10 in Terence, not at all in the other comedians). The exiguous remains
of tragedy on the other hand have as many as five cases. Vitruvius would admit it twice
(3.3.8 and 10.9.3).

[111] First here in the record. Tragedy had many such formations (e.g. *frondifer* at Naev. *Trag.*
25); comedy avoided them except in paratragic passages.

septemgeminus (v. 7),[112] *aequora* (v. 8),[113] *gradietur* (v. 9),[114] *-que* (vv. 11, 12, 17),[115] *caelitum* (v. 14),[116] *respectet* (v. 21).[117] Each of the other μέλη, apart from item 17, has much the same proportion of such vocabulary, a proportion rather smaller than the one to be found in the epic item 64, in Cicero's *Aratus* or in Lucretius' *De rerum natura*. The μέλη composed by Horace a generation later will similarly seem less 'poetic' than Virgil's *Georgics* or *Aeneid*. Of the other words of item 11 only *moechus* (discussed above pp. 347–8) would have given the orator qualms as being possibly unfit for a solemn public occasion.

The use of a pair of nearly synonymous words or phrases gave dignity to religious and legal injunctions and to formulae of social courtesy. Tragedy and the grander parts of comedy exploited the way of speaking.[118] Catullus' μέλη have it at v. 17 of the item under discussion (*uiuat ualeatque*); it also occurs at 17.9 (*praecipitem . . . per caputque pedesque*), 10 (*totius . . . lacus putidaeque paludis*), 30.3 (*prodere . . . fallere*), 10 (*uentos . . . ac nebulas aereas*), 51.14 (*exultas nimiumque gestis*). *uiuat ualeatque* looks like a formula of the ordinary language poeticised by the use of the particle *-que*.[119]

---

[112] First here in the record and never common. *tergeminus* (Lucret. 5.28, Virg. *Aen.* 4.511, 8.202, Hor. *Carm.* 1.1.8; doubtless coined by Ennius as a choriambic replacement of *trigeminus*) would have been the model.

[113] ≠ *mare*. An old word already restricted to tragic and epic poetry in the second century and rarely applied to anything but the sea. Catullus probably contrasts the calm of the sea in front of the Nile delta with the violence of the Indian shore-line.

[114] ≠ Liv. 21.38.6 *eo magis miror ambigi quanam Alpis transierit*. The simple form of the verb *gradi* appeared in old tragedy (Pacuv. 47) and in grandiose passages of comedy (Plaut. *Poen.* 632, *Pseud.* 859, 1236, *Truc.* 124). Cicero admitted it three time to his philosophical dialogues, twice in reference to the locomotion of four-footed animals (*Nat. deor.* 2.122, *Tusc.* 5.38) and once in a piece of grandiose imagery (*Tusc.* 1.110).

[115] ≠ *et*. Signs of a declining use of the old conjunctive particle *-que* are visible even in Plautus' comedies. Cicero used it more in his speeches than in his letters. In some speeches of a plain style (e.g. the *Pro Roscio Comoedo*) it is hardly to be found at all. The coupling of . . . *-que* . . . *-que*, whether original or modelled on . . . τε . . . τε, was outrightly paratragic in Plautus' time; see Fraenkel (1922: 209–11 = 1960: 199–201), Haffter (1934: 119 n. 4; 1956: 363).

[116] ≠ *deum*. *caeles* occurs five times in tragedy and only once in the remains of comedy (Plaut. *Rud.* 2). It remained restricted to the higher genres of poetry.

[117] ≠ *respiciat* (cf. Plaut. *Bacch.* 638a, *Rud.* 1316). The verb *respectare*, rare even in a frequentative sense, cannot have such a sense here. Tragedy had often used the frequentative form in *-tare* with no appreciable difference in sense from the base form (e.g. Ennius' *abnutare* (306), *aditare* (394), *aduentare* (37), *proiectare* (194), *raptare* (92)).

[118] See Haffter (1934: 53–85).

[119] Cf. Plaut. *Mil.* 1340 *bene ualete et uiuite*, *Trin.* 996 *male uiue et uale* (also *Bacch.* 246, *Stich.* 31, *Trin.* 52), Ter. *Andr.* 889 *immo habeat ualeat uiuat cum illa* (also *Haut.* 430).

g. Item 10: Substance and Tone

We move back for the purpose of linguistic analysis to the Phalaecian epigram item 10. It should not, however, be forgotten that the ancient reader moved the other way, coming from a lower to a higher style. The names of some of the persons involved in the incident which the epigram recounts and the references to the province of Bithynia and to certain landmarks of the Capital would have set the scene for the first readers of the poem in the Rome of the spring or summer of 56.[120] The absence of a specific addressee — the ten preceding items have one, likewise the next 31 — suggests that the poet presents himself as talking to a group of sympathetic friends. He describes, in part indirectly but in the main directly, a conversation between himself, one Varus, and a woman fancied by the latter. The low status of the woman prevents her being named, while it is no doubt the high status of the former governor of Bithynia which helps to keep him anonymous.[121] The ninth *sermo* of Horace's first book would not have been the first poem of its type to report a conversation with an obnoxious person at some length. Direct representation of dialogue has been posited for a number of the fragments of Lucilius' *Saturae*, but none is large enough to guarantee certainty. At any rate no other of the first sixty items of the *liber Catulli Veronensis* reports the two parts of a conversation. That needs to be remembered in considering the verbal style of item 10, which in many respects varies as much from its fellow epigrams as it does from the lyric item 11.

h. Item 10: Phonetic Features

There is very little phonetic repetition in item 10 that looks a matter of design. The only alliterations are the unremarkable *me meus* (1), *quibus quid* (6), *nihil neque* (9). Equally unremarkable are the assonances in *non sane illepidum neque inuenustum* (6), *in collo sibi collocare posset* (23), *insulsa male et molesta uiuis* (33) and the non-avoidance of homoeoteleuton in *irrumator praetor* (12–13) and *facerem beatiorem* (17). The triple anaphorae *quid esset iam Bithynia, quo modo se haberet, ecquonam mihi profuisset aere* (6–8) and *neque ipsis nec praetoribus esse nec cohorti* (9–10) had none of the force of the fivefold *siue* of 11.2–12. The recurrence of the verb in 5 *incidere* . . . 19 *incidisset*; 7 *haberet* . . . 28 *habere*; 13 *faceret* . . .

---

[120] C. Memmius (mentioned by name in 28.9) held a praetorship in 58 and was governor of Bithynia in the following year.

[121] The naming of him and Piso in item 28 (the latter also in item 47) made the attack there all the more scurrilous.

17 *facerem*; 20 *parare* . . . 30 *parauit* . . . 32 *pararim*[122] may be regarded as accidental or even as the result of studied unconcern. It certainly has no structural or semantic significance.

Catullus has *mihi* pronounced as a pyrrhic at vv. 3, 8, 18, 25, as a long monosyllable at v. 21, and as an iambus in the close of v. 32. The monosyllable was perhaps regular in ordinary speech. The iambus could hardly have not sounded archaic and artificial.[123] Likewise the dissyllabic *nihil* in the close of v. 9[124] and the trochaic *sibi* in the close of v. 32 (v.23).[125] The ithyphallic close of the hendecasyllabic verse gathered linguistic oddities.[126] The short forms *comparasti* (v. 15) and *pararim* (v. 32) have been labelled 'colloquial', but we cannot be entirely sure what the practice of ordinary speakers was at the time or what tone the corresponding long forms possessed.[127] The pronunciation of *Gaius* as a dactyl rather than a trochee (v. 30) looks artificial.[128] Nothing can be said about dactylic *illius*[129] or iambic *mei* (v. 31).[130] Pyrrhic *mane* (v. 27) would probably have been normal,[131] but dactylic *commoda* (v. 26) is hard to judge. Comedy shortened

---

[122] The *parare* of v. 20 picked up the compound *comparasti* of v. 15 according to an ancient pattern still alive in the ordinary language (on which see Adams (1992: 295–8)).

[123] The iambus is also found at 15.5. There are on the other hand in the Phalaecian epigrams against these two cases 18 of pyrrhic *mihi*, three of monosyllabic *mi*. The μέλη have the pyrrhic twice, the monosyllable three times and the iambus not at all. The iambus was already rare in comedy (at Plaut. *Pseud.* 192, 387, 934, 1314 against 33 cases of the pyrrhic, 21 of *mih'*, 24 of *mi*). Lucretius has the iambus once (1.845) against eight of pyrrhic *mihi* and two of *mi*. *mi* appears with great frequency in the letters of Rustius Barbarus, those of Claudius Terentianus and those from Vindolanda.

[124] Also at 6.12; 15.6; 16.6; 17.21; 23.8; 42.21; 51.7. Monosyllabic *nil* occurs at 30.2; 42.21. Terence has *nihil* at the end of the senarius *Phorm.* 940 and the trochaic septenarius *Haut.* 896. There is no clear trace elsewhere in comedy of dissyllabic *nihil. nihili* and *nihilo* on the other hand seem to have been regularly anapaests.

[125] Contrast also 36.4. The old form had already given way to the pyrrhic in comedy (cf. Plaut. *Pseud.* 23, 125, 186, 884). Lucretius has the iambus seven times against the pyrrhic 32 times.

[126] See Jocelyn (1995: 73–52).

[127] Catullus has in the Phalaecian epigrams also *norat* (3.6), *donarunt* (13.12), *cupisti* (19.3), *putastis* (16.3), *irrumasti* (28.10), *desissem* (36.5), *explicasset* (53.3); in the ἴαμβοι *nosti* (22.1). The first and third conjugation long forms seem not to occur anywhere. They are few in Lucretius in comparison with the short forms. The comic poets seem to have found at least some of them (e.g. those ending in a cretic) metrically useful. Quintilian thought that to use *conseruauisse* rather than *conseruasse* was pedantic (*Inst.* 1.6.20).

[128] Cf. dactylic *Troia* at 65.7.

[129] See above, n. 72.

[130] Monosyllabic or pyrrhic at Enn. *Scaen.* 60, Plaut. *Capt.* 765, 800, *Persa* 494, *Pseud.* 6, Ter. *Eun.* 801, Pacuv. *Trag.* 198 ≠ Plaut. *Amph.* 442, 601, 856, *Aul.* 244, *Bacch.* 379, *Vid.* 67, Ter. *Andr.* 869, *Eun.* 306, *Haut.* 951, 1026, Acc. *Trag.* 355.

[131] For the shortening of an originally iambic dissyllabic imperative see 50.18 *caue* (also in the lyric item 61 (145)). Contrast 1.8 *habe* (and 61.161 *subi*). The pronunciation of *aue* as an

such imperatives in anapaestic verse, while the rules of iambic and trochaic verse tended to the exclusion of words of dactylic shape. What happened in the ordinary language we just do not know.[132] Whether we relate the linguistic features of item 10 to its genre or to its particular theme, it remains curious that overall in the matter of the pronunciation of particular words the item was at least as artificial as item 11.

i. Item 10: Morphology and Syntax

In grammar item 10 shows less outright archaism and modernizing artificiality than item 11. On the other hand there are many more syntactic constructions of the kind that by the middle of the first century BC were being increasingly avoided in more formal Latin speech. Graecizing morphology like that of *Arabas* at 11.5 and of several proper names elsewhere in the Catullan corpus is absent. The Latinizing *Serapim* at v. 26 deserves note.[133] The item is strongly anchored in the life of the city of Rome. Archaising morphology appears only with the third person plural perfect *incidere* in the close of v. 5.[134]

Graecizing syntagms are no more evident in item 10 than in the other Phalaecian epigrams. The use of the supine *uisum* in vv. 1–2,[135] the position of the relative clause together with its lack of exact concordance with the main clause in vv. 14–16,[136] and the adnominal use of the prepositional phrase *ad lecticam* in v. 16[137] are easier to parallel in second- than in first-century BC literature. On the other hand various verbs of the general character of *ducere* certainly continued to be accompanied by the supine in some kinds of first-century writing, and the particular usage was possibly still alive in the ordinary language.[138] The same point could be made about the relationship between *ad lecticam homines* and *quod illic natum dicitur*

---

iambus (cf. Mart. 3.95.1, 5.51.7, 7.39.2) was regarded by some persons at the end of the next century as a pedantry (see Quint. *Inst.* 1.6.21).

[132] The problem is discussed from the angle of textual criticism by O. Skutsch (1976: 19) and Nisbet (1978: 93–4 = 1995: 78–9).

[133] Cf. Varro, *Men.* 128, Cic. *Verr.* II 2.160, *Nat. deor.* 3.47, Tert. *Nat.* 1.10; contrast Martial 9.29.6.

[134] Cf. 49.2 and contrast 12.15; 21.2; 24.2. Cicero felt some life in the form (*Orat.* 157) but used it rarely. It already had an expressive function in early comedy. See in general Bauer (1933), Pye (1963).

[135] Cf. (with *ducere*) Plaut. *Cist.* 90, *Poen.* 20, *Stich.* 139, frg. 89; (with *abducere*) *Pseud.* 520. Hor. *Serm.* 2.4.89 has *ducere me auditum . . . memento*.

[136] On the history of the Latin relative clause see Kroll (1912: 1–18).

[137] Instead of *lecticarii* (Cic. *S. Rosc.* 134, Sulp. Ruf. *ap.* Cic. *Fam.* 4.12.3).

[138] It appears with *mittere* at Cic. *Verr.* II 4.63; with *uenire* at ibid. 145 *et al.* Sallust has the phrase *uisum processerant* (*Iug.* 94.5). *cacatum uenire* was still in use at Pompeii in the next century (*CIL* IV 5242).

esse and about the use of *ad lecticam*.[139] Vv. 14–16 may therefore be regarded as parodying the talk of businessmen and managers rather than as indulging in literary archaism.

Syntax such as that in *quid esset iam Bithynia* (vv. 6–7), *nihil neque ipsis nec* (ed. Ven.: *neque nec in ipsis nea* V: *neque ipsis nunc* Westphal) *praetoribus esse nec cohorti* (vv. 9–10), *cur quisquam caput unctius referret* (v. 11), *irrumator praetor* (vv. 12–13), *ut puellae unum me facerem beatiorem* (vv. 16–17), *non . . . mihi tam fuit maligne* (v. 18), *at mi nullus erat nec hic neque illic* (v. 21), *in collo sibi collocare* (v. 23), *ut decuit (docuit* V*) cinaediorem* (v. 24), *quod modo dixeram me habere* (v. 28) and *istud . . . is sibi parauit . . . mihi pararim* (*paratis* Estaço) (vv. 28–32) flourished in the ordinary language of Catullus' time and was occasionally, despite its apparent illogicality or redundancy, accepted by users with ideals of correctness. Cicero's speeches have the double negative,[140] the use of *unus* to emphasize a superlative or quasi-superlative,[141] the adverb conjoined with *esse* in a predicate,[142] the formation in *-tor* functioning as an attributive adjective,[143] and the pluperfect exercising a simple preterite function.[144] His philosophical dialogues have the plural denoting a single person[145] and the formation in *-ior/-ius* performing something other than a comparative function.[146] Caesar's *commentarii* have the dative of the third-person reflexive pronoun preferred on at least two occasions to an employment of *suus*.[147] The semi-otiose use of the dative of the reflexive pronoun with *parare* occurs nowhere in Cicero's more formal productions nor in Caesar's *commentarii*, but it does with many other verbs of acquisition.[148] All the syntagms in question, it might be argued, were being

---

[139] For the use of a singular pronoun in regard to a plurality see v. 28 and Cic. *Att.* 4.15.7, 5.5.2, 11.11.2. For the use of *ad* phrases in definitions of slaves and the like see Cic. *Pis.* 61 *scriba ad aerarium*, Livy 34.6.13 *seruos ad remum* (hardly dependent on *dabamus*) and the non-literary material cited by Adams (1995a: 112–13).

[140] See *Verr.* II 2.60, *Phil.* 6.7.

[141] See *Prou.* 12, *Phil.* 2.7 for the superlative; *Sull.* 7 for the quasi-superlative. At Catull. 10.16–17 *beatiorem* is no more a genuine comparative than *unctius* at v. 11 or *cinaediorem* at v. 24.

[142] See *Verr.* II 4.95, *Cat.* 1.19, *Deiot.* 19. At Catull. 10.6–7 *quid* functions adverbially, as does *aliquid* at 1.4 (cf. Cic. *Diu. in Caec.* 48, 49).

[143] See *Cluent.* 40 (*uictor*), *Mil.* 50 (*occultator, receptor*).

[144] See *Caecin.* 15.

[145] See *Tusc.* 1.3.

[146] See *Tusc.* 4.47, *Cato* 41, 55. From the orations *Sest.* 59 can be cited. It is noteworthy that Catullus' Phalaecian epigrams frequently have such forms in the ithyphallic close (see Jocelyn (1995: 76–7)).

[147] See *Gall.* 1.7.3; 36.4. Cicero has *sibi* so used only at *Att.* 10.4.3 (contrast *Verr.* II 3.62).

[148] For *sibi habere* see Cic. *Verr.* II 1.148, 2.61, 4.151; for *sibi uelle Verr.* II 2.150, *Cluent.* 147; for *sibi uindicare Marcell.* 6.

increasingly avoided in the more ambitious literary genres. Nothing comparable is to be found in item 11 or in any of the other μέλη.

k. Item 10: Sentence Structure and Word-Order

The ten periods which form item 10 are comparatively brief. Nevertheless their constituents frequently overrun the boundaries of the hendecasyllabic verses. The longest of the periods (vv. 9–13) reports indirectly Catullus' first reply to the unnamed woman. It contains only 26 words. Its structure could hardly be called a structure at all.[149] Similar looseness marks what Catullus reports directly of his final reply (vv. 27–34). Someone speaking carefully on a formal occasion would hardly have dispensed with a verb as the poet does at vv. 6–8 and 31[150] or have employed only one in relation to two distinct temporal situations as the latter does at vv. 21–3.[151] The dropping of *si* in *utor tam bene quam mihi pararim* (v. 32) is of a piece with earlier apparent sloppiness.[152] The μέλη do not admit such inelegancies. We seem to be here as close as anywhere in the Phalaecian epigrams to the way speakers of Catullus' class used Latin on private occasions in the first century BC. The absence of extended participial phrases is also noteworthy.

Except in one case the order of the words of item 10 may be argued to have corresponded more with that of the spoken language than the order of those of item 11 did.

The placement of an accusative complement after a finite transitive verb, something perhaps already approaching the normal in the ordinary language, at least where principal clauses were concerned, manifests itself five times (vv. 9, 13, 15–16, 24, 29) in eleven comparable cases (≠ 1–2, 7, 11, 17, 26, 28–30). This set of figures coheres with those derivable from

[149] The early alteration of the paradosis *nihil neque nec in ipsis nec praetoribus esse* to *nihil neque ipsis nec praetoribus esse* has not been improved upon but is not without its difficulties. Hence some editors print Westphal's *nihil neque ipsis nunc praetoribus esse*. For the grammar see above, n. 140. The coherence of *cur quisquam caput unctius referret* with what precedes is a question more for the logician than the linguist. For the plural *(ei) quibus* following on from *quisquam* cf. Plaut. *Persa* 55–6, *Poen.* 37–9, 483–5, *Pseud.* 134, Ter. *Andr.* 626–7. For the inconcinnity of *quibus esset irrumator praetor nec faceret pili cohortem* cf. Anon. *B. Afr.* 64.1, 97.3.

[150] In vv. 6–8 something like *rogatum est* has to be supplied; in v. 31 *sint* and *attinet* (Plaut. *Aul.* 770 *et al.*). For *quid ad me?* cf. Cic. *Att.* 12.17.

[151] Ellis compared Cic. *Att.* 9.7.2, which relates to the future.

[152] Estaço altered *pararim* to *paratis*. So too at least one recent editor. From the first-century BC record one can compare only the ellipse of *cum* after *quam* at Cic. *Att.* 1.16.11 and 7.21.3.

the preceding and following Phalaecian poems[153] and contrasts significantly with those from the μέλη.[154] Enclitic *me* is forced towards the front of *Varus... otiosum* (vv. 1–2), and the heavily emphasized *istud* cannot avoid the head of the chaotic *istud... parauit* (vv. 28–30). A desire for emphasis similarly causes *istos* to precede the imperative in *paulum... commoda* (vv. 25–6). Where the six subordinate clauses are concerned, the postposition of the complement in *nec... cohortem* (v. 13) may have to do with the looseness of the attachment of the clause to its predecessor. That in *ut... cinaediorem* (v. 24) looks on the other hand to be the result of metrical compulsion.

The item contains no purely decorative epithets. Many nouns have no attribute of any kind. Of the sixteen attributes nine precede and seven follow; of the nine preceding only three are disjoined; of the seven following again only three. We might attribute a large degree of ordinariness to the poem in respect both of the positioning of the attributes and the employment of disjunction were it not for the pair of epithets preceding a pair of nouns in vv. 21–3. *fractum* and *ueteris* are attributes which might ordinarily have been expected to follow their nouns. The only parallel for the arrangement in comedy seems to be a passage of a highly elaborate canticum, *num quoipiam est hodie tua tuorum opera conseruorum nitidiusculum caput?* (Plaut. *Pseud.* 219–20); in first-century oratory a sentence of an ἠθοποιία of a man pretending to wealth he does not have, which is cited in the rhetorical treatise addressed to Herennius (4.63): *ei dicit in aurem aut ut domi lectuli sternantur, aut ab auunculo rogetur Aethiops qui ad balneas ueniat, aut asturconi locus ante ostium suum detur, aut aliquod fragile falsae choragium gloriae comparetur.* Ten examples occur, however, in the lyric items 17 (v. 5), 34 (vv. 19–20, 22–4), 51 (vv. 5–6), and 61 (vv. 9–10, 19–20, 54–5, 102–3, 154–5, 202–3), and they swarm in the epic item 64 (v. 7 *et al.*) and the elegies (66.1 *et al.*). At 6.10–11 an absurdly bloated

---

[153] Item 1: two in two cases; 2: ___; 3: none in four; 5: two in four; 6: none in three; 7: none in one; 9: one in two; 12: two in seven; 13: two in seven; 14: one in ten; 14b: ___; 15: three in ten; 16: three in eight; 21: one in four; 23: one in four; 24: none in three; 26: ___; 27: one in one; 28: one in five; 32: two in five; 33: ___; 35: one in five; 36: one in three; 38: none in one; 40: none in three; 41: none in two; 42: seven in eight; 43: ___; 45: three in eight; 46: none in one; 47: one in three; 48: none in one; 49: none in one; 50: two in six; 53: two in three; 54: ___; 55: one in six; 56: two in three; 57: ___; 58: one in one; 58b: one in one. Many of the cases of the object preceding the verb occur in subordinate clauses, where the ordinary language seems to have been almost as conservative as the more formal registers.

[154] The figures for the μέλη are: item 11: none in three cases; 17: one in six; 30: one in four; 34: none in two; 51: none in four; 61: twelve in forty (on the figure see above, n. 88).

climax is achieved by the words and their order. What effects the poet
seeks at 10.21–3 and 53.2–3 elude me.[155]

A very large number of words which were normally or frequently
enclitic inhabit the constituents of the periods of item 10. They all behave
as they might have done in the ordinary language. The position of *esse* in
v. 10 suggests that *praetoribus* is being contrasted with *cohorti*. We may
wonder whether the end of v. 9 has yet been correctly restored. In *quod
illic natum dicitur esse* (vv. 14–15) the auxiliary *esse* hooks in a fairly
common way[156] onto the principal verb rather than the apparently focused
participle. A strong emphasis rests on initial *ego* in vv. 16–20 (*ego . . .
inquam* contrasting with *inquiunt* in v. 14) and on initial *quaeso* in vv.
24–26.[157] Where the punctuation of the latter passage is concerned, editors
wrongly attach unemphatic *mihi* to *commoda* rather than to *inquit*.[158] In
the parenthesis *Cinna est Gaius* (v. 30) the *est* is where we should expect
it to be. Catullus' first thought was to stress the identity of the actual owner
of the *lecticarii*, giving the cognomen by which he commonly addressed his
friend.[159] He added the praenomen in order to be more specific to persons
less intimate. Since the praenomen normally precedes the nomen or the
cognomen or both, the disjunction gives Gaius a particularly strong
emphasis. Commentators should not talk of metrical compulsion.

The position of *ut* in v. 5 contrasts with that in vv. 3, 16, 19, 24 and
elsewhere in the Phalaecian epigrams.[160] Similarly the position of the relative pronouns in vv. 19 and 22 with that in vv. 9, 14, 28 and elsewhere in
such epigrams.[161] In all three cases the ordering helps to highlight a word
on which the run of the poet's discourse places some emphasis. Often,
however, in item 10 where the subordinator comes first it is not easy to
see why it rather than another word of the clause should have done so, if
the poet had a completely free choice. Overall in the Phalaecian epigrams

[155] Nothing should be made of the disjunction *ecquonam mihi profuisset aere* in v. 8. At Plaut.
Merc. 844 the noun immediately follows *ecquinam*. So too at Cic. *Deiot.* 40, *Phil.* 10.19, *Vatin.*
26, *Brut.* 22, *Part.* 48, *Att.* 9.9.2. Contrast, however, *Fin.* 4.67, *Q. fr.* 1.4.2. Where *ecqui* is
concerned, Plautus disjoins the noun more often than not (*Bacch.* 235–6, *Curc.* 341, *Epid.*
441, *Men.* 135, 673, *Merc.* 390, *Mil.* 782, *Pseud.* 482, 971, *Rud.* 125, 971).
[156] See Adams (1994*b*: 28–31(30–1)).
[157] For *quaeso* + vocative + imperative see Plaut. *Asin.* 683–4, *Men.* 742.
[158] Lee (1990) takes no notice of O. Skutsch (1976: 18–20). Thomson (1978) and Goold
(1983) do.
[159] See 95.1, 113.1. *est* functions as the copula does in more orderly statements of the type of
Livy 8.25.10 *Charilaus fuit qui ad Publilium Philonem uenit* (on which see Adams (1994*b*:
65)).
[160] Cf. 13.14 and contrast 2.8; 15.11, 13, 16; 27.3; 40.5.
[161] Cf. 46.10 and contrast 2.2, 3; 3.5, 11, 14; 12.7, 12; 13.11; 14.7, 13; 15.4, 7; 16.3, 7, 11; 21.10;
23.1, 3, 26; 24.1, 5, 6; 28.7; 36.12–15; 41.5; 42.7; 45.5; 53.2; 55.8; 58.2; 58*b*.7.

subordinators have the initial position,[162] and very often one of the other words of the clause would seem to deserve as much emphasis as *huc, prouincia* and *fractum* receive in item 10. Epigrams tended to preserve a calm and even tone.

l. Item 10: Vocabulary

Among the 114 words of item 11 there are, I have argued, more than a dozen which would have been recognizable only through the higher genres of the poetry of the previous two centuries and just one which might have caused surprise if uttered on a public occasion. A number of common words of the ordinary language seem to have been consciously avoided. None of the 191 words of item 10 on the other hand has a clearly 'poetic' ring, while many would have been avoided in the more formal kinds of contemporary speech, one at least in any kind of polite social intercourse.

The presence in item 10 of a large number of enclitic words has already been remarked. Remarkable also is the presence of the anaphoric *is* (vv. 9, 30), the deictic *iste* (vv. 26, 28), the interrogative *uter*, the cardinal numeral *octo* (v. 20), the adjectives *beatus* (v. 17 in the sense of 'diues') and *molestus* (v. 33) and the adverb *sane* (v. 4). These were all avoided to one degree or another in the higher poetic genres of the late Republic and early Empire.[163] They may have already had an 'unpoetic' ring.[164]

e (v. 2) might be thought to have had the tone of high poetry. *ex foro* on the other hand occurs nowhere in the record, whereas *e foro* is found at Cic. *Verr.* II 5.33, *Sest.* 77, *Pis.* 7, 23, 30. The fixed phrase preserved the apparent archaism.

scortillum (v. 3), *illepidum* (v. 4), *inuenustum* (v. 4), *irrumator* (v. 12), *grabati* (v. 22) and *insulsa* (v. 33) were in all likelihood either absent from, or rare in, contemporary oratory despite a presence in the ordinary

---

[162] *cum* heads its clause at 1.5; 2.5; 5.5, 10, 13; 7.7; 53.2 and is never displaced. *si* is displaced at 13.6; 21.9; 23.22; 58b.1; contrast, however, 13.2, 3; 14b.1; 15.3; 16.7; 32.4, 9; 35.7, 11; 36.4, 17; 42.5, 14, 23; 48.2, 5; 55.1, 18; 56.6.

[163] On *is, iste, uter, beatus, molestus* and *sane* and classical verse see Axelson (1945: 70–1, 71–2, 90–1, 27, 60, 94). *octo* appears only in the astronomical contexts of Cic. *Arat.* 268, Manil. 3.578; 580, 4.483, 5.339, Germ. 473, in Cicero's translation of *Il.* 2.299–330 (*Diu.* 2.63–4) and at Virg. *Georg.* 1.171 (in a famously prosaic passage).

[164] On the rarity of *is* in Ennius' *Annales* see O. Skutsch (1985: 64). The epic poem has no certain instance of *iste. uter* occurs at vv. 78, 83. Archaic tragedy has instances of *is* and *iste* but much fewer proportionately than comedy. *uter* occurs in the fragments of Pacuvius (62) and Accius (479). *beatus* in the sense of 'diues', *molestus* and *sane* occur in neither epic nor tragedy. Only comedy among the archaic genres of verse has *octo* (Plaut. *Amph.* 160, *Asin.* 564, 574, *Cas.* 122, *Men.* 223, *Mil.* 831, *Persa* 504, fr. 51).

H. D. Jocelyn

language. The half-affectionate diminutive form of *scortum*[165] would have lacked an appropriate dignity. Something about the tone of adjectival formations in *in-*, especially those whose second element normally conveyed approval, disqualified them.[166] The meanness of the object and the Greek origin of the word put *grabatus* on a black list.[167] *irrumator* could have been (like *basiatio* at 7.1, *irrumatio* at 21.8 and *fututio* at 32.8) Catullus' own invention, but the existence at Pompeii of *cacator* (*CIL* IV 3782), *fellator* (*CIL* IV 1666), *fututor* (*CIL* IV 1503), *pedicator* (*CIL* IV 4008) and *perfututor* (*CIL* IV 4239) cautions against hasty conclusions from the literary record. The softened sense of *irrumare* which the formation implies[168] did not make it any less inappropriate for a formal occasion. Indeed the availability of polite synonyms (e.g. *contemnere*) increased its offensiveness. Such vocabulary marked off other Phalaecian epigrams almost as clearly from their lyric neighbours.

The use of *repente* (v. 3) in the sense of 'primo aspectu',[169] that of *huc* (v. 5) in the sense of 'ad aedes huius',[170] that of *aes* (v. 8) in the sense of 'pecunia',[171] that of *nullus* (v. 21) in the sense of 'nemo',[172] that of adjectival *cinaedus* (v. 24) in the sense of 'improbus',[173] that of *bene* (v. 32) in the sense of 'multum'[174] and that of *male* (v. 33) in the sense of 'valde'[175] are absent from, or rare in, extant contemporary oratory. In informal conversation such uses were doubtless not so offensive to the fastidious.

Cic. *Att.* 16.2.4 *ego enim in uarios sermones incidebam, Fam.* 9.3.1 *in*

---

[165] *scortum* is found often enough in oratory, e.g. at Cato *ap.* Gell. 10.13.2, Titius *ap.* Macrob. *Sat.* 3.16.14, Cic. *Cat.* 2.10; 24, *Har. resp.* 59, *Dom.* 49, *Mil.* 55, *Sest.* 39, *Phil.* 2.44; 105. Catullus has it in a Phalaecian epigram (6.5) with the same tone as in oratory. On this tone see Adams (1983: 324–7).

[166] Oratory has one example of *insulsus*, in a speech with many stylistic pecularities (Cic. *Cael.* 69; for *insulsitas* see *Rab. Post.* 36).

[167] Cicero has the word only at *Diu.* 2.129.

[168] An Ostian inscription, *amice fugit te prouerbium 'bene caca et irrima medicos'* (*Jahrb. d. Arch. Inst.* 51 (1936), 466; *Die Antike* 15 (1939), 103), indicates that neither at 10.12 nor at 28.9–10 was Catullus inventing his use of the verb.

[169] At 17.24 and 63.28 it has its usual sense of 'subito'.

[170] Cf. the use of *huc*, 'ad domum nostram' at Hor. *Serm.* 2.2.128.

[171] The use appears in Cicero's work only at *Rep.* 6.2, where it seems to be a question literally of brass coins. The phrase *aes paucum* was clearly a common colloquialism by the early second century AD (Epist. Claud. Terent. Pap. Mich. VIII 471.10, 13, 31, Gell. 9.4.5, 20.1.31).

[172] At 11.19 *moechum* is to be understood with *nullum*.

[173] Mart. 6.39.12 does not seem exactly parallel.

[174] Contrast Cic. *Verr.* II 4.30 *multum illorum opera consilioque usus est. bene* is more often so used with adjectives and adverbs (Cic. *Att.* 4.9.2 *et al.*).

[175] For *male* enforcing pejorative adjectives cf. Horace *Serm.* 1.3.45 *male paruus*, 1.4.66 *rauci male*, Sulpicia, Tib. 3.16.2 *male inepta*. A similar use with certain types of verbs is evidenced in comedy (*formidare, metuere, timere; macerare, mulcare, perdere; odisse; interire, disperire*).

sermonem incidemus, De orat. 1.111 *uidear . . . fortuito in sermonem incid-isse, Lael.* 2 *memini . . . in eum sermonem illum incidere* taken together suggest that *incidere nobis sermones uarii* is a poet's deliberate upturning of a stock phrase.[176] This is, however, the only such phenomenon in item 10. On the other hand the poem contains a number of locutions absent from extant oratory but either demonstrably or conjecturably present in ordinary speech: *cur quisquam caput unctius referret* (v. 11),[177] *nec faceret pili cohortem* (v. 13),[178] *fugit me ratio* (v. 29)[179] and *tu insulsa male et molesta uiuis* (v. 33).[180]

With *scortillum . . . non sane illepidum neque inuenustum* (vv. 3–4) the poet issued a compliment — not altogether contradicted by his later *tu insulsa male et molesta uiuis* (v. 33) — somewhat more grandly than he would have done in a real address to friends. Such nearly synonymous doublets are often to be found in the Phalaecian epigrams (6.2; 12.5, 8–9; 13.3, 10; 14.8, 10; 15.4, 14; 16.7; 23.15; 24.9; 32.2; 36.10, 17; 38.2, 4; 42.22, 24; 43.8; 45.15, 24; 46.11; 50.7–8; 56.1, 4) and in the ἴαμβοι (22.9, 17; 25.9; 29.6; 31.4; 37.14; 39.8). Although the μέλη, the elegies and the epic item 64 tend to be sparing of them, they seem to have had an elevated tone.[181]

m. Item 12: Substance and Tone

Item 12 has a theme of much lower emotional charge than its lyric prede-cessor. The situation is roughly parallel with that of the Phalaecian item 10. It is less, however, a narrative of a past incident than a statement of the poet's continued irritation. It addresses the object of irritation alone. Mid-first century BC readers would have been able to recognize the situ-ation and the persons involved. The theme was unimaginable in a μέλος.

---

[176] Livy 1.57.6 *forte potantibus his apud Sex. Tarquinium . . . incidit de uxoribus mentio* and 32.20.3 *cum de Philippo et Romanis mentio incidit* might suggest that Catullus had some earlier literary model.

[177] Cf. Plaut. *Pseud.* 219–20 *num quoipiamst hodie tua tuorum opera conseruorum nitidius-culum caput?*

[178] Cf. 17.17 *nec pili facit uni*, Petr. 44.17 (also Cic. *Q. Rosc.* 20, *Att.* 5.20.6, *Q. fr.* 2.16.5). A large number of variants were available for the locution *aliquid nihili facere* (Plaut. *Bacch.* 89): e.g. also *non nauci facere* (Plaut. *Bacch.* 1102), *non flocci facere* (Plaut. *Cas.* 332 *et al.*), *non assis facere* (Catull. 42.13), *non hettae facere* (Paul. Fest. p. 88.24–7), *non dupundi facere* (Petron. 58.4).

[179] For *fugit ratio* (the regular order) see Plaut. *Amph.* 386, Anon. Rhet. *Herenn.* 2.24.

[180] Cf. Plaut. *Bacch.* 615 *inamabilis illepidus uiuo*, *Men.* 908, *Trin.* 390, Afran. *Tog.* 253, Cic. *Att.* 3.5, *Fam.* 14.1.2, Catull. 8.10; Virg. *Aen.* 3.493, Tab. Vind. II 346 ii 5.

[181] See above, n. 118.

It had probably appeared in ἴαμβοι[182] and in comedy.[183] Perhaps too in sympotic epigrams.[184]

n. Item 12: Phonetic Features

None of the purely phonetic repetitions of item 12 seem deliberate. The only alliterations are *sudaria Saetaba* (v. 14) and *miserunt mihi muneri* (v. 15). The latter arises from the use of a set phrase,[185] perhaps also the former. None of the assonances draws attention to itself. Two of the three cases of homoeoteleuton (in vv. 6–7, 7, 10) involve the long final syllables of grammatically related words.[186] This signals a positive unconcern for phonetic pattern.

The anaphora *aut... aut...* in vv. 10–11 solemnizes to a degree the humorous threat.[187] The item concludes with a repetition of words already used earlier (17 *Veraniolum meum et Fabullum* ≠ 15–16 *Fabullus et Veranius*), as do many other Phalaecian epigrams (5.13 ≠ 7–9; 9.11 ≠ 10; 16.14 ≠ 1; 21.13 ≠ 8; 23.27 ≠ 24; 36.20 ≠ 1; 42.24 ≠ 11–12, 19–20; 45.26 ≠ 19; 50.21 ≠ 18, 19; 55.22 ≠ 19; 57.10 ≠ 1), three of the ἴαμβοι (8.19 ≠ 11–12; 44.21 ≠ 12; 52.4 ≠ 1) and none at all of the μέλη.

The reading of the item required no unusual pronunciation, unless it be that *mihi* (a pyrrhic at vv. 6, 11. 15)[188] and *mei* (an iambus at v. 13)[189] as a rule suffered synizesis in ordinary first-century BC speech.

o. Item 12: Morphology and Syntax

No feature of the morphology of item 12 diverges from the norm. We may note that the Greek borrowing *mnemosynum* is given a Latin termination.

Three syntagms would have been hard to find in first-century oratory: the use of a form in *-ior* without a comparative reference (v. 3); the attachment of a prepositional phrase to a noun lacking any verbal force (v. 14); and the attachment of a simple volitive subjunctive to *necesse est* (v.

---

[182] Cf. Catull. 25.
[183] Alciphron's speaking name for a parasite Μαππαφάνισος (3.12) may have originated in comedy.
[184] Cf. Mart. 8.59.8, 12.29. *mappae* were not the only objects stolen at parties (Lukillios, *A.P.* 11.315).
[185] Cf. Plaut. *Mil.* 710, 939, *Pseud.* 777, 781, *Truc.* 430–1, 443, Cic. *Verr.* II 4.62, *Parad.* 40.
[186] See above n. 67.
[187] Contrast Mart. 11.104.1 *uxor, uade foras aut moribus utere nostris.*
[188] Iambic *mihi* was a plain archaism; *mi* perhaps already the regular form. See above, n. 123.
[189] On the pronunciation of the pronominal adjective see above, n. 130.

16). All three nevertheless had firm roots in ordinary speech.[190] Textual uncertainty makes discussion of *est enim leporum* †dissertus† *puer ac facetiarum*[191] (vv. 8–9) fruitless.

p. Item 12: Sentence Structure and Word Order

The periods of item 12 are as brief as those of item 11. They are, however, all tidily, if simply, constructed. Their constituents frequently overrun the verse boundaries. The brevity of *me non mouet aestimatione uerumst mnemosynum mei sodalis* (vv. 12–13) dispenses with exact logic. The apparent ellipse in *fugit te* (v. 4) probably came with the phrase from the ordinary language.[192] The absence of extended participial phrases is again noteworthy.

The order of the words of the constituents of the periods of item 12 seems even closer to that of an utterance of the ordinary language than is that of item 10. The artificiality of the intervening item again comes out very clearly.

The seven finite verbs with accusative complements, even *mouet* (v. 12) and *amem* (v. 16), stand in constituents with a degree of independence. Two, *tollis* (v. 3) and *fugit* (v. 4), have their complements following. It is at first sight surprising that the complements of *exspecta* (v. 11) and *remitte* (v. 11) should precede, given the frequency of the opposite order where injunctions are concerned even in the lyric items. The reason is that the complements *hendecasyllabos trecentos* and *linteum* are more strongly contrasted than the imperative verbs. The position of *mihi* in v. 15 suggests that a fresh constituent begins with *miserunt* and that *sudaria Saetaba ex Hiberis* forms an extended accusative, the very focus of the whole statement. Concern for emphasis would explain the order in v. 12 and v. 16.

The pair of adjectives forming the predicate in *quamuis sordida res et inuenusta est* (v. 5) is separated by another word of the statement, as in 9.11 *quid me laetius est beatiusue?*, 10.33 *tu insulsa male et molesta uiuis*, 15.4 *quod castum expeteres et integellum*, 36.16 *acceptum face redditumque uotum* and 38.2 *male est* (*male si* V) *me hercule et laboriose*.[193] Such an

---

[190] With *sudaria . . . ex Hiberis* compare Plaut. *Merc.* 257 *navem ex Rhodo*. There may have been a growing pressure to use *ut* with *necesse est* (Cic. *De orat.* 2.129); cf., however, Cic. *Verr.* II 2.45 *et al.*

[191] Passerat's commonly accepted *differtus* leaves a genitive still hard to explain in Latin terms.

[192] Cf. Cic. *Att.* 7.18.3, 12.42.2.

[193] Similar pairs of attributes are disjoined in the same way (1.7; 56.1; cf. in the iambic items 22.9; 39.8; 60.3). Contrast the predicates at 6.2; 7.2, 10; 13.10; 36.17; 56.4.

order seems to have been common enough in the ordinary language, but the rationale is by no means clear.[194]

No adjectival attribute stands disjoined from its noun. Straightforward considerations of emphasis explain the position of *Marrucine* (v. 1), *tua* (v. 7), and *mei* (v. 13).

The several enclitics behave according to patterns visible in contemporary prose of both the formal and the less formal kind. *salsum* (v. 4) contrasts very strongly with *sordida* and *inuenusta* (v. 5). Hence it rather than *putas* offers *esse* a post to lean on.[195] *est* is the very focus of the statement made in vv. 8–9 ('he *is*, you must agree, . . .');[196] likewise of that made in v. 13 ('it *is* on the other hand').

The subordinators *qui* (v. 7), *quod* (v. 12) and *ut* (v. 17) all head their respective clauses.

q. Item 12: Vocabulary

Of the 86 words which make up item 12 none except *ac* (v. 9) and *atque* (v. 2) had anything of the tone of high poetry. Not that these were exclusively poetical. The use of *atque* before an initial consonant raised the tone. Significantly, both connectives stood in the close of a 'Phalaecian' verse, a position which tended to attract words and forms obsolete or obsolescent in the ordinary language.[197] *ex Hiberis* (v. 14) would have sounded

---

[194] Cf. Plaut. *Amph.* 33 *iustam rem et facilem esse oratam a uobis uolo,* 184 *bene quae in me fecerunt ingrata ea habuit atque inrita* (≠ 118, 348, 547, 640, 730), Cic. *Att.* 1.13.2 *consul autem ipse paruo animo et prauo tamen,* 17.9 *ut frequentissimo senatu et liberalissimo uterentur,* 18.1 *illae ambitiosae nostrae fucosaeque amicitiae,* 19.10 *me imprudente erit et inuito* (≠ 1.4.2; 16.2; 16.6; 17.8; 18.1; 19.1; 19.5; 19.8).

[195] In 10.14–15 (see above n. 156), although *natum* bears a certain emphasis, *esse* attaches to the principal verb. Dramatic texts usually kept *esse* with the predicate rather than after *puto* (Plaut. *Amph.* 170–2, 284, 886, *Bacch.* 1083, *Curc.* 557, *Persa* 609, Ter. *Andr.* 330, 717, *Haut.* 151, 912–13, 990, *Eun.* 489–90, *Phorm.* 21, Pacuv. *Trag.* 25, 176), but see Plaut. *Bacch.* 121, Ter. *Haut.* 842–3, *Ad.* 817.

[196] For *est enim* demanding a concession from the hearer see Adams (1994*b*: 80–1).

[197] Contrast the use on the one hand of *et* at vv. 5, 16, 17 and at 10.33 and on the other of *-que* at 11.11–12, 17. Cato used *atque/ac* frequently in his orations but rarely in his *De agricultura.* Cicero used it sparingly in his dialogues and letters. His epideictic speeches have it much more often than those of an argumentative or expository character. *atque* preceded a vowel in Catullus' Phalaecian epigrams at 5.1; 6.2; 21.9; 45.3; a consonant at 12.2; 13.3; 26.5; 50.6; 58.3. Four of the latter five cases occur in the close of the verse. On the 110 occasions in Plautus' scripts where it occurs before a consonant (≠ 1069 before a vowel) there is something special in the context. A large proportion of the cases in Cicero's writings help to form a clausula. On *atque* and the close of Catullus' 'Phalaecian' verse see Jocelyn (1995: 79).

more erudite, perhaps even more poetical,[198] than, say, *ex Hispania*.[199] *talentum* (v. 7), *hendecasyllabus* (v. 10) and *mnemosynum* (v. 13) were recognizably of Greek origin but had no specifically poetic associations.

As in item 10, there are in item 12 a number of words avoided in the high poetic genres of the late Republic and early Empire — *belle* (v. 2), *inepte* (v. 4), *inuenusta* (v. 5), *enim* (v. 8), *leporum* (v. 8), *facetiarum* (v. 9), *quare* (v. 10), *hendecasyllabos* (v. 10), *mnemosynum* (v. 13), *sudarium* (v. 14)[200] — and perhaps already endowed with a decidedly 'unpoetic' odour.[201] Some of these — *belle*,[202] *inuenusta*,[203] *hendecasyllabos*,[204] *mnemosynum*,[205] *sudaria*[206] — were also avoided in oratory. All of them flourished in the ordinary language. To be noted also are words given a sense avoided in formal modes of speech but admitted at other levels of the language: *tollis* (v. 3) that of 'furaris';[207] *salsum* (v. 4) that of 'lepidum' or 'festiuum';[208] *quamuis* (v. 5) that of 'ualde';[209] *mutari* (v. 8) that of 'compensari';[210] *puer*

---

[198] Greek poets and historians used the same word of the river Ebro and the inhabitants of north eastern Iberia. The Romans seem to have taken over the Carthaginian name of the peninsula. 11.2–8 talks of peoples rather than lands. The *Hiberi* rather than the land manufactured the *sudaria*.

[199] The magistrate under whom Veranius and Fabius served (28.1–3) had the province of *Hispania citerior*.

[200] On *belle, enim, lepos* and *quare* see Axelson (1945: 35, 122–3, 61 and 48). *facetus* is as rare as *facetia*.

[201] At Enn. *Ann.* 364 *enim* is usually emended away. In tragedy it appears with certainty only at Pacuv. 377. *quare* is transmitted in neither epic nor tragedy.

[202] Cicero has the adverb only twice in his speeches (*Mur.* 26, *Quinct.* 93), but 28 times in his letters.

[203] Cicero has it only at *Brut.* 237.

[204] Also at 42.1. Next at Sen. *Contr.* 7.4.7 (of Catull. 53). Outside technical writing on metre, *hendecasyllabus* always denoted the 'Phalaecian' verse. Poetry itself was a topic treated in a very gingerly way by orators.

[205] The word does not occur elsewhere in recorded Latin, which is not to say that men of Catullus' circle did not use it in the sense of 'pignus memoriae'. It would have come from contemporary spoken Greek (cf. Meleag. *A.P.* 5.136.4, Matt. *Eu.* 26.13, Mk. *Eu.* 14.9) rather than from literature.

[206] Also at 25.7. Next at Val. Max. 9.12.7, but clearly a term in common use (Petron. 67.5,13, Mart. 11.39.3 *et al.*).

[207] Cic. *Verr.* II 2.136 and Caes. *Gall.* 6.17.5 are not exactly parallel although they help to explain the semantic development. The date of *CIL* I² 2376 (≠ 498–501) is uncertain.

[208] Cf., of an act, Cic. *Att.* 16.12, Mart. 3.12.3.

[209] Cf. 103.2. Plautus has the usage at *Men.* 318, *Pseud.* 1175 (P: *quam uelis* A), Varro at *Rust.* 2.5.1, Cicero at *Rep.* 1.43, *De orat.* 2.228, *Tusc.* 3.73.

[210] Neither the *TLL* nor the *OLD* register the passage. Baehrens compared Plaut. *Bacch.* 1153, Ter. *Andr.* 40 and Hor. *Ars* 168. Neither these passages nor those cited at *TLL* VIII 1722.72–1723.12 and *OLD*, p. 1150, s.v. *muto* 7a offer any real similarity.

(v. 9) that of 'adulescens';[211] *trecentos* (v. 10) that of 'plurimos';[212] *aestima-tione* (v. 12) that of 'pretio'.[213] Veranius receives a form of his name in v. 17 which he may have received in private discourse but would never have on a formal occasion.[214] Thus the vocabulary of item 12 takes the tone of the collection very decidedly back to that of item 10 and the earlier Phalaecian epigrams and enforces from yet another aspect the stylistic isolation of the lyric item 11.

IV. CONCLUSION

Although many present-day scholars find it hard where the first 61 items of the *liber Catulli Veronensis* are concerned to separate those in stichically arranged Phalaecian hendecasyllabic verses from those in the longer units of old Aeolian verse and even from those in the three kinds of iambic verse, examination of the structure of Catullus' Phalaecian hendecasyllable and attention to the analyses of all the ancient theorists suggest that this verse had its own special character. The specialness of the character transferred itself to the poems formed from runs of the verse. The request made of Furius and Aurelius in Sapphic stanzas has, I hope, been shown to differentiate itself from the account of the behaviour of Varus' whore and the denunciation of Asinius' theft not only in its metrical pattern but also in its wording and phrasing and in the ordering of its words. The plea to the anonymous *colonia* for a certain entertainment (item 17) can also be shown to stand apart in similar fashion from the threats against Furius and Aurelius (items 16 and 21). So also the complaint about Alfenus' treachery (item 30) from the iambic attack on Caesar's generosity towards Mamurra (item 29) and the iambic salute to Sirmio (item 31). So also the hymn to Diana (item 34) from the curse on Vibennius and son (item 33) and the invitation to Caecilius (item 35). So also the description of the effect of looking at Lesbia (item 51) from the account of writing verses in the company of Calvus (item 50) and the expression of disgust at the political success of Nonius and Vatinius (item 52). Nevertheless, while the Phalaecian epigrams and the ἴαμβοι approached much nearer the

[211] The Pollio named in v. 6 is clearly one able to mix in adult society, i.e. a youth above the age of sixteen. Slaves above that age could be called *pueri*. Catullus must be talking condescendingly of the younger Asinius.
[212] Cf. 9.2, 48.3, Hor. *Serm.* 1.5.12, 2.3.115–16, *Epist.* 2.2.164–5, Mart. 2.1.1, 12.70.7. Contrast 11.18 (see n. 54).
[213] Vitr. 10 pr. 1 is not completely parallel.
[214] Cf. the way Cicero refers to his daughter (*Tullia*) at *Att.* 1.8.3, *Fam.* 14.1 (*Tulliola*). Fabullus would have been the affectionate form of the name of Catullus' other friend.

ordinary language than did the μέλη, it does not appear that they disdained entirely the archaisms of the high genres of the previous century's poetry or the novelties of contemporary poetry.

Word order and vocabulary enforced differentiation more strongly than patterns of sound or features of grammar, although, where word order was concerned, Catullus took a fairly scrupulous account of ordinary contemporary speech. Where he had room for a conscious decision, whether in syntax or the lexicon, the desire to avoid one form or another of current linguistic behaviour proved as powerful as any more positive consideration. Rarely can metrical exigency have been a very strong determinant. The theme and the tone of a particular poem had their effect, but these were as much tied to the genre as the metre and the type of language were. The extent to which the five μέλη in question all emerge stylistically from their respective contexts gives some support to the view that Catullus or an editor designed the order of items 1–60 of the transmitted collection, although with more attention to form than to substance,[215] and that the designer meant item 61 to stand with these rather than with items 62–68. The common use of the term *polymetra* of items 1–60 is deplorable not merely because it corresponds with no ancient usage but also because, like the term 'lyrics', it diverts attention from the diversity of the poems in question. At all events the notion of a single 'natural' variety of the Latin language informing them all should be discarded.

Note. I have not as a rule marked my thefts from the *Thesaurus Linguae Latinae* or the grammars of Kühner and Stegmann and of Leumann, Hofmann and Szantyr. J. N. Adams did more than pick nits from an early draft of the chapter. Some objections put by G. P. Goold to its approach and some of its theses led to sharper formulations.

---

[215] This is not to say that the tradition preserves exactly every detail of the original design. A tidy mind could suppose that between, say, item 46 and item 47 it lost the lyric hymn to Priapus cited by the metricians and that between item 51 and item 52 it lost a Phalaecian epigram. At any rate the problem which the hymn to Priapus poses for the student of the arrangement of the *liber Catulli Veronensis* cannot be circumvented by the notion that some grammarian found it without an author's name in a collection of *Priapea* and ascribed it on no objective grounds to Catullus, let alone by its dismissal from editions of the work ascribed to the poet by our tradition.

Proceedings of the British Academy, **93**, 377–398

Tibullus and the Language of Latin Elegy

R. MALTBY

Summary. Ovid shares with Tibullus a number of the features generally attributed to Tibullan *elegantia*. It is Propertius whose verbal exuberance and mythological complexity mark him out from the others. These differences are perhaps to be attributed in some degree to the influence of Messalla on Tibullus and Ovid, and of Gallus on Propertius. Finally the concept of Tibullan *elegantia* needs to be redefined. His style is not consistently restrained but is capable on occasion of considerable elaboration and variety, which are all the more effective in contrast with his overall linguistic purity.

I. INTRODUCTION

RICHARD BÜRGER (1911: 371–94) argued that Tibullus was an analogist, showing preference for one form of word or synonym over another, and avoiding all lexical peculiarities, be it excessive colloquialism or high-style phraseology. He pointed out that Tibullus pefers *seu* over *sive, neu* for *neve* and *atque* for *ac*; he uses *fessus* for the colloquial *lassus, ventus* not *aura, gaudium* not *laetitia*. He avoids diminutives, Greek loan-words and the intimate erotic vocabulary used by Catullus and Propertius of their mistresses, e.g. *lux, vita, deliciae*. Bürger was justly criticized by Axelson (1945: 114–33) for attributing these features of Tibullus' style to the influence of Caesar and the analogists. Axelson claimed that Tibullus' choice of one word or form over another was often metrically motivated and in line with the practice of the other Roman elegists. The fact that Tibullus did not avoid the alternative forms of the perfect *ĕrunt, ērunt, -ere* and the syncopated form of *-erunt*, and that he used the doublets *senecta* and *senectus*, *deorum* and *deum*, *quibus* and *quis*, *caeruleus* and *caerulus*, *vinculum* and *vinclum* did much to discredit Bürger's analogist theory. Murgatroyd (1980: 16) added to Axelson's objections that Tibullus made use of the synonyms *anguis* and *serpens*, *umens* and *umidus*, *porto* and *veho*, and *coma*, *capillus* and *crinis* without apparent distinction. In fact Tibullus makes an even wider use of synonyms than that shown by Murgatroyd.[1] Despite these criticisms, Bürger nevertheless provided a sound basis for later studies of the *elegantia* and cultivated style for which Tibullus was praised in antiquity.[2] The features of this style, which were derived ultimately from the λεπτότηs of Callimachus and his followers including, amongst the Romans, Virgil in the *Eclogues* and Horace in the *Odes*, are best summed up by J. P. Elder (1962: 68) as 'purity of... diction, straightforwardness of... syntax, and directness of... comparisons'.

Bürger and subsequent students of the style of Tibullus, including Axelson, rarely provide accurate comparative statistics from the other two elegists, Propertius and Ovid. This leaves their conclusions open to an objection. It could be said that emphasis, ancient and modern, on Tibullan *elegantia* has obscured the fact that in essence Tibullus' style is little different from that of Ovid in the *Amores*, so Lee (1975: 9), whereas Propertius' verbal exuberance, reminiscent of his Hellenistic literary forebears and probably also of Gallus, sets him apart from the others. My aim is to answer this potential objection by taking some features of Tibullan style and comparing them directly with Propertius and Ovid. Usually Tibullus emerges as the most restrained of the three, but in almost all cases Ovid is closer to Tibullus than to Propertius.

The stylistic similarities between Tibullus and Ovid and their differences from Propertius are, I shall argue, to some extent explicable by the tastes of their patrons. A further conclusion is that one of the advantages of Tibullan stylistic purity was that, when he did use a colourful, daring or out of the way expression, its effect would be all the more telling by contrast with his normal style.

---

[1] Add to Murgatroyd's list of Tibullan synonyms: *volucer / avis, verax / verus, bracchium / lacertus, flumen / amnis, velox / celer, unda / aqua, lectus / torus, cunctus / totus / omnis, tellus / terra, taciturnus / tacitus, sopor / somnus, sanguinolentus / sanguineus, ploro / fleo, letum / mors, uxor / coniunx, puella / virgo*. On the distribution of the last two pairs in Latin poetry see Watson (1983: 119–43; 1985: 431–4), Adams (1980a: 234–55).

[2] Ovid, *Amores* 1.15.28 *donec erunt ignes arcusque Cupidinis arma / discentur numeri, culte Tibulle, tui*; 3.9.66 *auxisti numeros, culte Tibulle, pios*; Quintilian *Inst.* 10.1.93 *elegia quoque Graecos provocamus, cuius mihi tersus atque elegans maxime videtur auctor Tibullus, sunt qui Propertium malint. Ovidius utroque lascivior, sicut durior Gallus*; Velleius Paterculus 2.36.3 *Tibullus ... et Naso, perfectissimi in forma operis sui*.

II. GREEK LOAN-WORDS[3]

Horace informs us that Tibullus' patron, M. Valerius Messalla Corvinus, had strong views on foreign loan-words. In his speeches he was careful to use pure Latin only.[4] Porphyrion ad loc. states that Messalla went so far as to invent *funambulus*, as a Latin equivalent for the Greek σχοινοβάτης.[5] Messalla's views on the avoidance of Greek in official speeches were no doubt widespread.[6] Whether they would apply to verse might be doubted by some, but the context in which Horace cites him, namely an attack on the heavily Graecizing nature of Lucilius' verse, only makes sense if Messalla's views extended to poetry also. Appendix A lists the Greek loan-words which I have found in the three elegists. The Tibullan examples not in Bürger's list (1911: 387) are asterisked — a warning, if needed, about the unreliability of material collected before proper word-indexes were available.

Greek loan-words as a group are not uniform in their associations. They enter the Latin language at different periods and belong to different registers. No doubt the elegists' audience would have recognized most as Greek, but a word such as *sandyx*, ('red dye' or cloth of that colour), recently introduced by Virgil in his *Eclogues*, would presumably have sounded more foreign and exotic than *coma* ('hair'), which had been at home in Latin poetic diction since Pacuvius' day.[7] Similarly, scientific and technical terms like *hippomanes* (again recently introduced by Virgil in his *Georgics*) would have learned or didactic associations absent from the names of common utensils such as *cadus* or *crater*. A gradation of 'Greekness' can be established, starting at the least Greek end of the scale with words where early vowel weakening, e.g. *canistrum*, or the addition of a Latin suffix, e.g. *gypsatus*, *euhans*, displays a high degree of integration, through words well-established in the ordinary language, e.g. *poeta* or in technical vocabularies *podagra*, to rare or unusual Greek borrowings, e.g. *catasta*, or *antrum*, often restricted to verse, and ending with words which retain their Greek terminations, e.g. *cometen* (Tib. 2.5.71), *beryllon* (Prop.

---

[3] On Greek loan-words in Latin see Weise (1882), Palmer (1954: 81–4, 186), Kaimio (1979), Biville (1990).

[4] Horace, *Satires* 1.10.27ff. *Latine / cum Pedius causas exsudet Publicola atque / Corvinus, patriis intermiscere petita / verba foris malis, Canusini more bilinguis?*

[5] Porphyrion ad 1.10.28 *Pedius Publicola et Messalla adeo curasse dicuntur ne Graeca Latinis verbis inmiscerent, ut Messalla primus funambulum dixerit, ne σχοινοβάτην diceret.*

[6] Cf. the anecdote in Suetonius, *Tiberius* 71 about Tiberius' avoidance of Greek in the senate and his rejection of the word ἔμβλημα from a senatorial decree; see further Kaimio (1979: 106).

[7] The commonly occurring *coma* and *poeta* are excluded from the list on the grounds that their Greek origin was no longer strongly felt.

4.7.9). This last type, inflected in Greek, is a rare category in all three elegists (Tib. 3 per cent, Prop. 6 per cent, Ov. 5 per cent). Quintilian 1.5.58ff. suggests they should be avoided by orators and gives as an example (1.5.61) Messalla's use of the Latinized form of the nominative *Euthia* for *Euthias*, probably in his *oratio Hyperidis pro Phryne in lat. versa*. From the practice of the elegists it would seem that such reticence about the use of Greek terminations in Latin also extended to verse.

To clarify the distribution of these types amongst the elegists Appendix A gives the author of first attestation for each loan-word and shows the main categories to which each poet's Greek borrowings belong.

The frequency of different Greek words in Tibullus (one in 40 lines) is slightly greater than in Ovid (one in 45 lines). Even Propertius, with one in 36 lines, is not markedly out of step. In occurrences, however, Tibullus is more sparing (one in 32 lines), as opposed to Ovid (one in 23) and Propertius (one in 16).[8]

Of course the author of first attestation can only give a rough guide to when a word actually entered the language, but, with this proviso in mind, all three elegists use in similar proportions Greek words borrowed early (Plautus or before) and Greek borrowings from the time of Cicero and the neoterics (Tib. early 46.5 per cent, time of Cic. 46 per cent; Prop. early 37 per cent, time of Cic. 41 per cent; Ov. early 38 per cent, time of Cic. 36 per cent) with near contemporary borrowings (from Horace on) forming the smallest category (Tib. 13.5 per cent; Prop. 22 per cent; Ov. 26 per cent). Tibullus, however, is noticeably more restricted in his recent borrowings, showing a marked preference for Greek loan-words established before the Augustan period. Propertius (23 per cent) has a much greater proportion of rare or unusual words or words restricted to verse than Tibullus (17 per cent) or Ovid (14 per cent); he also has more words with Greek terminations (Prop. 6 per cent, Tib. 3 per cent, Ov. 5 per cent). Propertius (14 per cent) makes greater use of Greek words with Latin suffixes than Tibullus (7 per cent) and Ovid (4 per cent).

As for the lexical categories of Greek loan-words, the most frequent type in all three authors are words connected with poetry and music. Only in Propertius is the traditionally productive category of words connected with the life of luxury equally important. Propertius also differs in making much greater use of technical terms from the lower registers connected with sport, shipping and, in particular, household equipment and utensils.

---

[8] Joan Booth reminds me that Tib.'s avoidance of Greek does not extend to proper names, where his *noms parlants* Pholoe and Nemesis are Greek. To these I would add Marathus (on which see Murgatroyd 1980: 9) and Delia. In fact the use of meaningful Greek names is well established in Latin literature of all genres, especially comedy, lyric and pastoral.

It is striking that this last category is completely absent from Ovid. Clearly Propertius was willing to go further than Tibullus and Ovid in extending the lexical range of elegy to include terms more at home in the lower genres of comedy and satire.

As the figures for the frequency of Greek borrowings over Propertius' four books show, this stylistic feature becomes more marked in his later books. There is a contrast here with his use of diminutives, which, as shown below, become less frequent in Books 3 and 4. As Norden (1910: 507) points out, Propertius has more Greek loan-words than Virgil, Horace and Tibullus put together. This feature may be intended to parallel in Latin poetry the varied use of lexical registers and Greek dialect forms in his Hellenistic forerunners. The increase in his later books may be due to his movement away from personal love elegy towards experiments with more consciously Hellenistic themes. What is certain is that this is not an area where Tibullan influence led him progressively to restrict his usage.

Greek loan-words in Tibullus are clearly concentrated in poems where Hellenistic influence is particularly noticeable.[9] These are: 1.7, a birthday poem for Messalla which also praises his patron for his military victories abroad — a combination of a genethliakon and an epinikion, with clear echoes from Callimachus frr. 383 and 384 Pf., which were probably epinikia; 2.5 an invocatory hymn to Apollo ($\kappa\lambda\eta\tau\iota\kappa\grave{o}s$ $\H{v}\mu\nu os$) on the occasion of the appointment of Messalla's son Messalinus as one of the *Quindecim-viri Sacris Faciundis*, a poem displaying much antiquarian and literary *doctrina*, and again containing echoes from Callimachus, especially *Hymn* 2 (to Apollo). Apart from these two poems Greek loan-words are very rare indeed in Tibullus. Of course, this rarity makes their effect all the more striking, especially if they are concentrated in a single passage. A particularly good example is:

> vota loquor: regnum ipse tenet quem saepe coegit
> *barbara gypsatos* ferre *catasta* pedes. (2.3.59–60)

Here three words of Greek origin in a single pentameter serve to empha-size the barbaric character of Tibullus' rival for Nemesis, a foreign ex-slave. The word *barbarus* on its own would perhaps by this date be scarcely recognizable as Greek, but here it gains significance through its occurrence in a cluster of Greek loan-words. The rare *catasta*, which occurs first here or at Livy 28.21.2 and then not in verse again until Persius (6.77), refers to a revolving platform on which slaves were exhibited for sale. When on the

---

[9] Concentrations of Greek words in Tibullus: 1.3.59 *chorea*, 61 *casia*, 66 *myrteus*; 1.7.12 *lympha*, 15 *aetherius*, 28 *barbarus*, 44 *chorus*, 45 *corymbus*, 48 *cista*, 49 *chorea*; 2.5.2 *cithara*, 3 *chorda*, 17 *charta*, 32 *calamus*, 48 *barbarus*, 71 *cometes*, 98 *calix*.

catasta, foreign slaves were distinguished from *vernae* by having their feet smeared with gypsum. The verb *gypso*, derived ultimately from the Greek γύψος, occurs before here only at Cicero, *Epistulae ad Familiares* 7.6.1. The verb is retained by Ovid in his imitation of this line at *Amores* 1.8.64:

> nec tu, siquis erit capitis mercede redemptus,
> despice; gypsati crimen inane pedis.

But in Propertius 4.5.51–2:

> aut quorum titulus per barbara colla pependit,
> cretati medio cum saluere foro

where the epithet *barbara* in 51 suggests an echo of Tibullus, the Greek *gypsatus* is replaced by the Latin *cretatus*. Finally the application of *barbarus*, the Greek for 'foreigner', to a Greek is an ironic reversal of the common Plautine joke by which the word is used in the mouths of Greeks to refer to Romans.[10]

To sum up: it is Propertius who stands out from Tibullus and Ovid both in his greater frequency of Greek loan-words and in his wider lexical range. It is perhaps worth recalling that Messalla, the aristocratic defender of pure Latinity, in addition to being Tibullus' patron also encouraged Ovid's first attempts at verse.[11]

III. '*VERSUS ECHOICI*'

If Tibullus is somewhat restricted in his use of Greek loan-words, this is not the case with his introduction into Latin verse of a number of Hellenistic Greek rhetorical figures. The device of repeating the beginning of the hexameter at the end of the pentameter, a feature of Hellenistic epigram, as exemplified from Callimachus and Meleager[12], is attested for the first time in Latin poetry in Tibullus 1.4.61–2:

---

[10] Plautus, *As.* 11, *Mil.* 211, *Most.* 828.
[11] For Messalla as the patron of Ovid's early work, see Ovid *Pont.* 2.3.75ff. (to Messalla's son, Cotta Maximus): *me tuus ille pater . . / primus ut auderem commitere carmina famae / impulit: ingenii dux fuit ille mei*, and cf. *Trist.* 4.4.27ff., *Pont.* 1.7.27ff., 2.2.97f.
[12] *versus echoici*, cf. Martial 2.86.3 *nusquam Graecula quod recantat echo*; *AP* 7.518.1–2 (Callimachus)

> Ἀστακίδην τὸν Κρῆτα τόν αἰπόλον ἥρπασε Νύμφη
> ἐξ ὄρεος, καὶ νῦν ἱερὸς Ἀστακίδης,

AP 5.176.1–2 (Meleager)

> δεινὸς Ἔρως, δεινός· τί δὲ τὸ πλέον ἦν πάλιν εἴπω
> καὶ πάλιν οἰμώζων πολλάκι, 'δεινὸς Ἔρως';

> Pieridas, pueri, doctos et amate poetas.
> aurea nec superent munera Pieridas.

It is significant that this occurs in a lecture on the art of homosexual love, delivered by a statue of the god Priapus — an elegy, which, like 1.7 and 2.5, displays a considerable degree of Alexandrian influence. There is no example of such a *versus echoicus* in Propertius, but it becomes a favourite trick of Ovid's style,[13] with perhaps the best known example occurring at *Amores* 1.9.1–2

> militat omnis amans, et habet sua castra Cupido;
> Attice, crede mihi, militat omnis amans.

It is then used rather excessively by later Latin poets, see Munari (1971: 350, n. 10).

Another version of this is where the opening of the second half of the pentameter repeats the opening of the first half.[14] This becomes something of a characteristic hallmark of Tibullan style, often giving emphasis to the end of an elegy:

> 1.1.78 despiciam dites despiciamque famem
> 1.4.82 deficiunt artes deficiuntque doli
> 1.7.64 candidior semper candidiorque veni
> 2.5.100 caespitibus mensas caespitibusque torum

In all the Latin examples -*que* is attached to the echoed word, which is always in penultimate position in the line. Three of the poems in which it occurs are characterized by marked Hellenistic influence: 1.4, 1.7 and 2.5. It is not found in Propertius, but is used occasionally by Ovid. Its Greek origin is emphasized by its combination with Greek proper names in *Heroides* 4.112 *Pirithoum Phaedrae Pirithoumque tibi*, while *Amores* 2.11.10 *et gelidum Borean egelidumque Notum* is a humorous variation on the type. According to Seneca (*Contr.* 2.2.12) this last line was judged by Ovid's friends to be one of his three worst and by Ovid himself to be one of his three best.

In their use of *versus echoici* Tibullus and Ovid again resemble each other, but differ from Propertius. Tibullus appears to have been the innovator, although given the loss of Gallus and of so much neoteric poetry certainty on this point is impossible. His techniques were then taken up and developed further by Ovid. Again a connection with the circle of

---

[13] Ovid *Amores* 1.4.13–14, 1.9.1–2, 3.2.17–18, 43–4, *Ars* 1.191–2, *Epist.* 10.11–2, *Rem.* 71–2, 705–6, *Fast.* 2.235–6, *Trist.* 4.3.77–8.

[14] For Greek pentameter echoes, cf. *AP* 5.159.4 (Simonides) καὶ πόθεν αἱ ζῶναι καὶ πόθεν οἱ πίνακες; *AP* 6.13.6 (Leonidas) τῷ δὲ διὰ δρυμῶν, τῷ δὲ δι᾽ ἠϊόνων.

Messalla suggests itself. If, as seems likely, the pseudo-Virgilian *Catalepton* 9.13ff.[15] refers to Messalla, then he composed pastoral and erotic verse in Greek. It is possible that Tibullus and other members of the circle, such as the young Ovid, could have been influenced by the Hellenistic techniques displayed in these poems and encouraged to adapt them to Latin verse. Tibullus could, of course, have taken them directly from Hellenistic poetry, but it is strange that these particular types are not also to be found in Propertius, who in other areas shows a mastery of Hellenistic verse technique.

IV. POSTPONED PARTICLES

The postponement of the particles *et, at, atque, aut, nam,* and *namque* develops in neoteric verse in imitation of a Hellenistic Greek poetic mannerism.[16] Examples of postponed καὶ in Hellenistic poetry are given in Haupt (1875: 136–7) and Norden (1957: 402 n. 4). It is possible that the postponement of *nam* and *namque* could have been based on the analogy of *enim*, see Janson (1979: 95–6), but if so, it is strange that no clear example of postponed *nam* is found until Catullus 23.7[17] and of *namque* until Catullus 64.384. Platnauer's figures (1951: 93–6) for postponed particles in elegy suggest that this is more frequent in Tibullus and Propertius than in Ovid's *Amores*. To test this hypothesis all the examples of postponed *et* in Tibullus, Propertius and Ovid's *Amores* were counted.[18] Tibullus is the most frequent user (one in 32 lines). Again poems 1.4 and

---

[15] [Virg.] *Catalepton* 9.13ff.

> pauca tua in nostras venerunt carmina chartas,
> carmina cum lingua, tum sale Cecropio.
>
> . . .
>
> molliter hic viridi patulae sub tegmine quercus
> Moeris pastores et Meliboeus erant.
>
> . . .
>
> felicem ante alias o te scriptore puellam
> altera non fama dixerit esse prior.

[16] On postponement of particles see Haupt (1875), Schünke (1906), Artymowicz (1909), Norden (1957: 402–4), Platnauer (1951: 93–6), Ross (1969: 67–9).

[17] At Plautus *Mil.* 1379, *Pers.* 379 and *Pseud.* 521 the text is unsound. The conjecture of *nam* for *non* in Valerius Aedituus fr. 2.3 (Buecheler) should be rejected.

[18] Postponed *et*: Tibullus 1.1:3, 1.2:3, 1.3:1, 1.4:5, 1.5:2, 1.6:1, 1.7:6, 1.8:0, 1.9:1, 1.10:4, 2.1:3, 2.2:2, 2.3:5, 2.4:0, 2.5:2, 2.6:1 39 occurrences = 1 in 32 lines.
Propertius, Book 1, 23 = 1 in 30 lines; Book 2, 31 = 1 in 45 lines; Book 3, 19 = 1 in 52 lines; Book 4, 23 = 1 in 44 lines; Propertius 96 occurrences = 1 in 42 lines.
Ovid, *Amores* 1.3.10, 1.9.22, 1.15.34, 2.1.32, 2.6.35, 2.9.10, 2.10.36, 3.8.21, 3.12.18, 9 occurrences = 1 in 273 lines.

1.7, where Hellenistic influence is strong, have the most examples (5 and 6 respectively); though 2.5 has a surprisingly low total of two. Propertius is next in frequency (one in 42 lines). In the first book, however, it is more frequent (one in 30 lines) than in Tibullus, perhaps because of strong Catullan influence on the *Monobiblos*.

In this case it is Ovid who stands out as making very infrequent use of the device, with only 9 instances in the whole of the *Amores* (one in 273 lines). How are these figures to be explained? Unlike the *versus echoici*, which occur for the first time in Tibullus, the postponing of these particles had been introduced into Latin poetry by Catullus and his neoteric contemporaries, poets who, according to Tränkle (1960: 22–9) were particularly influential on Propertius, especially in his first book. Now as Norden (1957: 402) argues the reason why this Hellenistic device commended itself to both Greek and Latin writers was mainly metrical convenience and the need to keep unimportant words from taking up the emphatic first position in the line. It could be that Ovid, with his greater metrical facility and fastidiousness, simply found other, less artificial ways of overcoming these problems.

However, Ovid does follow Tibullus in his extension of this Hellenistic device to the postponement of enclitic -*que* to follow four-syllable verbs in the second half of the pentameter.[19] As Schünke (1906: 114–5) shows, Tibullus was the first to make use of this figure with -*que*, of which he lists ten examples in Books 1 and 2. Propertius has only one example, in his second book, while Ovid uses it five times in the *Amores* and more frequently in his later works, so McKeown (1987: 83). Ovid's greater use of this figure in comparison with Propertius is perhaps to be explained on the grounds that Ovid is complimenting its inventor Tibullus, an author whose style as a fellow member of Messalla's circle he greatly admired. Tibullus and Propertius, on the other hand, were to some extent rivals, working in their own contrasting styles, and although undoubtedly they may echo one another's verse, and although Tibullus' first book may have influenced to some extent the style and particularly the metrics of Propertius' later work, so Murgatroyd (1980: 13–15), conscious imitation, of the type we can see in Ovid, particularly, for example in *Amores* 3.9 on Tibullus' death, is rare.

---

[19] e.g. Tibullus 1.1.25 *pocula, de facili composuitque luto*; 2.5.90 *accendet, flammas transilietque sacras*; also at 1.3.14, 1.3.38, 1.6.54, 1.6.72, 1.7.62, 2.3.54, 2.5.70, 2.5.72. Propertius 2.20.12 *ferratam Danaes transiliamque domum*. Ovid *Amores* 1.8.112, 3.7.10, 3.10.12, 3.13.30, 3.14.12.

V. COMPOUND ADJECTIVES

It would be all too easy in a study of this kind to be guilty of selectivity in chosing features to back up the thesis that Ovid shares many of the characteristics of Tibullus' *elegantia*, and that it is Propertius whose linguistic exuberance sets him apart from the other two. In the interests of a balanced view an attempt was made to find an aspect of Tibullan *elegantia* that did not conform to this pattern. The only one to emerge was his avoidance of compound adjectives (see Appendix B). As with Greek loan-words, compound adjectives are a very diverse category.[20] Some of them, e.g. *agricola, benignus, magnificus*, are well established in all registers and are not restricted to poetic language; others, particularly those based on the suffixes *-ger* and *-fer*, came to be regarded as characteristic of high-style epic and tragic diction. Ennius is credited with increasing Latin's native stock of compound adjectives by attaching standard suffixes, and occasionally prefixes, to a wide variety of nouns on the analogy of Greek poetic practice. In Catullus these compounds occur most frequently in the long poems, see Ross (1969: 17–22). Tibullus' use is particularly restricted,[21] with only eight occurrences of six words (one in 155 lines). None of the six was invented by Tibullus, and only *imbrifer*, which occurs for the first time at Virgil, *Georg.* 1.313, and *lanificus*, which is used adjectivally for the first time in Tibullus, are at all rare. Earlier, from Lucilius on, *lanificus* occurs only as a feminine noun *lanifica* 'woman spinner' or 'weaver'. There is a parallel here with *agricola*, which occurs as a noun from Plautus on, but is used adjectivally first in Tibullus. The only other point of note is the use of *naufragus* in the active sense of 'shipwrecking', a sense also attested in Horace, *Carm.* 1.16.10, cf. Virgil, *Aen.* 3.553.[22]

Propertius, with 28 occurrences of 21 words (one in 144 lines), is not notably freer in his use than Tibullus. What does mark him out from Tibullus is his willingness to invent new compounds. No fewer than eight of his 21 compounds are attested for the first time in Propertius. Furthermore, by far the majority of Propertius' compounds are rare or poetic, with only three, *agricola, artifex* and *sacrilegus*, occuring regularly in prose. There is a marked increase in these compounds in Propertius' later books, especially Book 3. Again, as with Greek loan-words, this corresponds with

---

[20] On compounds in general in Latin see Bader (1962).
[21] But not as restricted as Ross (1979: 19 n.8) suggests, where he finds only two.
[22] For other examples of the use of adjectives in such an active sense in Tibullus see Cairns (1979: 109).

a move away from more subjective elegy towards more general themes where Hellenistic influence is more noticeable.

Ovid is much less restricted than Tibullus and even than Propertius, with 28 occurrences of 26 words (one in 98 lines). Of these no fewer than ten are attested for the first time in Ovid. Only four occur commonly in prose, *benignus, carnifex, magnificus* and *munificus*. Such compounds were to become more common in the *Metamorphoses*. But already in the *Amores*, as Booth has shown (1981: 2696–7), they could be used to add a touch of high-flown poeticism, as with the reference to the river Po at 2.17.32 as *populifer*, or a note of mock solemnity as when the epithet *Martigenae* is used at 3.4.39 for Romulus and Remus, the result of an extra-marital *affaire*. This is a case then where Ovid's inventiveness and wit lead him beyond the bounds observed by the other elegists.

VI. DIMINUTIVES

Tibullus' *elegantia* involved avoiding not only words such as compound adjectives whose tone was too elevated for elegy, but also colloquial features such as certain diminutives, whose tone could have been too conversational. This is one of the few features for which Axelson (1945: 41–3) gives full figures from all the elegists. An analysis of his findings is set out in Appendix C. Diminutives are again a diverse class, used in a wide variety of contexts, not all of which are colloquial[23]. Of the three elegists Tibullus is the least frequent user (one in 177 lines) and none of his six examples is especially colloquial. He is careful to avoid 'affective' diminutives of the type *ocellus*, used frequently in erotic contexts by both Propertius (*ocellus* 18: *oculus* 18) and Ovid (*ocellus* 11: *oculus* 25). Of the diminutives he does use, *capella* is the regular word for 'she-goat' in Augustan poetry; it appears to have been the base-form *capra* that was the everyday word from which most Romance reflexes are derived (Axelson 1945: 44–5). *fabella* is used in its specialized sense of a story told to children (cf. Cic. *de Fin.* 5.42 *(parvi) ... fabellarum auditione ducuntur*) and adds an air of innocence to the story-telling scene at 1.3.85. *fiscella* 'cheese basket' is an item of technical vocabulary, with no diminutive force (cf. Virg. *Ecl.* 10.71). *novellus* is perhaps the most unusual of Tibullus' diminutives. It refers normally to the young of animals (e.g. Varro, *Rust.* 1.20.2 *novellos ... iuvencos*) and in its context at 2.2.22 *ludat et ante tuas turba novella pedes* perhaps likens the crowd of young children playing at their father's feet in an affectionate way to a litter of young animals.

---

[23] On diminutives see Gow (1931), Hanssen (1951), Hakamies (1951), Adams (1995*b*: 543–65).

Tibullus' two remaining diminutives, *tabella*, once of a writing tablet (2.6.45) and once of a picture in a temple (1.3.38), and *tigillum* (2.1.39) of a small rafter used in the constuction of a primitive house, are technical words with no particular affective or colloquial tone. Propertius has more diminutives (one in 75 lines) than either Tibullus or Ovid. In contrast with Tibullus he is not averse to using affective diminutives of the type *auricula*, *labellum*, *lectulus*, *ocellus*, *parvulus* and *vocula*. These are much more frequent in the first two books, where again Catullan influence could have been important.[24] Propertius' use of *auricula* in Book 1 is the only occurrence of this diminutive in elegy. The context is a shut-out lover's complaint:

> Prop. 1.16.27–8   o utinam triecta cava mea vocula rima
>   percussas dominae vertat in auriculas.

As Fedeli points out (1980: 389), the presence of the rare *vocula* (27) and of *ocellos* (31) in the same context argues for an affective use of the diminutive here.[25] Tibullus and Ovid in the *Amores* use only *auris* (Tib. 1; Ov. *Am.* 5). The distribution of *ocellus* in Propertius is instructive here. Whereas in Book 1 it is the only word for 'eye', it disappears completely in Books 3 and 4 (Book 1 *ocellus* 10 — *oculus* 0; Book 2 *ocellus* 8 — *oculus* 5; Book 3 *ocellus* 0 — *oculus* 5; Book 4 *ocellus* 0 — *oculus* 8 — see Axelson (1945: 41–2)). This drastic reduction in diminutives in Books 3 and 4 may to some extent be a result of the change in tone and subject matter of the last two books, referred to above, but it is also possible that the restraint displayed by Tibullus in his first book may have influenced Propertius' later practice. Ovid is more restrained than Propertius in his use of diminutives (one in 98 lines), but unlike Tibullus he does not avoid the affective use of *labellum* and *ocellus*. His other diminutives are not particularly colloquial in tone and in general his usage is closer to that of Tibullus.

To summarize the findings so far, it is clear that except in the case of compound adjectives the purity of diction displayed by Tibullus is also a characteristic of Ovid's style in the *Amores*. The main contrast is between these two, both protégés of Messalla, and Propertius, a poet much influenced in his early career by Gallus, who could actually have been his first patron.[26]

---

[24] On Catullus' use of diminutives see Fordyce (1961: 95–6).
[25] On specialized uses of *auricula* in the sense of 'inner-ear' or 'ear-lobe' see Hanssen (1951: 117), André (1980: 7–18), Önnerfors (1989: 130–57) and Adams (1995b: 550–1).
[26] See Cairns (1986) and cf. Cairns (1983).

VII. ETYMOLOGICAL WORD PLAY

A detailed investigation of this topic in elegy would go beyond the scope of this chapter. One point, however, does seem relevant to the present investigation. Such interest in the origins of words is well attested in Tibullus and in Ovid,[27] and although it is not entirely absent from Propertius, particularly when the word play involves proper names,[28] it does not appear to be characteristic of his style. This is another area where the interests of Tibullus and Ovid coincide and contrast with those of Propertius. Again it would be tempting to see in this difference the influence of Messalla on Tibullus and Ovid. Seneca's comment at *Contr.* 2.4.8 that Messalla was a *Latini . . . sermonis observator diligentissimus* suggests at least that Messalla was particularly careful in his own choice of language.

VIII. TIBULLUS 1.4 AND THE MOCK DIDACTIC STYLE

The linguistic peculiarities of Tibullus 1.4. are adduced here as a final illustration of the effect of Tibullus' occasional departures from his stylistic norm. As argued earlier, this imaginary dialogue between the poet and a statue of Priapus is one in which Hellenistic influence is particularly marked. Priapus' art of homosexual love is commonplace in its precepts, but they are delivered in an amusingly pompous, mock didactic style, tricked out with numerous linguistic peculiarities and literary allusions.[29] The contrast with the Tibullan norm is noticeable and effective. Priapus' speech is introduced and concluded by the mock-epic phrases *sic ego: tum Bacchi respondit rustica proles* (7) and *haec mihi . . . deus edidit ore* (73). For the first, cf. Virg. *Aen.* 1.325 *sic Venus: et Veneris contra sic filius orsus,* and for the mock-heroic effect of *proles,* see Norden on *Aen.* 6.784. For *edidit ore,* cf. Virg. *Aen.* 7.194 *haec . . . placido prior edidit ore* (of Latinus). Priapus' speech begins, significantly, with a syntactical Graecism, *fuge . . . credere,*[30] modelled on the Greek φεύγειν + inf. (cf. Herod. 4.76, Plato, *Apol.* 26A) and occurring for the first time in Latin in Lucretius 1.1052

---

[27] Tibullus: Cairns (1979: 90–9), Maltby (1993), Murgatroyd (1994: *passim*). Ovid *Amores*: McKeown (1987: 45–61).

[28] Propertius: e.g. *Vertumnus* 4.2.10, *Velabrum* 4.9.5, cf. Cairns (1984).

[29] To the mock-didactic elements listed in my discussion Professor David West suggests the following additions: 5–6 *nudus . . . nudus,* cf. Virg. *Georg.* 1.299 *nudus ara, sere nudus*; 31–2 the ageing horse, cf. Lucr. 5.886–7; 55 echoes the famous Sapphic tag 1.21, cf. Hor. *Carm.* 2.5.13, 2.12.27–8; the undermining of Tibullus' position at the end of the poem is a standard feature of Horatian mock-didactic, e.g. *Epod.* 1.2.

[30] Professor David West points out that the verb retains an element of its literal sense viz. *fuge turbam.*

fuge credere, Memmi. This is the first of a number of echoes of Lucretius' didactic style. The pentameter has a mock-legal solemnity; *causam habere* and *iusta causa* are frequent in legal texts, and there is irony in *iusti...amoris* with reference to homosexual love. The legal humour here, and the play on technical terms, is very reminiscent of Ovid. More Lucretian echoes follow in 18–21: for the proverbial wearing away of stone by water, *longa dies molli saxa peredit aqua* (18), cf. Lucr. 1.326 *vesco sale saxa peresa*, with *lucida signa* (20), cf. Lucr. 5.518, and with *Veneris... venti* (21), cf. the etymological play on *Venus* and *ventus* at Lucr. 1.22–4, *alma Venus... te, dea, te fugiunt venti*. At 27 Tibullus uses the form *transiet*. This is the only example of this form of the future (for *transibit*) of any compound of *eo* in the whole of classical verse. In literary Latin generally it is extremely rare and does not occur again until Seneca.[31] However, its occurrence in early Bible translations and in a highly colloquial letter from Vindolanda[32] suggests that it may have been current in colloquial speech. Priapus is fond of unusual forms: *atteruisse* at 48 is the only surviving example of this form of the perfect of *tero* or its compounds apart from Apuleius and the *Itala* (see Neue–Wagener 3.394). As Murgatroyd (1980: 148) points out, the form is vouched for by Charisius 323.9 (B) and Veleius Longus *GLK* VII 74.5, who describes it as archaic. At 28 *remeatque*, the disjunctive *-que* has caused difficulties and has been changed to *-ve* in later MSS, but again it becomes a feature of poetic language from Lucretius on (see Bailey on Lucr. 2.825) and is another example of Priapus' intentionally didactic and recherché style. *colores* (29) for flowers is a metonomy of Lucretian origin (5.740), which recurs at Virgil, *Georg.* 4.306 and Propertius 1.2.9 in a similar didactic context. In 33 *vidi*, with its emphasis on autopsy and its appeal to personal experience, though not exclusively didactic, is characteristic of the didactic attitude, see Smith (1913: 275) and cf. Lucr. 4.577–9, 6.1044–55. Ovid makes frequent use of it in his mock-didactic *Ars Amatoria* (2.169, 493, 547, 3.43, 487, 598) and *Remedia Amoris* (1, 227, 311, 499, 555, 609, 621, 663). In 36 is a reference to the snake preserving its youth by sloughing off its skin; again the only other occurrence of *exuit* in this context is Lucretius 4.61. At 44 the rare compound *imbrifer* occurs earlier only in a didactic context at Virgil, *Georg.* 1.313.

---

[31] Futures of this type are restricted mainly to the compounds of *eo*, and occur most frequently in Christian Latin and Bible translations. See Neue–Wagener (1892–1905) 3.327f. Outside that sphere the only examples of *transiet* are Sen. *N.Q.* 3.10.4 and Apul. *Ascl.* 28 p. 314 (Hildebrand). Examples with other compounds in the classical period are as follows: *inietur* Cic. *Leg. Agr.* 2.25.67, *redies* Apul. *Met.* 6.19, *iniet* Sen. *Ben.* 2.1.2, *exiet* Sen. *Epist.* 17.9, *exient* Iulius Modestus *ap.* Charis. *Gramm.* 1.125K.

[32] Professor Jim Adams informs me that the form *rediemus* occurs at Vindolanda *Inv. no.* 93.1544 (see Bowman and Thomas (1996)).

The use of the future indicatives *temptabis* and *dabis* in 51–2 as directives, though not exclusively a didactic feature, is found in contexts where the authority of the speaker gives him confidence that the addressee will comply with his request, see Risselada (1993: 169). The high frequency of this construction in Cicero's letters (Risselada (1993: 174–8)) suggests it may have been a feature of conversational Latin. At 9 *Venerem vendere* looks like another etymological play on Venus' name (cf. Ovid, *Amores* 1.10.29–34). The typically Hellenistic structure of the couplet 61–2, which Tibullus reproduces here for the first time in Latin, was discussed in section 3 above. The speech ends with an accumulation of short mythological references: 63–4 Nisus and Pelops, 68 Ops and the rites of the Phrygian Mother Goddess Cybele. Finally the rather odd use of *expleat* in 69 deserves some explanation. What does *expleat urbes* mean? *expleo* is normally used of completing a circuit, as in *Aeneid* 12.763. Tibullus could be thinking of completing a circuit of cities. But given Priapus' penchant for learned etymologizing seen elsewhere in this passage, it could be that the ancient derivation of *urbs* from *orbis* (Maltby (1991: 655)) lies at the root of the expression here. Priapus is using a verb *expleo* with *urbs* which would be more appropriate with the word from which *urbs* is derived, namely *orbis*. The aim is to hint at the etymology *urbs* < *orbis*. At the end of the poem, when Tibullus himself takes up the stance of teacher of love, this change of role is reflected in his adoption of Priapus' didactic style with the proverbial *gloria cuique sua est* in 77, and the epic *tempus erit cum* in 79 recalling the Homeric ἔσσεται ἦμαρ.

APPENDIX A

Greek Words

Greek Words in Tibullus

aetherius (αἰθέριος, Cic.) 1, *barbarus (βάβαρος, Naev.) 3, *cadus (κάδος, Plaut.) 1, *calamus (κάλαμος, Plaut.) 1, *calix* (κύλιξ, Plaut.) 1, *canistrum (κάναστρα, Cic.) 1, *casia (κασία, Plaut.) 1, *catasta (κατάστασις, Tib./Liv.) 1, *charta* (χάρτης, Cic.) 1, *chorda* (χορδή, Cic.) 1, *chorea* (χορεία, Lucr.) 2, *chorus* (χορός, Naev.) 3, *cista* (κίστη, Cic.) 1, *cithara* (κιθάρα, Var.) 2, *cometes* (κομήτης, Cic.) 1, *concha* (κόγχη, Plaut.) 1, *corymbus (κόρυμβος, Virg. Ecl.) 1, *elegi (ἔλεγοι, Tib./Hor. *Carm.*) 1, *fucus (φῦκος, Plaut.) 1, *gypsatus* (γύψος, Cic. *Epist.*) 1, *hippomanes* (ἱππομανές, Virg. *Georg.*) 1, *lympha (νύμφη, Pacuv.) 2, *myrteus (μύρτος, Cato) 1, *myrtus (μύρτος, Cato) 1, *nardum* (νάρδος, Lucr.) 1, *palma (παλάμη, Plaut.) 1, *podagra* (ποδάγρα,

Cic.) 1, *scyphus* (σκύφον, Plaut.) 1, *stola* (στολή, Enn.) 1, *zmaragdus* (σμάραγδος, Var. *Men.*) 2.

* words not in Bürger's list (1911: 387)

On the possibility that *canistrum* was derived from the form κάνυστρον and that both *fucus* and φῦκος derived independently from a semitic root see Biville (1990: 148, 195–6).

30 words = 1 in 40 lines
39 occurrences = 1 in 32 lines
Tibullus 1 and 2 = 1240 lines

Early borrowings: 14 = 46.5 per cent
Ciceronian period: 12 = 46 per cent
Near contemporary: 4 = 13.5 per cent
First in Tibulus: *catasta?*, *elegi*? 2 = 7 per cent
Latin suffixes: *gypsatus*, *myrteus* 2 = 7 per cent
Rare or unusual: *catasta*, *chorea*, *elegi*, *lympha*, *hippomanes* 5 = 17 per cent
Greek terminations: *cometen* 2.5.71, 1 = 3 per cent

Lexical categories

1 scientific/technical 6 = 20 per cent	*aetherius, catasta, cometes, gypsatus, hippomanes, podagra*
2 poetry/music/dance 7 = 23 per cent	*calamus, charta, chorda, chorea, chorus, cithara, elegi*
3 plants/trees 5 = 17 per cent	*casia, corymbus, myrteus, myrtus, palma*
4 luxury items 4 = 13 per cent	*concha, fucus, nardum, zmaragdus*
5 utensils 3 = 10 per cent	*cadus, calix, scyphus*
6 religion 2 = 7 per cent	*canistrum, cista*
7 clothing 1 = 3 per cent	*stola*
8 other	*barbarus, lympha*

Greek Words in Propertius

acanthus (ἄκανθος, Virg. *Ecl.*) 1 (Book 3), *adamantinus* (ἀδαμάντινος, 1 Lucr.) 1(3), *adamas* (ἀδάμας, Virg. *Aen.*) 1(4), *aer* (ἀήρ, Cato) 4 (Books 2234), *aetherius* 1(2), *amphora* (ἀμφορεύς, Naev.) 1(4), *antrum* (ἄντρον, Virg. *Ecl.*) 14(11223333344444), *astrum* (ἄστρον, Cic.) 7(2333444), *barbarus* 6 (233344), *baris* (βάρις, Prop.) 1(3), *beryllus* (βήρυλλος, Maecenas) 1(4), *bombyx* (βόμβυξ, Prop.) 1(2), *cadus* 2(44), *calamus* 6(233344), *calathus* (κάλαθος, Virg. *Ecl.*) 2(23), *calix* 1(2), *canistrum* 2(34), *carbasus* (κάρπασος, Enn.) 2(4), *cataphractus* (κατάφρακτος, Sall.) 1(4), *cathedra* (καθέδρα, Hor.

Serm.) 1(4), *cerastes* (κεράστης, Prop.) 1(3), *cerasus* (κέρασος, Var.) 1(4), *chalybs* (χάλυψ, Virg. *Aen.*) 1(1), *chorea* 5 (12223), *chorus* 17 (11122222333333344), *chrysolithus* (χρυσόλιθος, Prop.) 1(2), *cithara* 2(24), *clatra* (κλῆθρα, Cato) 1(4), *comicus* (κωμικός, Plaut.) 1(4), *concha* 3(134), *conopium* (κωνωπεῖον, Var.) 1(3), *contus* (κοντός, Var.) 1(3), *corymbus* 4 (2344), *costum* (κόστος, Hor. *Carm.*) 1(4), *cot(h)urnus* (κόθορνος, Andr.) 2(23), *crater* (κράτηρ, Naev.) 1(3), *crocinum* (κρόκινος, Plaut.) 1(3), *crocus* (κρόκος, Var.) 1(4), *crotalistria* (κροταλίζω, Prop.) 1(4), *crystallus* (κρύσταλλος, Cinna) 1(4), *cyathus* (κύαθος, Plaut.) 1(4), *cyclas* (κυκλάς, Prop.) 1(4), *cycnus* (κύκνος, Lucr.) 1(3), *cymbalum* (κύμβαλον, Cic.) 2(33), *cymbium* (κυμβίον, Var.) 1(3), *delphinus* (δελφίν, Acc. *Trag.*), 2(23), *discus* (δίσκος, Plaut.) 1(3), *draco* (δράκων, Enn.) 2(24), *elegi* 1(4), *ephemeris* (ἐφημερίς, Asel.) 1(3), *epistula* (ἐπιστολή, Plaut.) 1(3), *euhans* (εὐάζων, Catul.) 1(2), *fagus* (φηγός, Catul.) 1(1), *fides* (σφίδη, Plaut.) 1(4), *fucus* 1(2), *gymnasium* (γυμνάσιον, Plaut.) 1(3), *gyrus* (γῦρος, Cic.) 2(33), *herois* (ἡρωίς, Laev.) 1(2), *heros* (ἥρως, Cic.) 4(1113), *herous* (ἡρῷος, Cic.) 2(23), *hippomanes* 1(4), *historia* (ἱστορία, Cato) 7(1233344), *hyacinthus* (ὑάκινθος, Catul.) 1(4), *hydra* (ὕδρα, Cic.) 1(2), *isthmos* (ἰσθμός, Cic.) 1(3), *lilium* (λείριον, Var.) 4(1234), *lotos* (λωτός Nep.) 1(3), *lympha* 7(1133444), *lyra* (λύρα, Var. *Men.*) 12(111222233444), *magnes* (μάγνης, Var.) 1(4), *mitra* (μίτρα, Lucil.) 4(2344), *mitratus* (μίτρα, Prop.) 1(4), *moecha* (μοιχή, Catul.) 1(4), *murra* (μύρρα, Plaut.) 1(1), *murreus* (μύρρα, Hor. *Carm.*) 2(34), *nardus* 1(4), *nympha* (νύμφη, Cic.) 3(233), *onyx* (ὄνυξ, Catul.) 2(23), *orgia* (ὄργια, Catul.) 2(33), *paean* (παιάν, Cic.) 1(3), *palaestra* (παλαίστρα, Plaut.) 1(3), *pancratium* (παγκράτιον, Var. *Men.*) 1(3), palma 13(1112233444444), *parma* (πάρμη, Enn.) 3(244), *pelagus* (πέλαγος, Pacuv.) 1(4), *petasus* (πέτασος, Plaut.) 1(4), pharetra (φαρέτρα, Andr.) 3(244), *phaselus* (φάσηλος, Cic.) 2(34), *platanus* (πλάτανος, Cato) 1(2), *pompa* (πομπή, Plaut.) 2(22), *pontus* (πόντος, Enn.) 6(111233), *purpura* (πορφύρα, Plaut.) 1(4), *pyramis* (πυραμίς, Cic.) 1(3), *pyropus* (πυρωπός, Lucr.) 1(4), *rhombus* (ῥόμβος, Prop.) 2(23), *sandyx* (σάνδυξ, Virg. *Ecl.*) 1(2), *sceptrum* (σκῆπτρον, Lucr.) 1(4), *smaragdus* 1(2), *terebinthus* (τερύβινθος, Prop.) 1(3), *thalamus* (θάλαμος, Catul.) 5(1233), *theatrum* (θέατρον, Naev.) 6(223344), *thyius* (θυία, Prop.) 1(3), *thyrsus* (θύρσος, Catul.) 1(3), *tigris* (τίγρις, Var.) 1(1), *toxicum* (τοξικόν, Plaut.) 1(1), *tragicus* (τραγικός, Cic.) 1(2), *trochus* (τροχός, Hor. *Carm.*) 1(3), *tropaeum* (τρόπαιον, Acc.) 5(33344), *tympanum* (τύμπανον, Lucr.) 2(33), *tyrannus* (τύραννος, Plaut.) 2(22), *zona* (ζώνη, Plaut.) 1(4).

111 words = 1 in 36 lines
256 occurrences = 1 in 16 lines
Propertius 4044 lines

Book 1 29 occurrences in 706 lines = 1 in 24

Book 2 60 occurrences in 1396 lines = 1 in 23
Book 3 89 occurrences in 990 lines = 1 in 11
Book 4 78 occurrences in 952 lines = 1 in 12

Early borrowings: 41 = 37 per cent
Ciceronian period: 46 = 41 per cent
Near contemporary: 24 = 22 per cent
First in Propertius: *baris, bombyx, cerastes, chrysolithus, crotalistria, cyclas, mitratus, rhombus, terebinthus, thyius* 10 = 9 per cent
Latin suffixes: *adamantinus, euhans, mitratus, murreus* 4 = 4 per cent
Rare or unusual: *adamas, antrum, calathus, carbasus, cataphractus, cerastes, chalybs, chorea, chrysolithus, cithara, clatria, crotalistria, cyclas, elegi, hippomanes, lympha, nympha, orgia, pancratium, pontus, rhombus, sandyx, thalamus, thyius, thyrsus, trochus* 26 = 23 per cent
Greek terminations: *barida* 3.11.44, *beryllon* 4.7.9, *heroidas* 2.28A.29, *heroas* 3.11.27, *isthmos* 3.22.2, *lotos* 3.12.27, *paeana* 3.15.42., 7 = 6 per cent

Lexical categories:

1 scientific/technical 17 = 15 per cent	*adamantinus, adamas, aer, aetherius, astrum, cataphractus, cerastes, chalybs, cycnus, delphin/ delphinus, draco, hippomanes, hydra, magnes, pyramis, tigris, toxicum*
2 poetry/music/dance 18 = 16 per cent	*calamus, chorea, chorus, cithara, comicus, cothurnus, crotalistria, cymbalum, elegi, fides, historia, lyra, orgia, paean, rhombus, theatrum, tragicus, tympanum*
3 plants/trees 10 = 9 per cent	*acanthus, cerasus, corymbus, crocus, fagus, hyacinthus, lilium, lotos, palma, platanus.*
4 luxury items 18 = 16 per cent	*beryllus, bombyx, chrysolithus, concha, costum, crocinum, crystallus, fucus, murra, murreus, nardus, onyx, purpura, pyropus, sandyx, smaragdus, terebinthus, thyia*
5 utensils/household equipment 10 = 9 per cent	*amphora, cadus, calathus, calix, cathedra, clatra, conopium, crater, cyathus, cymbium*
6 religion 3 = 3 per cent	*canistrum, euhans, thyrsus*

7 clothing 6 = 5 per cent   *carbasus, cyclas, mitra, mitratus,*
                                     petasus, zona

8 ships/sea 6 = 5 per cent   *baris, contus, isthmus, phaselus,*
                                     pelagus, pontus

9 sport 6 = 5 per cent   *discus, gymnasium, gyrus, palaestra,*
                                     pancratium, trochus

10 other 17 = 15 per cent   *antrum, barbarus, ephemeris,*
                                     epistula, herois, heros, herous,
                                     lympha, moecha, nympha, parma,
                                     pompa, pharetra, sceptrum,
                                     thalamus, tropaeum, tyrannus

Greek Words in Ovid, Amores

adamas 1, *aelinos* (αἴλινος, Ov.) 1, *aer* 2, *aetherius* 1, *barbaria* (βάρβαρος, Plaut.) 1, *barbarus* 2, *cedrus* (κέδρος, Virg. Georg.) 1, *chorda* 1, *concha* 1, *corona* 3, *cothurnatus* (κοθόρνος, Ov.) 1, *cothurnus* 6, *croceus* (κρόκος, Virg. Ecl.) 1, *crocus*, 1 *electrum* 1, *elegi* 2, *ephemeris* 1, *graphium* (γραφίον, Ov.) 1, *gypsatus* 1, *gyrus* 1, *herois* 1, *heros* 2, *herous* 1, *historia* 1, *historicus* 1, *lilium* 1, *lyra* 8, *magus* (μάγος, Cic.) 1, *marmoreus* (μάρμαρος, Cic.) 2, *myrteus* 1, *myrtus* 3, *nympha* 2, *palma* 4, *pelagus* 2, *peltatus* (πέλτη, Liv.) 1, *pharetra* 3, *pharetratus* (Virg. Georg.) 2, *phaselus* 1, *phoenix* (φοῖνιξ, Ov.) 1, *poeniceus* 1, *pompa* (πομπή) 8, *pontus* 2, *psittacus* (ψίττακος, Ov.) 4, *rhombus* 1, *sceptrum* 4, *sistrum* (σεῖστρον, Ov.) 2, *stomachus* (στόμαχος) 1, *thalamus* 3, *theatrum* 3, *thyrsus* 2, *tigris* 1, *toxicum* 1, *tragoedia* (τραγῳδια) 1, *tyrannus* 1, *zmaragdus* 1, *zona* 1.

55 words = 1 in 45 lines
105 occurrences = 1 in 23 lines
Ovid, *Amores* 2460 lines

Early borrowings: 21 = 38 per cent
Ciceronian period: 20 = 36 per cent
Near contemporary: 14 = 26 per cent
First in Ovid, *Amores*: *aelinos, cothurnatus, graphium, phoenix, psittacus, sistrum* 6 = 11 per cent
Latin suffixes: *cothurnatus, gypsatus, historicus, marmoreus, myrteus, peltatus, pharetratus, poeniceus* 8 = 14 per cent
Rare or unusual: *elegi, graphium, nympha, pontus, rhombus, sistrum, thalamus, thyrsus* 8 = 14 per cent
Greek terminations: *adamanta* 3.7.57, *aelinon* 3.9.23, *heroidas* 2.4.33, 3 = 5 per cent

Lexical categories

1 scientific/technical 9 = 16 per cent	*aer, aetherius, gypsatus, marmoreus, phoenix, psittacus, stomachus, tigris, toxicum*
2 poetry/music/dance 11 = 20 per cent	*chorda, cothurnus, cothurnatus, elegi, historia, historicus, lyra, rhombus, sistrum, theatrum, tragoedia*
3 plants/trees 7 = 13 per cent	*cedrus, croceus, crocus, lilium, myrteus, myrtus, palma*
4 luxury items 3 = 5 per cent	*concha, electra, zmaragdus*
5 utensils/household equipment 0	
6 religion 1 = 2 per cent	*thyrsus*
7 clothing 1 = 2 per cent	*zona*
8 ships/sea 3 = 5 per cent	*pelagus, phaselus, pontus*
9 sport 1 = 2 per cent	*gyrus*
10 other 19 = 35 per cent	*aelinos, barbaria, barbarus, corona, ephemeris, graphium, herois, heros, herous, magus, nympha, peltatus, pharetra, pharetratus, poeniceus, pompa, sceptrum, thalamus, tyrannus*

APPENDIX B

Compound Adjectives

Compound Adjectives in Tibullus

agricola (adj. Tib., noun Plaut.) 1.1.14, 2.1.36; *imbrifer* (Virg. *Georg.*) 1.4.44; *lanificus* (adj. Tib., *lanifica* noun Lucil.) 2.1.10; *magnificus* (Cic.) 1.5.6, 2.6.11 adv.; *naufragus* (active, as here, first in Hor. *Carm.* 1.16.10, passive in Cic.) 2.4.10; *sacrilegus* (Plaut.) 2.4.26.

6 words = 1 in 206 lines
8 occurrences = 1 in 155 lines

First in Tibuilus: adjectival uses of *agricola* and *lanificus*.

Compound Adjectives in Propertius

agricola (adj.) 1 (2), *armiger* (Acc. *Trag.*) 2(33), *artifex* (Plaut.) 2(24), *corniger* (Cic.) 1(3), *gemmifer* (Prop.) 1(3), *grandaevus* (Lucil.) 1(2), *lauriger* (Prop.) 2(34), *longaevus* (Prop. Virg. *Aen.*) 2(24), *mortifer* (Enn.) 1(3), *naufragus* 3(233), *octipes* (Prop.) 1(4), *odorifer* (Prop. Virg. *Aen.*) 1(2), *palmifer* (Prop.) 1(4), *sacrilegus* 1(3), *silvicola* (Naev.) 1(3), *spumifer* (Prop.) 1(4), *tergeminus* (Lucr.) 1(4), *turriger* (Prop. Virg. *Aen.*) 1(3), *undisonus* (Prop.) 1(3), *velifer* (Prop.) 1(3), *versicolor* (Cic.) 2(33).

21 words = 1 in 193 lines
28 occurrences = 1 in 144 lines

Book 1: 0
Book 2: 6 (1 in 232 lines)
Book 3: 15 (1 in 66)
Book 4: 7 (1 in 136)

First in Propertius: *gemmifer, lauriger, longaevus, octipes, odorifer, palmifer, turriger, velifer.*

Compound Adjectives in Ovid Amores

armifer (Ov.), *aurifer* (Cic.), *bacifer* (Ov), *benignus* (Plaut.), *biformis* (Virg. *Aen.*), *bilustris* (Ov.), *carnifex* (Naev.), *centimanus* (Hor. *carm.*), *corniger* 2, *fatifer* (Virg. *Aen.*), *lanificus, legifer* (Virg. *Aen.*), *liniger* (Ov.), *magnificus* (2), *Martigena* (Ov.), *munificus* (Cato), *naufragus, palmifer, pomifer* (Ov.), *populifer* (Ov.), *quadriiugus* (Enn.), *ruricola* (Ov.), *semiadapertus* (Ov.), *semisupinus* (Ov.), *septemplex* (Virg. *Aen.*), *signifer* (Cic.).

26 words = 1 in 95 lines
28 occurrences = 1 in 88 lines

First in Ovid: *armifer, bacifer, bilustris, liniger, Martigena, pomifer, populifer, ruricola, semiadapertus, semisupinus.*

APPENDIX C

Diminutives

Diminutives in Tibullus

capella (1.1.31), *fabella* (1.3.85), *fiscella* (2.3.15), *novellus* (2.2.22), *tabella* (1.3.28, 2.6.45), *tigillum* (2.1.39).

6 words, 7 occurrences
1 word per 207 lines, 1 occurence per 177 lines

Diminutives in Propertius

asellus 2(44), *auricula* 1(1), *corolla* 4(1122), *facula* 1(2), *flabellum* 1(2), *labellum* 1(2), *lapillus* 3(113), *lectulus* 2(24), *libellus* 7(1122333), *masculus* 1(2), *ocellus* 18 (1: 10, 2:8), *parvulus* 2(12), *quasillus* 1(4), *sacellum* 2(24), *sirpiculus* 1(4), *tabella* 5(22334), *vocula* 1(1).

17 words, 54 occurrences
1 word per 238 lines, 1 occurrence per 75 lines

Book 1: 20 (1 in 35 lines)
Book 2: 21 (1 in 66 lines)
Book 3: 6 (1 in 232 lines)
Book 4: 7 (1 in 136 lines)

Diminutives in Ovid, Amores

asellus, capella, labellum (3), *lapillus, libellus* (5), *ocellus* 11, *quantuluscumque, tabella* (12).

8 words, 25 occurrences
1 word per 307 lines, 1 occurrence per 98 lines

See B. Axelson (1945: 41–3).

Note. I would like to express my thanks to Dr Joan Booth and Professors Francis Cairns, David West and Jim Adams for their detailed and helpful comments on an earlier version of this paper.

Addendum to note 28. On etymologising in general in Propertuis see now A. Michalopoulos *PLLS* 10 (1998) forthcoming, which will show it to be more frequent than originally thought.

Proceedings of the British Academy, **93**, 399–414

Vt erat novator:
Anomaly, Innovation and Genre in
Ovid, *Heroides* 16–21

E. J. KENNEY

Summary. R. S. Conway no doubt overstated the matter when he described Ovid as 'a chartered libertine in Grammar', but his poetry is indeed informed from first to last by linguistic innovation and experiment. Critics who have sought to impugn his authorship of *Heroides* 16–21 have tended to concentrate on what they perceive as anomalies of style and language. It is the thesis of this chapter that a positive approach is more rewarding. It is argued that most of the apparent departures in these poems from what is generally accounted normal poetic usage are either characteristic examples of Ovid's discreetly innovative way with the Latin language, or are generically appropriate to the poems as letters, or are specifically calculated to lend colour or force to the writer's case. In conclusion the need is underlined for more discriminating and finely nuanced discussion of these problems.

I. INTRODUCTION: THE NEED TO BEWARE OF
HYPERCRITICISM

THE CRITIC OF a text whose authenticity is in dispute must always be alert to the danger of hypercriticism. By this I mean the tendency to identify as significant — which for the purpose in hand means negative — anomalies phenomena which in a text not for other reasons under suspicion would pass unremarked, or at least unreprehended.[1] Singularity is not in itself a

---

[1] Cf. Kenney (1979: 395).

ground for suspicion. It makes no sense to require that a writer shall never do anything unless he does it at least twice. In the *Heroides* one need look no further than the letter of Penelope to discover two unique syntactical usages in an area which will presently concern us in this paper: of the gerundive in *uir . . . mihi dempto fine carendus abest* and of the gerund in *reuertendi liber*.[2] So, when one turns to the double epistles and finds, to take an example of a phraseological rarity which in 1893 excited the suspicions of a critic still heavily under the influence of Lachmann,[3] that the phrase *susurrare de aliquo* meaning 'whisper about somebody' occurs in the entire surviving corpus of Latin poetry only in Hero's letter (19.19);[4] or, to revert to questions of syntax, that the common idiom *causa* (abl.) + possessive adjective meaning 'for my etc. sake' is found in the entire works of Ovid (who uses the word *causa* some 300 times) only twice, both times in the letter of Acontius (20.108, 198[5]), I do not see why we should suspect the hand of [Ovid] rather than Ovid. The incidence of such phenomena does not seem to differ significantly from that in the poems of unquestioned Ovidian authorship.[6]

I believe that it is more instructive to approach the question positively: to consider, that is, the literary effect in their context of apparent departures, lexical, syntactical and phraseological, from the stylistic register

---

[2] *Her.* 1.50, 80; cf. e.g. the use of *potens* + preposition at 5.147 *potens ad opem*, unparalleled until late antiquity (*TLL* s.v. 286.75ff.); *iurare* + *in* at 10.117 = 'conspire against', unique in Latin. On these and other singularities see Knox (1995), ad locc. and Index s.vv. archaisms, diction. (It should be noted that Knox's selection, the *Epistula Sapphus* apart, is confined to epistles which are in his view indisputably Ovid's.) Commentators on *A.A.* 3.2 are seemingly untroubled by the fact that the elision there of the monosyllabic verb *dem* is, we are told, unique not only in Ovid but in the entire corpus of Latin poetry from Cicero to Silius Italicus (Soubiran (1966: 402–3)).

[3] Who inaugurated the argument over the authenticity of certain of the *Heroides* (Lachmann (1848)); cf. Knox (1995: 7–8 and n. 14). Some of his criteria of what constituted grounds for suspicion were inconsiderately formulated: a case in point is that of Ovid's metrical treatment of Greek feminine proper names in *-a* (Kenney (1996: 249)).

[4] Leyhausen (1893: 47).

[5] Convincingly restored by Housman (Kenney (1996: ad loc.)).

[6] Other syntactical and phraseological singularities include: 17.203 *cursibus in mediis* for the usual *in medio cursu*; 19.14 *diluitur posito serior hora mero* 'you dissipate (wash away) the evening over your wine', an apparently unique extension of the normal usage of *diluere* with care or the like as object of the verb (*OLD* s.v. 1b); 20.20 *dicta tulisse* 'received your words', paralleled only at Stat. *Theb.* 11.252 *mugitum hostilem summa tulit aure iuuencus* (however, after *uerba* in line 19 *dicta* is otiose, and the text may be corrupt); 20.99 *re careant* 'lack realization', an apparently unparalleled phrase; 20.163 *amborum . . . pericula = ambo pericula = utrumque periculum. ambo* for *uterque* is Virgilian (Norden on *Aen.* 6.540ff., Arusian. *GLK* vii. 455.10), but I have not been able to parallel the precise form of the expression here. For further discussion of passages not mentioned in this paper see Clark (1908) and Tracy (1971), who between them mount a more than adequate case for the defence. See n. 60.

generally accounted 'poetic' or specifically Ovidian. In some cases the
presumed anomaly may turn out to be positive rather than negative: that
is, it can be shown on careful examination to embellish or lend force to
the writer's argument, or to be appropriate to the epistolary genre and
(especially in the case of Acontius and Cydippe) the adversarial style of
these exchanges.[7] 'What matters for judging the use of words in Latin
is . . . the tone, the context, and the sense of appropriateness.'[8] Where the
effect in its context is adjudged to be neutral or negative, it is still relevant
to enquire whether the number of such instances is in itself anomalous
and a cause for justified suspicion as to authenticity.

Stylistic registers shade into one another across the whole broad range
of the texts that have come down to us. Critics of Latin poetry still tend,
I suppose, to operate with Axelsonian criteria, identifying as 'unpoetical',
that is inappropriate in the higher genres, words, expressions and usages
deemed to be at home in comedy, satire and prose: archaisms, vulgarisms,
colloquialisms and prosaisms. Axelson's *Unpoetische Wörter* (Axelson
(1945)) will always be a landmark in the history of Latin stylistics —
'seminal, indeed epoch-making', as one authority has described it[9] — and
not all the strictures of his critics are well founded.[10] One point taken by
reviewers and others is, however, well taken and is directly relevant to the
argument of this paper: Axelson's omission to take into account the context
and the effect that a word or phrase may have in its particular setting.[11]
It is not in principle a defect of his book that, as reviewers have pointed
out, his approach is essentially negative; but in applying the results of his
enquiry it becomes vital to appraise the texts and contexts positively, and
it is this which is attempted in what follows. What is needed is to assess
the quality and impact of apparent deviations from normal 'poetic' usage[12]
in their argumentative and affective settings. Before embarking on my
examples, to illustrate what was said above about hypercriticism I will

---

[7] Cf. Kenney (1996: 1–2 and n. 3).

[8] Williams (1968: 745).

[9] Lyne (1989: 4 n. 18).

[10] The most influential criticism remains that of Williams (1968: 743–50); *contra*, maintaining
Axelson's position on the effect of genre on diction, Watson (1985); cf. Lyne (1989: 8 and n.
30).

[11] Watson (1985: 430); Lyne (1989: 5); cf. Axelson's reviewers, e.g. Ernout (1947: 70) 'dans
les combinaisons multiples où il intervient, le mot contribue à produire l'impression poétique,
mais il ne la crée pas à lui seul; il faut qu'il soit à sa place'; Bömer (1951: 166) 'Jedes
Wort, jede Erscheinung bedarf einer speziellen Betrachtung'. For a useful bibliographical
conspectus of the modern literature on Latin poetic style see Booth (1981: 3686 n. 2).

[12] Well defined for Ovid by Booth (1981: 3686 n. 11): Ovid's Latin is 'poetic' in the sense
that 'it embraces forms, constructions and vocabulary which are found throughout the whole
spectrum of Roman poetry and with particular frequency in the elevated genres, but which
are not generally used by prose-writers except for special effect'.

discuss a passage which, though it has exercised the critics, turns out on close inspection to be a non-instance, to be classed, if classification is thought to be called for, as a singularity rather than anomaly.

1   uixque manu pigra totiens infusa resurgunt
        lumina, uix moto concutit igne faces. (21.159–60)

    concutit *Burman*: coripit π: *alii alia*

We need not be concerned here with the problem of line 160, where Burman's correction may be accepted *faute de mieux*. The sticking-place for the critics has been *infusa* in line 159. This has been assailed and variously emended on the grounds that in the sense required here of 'fill by pouring' *infundo* is attested in classical Latin only in technical writers.[13] The transmitted text has found a robust champion in Professor James Diggle, but it might be thought that he somewhat overstates his case when he asserts that 'Eur. *Hipp.* 853–4 δάκρυσι . . . βλέφαρα καταχυθέντα, together with Barrett's elucidation of the linguistic phenomenon in his Addendum, p. 435, should be sufficient to rout the emendators'[14] — though it is true enough that none of the corrections hitherto proposed is remotely persuasive. In the first place, one should not be unduly deterred by the label 'technical': Vitruvius' Latin seems to be generally accounted that of a rude mechanical, but there is nothing uncouth or rustic about Columella's prose. 'Columella writes clearly, neatly, even elegantly'; his style is 'unaffected and resourceful'. From Frank Goodyear that was not faint praise.[15] The usage is in fact so widespread in post-classical and Christian prose that it must have been common parlance (rather than colloquial) already in Ovid's day; that would certainly not exclude it from Augustan elegy. Moreover, analogous usages in both Latin and Greek suggest that it can hardly have been calculated to grate on the ears of his readers. *Infundo* = 'fill (by pouring)' is no more of a strain on the language than the common *perfundo* = 'drench (by pouring)' or the uncommon but unreprehended use of the simple verb *fundo* = 'drench (with)', attested only in Tibullus and his imitator Lygdamus.[16] And in looking to Greek for an analogy Diggle could have found a much closer one in ἐγχέω, for which 'fill by pouring' is a classical sense attested in Sophocles, Xenophon and Alexis.[17] In short, far from affording grounds for suspicion or emendation, what we have here is a not untypical example of Ovid's discreetly masterful way

[13] *OLD* s.v. 2, *TLL* s.v. 1509.20ff.; Phaedr. 3.13.9 and Mart. 5.64.1 are wrongly classified.
[14] Diggle (1972: 38).
[15] *CHCL* (1982: ii. 669) = *The Early Principate* (1982: 173).
[16] *OLD* s.v. 3; Mart. 3.82.26 (cit. *TLL* s.v. 1564.19) is doubtful: see Shackleton Bailey ad loc.
[17] LSJ s.v. II; cf. Pearson on Soph. fr. 563, noting a further extension at Pind. *Nem.* 9.50 ἐγκιρνάτω τις νιν, sc. the bowl just mentioned.

with his own language.[18] It may be added that the concrete sense of *lumen* required here, the lamp itself rather than 'a light', seems to be rare, but it is unimpeachably classical: Cic. *Sen.* 36 *nisi . . . lumini oleum instilles* (*OLD* s.v. 6a).

II. SOME APPARENT 'ANOMALIES'

I begin with what seems to me a real syntactical curiosity falling within the category of apparently unmotivated archaism.

2   idem qui facimus, factam tenuabimus iram,
               copia placandi sit modo parua tui. (20.73–4)

               placandi *PGω*: placandae *s*

Acontius looks forward to allaying Cydippe's indignation with him in bed, as recommended in the *Ars Amatoria*. Editors since Heinsius have generally printed *placandi*; the construction is explained as gerundival, *tui* being neuter from *tuum*, so that grammatical gender overrides the sex of the person referred to.[19] I should not venture to dispute the point, but the construction is spectacularly rare; in fact there is only one other example of it with *tui* neuter referring to a woman,[20] at Plaut. *Truc.* 370 *tui uidendi copia est*; and at Ter. *Hec.* 372 *eius uidendi cupidus*, where *eius* likewise refers to a woman, the construction is explained by Madvig (1869; 113) as due to false analogy. That being so, the claims of *placandae* seem to demand reconsideration. Though dismissed by Heinsius as a solecism ('Latine vix dicitur'), it cannot be scouted out of hand. In addition to Ter. *Phorm.* 880 *ait uterque tibi potestatem eius adhibendae dari*[21] we have in Ovid himself an analogy if not a parallel at *Her.* 11.106 *amissae memores sed tamen este mei*. About a dozen MSS have *amissi*; no editor prints it, but Housman in his lecture notes remarked that the 'fem. is constructio ad sensum, since *mei* is really genitive of *meum*; with gerundive the neuter

---

[18] Cf. the passages cited in nn. 2, 4 above. If *infundo* is modelled on ἐγχέω, we may note as analogous Ovid's use of *nympha* in the *Heroides* (9.50, 103, 16.128; not 1.27, where see Knox (1995): ad loc.; *contra* Casali (1995) on *Her.* 9.50), always with a Greek proper name, in the sense of νύμφη = 'young woman'. This was picked up by the poet of the *Ciris* (435). It is relevant to note that *Her.* 9 (Deianira) was one of those condemned by Lachmann (1848: 58–60) and subsequently by Courtney (1965) and Vessey (1969); *contra* Jacobson (1974: 231–4); Casali (1995: 227–33). Cf. also 21.178 *labra* = λουτρά, an Ovidian innovation.

[19] See e.g. Madvig (1869: 111–13), K–S (1955: i. 746), Risch (1984: 120 n. 160) (not noticing this passage).

[20] Referring to a man at Ov. *Tr.* 2.154, 182.

[21] Bentley emended to *habendi se dare*, citing this passage, but later editors have not followed his lead.

is preserved, as 20.74'. He added a reference to Madvig's classic note mentioned above, on *De Finibus* 1.60, which is indeed worth quoting: 'E contrario nescio, an Ovidius Epist. XI, 106, ut erat novator, dixerit in femina: *Amissae memores*' eqs. Since then *placandi* is supported by a parallel and *placandae* only by an analogy (though in Ovid himself), editors are no doubt right to plump for the former, though in a spirit of gloomy resignation, to echo Housman, rather than confidence. But the construction in this form[22] must presumably have sounded unfamiliar in the ears of Ovid's contemporaries? Possibly, however, since most examples of these uses of the gerund and gerundive are with *copia* or words similarly connoting choice or opportunity,[23] even in his day *placandi . . . tui* might have passed current as set phraseology. Though an aura of puzzlement persists, I see nothing here that suggests [Ovid] rather than Ovid — rather, *ut erat novator*, the reverse.

Within the broad spectrum of anomaly, that is ostensibly 'unpoetical' usages defined above, there can be distinguished a narrower band of specifically or characteristically Ciceronian lexis and idiom. These will be treated separately; first I discuss the other instances in the order of their occurrence:

3   hinc ego Dardaniae muros excelsaque tecta
           et freta prospiciens arbore nixus eram.   (16.57–8)

prospiciens . . . eram is here no more than a metrically helpful equivalent for *prospiciebam*.[24] This usage is generally classified as colloquial, at home in comedy and prose.[25] It is in fact sporadically attested in the poets: Catullus, Lucretius, Propertius, Manilius and Ovid himself. In many of

[22] The type *lucis tuendi copiam* (Plaut. *Capt.* 1008, on which see Lindsay ad loc., Risch (1984: 104 n. 141) or *nauis incohandi exordium* (Enn. *Scaen.* 201 J.), in the form with the dependent genitive in the plural, would be relatively familiar from Cicero (Roby (1896: lxviii); K–S (1955: i. 745)), but that it was by Ovid's time felt as archaic is evident from its disappearance and subsequent re-emergence in the prose of Fronto, Gellius and Apuleius (H–S 1965: 375).
[23] Roby (1896: lxviii); H–S (1965: 375).
[24] Professor Nisbet suggests that *prospiciens* should be taken as participial and *nixus eram* as the main verb: 'I was leaning against a tree as I contemplated from this spot . . .'. This use of the pluperfect is certainly Ovidian: cf. e.g. *A.A.* 2.129 *litore constiterant* 'they were standing on the shore', *al.* However, though this way of taking the couplet is syntactically possible, sense and rhetoric tell against it. The emphasis in Paris' recollection is on his thoughts at the time rather than his posture: it was as he contemplated (unwittingly) his future that it started to happen to him. The words *hinc . . . prospiciens . . . eram* articulate the couplet and frame his as yet uncomprehending survey of the topless towers whose destruction the events of the next half hour were to set in train, and the sea over which the agent of that destruction was to come. The referee draws my attention to Prop. 3.3.13–14 *cum me Castalia speculans ex arbore Phoebus | sic ait aurata nixus ad antra lyra*, which supports the construction argued for here.
[25] Blase (1903: 256–7); H–S (1965: 388–9).

these cases, however, including the other Ovidian examples, there is room for disagreement as to whether the function of the participle is adjectival or genuinely predicative.[26] Here I think it is clearly the latter, a pure periphrasis for the usual tense, not noticed as such by Eklund in his monograph on the subject; it might have helped to alleviate his doubts as to the existence of 'periphrases with verbal complements . . . in pre-Christian Latin'.[27] This instance is instructive as a preliminary reminder of something that will continue to emerge from this discussion, that language is constantly developing and that Ovid can often be found, where Virgil before him is to be found, at the cutting edge of development.

4   aut ego perpetuo famam sine labe tenebo . . . (17.69)

The idiom *famam et sim. tenere* in the sense of 'maintain one's good name' appears to be otherwise exclusively found in prose.[28] This is one of those cases that expose the limitations of the Axelsonian prosaic/poetic dichotomy. *A priori* it is difficult to detect anything in either diction or the combination of words that tends to place a phrase such as this in a specific register. In this sense its literary effect can be classified as neutral.

5   sic meus hinc uir abest, ut me custodiat absens. (17.165)

'Though my husband is away, yet he guards me even in his absence.' This limiting or stipulative use of *ut/ne* + subjunctive also occurs twice in Hero's letter (19.87–8, 181–2) and once in Acontius' (20.101–2), also at *Tr.* 3.4.55–6. It appears to be otherwise characteristic of comedy, argumentative prose and satire.[29] Given the argumentative quality of these epistles, it is perhaps not out of place; but its anomalous frequency perhaps suggests that it belongs in the class of what might be called authorial 'tics': expressions or constructions which for some reason or other appear to have been haunting the poet's subconscious mind. No single instance is in itself objectionable or even especially remarkable.[30]

---

[26] Catull. 63.57, 64.317; Lucret. 3.396 and Munro ad loc.; Prop. 3.7.21, 4.6.1; Manil. 1.858, 3.332 and Housman ad loc.; Bömer (1976: 222).

[27] Eklund (1970: 47).

[28] Caes. *B.C.* 3.55.2; cf. with *dignitatem* Cic. *Fam.* 4.9.3, Livy 39.37.18.

[29] Hor. *Sat.* 1.2.123–4, *Ep.* 1.16.5–6, 1.20.25 and Mayer ad locc., *A.P.* 151–2 and Brink ad loc.; Bennett (1910: i. 263–7); H–S (1965: 641–2). Cf. correlative *ut . . . sic* with concessive sense at 17.71–2, 109–10, 241–2, *al.*

[30] Examples are: *ut nunc est* (16.50, 17.169, 19.127); *si nescis* (16.246, 17.198, 18.39, 29.150). See Palmer (1898: 436–7); Kenney (1996: ad locc.). In view of the erotic character of the double epistles and their greater emphasis on wooing as compared with the single, the relatively frequent occurrence of *quod amas et sim.* (16.85, 18.179, 19.179, 20.32, 35, 21.57) is unsurprising and does not really belong in this category; cf. the *Ars Amatoria*, with four instances in the first 264 verses of book I.

6   et peream si non inuitant omnia culpam.   (17.183)

peream si, rather like English 'I'll be hanged if', is a colloquial expression
(*OLD* s.v. *pereo* 3b; Hofmann (1951: 31)). In Ovid it is found only here
and in Cydippe's letter (21.29), though *peream nisi* occurs in the *Epistulae
ex Ponto* (3.5.45–7, 4.12.43), and Propertius has *dispeream nisi* (2.21.9–10).
It is interesting to note that, whereas Cicero's correspondents Caelius and
Cassius use this idiom, Cicero himself in his letters prefers the presumably
more formal *moriar si*. Colloquialisms are not so rare in Latin elegy that
this one should occasion surprise.[31] Ovid's own epistolary practice here
agrees with that of his heroines and that of other educated Romans.

7   tu quoque qui poteris fore me sperare fidelem?   (17.213)

This is the only instance in Ovid of *qui?* in the sense of 'how?'. It is
frequent in comedy, elsewhere in verse only in Catullus, Lucretius,
Horace's hexameters and Phaedrus. As a one-off it can stand beside
quicum at Virg. *Aen.* 11.822, one of only three examples in 'solemn
poetry'.[32] It suits Helen's argumentative tone, and Ovid's options for
phrasing her question were limited by metre: he never uses *quomodŏ*,
only the disjoined *quo … modo*. In its context the phrase is admirably
concise and forceful writing.

8   longior infirmum ne lasset epistula corpus
                   clausaque consueto sit sibi fine, uale.   (20.241–2)

In line 242 *ut* must be understood from the preceding *ne*, as at *Met.*
13.271–2. This kind of ellipse is not uncommon in prose;[33] in the form
found here its next occurrence seems to be in Juvenal.[34] Ovid, like Horace
before him, makes frequent and enterprising use of ἀπὸ κοινοῦ constructions, of which this is a type — and somebody had to be first.

---

[31] Tränkle (1960); Knox (1986: 31). Cf. Wilkinson (1959: 190), on colloquialisms in Horace's
Odes: 62 in 3134 lines, 'quite a high proportion'.
[32] Skutsch on Enn. *Ann.* 268; the others are Catull. 66.77 and Stat. *Theb.* 8.279, this latter an
obvious Virgilian *furtum*. Compare *sane*, only in Ovid at *Her.* 17.13 and (*s.v.l.*) 21.213, and
before him only at Virg. *Aen.* 10.48 (Kenney (1996: 248)). On Virgil as setter of linguistic
precedents cf. Lyne (1989: 14).
[33] K–S (1955: ii. 563–4). In verse cf. Hor. *Sat.* 1.1.1–3 *qui fit, Maecenas, ut nemo, quam sibi
sortem | seu ratio dederit seu fors obiecerit, illa | contentus uiuat, laudet diuersa sequentes?*,
where in line 3 *quisque* must be supplied from the preceding *nemo* (Brown ad loc.; and see
Courtney (1980) on Juv. 6.18).
[34] Juv. 13.35–7, 16.7–10; Courtney (1980) cites no poetic parallels. [Tib.] 3.10 (4.4).5–8, cit.
Baehrens (1912: 321), is not a case in point.

III. CICERONIANISMS: AN EPISTOLARY FEATURE?

I now turn to prosaisms apparently characteristic of Cicero in particular, again in the order of their occurrence.

9   nec potui debere mihi spem longius istam . . .   (16.105)

'I could not go on withholding from myself the realization of that hope', sc. of winning Helen. This special sense of *debeo* = 'leave unpaid' seems to be otherwise peculiar to Cicero.[35]

10   hoc quoque enim dubito, non quo fiducia desit
          aut mea sit facies non bene nota mihi,
      sed quia credulitas damno solet esse puellis
          uerbaque dicuntur uestra carere fide.   (17.37–40)

      quo *s*: quod *PG* ω

Causal *quo* + subjunctive is found in Plautus and Terence,[36] but what might be called the full-blown classical construction with *non quo* + subjunctive giving an attributed or rejected reason, followed by *sed quod/quia* + indicative giving the actual reason, apparently occurs in earlier Latin poetry only in Lucretius.[37] It seems to be a favourite of Cicero's.[38] This is of course to assume that *quo*, restored to the text by Burman, and not *quod*, is indeed what the poet wrote; but *quo* is frequently corrupted to *quod* in MSS, whereas I should be hard put to it to find instances of the reverse.

11   sed nihil infirmo, faueo quoque laudibus istis.   (17.127)

Infirmo in this technical sense of invalidating a statement or disabling an argument is a favourite of Cicero's in the *De inuentione*, where he uses it some scores of times; in the *De oratore* thrice and in the *Orator* once only, a significant contrast.[39] Given the adversarial and rhetorical character of the correspondence it is an appropriate word enough; but it is tempting to suggest that its use here may embody a discreet and highly Ovidian stroke of wit. From Gorgias onwards praise and blame of Helen had been a stock theme of the rhetorical tradition. Her use of this technical term

---

[35] *OLD* s.v. 3b; see Shackleton Bailey (1965: 170) on *Att.* 4.2 (74).2.

[36] Bennett (1910: i. 319); Handford (1947: 68 n. 2); Martin on Ter. *Ad.* 270.

[37] 2.336–7, 6.71–8 (2.692–4, 723–4 are interpolated: Deufert (1996: 130–3, 152–5)). Like Lucretius, Helen is arguing a case. At *Tr.* 5.11.3–5 the first *quod*-clause is in the indicative and states a fact.

[38] K–S (1955: ii. 385–6), H–S (1965: 588).

[39] *Infirmo* occurs nowhere else in classical Latin poetry; in its technical sense it is found at Auson. *Epp.* 21.43 Green, Prudent. *Harmart.* 181, non-technically at *CLE* 1869.13. Cf. Knox (1995: 211), on *aequaliter* at *Her.* 7.49, used there in a technical sense otherwise attested only in prose.

perhaps implies an anachronistic awareness of the fact: 'So much will in
years to come be said and written about me to my credit and discredit;
here is a character of me to which I can give the seal of (technical)
approval.'[40]

12   uos modo uenando, modo rus geniale colendo
              ponitis in uaria tempora longa mora.   (19.9–10)

Pono in this sense (originally financial) of 'lay out', 'dispose of', with
tempus, dies and the like as object is relatively rare, occurring before Ovid
apparently only in Cicero.[41] In Ovid it is elsewhere found only in the exile
poetry.[42] That is another reminder that it is a matter of chance whether a
usage comes down to us as an apparently isolated departure from the
norm or a development in a stylistic continuum. More than one ostensible
singularity might turn out to be nothing of the sort if we had more of the
work of Ovid's immediate predecessors and contemporaries — not to
mention his own lost works.[43]

13   inque caput nostrum dominae periuria quaeso
              eueniant.   (20.127–8)

The usual construction with *euenio* in the sense of 'happen to' is with the
dative. The only other classical example of *in* + accusative is in Cicero.[44]

Of these Ciceronian usages no. **11** stands on its own as specifically
technical; it is possible, as I have suggested, that Ovid was having a little
quiet fun with it. Nos. **9, 10** and **12** are attested both in the letters and in
other parts of the Ciceronian corpus; no. **13** is found once only in the
letters. This is admittedly a somewhat slender basis for the suggestion of
Ciceronian influence, and *infirmo* is in any case a word that Ovid might
have heard on the lips of his teachers in the declamation schools; he need
not have resorted to Cicero's rhetorical works to encounter it. Nevertheless
the possibility that he might have read Cicero's letters, or some of them,
must be left open. Though the publication of those *Ad Atticum* is generally

---

[40] For self-conscious awareness by Ovid's heroines of the literary tradition of which they are
a part see Knox (1995: 18–25).

[41] *Brut.* 87, *Att.* 1.13.1, 6.2.6, *Fam.* 5.21.1, *De or.* 3.17 Cf. however Hor. *Sat.* 2.7.112–13 *otia
recte | ponere*.

[42] *Tr.* 4.8.14, *Ex P.* 1.5.36, 48, 1.8.66.

[43] The Gallus fragment has engendered more questions than answers, but it is relevant to
note that it at least demonstrates that the collocation *Romana . . . historia* was not introduced
into elegy by Propertius (Anderson–Parsons–Nisbet (1979: 141)). This line, by the way, also
reminds us that we are not always well served by the lexicographers. Neither *OLD* nor *TLL*
distinguishes the sense of *mora* which is required here, 'distraction', 'pursuit', 'pastime',
though Planudes evidently grasped it, rendering ἐν ποικίληι τριβῆι. Cf. Booth (1991: 148) on
Am. 2.11.14.

[44] *Fam.* 2.10 (86).1 and Shackleton Bailey (1977: 409).

thought not to antedate the Neronian period, and though the earliest extant citation from those *Ad familiares* is by the elder Seneca, who outlived Ovid by some twenty years, we know too little about the pre-publication history of Cicero's correspondence to rule out altogether the possibility that Ovid may have had access to it.[45] We are certainly not entitled to assume that he never opened a prose book.[46]

IV. MISCELLANEOUS

Lastly, some passages which do not seem to fit neatly into the 'unpoetical' category but which seem to deserve remark.

> **14**   portubus egredior uentisque ferentibus usus
> applicor in terras, Oebali nympha, tuas.   (16.127–8)

Applico in the sense of 'put in at' is generally constructed with *ad* (e.g. *Met.* 3.598) or dative (e.g. *Her.* 7.117, *Tr.* 3.9.10). The only other instance with *in* is at Livy 37.12.10 *Romani et Eumenes rex in Erythraeam primum classem applicuerunt*. The passive in this sense is, however, specifically Ovidian (*Her.* 7.117, *Met.* 3.598).[47]

> **15**   digna quidem es caelo, sed adhuc tellure morare.   (18.169)

All the other instances of *adhuc* referring to the future in the sense demanded here of 'awhile' which are recorded in the dictionaries are post-Ovidian,[48] and the construction with the imperative is apparently otherwise unexampled. But the expression, to my ear at least, reads naturally; and, as has already been said, somebody has to take the lead in any extension of usage. In this case Ovid had before him analogies in the usage of Virgil, who introduced into high poetry both *olim* and *quondam* with reference to future time.[49]

> **16**   (*a*) cur totiens a me, lente morator, abes?   (19.70)
>
> morator *PW*: natator *ρω*: uiator *rec. unus*: de G incert.
>
> (*b*) otiosis locus hic non est, discede morator.
> (*CIL* iv. 813 = *CLE* 333 = 704 Diehl)

---

[45] See Nagle (1980: 33–4), for possible 'reminiscences of Ciceronian thought and expression' in the exile poetry.

[46] See below on the *De officiis*, n. 56.

[47] Otherwise only at Justin. 11.10.12 *exercitu insulae applicito*; see *TLL* s.v. 296.65ff.

[48] *OLD* s.v. 6a (four examples, all from the younger Pliny; this one not noticed), *TLL* s.v. 661.39ff.

[49] See Harrison (1991: 61), on *Aen.* 10.12, Austin (1977: 271), on *Aen.* 6.876; and cf. above, n. 32.

In the intransitive sense of 'loiterer' required here[50] the word *morator* is
otherwise attested only in this Pompeian graffito, an elegantly euphemistic
prohibition against committing a nuisance. The word in this sense was
evidently colloquial. It must be what Ovid wrote; the alternatives offered
by the tradition are clearly inferior.[51] His use of verbal nouns in *-tor* may
be described as relatively restrained but not unenterprising.[52]

Finally under this heading we have an instance, which turns out if
carefully examined to be exceptionally revealing, of what was described
above as Ovid's 'discreetly masterful' way with the Latin tongue. In three
passages of her letter Cydippe dwells on her oath and on what was — or
rather was not — in her mind when she read it out.

17   (*a*) quae iurat, mens est: nil coniurauimus illa;
                   illa fidem dictis addere sola potest.   (21.135–6)

              nil tum iurauimus *rec. unus*: nil nos i. *Heinsius*: sed nil i. *Palmer*

              (*b*) non ego iuraui, legi iurantia uerba:
                   uir mihi non isto more legendus eras.   (21.143–4)

              (*c*) nil ego peccaui, nisi quod periuria legi
                   inque parum fausto carmine docta fui.   (21.181–2)

Critics have taken exception in the first and third of these passages to
what they see as an unOvidian straining of language; and the first has
been variously and unconvincingly emended. So far, however, from doing
violence to the language, Ovid is here making his heroine make her point
by drawing a distinction founded on insistence on linguistic accuracy and
exact meaning. In (*a*) Cydippe is saying 'iuraui, sed non *coniuraui*', 'I
uttered (the words of) an oath, but I did not join in it (with my mind)',
emphasizing the prefix which distinguishes the compound and its special
senses. This is a specifically declamatory ploy noticed (and deplored: not
that this would have put Ovid off) by the elder Seneca as a kind of
affectation, *cacozeliae genus, quod detractu aut adiectione syllabae facit
sensum* (*Suas.* 7.11).[53] The implied opposition between *mens* and

---

[50] *TLL* s.v. 1475.60–5 fails to remark the distinction between the transitive and intransitive
senses.

[51] *natator* recurs at line 90 *magnus ubi est spretis ille natator aquis?*, where it is pointed; *uiator*
is purely inept.

[52] Cf. Linse (1891: 27–8).

[53] The example he gives is closely analogous to that under discussion: *peribit ergo quod
Cicero scripsit, manebit quod Antonius proscripsit?* Cf. Sen. *Ep. Mor.* 100.1–2, insisting on
the difference between *effundere* and *fundere*; and see Summers (1910: lxxxvi), Bonner (1949:
69–70).

uerba[54] is then made explicit, as so often in Ovid, in the following penta-meter, so epitomizing the issue (*status* = στάσις) on which Cydippe's case turns, that of *scriptum* vs *uoluntas*. This crucial distinction is then picked up, repeated and varied in (*b*): merely to read the words of an oath is not to swear, a point ingeniously developed and expanded in the word-play of line 144, 'I ought to have been allowed to *choose* a husband, not forced to "read" one.'[55] In (*c*) she pursues the distinction: 'peccaui, sed non peieraui'. She has indeed offended Diana by breaking her oath, but this was not a real perjury. Without what has preceded the words *periuria legi*, which some have found difficult to swallow, might indeed be puzzling: as a summary of Cydippe's case the phrase is brilliantly effective — 'point, all point'. Ovid had read the *De officiis*,[56] in which Cicero had drawn precisely the distinction which is in question here: *non enim falsum iurare periurare est, sed quod ex animi tui sententia iuraris, sicut uerbis concipitur more nostro, id non facere periurium est* (3.108). There is indeed an echo of those very words elsewhere in Cydippe's pleading: *consilium prudensque animi sententia iurat* (137). In Ovid's formulation the distinction is implied rather than stated, but it is none the less clear: 'non feci periuria, legi tantum'. Critics who have boggled at these lines have done so because they have failed to read them with the attention and respect for linguistic nuance that they require and deserve. Like his own Ulysses Ovid rings all the possible changes on the one point of substance that poor Cydippe can muster against her unscrupulous suitor: *illa referre aliter saepe solebat idem*. One lays down the double epistles to the echo of E. K. Rand's unanswerable challenge: 'if they are not from Ovid's pen, an *ignotus* has beaten him at his own game'.[57]

V. CONCLUSION

Of the ostensible or putative anomalies reviewed in the preceding dis-cussion no. **17** and perhaps also no. **7** can be shown to have an identifiable and designed literary effect in their contexts, and in that sense may be classed as positive (non-damnatory). Leaving nos. **9–13** aside for the moment, of the remainder nos. **3**, **8** and **15** can be classed as constructive

---

[54] Cf. e.g. Scip. min. *orat.* 11 *uerbis conceptis iuraui sciens*. For the idea of intention implied in *coniuro* cf. *Met.* 5.149–51 *namque omnibus unum | opprimere est animus, coniurata undique pugnant | agmina* eqs., where no actual oath is in question. For a unique use of *iuro* elsewhere in *Her.* see above, n. 2.

[55] Schawaller (1987: 206).

[56] Kenney (1958: 207 and n. 2); D'Elia (1961); Labate (1984: 121–74).

[57] Rand (1925: 27).

linguistic innovations, extending the range of Latin usage; in the last
instance the Virgilian analogies again remind us that this sort of thing was
part and parcel of the continuous process of development of the literary
registers of the language from Ennius onwards. Nos. **4, 5** and **6** may be
classed as neutral. This leaves the instances, nos. **9–13**, of specifically
Ciceronian diction and usage. The most plausible explanation of this very
light, and some might say statistically insignificant, Ciceronian coloration
is that it reflects the more adversarial tone of these epistles as compared
with the single *Heroides*.[58] It is an oversimplification, as Jacobson has
pointed out, to characterize the single letters *tout court* as *suasoriae* or
ethopoiae in verse and the double as *controuersiae*.[59] Nevertheless, *Heroides* 16–21 clearly do have a good deal in common with the *controuersia*.
This is most marked in the two outer pairs, in which the correspondents
are vigorously maintaining, or in Helen's case purporting to maintain,
diametrically opposed sides of a question, than in the epistles of Hero and
Leander. It is therefore perhaps not entirely accidental that most of my
examples of prosaisms and Ciceronianisms come from 16–17 and 20–21,
the pseudo-forensic tone of the *controuersia* being of course especially
prominent in the letters of Acontius and Cydippe — who, as we have
seen, all but quotes Cicero in her defence. At lines 145ff. of her letter,
immediately following on passage **17** (*b*), she resorts in desperation to a
sarcastic *reductio ad absurdum* of Acontius' tactics: why stick at entrapping
girls? Why not use this device to trick millionaires out of their wealth or
kings out of their kingdoms? This is in effect an exaggerated version of
the pleading actually recommended by Cicero in the *De inuentione* to the
speaker who is pleading for *aequitas* against the strict letter of the law:
*deinde nullam rem neque legibus neque scriptura ulla, denique ne in
sermone quidem cotidiano atque imperiis domesticis recte posse adminis-
trari, si unus quisque uelit uerba spectare et non ad uoluntatem eius qui ea
uerba habuerit accedere* (2.140). There is nothing to my mind inherently
improbable in the idea that Ovid turned over a few Ciceronian texts while
he was incubating these poems.

This leaves a residue of one non-starter (no. **1**) and one puzzle (no. **2**).
I am left wondering how *placandi*, if that is what Ovid wrote, sounded in
contemporary ears. Is it the sort of thing that, had the poems been given
a preliminary airing in private to a circle of critical friends, would have
provoked objections? If so, would the objection have been that the lan-

[58] Dr Horsfall points to an analogy in the case of the Council in *Aeneid* 11, where 'in his
portrait of Drances, and in his exchange with Turnus, Virgil drew on the language of
demagogy and polemic' (Gransden (1991: 14–15)).
[59] Jacobson (1974: 325–30).

guage was old-fashioned, or that it was correct but pedantic? Would the point have been taken that *placandae* was, strictly speaking, a solecism? But then, what of *amissae* at 11.106? Had that raised eyebrows, or was *constructio ad sensum* accepted in such cases? So far as the present instance is concerned, if I am right in my surmise that *Heroides* 16–21 never received the poet's final revision and were given to the world only after his death by some anonymous benefactor of mankind as they were found in his desk, there was no opportunity for any such discussion; and posterity is left to wonder.

It will, I think, have become clear that these so-called anomalies do not seem to me to add materially to the case for ascribing these epistles to an otherwise unknown poet of genius, which is what those who disbelieve in Ovid's authorship must necessarily postulate. That, however, is not really the point of this paper. What I hope to have shown is the need for finer discrimination in discussions of poetic style in such investigations. The Axelsonian dichotomy 'poetic/unpoetic' has its uses: it is certainly remarkable that in these poems Ovid should use four times a construction otherwise exemplified only in comedy, prose and satire and once in his exile poetry (no. 5); but when it comes to gauging its effect, and the effect of the repetition, on the ear of the contemporary reader we are again left guessing. To label every such case 'unpoetic', however, is unhelpful. The idea that even a great poet is bound to maintain a uniform quality and 'level' (to introduce another question-begging term) of style is an assumption which a nodding acquaintance with Shakespeare or Wordsworth should quickly dispose of. As regards the bearing of such departures from a postulated poetic norm on the *Echtheitsfrage*, the incidence of colloquialisms and prosaisms deserving to be noted as such does not appear to differ materially, as has already been implied, from that in the undoubted *Heroides*.[60] All that is of secondary importance; what matters is what these phenomena have to tell us about the literary art of *Ouidius nouator*.

Note. This paper has profited materially from the constructive comments of the Academy's referees. I am also grateful to Dr Robert Maltby for his help with the bibliography of the Axelsonian question.

[60] Above, n. 2. For the latest contribution to the debate on authenticity see Beck (1996) and my review in *CR* 48 (1998), 311–13.

ABBREVIATIONS

ANRW H. Temporini and W. Haase (edd.), *Aufstieg und Niedergang der römischen Welt.* Berlin and New York 1972–   .

CHCL E. J. Kenney and W. V. Clausen (edd.), *The Cambridge History of Classical Literature.* II *Latin Literature.* Cambridge 1982.

CIL *Corpus Inscriptionum Latinarum.* Berlin 1863–   .

CLE F. Bücheler and E. Lommatzsch (edd.), *Carmina Latina Epigraphica.* 3 vols. Leipzig 1894–1926.

GLK H. Keil (ed.), *Grammatici Latini.* 8 vols. Leipzig 1857–70, repr. 1961.

H–S J. B. Hofmann and A. Szantyr, *Lateinische Syntax und Stilistik.* Munich 1965.

K–S R. Kühner and C. Stegmann, *Ausführliche Grammatik der lateinischen Sprache.* 3rd ed. A. Thierfelder. 2 vols. Leverkusen 1955.

LSJ H. G. Liddell and R. Scott, *A Greek-English Lexicon.* New ed. by H. S. Jones. 2 vols. Oxford 1940 and repr.

OLD P. G. W. Glare (ed.), *Oxford Latin Dictionary.* Oxford 1982.

TLL *Thesaurus Linguae Latinae.* Leipzig 1900–   .

Bibliography

Adamietz, J. (ed.) (1986), *Die römische Satire* (Grundriß der Literaturgeschichten nach Gattungen) (Darmstadt).

Adams, J. N. (1971), 'A type of hyperbaton in Latin prose', *PCPhS* 17: 1–16.

—— (1976), 'A typological approach to Latin word-order', *Indogermanische Forschungen* 81: 70–99.

—— (1980a), 'Latin words for woman and wife', *Glotta* 50: 234–55.

—— (1980b), 'Anatomical terminology in Latin epic', *BICS* 27: 50–62.

—— (1982a), *The Latin Sexual Vocabulary* (London).

—— (1982b), 'Anatomical terms transferred from animals to humans in Latin', *Indogermanische Forschungen* 87: 90–109.

—— (1983), 'Words for "prostitute" in Latin', *RhM* 126: 321–58.

—— (1992), 'Iteration of compound verb with simplex in Latin prose', *Eikasmos* 3: 295–8.

—— (1994a), 'Wackernagel's law and the position of unstressed personal pronouns in Classical Latin', *TPhS* 92: 103–78

—— (1994b), *Wackernagel's Law and the Placement of the Copula* esse *in Classical Latin* (Cambridge Philological Society, Suppl. vol. 18) (Cambridge).

—— (1995a), 'The language of the Vindolanda writing tablets: an interim report', *JRS* 85: 86–134.

—— (1995b), *Pelagonius and Latin Veterinary Terminology in the Roman Empire* (Studies in Ancient Medicine, 11) (Leiden).

Allen, W. S. (1973), *Accent and Rhythm. Prosodic Features of Latin and Greek: a Study in Theory and Reconstruction* (Cambridge).

—— (1978, 2nd ed.), *Vox Latina. A Guide to the Pronunciation of Classical Latin* (Cambridge).

Alfonso, S., Cipriani, G., Fedeli, P., Mazzini, I., Tedeschi, A. (1990), *Il poeta elegiaco e il viaggio d'amore* (Scrinia, 3) (Bari).

Anderson, R. D., Parsons, P. J. and Nisbet, R. G. M. (1979), 'Elegiacs by Gallus from Qaṣr Ibrîm', *JRS* 69: 125–55.

Anderson, W. S. (1956; 1964; 1970; 1981), 'Recent Work in Roman Satire', *ClW* 50: 33–40; *ClW* 57: 293–301; 343–8; *ClW* 63: 181–94; 199; 217–22; *ClW* 75: 273–99.

—— (1961), '*Venusina lucerna*: the Horatian model for Juvenal', *TAPA* 52: 1–12. (Reprinted in Anderson (1982) 103–14.)

—— (1962), 'The Programs of Juvenal's Later Books', *CPh* 57: 145–60. (Reprinted in Anderson (1982), 277–92.)

—— (1982), *Essays on Roman Satire* (Princeton).

André, J. (1949), *Étude sur les termes de couleur dans la langue latine* (Paris).

—— (1967), *Les noms d'oiseaux en latin* (Paris).

_____ (1980), 'Deux remarques sur le volume du mot latin', *RPh* 54: 7–18.

_____ (1987), *Être médecin à Rome* (Realia) (Paris).

_____ (1991), *Le vocabulaire latin de l'anatomie* (Paris).

Arens, J. C. (1950), '-fer and -ger: their extraordinary preponderance among compounds in Roman poetry', *Mnemosyne*[4] 3: 241–62.

Argenio, I. (1963), 'I grecismi in Lucilio', *CRSt* 11: 5–17.

Artymowicz, A. (1909), 'Der Wechsel von *et* und *que* zu Beginn lateinischer daktylischer Verse von Ennius bis Corippus', *Wiener Studien* 31: 38–81.

Atherton, C. (1996), 'What every grammarian knows?', *CQ* NS 46: 239–60.

Austin, R. G. (ed.) (1964), *P. Vergili Maronis Aeneidos Liber Secundus* (Oxford).

_____ (ed.) (1971), *P. Vergili Maronis Aeneidos Liber Primus* (Oxford).

_____ (ed.) (1977), *P. Vergili Maronis Aeneidos Liber Sextus* (Oxford).

Avotins, I. (1980), 'Alexander of Aphrodisias on vision in the atomists', *CQ* NS 30: 429–54.

Axelson, B. (1945), *Unpoetische Wörter. Ein Beitrag zur Kenntnis der lateinischen Dichtersprache* (Lund).

Bader, F. (1962), *La formation des composés nominaux du latin* (Paris).

Baehrens, E. (ed.) (1885), *Catulli Veronensis liber* (Leipzig).

Baehrens, W. A. (1912), *Beiträge zur lateinischen Syntax*. Philologus, Suppl. 12 (Leipzig).

Bagnall, R. S. (1993), *Egypt in Late Antiquity* (Princeton).

Bailey, C. (ed.) (1947, corr. ed. 1949, 3 vols), *Titi Lucreti Cari de rerum natura libri sex* (Oxford).

Baratin, M. (1989), *La naissance de la syntaxe à Rome* (Paris).

Barnes, J., Mignucci, M. (edd.) (1988), *Matter and Metaphysics* (Naples).

Bartalucci, A. (1968), 'La sperimentazione enniana dell'esametro e la tecnica del saturnio', *SCO* 17: 99–122.

Bauer, C. F. (1933), *The Latin Perfect Endings '-ere' and '-erunt'* (Ling. Soc. America, Language Diss. 13) (Philadelphia).

Beck, M. (1996), *Die Epistulae Heroidum XVIII und XIX des Corpus Ovidianum. Echtheitskritische Untersuchungen* (Paderborn).

Bell, A. J. (1923). *The Latin Dual and Poetic Diction* (London and Toronto).

Benediktson, D. T. (1977), 'Vocabulary analysis and the generic classification of literature', *Phoenix* 31: 341–8.

Bennett, C. E. (1910), *Syntax of Early Latin, Vol. I—The Verb* (Boston).

Bentley, R. (ed.) (1711), *Q. Horatius Flaccus* (Cambridge).

Benz, L., Stärk, E., Vogt-Spira, G. (edd.) (1995), *Plautus und die Tradition des Stegreifspiels*. Festgabe für E. Lefèvre zum 60. Geburtstag (Tübingen).

Berkowitz, L. and Brunner, Th. F. (1968), *Index Lucilianus* (Hildesheim).

Binder, G. (ed.) (1988), *Saeculum Augustum II* (Wege der Forschung 512) (Darmstadt).

Biville, F. (1987), *Graphie et prononciation des mots grecs en latin* (Paris).

_____ (1989), (ed.) 'Grec et latin: contacts linguistiques et création lexicale. Pour une typologie des hellénismes lexicaux du latin', in Lavency and Longrée (1989), 29–40.

_____ (1990), *Les emprunts du latin au grec: approche phonétique* vol. I (Bibliothèque de l'information grammaticale, 19) (Louvain—Paris).

Blase, H. (1903), 'Tempora und Modi', in G. Landgraf (ed.), *Historische Grammatik der lateinischen Sprache*. 3. Band *Syntax des einfachen Satzes* (Leipzig).

Bloch, H. (1940), 'L. Calpurnius Piso Caesoninus in Samothrace and Herculaneum', *AJA* 44: 485–93.

Blümel, W. (1979), 'Zur historischen Morphosyntax der Verbalabstrakta im Lateinischen', *Glotta* 57: 77–125.

Boetticher, G. (1830), *Lexicon Taciteum* (Berlin).

Boldt, H. (1884), *De liberiore linguae Graecae et Latinae collocatione verborum* (Diss. Göttingen).

Bollack, J. (1965–69), *Empédocle* (3 vols; Paris).

Bömer, F. (1951), Review of Axelson (1945), *Gnomon* 23: 166–8.

—— (1952), 'Excudent alii . . .', *Hermes* 80: 117–23.

—— (1957), 'Beiträge zum Verständnis der augusteischen Dichtersprache', *Gymnasium* 64: 1–21.

—— (1965), 'Eine Stileigentümlichkeit Vergils: Vertauschen der Prädikate', *Hermes* 93: 130–1.

—— (1967), 'Ovid met. I 39', *Gymnasium* 74: 223–6.

—— (1969), *P. Ovidius Naso. Metamorphosen*. Buch I–III (Heidelberg).

—— (1976), *P. Ovidius Naso Metamorphosen*. Buch IV–V (Heidelberg).

—— (1982), *P. Ovidius Naso Metamorphosen*. Buch XII–XIII (Heidelberg).

Bonjour, M. (1984), 'Cicero nauticus', in R. Chevallier (ed.), *Présence de Cicéron*, 9–19 (Collection Caesarodunum 19 bis) (Paris).

Bonner, S. F. (1949), *Roman Declamation in the Late Republic and Early Empire* (Liverpool).

Booth, J. (1981), 'Aspects of Ovid's language', in H. Temporini (ed.), *ANRW* II.31.4 2686–700 (Berlin–New York).

—— (ed.) (1991), *Ovid. The Second Book of Amores* (Warminster).

Bourgeois, P. (1940), 'L'hellénisme, procédé d'expression dans les Géorgiques', *RÉL* 18: 73–94.

Bowman, A. K., Thomas, J. D. and Adams, J. N. (1990), 'Two letters from Vindolanda', *Britannia* 21: 33–52.

Bowman, A. K. and Thomas, J. D., with contributions by Adams, J. N. (1994), *The Vindolanda Writing-Tablets (Tabulae Vindolandenses II)* (London).

Bowman, A. K. and Thomas, J. D. (1996), 'New writing tablets from Vindolanda', *Britannia* 27: 299–328.

Bowra, C. M. (1952), *Heroic Poetry* (London).

Bramble, J. C. (1974), *Persius and the Programmatic Satire* (Cambridge).

—— (1982a), 'Martial and Juvenal', in Kenney and Clausen (1982), 101–27.

—— (1982b), 'Lucan', in Kenney and Clausen (1982), 533–57.

Braund, S. H. (1989a), 'City and country in Roman satire', in Braund (1989b), 23–48.

—— (ed.) (1989b), *Satire and Society in Ancient Rome* (Exeter Studies in History, 23) (Exeter).

—— (1992a), *Roman Verse Satire* (Greece and Rome New Surveys in the Classics, 23) (Oxford).

—— (1992b), *Lucan, Civil War, translated with introduction and notes* (Oxford).

—— (ed.) (1996), *Juvenal, Satires, Book I* (Cambridge).

Brenous, J. (1895), *Étude sur les hellénismes dans la syntaxe latine* (Paris).

van Brock, N. (1961), *Recherches sur le vocabulaire médical du grec ancien* (Études et Commentaires, 41) (Paris).

Brown, R. D. (1987), *Lucretius on Love and Sex: a Commentary on De Rerum Natura IV, 1030–1287, with Prolegomena, Text and Translation* (Columbia studies in the classical tradition, 15) (Leiden).

Bürger, R. (1911), 'Beiträge zur Elegantia Tibulls' in *XAPITEΣ. Friedrich Leo* 371–94 (Berlin).

Brunér, E. A. (1863), 'De ordine et temporibus carminum Valerii Catulli', *Acta Soc. Scient. Fennicae* 7: 599–657.

Bülow-Jacobsen, A., Cuvigny, H. and Fournet, J.-L. (1994), 'The identification of Myos Hormos. New papyrological evidence', *BIFAO* 94: 27–42.

Burnyeat, M. F. (1978), 'The upside-down back-to-front sceptic of Lucretius IV 472', *Philologus* 122: 197–206.

Cairns, F. (1972), *Generic Composition in Greek and Roman Poetry* (Edinburgh).

_____ (1979), *Tibullus: a Hellenistic Poet at Rome* (Cambridge).

_____ (1983), 'Propertius 1.4 and 1.5 and the 'Gallus' of the Monobiblos', *PLLS* 4: 61–104.

_____ (1984), 'The etymology of *militia* in Roman elegy' in *Apophoreta philologica Emmanueli Fernandez-Galiano a sodalibus oblata* 2.211–22 (Madrid).

_____ (ed.) (1986), *Papers of the Liverpool Latin Seminar 5, 1985* (Liverpool).

_____ (1986), 'Stile e contenuti di Tibullo e di Properzio' in *Atti del Convegno Internazionale di Studi su Albio Tibullo* 49–50. (Rome).

Callebat, L. (1974), 'Le vocabulaire de l'hydraulique dans le livre VIII du *De architectura* de Vitruve', *RPh* 48: 313–29.

_____ (1982), 'La prose du *De Architectura* de Vitruve', in H. Temporini (ed.), *ANRW* II.30.1: 696–722 (Berlin).

_____ (ed.) (1995), *Latin vulgaire, latin tardif. IV.* Actes du 4ᵉ colloque international sur le latin vulgaire et tardif. Caen, 2–5 septembre 1994 (Hildesheim, Zurich, New York).

Campanile, E. (1985), art. 'grecismi', in *Enciclopedia Virgiliana* ii.805–7 (Rome).

Casali, S. (ed.) (1995), *P. Ovidii Nasonis Heroidum Epistula IX. Deianira Herculi* (Florence).

Caspari, F. (1908), *De ratione quae inter Vergilium et Lucanum intercedat quaestiones selectae* (Diss. Leipzig).

Cavenaile, R. (1958), *Corpus Papyrorum Latinarum* (Wiesbaden).

Cèbe, J.-P. (1966), *La caricature et la parodie dans le monde romain*, (Bibl. des Écoles françaises d'Athènes et de Rome, 206) (Paris).

Charpin, F. (ed.) (1978, 1979, 1991), *Lucilius, Satires. Texte établi, traduit et annoté* (Paris).

Christ, W. (1879, 2nd ed.), *Metrik der Griechen und Römer* (Leipzig).

Christes, J. (1971), *Der frühe Lucilius. Rekonstruktion und Interpretation des XXVI. Buches sowie von Teilen des XXX. Buches* (Heidelberg).

_____ (1972), 'Lucilius. Ein Bericht über die Forschung seit F. Marx (1904/5)', in H. Temporini (ed.), *ANRW* I.2. 1182–1239 (Berlin).

_____ (1986), 'Lucilius', in Adamietz (1986), 57–122.

Cichorius, C. (1908), *Untersuchungen zu Lucilius* (Berlin).

Clark, S. B. (1908), 'The authorship and the date of the double letters in Ovid's Heroides', *HSCPh* 19: 121–55.

Coffey, M. (1989, 2nd ed.), *Roman Satire* (Bristol).

Coleman, R. G. G. (1977) 'Greek influence on Latin syntax', *TPhS* 1975: 101–56.

―――― (1987), 'Vulgar Latin and the diversity of Christian Latin', in J. Herman (ed.), *Latin vulgaire—latin tardif* 37–52. (Tübingen).

―――― (1989), 'The formation of specialized vocabularies in grammar and rhetoric: winners and losers', in Lavency and Longrée (1989: 77–89).

―――― (1991), 'Latin prepositional syntax in Indo-European perspective', in Coleman (ed.), *New Studies in Latin Linguistics* 323–38 (Amsterdam).

―――― (1995), 'Complex sentence structure in Livy', in D. Longrée (ed.), *De Vsu. Études de syntaxe latine offertes en hommage à Marius Lavency*, 71–84 (Louvain-la-Neuve).

Collinge, N. E. (1962), 'Medical terms and clinical attitudes in the tragedians', *BICS* 9: 43–7.

Conrad, C. (1965), 'Word order in Latin epic from Ennius to Virgil', *HSCPh* 69: 194–258.

Conte, G. B. (1970), 'Ennio e Lucano', *Maia* 22: 132–8.

Contino, S. (ed.) (1988), *A. Cornelii Celsi, De medicina liber VIII* (Bologna).

Coppel, B. (1976), review of Ross (1969), *Gnomon* 48: 559–66.

Cordier, A. (1943), 'La langue poétique à Rome', *Mémorial des études latines...offert à J. Marouzeau* 80–92 (Paris).

Courtney, E. (1965), 'Ovidian and non-Ovidian Heroides', *BICS* 12: 63–6.

―――― (1980), *A Commentary on the Satires of Juvenal* (London).

―――― (ed.) (1993), *The Fragmentary Latin Poets* (Oxford).

Cutt, T. (1936), *Meter and Diction in Catullus' Hendecasyllabics* (Diss. Chicago).

Dagron, G. (1969), 'Aux origines de la civilisation byzantine: langue de culture et langue d'état', *Rev. Hist.* 241: 23ff.

Daube, D. (1956), *Forms of Roman Legislation* (Oxford).

De Decker, J. (1913), *Juvenalis Declamans* (Ghent).

Deichgräber, K. (ed.) (1935), *Hippokrates über Entstehung und Aufbau des menschlichen Körpers*, Περὶ σαρκῶν mit einem sprachwissenschaftlichen Beitrag von Eduard Schwyzer (Leipzig–Berlin).

―――― (1971), *Aretaeus von Kappadozien als medizinischer Schriftsteller* (Abh. d. Sächs. Akad. d. Wiss. zu Leipzig, Philol.-hist. Kl., 63, 3) (Berlin).

D'Elia, S. (1961), 'Echi del "de officiis" nell' "Ars amatoria" ovidiana', in *Atti del I congr. int. di studi ciceroniani*, ii. 127–40 (Rome).

Della Corte, M. (1958), 'Le iscrizioni di Ercolano', *Rendiconti della Accademia di Archeologia, Lettere e Belle Arti*, n.s. 33: 239–308 (Naples).

Delatte, K. (1967), 'Keywords and poetic themes in Propertius and Tibullus', *RELO* 3: 31–79.

Delz, J. (ed.) (1987), *Sili Italici Punica* (Stuttgart).

De Meo, C. (1983), *Lingue tecniche del latino* (Testi e manuali per l'insegnamento universitario del latino 16) (Bologna).

Denniston, J. D. (1952), *Greek Prose Style* (Oxford).

Deufert, M. (1996), *Pseudo-Lukrezisches im Lukrez. Die unechten Verse in Lukre-*

zens *'De rerum natura'*. Untersuchungen zur antiken Literatur und Geschichte 48 (Berlin and New York).

Diggle, J. (1972), 'Ouidiana', *PCPS* NS 18: 31–41.

Diggle, J. and Goodyear, F. R. D. (edd.) (1972), *The Classical Papers of A. E. Housman* (Cambridge).

Dingel, J. (1997), *Kommentar zum 9. Buch der Aeneis Vergils* (Heidelberg).

Dionisotti, A. C. (1995), 'Hellenismus' in O. Weijers (ed.), *Vocabulary of Teaching and Research Between Middle Ages and Renaissance* (Civicima. Études sur le vocabulaire intellectuel du Moyen Age 8) (Turnhout).

Domínguez Domínguez, J. F. and Martín Rodríguez, A. M. (1993), '*Dare* con infinitivo en latín clasico', *Cuadernos de filología clásica*, 4: 9–22.

Dover, K. J. (1963), 'The Poetry of Archilochus', in *Entretiens sur l'Antiquité classique* 10: 183–212 (Geneva).

_____ (1968, corrected reprint of 1960 ed.), *Greek Word Order* (Cambridge).

Draeger, A. (1882, 3rd ed.), *Über Syntax und Stil des Tacitus* (Leipzig).

Drexler, H. (1967), *Einführung in die römische Metrik* (Darmstadt).

Dubois, J. (1966), 'Les problèmes du vocabulaire technique', *Cahiers de lexicologie* 9: 103–12.

Dumortier, J. (1935), *Le vocabulaire médical d'Eschyle et les écrits hippocratiques* (Paris).

Easterling, P. E. (ed.) (1982), *Sophocles, Trachiniae* (Cambridge).

Eich, M. (1925), *De praepositionum collocatione apud poetas Latinos inde ab Ovidio* (Diss. Bonn).

Eklund, S. (1970), *The periphrastic, completive and finite use of the present participle in Latin. With special regard to translation of Christian texts in Greek up to 600 A.D.* (Acta Universitatis Upsaliensis. Studia Latina Upsaliensia, 5) (Uppsala).

Elder, J. P. (1962), 'Tibullus: Tersus atque Elegans' in J. P. Sullivan (ed.) *Critical Essays on Roman Literature: Elegy and Lyric*, 65–106. (London).

Eliot, T. S. (1932 [1917]), 'Tradition and the individual talent', in *Selected Essays*, 13–22 (London).

Ellis, R. (1876; 2nd ed. 1889), *A Commentary on Catullus* (Oxford).

Erbse, H. (1953), 'Homerscholien und hellenistische Glossare bei Apollonios Rhodios', *Hermes* 81: 163–96.

Ernout, A. (1946), 'Infinitif grec et gérondif latin', *Philologica* (Paris).

_____ (1947), 'Le vocabulaire poétique', rev. of Axelson (1945), *RPh* 21: 55–70 (= 1957*b*: 66–86).

_____ (1956), 'VENVS, VENIA, CVPIDO', *RPh* 30: 7–27 (= 1957*b*: 87–111).

_____ (1957*a*), 'METVS — TIMOR. Les formes en -*us* et en -*os* (-*or*) du latin', in 1957*b*: 7–56

_____ (1957*b*), *Philologica* II (Paris).

Ernout, A. and Meillet, A. (1959; 4th ed.), *Dictionnaire étymologique de la langue latine. Histoire des mots*, augmenté d'additions et de corrections nouvelles par J. André (Paris).

Ernout, A. and Thomas, F. (1953), *Syntaxe latine* (Paris).

Evans, W. J. (1921), *Allitteratio Latina* (London).

Évrard-Gillis, J. (1976), *La récurrence lexicale dans l'oeuvre de Catulle: étude stylistique* (Paris).

Fantham, E. (1972), *Comparative Studies in Republican Latin Imagery* (Toronto).

Farrell, J. (1991), *Virgil's 'Georgics' and the Traditions of Ancient Epic* (New York and Oxford).

Fedeli, P. (ed.) (1965), *Properzio, Elegie libro IV: Testo critico e commento* (Bari).

_____ (ed.) (1980), *Sesto Properzio, Il primo libro delle Elegie: Introduzione, testo critico e commento* (Florence).

_____ (ed.) (1985), *Properzio, Il libro terzo delle Elegie: Introduzione, testo e commento* (Bari).

Ferguson, J. (1987), *A Prosopography to the Poems of Juvenal* (Brussels).

Fiske, G. C. (1919), 'The plain style in the Scipionic Circle', in *Studies in Honor of Ch. Forster Smith* (Madison).

_____ (1920), *Lucilius and Horace. A Study in the Classical Theory of Imitation* (University of Wisconsin Studies in Language and Literature 7) (Madison).

Fitch, J. G. (1981), 'Sense-pauses and relative dating in Seneca, Sophocles and Shakespeare', *AJP* 102: 289–307.

Flashar, H. (ed.) (1971), *Antike Medizin* (Wege der Forschung 221) (Darmstadt).

Fluck, H.-R. (1980), *Fachsprachen: Einführung und Bibliographie* (Munich).

Flury, P. (1968), *Liebe und Liebessprache bei Menander, Plautus und Terenz* (Heidelberg).

_____ (1990), 'Beiträge aus der Thesaurus-Arbeit, XXV: *occurrere*', *MH* 47: 225–6.

Fordyce, C. J. (ed.) (1961; repr. with corrections and additional notes 1973), *Catullus: a Commentary* (Oxford).

_____ (ed.) (1977), *P. Vergili Maronis Aeneidos libri 7–8*, with a commentary ed. by John D. Christie (Oxford).

Fraenkel, E. (1922), *Plautinisches im Plautus* (Philologische Untersuchungen 28) (Berlin)

_____ (1928), *Iktus und Akzent im lateinischen Sprechvers* (Berlin).

_____ (1960 = transl. of [1922] with addenda), *Elementi plautini in Plauto* (Florence).

_____ (1968), *Leseproben aus Reden Ciceros und Catos* (Rome).

Freudenburg, K. (1993), *The Walking Muse: Horace on the Theory of Satire* (Princeton).

Friedländer, P. (1941), 'Pattern of sound and atomistic theory in Lucretius', *AJP* 62: 16–34.

Gaisser, J. H. (1993), *Catullus and his Renaissance Readers* (Oxford).

Gardner-Chloros, P. (1991), *Language Selection and Switching in Strasbourg* (Oxford).

Garvie, A. F. (ed.) (1986), *Aeschylus, Choephori, with Introduction and Commentary* (Oxford).

Geymonat, M. (ed.) (1973), *P. Vergili Maronis Opera* (Turin).

Gianfrotta, P. A. (1987), art. 'Navis', in *Enciclopedia Virgiliana* iii. 670–4 (Rome).

Gigante, M. (1981), *Scetticismo e epicureismo* (Naples).

Gigon, O. (1978), 'Lukrez und Ennius', in *Entretiens sur l'Antiquité classique* 24: 167–91 (Geneva).

Godwin, J. (ed.) (1986), *Lucretius: 'De Rerum Natura' IV* (Warminster).

_____ (ed.) (1991), *Lucretius: 'De Rerum Natura' VI* (Warminster).

Gow, A. S. F. (1931), 'Diminutives in Augustan Poetry', *CQ* 26: 150–7.

Goodyear, F. R. D. (ed.) (1972), *The Annals of Tacitus, I: Annals 1.1–54*, (Cambridge Classical Texts and Commentaries 15) (Cambridge).

—— (ed.) (1981), *The Annals of Tacitus, II: Annals 1.55–81 and Annals 2*, (Cambridge Classical Texts and Commentaries 23) (Cambridge).

Goold, G. P. (1974), *Interpreting Catullus* (London).

—— (1983), *Catullus, edited with introduction, translation and notes* (London)

—— (1990), *Propertius* (Cambridge, Mass.).

Görler, W. (1982), 'Beobachtungen zu Vergils Syntax', *Würzburger Jahrbücher* 8: 69–81.

—— (1984), 'Zum Virtus-Fragment des Lucilius (1326–1338 Marx) und zur Geschichte der stoischen Güterlehre', *Hermes* 12: 445–68.

—— (1985), art. 'Eneide, 6. La lingua', in *Enciclopedia Virgiliana* ii. 262–78 (Rome).

Gransden, K. W. (ed.) (1991) *Virgil Aeneid Book XI* (Cambridge).

Gratwick, A. S. (1982), 'The Satires of Ennius and Lucilius', in Kenney and Clausen (1982), 156–71.

Griffin, J. (1985), *Latin Poets and Roman Life* (London) (pp. 1–31 = *JRS* 66 [1976], 87–105).

Grilli, A. (1978), 'Ennius podager', *RFIC* 106: 34–8.

Groeber, G. (1884), 'Vulgärlateinische Substrate romanischer Wörter', *ALL* 1: 204–54.

Guilbert, L. (1965), *La formation du vocabulaire de l'aviation* (Paris).

Haffter, H. (1934), *Untersuchungen zur altlateinischen Dichtersprache* (Problemata, 10) (Berlin).

—— (1956), 'Zum Problem der überlangen Wortformen im Lateinischen', *WSt* 69: 363–71.

Hahn, E. A. (1958), 'Vergil's linguistic treatment of divine beings, part II', *TAPA* 89: 237–53.

Hakamies, R. (1951), *Étude sur l'origine et l'évolution du diminutive latin et sa survie dans les langues romanes* (Helsinki).

Halm, C. (ed.) (1863), *Rhetores Latini Minores* (Leipzig).

Handford, S. A. (1947), *The Latin Subjunctive. Its Usage and Development from Plautus to Terence* (London).

Hanslik, R. (1969), art. 'Lucilius', in *Der kleine Pauly*, vol. III (Stuttgart).

Hanssen, J. S. T. (1951), *Latin Diminutives: a Semantic Study* (Bergen).

Hardie, P. R. (ed.) (1994), *Virgil, Aeneid, Book IX* (Cambridge).

Harrison, E. L. (1960), 'Neglected hyperbole in Juvenal', *CR* NS 10: 99–101.

Harrison, S. J. (ed.) (1990), *Oxford Readings in Vergil's Aeneid* (Oxford).

—— (ed.) (1991), *Vergil, Aeneid 10*, with introduction, translation, and commentary (Oxford).

Hartung, H. J. (1970), *Ciceros Methode bei der Übersetzung griechischer philosophischer Termini* (Diss. Hamburg).

Haupt, M. (1841), *Observationes Criticae* (Leipzig) (= 1875: 73–142).

—— (1875), *Opuscula* I (Leipzig).

Heck, B. (1950), *Die Anordnung der Gedichte des C. Valerius Catullus* (Diss. Tübingen).

Henry, A. (1971), *Métonymie et métaphore* (Paris).

Herescu, N. I. (1960), *La poésie latine. Étude des structures phoniques* (Paris).

Heraeus, W. (1937), *Kleine Schriften* (Heidelberg).

Hermann, G. (1796), *De metris poetarum Graecorum et Romanorum libri III* (Leipzig).

———— (1816), *Elementa doctrinae metricae* (Leipzig).

Hettrich, H. (1988), *Untersuchungen zur Hypotaxe im Vedischen* (Berlin – New York).

———— (1990), *Der Agens in passivischen Sätzen altindogermanischer Sprachen* (NAWG, 1. Philologisch-historische Klasse, Nr.2) (Göttingen).

Heusch, H. (1954), *Das Archaische in der Sprache Catulls* (Diss. Bonn).

Heurgon, J. (1959), *Lucilius* (Paris).

Heyne, C. G. and Wagner, G. P. E. (edd.) (1830–33, 4th edn.), *P. Virgili Maronis opera.* (Leipzig).

Highet, G. (1951), 'Juvenal's Bookcase', *AJP* 72: 369–94.

———— (1954), *Juvenal the Satirist. A Study* (Oxford).

Hillen, M. (1989), *Studien zur Dichtersprache Senecas. Abundanz. Explikativer Ablativ. Hypallage* (Untersuchungen zur antiken Literatur und Geschichte 32) (Berlin – New York).

Hinds, S. E. (1987), 'Language at breaking point: Lucretius 1.452', *CQ* NS 37: 450–3.

Hofmann, J. B. (1951), *Lateinische Umgangssprache*. 3. Auflage (Heidelberg).

Hofmann, J. B. and Szantyr, A. (1965), *Lateinische Syntax und Stilistik*. (Handbuch der Altertumswissenschaft II 2.2) (Munich).

Holford-Strevens, L. (1988), *Aulus Gellius* (London).

Hollis, A. S. (ed.) (1977), *Ovid, Ars Amatoria Book I, edited with an introduction and commentary* (Oxford).

Horsfall, N. (1971), 'Numanus Regulus. Ethnography and propaganda in *Aen.* IX.598f.', *Latomus* 30: 1108–16 (= Harrison (1990: 127–44)).

———— (1981), 'Some problems of titulature in Roman literary history', *BICS* 28: 103–11.

Housman, A. E. (1907), 'Luciliana', *CQ* 1: 51–74, 148–59. (= Diggle and Goodyear (1972) ii.662–97.)

Hunter, R. L. (ed.) (1989), *Apollonius of Rhodes, Argonautica Book III* (Cambridge).

Hupe, C. (1871), *De genere dicendi C. Valerii Catulli Veronensis. Pars I* (Diss. Münster).

Hutchinson, G. O. (1988), *Hellenistic Poetry* (Oxford).

———— (1993), *Latin Literature from Seneca to Juvenal. A Critical Study* (Oxford).

Ilberg, J. (1907), 'A. Cornelius Celsus und die Medizin in Rom', *Neue Jahrbücher* 19: 377–412 (= Flashar (1971), 308–60).

Jacobson, H. (1974), *Ovid's* Heroides (Princeton, N.J.).

Jal, A. (1861), *Virgilius nauticus. Études sur la marine antique* (Paris).

Janni, P. (1967), 'Due note omeriche', *QUCC* 3: 7–30.

Janni, P. and Mazzini, I. (edd.) (1991), *La traduzione dei classici greci e latini in Italia oggi. Problemi, prospettive, iniziative editoriali* (Atti del Convegno Nazionale, Macerata, 20–22 aprile 1989) (Macerata).

Janson, T. (1979), *Mechanisms of Language Change in Latin* (Stockholm).

BIBLIOGRAPHY

Janssen, H. H. (1941), *De kenmerken der romeinsche dichtertaal* (Nijmegen – Utrecht).

Jenkyns, R. (1982), *Three Classical Poets: Sappho, Catullus and Juvenal* (London).

Jocelyn, H. D. (ed.) (1969a), *The Tragedies of Ennius: the fragments edited with an introduction and commentary* (Cambridge).

――― (1969b), 'The fragments of Ennius' Scenic Scripts', *AC* 38: 181–217.

――― (1971), 'The Tragedies of Ennius', *Entretiens sur l'Antiquité classique* 17: 41–95 (Geneva).

――― (1972), 'The Poems of Quintus Ennius', in H. Temporini (ed.), *ANRW* I.2.987–1026 (Satires and minor works: 1022–6) (Berlin).

――― (1977), 'Ennius, Sat. 6–7 Vahlen', *RFIC* 105: 131–51.

――― (1979), 'Catullus 58 and Ausonius, *Ep.* 71', *LCM* 4: 87–91.

――― (1980), 'Marcello Zicàri and the poems of C. Valerius Catullus', *RPL* 3: 55–72.

――― (1986), 'The new chapters of the ninth book of Celsus' *Artes*', *PLLS* 5: 299–336 (Liverpool).

――― (1995), 'Two Features of the Style of Catullus' Phalaecian Epigrams', *Sileno* 21: 63–82.

Jouanna, J. (1970), review of Lanata (1968), *REG* 83: 254–7.

Jouanna, J. and Demont, P. (1981), 'Le sens d' ἰχώρ chez Homère (*Iliade* V, vv. 340 et 416) et Eschyle (*Agamemnon*, v. 1480) en relation avec les emplois du mot dans la *Collection hippocratique*', *REA* 83: 197–209.

Kaimio, J. (1979), *The Romans and the Greek Language* (Commentationes Human. Litterarum Soc. Scient. Fenn. 64) (Helsinki–Helsingfors).

Kaster, R. A. (ed.) (1995), *C. Suetonius Tranquillus, De Grammaticis et Rhetoribus, edited with a translation, introduction and commentary* (Oxford).

Kenney, E. J. (1958), 'Nequitiae poeta', in N. I. Herescu (ed.), *Ovidiana. Recherches sur Ovide*, 201–9 (Paris).

――― (1962), 'The First Satire of Juvenal', *PCPS* NS 8: 29–40.

――― (1963), 'Juvenal: Satirist or Rhetorician?', *Latomus* 22: 704–20.

――― (ed.) (1971), *Lucretius De Rerum Natura Book III* (Cambridge).

――― (1979), 'Two disputed passages in the Heroides', *CQ* NS 29: 394–431.

――― (ed.) (1996), *Ovid Heroides XVI–XXI* (Cambridge).

Kenney, E. J. and Clausen, W. V. (edd.) (1982), *The Cambridge History of Classical Literature*, ii, *Latin Literature* (Cambridge).

Kingsley, P. (1995), *Ancient Philosophy, Mystery, and Magic: Empedocles and Pythagorean Tradition* (Oxford).

Knoche, U. (1982; 4th ed.), *Die römische Satire* (Göttingen).

Knox, P. E. (1986), 'Ovid's *Metamorphoses* and the traditions of Augustan poetry', *PCPS* Suppl. 11 (Cambridge).

――― (ed.) (1995) *Ovid Heroides. Select Epistles* (Cambridge).

Koch, P. (1995), 'Latin vulgaire et traits universels de l'oral', in Callebat (1995: 125–44).

Korfmacher, W. Ch. (1935), 'Grecizing in Lucilian Satire', *CJ* 30: 453–62.

Korzeniewski, D. (ed.) (1970), *Die römische Satire* (Wege der Forschung 238) (Darmstadt).

Krenkel, W. (ed.) (1970; 2 vols), *Lucilius, Satiren. Lateinisch und Deutsch* (Leiden).

Krause, H. (1878), *De Vergilii usurpatione infinitivi* (Diss. Halle).

Kroll, W. (1912), 'Der lateinische Relativsatz', *Glotta* 3: 1–18.

——— (1913) (repr. 1958), *M. Tullii Ciceronis Orator*. Als Ersatz der Ausgabe von Otto Jahn. Erklärt von W. K. (Berlin).

——— (1924), *Studien zum Verständnis der römischen Literatur* (Stuttgart).

——— (1925), 3rd ed., repr. 1969, *Die wissenschaftliche Syntax im lateinischen Unterricht* (Dublin).

——— (1929), 2nd ed., 1st ed. 1922, reprinted with addenda, 1968), *C. Valerius Catullus* (Stuttgart).

Kudlien, F. (1963), *Untersuchungen zu Aretaios von Kappadokien* (Mainz).

Kühner, R. and Stegmann, C. (edd.) (1955; 3rd ed. by A. Thierfelder, 2 vols), *Ausführliche Grammatik der lateinischen Sprache* (Darmstadt).

Labate, M. (1984), *L'arte di farsi amare. Modelli culturali e progetto didascalico nell'elegia ovidiana*. (Biblioteca di 'Materiali e discussioni per l'analisi dei Testi classici', 2) (Pisa).

Lachmann, K. (1848), 'De Ovidii epistulis', *Prooemium indicis lectionum aestivarum a. 1848 = Kleinere Schriften zur classichen Philologie*, ed. J. Vahlen, 56–61 (Berlin).

Lakoff, G. and Johnson, M. (1980), *Metaphors We Live By* (Chicago).

Lakoff, G. and Turner, M. (1989), *More than Cool Reason: a Field Guide to Poetic Metaphor* (Chicago).

Lanata, G. (1966), 'Sul linguaggio amoroso di Saffo', *QUCC* 2: 63–79.

——— (1968), 'Linguaggio scientifico e linguaggio poetico. Note al lessico del *De morbo sacro*', *QUCC* 5: 22–36.

Landgraf, G. (1898), 'Der Accusativ der Beziehung (determinationis)', *ALL* 10: 209–24.

——— (1914, 2nd ed.), *Kommentar zu Ciceros Rede Pro Sex. Roscio Amerino* (Leipzig—Berlin)

Langslow, D. R. (1989), 'Latin technical language: synonyms and Greek words in Latin medical terminology', *TPhS* 87: 33–53.

——— (1991), 'The development of Latin medical terminology: some working hypotheses', *PCPS* ns 37: 106–30.

La Penna, A. (1951), 'Note sul linguaggio erotico dell'elegia latino', *Maia* 4: 187–209.

——— (1956*a*), review of Heusch (1954), *Gnomon* 28: 291–4.

——— (1956*b*), 'Problemi di stile catulliano', *Maia* 8: 141–60.

Lateiner, D. (1977), 'Obscenity in Catullus', *Ramus* 6: 15–32.

Lausberg, M. (1990), 'Epos und Lehrgedicht. Ein Gattungsvergleich am Beispiel von Lucans Schlangenkatalog', *Würzburger Jahrbücher* 16: 173–203.

Lavency, M. and Longrée, D. (edd.) (1989), *Actes du Ve Colloque de Linguistique latine* (Louvain-la-Neuve / Borzée, 31 March–4 April 1989) (*Cahiers de l'Institut de linguistique de Louvain* 15.1–4) (Louvain-la-Neuve).

Leavis, F. R. (1948, 2nd ed.), *Education and the University, a sketch for an 'English School'* (London).

Lebreton, J. (1901), *Études sur le langage et la grammaire de Cicéron* (Paris).

Lee, A.G. (1975), *Tibullus: Elegies* (Cambridge).

—— (ed.) (1990), *The Poems of Catullus, Edited with an Introduction, Translation and Brief Notes* (Oxford).

Lehmann, C. (1979), 'Der Relativsatz vom Indogermanischen bis zum Italienischen. Eine Etüde in diachroner syntaktischer Typologie', *Die Sprache* 25: 1–25.

—— (1984), *Der Relativsatz* (Tübingen).

Lehmann, Y. (1982), 'Varron et la médecine', in Sabbah (1982), 67–72.

Leishman, J. B. (1956), *Translating Horace* (Oxford).

Lelièvre, F. J. (1958), 'Parody in Juvenal and T. S. Eliot', *CPh* 53: 22–6.

Leo, F. (1896), *Analecta Plautina de figuris sermonis I* (Progr. Göttingen) = Fraenkel, E. [ed.], [1960] *Friedrich Leo. Ausgewählte kleine Schriften*. Erster Band: *Zur römischen Literatur des Zeitalters der Republik*: 71–122 (Rome).

—— (1906), 'review of Lucilii carminum reliquiae ed. Marx, vol. I–II, *GGA*: 837–61 (= Fraenkel, E. [ed.] [1960], *Friedrich Leo. Ausgewählte kleine Schriften*. Erster Band: *Zur römischen Literatur des Zeitalters der Republik*: 221–247 (Rome)).

—— (1967), *Geschichte der römischen Literatur*. Erster Band: *Die archaische Literatur*. Im Anhang: 'Die römische Poesie in der Sullanischen Zeit' (Darmstadt) (= Unveränderter Nachdruck der Ausgabe Berlin 1913).

Leumann, M. (1947), 'Die lateinische Dichtersprache', *MH* 4: 116–39 = *Kleine Schriften* (Zürich-Stuttgart 1959) 131–56 = Lunelli (1980) 131–78.

—— (1950), *Homerische Wörter* (Basel).

—— (1977, 6th ed.), *Lateinische Laut- und Formenlehre* (Handbuch der Altertumswissenschaft II 2.1) (Munich).

Levinson, S. C. (1983), *Pragmatics* (Cambridge).

Lévy, C. (1992), 'Cicéron créateur du vocabulaire latin de la connaissance: essai de synthèse', in *La langue latine, langue de la philosophie* (École française de Rome, 161) (Rome).

Lewis, N. (1959), *Samothrace, the Ancient Literary Sources* (London).

Leyhausen, J. (1893), *Helenae et Herus epistulae Ovidii non sunt* (Diss. Halle).

Linde, P. (1923), 'Die Stellung des Verbs in der lateinischen Prosa', *Glotta* 12: 153–78.

Lindsay, W. M. (1893), 'The Saturnian metre', *AJP* 14: 139–70, 305–34.

—— (1907), *Syntax of Plautus* (Oxford).

—— (ed.) (1913; repr. Hildesheim 1978), *Sexti Pompeii Festi de verborum significatu quae supersunt cum Pauli epitome* (Leipzig).

—— (1922), *Early Latin Verse* (Oxford).

Linse, E. (1891), *De P. Ovidio Nasone vocabulorum inventore* (Progr. Dortmund).

Löfstedt, B. (1990), 'Notizen zu Sprache und Text von Celsus, De medicina', *MH* 47: 60–2.

Löfstedt, E. (1911), *Philologischer Kommentar zur 'Peregrinatio Aetheriae'. Untersuchungen zur Geschichte der lateinischen Sprache* (Uppsala).

—— (1928 [vol. 1]; 1933 [vol. 2]; 1942 [2nd ed. of vol. 1]), *Syntactica. Studien und Beiträge zur historischen Syntax des Lateins I & II* (Lund).

—— (1959), *Late Latin* (Oslo).

Lohmann, A. (1915), *De Graecismorum Vergiliano usu quaestiones selectae* (Diss. Münster).

Long, A. A., and Sedley, D. N. (1987, 2 vols.), *The Hellenistic Philosophers* (Cambridge).

Lot, F. (1946), 'La langue du commandement dans les armées romaines', in *Mélanges dédiés à la mémoire de F. Grat* (Paris).

Luck-Huyse, K. (1996), *Der Traum vom Fliegen in der Antike* (Palingenesia 62) (Stuttgart).

Lunelli, A. (ed.) (1980, 2nd ed.), *La lingua poetica latina* (contains Italian versions of Janssen (1941) and Leumann (1947) with updated bibliography and annotations) (Bologna).

Lyne, R. O. A. M. (1980), *The Latin Love Poets: from Catullus to Horace* (Oxford).

—— (1989), *Words and the Poet: Characteristic Techniques of Style in Vergil's Aeneid* (Oxford).

McGlynn, P. (1963, 2 vols), *Lexicon Terentianum* (Glasgow).

McKeown, J. C. (ed.) (1987), *Ovid: Amores. Text, Prolegomena and Commentary* (Liverpool).

McKie, D. (1984), 'The horrible and ultimate Britons: Catullus, 11.11', *PCPS* NS 30: 74–8.

Madvig, J. N. (ed.) (1869), *M. Tullii Ciceronis De finibus bonorum et malorum.* 2nd ed. (Copenhagen).

Maltby, R. (1991), *A Lexicon of Ancient Latin Etymologies* (Leeds).

—— (1993), 'The Limits of Etymologising', *Aevum Antiquum* 6: 257–75.

Marache, R. (1964), 'Rhétorique et humour chez Juvénal', in Renard and Schilling (1964), 474–8.

Marganne, M.-H. (1993), *L'ophtalmologie dans l'Égypte gréco-romaine d'après les papyrus littéraires grecs* (Studies in Ancient Medicine, 8) (Leiden).

Marichal, R. (1992), *Les ostraca de Bu Njem* (Suppléments de 'Libya Antiqua' 7) (Tripoli).

Mariner, S. (1963), '*Traiectus lora* (Virg. *En.* II 273)', *Estudios Clasicos* 7: 107–19.

Mariotti, I. (1954), 'I grecismi di Lucilio', *Stud. Urb.* 28: 357–86.

—— (1960), *Studi Luciliani* (Florence).

Mariotti, S. (1991, 2nd ed.), *Lezioni su Ennio* (Urbino).

Marouzeau, J. (1907), *Place du pronom personnel sujet en latin* (Paris).

—— (1922), *L'ordre des mots dans la phrase latine, I: Les groupes nominaux* (Paris).

—— (1949*a*), *L'ordre des mots dans la phrase latine, III: Les articulations de l'énoncé* (Paris).

—— (1949*b*), *Quelques aspects de la formation du latin littéraire* (Collection linguistique 53) (Paris).

—— (1962; 4th ed.), *Traité de stylistique latine* (Paris).

Marshall, P. K. (ed.) (1968, 2 vols), *A. Gellii Noctes Atticae* (Oxford).

Martyn, J. R. C. (1979), 'Juvenal's Wit', *Grazer Beiträge* 8: 219–38.

Marx, F. (1882), *Studia Luciliana.* Diss. Bonn.

—— (ed.) (1904, 1905), *C. Lucilii carminum reliquiae.* Vol. prius: Prolegomena, testimonia, Fasti Luciliani, carminum reliquiae, indices, Vol. posterius: Commentarius (Leipzig).

—— (1909), 'Die Beziehungen des Altlateins zum Spätlatein', *NJb. f. d. class. Altertum*: 434–48.

BIBLIOGRAPHY

—— (ed.) (1915), *A. Cornelii Celsi quae supersunt* (*CML*, i; Leipzig–Berlin).

Mason, H. A. (1963), 'Is Juvenal a Classic?', in Sullivan (1963), 93–176.

Maurach, G. (1975), 'Ovid. Met. I, 48 und die Figur der "Umkehrung" ', *Hermes* 103: 479–86.

Mayer, R. G. (1983), 'Catullus' divorce', *CQ* 33: 297–8.

—— (ed.) (1994), *Horace, Epistles, Book I* (Cambridge).

Mazzini, I. (1988), 'La medicina nella letteratura latina. I. Osservazioni e proposte interpretative su passi di Lucilio, Lucrezio, Catullo e Orazio', *Aufidus* 4: 45–73.

—— (1990), 'Il folle da amore', in Alfonso *et al.* (1990), 39–83.

—— (1991*a*), 'La medicina nella letteratura latina. II. Esegesi e traduzione di Horat. *Epod.* 11, 15–16 e *Od.* I 13, 4–5', in Janni and Mazzini (1991), 99–114.

—— (1991*b*), 'Il lessico medico latino antico: caratteri e strumenti della sua differenziazione', in Sabbah (1991), 175–85.

—— (1992*a*), 'La medicina nella letteratura latina. III. Plauto: conoscenze mediche, situazione e istituzioni sanitarie, proposte esegetiche', in Mazzini (1992*b*), 67–113.

—— (ed.) (1992*b*), *Civiltà materiale e letteratura nel mondo antico* (Atti del Seminario di Studio, Macerata, 28–29 giugno 1991) (Macerata).

Meillet, A. (1965; 7th ed.), *Aperçu d'une histoire de la langue grecque* (Paris).

Menière, P. (1858), *Études médicales sur les poètes latins* (Paris).

Mette, H. J. (1956), rev. of E. V. Marmorale, *L'ultimo Catullo, Gnomon* 28: 34–8 (part repr. in R. Heine (ed.) [1975] *Catull* [Wege der Forschung 308, Darmstadt]: 19–23).

Meyer, W. (1889), 'Caesur im Hendekasyllabus', *SB Bayr. Ak., philosoph.-philol. und hist. Cl.* 2: 208–27.

Migliorini, P. (1990), *La terminologia medica come strumento espressivo della satira di Persio* (Quaderni di Anazetesis 2) (Pistoia).

Mignot, X. (1969), *Les verbes dénominatifs latins* (Paris).

Miller, H.W. (1944), 'Medical terminology in tragedy', *TAPA* 75: 156–67.

—— (1945), 'Aristophanes and medical language', *TAPA* 76: 74–84.

Mohler, S. L. (1948), 'Sails and Oars in the Aeneid', *TAPA* 79: 46–62.

Momigliano, A. (1957), 'Perizonius, Niebuhr and the character of the early Roman tradition', *JRS* 47: 104–14.

Morford, M. P. O. (1972), 'A Note on Juvenal 6.627–61', *CPh* 67: 198.

Mras, K. (1927/28), 'Randbemerkungen zu Lucilius' Satiren', *WS* 46: 78–84.

Mudry, Ph. (1982), *La préface du* De medicina *de Celse: Texte, traduction et commentaire* (Bibliotheca Helvetica Romana 19) (Rome).

Mühmelt, M. (1965), *Griechische Grammatik in der Vergilerklärung*, (Zetemata 37) (Munich).

Müller, C. F. W. (1869), *Plautinische Prosodie* (Berlin).

—— (1908), *Syntax des Nominativs und Akkusativs im Lateinischen* (Leipzig and Berlin).

Müller, C.W., Sier, K. and Werner, J. (edd.) (1992), *Zum Umgang mit fremden Sprachen in der griechisch-römischen Antike* (Palingenesia 36: Kolloquium der Fachrichtungen Klassische Philologie der Universitäten Leipzig und Saarbrücken am 21. und 22. November 1989 in Saarbrücken) (Stuttgart).

Müller, H. M. (1980), *Erotische Motive in der griechischen Dichtung bis auf Euripides* (Hamburg).

Müller, K. (ed.) (1975), *T. Lucreti Cari: De rerum natura libri sex* (Zurich).

Münscher, K. (1921), 'Metrische Beiträge II. Erstarrte Formen im Versbau der Aiolier', *Hermes* 56: 66–103.

Munari, F. (1971), 'Textkritisches zu mittellateinischen Dichtern' in Coseriu, E. and Stempel, W.-D. (edd.) *Festschrift für Harri Meier zum 65. Geburtstag* (Munich).

Murgatroyd, P. (1980), *Tibullus I: A Commentary* (Pietermaritzburg).

―――― (1994), *Tibullus: Elegies II* (Oxford).

Myers, R. and Ormsby, R. J. (1970), *Catullus. The Complete Poems for Modern Readers* (New York).

Myers-Scotton, C. (1993), *Duelling Languages. Grammatical Structure in Code-switching* (Oxford).

Mynors, R. A. B. (ed.) (1958), *C. Valerii Catulli Carmina* (Oxford).

―――― (ed.) (1990), *Virgil, Georgics, edited with an introduction and commentary* (Oxford).

Nagle, B. R. (1980), *The Poetics of Exile: Program and Polemic in the Tristia and Epistulae ex Ponto of Ovid.* (Collection Latomus, 170) (Brussels).

Naiditch, P. G. (1988), 'Three notes on "Housman and Ennius"' *Housman Society Journal* 14: 46–9.

Naylor, H. D. (1922), *Horace, Odes and Epodes: A Study in Poetic Word-Order* (Cambridge).

Neue, F. and Wagener, C. (1892–1905; 3rd ed.), *Formenlehre der lateinischen Sprache* (Berlin).

Neumann, G. (1968), 'Sprachnormung im klassischen Latein', *Sprache der Gegenwart* 2: 88–97.

Newman, J. K. (1990), *Roman Catullus and the Modification of the Alexandrian Sensibility* (Hildesheim).

Nilsson, N.-O. (1952), *Metrische Stildifferenzen in den Satiren des Horaz* (Stockholm).

Nisbet, R. G. M. (1978), 'Notes on the text of Catullus', *PCPS* NS 24: 92–115 (=1995: 76–100).

―――― (1995), S. J. Harrison (ed.), *Collected Papers on Latin Literature* (Oxford).

Nisbet, R. G. M. and Hubbard, M. (1970), *A Commentary on Horace: Odes Book 1* (Oxford).

―――― (1978), *A Commentary on Horace: Odes Book II* (Oxford).

Norden, E. (ed.) (1903; 1957, repr. of 2nd ed., 1915), *P. Vergilius Maro, Aeneis Buch VI* (Leipzig and Stuttgart).

―――― (ed.) (1910), *Einleitung in die Altertumswissenschaft* (Berlin).

Nowottny, W. (1962), *The Language Poets Use* (London).

Nutton, V. (1993), 'Roman medicine: tradition, confrontation, assimilation', in H. Temporini (ed.), *ANRW*, II.37: 1, 49–78 (Berlin).

Önnerfors, A. (1963), *In Medicinam Plinii studia philologica* (Lunds Univ. Årsskrift. N.F. Avd. 1. Bd 55, Nr 5) (Lund).

―――― (1989), '*Dare* und *Auris/Auricula* im Spätlatein', *Symb. Osl.* 64: 130–57.

———— (1993), 'Das medizinische Latein von Celsus bis Cassius Felix', in H. Temporini (ed.), *ANRW* II.37: 1, 227–392 (Berlin).

Ortony, A. (1979), *Metaphor and Thought* (Cambridge).

Paganelli, D. (1961), *Properce: Élégies* (Paris).

Page, D. L. (1936), review of Dumortier (1935), *CR* 50: 17–18.

Palmer, A. (ed.), (1898) *P. Ovidi Nasonis Heroides with the Greek translation of Planudes* [Completed by L. C. Purser.] (Oxford).

Palmer, L. R. (1954), *The Latin Language* (London).

Paludan, E. (1941), 'The development of the Latin elegy', *ClMed* 4: 204–29.

Pascucci, G. (1961), '*consens, praesens, absens*', *SIFC* 33: 1–61.

Pasquali, G. (1981), *Preistoria della poesia romana: con un saggio introduttivo di Sebastiano Timpanaro* (Florence).

Patzer, H. (1955), 'Zum Sprachstil des neoterischen Hexameters', *MH* 12: 77–95.

Pearce, T. E. V. (1966), 'The enclosing word order in the Latin hexameter' *CQ* NS 16: 140–71; 298–320.

Peppler, C. W. (1910), 'The termination –κος, as used by Aristophanes for comic effect', *AJP* 31: 428–44.

Peter, H. (1901), *Der Brief in der römischen Literatur* (Leipzig).

Petersmann, H. (1986), 'Der Begriff *satura* und die Entstehung der Gattung', in Adamietz (1986), 7–24.

———— (1989), 'Die Urbanisierung des römischen Reiches im Lichte der lateinischen Sprache', *Glotta* 96: 406–28.

———— (1992), 'Vulgärlateinisches aus Byzanz' in Müller, C. W. *et al.* (1992), 219–31.

———— (1995a), 'Soziale und lokale Aspekte in der Vulgärsprache Petrons', in Callebat (1995), 533–47.

———— (1995b), 'Zur mündlichen Charakterisierung des Fremden in der Komödie des Plautus', in Benz *et al.* (1995), 123–36.

———— (forthcoming), 'Language and style as means of characterization in the comedies of Plautus', *Papers of the Leeds International Latin Seminar*.

Phillips, J. H. (1984), 'Lucretius and the (Hippocratic) *On Breaths*: Addenda', in Sabbah (1984), 83–5.

Pigeaud, J. (1980), 'La physiologie de Lucrèce', *REL* 58: 176–200.

———— (1982), 'Virgile et la médecine. Quelques réflexions sur l'utilisation de la pensée physiologique dans les Géorgiques', *Helmantica* 33: 539–60.

———— (1988), 'Die Medizin in der Lehrdichtung des Lukrez und des Vergil', in Binder (1988), 216–39.

Pinkster, H. (1987), 'The pragmatic motivation for the use of subject pronouns in Latin: the case of Petronius', in *Études de linguistique générale et de linguistique latine offertes en hommage à Guy Serbat*, 369–79 (Paris).

Pinotti, P. (ed.) (1988), *Publio Ovidio Nasone, Remedia Amoris* (Edizioni e saggi universitari di filologia classica, 39) (Bologna).

Platnauer, M. (1951), *Latin Elegiac Verse* (Cambridge).

Ploen, H. (1882), *De copiae verborum differentiis inter varia poesis Romanae antiquioris genera intercedentibus* (Diss. Strasbourg).

Poncelet, R. (1957), *Cicéron traducteur de Platon. L'expression de la pensée complexe en latin classique* (Paris).

Powell, J. G. F. (1987), 'The *farrago* of Juvenal 1.86 reconsidered', in Whitby, Hardie and Whitby (1987).

———— (ed.) (1988), *Cicero: Cato Maior De Senectute* (Cambridge).

———— (1995*a*) 'Cicero's translations from Greek', in Powell (1995*b*), 273–300.

———— (ed.) (1995*b*), *Cicero the Philosopher* (Oxford).

Puelma Piwonka, M. (1949), *Lucilius und Kallimachos. Zur Geschichte einer Gattung der hellenistisch-römischen Poesie* (Frankfurt am Main).

Pye, D. W. (1963), 'Latin 3rd plural perfect indicative active — Its endings in verse usage', *TPhS*: 1–27

Radermacher, L. (1951), *Artium Scriptores (Reste der voraristotelischen Rhetorik).* (Österr. Akademie der Wissenschaften, phil.-hist. Kl., Sitzungsberichte, 227. Bd., 3. Abh.) (Vienna).

Ramage, E. S. (1957), *Urbanitas, rusticitas, peregrinitas: the Roman view of proper Latin* (Cincinnati).

Rand, E. K. (1925), *Ovid and his Influence* (London, Calcutta, Sydney).

Rawson, E. D. (1969), *The Spartan Tradition in European Thought* (Oxford).

———— (1985), *Intellectual Life in the Late Roman Republic* (London).

Reichenkron, G. (1961), 'Zur römischen Kommandosprache bei byzantinischen Schriftstellern', *Byz. Zeitschr.* 54: 18–27

Reitzenstein, R. (1893), *Epigramm und Skolion. Ein Beitrag zur Geschichte der alexandrinischen Dichtung* (Giessen).

———— (1907), art. 'Epigramm', *RE* 6.1: 71–111.

———— (1912), *Zur Sprache der lateinischen Erotik* (Sitzungsb. d. Heidelberger Ak. d. Wiss., Phil.-hist. Kl., 12. Abh.) (Heidelberg).

Renard, M., and Schilling, R. (edd.) (1964), *Hommages à Jean Bayet*, (Collection Latomus 70) (Brussels).

Riemann, O. (1885; 2nd ed.), *Études sur la langue et la grammaire de Tite-Live* (Paris).

Risch, E. (1984), *Gerundivum und Gerundium. Gebrauch im klassischen und älteren Latein. Entstehung und Vorgeschichte* (Berlin–New York).

Risselada, R (1993), *Imperatives and Other Directive Expressions in Latin* (Amsterdam).

Roby, H. J. (1896), *A grammar of the Latin language from Plautus to Suetonius.* Part II *Syntax* (London).

Romaine, S. (1995; ed. 1, 1989), *Bilingualism* (Oxford).

Romano, A. C. (1979), *Irony in Juvenal* (Hildesheim and New York).

Ronconi, A. (1938), 'Stile e lingua di Catullo', *A & R* III 6: 139–56 (= 1950: 23–47).

———— (1939), 'Allitterazione e stile in Catullo', *Stud. Urb.* 13B: 1–77 (= 1953: 9–82 = 1971: 11–86).

———— (1940*a*), 'Per la storia del diminutivo latino. Studi esegetici e stilistici', *Stud. Urb.* 14B: 1–45 (= 1953: 107–50 = 1971: 87–130).

———— (1940*b*), 'Atteggiamenti e forme della parodia catulliana', *A & R* III 8: 141–58 (= 1953: 193–212 = 1971: 173–92).

———— (1950), *Da Lucrezio a Tacito* (Messina—Florence).

———— (1971; ed. 1, 1953), *Studi catulliani* (Bari—Brescia).

van Rooy, C. A. (1965), *Studies in Classical Satire and Related Literary Theory* (Leiden).

Rösler, W. (1989), 'Typenhäuser bei Aischylos?', in Schuller *et al.* (1989), 109–14.

Ross, D. O. (1969), *Style and Tradition in Catullus* (Cambridge, Mass.)

Rothstein, M. (1966; 3rd ed.), *Sextus Propertius: Elegien* (Dublin — Zurich).

Rudd, N. (1960), 'Horace on the origins of satura', *Phoenix* 14: 36–44.

—— (1986), *Themes in Roman Satire* (London).

Ruijgh, C. J. (1957), *L'élément achéen dans la langue épique* (Assen).

Sabbah, G. (ed.) (1982), *Médecins et médecine dans l'antiquité* (Centre Jean Palerne: Mémoires, iii) (Saint-Étienne).

—— (ed.) (1984), *Textes médicaux latins antiques* (Centre Jean Palerne: Mémoires, v) (Saint-Étienne).

—— (ed.) (1991), *Le latin médical. La constitution d'un langage scientifique* (Centre Jean Palerne: Mémoires, x) (Saint-Étienne).

Safarewicz, J. (1965), 'Uwagi o jezyku Lucyliusza', *Eos* 55: 96–105.

Sager, J. C., Dungworth, D. and McDonald, P. F. (1980), *English Special Languages: Principles and Practice in Science and Technology* (Wiesbaden).

de Saint-Denis, E. (1935), *Le rôle de la mer dans la poésie latine* (Paris).

—— (1965), *Essais sur le rire et le sourire des Latins* (Paris).

Schäublin, C. (1988), 'Housman and Ennius', *Housman Society Journal* 14: 42–5.

Schawaller, D. (1987), 'Semantische Wortspiele in Ovids Metamorphosen und Heroides', *Gräzer Beiträge* 14: 199–214.

Scherer, A. (1963), 'Die Sprache des Archilochos', in *Entretiens sur l'Antiquité classique* 10: 89–107 (Geneva).

Schmid, P. (1964), 'Juvénal. Essai d'une définition stylistique'. Résumé, in *REL* 42: 57–9.

Schmid, W. and Stählin, O. (1929), *Geschichte der griechischen Literatur*, I: i (Munich).

Schmidt, B. (ed.) (1887), *C. Valeri Catulli Veronensis carmina* (Leipzig).

—— (1914), 'Die Lebenszeit Catulls und die Herausgabe seiner Gedichte', *RhM* 69: 267–83.

Schmidt, E.A. (1977), 'Lucilius kritisiert Ennius und andere Dichter. Zu Lucilius fr. 148 Marx', *MH* 34: 122–9.

—— (1985), *Catull* (Heidelberg).

Schmitt, R. (1967), *Dichtung und Dichtersprache im indogermanischer Zeit* (Wiesbaden).

Scholte, A. (ed.) (1933), *Publii Ovidii Nasonis Ex Ponto Liber Primus commentario exegetico instructus* (Amersfoort).

Scholz, U.W. (1986a), 'Der frühe Lucilius und Horaz', *Hermes* 114: 335–65.

—— (1986b), 'Die *satura* des Q. Ennius', in Adamietz (1986), 25–53.

Schreiber, G. (1917), *De Lucili syntaxi* (Diss. Greifswald).

Schünke, E. (1906), *De traiectione coniunctionum et pronominis relativi apud poetas Latinos* (Diss. Kiel).

Schuller, W., Hoepfner, W. and Schwandner, E. L. (edd.) (1989), *Demokratie und Architektur: Der hippodamische Städtebau und die Entstehung der Demokratie* (Konstanzer Symposion vom 17. bis 19. Juli 1987) (Munich).

Schulze, K. P. (1920), 'Bericht über die Literatur zu Catullus für die Jahre 1905–1920', *Bursians Jahresb.* 183: 1–72.

Schuster, M. (1948), art. '(123) C. Valerius Catullus', *RE* II.7.2: 2353–410.

_____ (ed.) (1949), *Catulli Veronensis liber* (Leipzig).

Schweizer, H. J. (1967), *Vergil und Italien* (Aarau).

Sconocchia, S. (ed.) (1983), *Scribonii Largi Compositiones* (Leipzig).

_____ (1993), 'L'opera di Scribonio Largo e la letteratura medica latina del 1. sec. d. C.', in H. Temporini (ed.), *ANRW* II.37: 1, 843–922. (Berlin).

Scott (Ryberg), I. G. (1927), *The Grand Style in the Satires of Juvenal* (Smith College Classical Studies 8) (Northampton, Mass.).

Sebeok, T. A. (ed.) (1960), *Style in Language* (Cambridge, Mass.).

Sedley, D. N. (1988), 'Epicurean anti-reductionism', in Barnes and Mignucci (1988), 295–327.

_____ (1989), 'The proems of Empedocles and Lucretius', *GRBS* 30: 269–96.

_____ (1992) 'Sextus Empiricus and the atomist criteria of truth', *Elenchos* 13: 21–56.

Segal, C. (1990), *Lucretius on Death and Anxiety* (Princeton).

Segebade, J. (1895), *Vergil als Seemann. Ein Beitrag zur Erklärung und Würdigung des Dichters.* Progr.d.Gymn. (Oldenburg).

Shackleton Bailey, D. R. (ed.) (1965), *Cicero's Letters to Atticus.* II *58–54 B.C. 46–93 (Books III and IV)* (Cambridge).

_____ (ed.) (1977), *Cicero: Epistulae ad Familiares.* I *62–47 B.C.* (Cambridge).

_____ (1992), 'Homoeoteleuton in non-dactylic Latin verse', *RFIC* 120: 67–71.

_____ (1994), *Homoeoteleuton in Latin Dactylic Verse* (Stuttgart—Leipzig).

Sharrock, A. R. (1994), *Seduction and Repetition in Ovid's Ars Amatoria 2* (Oxford).

Shipley, F. W. (1911), 'The heroic clausula in Cicero and Quintilian', *CPh* 6: 410–18.

Silk, M. S. (1974), *Interaction in Poetic Imagery with Special Reference to Early Greek Poetry* (Cambridge).

Simpson, F. P. (1879), *Select Poems of Catullus* (London).

Skutsch, F. (1892), *Plautinisches und Romanisches. Studien zur plautinischen Prosodie* (Leipzig).

Skutsch, O. (1934), *Prosodische und metrische Gesetze der Iambenkürzung* (Forschungen z. griech. u. latein. Grammatik 10) (Göttingen).

_____ (1964), 'Rhyme in Horace', *BICS* 11: 73–8.

_____ (1969), 'Metrical variations and some textual problems in Catullus, *BICS* 16: 38–43.

_____ (1976), 'Notes on Catullus', *BICS* 23: 18–22.

_____ (1980), 'Catullus 58.4–5', *LCM* 5: 21.

_____ (1985), *The 'Annals' of Quintus Ennius edited with Introduction and Commentary* (Oxford).

Smith, K. F. (1913), *The Elegies of Albius Tibullus* (New York).

Smith, W. S. (ed.) (1989), 'Heroic models for the sordid present: Juvenal's view of tragedy', in H. Temporini (ed.), *ANRW* II.33.1: 811–23 (Berlin).

Soubiran, J. (1966), *L'élision dans la poésie latine* (Paris).

Spies, A. (1930), *Militat omnis amans* (Diss. Tübingen).

von Staden, H. (1989), *Herophilus: the Art of Medicine in Early Alexandria* (Cambridge).

Stevens, E. B. (1953), 'Uses of hyperbaton in Latin poetry', *ClW* 46: 200–5.

Sullivan, J. P. (ed.) (1963), *Critical Essays on Roman Literature: Satire* (London).

Summers, W. C. (1910), *Select Letters of Seneca edited with introductions and explanatory notes* (London).

Svennung, J. (1935), *Untersuchungen zu Palladius und zur lateinischen Fach- und Volkssprache* (Uppsala).

—— (1945), *Catulls Bildersprache. Vergleichende Stilstudien* I (Uppsala Universitets Årsskrift 3) (Uppsala—Leipzig).

Swanson, D. C. (1962), *A Formal Analysis of Lucretius' Vocabulary* (Minneapolis).

Syndikus, H. P. (1984), *Catull. Eine Interpretation. Erster Teil. Die kleinen Gedichte (1–60)* (Darmstadt).

Terzaghi, N. (ed.) (1934, 2nd ed.), *Lucilio*, (Turin) (Repr. Hildesheim, New York 1979).

—— (ed.) (1966), *Saturarum Reliquiae* (Florence).

Thierfelder, A. (1955), 'De morbo hepatiario', *RhM* 98: 190–2.

Thill, A. (1979), *Alter ab illo. Recherches sur l'imitation dans la poésie personnelle à l'époque Augustéenne* (Paris).

Thomas, R. F. (ed.) (1988, 2 vols), *Virgil, Georgics* (Cambridge).

Thomson, D. F. S. (ed.) (1978), *Catullus. A Critical Edition. Edited and Introduced* (Chapel Hill).

Tovar, A. (1969), 'Lucilio y el latín de España', in *Studi linguistici in onore de V. Pisani*, ii.1019–32 (Brescia).

Townend, G. B. (1973), 'The literary substrata to Juvenal's satires', *JRS* 63: 148–60.

Tracy, V. A. (1971), 'The authenticity of *Heroides* 16–21', *CJ* 66: 328–30.

Tränkle, H. (1960), *Die Sprachkunst des Properz und die Tradition der lateinischen Dichtersprache* (Hermes Einzelschriften 15) (Wiesbaden).

—— (1967*a*), 'Ausdrucksfülle bei Catull', *Philologus* 111: 198–211.

—— (1967*b*), 'Neoterische Kleinigkeiten', *MH* 24: 87–103.

—— (1981), 'Catullprobleme', *MH* 38: 245–58.

Traina, A. (1975), 'Orazio e Catullo' in *Poeti latini (e neolatini). Note e saggi filologici*: 253–75 (Bologna).

Untermann, J. (1971), 'Entwürfe zu einer Enniusgrammatik', *Entretiens de la Fondation Hardt* 17: 209–51 (Geneva).

—— (1977), 'Zur semantischen Organisation des lateinischen Wortschatzes', *Gymnasium* 84: 313–39.

Väänänen, V. (1966, 3rd ed.), *Le Latin vulgaire des inscriptions pompéiennes* (Berlin).

Vairel-Carron, H. (1975), *Exclamation. Ordre et défense* (Paris).

Van Sickle, J. B. (1968), 'About form and feeling in Catullus 65', *TAPA* 99: 487–508.

Vechner, D. (1610, ed. 1, Frankfurt; ed. 2 Strasburg 1630; ed. 3 Leipzig 1680; ed. 4 Gotha 1733 (Heusinger)), *Hellenolexia*.

Vessey, D. W. T. C. (1969), 'Notes on Ovid, *Heroides* 9', *CQ* ns 19: 349–61.

Vetter, E. (1953), *Handbuch der italischen Dialekte*, I. Band: Texte mit Erklärung, Glossen, Wörterverzeichnis (Heidelberg).

Vollmer, F. (1923), *Römische Metrik*, in A. Gercke and E. Norden (edd.), *Einleitung in die Altertumswissenschaft*. I. Band: 8. Heft (Leipizig & Berlin).

Wackernagel, J. (1892), 'Über ein Gesetz der indogermanischen Wortstellung', *Indogermanische Forschungen* 1:333–436 (= *Kleine Schriften* (1955) i. 1–104 (Göttingen)).

—— (1926 [vol. 1], 1928 [vol. 2]), *Vorlesungen über Syntax* (Basel).

Walde, A. and Hofmann, J. B. (1930–1956, 2 vols), *Lateinisches etymologisches Wörterbuch* (Heidelberg).

Waszink, J. H. (1971), 'Problems concerning the Satura of Ennius', *Entretiens sur l'Antiquité classique* 17: 97–147. (Geneva).

Watkins, C. W. (1982), 'Aspects of Indo-European poetics', in E. C. Polomé (ed.), *The Indo-Europeans in the fourth and third millenia*, 104–20 (Ann Arbor).

—— (1989), 'New parameters in historical linguistics, philology and cultural history', *Language* 65: 783–99.

—— (1995), *How to Kill a Dragon. Aspects of Indo-European Poetics* (New York – Oxford).

Watson, P. (1983), '*Puella* and *Virago*', *Glotta* 61: 119–43.

—— (1985), 'Axelson revisited: the selection of vocabulary in Latin poetry', *CQ* NS 35: 430–48.

Weinreich, O. (1959), 'Catull c. 60', *Hermes* 87: 75–90.

—— (1960), *Catull. Liebesgedichte und sonstige Dichtungen* (Hamburg).

—— (1962; 2nd ed.), *Römische Satiren* (Zürich und Stuttgart).

Weis, R. (1992), 'Zur Kenntnis des Griechischen im Rom der republikanischen Zeit', in Müller, C. W. *et al.* (1992), 137–42.

Weise, F. O. (1882), *Die griechishen Wörter in Latein* (repr. 1964 Leipzig).

Wellmann, M. (1931), *Hippokratesglossare* (Quellen und Studien zur Geschichte der Naturwissenschaften und der Medizin, 2) (Berlin).

West, D. A. (1969), *Imagery and Poetry of Lucretius* (Edinburgh).

West, M. L. (1982), *Greek Metre* (Oxford).

Westphal, R. (1867), *Catulls Gedichte in ihrem geschichtlichen Zusammenhange* (Breslau).

Whitby, M., Hardie, P., and Whitby, M. (edd.) (1987), *Homo Viator. Classical Essays for John Bramble* (Bristol).

Wiesen, D. S. (1989), 'The verbal basis for Juvenal's satiric vision', in H. Temporini (ed.), *ANRW* II.33.1: 708–33 (Berlin).

Wifstrand, A. (1933), *Von Kallimachos zu Nonnos* (Lund).

Wilamowitz-Moellendorff, U. von (1898), 'De uersu Phalaeceo' in *Mélanges Henri Weil* (Paris), 449–61 (revised in 1921: 137–53).

—— (1921), *Griechische Verskunst* (Berlin).

Wilhelm, F. (1925), 'Zu Ovid Ex Ponto I,3', *Philologus* 81: 155–67.

Wilkinson, L. P. (1959), 'The language of Virgil and Homer', *CQ* NS 9: 181–92.

—— (1963), *Golden Latin Artistry* (Cambridge).

Williams, G. W. (1968), *Tradition and Originality in Roman Poetry* (Oxford).

Williams, R. D. (ed.) (1960), *P. Vergili Maronis Aeneidos Liber Quintus* (Oxford).

Wills, J. (1996), *Repetition in Latin Poetry. Figures of Allusion* (Oxford).

Winterbottom, M. (1977*a*), 'A Celtic hyperbaton?', *The Bulletin of the Board of Celtic Studies* 27: 207–12.

—— (1977*b*), 'Aldhelm's prose style and its origins', *Anglo-Saxon England* 6: 50–1.

Wiseman, T. P. (1969), *Catullan Questions* (Leicester).

—— (1974), *Cinna the Poet, and Other Roman Essays* (Leicester).

_____ (1979), 'On what Catullus doesn't say', *Latin Teaching* 35 n. 6: 11–15.

Wölfflin, E. (1882), 'Über die Aufgaben der lateinischen Lexikographie', *RhM* 37: 83–121.

_____ (1885), 'Das adverbielle *cetera, alia, omnia*', *ALL* 2: 90–9.

_____ (1886), 'Der substantivierte Infinitiv', *ALL* 3: 70–91.

Wyke, M. (1989), 'Mistress and metaphor in Augustan elegy', *Helios* 16: 25–47.

Zanker, G. (1987), *Realism in Alexandrian Poetry: a Literature and its Audience* (London–Sydney–Wolfeboro, NH).

Zicàri, M. (1964), 'Some metrical and prosodical features of Catullus' poetry', *Phoenix* 18: 193–205 (= 1978: 203–19).

_____ (1978), *Scritti catulliani* (Urbino).

Zwierlein, O. (1986), *Kritischer Kommentar zu den Tragödien Senecas* (Akad. d. Wiss. u. d. Literatur Mainz, Abhandlungen der geistes- und sozialwissenschaftlichen Klasse, Einzelveröffentlichung 6) (Wiesbaden).

Index verborum

Index locorum

Index rerum

ablative absolute, 150–1; of comparison, 79–80; of quality in Lucilius, 303; singular in *i*, 42–3

accusative: adnominal, 82; of direction, 79, 261–2; internal, 78–9; morphology of, 43; of object with participle in *-nt-*, 353; perlative, 79, 82; position of acc. of obj., 354–5, 364–5, 371

adjectival use of proper noun, 353

adjectives from proper names, placement of, 141–2; possessive, 142

'alienation', 269, 279, 282

alliteration, 40, 47–8, 53, 70, 82, 89, 90, 103, 259; in Catullus, 66, 349, 360, 370; in Ennius, 294; in Naevius, 290

analogical morphology, 303, syntax, 171–5, 178–9

anaphora, 350, 360, 370

anastrophe of preposition, 159

antithetical/focussed term attracts enclitics, 104–5

ἀπὸ κοινοῦ, 144, 152, 406

apostrophe, 88

archaism, 10–11, 31, 33 (final *s*), 41 (morphology), 57–8 (revivalist diction), 58 (avoided by Ovid), 173, 181, 182, 249–68 *passim*; 293, 295 (in Ennius), 302, 304 (in Lucilius), 352, 362 (morphology), 353 (syntax), 356–7, 367, 403, 404 n. 22

Aretaeus of Cappadocia, 187–8

'asserting/revealing' verbs with personal pronouns, 122–3

assonance, 49, 53; in Catullus, 349, 360

attractio inuersa, 251–2

Axelson criticized, 323, 343 n. 36, 378, 401 nn. 10, 11

bathos, 329

bilingualism, 45, 177–8

calque, 61–2, 69–70, 73, 181

chiasmus, 139, 140, 142

Cicero's influence on Ovid, 407–9, 411–12

'code switching', 300

'collective' plural, 353

colloquialism, 5–10, 38 (*uiden*); in Catullus, 115–16, 118; in Lucilius, 304–6, 307–8; in elegy, 406

colometry and word order, 149–50

Columella's prose, 402

compound words, 2, 60–3, 239, 242 n. 39, 358 n. 111, 386–7

dative of direction, 80, 262–3

demonstrative preceding personal pronoun, 101, 105, in Catullus, 113–14; in Augustan poets, 130–2

'dialects' used in Latin poetry, 3, 27 (§2.6), 64 (§27.4), in Ennius, 291–2, in Lucilius, 308–9

didactic/scientific poetry, 22–3, 60

diminutives, 59–60, 387–9; in Lucilius, 306–8

elision, 33; of monosyllabic word, 400 n. 2

Empedocles as model for Lucretius, 235

enallage, 85

'enclosing' word order, 127–30

enjambment, 146–8, 354

etymology, 180, 389, 390

final *o* shortened in pronunciation, 9, 38

final *s*, how treated in verse, 33–4

focussed term preceding personal pronoun, 102–3

genitive: emphasized, 141; plur. in *-um*, 43; in poetry, 80–1; of quality avoided by Lucilius, 303

gerund(ive) (impersonal with object), 215 n. 89, 259–60

grecism: lexical, 11, 64–66, 158, 161, 299 n. 12 (Lucilius), 373, 379–82; morphological, 12, 46–7, 158, 300–1 (Lucilius), 352, 380; syntactic, 12; revivals under Greek influence, 79 (adverbial neuter), 82 (accusative), 8, 83 (aspect of verb); syntactic (in Catullus), 353, (in Tibullus), 389; word order, 159

DATE DUE

UPI 261-2505 G   PRINTED IN U.S.A.